# THE SULPHUR WELL CORRESPONDENT

Compiled and edited

by

Ray Miller Ware

June 14, 1997

MAILING ADDRESS
Ray M Ware
3521 Greentree Road
Lexington, Ky 40517

Tel 606-272-3797

Copyright 1997
Library of Congress
Control number 98-102310

# TABLE OF CONTENTS

| | |
|---|---:|
| PROLOGUE | 1 |
| THE FIRST YEAR - 1887 | 10 |
| THE SECOND YEAR - 1888 | 43 |
| THE RAILROAD - 1889 | 71 |
| FAMILY DEATHS - 1890 | 95 |
| A NEW CONSTITUTION - 1891 | 112 |
| FAMILY HISTORY - 1892 | 135 |
| FINANCIAL PANIC - 1893 | 151 |
| MODERN TIMES - 1894 | 167 |
| MARRIAGE - 1895 | 183 |
| UNCLE RAY'S BIRTH - 1896 | 219 |
| CLOTHING STORE - 1897 | 241 |
| THE WAR - 1898 | 265 |
| STORE CLOSING - 1899 | 299 |
| SUSAN NAVE - 1900 | 329 |
| MILLERS SETTLE IN OKLAHOMA - 1901 | 358 |
| DR HENDREN IN OKLAHOMA - 1902 | 381 |
| PASSING OF A LANDMARK - 1903 | 409 |
| EARLY HISTORY - 1904 | 421 |
| CORRESPONDENCE ENDS - 1905 | 431 |
| EPILOGUE | 441 |
| ABOUT THE COMPILER | 459 |
| THE GEOGRAPHICAL SETTING OF THE STORY | 469 |
| FAMILIES THAT APPEAR FREQUENTLY IN THE STORY | 470 |
| BIBLIOGRAHY | 482 |
| INDEX | 484 |

## PROLOGUE

Correspondents for local newspapers filled a need to tie individuals to their own and other communities. In the late nineteenth century people traveled more, read more, wrote more, and thought more, than most people today would believe. The more isolated communities and individuals were, the greater their need to connect with others outside those areas. Village correspondents helped by personalizing local events, and by telling others that their residents were visiting relatives, attending expositions, working, suffering hardship, enjoying milestones such as weddings and births, as well as grieving over family tragedies. People in other communities, even in other states were interested in these events. This story covers the last part of the nineteenth century, beginning in 1877, and ending in the twentieth century, about 1905 (with epilogue, 1921). This was a time of incredible change, during which the Sulphur Well correspondent wrote about the events of his time.

The United States was a relatively young, growing and developing country. There was rapid population growth, affected by an European migration from 1850 to 1920. There were still free western lands, and opportunities caused a continuing western movement of the population. Technology led to great changes in the development of the country. Steam power was, by the 1870s, most important for industrial development in the east. Then, later, electrical power emerged. Petroleum was found at Titusville in the 1850's, and kerosene provided the fuel for the coal-oil lamp. Gas became important when, in 1880, it was discoved as a by-product of coke, and subsequently became the first central lighting system.

The process of industrialization displaced labor. There was an immense industrial transformation between 1870 and 1914. With advancing technology, fewer people were needed on the farm, and more were needed in the factories in the cities. While creating opportunities, it also disrupted the rural way of life. It affected women as well as men. Even as late as 1870 only one in seven workers outside the home were female. The lack of a retirement system meant that in 1890, there were still two-thirds of the all persons over sixty-five in the workforce.

In the early nineteenth century rivers and canals greatly influenced the development of the country, and many of the early commercial centers were located near navigable waterways. By 1830 Cincinnati was a national meat-packing center, and by the 1870's Cincinnati was the population center of the country. Thus, by virtue of its location, and its position as a transportation center, it drew livestock and other agricultural products. Railroads were just beginning in the United States by around 1830, but networks mushroomed, and by mid-century the United States had the most extensive system in the world. Railroads passed though many small towns and changed their mode of transportation overnight. There were many technological improvements that aided this expansion. The Bessemer steel process allowed the cost of rails to fall from $120 per ton in 1874 to $18 per ton in 1898. Railroad technology was also surrounded by the steam engine, T-rails, new road base, and civil engineering advances in cutting, filling, and grading. There were air-brakes and coupling systems invented in the 1870's, and track guage was standardized.

Turnpikes and highways were not important to the national movement of goods and people until the advent of the motor vehicle. However, turnpikes were very important locally for such movement, and linked the farming communities to the nearest cities.

The technological advances didn't come over night. Knowledge of the possibilities existed for years before the commercial application of the concepts or inventions. There were fairs and expositions that people attended regularly. There were also well-publicized failures, so the coming of electric lights and motor cars, while many may have scoffed, were not unexpected.

A large segment of the economy was engaged, directly or indirectly, in agriculture which is very capital-intensive, and farmers tended to be debtors. Consequently, there was a natural disposition toward low interest rates. They blamed the banks and the government when money wasn't available or interest rates were high. This tended to make the farmers very interested in politics. The Grange was organized in 1870, and the populist movement was well under way by 1890. They also blamed monopolists and tariffs for low prices for their produce, and high prices for what they needed to buy. Typically, the farmers produced a narrow range of cash crops, and used the proceeds to buy their seed and equipment, support their families, and pay their debts.

The farmers were not just being paranoid about the banking system. The National Banking Act of 1863 permitted federal chartering of banks, minimum reserve standards, and a national currency. However, the problem of reserves had not been solved. Smaller banks kept funds with larger banks in the financial centers of the country. Whenever there was economic instability, the funds flowed out of the financial centers, thus restricting the reserves upon which a banks ability to lend were based. This process caused what in those days were called panics. There were panics in 1873, 1884, 1893, 1903, and 1907 which led to establishment of the Federal Reserve System in 1913. The entire period from 1866 to 1896 was characterized by falling prices, and the depression that lasted from 1873 to 1877 set the stage for the last quarter of the nineteenth century. The preceeding economic setting came largely from Davis, Hughes, and McDougall, <u>American Economic History: The Development of a National Economy</u>. Revised Edition, 1965. Richard D Irwin, Inc., Homewood, Illinois.

To narrow the focus from the nation to state and local affairs, we move to the formation of Jessamine County in 1798. It was formed out of the southern part of Fayette County, and is bounded by the Kentucky River from the east to the southwest part of the county near High Bridge. While Jessamine is a part of the Bluegrass, and indeed some of the northern part is in the horse country, the parts bordering the river are quite rough and hilly. The county seat, located in Nicholasville, was first surveyed in 1798 and chartered in 1812. Its population was stagnant and still had only about three thousand people as late as the 1930's. Nicholasville did became the hub for most of the smaller communities in the county. You will see from various news items that Jessamine County was strictly a farming area, and never able to establish an industrial base. Nicholasville was mainly the site of "court days" activity, and some retailing and services. It was quite a center for schools and churches, and the place for the farmers in surrounding communities to shop on Saturdays. The proximity of Lexington was such that even in the nineteenth century, people preferred to buy their clothing in Lexington.

Sulphur Well is about three and one-half miles from Nicholasville on Ky 39. The road continues to the river at Paint Lick, where there was once a ferry that crossed over into Garrard County. The road then goes on to Lancaster. Sulphur Well was also known as Ambrose. It received this name for its post office, named for Ambrose Cobb. There are a number of other small communities that are in the area, and their residents often pass through Sulphur Well on their way to Nicholasville. These communities include Little Hickman and Pink, Elm Fork, and Black Bridge. Pollard, Mt Lebanon, and Chrisman Mill are in an adjacent area, and mostly take a different route to town. These communities are identified as communities because of their churches and schools, and their general stores that in the old days usually contained a post office. Farmers claim residence in one community or another as much by which school or church they attend as by their physical location. There were ferries along the river which permitted considerable travel in the tri-county area of Jessamine, Garrard, and Madison. I have enclosed a map of the area in one of the appendices. The people often went to Nicholasville for court days, and there was considerable business and social visiting.

The people of Kentucky, Jessamine County, and Sulphur Well, were deeply involved in race relations, politics and religion. The Civil War had been over only twelve years when this journal begins. Many people who served in the war were alive and active in society. There were also many African Americans living who had been slaves, or who were acculturated in the Antebellum South. The political parties were shaped by the Civil War and the Reconstruction. Religion is a major building block in society. It dictates ways of thinking about extra-marital relations, use of alcohol, working on Sundays, and relations among people of different races and genders. In other words, suffrage, prohibition, "blue laws", and racial attitudes are interrelated with religion and politics, and are reflected in everyday lives.

This background is not intended to be comprehensive, but offered to provide the context for the correspondent's weekly reports from Sulphur Well. When supplemented by news items, his story becomes more complete. I refer to the correspondent as "he", but based upon pseuodnyms there may have been as many as six different correspondents between 1877 and 1892, and the one who signed as Ivy may have been female. Our correspondent, who I will identify later, said in one of his articles that he had been the correspondent for twenty-five years, since the inception of the <u>Jessamine Journal</u>, but it is clear that others filled in for him at various times. I hope you read his accounts with as much interest as I have, although my interest is heightened by his frequent reference to my ancestors. The Millers were residents of Sulphur Well for almost two hundred years, beginning in the 1780's. I will frequently enlarge upon the events pertaining to them, to the Hendrens because my grandmother was a Hendren, and to various individuals whom I find interesting. I will also recount some humorous stories that I believe are timeless.

The material is presented to you as a chronical of the Sulphur Well correspondent. His first article, that remains in existence, was not printed in the <u>Journal</u> until February 18, 1887, but I will "keep his diary for him" until he speaks for himself.

September 7, 1877

The West is open for settlement, and the railroads are providing the transportation. A large group of African-Americans were provided transportion from Lexington to Kansas to settle, indicating that the movement of persons displaced after the Civil War is still in progress.

The farmers are continuing to have economic problems. They carried over a surplus of corn that they are willing to sell at almost any price in September just before the new crop is harvested. They are dissatisfied with the price of wheat, and some are holding back their supply to obtain a better price.

People place a very high value on education. There is an "English and Classical" high school in Nicholasville, and a "Female Institute".

Horses play a large part in local entertainment. There is a "driving park" in Nicholasville for trotting horses, and races are arranged periodically. People also arrange outings. One local group traveled to Frankfort to visit the capital. While there they toured the prison, and later had a "sumptuous" meal at the Capital Hotel. Eating out, particularly eating delicacies, was much in vogue. One Nicholasville restaurant features fresh oysters.

Matters of health are of great concern. Salves and ointments covering a variety of ailments are advertised, and there are treatments for digestive complaints. While doctors are readily available, there is a great deal of self-treatment for common health problems.

There is more knowledge of the "outside world", than we might imagine. The back page of the Journal is devoted to news from Washington, and the rest of the world. There is interest in national as well as local politics.

Because of a fire at the <u>Jessamine Journal</u>, there is a five-year break in our knowledge of what went on in Jessamine County between 1877 and 1882.

October 27, 1882

Railroads and migration are "in the news". The Mississippi Railroad advertises a ten-hour schedule from Cincinnati to St. Louis. The local ticket agent sold a dozen tickets to parties going West during the week. Emigration from the county is said to be growing in numbers. Over 9,000 new farms were established in Minnesota and Dakota in the past year. Two prominent young men are off to Texas with the intention of exploring business opportunities. Sidings are being added to facilitate freight loading and unloading at the depot. Officials from the Louisville Southern Railroad were entertained in Nicholasville, to induce them to route their line through Nicholasville. Inventors are busy. One Kentuckian is working on a means to telegraph a train while en route. There are apparently enough business visitors to Cincinnati to warrant an item that the Crawford House is centrally located and a good place to eat.

Farmers are always finding problems with the prices of their produce. The Winchester cattle market was so "dull" this week that half the entries were kept by their owners.

## Weekly Courier Journal

This story is about the Sulphur Well correspondent for the Jessamine Journal. However, the following items supplement the Journal during the period in which there are few issues available.

October 12, 1882: A New York State man who tried a flying machine of his own invention had no advice to those people who were crowding around him. All he said was "work in `durned fool' somewhere on my tombstone." We tend to think of the date of an invention as though that is the beginning, when actually it is the culmination of the imagination and persistence of many people that allowed the success to occur. It is hard to imagine that some people were trying to fly when almost everyone else drove horse and buggies!

October 19, 1882: Dr J C Miller sold a two-year old bay colt by Halsora that was said to be one of the best trotting horses bred in the county. Dr John C Miller is the son of Merriman F Miller and Celia Sageser. He was born on the family farm in Jessamine County in 1841. According to his biography in Perrin's Kentucky. A History of the State, Dr Miller began his medical studies in 1862 under Dr S D Welch. He graduated from the Ohio Medical College in 1864, and attended Bellevue Medical College in New York the following year. He married Nanie Rice of Madison County in 1868. Dr Miller practiced medicine in Jessamine County, except for the four years, 1873 to 1877, that he spent in Madison County. He obviously had some success as a breeder of trotters as early as 1882.

November 9, 1882: Mr Wm Hendren sold his homeplace at Sulphur Well, 83 acres with a good house and outbuildings, to Mr George Gray at $55 per acre. Mr Gray sold his house and lot to Mr B Wolf for $600. The next article is from the Jessamine Journal.

November 2, 1883

Travel, crops, food and entertainment are of great interest. So is knowledge. Many people travel to expositions because they see the latest in technology, and displays of products. The expositions also became family vacations and social events. There are excursion fares on the railroads that made travel relatively inexpensive. People also travel to other states, either on business or to see relatives as far away as New York. They can take a scenic route through Washington, Baltimore, and Philadelphia. Some people travel abroad. One group is going to Rome, Egypt and the Holy Land. There is also constant migratory movement of people in search of land and opportunity.

Whatever the prevailing national economic conditions, in the Fall of 1883 there is an abundance of foodstuffs from the farms in Jessamine County. The chief cash crops are tobacco and hemp, along with livestock. Farmland is selling for $15 to $35 per acre, tobacco for 12 cents per pound, and a "square" meal in a Lexington restaurant can be obtained for 35 cents.

Kentucky is 34th of the 38 states in literacy. Even so, the Female Institute has attracted the daughter of a Mississippi couple who visited her the past week. People who want to improve their knowledge can do so with the help of The Century magazine that features articles on architecture, religion, astronomy, outdoor England, novels and novelettes.

Weekly Courier Journal

The Courier is again being used to supplement the few issues of the Journal that are available during this period. It tells something about the customs of the time, and shows that travel times to distant places weren't all that bad!

January 18, 1884: This article pertains to etiquette for men, copied by the Courier from the New York World, that gives men some advice:
  Don't wear clothes that attract attention.
  Don't wear business clothes to an afternoon reception.
  Don't wear a white tie with anything but a dress suit.
  Don't wear much jewelry. Small gold studs are preferred. No diamonds.
  Don't smoke in the presence of ladies. Remove your cigar before bowing to a lady. It's questionable to smoke on the streets.
  Don't bow to a lady until she bows to you.
  Don't shake hands with a lady on your first introduction, unless she evidences a desire to do so.
  Don't call on a lady unless you have permission to do so.
  Don't make your calls or visits too long--one hour is long enough.
  Don't fail to send in your card on your first visit.
  Don't forget to raise your hat when you bow to a lady or an older gentlemen.
  Don't fail to answer all notes.
  Don't be late for a dinner party.

Don't drink too much wine, either at dinner, or later.
Don't express yourself ungrammatically.
Don't introduce business affairs into private conversations.
Don't discuss your likes and dislikes, and above all don't discuss your personal affairs.
Don't adopt affectations of speech. Don't boast. Don't swear.
Don't appear extravagant or miserly.
Don't show affection unless you are serious.
Be courteous and always respect the rights of others.

May 16, 1884: Rail transportation is pretty good by this time. This is one train schedule of the Cincinnati, New Orleans, and Texas Pacific Rail Road Company: Depart Nicholasville at 11:55am; arrive at Chattanooga at 9:10pm; arrive in Atlanta at 4:00am; and arrive in New Orleans at 8:50 pm. The next article is in the Jessamine Journal.

April 4, 1885

It is Spring, and there is great interest in the breeding season for horses. Many stallions are advertised, and there was an exhibition of several stallions in Nicholasville. There is interest in all kinds of horses: mules for work, saddle-horses, trotters that may have been used for buggies, or for sport, and thoroughbreds. The horse farms are south of town on the Danville Road, on the Chrisman Mill Road between Sulphur Well and Nicholasville, and along the Harrodsburg road. The times appear to be unsettled socially and economically. Saying that the land is overrun with tramps and criminals, an article summarizing a survey of men in prison, found that some were incarcerated for reasons relating to alcohol, others lacked education, but primarily they lacked a trade.

Mrs J E Nave of Danville visited her brother, Dr John C Miller, whose wife Nanie Rice died on April 15, 1885. Susan Miller Nave and John are children of Merriman Miller. Susan is buried in the family cemetary on the Miller farm.

June 19, 1885

The annual cost of food is incredibly low, being estimated at $4 billion for the country as a whole, or about $87 per person per year! Cans and canning is of recent origin. The food packed in this manner is of very poor quality. Tomatoes are said to be a few seeds floating in colored water. Peas, corn and succotash, known as "soaks", are as nutritious and palatable as wood chips. Meat already too old, and often diseased, when canned often caused nausea and stomach poisoning. The public is asking for protection, so legislation is being sought to protect consumers against dishonest manufacturers and merchants. The wheat crop for 1885 is expected to very poor, based upon wheat-growing states of the West and South.

A scene at the Lexington train depot is of children "gathered from the streets and garrets" being sent West to new homes.

## October 2, 1885

Times are unsettled. The editor proclaimes "We are in favor of convict labor.... These vagabonds around town need to be sold and we intend to give the grand jury the benefit of them". He also said that tramps have become such a nuisance that some days there would be four or five that visited houses in town begging food or money. He also laments that an escapee from the workhouse was arrested in Cynthiana and returned, saying it would have been better to leave him there and rid the county of such a character! A mob of twenty-seven masked men rode onto a Cynthianna man's farm and destroyed seventeen head of diseased cattle. The animals were then burned. While some in Pendleton County, believed to be the home of the mob members, wanted to make restitution, some leading citizens opposed it.

## November 13, 1885

Emigration, travel, clothing, food and entertainment, and the status of African-Americans are the topics of the week. The flow of emigrants through New York is very great. Most are destined for New York, Illinois, Michigan, Minnesota and Wisconsin.

From Spears: Lonzo Mitchell visited relatives in Texas, and came back by way of New Orleans to see the Exposition there.

It is Fall and time for winter clothing. The style for men and boys is a four-button, cutaway jacket. Those whose purchases are $15 get a Waterbury watch with their suit. I remember my grandfather, Luther Ware, sometimes asking me when I was a youngster "Ray, what does your Waterbury say?"

As to food, Smithwick's Confectionery and Bakery is the best in Nicholasville! It has homemade candies made daily including Boston chips, cream caramels, cream chocolate sticks and drops, and cocoanut bars. The bakery has fresh bread, and delicacies such as oysters direct from Baltimore, and a nice line of fruits, nuts and tobacco. They also cater weddings and other special events.

It is significant to note that some African-Americans are doing well. Lancaster has a colored lawyer and Harrodsburg a colored physician. Also, in Frankfort, local blacks have created a reading room to improve themselves.

## July 2, 1886

It's summer and the topics are weather, crops, clothing, and visiting. It has been a wet late Spring and early Summer. The wheat crop is better than expected, but some rust is experienced. At Little Hickman, a wind and rain storm leveled fields of corn and tobacco.

As July 4th approaches, merchants are anxious to sell their summer goods. One store featured satteens, French patterns, silk velvets, calico, India linen, ginghams, cottonade, summer jeans, and all wool summer cashmeres for boys in the dry goods department; chinele fringes, oriental flouncing laces, silk gloves, Kidd gloves, Lisle hose, bustle and dress steels, parasols, and corsets in the notions department; and in the shoe department there are opera slippers, Dongola Kidd button shoes, men's and boy's buttons with front lace, and Congress shoes.

Various towns are advertising their fairs. People are visiting friends and relatives in other towns or communities, and one family returned from Florida. Some are going to spas for a month, or other places for the summer.

In the Personals: "Mrs Frank Miller and her little son Forest of this county are visiting relatives in Estill." Her husband, Francis S Miller operated a store in Wisemantown for many years. It is not clear whether he retired, and returned to the family farm, bringing his wife and unmarried children with him; or if, following his death in March, 1885 that his widow decided to come live with her father-in-law, Merriman Miller, whose wife Celia had died three years earlier. In any case, one son, John Pink Miller continued to operate the store in Wisemantown. Another son and three daughters were married and living in Wisemantown or Irvine. One daughter remained a spinster and spent her life with relatives in both Estill and Jessamine County. The youngest daughter is Nannie Rose, who at this time is about sixteen, and unmarried. Forest is about fourteen. Francis S Miller (Frank) is buried in the family graveyard on the farm, not far from where the old house was located. Several other family members are buried there also. Frances M Miller received the farm of approximately 205 acres for service during the Revolutionary War. His son, Merriman, inherited the farm and operated it until his death. You can find a copy of the Miller family tree in one of the appendices, along with a list of the family members buried in the family cemetery on the farm. A family tree for the Hendren family is in the same appendix.

I have also prepared an index of names, logical to my way of thinking, for those who are familiar with Sulphur Well people. Women's married name appears first, followed by their maiden name, e.g. Miller, Scottie Hendren. There were innumerable decisions required because of juniors and seniors, middle initials, abbreviations, and nicknames. I mostly avoided Mrs except when the husband's name was used. I have maintained that religion was one of the most dominant influences on the life of people at this time. Therefore, the ministers are listed first as Brother, Elder, or Reverent. There are a lot of them! I also considered the Sulphur Well correspondent as a "person" and all his articles are indexed under that title. This is a good place to inform the reader that there is an appendix that summarizes a short biographical sketch about the most active families in Sulphur Well, and when they get lost in the hundreds of people that flow throught the story, they can refer to that appendix to reestablish family relationships.

## THE FIRST YEAR - 1887

The <u>Jessamine Journal</u> was destroyed by fire, so the first issue containing an article by the Sulphur Well correspondent was in 1887.

### February 18, 1887

Some insight into what city life in a small town is like can be seen by what they felt needed to be prevented. These are some of the by-laws and ordinances of the town of Nicholasville, which I have paraphrased:

> Hog pens, privies, and dead animals are declared public nuisances. Disorderly houses (prostitution) are prohibited. Public drunkenness is not allowed. No gum slings (sling-shots) are permitted. No fireworks are allowed within the city limits. Obscenity is prohibited. No slaughterhouses are allowed within one hundred yards of any residence. No fighting animals are permitted. Vagrants can be fined. No ballplaying in the court house yard is allowed. Breach of peace is subject to fine, as is disturbing religious worship. Throwing filth in the streets is not allowed. Hitching horses to trees is prohibited, as is allowing animals to be at large. Shooting anywhere in the city is subject to fine. Fast driving is not allowed, horses can only go at a trot. Standing stallions (breeding) in the streets is not permitted. Damaging lamp posts is an offence. Citizens are required to build sidewalks upon order. Saloons have to be licensed, and Sunday laws observed. p1c4

This gives the picture of people trying to do in the city the same things they had done in the country where there were fewer neighbors. It shows a lack of playground for youth, and a great deal of idleness among adults, at least on occasions such as Saturdays, Sundays, court days, holidays, and days when farm work was slow.

It is traditional for farmers to gather at general stores, or other public places where you can gather around a fire, or in good weather sit on a rock wall such as around the courthouse in Nicholasville, or around the pump at Sulphur Well. In such groups, there was always at least one person who liked to be the center of attention, usually talking in a loud voice, and telling one story after another, often to the embarrassment of someone present. It is probably in this context that from Little Hickman's J W Overstreet came a letter to the editor:

> While we were in your city last week it was circulated here that myself and wife had parted. The one who started the tale is an infamous liar.... I had started to Barboursville, Ky, to visit friends, but missed the train, and the next day I was out of the notion. p3c3

However, it may have originated with Overstreet himself because some years earlier, Mr Overstreet, who was deaf was reported to have offered to place $100 in escrow at the bank for a traveling "doctor" who claimed to have a cure for deafness, if he were indeed "cured".

Travel between communities is not always uneventful, and sometimes road conditions caused accidents. People complained that the turnpikes were in poor condition, saying that owners of pikes who extort such exorbitant revenue should keep the roads in safe condition. Nevertheless, people did travel a great deal by horse and buggy, and often made "flying trips" to other communities. My aunt, Edith Jesse, remembers on cold winter nights hearing horse hoofs hitting the frozen ground "a mile away".

This brings me to the first extant article of "The *Sulphur Well Correspondent*" reproduced below:

> Notwithstanding the bad weather our merchants are having a fair trade.
> 
> We are glad to see the Journal increase in size. May it live long and prosper.
> 
> Some of our farmers are through breaking hemp and a few have commenced ploughing for corn.
> 
> The election continues the subject of conversation, both sides claim their man to be in the lead.
> 
> There is much sickness in the community and our doctors are having all they can do.
> 
> Mr and Mrs Giles Saunders, after some months absence, have moved back to our village and gone to housekeeping in the Taylor property.
> 
> J H Murphy and J P Turner were in Lancaster several days last week attending Circuit Court.
> 
> Miss Ida Gray, accompanied by your correspondent, paid a flying visit last Saturday and Sunday, to Miss Mary Ray and other friends at Buckeye.
> 
> C J Taylor, the prince of drummers, was in Cincinnati last week, selecting his samples. He will leave in a few days on a trip to other counties.
> 
> J T Berry, of Madison, was here Monday and Tuesday on business.
> 
> Mr and Mrs John Bourne, of Garrard County, spent several days here this week visiting E E Bourne and other friends.
> 
> Mrs H C Hemphill, who has been sick for some time, is very low at present writing. p3c5 White Cloud

The correspondent called himself White Cloud. The correspondents frequently used pseudonyms in these days. Sometimes they seemed to have meaning, and other times the meaning, if any, was obscure. The correspondent this week accompanied Ida Gray to Buckeye to visit friends. Both appear to be single at this time. I will let the correspondent further indentify himself as time goes by. Ida Gray is the daughter of the local distilleryman, and Mary Ray is the daughter of a doctor in Buckeye. The Rays are a prominent family in that neighborhood.

February 25, 1887

J B Logan, evidently a turnpike operator, responded to the complaint of the previous week about one section of the turnpike as being unsafe by saying the road looked solid until it fell in, and that it was quickly filled in afterward. Also relating to last week: some boys ran afoul of the aforementioned ordinances of Nicholasville and were sentenced to the work house for being drunk and disorderly.

One public sale may not reveal the possessions of a typical farm family, but this what one farmer offered at public sale:

> All my private property consisting of 20 head of cattle, some of which are extra milch cows; stock hogs; one buggy mare safe for a lady; one well broke mule; buggy harness; one blue grass stripper; corn in the crib; and fine timothy hay. Also, the entire lot of household and kitchen furniture. p2c5

Some Jessamine crops may have been sent abroad. It was reported that German agents were in the county "for the purpose of purchasing corn, oats, and red winter wheat in large quantities." p2c4

There are published reports of patents. Apparently there is a great deal of research into the uses of electricity because many of the inventions are related. For example, patents that were granted included an electric heater; an engine governor; a reclining chair; a clothes drier; a corn harvester; a fruit picker; a saw guide and band saw mill; a spindle; a stove pipe crimper; and an electric clock.

An event occurred in the Miller family: "Last Tuesday at the home of her mother, Miss Rosa Miller and Andrew Sageser were married by Rev W W Spates. The couple left in the afternoon for a three weeks trip to Springfield, Illinois." p3c1 This was Nannie Rose, the youngest daughter of the late Francis S Miller and Elizabeth Jane Miller. The home referred to would be at the family farm now on Snowden Lane.

The above event was not reported by the *Sulphur Well Correspondent*, perhaps because he considered the lane off the Hoover Pike to be outside his district, or because he had a lot of other things to report. His report is as follows:

> *The election passed off very quietly here Saturday.*
> *Small grain looks well through this section. The farmers (are) expecting a large yield.*
> *Several loads of tobacco were weighed here last week to go to Henry Nichols near Hanley. The price paid was 4c.*
> *Eld. Black, of Lexington will preach here Saturday night and Sunday.*
> *Mrs H C Hemphill of whose sickness we spoke last week is still very low. She desires to return her thanks to those of the community who have shown her so much kindness during her illness.*
> *Mrs Sallie Saunders who has been very sick for several days we are glad to know is improving.*
> *After several days sickness Dr G M Hendren is able to be out again.*
> *Miss Sallie Woolfolk, of Buckeye, and Mr Clell Johnson, of Lancaster came over last Friday and spent several days with friends at this place.*
> *Miss Jennie Walker of Hanly, is visiting Mrs Wm Walker.*
> *Prof. George Burton, of Kirksville, has secured a three months school at this place and will commence on the 28th. From the recommendations Mr Burton brings we are satisfied the people have made a good selection.*
> *Joe Woodward, of Midway spent Saturday and Sunday among his many friends here. Joe seems to have a great fondness for his old home. Wonder if anybody can tell why it is?*

*Most of our farmers were in town Monday and heard the views of the different candidates for Governor. All we have heard express themselves are in favor of Hon. J D Harris as the man. We know Mr Harris personally and have no hesitancy in saying he is in every way fitted for the place and will give the people a good administration. We would be glad to see this county instruct for him as first choice.*

*J T Bright, of Louisville is visiting his brother W H Bright.    p2c2*

The Sulphur Well correspondent may know J D Harris by way of family connections in Madison, where Harris lived. Also, it is clear he has strong ties to Garrard County. It is probable that it is he that Miss Sallie Woolfolk of Buckeye and Clell Johnston of Lancaster came to visit. There are several variations of this name: Wm McC Johnston; McClellan Johnston; Wm McClellan Johnston. In any case, his name is Johnston, and perhaps the printer made an occasional error.

March 4, 1887

From events abroad to local politics. The Suez Canal is getting electric lights to facilitate night passage. In Washington, D.C. the Interstate Commerce Commission has just been authorized, and the President is seeking candidates for nomination to the Commission. One well-qualified candidate is concerned that the Commission will not be able to satisfy either the public or the railroads, and therefore appear incompetent.

Two Nicholasville entrepreneurs are trying to promote the building of a flour mill in time for the coming wheat harvest. The race for Senator in the district (Woodford, Scott, and Jessamine) is becoming heated, with five candidates in the race. And, from Jessamine Station the correspondent says that "politics is the all-absorbing question at this time." "Tariff, taxation ..., and other issues are discussed", he said, "but not one word is said in defense of our schools." He said that education of the children of the state had been neglected and Kentucky was near the foot of the class among the other states. p2c4

And, how were young ladies dressing these days? According to one source from Nicholasville, of the two prettiest ladies at the Danville hop the previous week, one wore black silk with jet trimmings and natural flowers, while the other wore blue velvet and natural flowers.

During the session of Circuit Court John Pink Overstreet "appointed a committee to take charge of Merriman Miller's estate." p2c3 Overstreet is Merriman's son-in-law, having married Sarah Miller. This is due to incompetency, more about this in July when he dies. During the same court proceeding the "Rev S Noland appointed a committee to manage the estate of Matilda Miller." p2c3 Matilda, later known as Aunt T, was somewhat hard of hearing, had a speech impediment, and perhaps was somewhat "slow". She is the granddaughter of Merriman.

So, on March 4, 1887, the *Sulphur Well Correspondent* writes:

*Several of our citizens are attending Bro. Bronston's meeting in Nicholasville this week.*
*Prof Burton opened his school Monday morning with good attendance. This is a good point to build up a first-class school and we think Prof. Burton the right man in the right place.*
*Elders Black and Neal preached to good congregations here Saturday night and Sunday.*
*J H Murphy has been right sick for several days, but some better at present.*
*W H Bright has moved to his residence recently vacated by Squire Stotts. The Squire has gone down on the river at Saunders Ferry.*
*John Taylor of Midway spent Sunday at home.*
*Misses Carrie and Mattie Woodward paid a visit to friends at Hanly and Camp Nelson last week.*
*Our friend, R A Mosley has a very large boil on his face. Bob says the first fellow that makes him laugh, gets a John L Sullivan lick.*
*J H Brumfield sold his fancy buggy mare to parties at Birmingham, Ala. for $200. p2c3*

The Russell's Cross Roads' correspondent signed himself "Black Cloud". A poke at the Sulphur Well correspondent who signed himself White Cloud the previous week, I suppose.

March 11, 1887

The period has been characterized by rapid change. One young man, on his twenty-sixth birthday commented on what had occurred within the span of his life time. He said:

> (He) was born just the day before the inauguration of Abraham Lincoln ... and have consequently lived through the greatest Civil War.... I have seen the population of the United States double, and seen them celebrate the 100th anniversary of the nation's independence. During my recollection four great Pacific railroads have spanned the continent, and the Atlantic cable had put the old and the new world in constant telegrapic communication. Slavery has been forever abolished. Two presidents have been assassinated.

He felt that the changes in the intellectual world had been even more impressive; that the sciences had been revolutized. He said that astronomers had learned more about the sun thought the use of the spectroscope in the past 25 years that in all the centuries previously. He believed that:

> Recent discoveries in chemistry, physiology, in microscopy, have materially altered our views of physical science. Archaelology, ethnology, and even ancient history have been remodeled by discoveries in recent times.

He said that "it would take all day" to enumerate all the inventions in the application of science to human industry. "The discoveries in electricity alone", he thought, were "enough to make the quarter century forever famous." p1c7

On March 11, 1887 the *Sulphur Well Correspondent* penned the following events:

*The desks for the new school house have arrived and been placed in. We have now one of the best arranged and most comfortable houses in the county.*

*Mat Cobb of this place and Benedict Baker near Lebanon have swapped farms. They moved Wednesday.*

*We neglected, unintentionally last week to mention the severe burning of Mr. and Mrs Henry Hare's little daughter Nannie.*

*It is with much regret that we announce this week the death of Mrs Ella Hemphill, which occurred after a long and painful sickness at the residence of her husband H. C. Hemphill on Sunday morning. She leaves a husband and three small children with numerous other friends to mourn her loss.*

*Clell Johnston of Lancaster came over last Saturday on business and to bid his many friends at this place good bye. He left Monday morning for Birmingham, Ala., to make that place his future home. We wish him success in his new field of labor.*

*C.T. Taylor returned from a trip to several other counties, and reports good sales. He says the general outlook for business is encouraging.*

*Mrs Annie Wagner, of Maysville, is visiting her mother Mrs Wm Hendren.*

*Miss Mary Ray and brother Bronson, visited Misses Texie and Ida Gray and other friends. Miss Texie returned home with them Monday morning for a two weeks visit.*

*On the 8th inst., the Sulphur Well vagrant's club was called together in secret session to pass resolutions on the loss of two of its most prominent members, Squire Arch Stotts and Mat Cobb, whose presence now loom up elsewhere. From what your correspondent can learn the Club is getting in a fearful shackled condition of late. It is also rumored on our streets that there will be a sale at public outcry of the remainder of this order in a few weeks. We are glad to report the sick of our community improving.* p3c5

The Sulphur Well correspondent overlooked some personal items pertaining to the Miller Family, that were considered noteworthy by the correspondent from Cosey Corner. "Mr Andrew Sageser and bride (nee Miller) have returned from their wedding trip to Illinois...." p3c5 "Mrs E Miller and son Forest left Wednesday for Estill County to visit relatives." p3c5

March 18, 1887

An advertisement of Wolf & Butler gives some indication of economic activity in Nicholasville and surrounding communities. They offer to "pay cash for hemp, wool, cattle, sheep, hogs, wheat, corn, oats, etc." and offer to sell, for cash, "coal, lime, cement, salt, shingles, and various other articles." p1c1

The *Sulphur Well Correspondent*, on March 18, 1887 writes:

*The nice weather of the last week put our farmers to work.*
*Our colored friends are preparing to build a school house here this spring.*
*Elder Wright preached at this place several nights last week.*
*Charley Horine paid a visit to Buckeye Sunday. He seemed to be highly pleased with his trip.*
*Frank Rettig went to Midway Tuesday.*
*Miss Julia Hare has gone on a two weeks' visit to friends and relatives at Keene.*
*Miss Carrie Woodward spent last week in Nicholasville.*
*Frank Horine shipped about 300 bushels of rye to Cincinnati this week to be put on the market.*
*N.D. Davis and George S Diamond attended court at Lexington Monday. They report business very dull.*
*Mrs M.W. Spruce is having her store room ceiled and making other improvements.*
*Mrs Dr Hendren visited her parents near Watts Mill, Sunday. p2c3*

## March 25, 1887

Apparently Kentuckians, and perhaps, mid-westerners and southerners alike have always felt an antipathy toward New York. A dispatch from New York containing an interview with Mr E J Curley, a distiller from Kentucky, quoted him as saying:

> Do you know this is one of the most un-American cities in America? Its people have no great love of country, and patriotism with them is measured by what it will pay....New York may be classed as the vulture. It cares nothing for the West except to pluck it. Its representatives have opposed invariably the River and Harbor Bill. This because the West rather than the East, is the beneficiary of the bill.

He concluded: "They want everything going out of the country to pass throught their hands, as well as everything coming into it." p3c3 The goals of the east and the other parts of the country were clearly at odds.

Every part of the country wants to grow and be prosperous, even Nicholasville, a town that has stagnated for over one hundred years. The editor of the <u>Jessamine Journal</u> is forever mentioning the successes of other towns and cities, calling them booms, and beseeching entrepreneurs to step forward. One perceptive farmer wrote a letter stating why he thought Nicholasville would never grow. He said there was nothing in Nicholasville to boom with. There was "no business, and no prospects of business." And, he said, "those who have a little money have no enterprise". He said that there were good churches and schools, but nothing else. p2c4 The farmer may have been right, for many letters and reports back from former residents who went on to other cities, particularly Birmingham and Dallas, wrote back, telling, usually in superlatives, about opportunities that they found.

Life in these days seems to revolve around court days and religion. Court days are important days for buying and selling horses and other livestock, and quoted prices are readily obtainable. For example "last Monday was court day. Cattle sold a little higher than usual. Horses $50-100; cows and calves from $25-100; hogs 5c a pound." p2c2 While Dr Welsh was away Dr J L Wilds, "the successful and genial doctor from Ambrose" took care of his practice.p2c4 Dr Wilds took the opportunity on court day to purchase a harness-broken four year old colt. p2c2 A humorous, but perhaps pathetic, example of the importance of religion was this note:" John Wait, aged 70, got a divorce from his wife of 50 years. "He was a Methodist, she a Baptist, which was the cause." p2c3

So, in this day and age, the *Sulphur Well Correspondent* writes his commentary:

*Miss Texie Gray has returned from a visit to Garrard.*
*J.F. Horine and lady spent Sunday with friends at this place.*
*Elder Black, of Lexington, will preach here Saturday night and Sunday.*
*W. Grant Berry, representing the boot and shoe firm of F.G. Ringgold & Co., Cincinnati, was in our village Monday.*
*Horace Turner is on the sick list this week, and is not able to attend school.*
*Will Hendren, Jr., spent Sunday at Buckeye. It seems as though some of our boys have taken a great fancy to that place of late.*
*Miss Mary Ray paid us a short call Monday on her way to and from Nicholasville.*
*We are glad to see Mrs T J Horine out again after several day's illness.*
*C T Taylor will leave for Cincinnati next Monday, to be absent three or four weeks.*
*H S Parks and W T Walls, candidates for State Senator, were in our village last Friday presenting their claims to the voters.*
*Madam Rumor says there will be two or three weddings in this community at an early day.*
*A certain young man living in the suburbs of our place sat on the fence all day Monday without dinner waiting for his girl, who lives over the river, to return from Nicholasville. Poor fellow, he left just a few moments too soon.p2c5*

The fence, in all probability, is a rock fence adjacent to the Sulphur Well pump, that is fairly low, with large flat stones, that always was a favorite "loafing" place. It is located at the junction of the Elm Fork road and Ky Highway 39 that passes through Sulphur Well, crosses the river at Paint Lick, and leads to Buckeye, and Lancaster.

One last note, again perhaps considered outside Sulphur Well proper since this would be at the farm on what is now Snowden Lane."On Monday, at the residence of Mrs Frank Miller, Mr Samuel Tillett was married to Miss Jane Hunt, Rev T J Overstreet officiating." p2c2

## April 1, 1887

Not much occuring at this time except farmers beginning spring activities. Visiting, especially on Sunday, is always in season. Undoubtedly, the changing seasons promotes interest in new clothes. The fashion for young men includes "Cheviot suits in 4-button cutaways", with either straight or round cut sacks. Said to be the "nobbiest suits made"! Hats, with either soft or stiff brims are in style. p2c6-7

Thus, it is when the *Sulphur Well Correspondent* writes:

> *Farmers say the heavy rains of two weeks have done much damage to the wheat crop.*
> *Gardening was in full blast last week.*
> *Measles are prevailing to a considerable extent in our neighborhood.*
> *Mary Saunders, colored, died on the 26th inst., of typhoid fever, aged about 30 years.*
> *Robert Masters of Midway spent Sunday and Monday with his many friends at this place.*
> *Miss Carrie Woodward is spending the week in Nicholasville.*
> *Miss Julia Hare has returned from a visit to friends and relatives at Keene.*
> *Mrs Wm. Hoover, Jr., returned home Sunday after a visit of several weeks to her parents.*
> *Mr and Mrs Richardson of Irvine, returned home Monday after a visit of several days to Mrs Frank Miller near this place.*
> *J T and W H Bright attended court at Lancaster Monday. They reported business fair.*
> *Mrs Sallie Saunders is still confined to bed.*
> *C T Taylor left for Cincinnati Monday.*
> *Mrs Hattie Davis attended church here Sunday.*
> *Capt. J P L Jennings, of Cincinnati, was here buying cattle.*
> *Mrs Jessie Terhune, of Mercer County, is on a visit to her parents, Mr and Mrs Jas. Woodward.*
> *Most of the hemp in this community is ready for market.*
> *Miss Emma Dorman, one of Nicholasville's most charming young ladies spent Sunday and Monday with Misses Texie and Ida Gray. p3c5*

There is no question that Texie and Ida Gray are the swinging singles of the day. They receive visits from other young ladies from Nicholasville and Buckeye, and, apparently young men from all over. According to the 1880 Census, Texie would be about 21 at this time, and Ida about 19. They are the oldest of six children of George Gray, who was born in North Carolina, and a distiller by trade.

A measle epidemic generally prevailed, not just in Sulphur Well, but was reported to be serious in other communities as well. While thought of as a child's disease, it can be fatal.

In other notes, two young ladies that will in years to come be connected to the Miller family are also visiting: "Misses Scottie and Bertha Hendren, of Lexington, who have been visiting their sister, Mrs Adam Adcock, of this place (Nicholasville), for several days, returned home Sunday." p3c4 Scottie is to marry Forest Miller several years later.

From Cosey Corner: "Mr Wm Richardson and wife accompanied by Mrs Lucy Snowden and children of Estill County, are guests of Mrs Frank Miller. On last Thursday, G B Taylor sold his house and farm to Andrew J Sageser."p3c4 Andrew and Nannie Rose just married in February, two months previously. Also, Susan (Aunt Sudie) Miller Richardson, Lucy Miller Snowden, and Nannie Rose are all daughters of Mrs Francis S Miller (Elizabeth Jane).

April 15, 1887

A man one hundred years ahead of his time! He claims:
> I am a firm believer in woman suffrage. Women preachers edify me, women lecturers delight me, women doctors thrill me, women telephone clerks enchant me, and women barbers are to me a source of fifteen-cent joy. Women's rights should be respected. In the pulpit and in tights, before the bar and behind it, woman must have her place....however, in the name of humanity and eyes, I must protest--the right of women to carry umbrellas! Supplement, p1c5

Against this background, the *Sulphur Well Correspondent* writes:

*Miss Lena Bright, of Lancaster, is visiting friends and relatives at this place.*
*Mrs Moseley and friends of Missouri are visiting Mrs W H Hare.*
*Farmers are busy planting corn.*
*Newton Davis sold last week a lot of fat hogs at five cents.*
*Mr and Mrs Hare's little daughter Nannie who was burned sometime since is still quite sick.*
*The measles have about gone the rounds in this community and the children are all now back in school.*
*W H Bright felled a large tree in his yard Monday, and in falling some limbs struck the front of his house doing considerable damage.*
*A Sunday School was organized here last Sunday with Prof. Geo. Burton, Superintendant, Will Hendren, Secretary and Treasurer, Miss Carrie Woodward, Mrs M W Spruce, Mrs W H Bright, and Frank Rettig as teachers. We look for a good work in this direction as it was badly needed.*
*The turnpike from this place to Hanley will soon be completed.*
*J H Murphy was at Wilmore this week surveying the route for a new turnpike.p3c4*

The Correspondent again signed as "White Cloud".

There are two more family notes to record. "Mrs Adam Adcock visited her parents at Lexington this week." p3c3 This was Scottie's sister visiting Will D and Levisa Hendren. They lived in (rented) what is now the Bank of the Bluegrass building. Their mother died in 1889, and their father went to Nicholasville to live with Addie Adcock until his death in 1891. This is how Scottie came to be in Nicholasville. It was her mother's death and their leaving Lexington that kept her from using a scholarship to attend college in Lexington. She always said that she attended Dudley School from the time that she was six until she was sixteen. She would have been about fourteen at this time.

Dr Hendren practices medicine in Sulphur Well, and Will Hendren, his brother, is mentioned by the correspondent in the above article. Their father William Hendren, and Scottie's grandfather Harrison Hendren are brothers.

And from Canton, near Little Hickman: "Dr John Miller spent Sunday with his brother-in-law, Mr P Overstreet, at this place." p3c4 Pink Overstreet and his wife Sarah Miller and her brother, John Miller, are children of Merriman Miller. Dr John Miller has a successful practice and is a noted horse breeder. He has a standard-bred stallion by the name of

Graftonian. Pink Overstreet has a general store, and is the postmaster of the area that became known as "Pink".

April 29, 1887

This is a period when politics, religion, social disorder, and economics are of concern. Sometimes this comes out in the form of humor, sometimes in rather stark reports. The people seem to like tall tales. Freak occurrences are reported routinely, almost in Robert Ripley manner, so that it is really difficult to know when an article is tongue in cheek or factual. Lacking libraries, some people apparently like to read serialized stories. These stories involve (pseudo?) sophisticated people in large cities, even foreign countries, behaving in very soap-opera ways. Their interest in showing and maintaining their cultural attainments is demonstrated by the presence of Shakespearian groups in small farm communities. They are great believers in education, and respect those who become educated. They like nice things, home furnishings, clothes, and buggies. They like politics, want to know who the announced candidates are, and where they will speak. State political meetings are reported and there is a weekly correspondent in Washington. They have a great curiosity, and care little for others privacy in such matters. Apparently, everyone knows the price people receive when they sell houses, farms, and horses. They visit a lot, particularly the ladies and young folk. There are a lot of family visits, week-end, or for the week. Many people have migrated to other states, and they come back for visits periodically.

The (current) editor of the Jessamine Journal is someone who could bring a cosmopolitan perspective to the paper. John Kerr, editor of the Journal in 1887, was born in Canton, China. He came to America, went to school in San Francisco, then entered Wooster University. He worked for the Pittsburg Post, the Chicago Times, and the Cincinnati Post before coming to Nicholasville.

During this period of what one author has called "The Robber Barons", were the railroad builders, the bankers, the steel makers, and the oil tycoons. One of this number was Jay Gould. His "prayer" went like this:

> Our father who art in England, Rothchild be thy name; thy kingdom come to America; thy will be done in the United States as it is in England; give us this day our bonds in gold, but not in silver; give us plenty of laboring men's votes to keep monopoly in power and its friends in office. We know, our father, that we have done many things that were wrong; we have robbed the honest poor, and brought distress to many a door; we know that it was wrong to refund the bonds and make them payable in coin; we know it was wrong to water our railroad stock, but thou knowest that we made money by that. Now, our father, thou knowest we are above politics, it is the same with us whether Democrat or Republican rule, for thou knowest we are able to sway all parties in our favor. Lead us not in the way of strikers, and above all things deliver us from the hands of the Knights of Labor. Thus shall we have the kingdom, bonds, interest, power and gold until the republic shall end. Amen. p1c4

There was also time to poke fun at religion, as the following story (paraphrased) shows: The old missionary returned to a community after many years of absence. He accused the people of having lapsed back into paganism. The chief replied that after the missionary left, that a Catholic came and told them how bad Methodist were, so they converted to Catholicism. Then, the priest went away and a Presbyterian came along who told them about regeneration, adoption, and election, so they became Presbyterians. Then a Episcopalian arrived, and they burned their Westminsters and began using prayerbooks. After he left, a Baptist landed and walked everyone into the water and baptised them right. Then a New Congregationalist came along, and told them that as long as they were heathen that they were a dead cinch for Heaven, but that if they became Christians that they would have to walk the straight and narrow or go to an everlasting bonfire. So they ate him, burned the bibles, and returned to the old life. The old chief turned to the tribe and said "put the parson in the cage and fatten him up for Thanksgiving Day!" p1c6

May 6, 1887

There being little news the *Sulphur Well Correspondent* writes:

*Our farmers are considerably behind in corn planting, owing to the bad weather for the past two weeks.*
*We are glad to report but little sickness in our neighborhood at present.*
*Considerable damage was done by the high waters week before last in this community.*
*The new church known as Elm Fork, two or three miles from this place will be dedicated next Sunday. Dinner on the grounds and everyone cordially invited.*
*Misses Ida Gray, Lulie Spruce and Maggie Masters attended church at Lebanon Sunday.*
*Misses Carrie and Mattie Woodward are spending the week with friends in Nicholasville.*
*Eld. Grider of the Methodist church will preach here next Sunday night.*
*J H Murphy is at Camp Nelson this week surveying the Scott estate.*
*Mrs Wilds of Garrard, is visiting her son, Dr J L Wilds at this place.*
*Frank Horine is on duty this week as storekeeper at Gray's distillery.*
*Many thanks Mr Editor for the kind invitation to your wedding. May long life, happiness and prosperity be yours. p3c4*

May 13, 1887

Politics, religion, and the aftermath of the Civil War: Gen. Simon Bolivar Buckner is the Democratic nominee for governor of Kentucky, after State Senator Harris yielded his own nomination, and seconded that of the General. There was criticism from Columbus, Ohio denouncing the Democrats of Kentucky for nominating an ex-Confederate instead of an ex-Union soldier.p2c2 And, from the Richmond Register, a report that "the place is overrun by lazy negroes who have become a positive nuisance on the streets." The editor of the Jessamine Journal said "we are sorry to say Nicholasville is infested with the same nuisance." p3c6

More on religion: A Sunday School teacher told her pupils that as they put their pennies in the collection box, they should repeat a suitable Bible verse. The first dropped in his money saying "The Lord loves a cheerful giver". The second said "He that giveth to the poor lendeth to the Lord." The last little boy dropped in his penny saying "A fool and his money are soon parted." p4c3

The *Sulphur Well Correspondent* reports on May 13, 1887:

*Born to the wife of Lee Terhune, a son, James Isaac; also to the wife of Will Clark, a daughter.*
*Our efficient Surveyor, J H Murphy, has been kept busy for the last two weeks surveying turnpikes, etc.*
*Frank Rettig left Wednesday for a visit of several days to to his home at Louisville.*
*Miss Texie Gray spent several days last week with friends in Nicholasville.*
*A large crowd was in attendance at the dedication of the new church at Elm Fork, Sunday. Only about $20.00 of the debt which amounted to $118.00 was raised. Eld. O J Young preached the sermon.*
*C T Taylor left, Wednesday, for a business trip to other counties.*
*J P Turner attended the Republican Convention at Louisville, this week.*
*The very many friends here of Bronson Ray regret very much to hear of his serious illness.*
*Several of our young people attended the Indian show this week. Some of them are anxious to buy the short horn cow which two young men milked so gracefully, Tuesday night. p3c4-5*

May 20, 1887

Front page love - romantic, illicit, and perhaps unrequited: First, a classic romantic love story: "A Noble Girl's Love" set in the 1860's. A young man from the East, taking a "tour of recreation" from his study of law, finds his way to a boarding house in San Francisco. He is greatly fatigued, and takes his meals in his room. However, the daughter of the matron plays the piano each night in the parlor, and one evening he hears a beautiful, yet sad and poignant voice accompanying the piano. He is immediately drawn to meet the owner of the "voice". He becomes infatuated, and sees her daily. "One moonlight evening, when the stars studded the vaulted heaven with wonted brilliancy and bracing breezes stole softly through the trees and flowers..." he declares his love, and kisses her madly. She responds and he says "You will be my wife!". She gently disengages herself saying "that can never be...at the same time sobbing bitterly, as if in deep anguish." p1c2-5

At the other end of the spectrum the tragedy of illicit love, one affair involving race, the other righteous anger, and the resulting gossip: "Tom Crittenden, who killed the negro Rose Mosby, has at last been acquitted. The circumstances of the tragedy are well known and the verdict of the jury cannot fail to excite general comment."p1c5 Then there was "Jessie Buckner, who became noted for causing Congressman Phil Thompson to kill Davis as his wife's seducer, is now in a house of ill fame in Cincinnati."p1c5

The race for governor is in full sway. The platform of the Democratic Party in Kentucky, paraphrased, includes: support for honest money, i.e. gold and silver, and convertible paper currency; it views with alarm the growing tendency to seek the aid and bounty of the federal government; it denounces the present war tariff as a masterpiece of injustice; it supports reclaiming one hundred million acres of land granted to the railroads; it believes in the freedom of labor, and that working men should be protected against the oppression of monopolies; it wants laws to facilitate the collection and dissemination of information relating to the interest of labor; and it opposes importation of low cost labor from abroad. This seemed to be a rather broad statement of principles for a small, inland Commonwealth such as Kentucky, but this is how it was on May 20, 1887. p4c1-2

## May 27, 1887

School is ending for the year, some seasonal jobs ended while others began, and it was time to change to lighter clothing. The Jessamine Female Institute announced its commencement exercises. Men have the choice of rolling sacks, 4-button and 3-button cutaways, straight-front sacks, and single or double breasted Prince Albert suits. For summer there are black alapaca coats, moleskin pants, cottonade pants, seersucker coats and vests; hats either stiff or soft, and for summer there is straw. The stiff hats are in gold, coffee and cinnamon colors. p4c1-5 For the women there is a new stock of spring millinery, flowers, feathers, ornaments, trimmings, and all novelties in millinery. p2c6-7

While some trade is slow, cattle sales are pretty good. In Cincinnati fair to good cattle are selling for $4.00 to $4.35 per hundred-weight, and extra good cattle bring between $4.50 and 4.75. p4c2

Natural gas is not unknown in these times, but has largely been ignored in the past as this story from Jessamine Station indicates. Apparently natural gas is close to the surface in some instances. The correspondent says that his father told him of the story of workers blasting a (water) well (perhaps a cistern) on the property of the Female Academy, that caught fire and burned for several days. It was subsequently walled up and abandoned, because there was little importance attached to natural gas in those days. p3c4

In this context the *Sulphur Well Correspondent* on May 27, 1887 writes:

> *Our merchants say that trade is rather dull at present.*
> *Last Sunday was show day with the ladies, also with some of the boys who have new suits.*
> *The fine rains we have had the past few days were badly needed.*
> *The Distillery ware-house of Geo. S Gray was broken into last Sunday night by unknown parties, and several gallons of whisky taken.*
> *J H Murphy and J W Baker have about forty head of the finest cattle we have seen this season. They are sold to Cincinnati parties at 4 1/2 to be delivered the 1st of June.*
> *Joe Woodward, Robert Masters and John Taylor have returned from Midway, where they have been the past ten months working in the distillery of S J Greenbaum.*
> *The young folks had quite a pleasant little croquet party at this place on last Saturday evening.*
> *Elbert Walker and Willie Gray made a flying visit to Buckeye, Sunday.*
> *Ed Jackman, of Louisville, and Mr Stone, of Midway, spent several days last week visiting friends at this place.*

*Prof George Burton closed his school here on last Friday and left for home, Monday morning. The professor is a model teacher, and made many warm friends while in our midst. Come back soon to see us, George. Somebody seems very lonely since you left.*

*There is talk of organizing a stock company and boring for natural gas at this place. From the indications there is evidently gas at no great depth, and we think it the duty of our citizens to take the matter in hand at once.*

*Mr Fred Burton, of Kirkville, spent Saturday and Sunday in our village. p3c4*

June 3, 1887

This is the time for strawberry and ice cream suppers! The ladies are wearing black Lisle hose and gloves, and carrying silk umbrellas with gold handles. Politics is still in the air with frequent references to the two political parties and their candidates. There are also other single issue parties such as the Prohibitionist.

Sickness is a perpetual concern. Measles are especially bad. It appears that the doctors that serve Sulphur Well are quite good. Dr Wiles was called to Danville to assist in an operation there. It was said that he "was rapidly enlarging his practice, and, at the same time rising to the top of his profession!" p3c5

June 17, 1887

The Lexington barbecue kicking off the Democratic campaign for state offices drew 15,000 people from all over the state. Almost all the leaders and orators were present. The meeting began at 10 am with the band playing "My Old Kentucky Home." The Democratic candidate for governor, Gen Buckner then spoke for two hours!p2c1

So the *Sulphur Well Correspondent* writes:

*Some of our farmers are harvesting this week.*
*Murphy and Baker are overhauling their engine and separator preparatory to threshing wheat.*
*Geo. W Gray has sold his farm at this place to Andrew Sageser for $4,000 cash, possession to be given by Sept. 1st. Mr Gray thinks of moving to Tennessee.*
*Some of our boys attended the barbecue at Lexington, Wednesday.*
*Elder Grider, of the Methodist Church, preached here Sunday night.*
*Miss Texie and Ida Gray attended the wedding of their cousin, Miss Ollie V Hughes, to Mr Will Peel, on Thursday of last week.*
*Misses May and Clay Moseley, accompanied by their brother Forrest Moseley, of Louisville, are visiting Miss Julia Hare this week.*

This ties in with the sale of the Gray farm to Andrew Sageser, who had recently married Nannie Rose Miller. I have not yet fixed the location of the farm. p3c5

There are two items from the Buckeye Correspondent about people of whom the Sulphur Well correspondent often writes. One concerned Texie Gray visiting the Rays of Buckeye. The other was that Bronson Ray was still confined to bed without prospect of a quick recovery.p3c4-5 The nature of the illness was never indicated. A buggy ride over to Buckeye was not really very distant, but the climb up from the river, particularly on the Buckeye side, was pretty steep. The river has pretty good palisades in the Paint Lick area.

June 24, 1887

Politics became bloody in Rowan County. The Rowan County "war" originated with the election of 1884 when the ticket was split between Republicans and Democrats. The sheriff was a Republic and the Morehead city marshall, the county attorney, and others were Democrats. Finally, the sheriff resigned and the Democrats led by Craig Tolliver, took over the county. They were a criminal element and terrorized the entire area. A posse of approximately 300 men from several counties surrounded the town and a shoot-out occurred at the train depot. This ended the "war" and the citizens resolved to settle their disputes peaceably. p2c2

In Jessamine, the political battles were not just between Republicans and Democrats. "Never before in the history of this county have politics been more mixed up that at present. With a Republican, a Prohibitionist and a Henry George candidate to fight...." p2c1 And, that didn't include the "Union Labor Party" that also selected a slate of candidates.

Summer also brings the Chatauqua. The Chatauqua began in 1873 on the shores of the lake located just south of Erie as an outdoor Sunday School Institute, and quickly became known throughout the world. It was the greatest educational movement of that day, for it had 150,000 students enrolled in the Chatauqua Literary and Scientific Circle. The Chatauqua appealed to no sect or class. It was said to include "college presidents and servant girls, men 80 years old, and boys and girls...." It combined education and religion. p3c3

Merchants are attempting to close out their summer clothes to make room for the new fall stock. Women have the opportunity to acquire clothes at sale prices. There are lawns (thin cotton or linen fabrics) of black organdy and plain black; white crepe, white check muslins, and nainsooks (soft, lightweight cotton). There are chimizette collars, ribbon and crepe rushing, gauze underwear, summer corsets, silk and lace mitts, and fine hosiery. There are also box robe suits, plain and checked serges, and beige's with braid and buttons to match. p3c7

At the same time that wheat is being harvested in Kentucky there was wild speculation in the grain market in Chicago. "There was an extraordinary break in the price of wheat at Chicago last week, and financial disaster overtook the great clique. The decline of June wheat was twenty cents per bushel at one time...the most sensational collapse seen in that market in its history." It was said that sixteen million bushels of grain was being held by a mysterious combination of speculators. The wheat had to be sold "under the hammer", and several of the brokerage houses announced the suspension of trading. The effects also were felt closer home. "In consequence of the wheat speculation the Fidelity National

Bank of Cincinnati closed its doors Tuesday.... This is the outcome of investing money in the wheat gambling business at Chicago." p2c1

There may have been little local attention when it started, but something occurred with long run effects upon the transportation links between Sulphur Well and Kirksville (in southern Madison County) and Buckeye (in southern Garrard County). "Beattyville, the mountain town where the forks of the Kentucky meet, is reported to be on a young boom. Locks and dams are being built across the river...." As the dams and locks proceeded, the river became less easy to cross and in fewer places. There were regular ferries at Hunters Ferry and Paint Lick to reach these areas.

During the busy week preceeding June 24, 1887 the *Sulphur Well Correspondent* writes:

*Harvest is about over in our community. The wheat crop is not so heavy as was expected.*
*W H Bright has the finest prospect for water melons we have seen this season.*
*Miss Carry Woodward will teach school at Pleasant Hills, about two miles below this place.*
*Dr B Johns and sister, Miss Mattie, of Pleasureville, Henry county, are visiting their sister, Mrs N D Davis.*
*Walter Hendron (sic) left last Saturday for a three weeks's visit to friends and relatives at Cincinnati.*
*George Myers, of Clinton, Illinois, is visiting friends and relatives in the community.*
*George Burton, of Kirksville, spent Saturday and Sunday with his many friends here. He has secured the public school at this place and will commence about the middle of July.*
*Charley Horine and Frank Rettig visited friends in Madison and attended the commencement at Berea College this week. p3c5*

Walter Scott Hendren is a brother of Dr Hendren.

July 1, 1887

How the Hard Times Began. "In the United States the phenomena antecedent to the crisis were enumerated at the time to be `a rise of prices, great prosperity, large profits, high wages and strikes for higher; large importations, a railway mania, expanded credit, over-trading, over-building, and high living.' The failure began on the 17th of September 1873, by the failure of a comparatively unimportant railway company...", then by a bank and a succession of bankruptcies, and finally the default of railway bonds totalling over $789 million. p4c2

Locally, the weather is a factor, with an unusually dry June. In Little Hickman the wheat harvest is over and not very good. Very little tobacco has been put out and its survival is low. The continued dry weather is taking its toll on crops.p3c5

The *Sulphur Well Correspondent* writes:

*Murphy and Baker started their separator last Monday.*
*Eld. Cunningham preached to good congregations here Sunday morning and night.*
*Eld. Geo T Walden, of Lexington, will begin a protracted meeting at this place on the second Sunday in July.*
*Miss Viola Davis has been very sick with measles for some days, but is somewhat improved at present.*
*Misses Minnie and Carrie Prather, of Spearsville, spent Sunday with Mrs N D Davis.*
*Misses Cora and Lena Buley, of near Louisville, are visiting their aunt, Mrs J P Turner.*
*Mrs Wm Walker is on the sick list this week.*
*Miss Emma Quinn and Miss Lizzie Masters attended church here Sunday.*
*Miss Lulie Spruce is visiting friends at Hanly.*
*Robert Masters and John Taylor returned Monday from Shelbyville where they went to attend the wedding of Mr Ed Jackman.*
*Andrew Sageser has moved into our village and occupies part of the house which he recently purchased from Mr Gray.*
*Elbert Masters, Ham Dozier and Walter Bain, three of Nicholasville's fashionable dudes, seem to have a great fondness for our place. Can any one explain why?.*
*Miss Sybie Wilds paid a visit to this place last Monday. p3c5-6*

July 8, 1887

This has all to do about crops, weather, prices, and entertainment. The Journal carried a full list of all the towns having fairs from August to October. The Madison County Fair features trotting and running races each day. Crops are adversely affected by the lack of rain during the spring and early summer. It has reduced the wheat crop by as much as one-half in some communities, it is hurting corn and hemp, and the small amount of tobacco that had been set is doing poorly. To add to the farmers' woes of wheat short-falls, the prices are so low that some farmers are holding back their wheat for higher prices.

The Fourth of July holiday has just come and gone, apparently without much celebration! According to the Journal, the banks closed for the day, which was a Monday; a few fire-crackers were set off; but only the colored people of Nicholasville celebrated in a demonstrative manner.p3c2 Things must have been just as quiet in the communities, because not a single correspondent noted the holiday! However, people are ready for what may be called "religious entertainment". High Bridge plans a "camp meeting" featuring good scenery, walks, dining hall, evangelists, and the "best" in vocal and instrumental music.

So, the *Sulphur Well Correspondent*, on July 8, 1887 writes:

*Blackberry gathering in season.*
*J H Murphy has adopted the cash system in his merchandise business.*
*The dry weather has done considerable damage to the hemp crop in this part of the country.*
*Butler Giboney and family have returned from Wichita, Kansas, and are visiting friends in the community.*

*Mr and Mrs Taylor spent Sunday and Monday with relatives and friends in Lexington.*
*Miss Jennie Parrish and mother, of Cave City, are visiting Miss Julia Hare, at this place, and other relatives in the county.*
*Mrs Askins, of Bryantsville, visited Mrs W H Bright last week.*
*Miss Mamie McTyre spent Sunday in our village.*
*Mrs Dr Wilds, accompanied by Miss Sybell, left Tuesday for East Burnstadt to be benefitted by the springs and to visit relatives.*
*Eld. Walden will begin his meeting here on next Sunday.  p3c5*

July 15, 1887

Nothing but politics, and visiting. Another barbecue in Cynthiana; a rather inflammatory speech in Camp Nelson intended to arouse the colored people of that area to vote Republican. According to the correspondent from Windom: "Political chat can be heard at any time and any place in this community." p3c4

All the correspondents are reporting the visiting going on. The young ladies are making themselves known in other communities, the young men flocked to the pretty girls, and relatives are getting together.

This is what the *Sulphur Well Correspondent* has to say:

*The wheat crop is short about one-third.*
*Elder Walden failed to reach here Sunday according to appointment, but came Monday and is now preaching to crowded houses. The meeting will continue through this week and next. Elder Stanley filled the pulpit Sunday.*
*Mr George Gray and family moved to Lexington Wednesday to make that place their future residence. They have many friends here who regret very much to give them up, but wish them great success in their new home.*
*Miss Carrie Woodward began her school Monday at Elm Fork.*
*Clell Johnston, of Lancaster, spent Saturday and Sunday in our village, seeing the girls.*
*Miss Mary Ray is visiting friends here this week.*
*Miss Sallie Alverson, of Hanly, is visiting Miss Ola Davis.*
*Misses May and Ella Wheeler, of Cincinnati, accompanied by their mother, are visiting friends in this community.*
*Miss Emma Turner is visiting her uncle, J P Turner.*
*George Myers left for his home at Clinton, Ill., Thursday.*
*Miss Lizzie Masters is visiting her aunt, Mrs Wm. Walker.  p3c4*

There was no mention of the reason for the Grays selling their farm, but it was probably caused by the overproduction of whisky at the time. The distillers have agreed to suspend production for one year. This apparently put Gray out of business.

July 22, 1887

The weather, "dull" times, and credit. The weather is a chief topic of conversation. From Spears "It was never as hot here as it is now." p3c3 "There is less water and more toad frogs about here now than was ever known before." p3c4 And from Harrodsburg: "Thermometer 104 Sunday." p3c4 Wheat sales are down a third, crops are suffering, and merchants are having a hard time collecting their accounts. Settlement days are January 1 and July 1. The merchants "carried" accounts until July 1st, and several are publishing notices that they will sue if not paid immediately. J H Murphy, Sulphur Well store-keeper went on a cash basis the past week.

So, the *Sulphur Well Correspondent* writes on July 22, 1887:

> *Born--To the wife of T H Horine, a son. Tom is the happiest fellow in town.*
> *Miss Ida Gray spent several days here this week attending the meeting and visiting friends. She returned to her home at Lexington Wednesday.*
> *Miss Mary Ray left for her home Monday.*
> *Prof Geo. Burton spent Saturday and Sunday with his many friends at this place. He will begin his school here on Monday next the 24th.*
> *Misses May and Clay Mosley spent Sunday with Miss Julia Hare.*
> *Speed Taylor and lady of Madison visited friends and relatives here this week.*
> *Mrs W J Denman, of your city, and Mrs Woodie Davis of Kansas City visited Mrs C T Taylor and other friends this week.*
> *Miss Sallie Grimes is visiting friends at Lexington.*
> *Eld. Walden still continues his meeting at this place but will probably close Friday night.*
> *Up to present writing there have been 13 additions. p3c3*

The Correspondent didn't report the following death:

> Marion (sic) Miller, aged 70, one of the oldest, wealthiest and largest connected citizens of this county died Sunday. For some time his health had been poor and his mind was the first to be affected. Some time ago he gave away several thousand dollars to friends, and through the efforts of friends he was declared an imbecile and Dr J C Miller and J Pink Overstreet were appointed guardians of his estate. His wife died many years ago and his children are all grown and married. His circle of friends and acquaintances was a large one, and all mourn his loss. p3c1

The correct name of the decedent is Merriman F Miller. The court action on this was reported in March, 1887. The guardians are his son, Dr John C Miller, and his son-in-law Pink Overstreet.

## July 29, 1887

More fall-out from the suspension of production of whisky. "Jack Van Arsdale, a large distiller of Mercer county, has assigned; liabilities $40,000." p1c3 Another distillery was for sale - the W H Sellers Distillery with about 90 acres of land and a frame residence with ten rooms and fine cellars. The distillery had a three barrel per day capacity, with spring water, and a mill seat with facilities for grinding both wheat and corn. There were also corn cribs, stables, and a Fairbanks scale. p2c3

The High Bridge Camp Meeting has just concluded. It was reported that the ministers delivered excellent sermons. The crowds were large and for the most part orderly. The Sunday crowd alone was estimated at 12,000. Many of the people wandered around the cliffs and took trips up and down the river, but "few of them paid any attention to the religious services that were in progress." The editor said "at one time or another it is our firm belief that nearly every man, woman and child in the county was at the camp meeting." p3c2

Excursions trains are available to Mammoth Cave, and to Niagara Falls for vacationers and sight-seers. A special train was arranged for the fair at Danville.

There is no report from the Sulphur Well correspondent; however, his good friend, Bronson Ray, from Buckeye, who had been confined to his room for the past three months, is recovering and "getting about again." p3c4

### August 5, 1887

There is no report again this week from the Sulphur Well correspondent. Perhaps he went on one of the excursions! However, there is this notice of the sale of Merriman Miller's personal property by his Administrator:

> Public Sale. On next Tuesday, August 9th, at my residence, I shall sell the following property of M F Miller, deceased; One safe family combined horse; buggy; harness; gold watch and chain; 3 sets heavy silver spoons; large secretary; bed; bedsteads; trunks; chains; fishing tackle; cooking stove, etc, on 3 months credit. Sale at 3 o'clock pm. J Pink Overstreet, Administrator. p3c5

The news is not good for farmers: the price of livestock is down fifty cents per hundredweight. Extra good shipping cattle are only $3.50 to $4.00. p2c3

### August 12, 1887

Confederate General Simon Bolivar Buckner, the Democratic candidate, won the governor's seat with a 22,000 vote majority over three opposing tickets, including Republican William Bradley.

The *Sulphur Well Correspondent* returns after a two week absence, giving us the following information:

> *Wheat thrashing is about over in the neighborhood.*
> *Our physicians are having all they can do.*
> *Mr John Dickerson and Miss Mary Ray, accompanied by Miss Texie Gray passed through here Tuesday en route to Cincinnati where they were married Wednesday. May long life and happiness be theirs!*
> *Misses May and Clara Moseley spent Tuesday night with Miss Julia Hare.*
> *Mrs Arkie Diamond visited friends and relatives in Lexington this week.*
> *The Misses Wheeler of Cincinnati are visiting in the neighborhood.*

*Elder Grider is conducting a protracted meeting at Pleasant Hill some two miles from this place. He is assisted by Miss Belle Hunt, the lady preacher.*
*C T Taylor left Wednesday for a trip to other counties.*
*Miss Eula Taylor will attend school at Midway the coming session.*
*Mr Jason Tudor of Madison was in our village last week visiting friends and calling on the ladies.*
*Miss Sybie Wilds is visiting relatives here this week.*
*Miss Emma Reynolds of Cincinnati is visiting her sister Mrs T J Horine.*
*Perhaps the people generally are not aware of the fact that we have a spider legged Dude in our village, but such is the case.* p3c6

The Correspondent downplayed the marriage of Dickerson and Mary Ray. Mary Ray had been a frequent visitor in Sulphur Well, and she and her brother Bronson, are good friends with the Correspondent. Why so little comment? Contrast his report with this one from Nicholasville.

> Tuesday Mr Jno. H Dickerson, of Paint Lick, passed through town for the depot, accompanied by a most beautiful young lady and as he wore an unusually bright smile we suspected he was bent on matrimony. Sure enough we were right, for he was on his way to Cincinnati to wed Miss Mary Ray, of Buckeye, Ky., and we say for Mr Dickerson that we admire his taste, for he has selected as a companion, a lady of real Kentucky beauty. Miss Texie Gray, of Ambrose (Sulphur Well) accompanied them. p3c3

August 19, 1887

Preparations are being made for the inauguration of Governor-elect Buckner on Tuesday, August 30th.

The drought is having a serious effect upon tobacco. An expert visited several tobacco-producing counties and reported that the acreage planted is only about 35 percent of that of the previous year. He said that many fields had been abandoned, and that the prospects for harvest were for perhaps as little as 500 pounds per acre.

Monday was Court Day in Nicholasville. "Some horses and cattle were on the market but owing to the present stringency of money, there was very little demand and few were sold. Those sold brought low figures." p3c2

Aftermath of the Civil War:
> Mr Editor--Will you please say that I had two daughters, the oldest Mary E Ross, with bright complexion and straight hair and the younger one Saint Lue Fields, both born in Versailles; the one in 1847 and the other in 1849. I was sold to Mr Alexander Lisle of Nicholasville and they were sold at the same time, the older to Mrs Jacob Brown of Versailles, and the other to Mr Geo. Carter. Not heard from them since freedom and any one who reads this and knows anything about either of them will confer a great favor by letting me know where they are. Signed: Their Mother, Mrs Selina Halls. p3c2

"Mr Elbert Masters spent Sunday in Lexington. Elbert is trying fast to get Gray." p3c4 I don't know whether it was Texie or Ida, but think the latter.

The *Sulphur Well Correspondent* reported:

*Mr and Mrs Bart Taylor, of Lexington, spent several days here this week and last visiting friends.*

*J H Brumfield is tearing down and selling the empty warehouses on the place he recently purchased of S J Greenbaum.*

*Charley Horine and Mrs Ella Taylor are visiting their sister, Mrs Mattie Shearer at Kirksville this week.*

*Miss Fannie Ison, of Garrard, is the guest of Mrs Dr Wilds.*

*Wm. Gray, of Lexington, was down Sunday to see his girl. He has got to be a great ladies man of late.*

*Will Hendren, Jr., is on a visit to relatives at Cincinnati. He will probably go on to Kansas before he returns.*

*N B Long and wife of Madison, visited Mr and Mrs John West last week.*

*Miss Julia Hare is on a visit to friends at Keene.*

*Mrs Annie Wagner is visiting her parents and other relatives near this place.*

*Miss Sallie Grimes is visiting in Garrard.*

*Eld. Greenwood will preach here Saturday night and Sunday.*

*The meeting at Pleasant Hill still continues with great interest. There have been several additions. (This is Elm Fork, not Shakertown.)*

*There was a Reck on the road here last Sunday night. A certain young man at this place can tell you what kind it was. p3c5*

August 26, 1887

The rains came to Jessamine Station and the grass is becoming green once more and everything is looking well, but corn will still only make half a crop. Buckeye is still parched! "Some of our oldest citizens say that water is scarcer in this vicinity than it has been for a number years, Paint Lick Creek has almost dried up. Nearly all the wells and cisterns have given out...." p2c3 The newly weds returned to Buckeye. "Mr John Dickerson and Miss Mary Ray, have gone to housekeeping near Gunn's Chapel."p2c3

Windom reported "that 'Reck' that occurred at Sulphur Well last Sunday night happened at this place one night this week." p2c4 There is no report from the Sulphur Well correspondent this week, and the pun on the name Reck is not clear. The two correspondents are apparently friends as the next two weeks indicate.

"Mr and Mrs Adam Adcock and little daughter Bessie, are visiting in Knoxville, Tenn." p3c4 Mrs Adcock is Scottie Hendren's sister.

September 2, 1887

The *Sulphur Well Correspondent* returns with this article:

*Misses Texie and Ida Gray spent Saturday and Sunday with friends at this place.*
*The many friends of Geo. Peel are glad to see him back again.*
*Miss Ollie Davis is attending the Lexington fair.*
*Miss Lulu Taylor left Tuesday for Midway to attend school.*
*Miss Annie Rettig, of Louisville, is visiting her brother Frank.*
*John Taylor, of Lexington, visited friends here last week.*
*Hogs are selling at $3.50 to $4.00 in this community.*
*The hemp crop is shorter than it has been known for years.*
*J H Murphy is taking invoice (inventory) of his stock.*
*Mrs J P Turner visited friends in Garrard last week. p3c5*

September 9, 1887

The *Sulphur Well Correspondent* writes:

*The old well at this place continues to furnish water for the surrounding county, for over two miles.*
*Farmers are looking rather blue over the prospects for corn and fall grass.*
*J P Turner shipped a car load of fat hogs to market Wednesday. He also shipped a load of nice cattle last week.*
*Eld. Jesse Walden is holding a protracted meeting at Elm Fork with good success.*
*W A Hopkins, H Spralgmeir, Ben Robinson, and F W Fallett, U S Special Gaugers, were in our village this week, inspecting the whisky of S J Greenbaum and G W Gray. They found everything in apple pie order, and give the store- keepers, J F Barclay and Groom Taylor, great praise.*
*Mrs W H Bright is visiting in Garrard*
*Geo. M Berry spent Sunday in Lexington.*
*Mr and Mrs Lee Terhune are visiting relatives here.*
*Miss Julia Hare has returned from a visit to friends at Keene.*
*Jim Grimes has one of the best patent churn dashers in the market. Those who have tried it say they will use no other. p3c5*

The "old well" referred to is the well for which the village is named. While "city" people often came down to drink the water and gagged, residents never noticed the sulphur content. The fact that it served people for miles around during the worst drought in years testifies to the volume of the stream. Another everflowing stream in the area was known as "Big Spring". George Ware tells me that a distillery did operate at Big Spring and that one of the warehouses still exists and is presently being used as a tobacco barn. The Gray distillery was located there.

From Windom: "A friend of the Sulphur Well correspondent says the only reason that the above mentioned correspondent doesn't get `Gray' is because he is bald." p3c5  I believe that the "friend" is Joe Woodward of Midway. Look for the Sulphur Well correspondent's response to the Windom correspondent in two weeks.

September 16, 1887

Voter fraud apparently was prevalent in the May election in Jessamine County. It was reported that a farmer would bring as many as eighteen "bummers" from other counties to the polls, and state to the election officials that they worked for him on a year-round basis. This was enough to allow them to vote. p1c2-4

"The Governor this day remitted the following indictments returned by the Grand Jury of Jessamine County:

> One against Henry Welch, on receiving the vote of a person not qualified to vote.
> Two against L D Baldwin, for carrying a concealed deadly weapon.
> One against W T Jones, for carrying a concealed deadly weapon."p1c6

There were numerous other indictments for breach of peace, assault and battery, forgery, and one for failing to keep registration books. Baldwin was blamed for destroying the registration books, and as indicated above he was armed. These two things lead to his death on November 18th.

From Little Hickman: "The election fraud is still the topic of conversation." p3c5

September 23, 1887

Not all emigrants from Kentucky find their new homes more hospitable! "A former citizen of Barren County, Kentucky, now living in Kansas, writes to his brother that he will not make three bushels of corn per acre, and that every farm in ten miles of him is for sale." p1c1 For the record, the yield in Kentucky that year was four barrels (note: barrels not bushels). p1c6

"The Eastern wheat market is off again, dropping to a figure almost as low as has been reached this year." p1c6 "The crop of potatoes this year is the smallest that has been raised for years, owing greatly to the drouth...." p1c6

The *Sulphur Well Correspondent* is back at work, but this is the last letter written by the person whom I believe to be George M Berry. You will see, as time goes on, that he marries Ida Gray, makes his home in Lexington, and takes a "traveling" job with a Cincinnati firm. The next letter is written by "Joy" in December.

> *Farmers say this is the dryest season since 1854.*
> *Our physicians report sickness on the increase.*
> *Miss Lula Spruce gave a social to her friends on Friday night of last week.*
> *Miss Annie Rettig, after a visit of two weeks at this place, has returned to her home at Louisville.*
> *Miss Ella March is visiting friends in the neighborhood.*

*Miss Sallie Grimes has returned from a visit to friends in Garrard.*
*Another "Reck" on the road last Saturday night, but this time it got wrecked.*
*Charley Horine has gone into the merchandise business with J H Murphy.*
*Madam Rumor says there will be a wedding down this way soon.*
*The Windom correspondent must be terribly off when he speaks of us as being "bald". If your friend don't know the difference between a high forehead and a bald-headed man, send him down this way and we will try and "Spruce" him up a little.*
*Mrs Jas. Cobb spent Saturday and Sunday in Lexington visiting friends and relatives.*
*J T Berry and Woodson Masters, of Madison, were here Tuesday on business.* p3c5

Joe Woodward is the "friend" who later marries Lulu Spruce, so the Correspondent is probably making a pun.

## September 30, 1887

A view of Kentucky during this period by one of its congressmen: "...Kentucky coal-fields are more extensive than those of Pennsylvania, and .... five hundred miles of railroad have been built in the State during the past year; ... the State produces 40 percent of the tobacco raised in the country, and a great deal of the whiskey." He doesn't think that development of the South will not make Southerners protectionist, but he does feel "that they are in favor of a revision and reduction of the tariff." p1c4

A new hotel is under construction in Nicholasville. It has a brick exterior, and is trimmed with cut stone. It measures 90x150 feet, stands two and three stories high, and contains forty rooms plus halls, parlors, reception and dining rooms. p1c5

A break in the drouth. "A copious but quiet rain begun falling Monday afternoon and continued till Wednesday night, to the great relief of everybody and every thing, giving new life to vegetation and filling ponds, branches, cisterns and wells." p3c2 The weather must have been a little freakish. A light snowfall was reported in Lexington, and a "good size frost" was experienced in Nicholasville.

"Miss Texie Gray, of Lexington, visited Miss Emma Dorman last week." p3c3 Miss Texie is everywhere! She and Emma Dorman visited the "Misses Crow" this week. p3c4

The Windom correspondent responds: "The Sulphur Well correspondent claims to have a high forehead instead of a bald head. If such be the case, he certainly has an extensive fore head." p3c4 While he may have the last word, the Correspondent gets the girl!

## October 7, 1887

"Nearly all the large distilleries in this State have signed the agreement not to operate before July 1, 1888...." The small distillers are not in the agreement, but their output is considered inconsequential. p1c1

A raconteur tells of his growing up in Perryville. He asks
'Did you ever hear about the time that everybody in Perryville went to Danville to see the eclipse?' Of course I had not, so he said 'Well, the people of Perryville had been in the habit of going to Danville to attend court, to the circus, and in fact, Danville was their Mecca. I cannot recall the year, but at any rate there was to be an eclipse of the sun, so we people at Perryville made our arrangements to go to Danville to see it, never for a moment having thought that we could have the same opportunity for seeing at Perryville that they had at Danville. However, most everybody went and came home pleased with the success of the trip to Danville'. p1c4

### October 14, 1887

From Buckeye: "Bronson Ray is again smiling behind Mr Brown's counter." p2c2

"Miss Texie Gray and brother Willie, of Lexington, are visting friends in this place (Nicholasville)." p3c4

### October 21, 1887

"J B Stacy has bought the old W P Noland farm, from S F Miller's executor, at the price $2,050 cash." p1c6 This was from Madison County. I suspect that the initials are reversed and that the decedent is Francis S Miller.

### October 28, 1887

Farm report: Turnips are selling at "$1 per bushel in Lincoln County". Cattle are sold at $3.50, and hogs at $4.00 per hundred-weight. "The first load of new tobacco was sold ... for $5.10 for lugs and $1.00 (per hundred pounds) for trash. Hemp sold for $5.56 for 112 pounds, an unusual measure. Mules are selling well, a yearling colt brought $170. Harness horses sold at prices ranging from $185 to $225. However, "a handsome team of two year old geldings" was sold to Governor Buckner for $800. Fat ewes sold for $3.50. p1c6

The drought previously reported is general. "The present stage of the Ohio River is the lowest in seven years." p2c1

"Scarlet fever has appeared in violent form among the children of Hopkinsville." Typhoid fever is "raging", and three deaths are attributed to it in Elizabethtown. p2c4

There is a bill before Congress to aid in the establishment and to give temporary support of common schools. p4c1

November 4, 1887

Another sign of prices and produce. "Walnuts are selling for 50 cents per bushel in Georgetown." p2c4

Apparently the quality of breeding cattle in Kentucky is pretty good. "Mr J E Marcum, of Montana Territory, was at Burgin last week buying up a car load of young bulls to take West." p2c4

The correspondents read each other's columns, and sometimes mimic the others in style and content, and often make comments about the other correspondents or their items. From Windom: "Nothing from 'Jumbo' last week. What has become of him? Gone to Birmingham, I guess." p3c4 This was from "Dranreb". I reviewed the last few issues and found that the Pink correspondent signs as "Hawk Eye"; the Buckeye correspondent signs as "Vulcan"; the Little Hickman correspondent as "Pomp."; and the Mt Lebanon correspondent as "Unknown". I have previously mentioned that the Sulphur Well correspondent has at least twice signed himself as "White Cloud". To which the Russell Crossroads correspondent responded with "Black Cloud".

November 11, 1887

From other correspondents: "Jumbo", from Windom thanked "Dranreb" for reporting while he was gone, but said he had not been to Birmingham, as had been speculated. p3c4 Dranreb is Bernard spelled backward. From Richmond: "The Irvine stage now leaves Richmond in the morning and returns at night."p1c8 From Buckeye: "Mr N. Davis and Walter Harris came over from Jessamine last week to look at Mr Word's hogs. They offered him 4 cents per pound, which he refused."p2c3 "Mr Jno. M Dickerson, an enterprising, go-ahead merchant of Buckeye, was in town Monday on his way to Lexington."p3c4 Dickerson, you remember, married Mary Ray a few weeks ago. There are several reports of hunting activity from all the correspondents. They were mostly hunting birds - turkey, dove and quail - and rabbits. Some Nicholasville men went in groups to hunt in Tennessee.

"Elder J R Hoover will preach at the Christian Church, Sulphur Well, at 11 o'clock next Sunday." p3c1

November 18, 1887

From Richmond: "'Cattle are lower in price than they have been since 1841', remarked Mr Talton Embry, the well-known cattle man, the other day." p1c7 The low cattle prices are undoubtedly related to the continuing drought, as are several fires reported in this issue. They ranged from a forest fire in Estill County, to local building fires.

The ill feelings from the previous election are still strongly felt. Two men met on the street in front of the Phoenix Hotel in Lexington, and following an argument, shot each other, one fatally. The argument was over the disappearance of poll books. The deceased was Lew D Baldwin, of Nicholasville. p2c2

### November 25, 1887

The funeral of Lew D Baldwin was attended by a crowd of three to five thousand. The funeral cortege was said to be the largest ever witnessed in the county, and that there were 142 carriages and other vehicles in the procession. p2c2

From lower Garrard: "A M Askins has removed his family from Bryantsville to Sulphur Well, where he will take charge of a blacksmith shop." p1c4 This is Nancy Stacy Breiner's grandfather. Guy Stacy, Nancy's father, was a nephew of Forest Miller, my maternal grandfather. Luther Ware, my adopted grandfather, will later become an apprentice of Askins.

"Dr J L Wilds, of Ambrose, who is attending lectures in Cincinnati, was home on a visit last week." p3c4

### December 2, 1887

Concerning the recent death of Lew Baldwin, a friend writes:
> As to the frauds in the Jessamine county election, it is out of place to discuss them here. The grand jury found indictments against Lew Baldwin and others as guilty of complicity in those frauds.

He was pardoned by out-going Governor James P Knott before he came to trial. The friend goes on to state:
> There is hardly any exciting election in a county of Kentucky wherein men of good repute in the community do not, directly or indirectly, countenance fraud of sort. In this election I have no doubt that both sides used every effort to win and both sides technically violated the law in many instances. p1c4

Baldwin was accused of stealing the poll books after the election was over. The friend says that the county inherited this situation after the Civil War.
> At the close of the war political and race feeling was bitterer in Jessamine county than anywhere else in the State. The colored troops who were disbanded at Camp Nelson lingered about there. Many of the thugs and camp followers who infest large military posts remained. And the native politicians, who had their cohorts, were the most rabid and incendiary of their sort. It took nerves of steel and untiring energy to reclaim the county. These attributes Lew Baldwin had to a superb degree. p1c6

The friend telling this story was J Soule Smith, correspondent of the <u>Lousiville Times</u>.

The continued use of titles for men also indicates the continued memory of the Civil War. Governor Buckner had been "General Buckner". Many men were called Colonel, and some Captain. This is twenty-two years after the end of the war, and these titles are still being used.

"Mrs Tudor, of Madison county, died last Tuesday. She was the mother of Mrs W D Hendren, and grandmother of Mrs Adcock, of Nicholasville." p3c1 This is also Scottie Hendren's grandmother, thus my great, great grandmother.

It has seemed to me that most of the communities had a "Mite" society. The correspondents frequently mentioned them. I thought they were tongue-in-cheek references to snobbish cliques. It finally makes sense! "The Baptist Mite Society...." The biblical "widow's mite"!

Telephone service is near. "A gentlemen of Danville was in town Saturday arranging for telephone connection with Danville and Harrodsburg." p3c5

From Jessamine Station: "The majority of farmers are through butchering hogs, a few have had to wait on account of the scarcity of salt." p1c4

December 9, 1887

"Miss Texie A Gray entertained a delightful card party, Friday night, in honor of Miss Cordie Crow, of Nicholasville." p3c4 As stated earlier Texie is about twenty-one at this time. She seems popular with girls in at least Buckeye, Nicholasville, and other parts of the county. Obviously she was very happy and outgoing. Perhaps by this time a little desperate, as it appears that it was rather common to marry by eighteen. She certainly was making herself known and available to the young men of the county.

Better communications and travel: There have been more discussions on a telephone line from Lexington to Danville via Nicholasville. A new line is needed since the present line is fully utilized. The Cincinnati and Southern Rail Road put on a fast express train for Florida, leaving Lexington at 10:15am and arriving at Jacksonville at noon the next day.

> What are the poorer class of negroes of Nicholasville to do this winter? How are they to get clothes and food and coal? Nothing in the hemp line before spring. No factories, no public works of any kind in progress, and as few, if any, of the negroes are skilled laborers or mechanics, it becomes a serious question as to what is to become of them during the winter. p3c2

This is the first report from Sulphur Well for several weeks. It is different from past reports. There is a different relationship to the people being written about. Also, the previous reports were Sulphur Well, this one is called "Ambrose Neighborhood". Further, there is a sub-title of "Personals" that has not been used previously. Bob Moseley and the correspondent were good friends, here he is called "Bob" in quotes. There is a reference to Belle Hunt, who had previously been referred to as "a lady preacher", now referred to as an old friend. And, last, it is signed "Joy." We will probably never know who Joy is. My chief suspect is Mrs Spruce, the postmistress, who might be more inclined to use

Ambrose, the postal designation, than the community name. Here is what the *Sulphur Well Correspondent* has to say:

*The linen wedding last week at Mr and Mrs Wm. Hoover's proved a very enjoyable affair. Those present partook of a bountiful repast prepared by the host and hostess.*

*The dance at Mr Sageser's was postponed from Friday night to next Wednesday night, on account of the inclement weather.*

*Prof. Burton's school closes Friday, the 9th. The face of the school boy looks bright.*

*Askins Bros., who recently moved to our place from Bryantsville, are workmen of ability. We wish them much success.*

*Mr Robt. Moseley has been changed from Curley's distillery to this place. We are glad to have you among us again "Bob".*

*Mr N D Davis bought eight head of two-year old cattle from J P Turner last week, at 3cts.*

*Miss Belle Hunt will preach Saturday night at the M E Church. Let her old friends come out and hear her.*

              Personals

*Mr Thos. Bright, of Cincinnati, is visiting his brother, Wm Bright, our polite and obliging merchant of this place.*

*Miss Emma Reynolds returned home last week after an extended visit to her sister.*

*Mrs Bettie Murphy is visiting her son, J H Murphy.*

*Ham Dozier was in town Sunday night. We will soon have lots of ham around here.*

*Mr Harland Cobb is in town again with his wife. We wish them much success in their wedded career.*

*Why have all our young people put off marrying until so late in the year? We learn there are two more marriages contemplated in our neighborhood. Joy. p3c5*

An explanation of Miss Belle Hunt's role in the church might be helpful. It is said that she is a lady of culture, ability and piety, but that she is a lay teacher, not an ordained minister because the Methodist Church does not permit the ordination of women. It is common practice for women to assist by both preaching and praying in services.

              December 16, 1887

The editor said that the Ambrose correspondent meant to sign as "Ivy", but the printer put "Joy" instead. Here is what the *Sulphur Well Correspondent* says this week:

*Our town is on the boom. We now have three general stores, four blacksmith shops, two churches, four doctors, and couple of preachers.*

*H G Turner received a number of fine specimens of gold and silver ore from Gold Hill, Nevada. He is collecting a geological cabinet.*

*Dr Miller sold eight young mules to Madison county parties for $100 each.*

*The members of the M E Church at Pleasant Hill are putting a new roof on the house.*

*Elijah Stennett sold his entire hemp crop to Brown & Bros., of Nicholasville for 4 1/2c.*

*Will we have a school this spring? Surely our children are not to waste their best time for study.*

*There were several bunches of stock hogs sold in town last week. They averaged from $3 to $3.30.*

*Prof. Burton has returned to his old home at Kirksville, Ky.*

*Richard Fox, from Madison, was in town last week.*
*Miss Nannie McTyre, from Keene, and some other charming young ladies are the guests of Miss Julia Hare.   Ivy. p3c4*

I believe that the doctors are: Miller, Wilds, Hendren, and Peel. The stores are owned by Murphy, Wm Bright (see last week), and Mrs Spruce. The blacksmith shops are owned by Atkins, who just arrived from Bryantsville a week earlier, and others. I am not aware that there are any resident preachers, or that there is more than one church, which has always been Christian. I suspect the correspondent means that there were two congregations. The Methodists held meetings at least periodically, many of them in Mrs Miller's home. Pleasant Hill later became known as Elm Fork.

December 23, 1887

The *Sulphur Well Correspondent*'s notes are short this week, with some mention of the season:

*Our young people are anticipating most delightful times Xmas. Several parties, weddings, etc., are expected. It seems as though the last part of the year will be the most enjoyable.*
*J P Turner bought one of the race mares owned by the late  L D Baldwin for $76.*
*Wilson Baker sold Robt. Quinn five two-year-old cattle at 3 cts.*
*Some of our people are attending the revival meetings in your town. They express themselves as being most highly pleased with the meetings.*
*Dr Fountain Dickerson, of Madison county, is over to spend a few days in town.*
*J H Bogie, of East Hickman, was in to town Tuesday.*
*Mrs Joe McDonald and little daughter, Hattie, of Spencer county, are the guests of Mrs J P Turner.  Ivy p3c4*

December 30, 1887

The tariff question is still being discussed. Each state wants protection for its major products. "So on through the list of States, there is a demand for the protection of local interest, and this demand is made alike by Democrats and Republicans. Politicians may talk about free trade, but when it come to the test it will be found they want protection for their home products." p1c3 Kentucky is predominately Democratic. "Ten years ago there was but one Republican in the State Senate. When that body meets today it will contain seven." p1c3

This is a report card on public education. "The average wages (per month) for male teachers of Jessamine county" for 1887 is $39.32; for women $29.66; for colored males $37.41; and for colored females $33.75. "The cost of tuition of each child is 96 cents per month." The total revenue from all sources is $5,272.88. There are 2,071 white children according to the census report of the trustees, but only 1,136 attended school. The value of all the school houses in the county is $8,600, and all but three of them are in good condition. There are 1,213 colored children in the census, with 612 attending school. The value of the colored schools is $2,700, and total revenue for the schools is $2,521.23. "Jessamine has 12 colored schools, all in good working order." p1c4

This is a brief statement about Nicholasville by the editor: The new hotel is nearing completion, one that would rival those in larger cities; the Female Institute has gained "almost a national reputation"; there is also a public school; one railroad, the Cincinnati Southern, however Lexington provides east and west connections; a fire department; a well-kept cemetery; one private bank and the First National Bank; "one newspaper ... Democratic in politics, but conservative in all things"; and one roller mill. p1c5

The editor also says that "for the week past we have been in the midst of the Christmas holidays. In spite of hard times, there has been much good cheer and many rejoicings." p2c1 He goes on to say that during such festivities that those who are fortunate should not forget the less fortunate, many of "whom are absolutely suffering for the commonest necessaries of life".

"Sister Hunt has been holding meetings some three years and has five hundred or more conversion testimonials of her call to the work." p3c2 The editor says that at first there was some prejudice, but that "her plain, faithful and loving addresses won everyone's hearts." She is much in demand. Even though she is a member of the M E Church South the northern church "has engaged her for months to come."p3c2

A word from the Bowling Green Democrat: "A female evangelist is stirring up the natives and causing a rattling of dry bones in Nicholasville, and there is now some hope for Brother McCarty, of the Jessamine Journal, who is not in love with male preachers!" p2c1 The editor has been carrying on a running feud with several ministers for weeks after he ran an article about a fallen minister, and made some unkind comments that several ministers interpreted as painting all of them with the same brush. It is obvious that he doesn't include Belle Hunt in that number!

After having served on a search committee for my church, seeking a replacement for a minister who served for twenty-five years, I can empathize with the church that is trying to find a replacement for Henry Ward Beecher.
> They seem to have some difficulty in finding a pastor of Plymouth Church to supply the vacancy made by the death of Beecher. A learned and brilliant man is wanted -- a `star' preacher. It is not essential that he have any religion if he otherwise fills the bill. p2c1

The correspondents had to be admonished by the editor to give the news, but to avoid all personalities. I suppose he meant making comments about the people mentioned. Once before the editor had said that puffery (excessive praise) would not be printed. I don't believe that any mean-spirited comments are published, although a correspondent occasionally twited another.

There is no report from Sulphur Well to close the year. This has been the first full calendar year that we have covered. It also ends a decade that began in 1877 with a single issue, skipped five years, then four more years of hit and miss issues.

## THE SECOND YEAR - 1888

In 1888 we have a few intermittent reports from what appears to be three different correspondents. However, there is a fair amount of local history to enrichen our story.

### January 6, 1888

The front page of the Journal carries a letter from Edmund A Lord to S M Duncan, of Nicholasville. He is writing from St Thomas, VI and is on his way to England, after having just come from Bermuda.

These are just some stray facts: There are 633 prisoners in the Frankfort penitentiary. p1c6 Estill Springs was sold in bankruptcy for $11,350.p1c6 The Ohio River is frozen over and navigation suspended. A Swiss colony tried to raise grapes in Jessamine County from 1790 to 1801; however, the European grape was too tender for the Kentucky climate and it was susceptible to root louse. p1c7 The Jessamine Journal is beginning its sixteenth year. p2c1

This is an inventory of horses and livestock in Jessamine County: There are 4 thoroughbred stallions; 54 thoroughbred mares and foals; 38 common stallions and 3,096 common horses; 795 mules; 315 purebred cows and calves, and 2,964 common cattle; 5,219 sheep; and 5,034 hogs. p2c4

From Buckeye:"William and Bronson Ray are improving" p2c3 This is either a continuation of the long illness, or another one for Bronson.

"On Monday night last Mr Joe Woodward and Miss Lulu Spruce, eloped from Sulphur Well and were married at Cincinnati. They were accompanied by Will Hendren and Miss Carrie Woodward." p3c3

There is no mention of Joe Woodward's marriage in the *Sulphur Well Correspondent*'s column this week.

*The dinner given by Andy Sanders for the benefit of the colored Baptist church was well patronized.*
*It is rumored that Rev. Owen Young will preach at Elm Fork this coming year. Looks as if there are a good many young preachers around here.*
*Benedict Baker died very suddenly last Friday night. He was apparently well and healthy at 4:30pm, and at 10 o'clock the same night was dead. The cause of his death was believed to have been congestion. In the death of Mr Baker our county loses a worthy citizen and true Christian.*
*Dr J L Wilds has been home several days visiting. He left for Cincinnati Monday.*
*Walter Hendron (sic) has returned home from an extended tour through Kansas.*
*The Misses Warren from Windom have been visiting Mrs J H Murphy for the past week.*
*Frank Rettig has been home on a short visit during the holidays.*
*Miss Hunt, the evangelist, is spending several days in town.*

*Carr Willis and family are spending several days in town. It is reported that they will make this place their future home.*     *Ivy p3c4*

### January 13, 1888

Here is more about the fraud in Jessamine in the recent election. During court hearings one witness in the Plaquemine District, that includes Sulphur Well and Little Hickman, said that there were four pages in the poll book containing 120 names of non-residents of Jessamine County, or else were fictious names. These votes were for Jones, the Democratic candidate for state representative. The books then disappeared and were never found. Lew D Baldwin was responsible for their loss, and the dispute over their disappearance led to his death. p2c2

J H Murphy, of Sulphur Well, is the Chairman of the Republican County Committee at this time.

### January 20, 1888

A heavy sleet fell. Several injuries were reported by people slipping on ice, and the roads were too slick to drive.

### January 27, 1888

Magazines were available to inform anyone with an inquiring mind about technological changes. For example, "The Scientific American...presents weekly to its readers the best and most reliable record of various improvements in machinery, while the scientific progress of the country can in no other way be gleaned so well...." p1c3 While not everyone could afford such magazines, the public library in Nicholasville was available, and those who read could pass along interesting tidbits in conversation.

Several wrote in favor of the "Blair Educational Bill" that would provide federal aid to education.

The Kentucky legislature is in session, and is in the process of redistricting the state. The Democrats are gerrymandering as usual, and the Bardstown editor says "The history of gerrymanders is that the party resorting to them always loses...." p1c7 Maybe in the next life!

The paper has been carrying letters from people living in other parts of the country telling about life there. The one this week is from Sittie Fritzlen, a schoolteacher in Taos, New Mexico, who is the daughter of a Nicholasville merchant. p1c4-6

There are more divorces during this century than I would have suspected. There are seven suits for divorce in this term of the Circuit Court.

"Free" turnpikes are being discussed. There is a general feeling that the expense of using turnpikes restricts trade.

"Coasting" has become the rage -- sleigh-riding down the hill on the Danville Pike, south of Nicholasville. All classes and ages are doing it! "The merchant, mechanic, physician and lawyer all ride upon the same sled and bring along with them their wives, sisters, and sweethearts." p3c3

February 3, 1888

Edmund A Lord, the letter writer who was in the Virgin Islands, is now in Plymouth, England. At one time he was a minister at Bethany and Sulphur Well, although his home was apparently in Lexington.

By this time Mrs E J Miller (Elizabeth Jane) has become one of the wealthiest people in Jessamine County. In a published list of the people paying the most county taxes she and her brother-in-laws, Dr John C Miller, and John Pink Overstreet, husband of Sarah Miller who is the sister of John C Miller, all made the list. p1c6-7

Governor Buckner dispatched General Hill to Pike County to make a comprehensive study of the Hatfield and McCoy feud.

A major topic of conversation is whether Jessamine County should meet the terms of the Louisville Southern Railroad. It wants to build a road from Louisville to Beattyville that would come through Nicholasville. The railroad needs each county to help finance the construction costs of the road. Jessamine is requested to provide $150,000 in bonds, which would be exchanged for stock in the road. In return the railroad would "guarantee coal delivered into Jessamine at a maximum of eight cents, to give a lumber rate not to exceed $2 per thousand from any point in Eastern Kentucky to Nicholasville...." p2c2 If the terms are not met, officials say that the line will go instead through Burgin and Lancaster. A tax will have to be imposed to retire the bonds. The state senator from the district opposes such a tax and says that taxpayers money should not be used in a speculative private enterprise, and that if the railroad did not have enough money to build the road, then it should not be built.

February 10, 1888

Despite the state senator's warning, it is said that the county is almost unanimously in favor of the project.

J H Murphy, resident of Sulphur Well, and a former county surveyor and sheriff, offers his opinion as to the best route for the proposed railroad. According to him the route should go from Nicholasville to Sulphur Well, then to Richmond. He says that it should go through the farms of J P Turner, J T West, and Dr John C Miller, and then on to Hickman

Creek. Dr Miller's farm is at, or near, the intersection of West's Lane and Chrisman Mill Road. p1c8

There are rumors about the state capital being moved elsewhere. Indeed, several other cities have aspirations. They are also in the process of selecting delegates to a constitutional convention. The legislature has been in session for weeks, and the state is in a political turmoil. The legislature took a junket to Lexington one evening for dinner at the Phoenix Hotel, and while there one legislator happened to see a friend in the dining room. He asks what the friend is doing there, and the friend answers that he is on the Munday jury. The legislator responded that "he hoped that they would be kept there until they hung that old woman". p2c4 This was taken by the deputy sheriff accompanying the jurors as jury tampering, and the legislator was taken before the judge. Fortunately, for him, the judge accepted his plea of innocence. This trial, by the way, was the O J Simpson trial of its day in Jessamine. Mrs Munday was accused of poisioning her husband for his insurance of $20,000, which was quite a sum in those days! For your information, she was acquited also.

Here is an update on the retail prices of groceries and produce: Flour $3 per cwt; meal $1 per bushel; bacon 14 cents per pound; coffee 25 cents per pound; sugar 7 cents per pound; lard 10 cents per pound; coal oil 20 cents per gallon; butter 25 cents per pound; and eggs 20 cent per dozen. p2c5

February 17, 1888

A little gem of wisdom: "...it is not always the barking dog that is the best hunter." p1c4 This is another way of saying that politicians who made the best speeches are not necessarily the best legislators!

There is a strong possibility that three new states will be added to the union - New Mexico, Montana, and Dakota which is yet undivided. p2c1

One of the local citizens, A B Duncan, writes back concerning his view of New Orleans. "I have taken in most of the city, and a more dilapidated and run down old city I have never seen." p2c2 That is just the beginning of his highly critical letter!

The new hotel in Nicholasville has been officially named the "Hotel Nicholas".

George M Berry and Ida Gray got married:
> Gray-Berry.-At the residence of the bride's parents in this city (Lexington), on February 14th, Mr George Berry and Miss Ida Gray, Rev. Mr Walden officiating. Mr Berry was formerly of Sulphur Well, Jessamine County, and is now a clerk in T J Pilcher's dry goods house. By a course of exemplary conduct, endowed with many amiable qualities, he has won many friends. Miss Gray is a daughter of G W Gray, the well-known distillery man, formerly of Jessamine County. She is a

charming brunette, possessing all the beauty and accomplishments which make a loving and dutiful wife. May their pathway be strewn with unfading flowers. p3c6

If you tie all the pieces together as I have, you will conclude that George Berry was the Sulphur Well correspondent prior to Joy/Ivy. You will see in later years a reference that George Berry was bald.

February 24, 1888

The fruits of the Civil War are evident in the paper almost weekly. "Twelve negro men were arrested in Nicholasville last week for vagrancy, and taken before the court...."p1c6 Within the past couple of weeks, the negroes were trying to get fifteen cents, because they had heard that the judge was going to have any of them arrested that didn't have that much on them.

The Journal editor says that the legislature has done so little the past week that he finds it unnecessary to give his usual summary.

This tongue in cheek advertisement got my attention:
> A complete failure. My new stock of goods has just arrived and I find on examination they are not good. My Columbus Buggies and Surreys Phaetons and Barouches have paper tops and poplar wheels. The Solid Comfort Plows, Old Hickory Wagons and Evans' Corn Planters are so inferior, and my Hemp and Manilla Twine are so rotten, that I will not be able to use any of it this season, and my house is leaking all over my should-have-been Steel Binders and other worthless goods, making my condition a deplorable one. Please don't call on me in this sad condition. W G Moseley. p2c5-6

I wonder if this reverse psychology worked? I suppose it got people's attention, anyway.

On the surface this seems like an odd combination. "Notice. I will from this date give my personal attention to the Undertaking Department of my Business. My stock of Furniture, Carpets, and Wall-paper will be found complete and offered at the lowest possible price. F P Taylor." p2c6-7

Family linen: "Adam Adcock, selling liquor to minor, $50 fine." p3c2 Adcock is a saloon-keeper. The editorial comment was that the indictment was for selling liquor to a colored youth on the verbal order of his father. Mr Adcock paid his fine without trial. Two others were charged for the same offense, stood trial and were acquited. Adcock must have been an interesting individual. He owned trotters. He was a city councilman, and later, a school board member. "Miss Lizzie Hendren, of Lexington, is visiting her sister, Mrs Adcock." p3c3 She later marries a Van Winkle and lives in Frankfort.

## March 2, 1888

Work on the railroad has been delayed by bad weather. However, "the masonry has been completed from Harrodsburg to Louisville." p1c7 There are still several bridges to build, and only twenty-eight miles of track has been laid.

It appears that the short tobacco crop of 1887 is encouraging farmers to plant large acreages in 1888. One farmer alone planned to put out fifty acres. Many farmers planned to "put out every foot" they can in tobacco. The editor predicts the biggest crop of all times, and falling prices. He advises producing grain, cattle and hogs instead.

There is some questioning of the "Sunday laws" because of their inconsistent interpretation and application. It is sometime tough to be a Christian: "The students suspended from the Bible College at Lexington, Ky, for attending a theatrical performance, have been reinstated by the faculty." p2c3

The editor's admonishes the correspondents to "give nothing but news of general interest, we don't want anything about the young people sparking; wait till they go to marry, then fall on 'em." p3c3

Some confusion in the reports, but she is still married. "Mr George M Berry, of Madison county, traveling for a Cincinnati house was married to Miss Ida Gray, in Lexington."p3c5

## March 9, 1888

The tariff bill is now before Congress, but its passage is in doubt because many states have products that will be adversely affected by a lower rate.

John Dickerson, who married Mary Ray, of Buckeye isn't doing well. "Dr William Ray is closing out Jno. M Dickerson's stock of goods this week. Luther Spears is the auctioneer." p2c3 John was a civil war soldier, and married late in life. After this apparent failure he became a traveling salesmen, and apparently was well liked. It is my understanding that he was originally from Sulphur Well.

The editor is promoting the establishment of a savings and loans association. Nicholasville is chronically short of affordable housing. Sound familiar? And, by the way, the new hotel has just opened. This was no small thing; a good restaurant, a meeting place, and a place for "traveling men" to stay was very important in a small town!

## March 16, 1888

The Kentucky Legislature must have always been inept! "The present body may not be any worse than its predecessors, but if a bigger lot of monumental jackasses ever assembled at Frankfort the fact is not recorded." p1c8

The Greenbaum Distillery (co-owned by George Gray at Big Spring, near Sulphur Well) was robbed. Six men were arrested. They included a nephew of Groom Taylor, a Federal Gauger at the distillery, and Joe Woodward, "a young man of good character and family". p3c2 Woodward had just married Lulu Spruce a few weeks before. Another account of the arrest went as follows: "For six months past the distillery of Mr G W Gray, at Sulphurville (sic) near Nicholasville, has been robbed of large amounts of whisky." p3c2 All efforts by Gray to catch the thieves had been unsuccessful, so he hired a Cincinnati detective agency. The detective sent to the area posed as a tobacco grower. He associated himself with two of the suspects, intercepted an incriminating letter, and got confessions from two of the accused men. They incriminated the others. All were then taken to Richmond to await trial. p3c2 The result of their trial will follow later.

Gardens are quite large at this time. A rather modest house of four rooms for rent features a three acre garden.

Dr John C Welch died. He was born on a farm just a mile south of Nicholasville. He was a graduate of Transylvania's medical school. Dr Welch practiced medicine for 41 years, much of which he did without charge. He was a surgeon for the Union Army in the Civil War. Dr Welch was associated with many charitable organizations, held high offices as a Mason, and was a trustee of the schools for many years. He had three sons who became doctors. p4c1

## March 23, 1888

Another letter has been received from a former resident, this one now in California. He speaks of the charm of the sea coast, and the view of the mountains. He tells of the variety of fruit trees, and is especially taken with oranges. He is impressed by the thousands of acres of wheat grown there.

The <u>Chicago Tribune</u> described Kentucky's Senator James Beck as being 66 years old, but not appearing over fifty. "He is a solidly built man, with a big Scotch head, a ruddy complexion, chin whiskers of a silvery gray and a vigorous mustache." p1c8

The race for sheriff has been talked about for weeks already even though the race is months away. The contest is between the Democrat, Moseley, and a citizen's ticket made up mostly of Republicans. There was an unusually large crowd in town for court day, and the sheriff's race was a major topic. They were also talking about crops, livestock, the proposed railroad, and the new hotel.

James W Tate, the Kentucky State Treasurer for twenty years, has been "found short in his accounts to the amount of $197,000..." and has fled the state. He is believed to be in Canada, and there is a $5,000 reward for his arrest. p2c2

A wealthy woman of the county died, and her probated will was published in the paper. She had quite an extended family, and remembered everybody. She left the balance of her estate to the M E Church, South.

William Huddleston and Francis Brumfield were married at the Sulphur Well Christian church, by the Rev J G Perkins.

It appears that the Cincinnati detective agency sent a rogue to investigate the distillery robbery. Part of the evidence against the suspects were two letters, which the trial commissioner found to be in the detective's own handwriting. He also answered "yes" to questions concerning his turning state's evidence against his partner in the theft on a car load of cattle; his arrest on a charge of rape; and his arrest for selling whisky without a licence. The suspects were "released and returned home on the afternoon train". p3c3

Women's clothing appears to be a fire hazard. This week is the second in which women have been severely burned when their clothing caught fire. Apparently it is common for the women to burn trash or garbage in the spring. One had been cleaning the chicken house.

From Hanly: "Miss Kate Hunter, Ambrose, is the guest of Miss Mollie Carter." p3c4

Finally, another report from the *Sulphur Well Correspondent*:

*H G Turner closed his subscription school last Friday. He will resume his studies at Bethel Academy.*
*Elder Owen Young has resigned his position at Elm Fork. It is reported the vacancy will be filled by Elder J H Perkins.*
*Thos. Peele sold his house and barn to a party from Tennessee. Mr Peele will remain in the house through the summer.*
*Pneumonia and measles are still in our neighborhood. Several cases have proved fatal.*
*The many friends of Dr Peele will be sorry to hear of his serious illness.*
*Ambrose must be an exception to other parts of the county. We are in for fat stock and good crops of wheat; no tobacco.*
*Master Jimmie Woodward and sister, of Bohon, were home for a short visit.*
*Miss Arkie Diamond is visiting friends in Lexington.*
*Wm. McC. Johnston, a dashing young lawyer of Lancaster, was in town Saturday.*
*Mr Melvin Harris, of Lexington, made us a flying call last week.    Ivy         p3c4*

It seems strange that the correspondent didn't follow up on news such as the distillery robbery. I'm sure Sulphur Well was buzzing. I doubt if there was anything else was discussed for the past two weeks. However, it would make sense if the correspondent were Mrs Spruce, and Joe Woodward her son-in-law. It might help if we knew who Melvin Harris is, and his relationship to the correspondent.

March 30, 1888

"Another old soldier has fallen." p1c5 Thus began a biographical narrative of Major Allen L M'Afee, a veteran of two wars. It has become more clear to me with every issue how deeply the Civil War imprinted the people of Jessamine County. I suppose some of the younger veterans of the Civil War lived to see the next century, but many of them are now growing old. I am amazed at how their rank became a lifetime emblem.

Decatur, Alabama became a boom town as a result of the railroads, and the making of steel. Kentuckians, and others were drawn there in seach of wealth and opportunity. The Journal now has a special correspondent writing from Decatur. Part of the excitement in Jessamine County over the railroad is based upon the belief that Beattyville would become another "Birmingham", and that with the railroad connecting Beattyville to Nicholasville, that they would share in the prosperity.

The legislature is busy passing resolutions concerning the absconded State Treasurer. "Of course the office will be declared vacant, and the treasury vaults pretty much the same way." p2c2 "The Courier Journal's insinuation that the Legislature has lost it head over the Tate matter is unjust, if not libelous. How could that honorable body lose what it never possessed?" p2c2 The bondsmen for the State Treasurer are also busy getting judgments against any property of Tate's they can find. A notice of sale of some land in Jessamine appeared this week. They found about one hundred barrels of whiskey he had stored last week.

The new hotel has been leased to Mr H C Rodenbaugh, a local businessman, who will operate the property. Cook Bros., one of the leading clothiers is going out of business. Bronaugh & Dickey also announced the dissolution of their hardware business.

From Buckeye: "N D Davis, of Sulphur Well, was in this neighborhood last Thursday, buying fat cattle for the Nicholasville market." p4c2 "Mr J M Dickerson, of the Chapel neighborhood, will move to our town in a few day. Come along, John, you are welcome." p4c2

The code of honor is strong. Ballard Bronston, of Richmond, shot Gilbert Dudley because of "...undue inimacy between the deceased and Bronston's wife; and report has it that whilst acting as Deputy Sheriff Dudley went to Bronston's house to levy an attachment whilst the latter was from home and acted in a scandalous manner." p2c2 The shooting took place in a bar room on First Street in Richmond.

There has been a lot of gunplay. It is now a $100 fine to carry a concealed weapon in Nicholasville. Everyone, including young men, seem to be carrying weapons. The operator of the ferry at Paint Lick was shot at five times while ferrying a passenger across the river. One shot grazed his head, but he was otherwise unhurt.

## April 6, 1888

"Wilson Willis, who is charged with amusing himself by playfully shooting at George Snell, the ferryman at Paint Lick..." is now in jail. p3c1

The vote for the proposed railroad is next week as to whether of not for Jessamine County will subscribe to $150,000 of bonds in the company.

Tate's dishonesty shocked everyone. It was said of Dick Tate that if everyone in the state were asked to name an honest man, he would have received the most votes. His name had become the symbol of integrity. p1c8

It is reported that Treasurer Tate lost heavily in the wheat deal that wrecked the Fidelity Bank at Cincinnati last Spring. An investigation of the vouchers in the Auditor's office and the bank account shows a discrepancy of $100,000 that month. It is well known that Mr Tate made frequent trips to Cincinnati at that time. He was a member of the Cincinnati Chamber of Commerce. p1c8

The Sulphur Well Correspondent speaks again, but for the last time as Ivy:

*Another newcomer in town. He was born on the 30th, in the home of Mr W H Hare.*
*Dr Peele is recovering from his illness.*
*J P Turner bought five yearling mules at $45 per head.*
*T J Smiley was in town last week, buying horses.*
*Notwithstanding "Fools Day" came on Sunday our people suffered some severe jokes.*
*There are three parties in town who are trying to make up a select school. Surely we will have a good one.*
*Dr Johns, of Danville, has been visiting his sister, Mrs. N Davis.*
*Mrs Green Wheeler, of Cincinnati, has been spending a few days with her mother, Mrs W Hendren.*
*Miss Julia Hare visited friends in the south last Sunday.*
*Miss Sibbie Wilds has returned from her visit to her folks in Garrard.*    p3c2        Ivy

## April 13, 1888

The bonds that Jessamine County is to trade for stock only will occur if the line is actually built and operating. The reason for the road is to connect the resources (coal and timber) of eastern Kentucky with the agriculture of the Bluegrass, and the industry and markets of Louisville. p1c6

## April 20, 1888

A merchant says "Times are hard and money is scarce, but I have a full line of Spring Goods...." p1c2

## April 27, 1888

"If Dick Tate will only come back and get the rest of the money out of the treasury and so compel the Legislature to quit and go home, all will be forgiven." This was reprinted by the Journal from the Owensboro Inquirer. p1c6

"The line of the railroad in Anderson County is thronged with spectators who have come miles to see the railroad, never having seen one before, and the appearance of the locomotive is heralded with delight." p2c2 The L & N has arranged to run special vegetable trains to the northern cities as soon as the season opens.

## May 4, 1888

Dr Willis L Kenley, who practiced in Sulphur Well from 1852 to 1855, died in Missouri on May 2, 1888.

## May 11, 1888

"Hard Shell" says that there are several advantages to having a circus come to town. First, the health benefits are remarkable. "A number of excellent women, who for months past have been martyrs to neuralgia, rheumatism, and other chronic ailments, which had defied the medical skill of our city physicians, and had prevented the good sisters from attending their beloved church, were suddenly cured of their complaints, and turned out...to see the circus." Second, he said "The decided improvement in our people's facilities for transportation was quite a notable circumstance. Church members who had not been to their churches for nearly a year, because they 'had no conveyance, and it was too far to walk' found, upon further consideration, that they could...make a perfectly safe and highly enjoyable trip to Nicholasville to see the circus." He also said "A manifest improvement took place in the financial condition of the community." People who had been unable to pay the banker, the grocer, or their church dues, suddenly had money to go to the circus! p1c6

Jessamine County got its flour mill! It is 40x40 feet, with a basement, and is four stories high. It has its own railroad spur, and a macadamized road from the mill to the Versailles and Nicholasville turnpike. It makes four grades of flour, and grinds meal as well. p3c2

There's a "Neighborhood Sayings and Doings" that sounds much like the Sulphur Well correspondent. If you recall he once wrote that there was a terrible Reck on the road. In this article the correspondent writes: "There was a terrible Reck in our Sunday School the other Sunday, and we are glad to say Miss Jennie W. escaped uninjured, although she was very close to the Reck." Supplement, May 11, 1888 p2c1 The article was signed W.H.A.

May 18, 1888

Women have the opportunity to keep up with fashions. A special correspondent regularly reports from New York: "Darkness is prominent in millinery"; the colors are usually mahogany or green. Some bonnets "show the natural yellow of the straw" and are trimmed in pink or blue. "Net, tulle or crepe lisse are much used" as materials with pleats and embroidery on the edges. "Uniformity is very noticeable, and each part of the costume conforms to the other parts." Tan or gray gloves are still standard. Plaid parasols are "conspicuous", with some stripes favored. Supplement, May 18, 1888 p1c2

The local girls have a good school that attracts wide attention. The graduates of the Female Institute in Nicholasville come from Fort Worth, Quincy (IL), Washington County (MS), and Kentucky towns such as Georgetown, Frankfort, Ashland, Cloverport, Danville, Nicholasville, and Fayette as well as local girls from Jessamine County. p3c3

The weather is unpredictable as usual. A heavy frost fell Monday night that was very destructive to vegetables. Tobacco plants are scarce and many predict that the tobacco crop will not be as large as expected for that reason.

From Buckeye: "Born to the wife of John M Dickerson, a daughter, Lucy Ray. All are doing finely and John is as well as could be expected." p1c8

"No new developments regarding natural gas at Sulphur Well, but it is believed that some investigations will be commenced within a few weeks." p3c2 Unfortunately, nothing came of any investigations that may have occurred. No report from Sulphur Well, but there is some family news. "Miss Lizzie Hendren, of Lexington, is visiting Mrs Adam Adcock. p3c4

May 25, 1888

A strawberry festival is planned at Roberts Chapel. There will be two rooms "for married folks, while the parlor and yard will be at the disposal of the young people." p3c2 East Hickman Baptist Church features "croquet, swings, and pleasant entertainment for the children" for 50 cents at the gate for adults, 10 cents for children. Proceeds will be used for furnishing the new church building.

"A party of gentlemen from Shelby County... accompanied by several from Keene, gathered at Wilson's Landing on the Kentucky River" for several days fishing. p3c2 Fishfrys are considered pleasant social occasions, especially when accompanied by pitching horseshoes.

There was a good crowd for Court Day as the weather was cool and the ground too wet to work. Hotel Nicholas had 120 guests for dinner. Jesse Neal supplies the strawberries to the hotel from a half-acre field. There will be an organizational meeting at Hotel Nicholas for the Jessamine County Fair. The talk of the railroad has changed the price of property by the acre to the front foot. A corner lot next to the hotel brought $24.65 per foot at auction. Residential lots are going for $2 to $4 per foot.

This isn't a very good year. Cut-worms are particularly bad. Corn is bringing $3.50 per barrel and farmers refuse to accept that price. Isaac Levy, proprietor of the Kentucky Clothing House, admits to being "in a bad fix" and must raise $6,000 by the end of the month, and will therefore offer ever article at 75 cents on the dollar. p4c3-5

June 1, 1888

"Mrs A K Adcock has been visiting her father's family in Lexington this week." p4c2 This is Addie Hendren. There will be a lot of visitation though the years.

Jessamine farmers raise a fair amount of sheep. There was a car-load of lambs shipped from Nicholasville, and one from Wilmore this week. Dairying has also become a growing industry. Three local farmers are keeping around thirty cows each, with about one-half in production at any one time. One of them runs a wagon regularly between his farm and town. "Many farmers have peas and beans they would like to sell, but they can't afford to pay tolls to come to town...." Supplement p1c1 Opposition to toll roads is gathering strength. Most people want them to be made free, and be supported by tax revenue. Office seekers are being asked to express themselves. "As the railroad is the great national civilizer and educator, so the turnpike is the great civilizer of the county and neighborhood." p1c6 This is a very perceptive statement from someone who merely signed himself as a "farmer" in a small town!

The Jessamine Station correspondent writes that there is a spirit of emigration among the young men of the community who are speaking of going west in search of higher wages and regular work.

At last! Another article from the *Sulphur Well Correspondent*, but a different one:

*Andrew Sageser has commenced setting out tobacco and expects to put out about six acres.*
*B F Wilds has returned from Missouri and is the guest of his brother, Dr J L Wilds.*
*We can compliment J H Broomfield and Elbert Walker as being the best overseers we have had for years on our county roads.*
*J H Broomfield and J H Murphy are erecting a new pair of scales.*
*Miss Syb Wilds, of Garrard, is the guest of her brother, Dr J L Wilds.*
*The schools of Misses Julia Hare and Minnie Hemphill's closes Friday, June 1st.*
*Farmers report the wheat crop short.*
*Stock hogs are selling at 4 1/2 per cwt.*
*Joseph Woodward has accepted a position in Louisville as engineer.*
*A M Askins and James Cobb have the reputation of being the best gardeners in town.*
*T J Horine has a fine Wilk's colt, for which he has refused $100.*
*G C Hemphill has the best field of corn we have seen this year.*
*Mr Flariday Stafford was fortunate enough to kill two mad-dogs last Friday.*
*Some think Sparks and Davis will be the next sheriff, and deputy, while others think Moseley and Rutherford will win. We are inclined to think the latter will get there.*

*The popular salesman, J C Hunt, of Lexington, was in the village this week.*
*W H Bright was in Lexington this week buying goods.*
*We, of this neighborhood, propose to stand by the good old Jessamine Journal that has always treated all our citizens with the greatest respect.     Alaric     p3c4*

The correspondent has signed himself Alaric. So far we have had White Cloud, Joy/Ivy, and now Alaric. I might also mention that the Joe Woodward above who has become an engineer in Louisville, is the one who married Lulu Spruce, and who was suspected of robbing the distillery.

June 8, 1888

There is continuing anxiety about the route of the railroad--through Lancaster or Lexington rather than through Nicholasville.

The directors of the Fair Board are considering whether to raise enough money to attract good trotters for the half-mile track, or to have an "old fashioned" county fair featuring stock, vegetables, and arts and crafts.

The distillers met and agreed to limit production in 1888 & 1889, with quotas to be allotted to producers based upon capacity. p1c4

"Judge Hines, for the State, instituted suit against Tate, and his bondsmen, to recover $247,000 less credits yet to be determined." p2c1

From Versailles: "All the people, young and old, are out in their buggies on Sunday afternoon from noon till dark." And from Nicholasville: "Croquet playing occupies considerable time of some business and professional men during dull days." p3c2 I think this gives a picture of how people spent their leisure time during this period.

From Sulphur Well: "At the close of Miss Julia Hare's school last Friday she gave a picnic to her scholars and patrons, which was held in J P Turner's woodland, and all report a nice time." p3c3

From the *Sulphur Well Correspondent:*

*Messrs. Robert Masters and William Gray, of Lexington, were in the village Saturday and Sunday.*
*N D Davis and J H Broomfield were elected as school trustees last Saturday.*
*Mr Jerome Sparks was around last week, shaking hands with the boys. We would like to see Mr Moseley and give him the right hand of fellowship.*
*Dr Hendren was called to Madison last Friday to see a patient.*
*Work hands are plentiful but work scarce.*
*McClellan Johnston and Miss Palmer were visiting friends here last Sunday.*
*Thomas Peel had his garden destroyed by a cow one night last week.*
*Miss Sallie Grimes, of this place, is visiting friends in Garrard this week.*
*Dr Wilds reports Mrs Tom Turner (who has been quite ill for some time) improving.*

*Mr Louis Clark came very near loosing his eye while at work on the road last week.*
*Messrs Charley Horine and Frank Rettig spent Sunday and Monday in Madison.    Alaric p2c8*

### June 15

Trimble County is expecting to produce 200,000 bushels of peaches this year. p3c3 A crop of 300 to 500 gallons of raspberries sold at 40 cents per gallon. p3c3

### June 22, 1888

People lived by their wits then as well as now. A man stopped his buggy on Main Street in Nicholasville. He began by offering sleeve buttons for sale for prices ranging from 10 cent to a dollar. Then he asked all those who had made purchases, to hold up their buttons. For those who had paid $1, he gave $2; to those who paid 10 cents, he paid 25 cents. Then "he offered watch chains at $1 each. After selling several, he took each silver dollar he had received and wrapped it in a one dollar greenback and placed (them) in a conspicuous place in front of him." Then he offered watches for $10 and sold several. As he sold, he never claimed what the value was of his merchandise, and cautioned purchasers not to buy if in their opinion it was not worth the sales price. When everyone had finished purchasing, he asked if there was "anyone who thought that he had not done all he promised", and not a single hand went up! "He then said `All satisfied? Well I am too,' and making a polite bow drove off some $200 richer". p3c4

"The most fashionable hop ever given in Nicholasville took place at Hotel Nicholas ... under the auspices of the Jessamine Social Club. It was attended by belles and beaux from all the surrounding towns, as well as our young people from the city and county." p4c2

The *Sulphur Well Correspondent* reports:

*The Rev. H E Ward, of Lexington, has preached for us for the last time, as he expects to go to Virginia to evangelize.*
*J W Miller, of this place, has the reputation of being the best cabbage grower in this end of the county. He informs us that he has one that measures three feet across. The variety is known as the late Shaker Russet.*
*H C Hunt, salesman of Curry, Howard and Co., Lexington, was in our village again recently.*
*Mr Jess Fox, of Garrard, of the firm of Rice & Fox, was here last week for the purpose of buying mules.*
*Mr Michael Robinson, of Garrard, was lately the guest of Mr A M Askins.*
*Mrs Lula Woodward left for Louisville to join her husband, where they will make their future home.*
*Mrs Dr J L Wilds has returned home from a visit to friends and relatives in Garrard.*
*J H Murphy and Wilson Baker are having their thrasher overhauled and are peparing to do the people some good work.*
*The hog cholera is raging in this section. Alaric p2c8*

The J W Miller, above, is not James William Miller, son of Francis S and Elizabeth Jane Miller, and older brother of Forest Miller. He was known as Jim, ran a general store in Sulphur Well, and was postmaster at the time of his death in 1898. Alice Kirk, of Knoxville, has his personal bible.

"W H Bright, dealer in groceries and family supplies. Country produce a specialty. Sulphur Well. Jessamine County, Ky." This ad appeared for the first time. p4c3

June 29, 1888

The *Sulphur Well Correspondent* writes:

*The farmers are all busy in their harvest.*
*We are greatly in need of rain.*
*Frank Rettig was called to Memphis, Tenn., to attend his brother-in-law's funeral.*
*S M Miller, deputy collector, made a levy on a lot of S J Greenbaum's whisky, which will be sold July 7.*
*Miss Syb Wilds has returned to home in Garrard.*
*Farmers report their wheat crops better than they expected.*
*Moseley and Rutherford are still ahead. So say the boys.*
*Mrs Spruce is on the sick list this week.*
*A M Askins & Bro. are kept busy in their blacksmith and wood shops.*
*Nicholasville, Lexington and Sulphur Well young folks report having a nice time at Little Hickman last Sunday.*
   *Alaric      p3c3*

The Correspondent next week will make reference to this article about the Rev George O Barnes, often called the "Mountain Evangelist". Rev Barnes was once a missionary in India, who has since traveled in America and abroad "proclaiming a gospel that, somehow, appears familiar and welcome to the few, but strange to the many--the story of God's universal and unconditional love, holding out eternal salvation to the sinner once confessing." However, he began speaking out on issues related to the Civil War, construed by some as being at variance with the decrees and traditions of the Presbyterian Church. He separated himself from the old church and began preaching "...independent of creeds, standards, or traditions, and presented the gospel...from a source higher than earthly will or power." p1c6-7. He traveled the mountains of Kentucky and at least on one occasion, was denied the pulpit of any church in that town, yet the churches all dismissed their services when he secured the use of the county court house. This was regarded by some as being hypocritical.

July 6, 1888

New York fashions: "It is the summer of plastrons, plaits and puffings, of full vests, of redundant sleeves and ample drapery, to say nothing of bright colors, large figures and conspicuous plaids." p1c7

The American Wheelmen, 100 strong, are making their fifth annual tour. They will begin in Indianapolis, ride to Cincinnati, boat to Maysville, then ride to Lexington, Nicholasville, Pleasant Hill, Bardstown, and end in Louisville. They made arrangements to have breakfast at the Hotel Nicholas.

Work commenced on the new railroad from Lawrenceburg to Lexington. The Louisville Southern is connecting with the Cincinnati Southern, and will put on a new line of Pullman coaches between Chicago and Chattanooga.

From Woodford: "The wheat crop is probably the finest ever raised".p2c7 "Barley is also very fine." p2c7 A full crop of corn is expected.

From the *Sulphur Well Correspondent*:

*The hum of the thresher can be heard, and everybody is busy.*
*We have had good rains and those who had tobacco to set got through.*
*Mr T J Horine made about fifteen bushels of wheat per acre.*
*Butter is selling at 10 cents per lb., eggs 10 cents per dozen.*
*Mr B F Wolf was in the village this week, buying wheat, and he succeeded in buying several crops at 70 cents per bushel.*
*We would like to know what kind of religion people have who abuse Mr Barnes.*   Alaric p3c4

## July 13, 1888

The Cincinnati Centennial Exposition runs from July 4th through October 27th. It features a grand jubilee celebrating the Northwest Territory. It also offers exhibits, "novel" entertainment, and "dazzling effects".

Railway engineers were in Nicholasville locating the line between Lawrenceburg, Nicholasville and Lexington, and another line from Nicholasville to Richmond and Beattyville. A crew of ten surveyors were in Lancaster surveying a line from Burgin to Lancaster, and on to Madison County. p1c6

The editor received a letter just after the publication of an article on Rarus, a trotting horse, saying that it was the writer's belief that "Dr J C Miller could give some interesting facts regarding that celebrated horse. In answer to a query on the subject, Dr Miller writes:

Nicholasville, Ky., June 27, 1888

Dear Sir--Your favor of the 19th inst. received a few days since. Mr Frederick got Rarus and Grafton mixed. I bred Grafton and practiced medicine on him. Mr Bonner drove Rarus and Grafton double. I sold Gyp, the dam of Grafton, to Mr Bonner. Grafton was the fastest running walker I ever saw. He also paced and racked naturally, but would do neither unless forced. He loved to 'run', walk and trot. It was very difficult to keep him from running when going fast. I have a number of fillies closely related to Grafton. Very respectfully, Jno. C Miller." p1c6

From Little Hickman, Pomp says "In this vicinity there are 14 Mugwumps, 13 floaters, and a good sprinkling of Jacksonian Democrats; the balance is what some cranks term 'them disrespectful Radicals'". p3c4

Pomp also said "It appears like Bro. Barnes, Sam Jones (another evangelist), resident cranks, picnics, sickness, rain, thunder and lightning, death, roasting ears and colic is going to attack this county in rotation and some all at once." p3c4

Sam Small, at a revival he was conducting, got himself in some hot water by maligning the local clergy for not properly tending their flocks, while they were on the platform with him. First one got up and demanded an apology, and Sam replied that he certainly didn't mean him. Then another minister arose and also asked for an apology, and Sam replied that he didn't mean him any more than he had meant the first minister. Then the other ministers rose and he apologized to all of them, leaving his audience somewhat disgusted. p2c8

The *Sulphur Well Correspondent* then writes his last article as Alaric:

*Mr Lee Terhune and wife, of Mercer, were the guests of James Woodward.*
*Mrs T J Horine has returned from Cincinnati, where she has been visiting her sister.*
*Misses Julia and Mamie Hare visiting friends in Garrard this week.*
*Mr William Gray and his mother, of Lexington, were the guests of Mr and Mrs George Diamond.*
*Mr Wilson Masters reports his fruit crop good.*
*Everyone who has heard Mr Barnes likes him.  Alaric p3c5*

July 20, 1888

Popular summer resorts: Rockcastle Springs is billed as a "model family resort", not for transients or sportsmen. Crab Orchard Springs, open the year round, features a brass and string band from July through August. Estill Springs has a bowling alley, billiard rooms, boating and bathing. The waters are blue and black sulphur. The rates are $2 per day, or $10 per week at Estill Springs. p1c1 The rate at Dripping Springs is even cheaper, $30 per month. p3c1

The exact route of the Louisville Southern to Lexington has not yet been determined, and that is troubling quite a few citizens.

There was a great deal of talking about politics and several speeches were made at Court Day. Dr Miller had his purebred Holstein bull on exhibition during Court Day, and Bernard Wolf bought 800 bushels of wheat from Dr Miller.

### July 27, 1888

More on the George O Barnes story. An "orthodox" minister commenting on Barnes said "He may call his anger by a holy name; but it is there, and very discernable." He said that by this means Barnes gets hundreds of sinners enlisted in his behalf. "He let us know that every man had a different God. He had an inferior one fifteen years ago when in Nicholasville (when he was still a minister in the Presbyterian Church), now he has a better one...." p3c3

The High Bridge Camp Meeting did well again this year. An estimated crowd of ten to fifteen thousand attended last Sunday. Sam Jones got $750 for his week's services! To put this in perspective, teachers and workers earned less than this in a year!

The editor complained that Madison County had arranged three fairs, while Jessamine couldn't arrange even one! He said they needed to pull together.

### August 3, 1888

An interesting bit of history of the locks and dams on the Kentucky River. Five locks were completed by this time beginning from the Ohio River at Carrollton, with a sixth under construction in Mercer County. The dam at Beattyville was slipped into an appropriation bill undetected. The bill passed and the dam was built even thought it has no practical effect upon navigation!

The vote in Estill County on the railroad will be taken on August 11th. The general election comes in two weeks and the sheriff's race has been going on for months in Jessamine. The tariff is the national issue.

From Little Hickman: "J H Easley and wife, of Sulphur Well neighborhood, visited relatives here last Sunday." p2c7

### August 10, 1888

Pete Mosely, the Democratic candidate for sheriff, had an unexpectedly close race, winning by only seventeen votes. The editor said it was because "he was handicapped from the start by bad management and indiscreet partisans." p2c1

### August 17, 1888

Estill County voted to buy stock in the railroad to Beattyville. This closed the subscriptions that were needed to build the road from Louisville to Beattyville, through Nicholasville.

August 24, 1888

"Miss Susie Hendren, of Lexington, is visiting her sister, Mrs Adam Adcock." p2c8

August 31, 1888

The *Sulphur Well Correspondent* began signing himself "Alaric" on June 1st, and continued to do so until July 13th. I don't believe that his identification will ever be possible. This article is unsigned, and begins as thought he has just undertaken the assignment.

*According to promise, I will endeavor to write you a few items from time to time and hope they may be interesting.*
*Mr Wm. Carter and wife, of Lexington, passed through our village last week on their way to Garrard, to visit his brother-in-law, Mr. Teater.*
*We are glad to see the smiling face of Miss Fannie Johns in our midst again after an absence of several months.*
*Miss Mary Deitrich, of Hanly, spent several days with Lula Taylor, last week, and left with a very severe heart trouble caused by one of Cupid's darts. Hope it may not prove fatal.*
*Dr J C Miller is confined to his bed with flux.*
*Mr Charlie Hudson is reported dangerously ill with typhoid fever.*
*Mr Baird, from Camp Nelson, has moved to this place and will take charge of the public school here, beginning Sept. 10. Mr Baird comes well recommended and is a gentleman of high culture and good morals, and we hope by the aid of the patrons in this district that he will be able to build up our school.*
*Mr Alex Askins has rented Mr Geo. Diamond's property and will move to it in a few days; he also has rented C F Taylor's blacksmith shop for another year. We are glad to know Mr Askins will remain with us, as he is an excellent smith, and his brother Sam is a natural mechanic. They are both deserving workmen.*
*W H Bright has plowed up some sod land and is preparing to set out a large onion bed. Willie is a good gardener and we hope he will succeed in the onion business.*
*N D Davis bought a fat cow of Mr Baird for the Nicholasville market. Price paid 3 cents.*
*W H Hare sold some of his hogs for the Cincinnati market at 5 cents.*
*J W Poor, of Garrard, bought 100 head of hogs for the Cincinnati market at 5 cents.*
*J H Brumfield and wife, visited her parents in Madison Saturday and Sunday.*
*Mr Brumfield has rented his farm of 40 acres on the Sulphur Well pike to Mr Handy from Casey County, to be cultivated in tobacco and other crops.*
*The funeral procession of J H Bogie passed through our little village Sunday afternoon, reminding us of one of the most stubborn facts which man has to learn, viz., that he must die.*
*The civil engineers for the Louisville Southern were around last week viewing this route, taking J W Baker and James Cobb along as guides to point out the old survey made by J H Murphy, he being absent. They seemed well pleased with the route on this side of the river, but not so well with the Madison side. They will be back however this week to re-survey it. While many here are wishing that it may go this way, there are many others who hope it may not; the business men belong to the first class and the farmers to the latter.*
*Mr Wm. McDowell, of Nicholasville vicinity, spent the day with N D Davis Sunday.*
*Mr Stephen Snowden and family, of Estill county, are visiting Mrs Frank Miller, and other relatives.* p2c5

The J H Bogie referred to in the article above was a well-known farmer and trader of the East Hickman neighborhood, who died on August 25th of typhoid fever. He came from Garrard County, and was taken to Buckeye for burial.

And from Little Hickman: "Miss Carrie Woodard, of Ambrose, is teaching school at Sweet Home." p2c5

September 7, 1888

The *Sulphur Well Correspondent* writes this day:

*N D Davis, our energetic and popular tradesman, has of recent date, embarked into the cattle business very extensively. He has at present about 150 head and paid from 3 to 4 cts; one lot of 30 head bought of Mr John Perry, of Hanly, bringing $900. Other purchases were made in Madison and Garrard counties. Also a lot of fine long yearlings from Dr J C Miller at 3 3/4 cts.*

*Mrs Miranda Spruce, our clever postmistress, has returned from a pleasant visit to her daughter, Linnie, whom she left in Louisville to attend school. Mrs Lizzie Walker tended the store and postoffice while she was absent, assisted by Mr Frank Rettig.*

*Dr E B Johns paid a short visit to his sister, Mrs N D Davis, last week.*

*Mr Frank Horine has returned from a visit to Madison County.*

*Miss Ola Davis, who has been visiting in Henry County for several weeks, has returned. She was accompanied by her grandmother, Mrs Rev Wm. Johns, who will remain until after the Methodist Conference, which meets next week in your city.*

*W H Bright sold a work mule 4 years old to a farmer of Fayette county for $100 cash. A good price Willie.*

*Mrs Dr J C Welch, was the guest of her daughter, Mrs Dr Wilds, this week.*

*Dr J C Miller is some better at present.*

*Mr Charles Hudson is improving, and will be out again soon, we hope.*

*Mrs Maggie Cook, of Keene, is visiting her father, J W Baker. We are glad to see she is looking much better than she did a month or two ago.*

*Messrs. Murphy and Baker after a rest of a week or ten days, are out again with their fine traction engine; threshing the remainder of the wheat crop.*

*Mr Andrew Sageser is building a veranda to the house lately bought of Mr George Gray, and making other improvements that were much needed, such as fencing, papering, &c, and will paint soon.* p2c4

Here are some additional items not mentioned by the Sulphur Well correspondent:

From Pomp of Little Hickman: "Elbert Walker, of Ambrose, was down Sunday. His batchlerhood is status quo and he still looks well." p2c4

The Louisville Southern's surveyors are still searching for a route from Nicholasville to Richmond. The Murphy route (see February 10, 1888 for the farms it crossed) went through Sulphur Well as was stated by the correspondent last week.

"Miss Scottie Hendren, of Lexington, is visiting Mrs Adam Adcock." p3c4 Scottie is my maternal grandmother.

Dr J W Wilds, Sulphur Well physician, received three royal degrees from the I.O.O.F. He has been a member for ten years.

## September 14, 1888

The Louisville Courier Journal chided the Jessamine Journal for appearing to side with Cincinnati against Louisville. In response the editor said that the "Journal was for Kentucky against the world, and Kentucky towns against towns in any other state...." But, when Louisville merchants didn't advertise in local papers, didn't sent "drummers to compete with (those of) Cincinnati houses", it had to draw attention to those facts. p1c4 Perhaps because of the importance of the livestock market in Cincinnati, Jessamine was much more oriented toward Cincinnati than Louisville. No one ever eloped to Louisville, but they did to Cincinnati!

The *Sulphur Well Correspondent* writes:

*Miss Mayme Hare has returned from a pleasant visit to friends and relatives at Keene.*
*Miss Florence Hutchison, of your city, spent several days last week with Mrs L E Baird, returning home Sunday, accompanied by Miss Lizzie Peyton, of this place.*
*Mrs Julia Moseley and daughters, Misses May, Clay, and Irene, of Keene, were the guests of Mrs W H Hare Saturday and Sunday.*
*Miss Sybelle Wilds has returned to her home in Garrard County, after an extended visit to her brother here.*
*Mr Wm McC. Johnson, a rising young lawyer, of Lancaster, and his charming little niece, Miss Willie Belle Burnsides, visited friends here Saturday and Sunday. Come again Clel. there is always a welcome here for you.*
*Master Marshall Davis, son of N D Davis, had his finger badly mashed in a cider mill last Thursday, but it is healing up nicely.*
*Mrs C A Kenney, of Princeton, Ind., was the guest of her cousin, Mrs Wilds, one day this week.*
*We are glad to report Dr J C Miller getting well, but his son, Rice, was taken Saturday with the same disease, dysentery, though is better at this writing.*
*Mr Mann Miller, brother of Dr Miller, from Irvine, is here on a visit.*
*Our public school opened Monday morning with a full attendance.* p2c4

An additional Sulphur Well item not covered: "Murphy & Baker, Sulphur Well, have purchased a large and fine clover huller." p3c1

## September 21, 1888

The *Sulphur Well Correspondent* writes:

*J P Turner, who is a shrewd and careful trader, purchased a fine young jack at the sale of Esq. Mitchell, last Thursday, with a view of raising mules. Price paid, $391.*

Messrs. Horace and Jimmie Turner, sons of J P Turner, and young men of good morals and industrious habits, left this place Monday for Delaware, O., where they will finish their literary education. They were accompanied by their father who will return in a few days.

Mr Russell Woodward, one of the oldest citizens of Little Hickman, was visiting friends at this place this week.

Miss Janie Walker, and industrious young lady from Hanly, visited relatives here last week.

Mr Tom Moseley and wife, of Keene, and Mr George Mosely, of Missouri, were the guests of W H Hare last week.

Glad to see the smiling face of Mr Wm McC Johnson in our midst again Sunday and Monday.

Born to the wife of W H Hoover, a fine daughter, Thursday Sept. 13.

Rev. Johns, brother of Rev. Wm. Johns, decd., was the guest of his niece, Mrs N D Davis, Thursday night.

J J Poor and daughter, Ora, and Miss Florence Christopher, of Garrard, visited relatives and friends here last week and attended Conference.

Miss Suinie Turner, of Garrard, has come here to live with her uncle, J P Turner, and will attend the public school. All seem pleased with the new teachers.

E E Bruner, of Little Hickman, passed through this place Saturday on his way home with 150 poor hogs, which he had bought in Scott and Owen counties, to fatten. Price paid 5 1/2 cents.

Mrs Wm Vince is visiting her daughter, Mrs W H Hoover.

Misses Julia and Mayme Hare, two of our prettiest girls, spent Court Day in your city, attending Conferences. p3c5

September 28, 1888

The *Sulphur Well Correspondent* writes:

Miss Belle Hunt, the evangelist, paid a short visit to Mrs Nancy Baker, of this place, last week.

Mrs J E Nave, of Danville, is visiting friends and relatives in the county this week.

Mrs Sallie Shy, of Texas, visited her sister, Mrs W H Hoover, last week.

W H Hare has been somewhat indisposed for the last week or two.

Mrs J C Welch visited friends and relative here this week.

Mr Thomas Crawl was in our vicinity last Sunday driving around with the girls. Come again, Tom. She will be glad to see you.

Mr Andrew Sageser and wife, are visiting relatives in Irvine, Estill County.

J H Murphy, an enterprising and leading business man, has about completed the erection of his Fairbanks Scales.

Messrs Frank Rettig and Charles Horine took advantage of the cheap rates and visited the Falls City last week.

Mrs J P Overstreet of Pink was to see her brother, Dr J C Miller, last week. The doctor continues to improve, and will soon be out again, we hope.

Mrs W H Hare and daughter, Miss Julia, and Mrs J L Wilds spent Sunday in Keene with friends and relatives.

Messrs Joe McDonald and John Lovel, of Spencer County, visited their brother-in-law, J P Turner, last Monday and Tuesday.

> *J P Turner was not so well pleased with the school at Delaware, O., as he expected, so he brought his sons home with him; sending Horace to school to Center College at Danville, and James to Bethel Academy.*
>
> *Mrs J H Dean visited friends in Danville this week, and went to Lawrenceburg to attend the Neiding-Bourne wedding, which took place Tuesday afternoon at 5:30 o'clock.*
>
> *Bro. Ward, of the Theological school at Lexington, came down Saturday afternoon and preached for us that night and twice on Sunday. He is a young devine of great ability and all were favorably impressed with his sermons. Come often Bro. Ward, for we need your services.*
>
> *Bro. J S Young, of the M E Church, preached at the Christian Church here Tuesday night the 20inst. But few attended on account of the threatening rain. Subject of sermon, "God's Unreciprocated Love." Bro. Young is an able and earnest preacher full of good thoughts and is fast gaining an enviable reputation. p3c5*

It appears that Mrs J E (Susan Miller) Nave was in Sulphur Well at the same time as Mrs J P (Sarah Miller) Overstreet, both visiting their brother, Dr Miller during his illness.

### October 5, 1888

According to the Owensboro Inquirer political party lines are being readjusted according to individuals views of the tariff. However, the Jessamine Journal editor feels that few would change parties over that one issue. p2c1

The directors of the Louisville Southern Railroad awarded the contract for the construction of the road from Versailles to Beattyville. This included stations and other buildings as well. The route from Nicholasville to Richmond was not decided, there being two possible routes; one through Sulphur Well, the other by way of Marble Creek to the mouth of Tates Creek, and then on to Richmond. p3c2

Texie did it! "Mr Thos. Cooley, who has been located at Omaha, Nebraska for several months, came home last week, he said, to see his friends, but the smile which Tom wore, indicated that other attractions more important were the cause of his return. On Thursday of last week he hied himself away to Lexington, the home of his affianced, and procuring marriage license, was married at the residence of Eld. Mathews, to Miss Texie Gray, a well-known beauty recently of this county. The groom is a young man well liked in Jessamine and everybody joins with us in wishing the newly married pair a happy voyage through life. They left last Saturday for Omaha, where the groom has a lucrative position. Mr Dick Pilcher and Miss Emma Dorman of this place, were the attendants." p3c3

### October 12, 1888

Ground was broken on the Versailles-Beattyville route. Work is also progressing on the Lexington branch of the railroad.

From Garrard: "William Best says he sold two hundred barrels of corn to J W Miller at $2.00 per barrel shucked down in the field." p1c8

October 19, 1888

"The Democratic Party is for (the) protection of labor." Governor Hill, speaking in Indianapolis, said that "the Democratic party is not a free-trade party." p1c6

Court Day was rainy, "the streets were muddy, and the air chilly. Notwithstanding, a fair crowd was in town from the country, and many from a distance to attend the large sales of property which had been extensively advertised." p3c2 The I. Levy store was crowded all day.

The distilleries will resume operations again, but on a limited basis. I might mention that the distilleries are major factors in the economy of Jessamine County. Not only do they directly employ workers, but farmers sell the corn to make the whiskey, and then the resulting mash feeds hundreds, perhaps thousands, of cattle and pigs.

October 26, 1888

Rabbit hunting is entertaining the local sportsmen, but rain is preventing farmers from stacking hemp and threshing the seed.

From Union Mills: "Willard Davis, of Sulphur Well, spent Saturday and Sunday with friends in this community." p3c5 This is according to "No Nothing".

November 2, 1888

There is a rumor that the former State Treasurer is now in Japan, after passing through Vancouver. Although the loss was put at around $200,000, it is believed that Tate took no more than $50,000 with him. At least some part was probably lost on speculation in wheat a year earlier. p1c5

The presidential election is next Tuesday.

November 9, 1888

Republican William Henry Harrison defeated Democrat Grover Cleveland for president. Harrison carried all the Northern states, and the West, while Cleveland carried the "Solid South". Unfortunately for Cleveland, the North had more electoral votes. The Democrats carried Kentucky by about 40,000 votes. p2c2

The eleven year old daughter of Dr and Mrs J L Wilds died. Her funeral was held at the Baptist Church in Nicholasville, and she was buried in the Welch plot of Maple Grove Cemetary. p2c3

Tramps and burglars are numerous. As the weather worsens they are looking for food, clothing and supplies.

Irish pototoes are plentiful and are being taken by the wagon load to the city to be sold for 40 cents per bushel.

### November 16, 1888

The only incumbents before Cleveland to lose the presidency had been John Quincy Adams and Martin Van Buren. From the New York Sun:

> When a party deliberately buries out of sight the principles on which it was founded, and of which it was founded, and of which it has been for a century the custodian and trustee, when it sends some of it best men to the rear and surrenders the management of it affairs to a syndicate of cracked intellects and theorist enthusiasts with just enough shrewdness to half disguise their ultimate purpose: when it abandons politics, in the sane sense, and makes itself an engine for propagation of a theory--in short, when it goes in for a educational canvass, somebody is bound to be educated. p1c8

This piece lacks specifics, but certainly indicates a poorly run Democratic campaign.

From the Lexington Gazette: "Partly, in our opinion, it (the reason for the defeat) was forcing tariff reduction as the sole and prominent issue of the campaign." p2c2 "The Mills Bill was so sweeping and radical and instantaneous in its operation as to threaten destruction to many vested interests..." p2c2

They didn't learn from experience! "In the late congressional election no names were recorded on the poll books at Keene and Sulphur Well, consequently those precincts are thrown out." p3c3

From Nicholasville: "Miss Lulu Taylor, of Sulphur Well neighborhood, has returned home from school at Midway."
p3c3

From Buckeye: A revival at Gunn's Chapel was extremely successful. Belle Hunt assisted, and was described as follows:
> Her very manner, as well as her words, carry conviction to the hearts of her hearers, and no one can doubt the sincerity of religious zeal and fervor or the truthfulness of the assertion that she has consecrated her life to the Lord, 'turned her back on the world and her face to the cross', and is always and under all circumstances 'happy on the way' in the path she has chosen. p1c6

### November 23, 1888

Dr John C Miller's farm has been placed on sale. It is located four miles east of Nicholasville. The farm contains 218 acres, has a brick residence, stock barn, cow stable, mule shed, "never-failing springs", a trotting track, carriage house, smoke-house, hen house, milk house, cistern, tenant house, fish pond, and a young orchard. The "fencing is nearly all stone." p1c2 Dr Miller's farm in on the Chrisman Mill Road, and is not the "Miller Farm" that is located on what is now known as Snowden Lane, off the Hoover Pike.

### November 30, 1888

Ground was broken and the grading work on the Madison route commenced. The Tates Creek line was selected over the Silver Creek route because it was shorter, and the landowners gave almost all the right-of-way to the railroad. p2c2

### December 7, 1888

The line of the Richmond, Irvine, Nicholasville and Three Forks Railroad has been located in Madison County. There will be a bridge built at the mouth of Tates Creek.

### December 14, 1888

The evangelists of the day are well paid, the best receiving as much as $200 per day. p1c6 However, some feel that they have peaked in popularity. p1c4

### December 21, 1888

The Louisville, New Albany & Chicago Railroad leased the Louisville Southern, the company that is building the road through Nicholasville.

### December 28, 1888

There is concern about the take-over of the Louisville Southern. From the Lexington Press: The L & N "practically owns the Louisville Southern", which has been leased to the L N & A Railroad, "commonly known as the Monan Route". The lessee has no obligation to extend the present Southern line. p4c5

The River and Harbor bill before Congress is expected to provide $100,000 for the improvement of the Kentucky River.

"Miss Jennie Parrish, of Louisville, is visiting Miss Julia Hare, Sulphur Well." p3c3

The year ends without a report from Sulphur Well. Ivy continued a series of six articles that began in December, 1887, and ended in April, 1888. Alaric penned a series of six articles in June and July. Then, what appears to be another correspondent commenced writing in August, 1888. After a few more articles in September there were none for the remainder of the year. From all appearances, the correspondents--Ivy, Alaric, and Unsigned --are three different people. Ivy refers to Sulphur Well as Ambrose, the others do not. Ivy refers to Wm Bright rather than W H Bright as the others do. Alaric says Mamie, and Unsigned says Mayme; in referring to Mayme Hare who marries McClellan Johnston. Ivy and Unsigned refer to him as Wm McC Johnston, while Alaric writes McClellan. In referring to Dr Wilds sister, Ivy writes Sibbie, Alaric writes Syb, and Unsigned writes Sybelle. Its quite possible that a writer is not always consistent in using names. Ivy writes that Johnston is a dashing young lawyer, which sounds feminine; while Unsigned writes that he is a rising young lawyer, which sounds like someone older. Alaric spells the name Broomfield, while Unsigned spells it Brumfield; both spellings were used in those days.

## THE RAILROAD - 1889

Building the "Riney B" Railroad through Nicholasville is an important part of the local history. Also, the Sulphur Well correspondent appears to identify himself this year.

### January 4, 1889

Pomp says that its "a very dull Christmas at this place. Some miserable thief stole a few things from Overstreet's shoe case Christmas night." p3c4 Pomp runs the general store in Little Hickman.

Pretty incredible, but it happened! "The Carlisle Christian Church expelled four members, and the pastor, Elder Edmonds, created a sensation by announcing that he had about seventy others on his list, and that unless a reformation was shown in their lives there would be more to follow". p1c3

Edmund A Lord, last in England, again writes to S M Duncan from Odessa, Russia! He is studying the history of the Greek Church which he says is strongest in Russia. p1c4-5

Beattyville is preparing for the railroad. The Corps of Engineers is engaged in laying out streets and parks, anticipating that Beattyville will become the "Birmingham of Kentucky". p2c2

Dr Miller is still advertising his farm for sale.

### January 11, 1889

Bennett Young says that an army of men are waiting to begin the Lawrenceburg and Lexington roadway. p1c3

There was a real estate transfer of a town lot to W D Harris and Dr Miller. p2c4

Dick Pilcher and Emma Dorman got married."Miss Emma Dorman is the third daughter of Mrs Nannie Dorman. She has for the past two years occupied a position as saleslady in the dry goods establishment of R E Cannon, and by her pleasing dispositon has made inumerable friends throughout the county." p3c4 This is one of the many friends of Texie.

Here is a bit of philosopy that I couldn't pass up:
"He who scorns wine, women and song
Lives a fool his whole life long!"p3c3

### January 18, 1889

From Nicholasville: "Miss Lizzie Hendren, of Lexington, and Miss Sallie Woolfolk, of Garrard, were the guests of Mrs A K Adcock last week." P3c3 This the Sallie Woolfolk who accompanied Wm McC Johnston to Sulphur Well and is well known by the Sulphur Well correspondent.

### January 25, 1889

Prices of agricultural goods have tended to remain low. The price of hemp has dropped even lower, to $4 per 112 pounds.

### February 1, 1889

Dr Miller is still trying to sell his farm.   "Mrs Betsy Bourne, of Sulphur Well neighborhood", died on January 24th. p3c3 From Pink: Elbert Walker visited Runyon's last week.

"Tramps and theives are getting numerous in and out of the city. Keep a lookout for them." p2c2

Kentucky just passed a Medical Practices Act that goes into effect in April, and "...no one can practice medicine in the State without a diploma from a reputable medical college, (is) endorsed by ... the State Board of Health, and registered ... (by) the County Clerk." Physicians with 24 years practice are exempted.p4c4

### February 8, 1889

Farmers in Ohio and the upper counties of Kentucky are organizing a tobacco trust.

After several months, another article from the *Sulphur Well Correspondent*:

*Much has transpired since our last writing that might have been of interest to the time-honored Journal, but for reasons best known to your humble correspondent we have failed to report the same, but again, at your request, we resume our correspondence.*

*The past week has been quite a sad one with us as several of our citizens have been called to their long homes, and others not expected to live many days.*

*Mr Wm. Lay, an honest, well-to-do, and hard-working farmer, son-in-law of Mr Moraney Moore, departed this life Friday, Feb. 1st. He was sick but a few days, having a complication of diseases, chief of which was pneumonia. Drs. Miller, Hendren and Squire Welch attending him.*

*Mrs Fountain Switzer died Sunday evening, Feb. 3, of consumption.*

*Mrs John Peele died Monday morning at 4 o'clock of pneumonia.*

*Mrs Lay, mother of Wm. Lay, deceased, is very ill at the home of her son, and not expected to live. Mr Moraney Moore is also reported to be dangerously ill.*

*(Mrs Lay, died on Wednesday, and was buried in Madison County Tuesday.)*

*Two of our brightest and prettiest young ladies are visiting friends in Garrard - Miss Carrie Woodward is visiting Miss Sallie Woolfolk, of Buckeye, and Miss Julia Hare is visiting her sister, Mrs W M Johnston, of Lancaster.*

*Rev. T. Warn. Beagle will preach for us again in the Christian Church at this place on the first Sunday in March, at 3 o'clock, p.m. We hope all who can will attend, that they may receive the benefit of a true gospel sermon.*

*Mr J H Murphy paid a short visit to his friends, W O Bradley and Wm McClellan Johnston, of Lancaster, Sunday and Monday.*

*Mr H C Hemphill shipped his hogs to Cincinnati last week. He also had an offer for his farm by some parties from the mountains, but declined, and we are glad he did, for Hugh would be very much missed by all in this vicinity.*

*Messrs. Walker and Bourne are slaughtering some very fine beef cattle now for this village and your town market; you only need to give them a trial and be convinced.*

*The public school at this place closed Friday afternoon with quite a variety of speeches and compositions; notably among those of special interest were those of Messrs. Hugh Miller and Clayton West, which contained much sound advise and worthy to be followed. There were others that deserve mention, but we must not intrude on the liberality of our kind editor, if he is a widower and has the patience of Job. But just a word for our faithful teachers. Considering the many disadvantages under which they labor they have done a remarkably good part by the school as a whole, and the younger ones over whom Mrs Baird had charge have exceeded all expectation in the wonderful and rapid advancement they have made. Some that scarcely knew their A B C's at the beginning of the school, can now read well in the Second Reader, and have spelled the old blue-back spelling book through the second time. Now, in consideration of all this, and since Mr Baird has given us double work for the public money, we think it nothing but our reasonable duty to give him and Mrs Baird, as an expression of our gratitude, the full attendance of all who had the benefit of the public school for the next five months, as it was with this object in view that Mr Baird and his wife made such a sacrifice of their time.*

*Misses Ella March, of Richmond, and Sallie Patton, of your city, visited friends at this place last week.*

*Mr and Mrs C T Taylor and Mr and Mrs Milton Horine were the guests of their mother, Mrs Margaret Horine, last Sunday.*

*We are glad to report that Mrs Maggie Cook is still improving, and we hope by early Spring she will be able to be out again.*

*Mrs Sarah Foster, who was partially paralyzed last week, is rapidly improving. p3c4*

This has to be the longest single article that the Correspondent has submitted!

## February 15, 1889

From Irvine: Work on the rail line commenced. The teams and men are on hand, and ground was broken four miles above Irvine. "The engineers have completed the survey to the river at Irvine...." They are "running a line on the northeast side of Irvine, by Estill Springs, to a crossing of the Kentucky River at the foot of Sweet Lick Mountain.p2c2

Nicholasville now has telephone service to Harrodsburg through Danville. It appears likely that service will soon be extended to Stanford, Lancaster, and possibly Richmond.

From Decatur, Ala, Feb 9, 1889.
   To the Editor of the Journal: I have seen a copy of your paper at the Tavern and I like it. Enclosed find $1. Send paper as long as the dollar lasts and then I will send another. Yours truly, Ben Bledsoe. p3c3

From Nicholasville, Ky Feb 13, 1889:
   Dear Sir; That dollar didn't last long. I paid it to Hotel Nicholas for board. Send another. Don't grumble, for you know how it is to B Bled-so. Ed. Journal." p3c3

The railroad is advertising tickets for the Marti Gras in New Orleans, with trains leaving every morning and night. The travel time is twenty-seven hours.

Still settling the Merriman Miller estate, I suppose:"M F Miller's Adm'r vs Samuel Barkley, Equity." p4c2 Barkley married Catherine Miller, daughter of Merriman F Miller, on January 2, 1879. She was 37 at the time. She is variously known as Kate or Kitty. Kitty is on her tomb stone. She is buried in Maple Grove Cemetery, Section L, and not with Barkley, but in the Allen Clay Watts lot. Kitty was born December 14, 1843, and died June 13, 1923.

February 22, 1889

There has been some progress on the railroad. A contract was let for 25 miles of track.

Dr Miller purchased a twelve year-old stallion by Old Almont, name not given.

A guager suffered a painful accident from stepping in a hole in the floor of Greenbaum's warehouse near Sulphur Well.

"Bright--on the 13th, to the wife of W H Bright, near Sulphur Well, a 10 pound daughter." p3c3

The *Sulphur Well Correspondent* writes:

*Mrs Ophelia Berkie and daughter, of Harrodsburg, made a short visit to her brothers, Messrs. Alex. and Sam Askins, last week.*
*Mr and Mrs W McC. Johnston, of Lancaster, were the guests of her father, W H Hare, last Sunday, returning home Monday. Mr Mills Parish, of Louisville, was also the guest of Mr Hare several days last week.*
*We are sorry to report Mrs Dr Hendren very ill with pneumonia. She was taken sick while waiting on her father, Mr G Jasper, who is not expected to live. Mrs Hendren is still at her fathers, not able to come home.*
*Miss Ella Woodward, of Daughter's College, Harrodsburg, is at home for a few days visit, not feeling well enough to attend school.*
*Mr Ben Grimes, of Lexington, is visiting his brother and sisters at this place.*
*B F Wilds, of Garrard, was over here Monday with the view of buying work stock. He succeeded in getting a good mare mule 3 years old, broke, from J P Turner, at the low price of*

$110. He was very much pleased with one of our pretty girls. We may look for him over again very soon.

   Miss Julia Hare returned home Sunday from a very pleasant visit to friends and relatives near Lancaster. She was accompanied by Mr John Johnson, who is a clerk in Robinson's hardware store at Lancaster, and is a very promising young man.

   Miss Rhoda Peel, of Hanly, entered school at this place Monday, and will board with Mrs L E Baird. We are glad to have Miss Rhoda with us and it is encouraging to Mr Baird to receive scholars out of his district.

   Mr James Woodward has returned home from Harrodsburg, where he has been for several months, to enter school here. We are glad to know Mr Baird has a full school, for he deserves it.

   Mr Groom Taylor was very worthily elected county committeeman of the Democratic party for the precinct last Saturday.

   Mr Frank Rettig and other employees have been kept quite busy at Greenbaum's warehouse for some time past, having shipped 100 barrels last week, and orders are out for as many more this week. They are rushing matters for their time on bonded whiskies expires the first of June or July.

   Thanks to H G Turner, of Centre College, for an invitation to attend the annual celebration of Washington's Birthday, Friday, Feb. 22, at the Second Presbyterian Church, Danville, and we are glad to know that Horace is one of four chosen by the faculy to enter an oratorical contest which takes place at Lexington in the near future, and it would be highly gratifying to us should he win the laurels of the occasion; for he is possessed of more than ordinary intellect, and we predict for him a brilliant future.

   We are sorry to report Mr Moraney Moore no better, and his physician, Dr S D Welch, entertains no hope of his recovery. p2c4

March 1, 1889

Nothing wrong with price-fixing in these days! The millers of central Kentucky decided to raise the price of flour by ten cents per hundred pounds. p1c4

Several crops of tobacco sold for seven cents a pound.p1c8 This is a very low price. The Kentucky Burley Tobacco Growers proposed raising half a crop in 1889, and indeed, that position was endorsed at a convention held in Lexington. However, this was unsatisfactory to the Ohio growers. p1c8

Moraney Moore died on February 21, 1889 leaving "a large family well provided for. He was buried at his home." p3c3 "Home" was the farm on the road to Black Bridge, just south of the Hoover Pike intersection. It adjoins the farm that belonged to Newt Davis.

Let me list the merchants adverting at this time, showing the type of goods offered: W G Moseley sold buggies, wagons, and farm equipment; W N Alliband did repairs of all kinds, both blacksmithing and woodwork, and made vehicles to order; H H Lowry sold groceries, glassware, and lamp goods; Chas. Deering sold dry goods; Mitchell & Davis sold hardware, stoves and tinware; E J Young had a livery, feed, and sales stable; Harris & Co. sold furniture, carpets, and conducted a undertaking establishment; H W Rose was a tailor and clothier; Mrs M Kilvington sold dry goods and notions; Hadley sold watches, jewelry, and spectacles; I Levy, prop. Ky Clothing House sold men's clothing; A G Woods had a pharmacy; B Wolf dealt in coal, wood, salt, lime, cement, plaster; Masters & Son sold fresh fruits and bread; J J Bronaugh sold boots and shoes. This gives a pretty good view of the goods and services available.

March 8, 1889

This week is devoted mostly to Miller Family history!

From Nicholasville: "M M Miller, one of the leading business men of Irvine, visited his brother, Dr J C Miller, last week." p3c3

M M Miller is Merriman (Mann) Miller, son of Merriman F and Celia Miller, born November 23, 1846. He went to Irvine as a young man, where he met Bettie Anderson. They were married on December 24, 1874. For many years he was in the banking and mercantile business in Irvine. Mann retired soon after 1900, and moved to Lexington, where he bought and sold rental property, accumulating a relatively large estate. Both he and Bettie are buried in the Lexington Cemetary. They had a son and two daughters, and I will give a more complete account of them later.

From Nicholasville: "Rice Miller, who is attending Estill Seminary, at Irvine, made a brief visit last week to his home in this county." p3c3 Rice Miller is the oldest of Dr John C Miller's children, and I will report a lot more about him later also.

Dr Miller's farm, for sale privately for several months, is now listed by G W Lyne & Co. as being four miles from Nicholasville, on the Nicholasville and Ky River pike (Chrisman Mill).

"The Estill Eagle says that James W Miller, of Irvine, has sold his farm to R M Quinn for the sum of twenty-eight hundred dollars, cash. It is reported that he will locate in Jessamine County, and open up a merchandise business, which will suit Jim much better than farming. We all wish him success." p3c5 . The store that he established was in the corner of Dr Hendren's yard, which is across from the Askins blacksmith shop and adjacent to the store operated by J H Murphy. Jim is a brother of Forest Miller, my grandfather.

There is some "correspondent" news. Richard Bricken, from Harrodsburg, but now the barber at the Hotel Nicholas, and Beatrice Funk, the Union Mills school teacher and Jessamine Journal correspondent have eloped. He "was seen getting into a buggy and driving rapidly out the Union Mills pike." Somewhat later he was joined by Miss Funk at the Red Oak schoolhouse. They came throught Nicholasville on their way to Lexington, and were met there by Andy Haggin and Fount Hendren who had gone on ahead on the train to make arrangements for the wedding at the Ashland House. The couple was married by a Lexington minister. p3c3 Her article in this week's Journal said "Look out for a wedding in this neighborhood soon." p4c2

From Spears: "Miss Emma Davis, accompanied by Miss Emma Reynolds, of Sulphur Well, was visiting friends and relatives in Richmond last week." p4c2

## March 15, 1889

There was a considerable furor in Louisville when several tobacco manufacturing companies sought to impose rules upon the warehousemen of Louisville. One of these rules pertained to having a single uniform inspection. Another concerned identifying shippers, and assessing damages, where lower quality tobacco was found in hogsheads not found by samples taken from the hogshead (a practice known as "nesting"). The latter demand was not met, and three or four buyers left the market. A tobacco tax was also a continuing problem. The Cowles Bill was proposed to repeal the tax. p1c5

From Logan Station: "Mr William Hendren sold his place in this neighborhood to relatives in Garrard County." p2c3

A steamboat from Frankfort went up the Kentucky River loaded with cement to be used in the construction of the lock at Beattyville.

## March 22, 1889

"Welch Hughes, son of Dr Dimer Hughes, of Ambrose, was shot and dangerously wounded ... by Green Harvey", ferryman at Boone's Ferry. The argument was either interference with his domestic relations, according to Harvey; or the result of an argument about waiting for service according to Hughes. p2c3 Boone's Ferry is at the end of Cobb's Lane in Jessamine County.

The *Sulphur Well Correspondent* writes:

*Miss Mattie Johns, of Pleasureville, after vising her brother, Dr. E B Johns, of Danville, called by to see her sister, Mrs Belle Davis, and other friends of this place, one day last week. She is a charming young lady, and another soul was made happy by her friendly call.*
*Miss Helena Bright, of Lancaster, a most devoted friend and sister and a highly accomplished young lady, arrived in our village on the 13th inst; and we are glad to learn that she will remain several weeks, spending most of the time with her brother, W H Bright, and Mrs Dr. Wilds.*
*Hon. Wm McC. Johnston, of Lancaster, visited his father-in-law, Mr W H Hare, Saturday and Sunday, and attended our County Court on Monday, returning home Tuesday, taking his wife, who had been here since the week before, with him. Mr Johnston is a good Republican and a promising young attorney, and from his past favors to his party and other commending qualities, we predict that when the great distribution of Republican wealth is made, he will get a share. `So might it be.'*
*Mr James Woodward, Jr., visited his sister, Mrs Lee Terhune, at Harrodsburg, last week. Jimmie has a fine little saddle mare by Clay Wilkes, which he rode; indeed she is a daisy under the saddle.*

*Master Welch Wilds rode his fine Clay-bank colt to Garrard County Friday evening, visiting his grandmother and other relatives, and returned home Sunday much pleased with his trip.*

*Dr G M Hendren has moved into the residence of Mrs Nancy Baker, and Mrs Frank Miller moved into the house vacated by him. Mrs Miller recently purchased the property from Mr Giles Saunders, of Danville, paying $1,250 cash.*

*Mr Charles Hemphill sold an alderny milch cow with young calf in town Monday at $50. p3c4*

It appears that the identity of the current Sulphur Well correspondent is W H Bright. His family is from the Lancaster area.

My great-grandmother, Elizabeth Jane Miller moved into a house in the crossroads of Sulphur Well. It was a rather large frame house, of which we still have a pretty good picture. Unfortunately, as was the case with many frame houses, it eventually burned. She had her son, Forest, and daughter, Matilda living with her at this time. I don't know whether her brother-in-law, Jim Miller, who had a store nearby, lived with her or not.

The *Sulphur Well Correspondent* wrote for the second time in this issue. When they were received late, or there wasn't enough room in a particular issue they were sometimes carried over:

*Verily the busy time has come, and the lounger is no longer seen around our groceries, telling his long-winded tales and discussing flippantly the character of his neighbors, for work is the order of the day.*

*Miss Carrie Woodward is visiting her sister, Mrs Lee Terhune, of Harrodsburg.*

*Mr Ollie Grimes and family, of Lexington, visited friends and relations here last week.*

*Mrs Mayme Johnston, of Lancaster, has been spending the week with her parents, Mr and Mrs W H Hare.*

*Mr John Johnston, of Lancaster, was over again last week. Surely he is in earnest.*

*Rev. Jos. Ison dined with Dr J L Wilds the other day. He leaves this week for the Methodist Convention to be held at Louisville, and will be absent about two weeks.*

*Miss Emma Reynolds, of Cincinnati, has returned from a visit to Richmond and is now with her sister, Mrs T J Horine, of this place. We are always glad to have Miss Emma with us.*

*Miss Mollie Myers, of Madison, is visiting her sister, Mrs J H Brumfield.*

*Miss Irene Bourne celebrated her eleventh birthday by giving a pound party to her little friends at the home of her grandfather, Mr James Woodward. The little ones seemed to enjoy themselves very much, and said the ice cream and cake were just splendid. No pains were spared to make all happy who attended.*

*Mr B F Wilds, of Buena Vista, was over again last week, taking back with him some nice stock hogs.*

*Miss Delia Grimes went home with her brother Ollie, and will remain there some time. Miss Delia is a favorite here, and will be missed by her many friends.*

*Mr Green B Preston, who has been confined to his room all the winter, is able to ride out again, and made us a visit one day this week. p4c3-4*

From Logan Station: "Mr Welch Hughes, who was recently shot at Boone's Ferry, is not considered out of danger." p3c4 The correspondent there also reports that the farmers are delivering corn for the construction crew of the railroad, and that the work is moving along. Two loads of lumber passed through on their way to the worksite. Several lots were sold by J L Logan, and it appears that a town is coming into being. Logan sold his dairy to John Schenk.

Communication between towns is rapidly improving. The telephone line from Harrodsburg to Danville, Nicholasville, Lexington, and other towns is successful, and "will be extended to Burgin ... and shortly to Lawrenceburg and Shelbyville. p4c1 Lighting is also improving. "They are talking of electric lights at Richmond and Paris." p4c1

### March 29, 1889

The railroad is moving along. They have divided the work into several work-parties. "Chief Engineer Pearson is out upon the line and we understand is putting the finishing touches to the location from Irvine on up Miller's Creek." p2c1 Proposals have been made to make use of existing track so that Lexington and Harrodsburg can be reached by existing lines. The Versailles extention is in question. The new railroad will enter Nicholasville north of the old depot, and cross Main Street above the Cemetery. A large force of negro workmen passed throught Lexington, going out the Tates Creek pike. Richmond reports sounds of blasting, and men and machinery arriving daily.

There is a rumor that I. Levy will close his Nicholasville store and move to St Louis where he has purchased a controlling interest in a large clothing establishment.

According to Pomp "Mr Murphy will soon complete over a half mile of our pike. The pike is nearing the river, and when completed will be the nearest cut from your city to Lancaster." p3c4

Registered under the new Medical Registry Act:
    George M Hendren, age 43, of Madison County. Medical College of Ohio, Cincinnati. March 1, 1875.
    John C Miller, age 48, Jessamine County. Bellevue Hospital Medical College, New York. March 1, 1865.
    James L Wilds, age 37, of Garrard County. Homeopathic Medical College, Cincinnati, Ohio. March 1888.
    Thomas Peele, Age 52, of Jessamine County. Certificate to State Board that he had been practicing since May 9, 1857. p4c1
There were many others, but these four doctors practiced in Sulphur Well at one time or another.

### April 5, 1889

Property transfers: "Giles Saunders and wife to Elizabeth J Miller, 7 acres, $1,200." p1c6 This is the house at the crossroads of Sulphur Well, where Dr Hendren lived before moving to the Baker house. It was across the road from where I was born.

The *Sulphur Well Correspondent* writes:

Mr Horace G Turner, of Centre College, Danville, made his parents a visit last week, accompanied by one of the college students whose name we did not learn.

Mrs Julia Hersberger and children, of Missouri, and Miss Irene Moseley, of Keene, spent last week with their aunt, Mrs W H Hare.

Mrs Hersberger will move to Colorado in a short time.

Mr W H Hare, for some time has devoted his time to improving his land, building a new fence and making other improvements which will add much to the general appearance of his valuable farm.

Mrs E G Wilds and grandson, of Garrard, were the guests of her son, Dr Wilds, several days last week.

Mr H C Hemphill, who has been confined to his room for several days with nasal catarrh, is enquired after every day by his numerous friends, and they are anxious to see his jovial countenance again.

Miss Helena Bright and Mrs Dr Wildes were in Lexington Tuesday, visiting friends, and while there called at the Asylum to see Mrs John Masters and Miss Adams, of Garrard, both of whom seemed glad to see them and asked about their many friends.

We are sorry to report Mrs Maggie Cook not so well again. She has been riding around lately, was at the Well and Hanly, and remained standing on the ground for sometime and caught cold.

We called at the stables of Chrisman Bros. this week and found them busy fitting up their stables in the best of style, to accomodate their increasing business. They have four fine stallions at present, and are making a 7/8th mile track. These gentlemen are wide-awake business men, and deserve the patronage of the public in their line of business. p1c8

"Born - To the wife of Granville Sanders, near Sulphur Well, March 6th, a daughter." p2c3

Another twofer, a second article from the *Sulphur Well Correspondent*:

A rabid dog passed through this section of the country some twenty days ago, putting in his lethal work among the stock and his canine brothers. Mr J H Brumfield lost a fine brood sow and two hounds, and Mr Chas. Hemphill lost two head of fine cattle, and there may be more to succumb to the dread hydrophobia.

Mr Everett Bourne and Mr W H Bright went to Lancaster this week, taking with them Miss Lena Bright and her little niece, Birtie May. We are sorry to have Miss Lena leave us so soon, but will look forward with pleasure for another promised visit in the near future.

Misses Fannie Grow and Sybelle Wilds, of Garrard, are visiting friends and relatives in this county.

Miss Delia Grimes returned home last Saturday from a very pleasant visit to her brother in Lexington.

Sorry to learn that Miss Mary Preston, daughter of Mr Berryman Preston, is confined to her room with affection of the hip.

Mr Charlie Hudson sold his combined mare last week for a good price. p3c3

April 12, 1889

The merchants are having their day. The rumor is true. I. Levy is leaving town by August 1st. He has a wholesale establishment in St Louis. This is the Grand Opening of Bush Cook's Clothing Company. Croquet sets and hammocks have just been received by Mitchell & Davis.

A few drunks shot up the Shakers at Pleasant Hill! One of the drunks, a man by the name of Ed Lait, was angry because his wife left him to live there. p2c5

The *Sulphur Well Correspondent* writes:

*In last week's issue we reported Mr Chas Hemphill as having lost two fine cows from hydrophobia, but we were misinformed, as it was Mr L T Hemphill, and he has since lost a fine steer; and Mr Brumfield is reported to have lost another hog and one or two more dogs with the same dread disease.*

*Mr Wm. McClelland Johnston and wife, of Garrard, were over again Saturday and Sunday. Mr Johnston has applied for the post office at Lancaster, and we hope he may meet with success in his application.*

*Drs Welch and Wilds visited Buena Vista last Wednesday on professional and other business.*

*Mr Jimmie Turner has been confined to his bed with rheumatism for the last week, but it is not of a grave type, and we hope he will soon be out again. He is much better at present.*

*We are glad to see Mr F M Horine suggested as a candidate for Representative, and we think the Democrats of Jessamine would do well to consider his case in making their choice for same.*

*Well, the protracted meeting in your town has closed, much to the regret of some of our young (?) folks, who seemed to enjoy the ride there and back, almost as much as they did the sermons. Will not call any names as they are so timid.*

*As this is a good day for fishing, and we have nothing of any special interest to write, we will close our communication for the present, and hope for better results in the future, as matrimony seems to be the absorbing topic with some of our widows and widowers.* p3c4

April 19, 1889

Evidently yellow fever took its toll in Decatur, Alabama. People were scared, investors left, and factories closed. However, business is reviving. A former Kentuckian says that the town is extremely clean, the result of the work of the sanitary and health officials. p1c7

The work on the railroad is going well in the Tates Creek area. The approaches on the Madison side have been prepared for a tunnel expected to be about 650 long. The contract for the iron work for the bridge has not been let. Some of the negro workers are from Richmond, Va. and have worked on several other roads. p2c3

Court Day has been designated "Horse Show Day".

"Settlement with committee Matilda Miller and guardian of F F Miller. Filed and continued." From the County Court. This must have something to do with their share, as grand-children, of the Merriman Miller estate. p3c4

### April 26, 1889

High Bridge reported good fishing, with the shores lined with anglers. Several correspondents report that fishing parties are being arranged.

Oklahoma was opened for settlement Tuesday, and the territory is said to be overrun with squatters, speculators, gamblers, and adventurers. There is a lot more to come about Oklahoma.

From Nicholasville: "Miss Scottie Hendren, of Lexington, is visiting Mrs A K Adcock." p3c3

### May 3, 1889

Educational opportunities for women are improving. Kentucky University, in Lexington, will admit female students for the fall term.

### May 10, 1889

According to the Journal editor a large number of people in the Blue Grass area are illiterate, both black and white. He says that even candidates for public office can scarcely write their names, and that reading a book would be out of the question.

By way of contrast, it's time again for the Lexington Chuatauqua, commencing on June 25th, and lasting for ten days. Those who were educated reveled in it, heard speakers on many issues, both religious and secular, listened to music, and socialized.

### May 17, 1889

Dr Wilds left Sulphur Well. "Dr J L Wilds, of Ambrose, has bought of Mrs Mary Oxley her two-story brick residence on Mulberry street. Price paid, $3,500." p3c3

Miss Sittie Fritzlen, daughter of a Nicholasville merchant, who has spent the past year or two in New Mexico, teaching, has returned. p3c4 She has published an interesting article on her experiences in the Journal.

### May 24, 1889

The Railroad has decided to make the bridge over the Kentucky River entirely in iron. The span will be 300 feet with long approaches on each side.

From the *Sulphur Well Correspondent*:

*Miss Lizzie Peyton, who has been in a very critical condition with complication of troubles caused by falling down stairs, is thought by her physicians, Drs Mann and Wilds, to be some better at present.*

*Dr John S Welch, becoming weary of town life, came to our little village last week to get the benefits of the sulphur water and country air, and reports himself much improved.*

*Mrs Sallie Grimes came from Lexington last week to assist Mrs Baird in waiting on Miss Lizzie Peyton. She is an experienced hand, and the family is very glad to have her assistance in this, their trying hour.*

*Dr Fritz Askenstedt, of Cincinnati, is visiting Dr Wilds this week. They were room-mates at Pulte Medical College, where he graduated this spring. He has been associated with Dr Phil Porter, of Detroit, Mich., for several years, and this accounts for his proficiency.*

*Mrs Frank Miller and daughter have returned from a visit to relatives in Estill County. Miss T. Miller was quite sick while she was in Estill, having two physicians waiting on her at one time.*

*Mrs Mahala Foster is still very feeble, not expected to live long. She is 88 years old.*

*Mr N D Davis bought a fine lot of hogs from Mr Cal Crow last week. Price paid $4.25 per cwt.*

*Dr S L Wilds sold his fine saddle and harness mare, which he recently bought from Mr Charles Hudson, to Mr J F Ruble, of Garrard County for $125. He also sold a 4-year old gelding to Mr Sadler, of Tennessee, for $100.*

*The ladies of the Christian Church at this place will give an ice-cream and strawberry supper Saturday evening, May 25, for the benefit of the church. All come and bring your 25 cents, and we assure you, you will get the worth of your money.*

*Glad to see the smiling countenance of Mr H G Turner, of Centre College, in our midst last week.* p3c4

May 31, 1889

From Nicholasville: "Dr J L Wilds and family, of Ambrose, will move to Nicholasville about the first of next month, where the Doctor will practice his profession. He is a genial, cultivated gentlemen, and we will be glad to have him and his family among us." p4c1

June 7, 1889

The fashion report from New York indicates that black and white are particularly popular colors. Women are wearing black sashes on colored dresses. "India silks showing colored figures on a black background are very fashionable." Black hats and black gloves worn with colorful dresses, are very popular. p1c6

The Johnstown flood, that we still remember a century later, has just occurred! The water rushed down the Allegheny mountains and completely submerged the town of Johnstown, Pa. Over 1500 buildings were swept away, and there were estimates of 5,000 fatalities. p2c3

The Decatur, Ala. Bridge Company has been awarded the contract for the bridge over the Kentucky River.

June 14, 1889

Another new store has opened, just opposite the Hotel Nicholas. Jacob Frankel & Co. has general merchandise, clothing, notions, and shoes. However, the steam laundry in Nicholasville failed.

The strawberry crop is the finest in years!

From the Irvine Eagle: "Dr J C Miller, of Jessamine, was a guest of his brother, M M Miller, this week." p4c2

The census of school children at Ambrose was 104 for the year 1890. That was pretty large. Nicholasville had only 327. Notice the shift as time goes on.

June 21, 1889

A society wedding: The daughter of Dr S D Welch of Nicholasville and the son of Judge T J Scott of Richmond were just married. She is described as: "a young lady of beauty and intellect, ... excellence of character and womanly attainments...." He is "a lawyer and jurist of marked ability and a gentlemen of culture and universal popularity." After the wedding they departed on their wedding tour of Washington and New York. p3c2

"Earnest Duncan, near Sulphur Well, bought a horse in Madison last week, for which he paid $100." p3c2

Deering is selling his merchandise at cost. He has dry goods, notions, etc. He says the unseasonable weather hindered the sale of spring and summer merchandise.

From High Bridge: "Rain, rain, rain!" "The river is booming-thirty feet of water in the channel, and still rising. The lower bottoms are submerged...."p3c5

June 28, 1889

The editor instructs the correspondents: He tells them not to say convalescing, but to say getting well or recovering; to say Sunday when them mean Sunday, and not to use the Sabbath which could mean Saturday or Sunday; not to use evening when they mean afternoon; and "for Heaven's Sake don't say Mr Smith and lady, say Mr and Mrs Smith." p1c5

The liquor men were taunting the Prohibitionists that Jesus made wine for the people to drink. This caused the Lexington Blade, a Prohibitionist paper, to say that they didn't believe that Jesus turned water into wine, and if he did that it was an improper thing to do! p1c5

A little sarcasm from the editor about some self-rightous citizens: "The Pope is said to be very sick. Should he die, his successor might be found right here in Nicholasville ...." p2c2

Part of the inducement to vacation at Dripping Springs was a musical band, and an instructor who would teach all the latest society dances. p2c4

J W Overstreet, the Little Hickman correspondent known as Pomp, has invented a type of pliers, and has gone on a selling and demonstration tour. His column from Little Hickman is being written this week by L.O., and according to L.O., J W is fed up with selling on credit, and intends to sell at a lower price for cash only. p3c5

July 5, 1889

Lizzie Peyton, who had fallen down the stairs at the Baird residence in Sulphur Well, died at the age of 62. She suffered a "concussion and compression of the spine" that resulted in partial paralysis. p3c2

July 12, 1889

Estill Springs is at the foot of Sweet Lick Knob. Sweet Lick Creek is bounded by the "towering forms of California Ridge, Rock House and Hardwick's Chain." There are three springs--white, red, and chalybeate. p1c8

The editor of the Journal took a week off to vist Estill Springs, and this is his description of the journey: He left Nicholasville in the morning "with a good horse, and comfortable phaeton", making Richmond by noon in time for "dinner". He took the stage from Richmond to Irvine. It seated nine on the inside, and four on top.
> The road from Richmond to Irvine is fully as good as from Nicholasville to Richmond, through a good farming region, well cultivated, and embellished with tasteful improvements in the way of neat cottages and substantial farm houses. The scenery is pleasant and picturesque, and the eye is relieved by more woodlands and forests than we are accustomed to see in the regions around Nicholasville and Lexington. It is finely watered country--streams crossing the road every mile or so. p2c1

They arrived in Irvine in time for supper. He said that several Jessamine County people had settled there and seemed satisfied. Among those he mentioned was M M (Mann) Miller, who he said was doing well in the dry goods business. He said that there was no liquor sold at the Springs, and that those who mixed liquor with the sulphur water usually got sick.

A local girl, Mary Bradshaw, married Rudolph Weiser, who was thought to be a millionaire. He made his money as an engineer and contractor in Mexico. He bought an estate in Lexington for $60,000 and gave it to his wife. It shocked local society when she sued for divorce charging cruel and inhuman treatment. This was a surprise since there had been no rumors of problems in the marriage, although he had been in Mexico for the past two years. p2c3

John L Sullivan whipped Kilrain in 75 rounds. p2c3

The Republicans and Democrats are holding meetings to select their candidates for the coming election.

From Nicholasville: "Misses Susie and Scottie Hendren, of Lexington, are visiting their sister Mrs A K Adcock". p3c3

From the *Sulphur Well Correspondent*:

*Considering the long continued rains and other disadvantages, the crops in our "neck of the woods" are fair. Wheat will average fifteen to twenty bushels per acre. Corn is looking well.*
  *Mr and Mrs T J Horine entertained a few friends at their residence one evening last week. All expressed themselves as delighted.*
  *Mr Geo. Diamond who has been ill for some days is better at this writing.*
  *Messrs. J H Murphy and G M Hendren were in Richmond last week on business.*
  *Rob't Pulliam, A.M., recently of Centre college, but now of Central University (Richmond), was in town Monday laboring in behalf of the latter school. "Bob" was lately elected Principal of the preparatory of Central University. Quite and honor for a four years graduate.*
  *Here of late our little village has put on something of its old time look of gaiety. For several days past our streets have been filled with visitors. Among the number were Mrs N D Brewer and family, of Danville; Mr Hendrick, of Cincinnati; Misses Shearer and Willis, two charming young ladies of Richmond; Master Preston Sea, of Louisville; and Miss Fannie Hoskins, of Campbellsville.*
  *Mr and Mrs J P Turner entertained a few young people at their home on Wednesday evening. Among those present were Misses Julia Hare, Celia Matthews, Virginia Hemphill, of this county; Fannie Hoskins, of Campbellsville and Mamie Brewer, of Danville; Messrs. Dan Miles, Tom Welch, Dan Hemphill and Joe Matthews of the county, and Will Brewer, of Danville.*
  *A large number of our people (your scribe included) have expressed a desire to attend camp meeting Sunday. "What fools these mortals be." p3c5*

July 19, 1889

No good news for farmers, or their creditors. A tobacco trust has been formed with a capital of $36 million. Its purpose is to prevent competition in buying leaf tobacco. The lamb market continues "dull", and shippers have barely covered expenses. Collecting accounts is difficult. As one merchant put it "the first of July has come, and your account is due...." p3c1

The paper has been full of articles concerning prohibition. Despite any doubts concerning prohibition, the editor says there is "one policy (on which) all good people can agree, and that is the organizing of public sentiment against drunkenness." He continues "the chief aim of all good citizens ... should be to make drunkenness constantly more odious, and thus less and less common." p2c1

The Camp Meeting at High Bridge was attended by a great number of people coming from every town in Central Kentucky. Trains were completely full. p3c1 A heavy rainstorm occurred Sunday when people were returning from the meeting "some walking, others on horseback or in vehicles, and the expression of discomfort marked in their faces...." p2c3

### July 26, 1889

Dr Miller's farm is still for sale, $65 per acre. Farmers are advised to hold their wheat. They are told that exporting countries such as Russia and Hungary have no wheat to spare, and that the India crop is poor. The United States overall has a fair crop, and it is felt that Europe will want all that can be spared. A cattleman says there is no money in feeder cattle at this time. They cost $4 (per hundred) to purchase, and after feeding them they are worth only $4.30-$4.35.

There are several political articles since the election will be August 5th. The state is changing, says the editor. "Indifference to all progressive measures is giving way to an active interest in the development of the resources of the Commonwealth."p1c4

Work on the Kentucky River dams is progressing slowly. Work is presently underway on the new lock, No 6. The other dams have been repaired and are declared to be in good shape.

### August 2, 1889

From the *Sulphur Well Correspondent*:

*The contractors have begun repairing the Black bridge over Hickman Creek.*
*Messrs Chas Horine and Walter Hendren attended the Kirksville Fair on Friday and Saturday.*
*Misses McMinowey and Holman, of Harrodsburg, were the guests of Miss Carrie Woodward, Saturday and Sunday.*
*Mr Joe Brumfield is now occuping the house recently vacated by Dr Wilds.*
*Messrs Derb Sugars and Frank Johnston, of Lancaster, paid our place a flying visit on Sunday.*
*Miss Julia Hare is visiting her sister, Mrs McClellan Johnston, of Lancaster.*
*Miss Ella Wheeler, of Cincinnati, is visiting Mrs Dr Hendren.*
*Our farmers are having a great deal of trouble with the hay harvest. The crop will be very much damaged by the long continued rains.*
*Miss Mattie Woodward and brother James of Mercer, visited their parents at this place during the week.*
*Our people disapprove the collection of the railroad tax. Of course we cannot tell what the result will be. p3c6*

August 9, 1889

There was an attempt made to get Judge Phillips and the magistrates to meet, and reconsider the railroad tax that they had imposed, the one referred to in the Sulphur Well correspondent's last item above. p2c1

One of the leading evangelist in the area is George O. Barnes. General Landram writes that the record of Brother Barnes in the Mexican War was that "he blew the fife with great vigor." In any case he was awarded $8 per month for his "distinguished" service in the Mexican War. p1c6

"Two persons were struck by lightning at Sulphur Well, near the church, last Sunday. They were John West and John Baird. West was stunned and rendered senseless for some time, and Baird was so shocked that it is thought his hearing is impaired." p4c1

August 16, 1889

One would have scarcely thought that Nicholasville would have a "green grocer" in 1889, but it did! Masters & Son.

From the *Sulphur Well Correspondent*:

*The farmers have begun cutting tobacco. There is a tolerable fair crop.*
*Miss Etta Gray, of Lexington, is the guest of Miss Viola Davis.*
*Mrs J P Turner accompanied by her sons, Horace and Luther, spent last week with friends in Danville and Lancaster.*
*Miss Julia Hare returned home Sunday after a pleasant visit of two weeks in Lancaster.*
*J P Turner and son are attending the District Conference of the M E Church at Brown's Chapel, Garrard county, this week.*
*Hogs are very scarce, and worth five cents. The corn crop is so abundant that most persons are feeding what they have instead of selling.*
*Our public school is being taught by Prof Baird, an able and experienced teacher.*
*Hon McClellan Johnston, of Lancaster, was in town Sunday. He is a rising young lawyer, and was recently appointed Stamp Agent of this district.*
*Dr G M Hendren bought of Mitchell Masters one gray gelding. Price paid, $150.*
*Mr Jas. Cobb fell from a loaded wagon last week and was painfully, though not dangerously hurt. Both arms were sprained, and he was otherwise bruised.*
*Mr J T West recently refused $95 for a mule colt. They are very high this season.*
*Rev. Joe Ison, of Buena Vista, and Rev. Jas Young, of your city, visited friends here last week.*
*Many of our people are attending the protracted meeting at Little Hickman. The preacher, Bro. Ferrell, is an old Sulphur Well boy, and his old friends like to hear him.* p3c4

Please keep Bro. Ferrell's name in mind. You will see more about him on October 4 and November 1. Seems to be a very kindly old gentleman.

August 23, 1889

From Logan Station: "The railroad is beginning to look natural and seems very near completion at this place...." p3c5 From Nicholasville: The depot is lively. "Wagon after wagon of wheat is being hauled there every day." p4c1

From the *Sulphur Well Correspondent*:

*Mr Edmund Davis, of Shelbyville, is visiting Millard and Willard Davis.*
*Mrs Geo. Berry and infant daughter, of Lexington, are the guests of Mrs Geo. Diamond.*
*Miss Emma Reynolds, of Cincinnati, is visiting her sister, Mrs T J Horine, of this place.*
*Mrs A N Rice, of your city, spent Sunday with relatives here.*
*J P Turner bought of M L Johns, nine yearling mules at $65 per head.*
*Mr Robt Beasley, formerly of Lancaster, but now of Pineville, was in town this week, trying to induce some of our people to invest in Eastern Kentucky mining lands.*
*Our people are now attending the protracted meeting at Pleasant Hill, which is conducted by Rev James Young. He will be ably assisted in the work, and we predict that much good will be done in the name of the Lord. p3c6*
The Mrs George Berry mentioned above is Ida Gray.

August 30, 1889

The Circuit Court is in session, and several have been charged with violating the Sabbath, the so-called "blue laws".

There is a money "stringency" in the county. "Although crops are good and prices of all articles rule as high as could be expected, there seems to be a stringency in the local money market. Our business men are complaining of difficulty in making collections, and the sheriff is compelled again to call for payment of taxes." p3c2 The tin-ware firm of Patton & Derring "made an assignment", meaning they are insolvent. The editor says that they are good men, and that the failure was for causes beyond their control. The competing newspaper went out of business, and its assets were sold by the Master Commissioner.

M. B. Frazier, the Jessamine Station correspondent is a candidate for County Superintendent of Schools. His correspondence has frequently related to education.

From the *Sulphur Well Correspondent*:

*Most of the wheat in this vicinity is threshed.*
*Elder Ward, of Lexington, preached at the Christian Church Saturday and Sunday night.*
*Mr Jas. Woodward, Jr., of Mercer County, is home on a visit to his parents.*
*Mrs Frank Miller and son have returned home from a week's visit to relatives at Irvine.*
*Mr and Mrs McClellan Johnston, of Lancaster, spent Sunday with relatives here.*
*Mr Clayton West is attending the annual association of the Baptist Church at Buckeye, Garrard County, this week.*
*Mrs Julia Hersperger, of Colorado, is the guest of Mrs Wm Hare. p3c5*

From Little Hickman: "Mrs Foster, widow of the late David Foster, was buried at this place on Wednesday, 21st. Her residence was near Sulphur Well." p4c2

September 6, 1889

Fall is reflected in the colors of women's clothing. "A peculiar rust color ... is a prominent shade in Fall importations and is expected to displace the terra cottas, yellowish browns and other kindred hues...." Shoulder capes are also in vogue. p1c6

Last week I. Levy went East to get Fall and Winter merchandise. He is back with the goods, claiming he bought wholesale (what else?), and is passing a 25 to 33 percent saving to the customers. He still promises to leave town by January 1st. He had previously said August 1st.

If you remember a few weeks ago the Sulphur Well correspondent said the local citizens weren't very happy with the imposition of the railroad tax. This appears to have been the popular sentiment. A meeting was held at the courthouse, and a resolution passed, asking the County Court to rescind the tax. The court met as requested, and did in fact rescind the tax. It was felt that the levy was premature in that road had not been built, nor the bonds issued, for which the tax was imposed.

A barge-load of wheat sunk on the Kentucky River near Clifton.

A bicycle tournament was held at Welch's Track, one-half mile south of Nicholasville. Two hundred wheelmen attended. The program consisted of eight races of distances ranging from one-half mile to five miles. Some of the events were for novices, and others were open.

September 13, 1889

There is a report from Logan Station that the railroad tunnel on Tapp's Branch collapsed. The report however, proved to be false.

September 20, 1889

There are many, many articles on potential slates for the next election, still a year away. Also, there are religious articles almost always on the front page, often two or more.

"Mr & Mrs A K Adcock are home from a visit to relatives at Knoxville, Tenn." p3c3

September 27, 1889

The editor seems to be having an opinion change on the railroads. He carried a very unfavorable letter from Texas on the manner in which railroads charge excessive rates.

Adam Adcock sold his three-year old gelding, Little Grit, for $135. p2c4

### October 4, 1889

Mrs Weiser got her wish. Her divorce was granted. She was awarded custody of a daughter. However, she did not get alimony. She did get a farm of 392 acres, and all the personal property thereon.

Quite a letter was received from J W Ferrell, of Harrisonville, Mo. about his childhood and school days in Sulphur Well. His father and Dr Geo. S Brother went into business together (in Sulphur Well) in 1858.
> Eld Jesse Walden opened a high school in the neighborhood and gathered the young people from 'the regions round about' into one of the best schools ever conducted in Jessamine County. The school began in the old log school house that stood just back of the Christian Church.

Newt Davis was one of the students. He also named the Sparks, Reynolds, Robinsons, Horines, and others as attending. p4c2

### October 11, 1889

The route of the railroad through Richmond has been decided. The various contracts have been let along the road, for cuts, fills, tunnels and bridges. The grading work between Nicholasville and Richmond is nearly completed. There are camps of men working, totaling about a thousand men, and the work is on schedule. They are predicting an early completion of the entire road, perhaps by June of 1890.

Tollgates are unpopular, and it is believed that their days are numbered. Free turnpikes are expected in the future.

"Mr and Mrs J B Stacy, of Irvine, have removed to this county, where he will take charge of the farm owned by his mother-in-law, Mrs Frank Miller." p3c1  His wife is Sarah Belle Miller. I was never before aware that he came to farm the homeplace.

"Mr and Mrs A K Adcock and little daughter Bessie, are visiting in Cincinnati."     p3c3

A new bank, The Farmer's Exchange, is opening in Nicholasville. It will build on the corner lot opposite the Hotel Nicholas. The Farmer's Bank is still located in the same place. The hotel was torn down to make way for a new movie theater in about 1950.

### October 18, 1889

A good description of how they placed the piers for the railroad bridge is given in the paper, and the technology is impressive for the time.

The editor proclaims this is the time for pumpkin pies and cider!

October 25, 1889

Some work, some play. Farmers are making sorghum. The hunters are out in droves. Corn is being gathered and hogs are being fattened for slaughter. The corn is curing nicely in the shock. Some farmers are selling their corn at $1.50 (per barrel) in the field.

November 1, 1889

Turnips and cabbage crops are a bit short this year. Irish potatoes are so plentiful that they are selling for 20 cents a bushel. It's hard to make a buck, but they try. A Whitley County man invested $85 in sugar and blackberries and sold the wine by the barrel and realized $249, after spending about 15 days work in the process. People are being advised to keep apples in shallow bins, and to examine them frequently, to keep them in good condition. Farmers are opting for less tobacco, by sowing more wheat this fall.

J W Ferrell, minister and former resident of Jessamine County has become reminisent in his old age. I believe this is his third letter back to the Jessamine Journal. This one strikes a chord with my own feelings, so I will pass along a few lines: He says that just as a "passenger on an ocean steamer... stands on the deck and gazes at the land of his birth 'til it sinks beneath the old ocean's rim..." so too does one who has moved away from his birthplace. He attributes to a poet that "all distances are measured from home...." His was a humble "log cabin on the crest of a hill overlooking most of the farm." A short way from the house, under a giant oak tree, he says, was a bubbling spring with a gourd dipper. Cream and butter were kept in the springhouse. Almost surrounding the house, he says, was an old orchard which was a constant playground. Not far away was the family graveyard. He remembers the family gathering around the fireside in the evening, with his father reading the bible. After a prayer, his mother would tuck the children in bed, putting her hand on their heads, and telling them to be good boys. He says that since that time his "life has been a mosaic of light and shadow, with bright skies and rainy days." Some honors came his way and some burdens seemed greater that he could bear. Many times he longed for his mother "to come and lay her hand on his head and give him her evening blessing."p4c2

November 8, 1889

The work on the railroad between Nicholasville and the river is amost completed. The bridge piers are nearly done. On the Madison side the work is doing well, but the court has to determine damages for two landowners along the right of way. The engineers are really good. Putting in those piers was relatively easy. The tunnels also are done well. They used steam drills for this purpose.

From the *Sulphur Well Correspondent*, a short report:

*Miss Sallie Grimes has recovered from injuries sustained by tumbling into a goods box some time since.*
*J H Murphy, storekeeper for E J Curley, is off duty for a few days, and will spend the time looking after his large merchandise business at this place.*
*Messrs. F M and Charles Horine spent several days last week in Louisville visiting their friend Wm McClellan Johnston who is now Deputy Surveyor of the Port.* p3c3

The editor declares that partridges are plentiful!

November 22, 1889

The chief engineer of the railway is moving his office from Nicholasville to Richmond, since most of the work has been completed between those two cities, and the remaining work will be from Richmond to Irvine, and then to Beattyville.

From Nicholasville:
Mrs Louvisa Hendren, mother-in-law of A K Adcock, was found dead in her bed Wednesday morning. She had been suffering with asthma for several years and with paralysis for the last year, and the latter is thought to have caused heart failure, which resulted in death. Mrs Hendren has been living in Lexington, until recently, when she came here on a visit to her daughter, Mrs Adcock. She was the mother of eight children, five girls and three boys. Two of them are married--Mrs A K Adcock, of this place, and Mrs W H Van Winkle, of Frankfort. The eldest son, Fountain, also resides here. The others are Scottie, Susie, Bertha, Harry and Leo. Mrs Hendren was a member of the Christian Church. Her remains will be taken this morning to Madison County for burial. p3c2

Death was on November 20, 1889. She is buried in the Gilead Baptist Church Cemetery.

Harry P Hendren, was called "Pat". Edith tells me that Leo was in the asylum in Lexington for many years. Addie was Mrs Adcock, and Lizzie was Mrs Van Winkle. Scottie Hendren was my grandmother, making Levisa Tudor Hendren my great grandmother.

The first snow of the season fell on the 18th.

November 29, 1889

"Misses Delia Grimes, Mattie Woodward, and Linnie Spruce, of Ambrose, leave for the South this week to spend the winter." p3c3

December 6, 1889

The editor says that "the chief employment of farmers just now is gathering corn, cutting and hauling wood". p3c1 They are also killing hogs as the weather permits.

For entertainment the Jessamine Juvenile Comedy Company will present three farces, which will be performed by ten of the town's young people. p3c21

N D Miles, whom the editor ridiculed a week or two ago, replied: He said that the County had no right to issue bonds, even if they were placed in escrow. He said that the Louisville Southern had mortgaged the road in an amount equal to the value of its assets, and as a consequence the stock that the county would receive would be worthless. He argued that because the railroad had mortgaged its assets since entering into a contract with the county it had voided the contract. He also argued that the proper procedure in issuing the bonds had not been followed, and that their issuance was tantamount to approving the violation of the contract by the railroad. p4c2

December 13, 1889

Sam Small left the Methodist Church and joined the Episcopal Church. The editor says that he must have gotten rich because whenever a Methodist gets rich he inevitably became an Episcopalian! p3c1

Maybe she didn't go south after all: "Miss Delia Grimes, of Ambrose, Jessamine County, has been in Buena Vista during the week visiting some of her friends." p2c4

December 20, 1889

Singer sewing machines are advertised for $20. There are a lot of Christmas ads this year, more than usual.

December 27, 1889

The correspondent, after a break from September, 1888 to February, 1889, resumed his articles. He identified himself as William H Bright in one of those articles. His correspondence in early 1889 is long and newsy. By the end July the reports are of medium length. In August they become quite short. There is only one very brief article thereafter on November 8th.

# FAMILY DEATHS - 1890

Rose Sageser and Belle Stacy, daughters of Elizabeth Jane Miller, died during the year and were buried in the family cemetery. Their obituaries were written by B.T.

### January 3, 1890

Winter clothing is on sale: Men's suits range from $7-$15; boy's suits from $2.50-$7; Men's overcoats from $2.50-$15; boots are selling at cost; and shoes for men or women $2-$3.

An unusually warm winter is causing meat to spoil. This also explains the clothing sales so early in the season.

Farm prices are terrible. Hogs are selling for $3.45 per hundred; cattle $3.50; and corn $1.75 per barrel. Tobacco prices are severely depressed. They are at the lowest level remembered. One crop sold for 3 cents per pound.

First report since her marriage: "Mrs Texie Gray Cooley, of Omaha, Neb., is spending the week with Mrs Dick Pilcher." p3c3

"Mrs W Van Winkle, of Frankfort, and Miss Fatima Tudor of East Hickman were the guests of Mrs A K Adcock last week." p3c3 Sisters Lizzie and Addie Hendren are visiting.

### January 10, 1890

The warm weather continues. Wheat and grass is growing like in the spring of the year, and turnip greens are large enough to use. A lot of hog meat is spoiling.

The iron work on the bridge over the Kentucky River will be completed within a week.

Property: A Nicholasville lot was transferred to Geo. M Hendren, Walter S Hendren, and Wm L Hendren, all brothers. p4c2

### January 17, 1890

If the weather continues the Louisville Southern will be running into Richmond by May 1st. After two trials the jury awarded Wm. Arnold of Madison $20,000 for the right of way through his farm. $2,000 for the land, $2,000 for fences, and $16,000 damages.

James Barkley purchased half interest of Cook Clothiers and the firm will be known as Cook and Barkley. H W Rose is offering to sell his clothing business and residence. The clothing and accessory business has been very competitive.

Religion is a serious matter. The Methodist, Baptist and Presbyterian churches of Flemingsburg were holding joint prayer meetings. The Presbyterian minister, during his prayer, touched upon the "articles of faith in his church". The Baptist minister took exception, "and on their knees, the two preachers fought over the the doctrines of their respective churches". The members of the congregation rose to their feet and gathered around "the two combatants who bombarded one another with bible quotations, denominational arguments, and sharp retort." p4c2

January 24, 1890

The bridge over the river at Tates Creek has been finished. A large workforce is located at the Clay and Arnold farms where the work had been held up by the lawsuits. The tunnel in Estill was completed in record time, and the bridge at Irvine has commenced. All the work between Irvine and Beattyville is under contract. There were some delays while siting the line at Yellow Rock, and the decision was finally made to make a 650 foot long tunnel under it. p2c2

Texie gave birth! "Born-To the wife of Thos. Cooley, on the 15th inst., a daughter." p3c1

The pliars invented by J W Overstreet are pictured in the paper. According to the description they are 13 inches long, and weigh 1 3/4 lbs. They will cut, twist, stretch, draw and knot wire fence. They can be used as a screw driver, hammer, monkey and pipe wrench, hog ringer and stock marker.p4c7-8

A farmer borrowed the editor's volume of Darwin's Origin of Species. When he returned it he said it was sheer nonsense, that everybody knew that the best and brightest of the family die young, and that the no-goods live forever!

January 31, 1890

Modern lighting is gradually replacing gas lights in small town America! They have electric lights in successful operation in Harrodsburg.

There are some Sulphur Well-related news items, although there is no report from the Correspondent. J H Murphy, Sulphur Well merchant and surveyor, has been appointed Superintendent at E J Curley distillery. p3c1 "Miss Mattie Woodward, of Sulphur Well, spent several days last week with Miss Ida Smith, Harrodsburg." p3c2 "An infant child of Mr and Mrs Thomas Horine, of Sulphur Well, died last week." p3c3

February 7, 1890

"Miss Susie Hendren, a charming young lady of Nicholasville is visiting Miss Cynthia Roach, of E. Main Street." p3c2 I believe that Scottie went to Frankfort to stay with her sister Lizzie, so Susie must have been staying with the Adcocks in Nicholasville after her mother's death.

February 14, 1890

The former superintendent of the Greenbaum (and Gray) distillery in Sulphur Well was named postmaster in Nicholasville. The article says that the distillery burned two years ago, althought I did not see any such account. p3c2

February 21, 1890

Lexington is to have electric street lights by June 1st.

February 28, 1890

Estill Springs may be subdivided. The property including a 50 room hotel and 500 acres of mountain side was just sold to a Louisville firm. It is planning to sell lots on the side adjoining Irvine. p1c6

According to the Lexington Gazette agricultural land prices have fallen $10 per acre in the past year because of lower prices for farm products. The writer says that agriculture is the basis of the economy, and wonders if "...we are on a financial volcano". p1c7 Unfortunately, the writer was correct. There was a financial panic in 1893. One observer thought that there was a great danger of overstocking of trotters. He said that there were droves of weanlings and asked who was going to buy that many of them. One bright spot is sheep. Lambs are doing well, and will be ready for the market earlier than usual.

An Indiana man traded his hotel for the Logan farm at Logan Station for his son to operate. It was a dairy farm, and was apparently too much for the son to handle because the farm, equipment, dairy cattle are all to be auctioned off. I suspected the son was not a keen businessman when he purchased a pair of "aged" mules for $350, when the paper is full of young ones selling from $65-$100 each. p4c1

The editor is asking for someone to build an ice factory in Nicholasville. They have relied upon ice cut from Lake Mingo up to now. p3c3

March 7, 1890

Fashions from New York. "Short wraps (coats) for warm weather", said to be the prettiest seen for a long time, are "made of lace over colored silk linings". p1c6

The Kentucky River has been raging. It is reported to be ten inches higher than ever before recorded. Losses are heavy in the Little Hickman area. The Curley distillery at Camp Nelson had to shut down. It also lost 500 barrels that floated out of the cooper's area. Several houses are under water at the mouth of Paint Lick Creek. Spears reports the same condition at Tates Creek.

It looks as if H W Rose has been beaten out by I Levy. He is closing out his stock. Says he is going into the wholesale manufacture of cloth.

March 14, 1890

Measles and whooping cough are going around.

The auction of the old Logan farm went off as scheduled. All the personal property sold at reasonably good prices, but the farm did not meet its reserve price of $40 per acre. A crowd of over a thousand people attended from several counties.

March 21, 1890

The Schneck's (owners of the Logan farm) have all returned to their home in Seymour, Ind. p3c2

The bridge over the Kentucky River at Tates Creek collapsed, probably as a result of the recent flood. The masonry work sunk into the sandy soil and allowed a portion of the span to fall to the ground. This will of course delay the road. National events are shaping the railroads in Kentucky. Investors have quitely purchased a controlling interest in the stock of the Pennsylvania Railroad, which in turn owns the Monon. p1c7 The Monon owns the Louisville Southern that is building the Richmond, Nicholasville, Irvine and Beattyville line. None of the railroad officials will speculate upon how the new road will be affected.

Texie is still in town! "Mesdames Thos. Cooley, of Omaha, Neb., and Mrs George Berry, of Lexington, are visiting Mrs Al Rice." p3c2 This is Ida and Texie Gray.

March 28, 1890

There is a notice that the railroad will not only be completed, but extended into Virginia.

April 4, 1890

These are the Hendrens that owned property in Nicholasville, G M (Dr George M Hendren of Sulphur Well), William L, and Walter S Hendren.

April 11, 1890

Kings Tunnel in Estill County has been completed, leaving only one tunnel uncompleted on the line. There is a lot going on with the railroads, some of which I don't understand. The Louisville Southern has wrested control of their property from the Monon by "forceably" taking possession, and have established a connection with the O & M Railway after a "war-like tussel" with the Pennsylvania Railroad officials. p1c6

Everyone is trying to make a fast buck. The paper is full of ads and stories about how land prices are going up. Lots for speculation are offered for sale in Ashland and Middlesboro, Ky; Harrison, Tenn; and Big Stone Gap, Virginia.

## April 18, 1890

A temporary restraining order has been issued to prevent the railroads from repudiating a guarantee of the bonds of the Beattyville Railroad.

Fount Hendren, while in the company of others, was driving through Sulphur Well in a two horse wagon. "One of the wheels came off, throwing Fount to the ground. He received a very severe wound in the side by coming in contact with a sharp rock...; also one of his legs was badly bruised." p3c3 Fount is a brother of Scottie and Susie.

At a meeting of the stockholders of the Irvine Bank, M M Miller was elected cashier. According to the editor: "Mr Miller, the cashier of the new bank, is a native of Jessamine and a brother of our fellow countyman, Dr J C Miller. Mr Miller left this county some sixteen years ago, locating at Irvine, where he engaged in the mercantile business, and by his good management and thorough business qualifications has amassed a comfortable fortune of worldly goods. The directors exercised excellent judgment in securing him as their cashier." p4c2 This is "Mann" Miller.

## April 25, 1890

Texie finally went home, but not until the Nebraska winter was over! "Mrs Thos Cooley has returned to her home at Omaha, Neb." p3c2

## May 2, 1890

A lawn tennis club has been formed in Nicholasville. Three courts have been laid out near the new depot on North Main Street.

The recent sale of Estill Springs was recinded.

## May 9, 1890

Large quantities of tobacco has been changing hands at 3 to 9 cents per pound.

There is widespread dissatisfaction among the colored Republicans, more so at Keene than any where else, because they haven't shared in the fruits of the Republican victory in the presidential election last August. Many of the patronage jobs available are in the post office, and overseeing the distilleries.

Senator Beck's funeral was yesterday, and it is considered the most imposing ceremony witnessed in Lexington since the burial of Henry Clay. There is considerable speculation about his successor, who will serve out the four years of the incomplete term.

A training and trotting association has been formed in Nicholasville. The association hopes to put on an event and build a county fair around it.

Property transfers: "Thomas Peel and wife, town lot in Sulphur Well, $284." p3c4 I can't tell whether they bought or sold. Also, GM Hendren, WL Hendren, and Walter Hendren sold a lot in Nicholasville to I Levy.

May 16, 1890

The lamb trade is good, prices about 5 1/2 cents for June delivery.

The political pot is boiling. The Democrats are caucusing to select Senator James B Beck's successor. There are several aspirants, including former Governor James P Knott, and Representative James B McCreary. In every county of the state Democrats are meeting to pick their delegates to the state convention.

There was also a meeting in Nicholasville for the purpose of discussing the feasibility of organizing an electric light company.

I don't know who these Millers are: Mattie Miller married Squire Miller at the home of the bride in Sulphur Well.

May 23, 1890

John G Carlisle was selected by the legislature to succeed Senator Beck.

Ashland was crowded with people and the auctioneer sold 177 lots for $60,000. Speculation is rampant in almost every town with any faint hope of growth. People in Jessamine are investing in Tennessee, Alabama, and Colorado. p2c2

May 30, 1890

Schools are having their closing exercises; strawberry suppers are beginning; and the Kentucky River is finally back in its banks.

June 6, 1890

These advertised products give some insight into relative prices. Curd Brothers at Highbridge will sell you brogans (ankle-high mens' work shoes) for $1; Arm & Hammer soda sells for 5 cents per pound; and calico for 4 cents per yard. Adlers in Nicholasville sells "working men's shoes" for $2, and the price ranges upward to $5 for the best quality.

As I have said before, politics is always at the forefront of everyone's thoughts. Delegates are being selected for the constitutional convention. On June 21st a special election will be held for the late Senator Beck's seat in Congress. The spoils system is alive and well! The colored voters are disaffected because they have not received "their share" of public offices. "The men that do the voting should get some of the offices." p1c4 Kentucky Congressman McCreary, who has served long on the Foreign Affairs Committee, has introduced a bill to study the feasibility of a railroad that would connect the US with South America.

The 1890 Census is under way. Unfortunately, it was later destroyed by fire in Washington.

### June 13, 1890

The Democratic slate for the August election has been selected.

The editor visited the "coming cities" of Harriman, Cardiff, Rockwood and Spring City, all situated in the same valley of Tennessee. He was assured, by those who professed to know, that each would have 150,000 people within five years!

The Rivers and Harbors bill was passed by the House.

Property transfer: "William Hendren and wife to Rachel Hendren, 63 acres, $960." p4c2

### June 20, 1890

The Democrats are having a hard time selecting their representatives to the constitutional convention. Fayette County took 126 ballots and quit in disgust. They are being called back together on July 9th. p1c4

Dr Wilds took a "flying trip" to Buena Vista last week. His sister Sybelle just returned from spending several months in Missouri. p3c3

The Kentucky Wheelmen are quite active. They are planning a meet at Richmond in July.p4c2

### June 27, 1890

According to the editor, a strong Democrat himself, the Democratic party in Kentucky is demoralized, and is in the hands of "unscrupulous rounders and corruptionist". He says there is need for reform and purification. He urged all farmers and businessmen to attend the convention, become involved, and not let office holders, and office seekers take over the organization of the party. p2c1

The wife of Dr J L Wilds, gave birth on June 17th to a daughter.

Despite its problems, the railroad did finally get built. Gould McDowell, a long-time Nicholasville resident, remembers the R N I & B Railroad. It was called the Riney B. He said he had ridden it several times from Nicholasville to Irvine. Gould said he thinks the train operated until the 1930's. He believes that it was owned by the L & N Railroad, and at some point the L & N decided that the Kentucky Union going though Winchester was the better route, and discontinued the Riney B through Nicholasville and Richmond. He places the depot was on North Main Street in Nicholasville, about where the present municipal building now stands. The old depot building itself is now gone.

## July 4, 1890

Banks are closed for the fourth, but not much is made of the holiday in general. The First National Bank of Nicholasville reported that it had $271,000 in assets on July 1st. It had just over $5,000 in profits for the year.

Miss Johanna (Sittie) Fritzlen is home from Colorado, where she has been teaching. She has also taught in New Mexico. Johanna is the daughter of a local merchant. Other Jessamine folks are leaving town. The Rev. George O Barnes and family set sail for Scotland on July 10th.

Competition, or hard times, is taking its toll on some merchants. R E Cannon, who sells notions (dry goods), boots, and shoes, is quitting business. He has an inventory of $12,000 in dry goods, and $3,000 in boots and shoes. All is for sale at cost. No charge sales. Rose is still selling himself out at cost also.

The Shakers are in their preserving season, and are reporting a short supply of pears, apples, and cherries this year. Strawberries and raspberries are also less than usual.

When the meeting to choose delegates to the convention was held last Saturday, the floaters were out in force. p2c1

The new sub-division, Duncan Heights, has opened. Crowds may be seen in the park walking around the lake every evening. The editor says "let's all meet on the margin of the lake next Tuesday and buy a lot...." p2c1

Lucy Fathergill of Sulphur Well died at age 36, leaving four children, the eldest being eight years old.

## July 11, 1890

Twenty-seven of the lots in Duncan Heights were sold at the auction. Prices were lower than those that had been sold privately. p3c2

The Denman House, has been refitted and is now open for business. Rooms are $1.50 per day, meals 40 cents each. It is located on Main Street one block south of the courthouse. It was formerly known as the Baldwin House.

Rock Castle Spring advertises mountain scenery, fishing, boating, bathing, medicinal waters, good food, all at reasonable rates.

The editor of the Irvine Eagle says some of the finest honey he ever saw was selling for 12 1/2 cents per pound. p2c3 It is said that state-wide that barley is of fair quality; timothy and clover are good; the grape crop is fair; hemp came up well, but defective seeds caused failure in some areas; bluegrass seed is a complete failure; and only an average yield of corn is expected.p1c8

The High Bridge Camp Meeting will be July 18-28.

## July 18, 1890

There has been no report from Sulphur Well since November 1889.

## July 25, 1890

The joys of Rockcastle Spring! Rowing, bathing and fishing in the Rockcastle River. Plenty of boats available. The Springs are 18 miles from the railroad, but the editor says that "much of the road is smooth ridges, bordered by shady trees as on an avenue." The dress is decidedly informal. No jewelery is needed. Just something to walk in or row. Other amusements are hunting, pitching quoits (iron or rope rings pitched at a stake), croquet, euchre, and waltzes and cotillians. p2c2

From the *Sulphur Well Correspondent*:

*Mrs John West is on the sick list.*
*Rev. Mr Grinstead, of the M E Church, South, preached at the Christian Church Sunday afternoon.*
*Mr John Miller, Mr Will Richardson and wife, and Mr Snowden and wife, of Estill County, attended the funeral of Mrs Rosa Sageser.*
*Mr Wilson Baker was in Shelbyville last week to see his fast mare trot.*
*Misses Minnie and Ella Wheeler, of Cincinnati, are visiting friends and relatives at this place.*
*Mr Frank Rettig, of Louisville, is visiting Messrs. Chas. and Frank Horine.*
*Mrs Arkie Diamond is quite ill.*
*Mr James Sageser is residing with his son, Mr Andrew Sageser.*

*Mrs Han Stacy is suffering great pain from a rising in the throat.*
*Mortuary*
*"There is a reaper whose name's death*
*And with his sickle keen,*
*He cuts the bearded grain at a breath*
*And the flowers that grow between."*

*Died, on Thursday, July 17, after a lingering illness, Mrs Rosa Sageser, (nee Miller). Again we have been called to stand in the presence of the great mystery called death, and see one taken from our midst. This time the affectionate wife, the loving mother has been called, and the bereaved husband and orphan babe are left to mourn the loved one.*

*The same assemblage that met three years ago to hear words of congratulation from the hymeneal altar, met again last Friday to hear words of condolence. She, upon whom all eyes were turned then, was again the chief object of interest. Then she wore the bridal veil; this time a chaplet of flowers, which upon the cold, white brow, looked like an "April chorus on a ridge of virgin snow." Cut off in the full bloom of young womanhood, and while the shadows still were falling toward the setting sun, her death has cast a gloom over the whole community.*

*Her remains were interred in the family burying ground, where her ashes mingle with those of her forefathers.*

*The grief-stricken family have the sympathy of a host of friends, who would remind them that,*

*There is no flock however watched and tender,*
*But one dead lamb is there;*
*There is no fireside howsoe'er defended,*
*But has one vacant chair.*
*"B.T." p3c6*

Several of the people mentioned here are part of the family. Rosa's husband was Andrew Sageser; her sisters were Sarah Belle Miller, wife of Han Stacy; Susan Elizabeth Miller, wife of William D Richardson; and her brother John Pink Miller. The mother is Elizabeth Jane, now living in Sulphur Well. As you recall Han Stacy and his wife are tending the family farm. Rosa is buried in the family cemetary. Her original stone is missing, and we have just replaced it. BT says above that she had a lingering illness, and that she is survived by a child. Unfortunately the child died shortly thereafter.

August 1, 1890

Under the "Forty Years Ago" column: "The diet was more surcharged with grease, the winter breakfast usually being made of salted ham and hot cakes. Dinner was a hasty lunch at noon...." Bread was homemade, and coffee was freshly ground every morning. p1c7

The new cantilever bridge over the Kentucky River at Tates Creek has been completed. "It is two thousand feet long and over one hundred feet high." The road is now connected to the Cincinnati Southern and finished to the Marble Creek bridge. Trains will be running to Richmond in a few days. The grading to Irvine is nearly complete. In the other direction track-laying is progressing satisfactorily between Nicholasville and Versailles, and will be completed in three weeks. Nicholasville has been promised excursion trains from Louisville by the time of its fair August 13-15. p2c3

The following pertains to the death of Belle Miller Stacy: "Died - At her home near Sulphur Well Monday, July 28, of fever, Mrs Belle Stacy, aged 32 years. She was a daughter of Mrs E J Miller, and leaves a husband and five small children." p3c3 This is the wife of Han Stacy, and sister of Rosa who died the previous week. She and Han were tending the family farm, and she is buried in the family cemetary there. Her original stone is also missing, but the pedestal is there and we have replaced the stone. The obituary, written by B T follows:

## Obituary
## Mrs Belle Stacy

Died, on Monday, July 28, Mrs Belle Stacy (nee Miller) She leaves five small children and a host of sorrowing friends. She was well known and universally liked.

Mrs Stacy was a sister of Mrs Sageser, whose demise we mentioned last week. Another member of the family gone, another chair left vacant, another flower plucked on earth to plant beside the throne of God.

May the memory of her life strengthen the weak, and comfort the weary; may it hang sweet pictures of faith and trust in the silent galleries of sunless lives, and point the desolate, whose paths wind ever among the shadows and over rocks, where never the green moss grows, to the golden heights of the hereafter, where the palms of victory wave. B T p3c6

The *Sulphur Well Correspondent* reports:

*Charlie Horine was in Lancaster, Sunday.*
*Mrs M W Spruce is on the sick list.*
*Messrs. Frank Horine and Millard Davis attended the fair at Lancaster.*
*Elder Redmon preached at the Christian Church Sunday.*
*J P Turner bought of George S Diamond his farm of 200 acres. Price paid, $25 per acre.*
*Hon N D Miles addressed the citizens of Sulphur Well last week, on the needed changes in the Constitution of Kentucky. Mr Miles is not a spread-eagle, fourth of July, sky-scraper, but he presented his points in a forcible manner and made many friends. We think all his proposed changes would be good ones.*
*Mrs Ann Wagoner and children, of Ghent, are visiting friends at this place.*
*Some of our people are making active preparations for the picnic, which is to be at Little Hickman next Saturday, and are expecting a great time. It will pay everyone to go.*
*H G and J H Turner this week bought eight shares of stock in the Farmers' Exchange Bank, at $102.50 per share.*
*Crops in this section are short. Wheat made little more than half a yield. Corn is fair. The dry spell damaged the hemp, and as a result it is short. Fruit and vegetables are scarce and high. Tobacco is looking very well, though the acreage is small.*
*Elders Bush and Adcock, of your city, held services here Sunday afternoon.*
*Benj. Humphrey sold to J P Turner a mare and colt for $120. (signed) B.T. p3c5*

I'm not sure what to make of this "new" correspondent that signs himself "B.T." Several months went by without an article, and then they began anew with B.T. As mentioned earier, B T could be Dr Hendren, as he wrote a poem later featuring an empty chair.

August 8, 1890

A letter was sent to the editor from J B, Jr.(John Bronaugh), a Jessamine resident, concerning his trip to California. On his return he left Los Angeles, went through Sacramento and Nevada to Ogden, Utah, where he stopped to visit the Mormon Temple, Tabernacle and Assembly Hall. They were constructed from granite, and at a cost of some $4 million. He said he met some old classmates and a great many Kentuckians who treated him so nicely that it was difficult to leave. He continued on into the Rocky Mountains, and is working on a ranch. He calls himself a "cattle boy", and declares himself almost fully well, "having only a little part of his former sickness left." p1c5-6 I suspect consumption, for it was a common disease at the time.

The election was the most "peaceful and orderly ever conducted in the county." No one was hurt, and "no bad feelings were engendered. One or two friendly knockdowns here and there, but more in the spirit of fun than otherwise." p3c4 With good management floaters got $15 for their vote. The correspondent from Jessamine Station said that "a person would have supposed that prohibition had settled in that place." p3c5 This may be a good place to try to balance the items that I have taken from the Journal concerning politics and race. The Republicans had the black vote after the Civil War. There were several items after the presidential election that was won by the Republicans that the blacks were not being treated fairly in sharing the spoils. Prior to this election the Journal carried several articles where the Democrats called the Republicans hypocrites for not including any blacks on their slates.

August 15, 1890

The Jessamine County Fair is in progress. The adjacent counties are well represented, and the excursion trains are crowded each day.

August 22, 1890

The Democratic State Central Committee has designated September 6th for holding meetings in every county to select precinct committeemen. Farmers feel as if they have been neglected, and this is their opportunity to select a good representative.

August 29, 1890

The editor bemoans the fact that old-fashioned fairs are fading away. The pigs and poultry, handiwork, vegetables and flowers, are giving way to trotting races, accompanied by pool gambling.

Politicians are concerned over the growth of the Farmers Alliance movement in the South and West. Power was shown in Clark County where an endorsement of an ex-state senator was withheld because of the opposition of the Farmers Alliance.

A social problem is festering in Nicholasville. Upper Main Street is being blocked by Negroes on Saturday nights.

September 5, 1890

Dr Thomas Peel died, age 55. He was buried "on the home place, after the funeral services at the Elm Fork Christian Church." p3c3

September 12, 1890

The Farmers Alliance of Maryland is considering a cooperative to reduce the cost of getting produce from farm to market. The Grange and the National Farmers League, which is a union, are trying through political or other means to improve the lot of the farmer.

The delegates for the Constitutional Convention had their organizational meeting this week.

From Little Hickman: "William Miller, worthy and much-liked citizen of this place, died of typhoid fever on the 5th. He left a wife and children." I know of no connection with his family. p3c4

September 19, 1890

Sugar cane raisers are making molasses.

Many are attending the Richmond Fair on the new railroad. The train is composed of three coaches, all are canary (yellow) in color. Their interior "is of gold plush, brass finishings, and white ash woodwork." Each car has "air brakes and Janney couplers." The stations along the line from Nicholasville to Richmond are Perry, Daniels, Logana, Spears, Tates Creek, Million, and Newland. p3c2 Million and Newland are in Madison County.

Dr Miller held a colt show in Nicholasville last Monday, that was said to be the finest exhibition in recent years. Premiums were offered for the best horse and mule colts. Quite a number of the exhibitors were youngsters. p3c3

The Irish have experienced an almost complete failure of their potato crop.

## September 26, 1890

I thought that I might run across this item! "Miss Scottie Hendren has accepted a position at J. Adler's." p3c3 His first name was Julius. His ad this week offers dry goods, dress goods, cloaks, millinery, and notions. He claims "We offer the widest choice for taste or fancy. We offer the newest goods, patterns and styles, in the market. We offer the best values you ever received." p2c8

## October 3, 1890

A cold snap has caused fires to be lit at Jessamine Station, and women are trying to preserve their flowers. p2c4 Farmers are late getting in their tobacco crop, and they have been sowing their winter wheat, and cutting corn. Chestnuts are ripening. Lake Mingo has been leased by the Fishing Club and is in the process of stocking it with a variety of fish.

## October 10, 1890

"The first regular train between Louisville and Richmond ... arrived in this city yesterday...." The train was "cheered at every station, and the 104 mile run was made in just five hours...." p2c3-4 The road between Richmond and Irvine is nearing completion also. The route through Irvine will be "west of the residence of M M Miller" and then cross Main Street. p2c4

I was surprised that Dr Miller had this involvement. "The furniture and undertaking firm of Harris & Co., of this place, composed of W D Harris and Dr John C Miller, has been bought out by F P Taylor, the above firm's predessor in the business here." p3c1

From the Lancaster Record: "Mrs W H Bright and daughters, Misses Berta and Helena, of Nicholasville, are visiting at C J Doty's." p3c3 I wish I could discover the wife's name. The Sulphur Well correspondent, before BT, was the brother of Helena.

Miss Susie Hendren is with her aunt, Mrs Woolfork, of Lancaster.

## October 17, 1890

The railroad men are in town to get their bonds. Its not clear this week whether they have complied with all the terms yet or not.

The sweet potato crop is unusually large this year. There was a heavy frost last Tuesday, so I guess this is the end of fresh vegetables.

## October 24, 1890

"The new tariff law will add from 7 to 30 per cent to the cost of dry goods." p1c1 This is the McKinley Tariff.

"The struggle for the control of the next House of Representatives is now fairly on between the two great parties." p1c1

The editor satirizes his appeal to debtors to pay their bills at the paper for advertising and job work. He says that all his bills are paid, but that he needs money to buy a trotting horse! He says that the only way to command respect in the Bluegrass is to have a trotter, with a proper pedigree, that can do a mile in 2:30 or less. p2c2

### October 31, 1890

From the 1890 Census: "The population of Jessamine is 11,237, being an increase of 373 since 1880." p3c4 Although the U S population grew rapidly during the decade, Jessamine remained essentially the same.

Democratic County officers: From Sulphur Well-R E Sageser, Chas. Horine, Dr J C Miller, John W Cobb, Sr., LaFayette English, Hugh Hemphill, Hugh Peel, and John Perry. p3c4

### November 7, 1890

According to the editor the people have repudiated the McKinley Bill and voted Democratic in the general election.

### November 14, 1890

Thanksgiving is approaching and the the turkey crop is lighter this year. p1c6 Chicken thieves are so bad in the Buena Vista neighborhood that the correspondent there says that "since last spring there is scarcely a farmer in this vicinity who has not suffered a considerable loss of poultry by a mighty invasion in spite of watchfulness and care."p2c3

### November 21, 1890

John D Harris, a native of Madison County, a former State Senator, and once candidate for governor, has become President of the Convention of Tobacco Planters. He said in his opening address that he didn't mind the "warehousemen selling their own businesses", but he objected to their selling the farmers along with them. He said this meeting was called for planters "to band together for the promotion of their interests and protection against unscrupulous dealers and warehousemen." The Association plans to establish or select warehouses close to the growers on a co-operative plan. There is a call for a meeting of the Jessamine County farmers to consider collective action.p1c4

November 28, 1890

Thanksgiving services are being offered by the "M E Church, South at 10:30 am this (Thursday) morning. Sermon by T Warn Beagle." p3c2 I'll have to confess. While I wanted to mark the observance of the holiday, I also wanted to note the name of the minister.

December 5, 1890

There is still a shortage of turkeys. "Turkeys are not so plentiful this year as last and are higher. Dressed turkeys retail in the local market at 12 1/2 cents and in the cities sell as high as 15c." p1c6 Highbridge reports that "hog killing is now in order, but some fears are entertained that the weather is too warm to insure the safe keeping of meat." p3c4 A new game "putting the tail on the donkey" was introduced by the local school teacher at Jessamine Station, and it drew a large crowd. "If you wish to laugh try the game". p3c4

December 12, 1890

"In spite of the failures all over the country and the stringency in the money market, the president insists that money is plenty, that business is increasing and that prosperity is seen on every hand." p1c3 The economy undoubtedly dampened the holiday spirit, and the editor appears skeptical about the outlook.

December 19, 1890

Work had to be stopped on the railroad between Irvine and Beattyville "owing to the depression of the money market in New York, the construction company can not at present find sale for its bonds...." p4c2

J W Overstreet (Pomp), of Little Hickman, who became an avid wheelman, after his son got him started, has become the agency for the New Mail Bicycles.p3c2 Pomp's correspondence landed on the front page of the paper this week. His son and others "are attending the new college at Wilmore." This is Asbury that recently opened. He says that he is "contemplating building a large business house this winter...." Pomp tells at length of his memories of the old Mt Zion church that has been razed so that a new building could be erected. He mentions Dr J C Miller, among others, that "spent their palmiest days and vied with each other in waiting on the fair sex." p1c4

Property transfers: "George S Diamond and wife to J P Turner, 97 acres of land, $4,930. Wm Hendren and wife to Francis Hughes, 59 acres of land, $2,079." p4c2

December 26, 1890

The Shanahans, contractor for the railroad, lost their deposits of several hundred dollars when a Louisville bank failed. p1c3

At a meeting of the Board of the Riney B it was decided to increase the subscription by $500,000 and finish the road. p3c2

From Buena Vista: Dr Wilds and family visted Buena Vista. He rented his farm, and sold his cattle because his practice required "his undivided attention".p2c4

There was no report from Sulphur Well in 1890 until B.T. gave his eulogy for Rose Sageser. He then wrote the obituary of Belle Stacy the following week. There were no other reports in 1890. If not Dr Hendren, then it is difficult at this time to guess who B.T. might be. Whoever it is was a close friend of Rose Sageser's.

# A NEW CONSTITUTION - 1891

A revised state contitution is being presented to the people, and politicians are active. Unfortunately, the Sulphur Well correspondent submitted only a few reports.

### January 2, 1891

It is believed that there will be some relief from the "money stringency" after the payment of interest and dividends at the first of the year. It is claimed that "a few schemers" have jepordized all businesses. p1c3

The tobacco warehouses have been conveyed back from an association to the owners because of actions by the farmers. p2c2 The farmers had threatened to establish their own cooperative markets, so I guess that they won this round.

There were 2,584 legal voters in Jessamine County, of which 1802 were white, and 782 were colored.

A heavy sleet caused considerable damage to trees and blocked roads. p3c2 The Jessamine Station correspondent said that the rain and snow on Christmas Day curtailed a lot of turkey dinners and egg-nog parties. On the morning of the 26th the heaviest sleet in several years destroyed peach and apple trees. p3c5

### January 9, 1891

Buena Vista: "Miss Sybelle Wilds has accepted a situation in Louisville and left our village last Saturday." p2c3

They didn't have welfare, but they had thieves and burglars! Robbery is so rampant in Madison County, that they patrol the roads and arrest suspicious characters.

### January 16, 1891

The Fitzsimmons and Dempsey fight in New Orleans was won by Fitzsimmons in 13 rounds.

"Mr Adam Adcock is home from a visit to relatives in Tennessee." p3c3

### January 30, 1891

From Richmond: "Dr John C Miller, of Jessamine, was here last week. He owns a farm near Richmond, and there are many who would be glad to see him return to his former home to live." p3c3 This farm probably came to him from his wife's family.

## February 6, 1891

The weather is still cold! "Most of the farmers have already put up good ice two inches thick and a favored few were so lucky as to get it three inches thick." p1c5 Many farms had ice houses. They were dug several feet deep, lined with stone, and covered with a roof. When the ponds froze, ice was cut in blocks, and packed in layers of straw for insulation. The ice definitely was not purified, but to the extent that it was used to cool iceboxes in the house, it was probably safe. Its use in beverages would be the equivalent of drinking pond water.

The County has made a levy of 27 1/2 cents per hundred dollars on taxable property to pay for the interest on the railroad bonds. p3c2

The Silver question that runs throughout the nineties commenced with the "free coinage bill". It defines the dollar as the unit of value and states that it can be "coined of 412 1/2 grains of standard silver or of 25.8 grains of standard gold...." This establishes the ratio between the two metals at sixteen to one. The bill authorizes the coinage of silver dollars and restores silver to legal-tender status. The Treasury is directed to purchase whatever silver bullion that is offered at the price fixed by the bill, and to issue silver certificates based upon that bullion. p2c2

## February 13, 1891

Sybelle Wilds, after making a "flying trip to Buena Vista last Sunday" will "pursue her business in Cincinnati for the next two months." p2c2 Makes you wonder, doesn't it?

From Wilmore: "Chicken and turkey thieves are getting in their work very successfully". There is "hardly a night that someone's roost is not raided." p2c3

From High Bridge: Football has become popular! "Large crowds of men and boys gather nearly every Saturday afternoon to play." p3c3

"Mrs Wm Richardson, of Irvine, is visiting in this county." p3c3 This is "Aunt Sudie", Elizabeth Jane Miller's daughter.

The Denman House, newly renovated, is now for sale "cheap"!

The potato crop was poor, and potatoes are now selling for $2 per bushel.

Bears are rare in Kentucky in 1891, however one was killed in Powell County.

### February 20, 1891

"Miss Susie Hendren is attending the Normal Department of the State College, Lexington." p3c3 She was taking teacher training type courses, because she later does some teaching. It should also be noted that it was only in the fall of 1889 that women were allowed to attend.

### February 27, 1891

The Democratic State Convention is coming up in May in Louisville. The Democrats claim that the Republican Party has taken advantage of patriotic sentiment for 35 years. They say that "during that period farmers and producers have been robbed ... while bondholders and protected barons have grown richer and richer." p2c1 The leading Democratic candidates for governor for the 1892 election are John Young Brown of Henderson and Cassius Clay, Jr from Bourbon.

The editor says that after watching the delegates at the Constitutional Convention, "people are beginning to think that a new constitution was not as badly needed as previously imagined." p2c1

The war with Spain may have had its roots in 1891:
> Reciprocity with Spain is rendered impossible at present by reason of existing treaties between Spain and other governments that can not be abrogated in less than a year, some of which have been in force under different treaties nearly two centuries, and some of the admirers of Mr Blaine are attributing to him the practice of a shrewd political game for the acquisition of Cuba, by putting Spain in an embarrassing position, to relieve herself from which she will be compelled to either abrogate old treaties or invite revolt in Cuba by refusing to treat with the United States. In the latter case his favorite desire for the purchase of the island would be easily and cheaply realized. p2c1

### March 6, 1891

From Pink: "J H Easley bought a pair of work mules of Andrew Sageser for $250." p2c4

Mr Julius Adler is spending two weeks visiting the millinery markets to get the latest French and New York styles for his store in Nicholasville. p3c1

### March 13, 1891

The railroad got $600,000 in New York so that the line from Richmond to Irvine can be completed. p2c1

Pomp is completing the construction of his new store and post office. He says that it has the best layout of any in the county! p3c5

From Camp Nelson: There is something of a question over who is Superintendent of Curley's Distillery. J H Murphy has possession, but "Col. Wilmore (is) expectantly waiting Micawber-like `for something to turn up'." p3c5 I never saw the sequel to this, but Murphy did go on to other things.

March 20, 1891

Pie Parties are the lastest fad for raising money for the churches.

Harrodsburg has proposed a base ball league to include Danville, Nicholasville, Versailles, Lawrenceburg. This is the old Bluegrass League. The towns may change from time to time, but I watched many of their games in the late 1940's and early fifties. Their rules allowed them to hire a battery, that is, a pitcher and a catcher. This greatly improved the quality of play. I saw some former major and minor league players in this league.

There is still talk of electric lights, water works, and an ice plant for Nicholasville.

There is another letter from John Bronaugh, this time saying that he continues in ill health. This is the J B, Jr. who was the "cattle boy" in the letter a few months ago (August 8, 1890).

There is an advertisement for service to the stallion Alaric Almont. You may recall that the Sulphur Well correspondent once called himself Alaric, so the name may have been in common usage.

At last! Another article from the *Sulphur Well Correspondent*! No indication that he has been away, or why he hasn't written for over a year:

*Messrs. Gulley, Hardin and Whittaker of Lancaster, spent Sunday with friends here.*
*Mr Clayton West is reported to be quite ill.*
*Mr Richard Burton, of Buckeye, was the guest of Walter Hendren, Sunday.*
*Mrs Wm. Hoover, Sr., has been quite ill, but is now improving.*
*Jno. P Miller, of Estill County, visited his mother at this place last week.*
  *Farmers are taking advantage of the open weather, and are very busy plowing, while hemp-breaking progresses nicely.*
  *Our spring school is being taught by Miss Brown, a highly accomplished young lady of Lancaster, and all express themselves highly pleased.  p3c5  (unsigned)*

John P Miller took over his father's store in Wisemantown, and he is visiting his mother, Elizabeth Jane Miller.

115

March 27, 1891

The editor says that Jessamine folks take their politics too seriously and instead of just supporting their choice, they disparage the opposition and thereby create bad feeling. Things never change, do they?

New York fashions feature tailored suits in light woolens and bold plaids. Hats turn up in back and project in front. p1c5

A major bank has failed in Louisville, the Theodore Schwartz & Co bank. The failure of banks in South America and England has greatly handicapped new businesses, because investors refuse to lend.

Tramp "season" has opened. They probably start coming north as work or weather drives them.

Mrs Frank Miller subscribed to the Jessamine Journal.

April 3, 1891

Another sign of the economic conditions: The firm of Kimbrough Brothers, cigar and tobacco dealers in Lexington, was forced into assignment by the suit of a creditor.

"Mrs A K Adcock met with a painful accident last week by spraining her ankle, and is at present unable to leave her room." p3c3

David Newton Davis, age 61, died of pneumonia at the residence of his sister Mrs Diana Moore, of Sulphur Well. He was a batchelor and was buried in the family cemetary on the farm of his nephew, Newt Davis. p3c3

April 10, 1891

Two hundred thousand copies of Kentucky's new constitution are being printed and distributed to voters. p2c1

April 17, 1891

The editor says that copies of the "constitution, the new and the old, are now before us. Let us examine them both carefully and without predjudice and choose the one that we believe best...." p2c1

April 24, 1891

The gubernatorial candidates are beginning to circulate, giving their views on various issues such as the tariff, the free coinage of silver, the constitution, financial questions, etc.

As would be expected, they differ on some points. The editor says that it is bad enough to unjustly attack a Republican, but to do so to another Democrat was inexcusible! He also said that "there will be a circus in town today, but it would be a`patchin' to the one at the courthouse tomorrow week", when the Democrats make their choice for governor! p2c2

From Mt Lebanon: "Dr J C Miller lost a fine horse last week." p3c6

According to the editor spring is here, and the "martins have arrived and the honey bees are buzzing".

## May 1, 1891

From New York: "The most successful spring wrap is the single, long cape attached to pointed yoke." The most stylish are "in black cloth with gilt embroidered yoke." p1c5

## May 8, 1891

A very sad end of the life of John Schenk. He died at the age of 24 at his father's residence in Indiana. His father had bought the Logan dairy farm for John to operate, which he did for a year or two. The cause of death was "brain and nervous" trouble. He had been unconscious for several days, but shortly before his death he regained consciousness, and told the minister that "It will soon be over. I'm going home." He was married to Lulu Miller, who survives him. Her father was Henry P Miller. p3c6 I don't believe we are related in any way.

Hume Clay, of good family, was convicted of forgery. He is now in the Frankfort penitentiary, and has been made book-keeper of the broom factory.

Expressions of the day: "The tail goes with the hide." Once the Democrats chose a "Brown man" to be chairman of the meeting, they took everything else as well. The "Hardin and Clay men" were subjected to majority rule; or as the editor put it "the largest pole knocks down the persimmons." p2c1

## May 15, 1891

There was a big frost on the nights of the 5th and 6th that damaged gardens and orchards. Farmers are nearly though planting corn. Corn raised the prior year is selling at the very good price of $4 per barrel.

From Logana: "Misses Viola Davis, of Ambrose, and Addie Hendren, of Nicholasville, two of J F I's best students, visited Miss Lizzie Robinson from Friday to Monday." p3c4 This "Addie" is the daughter of Dr Hendren of Sulphur Well. Names get recycled a lot!

There was an "interesting" croquet party at Glasses Mill. Playing croquet was a prevalent party game, more often for the youth, but sometimes adults as well. We kids used to mow the grass and set up the wickets, and then get run off by the adults.

## May 22, 1891

The Democratic state ticket is headed by John Young Brown of Henderson County. In Shelby County the farmers "hogged the whole delegation". Party caucuses had been the rule, but the sentiment has swung to having precinct elections instead. The editor said "decent Democrats are becoming disgusted with the way those mass meetings (or rather mob meetings) are conducted. There is no decency, dignity, or fairness in them." p1c4 Scott and Jessamine are contending for who should get the next state senator. The counties in the district have been alternating the seat. However, this time there has been more sentiment toward getting "the best man".

The editor of the Jessamine Journal, H M McCarty, said that in response to tenders of support from Woodford and Scott, that he was available if called.

Nationally, the Democrats are expected to renominate Cleveland, and to support the free coinage of silver. The editor opines that "if silver should become so plentiful as to bring interest down to the legal rate of 6 per centum, or even less, we don't see any harm would result to the farming and laboring classes." p1c3

Jessamine is one of the top tobacco-growing counties in the state, ranking about eighth. It is also the second largest hemp producer in the state. There has been an increase in the prices of farm products since April 1890. Farmers have finished shearing their sheep. The wool is selling at 25 cents per pound. However, the farmers are finding that an early drought is becoming serious.

The question of free turnpikes is being discussed, and there is never-ending talk about new industry in Nicholasville. Right now it's about a new brick plant for the local market.

## May 29, 1891

Silver was demonetized in 1873, which was often called "the Crime of 73". However, monetizing the supply again eighteen years later, poses a new set of problems, in which there would be some large gainers, and the Treasury could lose control of the money supply. Anyone holding silver interests would gain because the market for silver would be expanded. The Treasury would lose control, because it would be forced to buy all the silver offered to it at a fixed price.

The Farmers' Alliance is making headway in Jessamine, with lectures and organizational meetings.

The Republicans have nominated A T Wood, of Mt Sterling, to head its slate of candidates.

The new constitution has split the Democrats, some for it and others against it, while the Republicans are united in their support for it.

There was a brazen thief in Stanford. He stole a pair of trousers. When he found they were too big, he returned them, and asked that they be exchanged for another pair!

The High Bridge Camp Meeting has become an institution of the Blue Grass.

Strawberries are ripe, but scarce!

The editor has ruled out all visits between neighborhoods in the county to be reported by correspondents. The paper has become increasingly commercial, in fact it is full of advertisements. So full, in fact, that it doesn't have room for the correspondent's articles. It has also become increasingly full of political articles, most recently, pertaining to the editor's becoming state senator. There has been a steady deterioration in the interest of the editor in the neighborhood reports, and in the journalistic quality of the paper.

"E T Lillard sold his farm on the Harrodsburg-Lexington Road and has purchased thirty acres of land from Mr Broomfield "in the Sulphur Well neighborhood, known as the Greenbaum Distillery property, for $2,500." p3c2 The property "is adjacent to one of the best streams of water for distilling purposes", and Lillard expects to rebuild the old distillery. p3c2 I don't know what happened to the plans, but they were never carried out.

June 5, 1891

This property transfer was recorded. "J H Broomfield sold to E T Lillard, 35 acres, $2500." p2c6 The more common spelling of this name is "Brumfield".

The Farmers' Alliance says it will not field a ticket, but will vote for the best man, regardless of the party. All indications are that there have been improvements in rural prospects, and that this will be a year of prosperity.p1c3

Sin in River City! The Little Hickman correspondent reported the arrest and conviction of two lewd women in that district. What they were doing, according to Pomp, was keeping a disorderly house. They were tried in the general store at Little Hickman by Squire Fain, and were fined $50 each. Since they were unable to pay, they were sent to the Nicholasville Workhouse. p2c5

The correspondents are reporting having considerable wind storms, but little rain. Wouldn't you know! The "largest crowd ever assembled" at Camp Nelson on Decoration Day placed a profusion of flowers on the graves. Unfortunately, a heavy rain dispersed the people before the ceremonies could begin. p2c6

The Pink correspondent reported that a fisherman sitting on the bank saw eight full-grown otters swimming down the river. p2c4 They soon became extinct in Kentucky. However, a restocking program began recently (the 1990's). Sue and I went to one of the locations that otter were being released in Taegert Creek near Grayson. They are interesting little creatures. One female sat, laid, and rolled on a fallen tree for an hour after being released, and many feet of film were shot capturing that sight! However, it was partly funny and partly pathetic how most of them sought some kind of cover in their strange environment.

### June 12, 1891

S M Duncan, local historian, described his walk from Nicholasville to Little Hickman: "The Hickman Spring is eight miles from Nicholasville on the Paint Lick pike. The hill and cliff scenery along the road from Sulphur Well is exquisitely beautiful and occasionally one is almost tempted to believe that he has passed beyond the bounds of an old settlement and plunged into unbroken forest of some unknown country." p1c4

> While the parson was out driving with a young sister of the flock, the horse kicked and ran away. His kick broke three of the pastor's fingers, and two of the sister's ribs. The good man is wondering what made the horse run away, and the rest of us are wondering how it happened that the sister's ribs and the pastors fingers were caught in the same kick!

### June 19, 1891

The County is in the midst of a wheat harvest. The weather has been pleasant all week, after a good rain on Monday, and gardens have been refreshed.

From Pink: "The rain last Monday was accompanied by considerable thunder and lightning, the latter killing a horse of Bob Wade's; struck a tree in Harvey Dean's yard, and also struck T J Hunter's house and played havoc with the stove pipe." p3c4

J W Overstreet (Pomp) is credited by the <u>Courier Journal</u> as being the champion bicyclist of Kentucky, for distance and time, "117 miles in twelve hours and thirty-five minutes!" p4c2 This is "Iron Man" distance if he actually did it!

### June 26, 1891

The election is coming in August. The new constitution will be voted upon at that time. They are trying hard to keep the issue nonpartisan. The state senatorial election is between McCarty and Branch, the candidates for state senator in the district, and it pits the counties, Jessamine and Scott, against each other. Brown appears to be the leading candidate in the gubernatorial campaign.

An interesting Sunday! A young man, aged about seventeen, hired a rig from the livery stable, and arranged to meet his true love, about fifteen, at the Little Hickman Church. They started for Lexington, but were overtaken in the vicinity of Sulphur Well by the girl's father, on "a foaming steed". It was reported that a "navy six in the hands of the girl's father was the persuading influence causing the young man to give up his seat in the surrey...." p3c3 While the father took the girl back to Little Hickman with him, and the young man was "crestfallen", the story doesn't end here.

At last, a report from the *Sulphur Well Correspondent*:

*There was a Holiness meeting held at this place last Saturday, June 20th. Good crowd in attendance--dinner on the ground.*
*A party of Lexingtonians, composed of boys and girls, passed throught this place last Sunday en route to Chalybeate Springs to spend the day, and on their way back stopped here with Mr James Cobb until the cool of the evening. They seemed to be enjoying themselves finely.*
*James Woodward, Jr., and Forest Miller have returned from a pleasant visit to friends in Mercer.*
*The Kansas cyclone speaker, M V B Bennett, made a very interesting and convincing speech on prohibition at this place last Saturday night to a crowded house. p3c4*

Evidently, Chalybeate Springs is in or near Pink. The Pink correspondent said that a party of about twenty young people spent the day there at the Springs.

### July 3, 1891

McCarty was not nominated for the state senate seat. His opponent from Scott won instead. The caucus was called rancorous, and some ill feelings were generated.

### July 10, 1891

"Eighty cents is the best offered price for wheat. Farmers are disposed to hold for a better price." p3c1

### July 17, 1891

The High Bridge Camp Meeting is underway. Special trains are available and thousands of people are attending.

### July 24, 1891

Farmers are this year coming to the front in politics. They are participating in the political meetings. The economy is improving too. The wheat crop is being sold, and money is easier. Previously, the price had been around 80 cents per bushel, which was considered too low, and farmers had been holding their wheat from the market. Also, fresh vegetables and chickens are plentiful.

The railroad still has financial problems. Work has stalled about five miles west of Irvine. The road is also coming upon its deadlines for completion in order to get the installment payments from Jessamine, Madison, and Estill.

The *Sulphur Well Correspondent* reports:

*Walter Scott Hendren, accompanied by his neice, Miss Minnie Wheeler, has returned from Cincinnati.*
*Mrs T C Reynolds, of Texas, is visiting Mrs T J Horine this week.*
*Mrs Katie Allen, of Franklin, Tenn., is visiting friends and relatives in this vicinity.*
*Misses Dora Murphy and Viola Davis have returned from a pleasant visit to friends and relatives in Lexington.*
*Mr and Mrs M P Horine, of Nicholasville, have been visiting Mr and Mrs J H Murphy this week.*
*Hunter-West--At the residence of the bride's father, near Sulphur Well, on Tuesday, July 16, 1891. Rev. J S Young joined in the holy bond of matrimony, Mr Wm. Hunter to Miss Jennie West. The newly married couple left for Garrard County where they will spend their honeymoon. They were accompanied by Mr Clayton West, a brother of the bride, and Miss Maggie Funk. Success and happiness to them, is the wish of their many friends.* p3c4

Walter Scott Hendren is the brother of Dr Hendren, and the son of William Hendren, Sr.

### July 31, 1891

Love triumphed over all! The young couple that was overtaken by the girl's father near Sulphur Well, were married in Tennessee, and are making their home with the bridegroom's father in Garrard County. p3c2

There is a lot of politics this week. Mr John C Hendren, of Kirksville, the Republican nominee for Representative from Madison, is the son of Tom Hendren of Nicholasville. p4c3 The floaters are against the new constitution because under the secret ballot system, you can only buy the promise of a vote, not the vote! p1c3 There is a problem in Hardin County. "The trouble lies in the methods of selecting candidates. Conventions and primary elections have become so corrupt that many Democrats have grown tired and disgusted with them." p1c4 In Covington "there is a hot and very scurrilous and disgraceful war being waged...". Some very dirty tricks have been charged to both sides. p2c1

At a board meeting of the Riney B it was reported that approximately $450,000 was needed to complete the road. A resolution was passed to apply $350,000 of county aid to the project, and obtain the remaining funds from other sources. p2c2

Even Valley View got into the speculation game! There was a sale of 200 lots on August 6th. As a community, Valley View has mail and express facilities, a flour mill, a distillery, stores, schools, and churches. It also has one saw mill that employs fifty men, and another that has twenty-five employees.

Samuel Barkley has been killed by George Burdine, a tenant on the Barkley farm, which is located on the Keene Pike about three miles from Nicholasville. The shooting occurred just inside the gate on the opposite side of the road from the Barkley residence. Both wives were witnesses to the affair. There had been trouble between the two, and Burdine had Barkley arrested for drawing a gun on him a few weeks ago. Barkley, who was born in 1822, was the last surviving son of Samuel Barkley Sr. He was buried in "the family burying ground." p3c3 Records show that he was 49 years old at the time of his marriage in 1879 to Kitty Miller, which would put his birth date in 1830. One or the other is in error.

## August 7, 1891

The Democrats easily won the election, and the new constitution was approved. Both houses of the legislature are Democratic.

The Jessamine County Fair runs from August 11th to the 14th.

The blackberry crop is heavier than usual.

## August 14, 1891

The sale of the Valley View lots was called a success, but it looks like a scam to me. One buyer purchased twenty lots, which he resold to the seller for a $300 profit. He then purchased a one-third interest in all the unsold lots. The average price of the lots sold was $110, which is equivalent to $1200 per acre. Prior to the laying out the lots, the farm had sold for $45 per acre. There was plenty of burgoo, *et cetra*. I suspect the "*et cetra*" was whisky! p2c5

The town was full of people and the county fair declared a success. The grandstands were filled, and the exhibits attracted great interest. Adam Adcock either drove, or owned, a horse in the first race at the Fair. He was entered again in the fourth race. Funny that Dr Miller has disappeared the last year or so after being in the paper regularly for so long. p3c2

## August 21, 1891

Bernard Wolf made an assignment for the benefit of his creditors. It was caused by a Jellico coal company that brought suit against him. The editor says "he has not been over venturesome or reckless. He is a good businessman, sober and industrious." "He is in the prime of life, with good health, untiring industry, and knowledge and experience in business ...." The coal yard is for sale or rent. p2c1

John Y Brown won the race for governor over Wood.

The *Sulphur Well Correspondent* is busy again:

Miss Ida Smith, daughter of Henry C Smith, of Harrodsburg, is visiting Misses Mattie, Ella and Carrie Woodward, of Sulphur Well. Miss Ida is an attractive young lady, who has made some impressions during her visit to the "Well".

The protracted meeting conducted by Elders Mills and Creighton is still going on. Three have become members of the church up to date. p3c4

August 28, 1891

The New York reporter says that chiffon is the leading material for evening dresses when thin silks are worn. China and India silks have replaced the traditional white which needed perpetual laundering. Colored fabric is always ready for wearing. p1c5

An unusual cold snap occurred and "fires, flannels and overcoats were very comfortable last Sunday and Monday."p3c1

From the Estill Eagle: "M M Miller has resigned (his) position of cashier of (the) Estill Bank." p2c3

There is plenty of corn, beans and potatoes on the market, but few buyers. p3c1

Dove shooting has commenced, and the hemp fields are full of hunters.

Hiter Lowery's new residence on Central Avenue in Duncan Heights, is termed the most elegant in the suburbs. It has nine rooms, two halls, two verandas, hot and cold water, and is located on a two acre lot that is the highest in the subdivision.

Tom Hendren's liquor licence was not renewed because of the crowds allowed to congregate in front of the saloon.

The song "Comrades" is having a tremendous run of popularity everywhere in the country. Singers are singing it; fiddlers, and piano-players are playing it. It rivals "Annie Rooney". p4c1

This was from Sulphur Well, but not in its usual position, so I'm not sure if its the "regular" correspondent. It is signed Senex, and if it is the *Sulphur Well Correspondent*,then he appears to have become quite religious!

For the last two weeks an abundance of rain has fallen and the farmers are jubilant over the prospects of one of the best of corn crops in our county. We are reassured that there will be bread for the eater and seed for the sower.

Recently I attended the Holiness Association meeting at Sulphur Well. There were but few present at the appointment for the meeting on the 15th of August. Was not announced in proper time for the people to know it. So far as I know the members of these Holiness Associations are composed of some of the best men and women of the Methodist Church; they are men and women whose character

*is above reproach,*
*and whose zeal for the cause of Christ is strictly sincere and honest. I saw not a single man or woman who belongs to these Holiness Associations at the horse races at our late fair. Every church in Nicholasville and Jessamine County was largely represented at that fair, and some are reported as betting on all sides and winning money. At night some would attend the dance in company of their mothers and dance till "broad daylight". The christian course in one of Paul's letters is represented as*

*a race.*

*How absurd would it be for a racer to stop at frequent intervals in his progress, or start with ardor and, then folding his arms deliberately, walk to the goal, as if no prize challenged him and no spectators gazed at him!*

*Do most christians exemplify the strong language of St. Paul, "Seeing we are compassed about with so great a cloud of witnesses, let us lay aside every weight, and the sin that doth so easily beset us, and let us run with patience the race that is set before us". What a spectacle would*

*the church of today*

*exhibit if each member maintained the progressive spirit of the pure principles of christianity. Let all ministers of the gospel purge the churches of their dancing and gambling members. The church will then regain her long lost influence. Senex. p4c2*

September 4, 1891

The editor reports that some people would not attend the Lexington Fair because it had horse racing. He said, however, that he saw many intelligent and conscientious people who were there, including two ministers of the gospel from Jessamine County. The Prosecuting Attorny created a sensation by complaining in court that the Grand Jury had failed to indict the Jessamine County Fair Company for allowing a gambling device to be run on the fair grounds. Actually, they paid a concessionary fee to be there.

Governor Brown was inaugurated last Tuesday with an "immense crowd in attendance." p2c1 Dr Woods made himself available for the Speaker of the House of Representatives of the State Legislature. The editor says that no one who "depends upon capacity and personal merit" could possibly succeed as Speaker. He said that the Speaker "must know how to hustle, and scramble, and bargain, and bribe!" p1c3

The editor says there is too much bloodshed, too much mob rule in Kentucky. He says that "anarchy and lawlessness, driven from the mountains, seems to have invaded the Blue Grass." p1c3 He may be referring to this: A mob from Stamping Ground took a man from the Georgetown jail and hanged him. The large mob from Stamping Ground scared away a smaller mob that was intent on lynching another of the inmates.

I want to insert a story, paraphrased, from another newspaper that is humorous and seems to be a sign of the times.

The Nicholasville Democrat , September 11, 1891

In Kingston, Ont. at a revival of "Free Methodists" the preacher criticized the mode of female dress, saying that women were born beautiful and die misshapen because they wore corsets. He was an earnest and powerful speaker, and his words caused great excitement among the women present.

"Throw off the accursed invention. Throw it off and go to God as you left Him. Burn them rather than burn your souls in everlasting fire!" He had hardly ceased speaking when an enthusiast piled up material for a bonfire and applied a match.

"Throw off the garment" shouted the minister.

"Burn them" cried a feminine voice in the crowd as she surged to the front.

There was a gleam of white shoulders as she flung her corset on the flames, saying that she would die as God had made her, not as she had made herself! Her example was contagious and in less than half and hour not a woman in the crowd wore a corset and nothing remained in the blaze but a mass of twisted corset steels! The excitement was great, and several women grew faint. The Free Methodists consider the revival a success and talk of carrying the war into the States! p2c2

September 18, 1891

There has been a lot of reports of "blue law" violations in recent papers, both locally and nationally. Religious fervor is pretty stong, not only concerning the use of liquor, but observance of the Sabbath as well. The Lexington baseball team disbanded because they were not allowed to play on Sundays. The Mayor of Philadelphia ordered all bootblack stands closed on Sunday. As usual there is a great deal of inconsistency in enforcement of the ordinances: street cars and trains still run, Sunday papers are delivered, and many other activities are permitted.

One of the "shrewdest capitalist" in Louisville remarked that "we are approaching an unexampled speculative era".

The Constitutional Convention reconvened after the election to "correct errors and inconsistencies" in the document. However, they now seem more intent upon making substantive changes instead.

The railroad is bogged down for the lack of money. A meeting was held in Versailles on Tuesday composed of prominent citizens of Louisville, Versailles, Nicholasville and Richmond, who determined that the money had to be raised, and the road finished. p2c2

Pomp, the correspondent from Little Hickman, has been complaining that the correspondent from Pink had been invading his "territory" in reporting news. The Pink correspondent said that Pomp hadn't been reporting lately, and that he had no desire to "steal his thunder". p2c3 Actually, Pomp has been running around all over the state on his bicycle. I don't know who he has "minding the store". He said that he could go back and forth to Danville, a distance of twenty-two miles in five hours on his bike. p2c3 Given the condition of the roads in those days, that is pretty incredible. I had "good legs" when I was a kid riding the hills around Sulphur Well, but I found trips of about ten miles on paved roads about all I could do. My son, who does triathilons, once called me to come bring him home one hot day, after doing twenty-odd miles. Pomp was evidently a fairly large man, at least for those days, and I remember earlier that someone described him as presenting something of a spectacle when he first started learning to ride. Once, he offered a reward for information as to the identity of the young driver of a buggy who had speeded up and ran him off the road.

The Adcocks are visiting in Cincinnati again. They have relatives both there and in Knoxville.

## September 25, 1891

New dress goods are very rough, because of "large twills, Astrahan weaves or bourette fleckings, the latter often bestrewn upon stripes, plaids, or figures...." p1c4

The Democrats are pumped up over the free silver question. They want to increase the money supply and lower interest rates. The Republicans are said to want to protect the position of gold, and keep rates as they are. There could be some fear of inflation also.

Average land prices by counties show Jessamine ranks tenth. The average in Jessamine is about $30.00 per acre.

Health problems are not just in the villages. Louisville reported ten deaths from typhoid fever last week.

Dr Miller had his second annual colt show on Main Street in Nicholasville. He offered prizes for the best looking colts that were offspring of his stallion, Big Jim Wilkes. p3c4

The young people are again offering a play "The Woven Web" at the New Opera House in Nicholasville. It is a war drama, and the authenic costumes were obtained from the East, and the stage settings are custom made. The past year's performance was a huge success. p3c3

The editor says that oyster suppers with celery trimmings will soon be in order.

Dancing is increasing in popularity. The waltz is "the most popular and prettiest of all the dances." Something new is added every year, but "eventually they all give way to the slow, easy, gliding, mazy waltz ." p4c2

Contrast these stories: "It is said that our police have lately arrested several idle negroes for vagrancy, which has had the effect of thinning the crowds around the saloon doors." p3c1 "With the majority of the colored brethern, it makes no difference whether they have flour, or meal, or meat in the house. If there is an excursion anywhere they are bound to join it." p4c2 "In Memory of Henry Bell, A very worthy and respected citizen." p4c3 He passed away at the age of 79. Henry was born a slave in South Carolina. His first owner was John Bell. He came to Kentucky at the age of 14. Afterwards he was sold, and then sold again. He joined the Christian Church at South Elkhorn, and after some time in Lexington, spent the last nineteen or twenty years as a member of the Christian Church in Nicholasville. "He was an Elder of the church at the time of his death...." He joined the army on April 25, 1865, and was honorably discharged. "Two years ago he joined the Miller Post of the Grand Army of the Republic, of which he became Chaplain...." He was buried with honors at a funeral "in the presence of hundreds of people." He was survived by his wife of forty years, Nettie Bowen, with whom he had sixteen children.   p4c3

October 2, 1891

"The man who is not a Baptist or a Democrat must feel lonesome in Owen County! There are two Baptist associations with 200 ministers and an enormous membership. According to the poll books there are 4,000 Democrats and 400 Republicans...." p1c5

September has been unusually hot and dry. Tobacco handled carelessly is being sunburned. One correspondent said that stock water was becoming scarce. p1c6

William Huls and his wife celebrated their sixty-second wedding anniversary in Mt Sterling. There were one hundred guests at their wedding, but none are still living. He is 83, she 81, and both are in excellent health. Huls' father fought in the Revolutionary War under Washington, moved to Montgomery County and surveyed the City of Mt Sterling. p2c2

Dr J L Wilds is the Chairman of the Committee of Arrangements of the Jessamine County Bible Society. p2c4

Last week Pomp started out for Louisville, but he had to give it up. He said the turnpikes were several inches in dust. He must have finished the trip by train, because he was the guest of the Louisville Cycle Club. p2c4

The young people didn't get a rave review for their dramatic effort this year. The reviewer said that the play was full of emotional parts, and the acting required was too difficult for amateurs. p3c3

A tin-type artist and photographer was arrested for plying his trade on Sunday. He was convicted, and fined $10. He refused to pay and was sent to the work-house for ten days. After one day with a pick and shovel he paid the fine. p3c3

"Dick Young, a colored inebriate from Sulphur Well, was fined three dollars and sent to jail for six hours by Judge Phillips last Saturday, for disturbing the court by loud talking." p4c1 I suppose that he was sitting in the court-room when this occurred.

From the Calhoun, Georgia Courier: The question for debate at the colored people's academy tonight will be "Which is of the Greater Advantage to the Country, Lawyers or Buzzards".

Dr L P Walter, Louisville surgeon, spends one day a month in Nicholasville. His advertisements specifically invite patients that have not benefited by treatment of other physicians, but state that he takes no incurable diseases. He appears to specialize in disorders of the eye, ear, nose and throat. p4c4

October 9, 1891

Col McCarty, the Senior Editor of the Journal, has suffered a stroke. He is paralyzed on the right side and is not able to speak. There will be more to follow on his illness. p2c2

Irish pototoes are selling for 40 cents per bushel, so the harvest was good. There are also plenty of hickory nuts and chessnuts for those who enjoy gathering them.

The townsite of Chandler, Oklahma was opened to the public. "Some 3,000 excited men and women were waiting to make a mad rush when the signal was given." p2c1

B Wolf, who recently made an assignment, has taken a position as salesman at the Frankel clothing store.

October 16, 1891

Dr Barnes, attending physician, says that Col McCarty's condition is as favorable as could be expected. p3c3

Extreme suffering in Russia from famines in thirteen provinces has been reported. A correspondent of the London Telegraph says that it is the most wide-spread distress for centuries. p1c6

"Miss Susie Hendren has accepted a position as cashier at Kaufman, Straus & Co., Lexington." p3c2

Corn cutting and wheat sowing is nearly over.

October 23, 1891

Friends of Col McCarty are now hoping for a partial recovery from his stroke. p2c2

"Mrs Richardson is visiting her mother...." p3c2 This is Susan Miller of Irvine.

Wild grapes, haws, hickery-nuts, and walnuts, are plentiful this year.

October 30, 1891

Two US sailors were killed, and others injured and insulted by a mob of 150, when they attacked a street car in which the sailors were riding in Valparaiso, Chile. This has created an international incident. p2c1

Nicholasville has a large number of tramps, which is believed to be an overflow from the Lexington races.

There has been no change in Col McCarty's condition. He has remained cheerful, and this has given some hope for further improvement. p3c3

"Tomorrow night is Halloween." p4c1

After years of insatiable demand and good prices, it is reported that there is no market, at any price, for weanling mules.

November 6, 1891

The old lawyer retired and left his business to his son. A few days later the son came home, and said proudly to his father "you know the old Gilpin estate that you have been trying for years to settle? "Yes, answered the father with the suggestion of a smile." The son then said "Well, it didn't take me two days to settle it...." "It was as easy as rolling off a log!" The father shouted "You infernal idiot! That estate has paid our living expenses for four years, and would have for four more if I hadn't left the business to a ninny!" p1c7

November 13, 1891

Fount Hendren is still in town. He killed a huge owl while hunting on the Sims property. p3c1

A. Broh couldn't make a go of it! He is closing out his stock and quitting business. He took over Rose's store.

November 20, 1891

A Mrs Arminta Miller, age 55, died near Mt Lebanon, and was buried in the Reynolds Cemetery. p3c2

November 27, 1891

The Colonel's condition appears to be permanent. Mr T H Morris, late of the Nelson Record, has purchased an interest in the Journal, and has moved his family to Nicholasville.

Sybelle, sister of Dr J L Wilds, is getting married. Her husband (E J Aldridge) is from Covington. The ceremony was performed in Nicholasville, and the couple left immediately for their home in Covington. p3c2

Centre and Central University of Richmond (Ky) played a football game in Nicholasville. A special train arrived from Richmond with their team and fans, about 150 strong. They marched into town with yells and songs. A little later the team and fans from Danville arrived. There were cheers and counter cheers. They were crowded around the hotels and street corners. At two o'clock they started streaming toward Price Field. Centre, "with better technique", won the day, 20 to 6. p3c4

December 4, 1891

The Riney B has been placed in receivership. Nevertheless, it is still expected that the road will be completed to Beattyville. p2c3

The Hendrens are everywhere. Miss Iva Hendren, of Richmond is visiting her cousin, Miss Myrtie Hendren. I don't know how they are related. Miss Susie Hendren, of Madison, is visiting relatives in Hanley.

The "cattle boy" died. John Bronaugh, age 24, died of consumption. He had been sick for more than two years, and had gone West for his health. He is buried in Maple Grove. p3c3

December 11, 1891

How to stop a long-winded attorney (paraphrased): An attorney had been summarizing his case in Federal Court for several hours. The judge and jury were tired out. Finally, in desperation, the Judge asked the Court Clerk if he could do anything to stop the attorney. The Clerk said that would be easy, that he could stop it within three minutes! He wrote a note to the attorney as follows: "My Dear Colonel, as soon as you finish your magnificant argument, I would like for you to join me in the clerk's office in a bumper of fine old bourbon." The note was handed the attorney, just as he concluded a soaring passage of his speech. He read it and said "And now, if it please your honor and you gentlemen of the jury, I leave the case with you." One minute later he was in the clerk's office. p1c5

More sin! Horrible revelations! "Elder J W Mcgarvey created a sensation" while addressing a crowd of more than a thousand people at the Lexingon YMCA. He said that in Lexington that were more than "six hundren lewd women, and that the police shut their eyes when bawdy houses were mentioned." He said that on the Democratic ticket that "there were five saloon-keepers, three ex-saloon keepers, twenty-one patronizers of saloons, six drunkards, and four race horse men!" He said that the morality of a community could be determined by the number of saloons, and that there were 275 saloons in Lexington. p1c6

Lock No 6 has just been completed and the Kentucky River is navigable approximately fifty miles above Frankfort, or about 110 miles from the mouth of the river at Carrollton.

December 18, 1891

Work on the railroad bridge at Irvine is progressing. It is scheduled for completion on February 28th.

The stores are all advertising Christmas merchandise.

The *Sulphur Well Correspondent* writes:

*Frank Horine bought a fine bunch of cattle from W L Hendren last week.*
*Miss Viola Davis is on the sick list.*
*Rev. Creighton preached here Sunday.*
*Miss Ida Smith, of Harrodsburg, spent a few days with friends here recently.*
*Miss Mattie Johns, of Pleasureville, who has been visiting her sister, Mrs N D Davis, left Wednesday for Harrodsburg to visit friends and relatives.*
*James Woodard left Monday for Louisville on a business trip.*
*Mr Forest Miller has returned from Irvine.*
*Miss Irene Moseley, of Keene, is the guest of Miss Julia Hare.*
*Our young people are anticipating most delightful times Christmas. Several parties, weddings, etc., are expected. It seems as though the last part of the year will be the most enjoyable.*
*Mr S. Snowden and daughter, of Irvine, are the guests of Mrs Frank Miller.*
*The young people of this place, will have a Christmas tree at the Christian Church, Thursday, Dec. 24th. Everybody is invited. p3c4*

W D Hendren, Scottie's father died. His obituary follows:

Hendren--At the residence of his son-in-law, A K Adcock, Sunday, Dec. 13th, at noon. W D Hendren died of pneumonia, aged 53 years. The deceased was a widower and father of eight children, all living, three sons and five daughters, two of whom, Mrs A K Adcock and Mr Fountain Hendren, are residents of this place. Mr Hendren was a native of Madison County, but for many years was engaged in business in Lexington and at one time was interested with his son-in-law Mr Adcock in business here. His remains were taken to Madison County Tuesday and buried beside his wife in the Gilead Church burying ground. p3c5

This raises the question of where Scottie was living at the time of her father's death. The last time she was mentioned in the paper was when she went to work as a clerk at Adlers in Nicholasville. I would guess that she was in Frankfort with her sister Lizzie. She says in her autobiography that she was living there when her sister, Addie Adcock in Nicholasville, wrote for her to come there to live, that she had found her a job at Duncan and Spears. She also says there were eleven children, three that died in infancy.

By coincidence, I received A History of Gilead Baptist Church in the mail yesterday! After visiting the graves last fall, I wrote to the Church and inquired as to whether there had been a denominational change in the past one hundred years. I wondered why the Hendrens, who were Christians (Disciples of Christ), had been buried in a Baptist Church cemetery, particularly since they had not lived in that neighborhood for about fifteen years. It's possible that I found the answer to that question in the history.

It says that there was a doctrinal crisis in the life of the church. In 1828 Alexander Campbell and his followers "invaded the whole section". According to the historian:

> This group gained considerable strength in a short period of time, and succeeded in leading many of the preachers of this area to accept their belief in baptismal regeneration. By 1830 the Tates Creek Association was dominated by Campbellites, and this situation led to the withdrawal of nine churches, as a result of which they 'dropped' correspondence with any and every association or church where the heresy of Campbellism was tolerated. Gilead was one of the nine to form a new Tates Creek Association." pp5-6.

It's probable that the Hendrens became "Campbellites", and when Will D Hendren and his family went to live in Lexington that they joined the Christian Church there. Scottie says in her autobiography that she "attended Sunday School at Main Street Christian Church (now Walnut Street). Old Bro. Van Pelt, taught the smallest children then. My two sisters also attended. They later joined the church there." After she was older, about sixteen, her mother died and she went to live with her sister in Frankfort. She says that she joined the Christian Church in Frankfort during a big meeting conducted by Bro. Mark Collis. She later joined the Christian Church in Nicholasville, when she moved. "Bro. Victor Dorris was pastor then. I sure did like to go to Church and Sunday School. A 'young peoples' meeting was organized, during my short stay." She says that Matt Nave and Sam Price were always there to see us (Susie, I think) home. "Good boys, they were too...."

December 25, 1891

The Rutgers College Glee Club will be in concert at the New Opera House in Nicholasville, on December 28th. p2c4

"Miss Carrie West, of Garrard, is visiting Miss Addie Hendren." p3c2 Addie is Dr Hendren's daughter.

Some of the leading men's clothiers are showing very high collars and very wide cuffs. The editor says they are both unbecoming and uncomfortable.

After having gone though the fad of souvenir spoons, the craze is now "dainty little after-dinner cups. They cost from $1 to $5 each. Only one cup is given at a time." At those prices I can see why! p4c1

There were not very many articles from the Sulphur Well correspondent this year. There were five unsigned articles in March, June, July, August, and December. There was one other article in August signed by Senex, who may or may not have been the Sulphur Well Correspondent. I think it likely that the unsigned articles this year are by the same correspondent who wrote the unsigned articles in 1888 and 1889.

# FAMILY HISTORY - 1892

There are many news items pertaining to the Millers and Hendrens during this year. There is little from the Sulphur Well correspondent, however.

### January 1, 1892

"Mr Fount J Hendren spent several days this week with his uncle, Mr Jas. M Hendren, of Speedwell." p3c2 Fount's father is Will D Hendren who just died in December.

"Miss Susie Hendren, of Lexington, Kaufman & Straus's popular cashier, visited her sister, Mrs A K Adcock this week." p3c2

"G R Moore, of Wilmore, has bought of Frank Hudson, of Sulphur Well neighborhood, a farm of 25 acres, for $575."

Everybody has the grippe! Even some weddings had to be postponed!

The latest "diversion" for men is a self-tied four in hand. The knot is made round and indented slightly. The fabric of the ties is soft, but heavy woven, silken material. p4c1

### January 8, 1892

"Miss Laura Hendren, of Bloomington, Ill. is visiting her cousin, Miss Scottie Hendren." It appears that Scottie is now (or still) living in Nicholasville, and that she has relatives living in Bloomington. p3c2

The paper is torn, but we can piece this story together: "Forest Miller and Ja..., pleasant young gents ... thought they w ... burg, but the ... Cynthiana. As they ... there they enjoyed the ... until they could leave .... p3c2 They must have wanted to go to Harrodsburg, but boarded a train bound for Cynthiana instead.

"Miss Lizzie Robinson gave one of the most enjoyable entertainments of the season at Logana on December 28th. The house was filled with guests from neighboring villages and towns." Dora Murphy and Marshall Davis, both from Sulphur Well, attended.

### January 15, 1892

The new Kentucky Wesleyan College at Winchester has been completed and opened.

"Tea cakes, apple and mince pies baked daily at Denman's City Bakery." p3c1

This is strange. B Wolf, who recently made an assignment of his coal yard, went out of business, and became a clerk at Frankels, advertises that he wishes to lend three or four thousand dollars on real estate mortgages!

The Riney B is still in receivership. The contractors have suits for payment, and the earnings appear to be meager.

## January 22, 1892

Julia Hare, daughter of W H Hare, and Ben D Spears were married in Sulphur Well at the bride's parents home. Julia was one of the gadflys of the Texie, Ida Gray era. Her sister Mayme married Wm McClellan Johnston of Lancaster.p3c5

"Monday was the dullest, meanest, gloomiest court day in years!" All the businesses suffered, but the saloons. Only one "poor old cow" was offered at auction. Even worse, "the county court transacted no business of interest."p3c5

## January 29, 1892

After several years of the railroads building everywhere, reality has set in. Mercer County has brought suit against the Louisville Southern to recover the $125,000 in bonds pledged to build the road through that county. The machine shops promised did not materialize. The connections are not good, and the freight rates are higher. The citizens are ready to have the rails pulled up. p2c2

## February 5, 1892

Dr Miller was the physician for the Poor House. His compensation is $40 for 1892. p1c7

Property transfer: "Sue Nave to Mary A Johnson, deed to correct title to lot on West Street, Nicholasville."

Duncan and Spears are putting in two large display windows in their store (clothing and shoes).

"The Kentucky River packet, City of Clarksville, is now making regular weekly trips from Louisville to Shaker Ferry (High Bridge), leaving Shaker Ferry, Monday morning at 7 o'clock and arriving at Louisville, Wednesday evening at 3 o'clock." p3c1

"There has been no material change" in the condition of the Senior Editor of the Journal, Col. McCarty, who suffered a stoke four months ago. "He still remains almost speechless, and there is very little action in his afflicted limbs." He is confined to his bed, and as soon as "the weather permits he is to be taken to the home of his son-in-law, Dr J J Rodman, at Owensboro." p3c4

February 12, 1892

There was a run on the Glasgow Deposit Bank that temperarily deranged the Cashier, who had to be restrained.

February 19, 1892

Col McCarty died last Monday morning. He was taken to Bardstown for burial, beside his first wife. p2c1

Pomp, Little Hickman correspondent, has passed the burden of corresponding to his wife. I don't know whether my remarks have made it clear or not, but Pomp and Col McCarty were very close friends. I'm surprised that there was no mention of McCarty's death in his last article.

This may be a good place to say that I have been frequently frustrated by what the correspondents do not say in their articles. The thesis of this work is that the correspondents view what is going on around them, and write in that context. Sometimes it seems that they are in their own little world and are ignoring what is going on elsewhere. Only one correspondent commented on McCarty's death in this issue of the Journal.

A bit of family news: "Mr A K Adcock, son-in-law of the late W D Hendren, received a check last Tuesday night from the Knights of Honor Insurance Company, St Louis, for $2,000.00 as insurance on the life of Mr Hendren. The check was payable to Mr Adcock because he had kept up the payments for the last several years." p3c1

And a bit of Sulphur Well news: "Fayette Brooks traded his fine stallion to George Diamond, of Ambrose, for other stock valued (at) three hundred dollars." p3c8

There is still some progress on the railroad. The first train with six cars of freight passed over the bridge at Irvine. p3c3

History repeats itself: "Public sentiment is demanding stricter immigration laws, not against honest, able-bodied, self-supporting people, but against paupers, criminals and the insane, who have been coming in alarming numbers." p1c7

Mosely's buggy and carriage business seems to be flourishing. I will view with interest what happens around the turn of the century. I wonder if he has any inkling of his situation?

February 26, 1892

It appears that Pomp has started his own paper, the Little Hickman Courier. It is a free publication, obtaining its revenue from advertisements. p1c4

Despite the extensive changes made to the new constitution after its submission to the voters, the Court of Appeals upheld its validity.

"Dr Geo. M Hendren has moved with his family from Jessamine County to Edenton, this county." <u>Richmond Register</u>. p3c2

Just in time! The Riney B is "sufficiently near completion for compliance with the contract between the railroad and Estill County" to secure the bonds committed by the county.
The arrival of the "official train" was "cheered lustily." "The engineer made the valley sound with the echoes of the whistle." "The train made several trips across the new bridge, carrying all those who wished to ride." p3c3

The Pink correspondent expressed his condolences for the death of Col McCarty. Jessamine Station added its praise. Pomp also weights in this week with a lengthy paragraph about McCarty, calling him an "intimate friend". p3c5-6

To complete my "editorial" from last week about how the correspondents wrote about events: We have to consider that it takes time for an event to occur, be reported in the paper, be read by the correspondents, for them to react to the news, and comment in their articles.

Its been a long time since we've heard from the Sulphur Well correspondent!

March 4, 1892

Broh, a clothier going out of business, will begin to auction his entire stock of goods on March 18th.

From Nicholasville: "Miss Scottie Hendren is the guest of Miss Ella Scearcy, Lexington." And this also: "Miss Susie Hendren, of Lexington, has been visiting her sister, Mrs A K Adcock." p3c2

March 11, 1892

The <u>Woodford Sun</u> and the <u>Versailles Clarion</u> are debating the question of women's suffrage.

"Miss Scottie Hendren is taking a course in book-keeping at the Capital City Business College, Frankfort." p3c2

Reported again: "Dr George Hendren and family have removed to Edenton, Madison County, where the doctor will practice his profession." p3c2

The grass isn't always greener! Little Hickman homecomings: "E B Evans arrived home last Sunday from Washington Territory, after an absence of ten years." p3c4 "Smith Tracy, who emigrated to Indiana several years ago, is expected back soon to run the farm of Mrs Lizzie Hocker." p3c4

I feel that I have been remiss in not reporting the innumerable instances of drunkenness that have appeared in the paper over the past few years. Its cumulativeness has made me conscious of my omission. While today "most" people are "social" drinkers, in the late nineteenth century people were either total abstainers, or drunks. This is obviously an overstatement, yet it is essentially true. It started with youths, both "fashionable" and poor, who drank in saloons, or privately. One recent article that I should have reported was of a drunken youth who vomited on the carpet in the parlor at a nice party. There are numerous stories of groups of men standing, actually blocking the sidewalks, in front of saloons. Many of the stories of shootings, stabbings, and fights, were in, or near saloons, or the result of heavy drinking on the part of at least one of the parties. Those who drank, did so to get drunk, and it was an almost exclusively male phenomenon. It had an immense impact on society, because it divided those who drank from those who hated drunks and the effects of drinking.

## March 18, 1892

Dr Miller purchased a bay yearling colt by Nutbreaker for $110 at the horse sales in Lexington. p2c3

The prices of other animals: Two year old cattle, $35-$40 per head; milk cows, $20-$45 per head; pairs of mules, $200 to $240.p2c4

Other prices: Corn, $2 per barrel; hemp seed, $1.70 per bushel; bacon, 6-7 cents per pound; hams, 9 cents; sides, 8 cents; wheat 85 cents per bushel; flour, $3 per hundred (I think); butter, 25 cents per pound; eggs, 12 1/2 cent per dozen; coal, 14 cents per bushel. p3c3

Kentucky is being Kentucky: "Wind, rain, snow, and cold weather have prevailed this week." p3c1

Three barge loads of coal arrived at the mouth of Little Hickman last Saturday. p3c1 This is news because when the river freezes, the coal doesn't get to Jessamine.

The Glass' Mill correspondent is just now recognizing the death of Col McCarty.

## March 25, 1892

Based upon the requests for stable room at the Fair Grounds, it appears that there will be two hundred or more horses trained over the Nicholasville track this season. That is a pretty large amount of activity. It is a one mile trotting track, and considered very safe.

April 1, 1892

"In the study of history, we learn that the world is indebted to the teachings of Jesus Christ for those grand truths of political science, which underlies modern liberty. The advent of Christ was the dawn of civil and religious liberty in the world." p1c4

The Republican Convention was termed "a large and harmonious gathering". The Eight District Republicans met in Nicholasville this past Friday. They passed resolutions favoring the McKinley bill and opposing the free coinage of silver; and they endorsed the administration of President Harrison and elected delegates that were instructed to vote for his renomination. p1c6

The editor of the <u>Lexington Blade</u>, a prohibitionist publication, was arrested and charged with criminal libel. He wrote:
> That shebang called the Christian Church of Paris is run by a Republican preacher in cahoots with a lot of whiskey-makers, sellers, and drinkers that never would have been heard of in the world except for the riches that have accumulated from money more illy gotten than that of Judas Iscariot.... p2c1

There is a bill before the Legislature to ban the playing of football and baseball on Sunday. There is never any rest from prohibition and blue-law activity. p2c1

April 8, 1892

There is a lengthy article about the coming exhibits at the World's Fair to be held in Chicago. It lists the nations that are coming, and the state organizations that will exhibit. This is followed by state political news, and then national news. These articles, plus the advertisements pretty much cover the front page. There appears to be subtle changes in the paper since the death of Col McCarty.

The editor of the <u>Blue Grass Blade</u>, who was indicted for libel, has been convicted. During the trial the editor turned his back on the proceedings and refused to offer a defense. The editor of the <u>Jessamine Journal</u> said that at various times he had considered the <u>Blade</u> editor a "crank and a knave", but noted that there were a lot of people that sympathized with him in his troubles. Those that know him say he is a "mild, gentle, and cultivated gentlemen". It is thought that the Paris church is not nearly as bad as despicted by the editor, yet believe "that in the main he is correct" in his assessment. p2c1

The water rose in the Kentucky River and the loggers have been busy rafting logs down the river to various sawmills. About 7,000 logs were purchased at High Bridge on the last tide. "Eight raftsmen from Breathitt County are reported drowned last Tuesday while attempting to pass three rafts of logs over the dam of Lock No 6, near Mundy's Landing." p3c1

April 15, 1892

Wouldn't you think that the lead item of the High Bridge correspondent would be the tragedy at the lock and dam? It wasn't mentioned. However, reports and the facts may differ!

April 22, 1892

No report from Sulphur Well. It's been a long time!

April 29, 1892

The front page, four columns wide was devoted to a plea for womens' suffrage by T W Shannon.

Labeled a "field day": The Democratic County Convention and Robinson's Circus, all on the same day! p2c1

Acts of incredible stupidity or meanness are not localized in time. There have been several instances of stretching barbed wire across roads. These wires cannot be seen in the darkness and have caused painful and critical injuries. A bill has been introduced in the legislature to make such an act a felony, and if a death should result, the person convicted of the offense would be charged with murder. p2c1

"Dr J L Wilds is putting a new front, and otherwise improving his residence". p3c1

Lexington's "running" races begin tomorrow and last for ten days.

May 20, 1892

The next World's Fair will be in Chicago in 1893, and it is front page news already. There is a great deal of information about exhibits, among them: a telephone exchange "with 600 instruments", a yacht regatta, a reproduction of Mt Vernon, etc. p1c6

May 27, 1892

Fire "destroyed the residence of George Moore, two miles below Sulphur Well on the Paint Lick pike." The Moores have eight children. p2c2

June 3, 1892

Excursions are available to the Republican National Convention in Minneapolis, and the Democratic National Convention in Chicago.

You may remember Mary (Bradshaw) Wieser, a local girl who married and divorced the mining engineer. Her divorce settlement included their farm, known as Donerail. It was sold recently. It is now rumored that she is about to be remarried, this time to a well-know Lexington politician. p3c2 I don't believe that ever happened.

## June 10, 1892

For traveling, ladies are advised to go for simplicity. At the stores, "ready-made costumes" of "coat, vest, and skirt" are available. Light weight silks with modest patterns are considered "excellent". p1c5

## June 17, 1892

Family news:"Mr & Mrs A K Adcock are attending the races at Latonia this week." p3c2 "Mrs W H Van Winkle and Miss Scottie Hendren, of Frankfort, and Miss Susie Hendren, of Lexington, visited their sister, Mrs A K Adcock, last week." p3c2

## June 24, 1892

Nicholasville is going to get its "water works" that it has been wanting for several years. A water tower was placed above Lake Mingo. The water is to be pumped from Jessamine Creek. p1c5

## July 1, 1892

The High Bridge Meeting Grounds has been purchased and renamed the Kentucky Palisades. A July 4th celebration featuring speakers and patriotic songs, with fireworks that night, is planned. The Camp Meeting will begin July 22nd and outstanding ministers are expected. p1c5

Henry Watterson, editor of the Courier Journal, went to the Democratic Convention as a delegate at large. He was opposed to the candidacy of Cleveland even though the Kentucky delegation was for him. He also refused any committee assignments, and in general irritated everyone. p2c1

## July 8, 1892

Blackberries are on the market for 25 cents for a water bucket full. Times have changed! Last Saturday I purchased a pint for $2.00 (July, 1996).

## July 15, 1892

I am struck by the increasing incidence of articles related to alcoholism. The effects upon family life, violence, community inconvenience, make me understand how a fed-up society could consider prohibition. A front page article pertains to a drunkard's home. p1c4

Ninety-five percent of the acreage in the US devoted to hemp is in Kentucky. This is the best description I have seen as to how the fiber is extracted, and what "breaking" hemp means: The land is prepared in the fall, and sowed the following March. The hemp matures in one hundred days. Kentucky and Illinois handle it differently. In Kentucky the hemp is cut by hand, and broken by hand, keeping the fiber straight. In Illinois, the hemp is cut with a mower, allowed to lay on the ground for some time before it is raked up, and "run through a power breaker to separate the fiber from the woody part of the stalk". They pay "no attention to keeping the fiber straight, and handle the crop with labor-saving machinery at much less expense. The improved cordage machinery does not require the fiber to be kept straight." p2c2

July 22, 1892

Wheat has been harvested, but threshing has been held up by rain. Tobacco planting was late, but indications are that the acreage will be at least as large as last year. p1c6

July 29, 1892

Several boys about town, all said to be under 21, were drunk last Friday night, and indulged in much loud profanity and obscenity on Main Street, in front of Hotel Nicholas. p3c1

The Camp Meeting at High Bridge is underway. The weather is hot as usual. The new owner of the camp grounds seems to be doing a good job of maintaining the facilitites. I had wondered before about security. Twenty-four policemen are on duty on Sundays, fewer at other times. The crowds seem to be smaller than usual this year, between 2,000 and 3,000 attended last Sunday. Sam Jones, a noted spell-binder, will be there Saturday and Sunday, and a much larger crowd is expected. p3c3

Contracts have been drawn for the construction of a water tower in town, and the intake and reservoir on Jessamine Creek. The intake is about one and a half miles from the Court House. p3c4

August 5, 1892

Not much was secret in this day and age! Dr Welch removed a ten-ounce tumor from the "right breast of Mrs W W Sageser." She is reported to be doing well. p3c2

Trenchs are being dug for the water mains to be installed along the streets.

"Miss Susie Hendren has resigned her position as cashier at Kaufman, Straus & Co., Lexington, and will take charge of Oak Hill School, in this county." p3c2

Seven men were arrested at High Bridge on Sunday. They were charged with a variety of offences. They were drunk and disorderly, carried concealed weapons, and one fired his pistol in the railroad car as the train passed through the tunnel near High Bridge. They were fined $50 each, and sentenced to ten days in jail. p3c4-5

August 12, 1892

Saratoga fashions are featuring entirely white outfits for day wear. "Nainsook or batiste are the favorite materials for dresses", which are most frequently finished with embroidry or lace. p1c5

Equal opportunity advertisement: "Cook wanted--Black, white, male, or female. Apply at this office." p3c1

The old steps of the Presbyterian Church are being replaced with concrete steps and pavement. The old steps are twelve feet long and are being offered for sale. p3c1

The Nicholasville Fair is underway. It features several horse races (trotting).

August 19, 1892

Surveys are being made to locate Lock Number Seven on the Kentucky River. It will be at Shakers' Landing, just below where Dix River empties into the Kentucky River. p1c4

From Glass' Mill: "Mr Howard Murphy, the merchant, of Sulphur Well, has gone in partnership with J H Glass in the milling business. They will buy up wheat at once and start their mill to running daily ...." p2c5

The Fair was quite successful, the weather was favorable and the attendance good. People from all the surrounding towns were represented. There were four trotting races each day. The pneumatic tire sulkies are now available, and one or two seconds faster on a one mile track, than the regulation sulkies. It is said that this is the last year for the old ones. p3c3

August 26, 1892

A fad for the young girls--wearing male suspenders with their skirts. Also faddish are corsets over ladies' costumes. Apparently they wore blazers over it all. p1c5 The mustache is becoming unfashionable for men. "Great men of all nations have clean faces...." p1c5

"Messrs J H Murphy and Jas. F Horine, two well-known and popular business men, have formed a partnership under the firm name of Murphy & Horine, and embarked in the clothing business, having bought of Mr Isaac Levy, of the Kentucky Clothing House, the latter's stock and fixtures. Mr Levy will remove to St Louis and engage in the furniture business." p3c1 This is the store that Forest Miller will later acquire an interest, in 1994.

Wm C Baxter is being sued for divorce by his wife, Amelia. She alleges drunkenness, cruel and inhuman treatment, and a failure to support his family. The couple have five children. At the time the suit was filed, he was in the workhouse in Lexington. p3c2

"Mrs A K Adcock and little daughter, Russie, left Tuesday for Knoxville, Tenn. to visit relatives." p3c2

## September 2, 1892

"Bicycling--Lexington is running wild over bicycling, boys and girls, old men and young men are all mounting wheels and the streets are lively day and night with them." p1c4

Fruit may be substituted on occasions when oysters aren't available for the first course. "The diner must therefore be aware of fruit etiquette! Bananas must be eaten with a fork; strawberries capped may be eaten with a spoon or a fork; uncapped, they are dipped into sugar and eaten with your fingers; pears must be divided, and the half eaten with a spoon; spoons should be used for mellons also." p1c4

What Sam Jones told the people at the Camp Meeting: "If you don't stop whisky drinking and horse racing in Kentucky the devil will get you ...." p1c5

Humor: An upset member of a private club complained that several other members had gone together and offered him $100 to resign his membership. His listener responded "don't you take it, Old Fellow, you'll get a better offer.

"Last Saturday, on Depot Street, the horse driven by Mrs A K Adcock became frightened at a traction engine, made a short turn and broke down a wheel of the surrey." p3c1

"Miss Lettie Brown, of Knoxville, Tenn., neice of Mr A K Adcock, returned this week with Mr Adcock and little daughter, Bessie, for a visit to Mr Adcock's family." p3c2 This may be when Scottie Hendren, Mrs Adcock's sister, first meets Lettie Brown. Lettie evidently made a long visit, see the next item on September 30th.

Murphy and Horine have just employed George Diamond as their new salesman. It is said that he is well-known, and would welcome his friends to his new place of business.

This is really a series of coincidences. Scottie Miller says in her autobiography that she and Susie had some distantly related cousins living in Nicholasville who had friends at Sulphur Well, and were often invited to parties there.
> One night a surprise party was being given to George Diamond, wife and son. Walter and Bertie Bain asked us to go. (They) said (it) didn't make any difference if we didn't know them, as was a surprise party. Somehow the family heard of the surprise party and left home, so everyone was invited to go to Mrs Miller's. Susie and I refused at first, saying we didn't know them, but we were begged to go, and did, so that was how I first met my future husband. I don't remember how Susie

met the fellow she married, Andrew Sageser, but his first wife was Forest's sister Rosie, who died soon after her baby was born. Forest and I continued to go together for almost three years.

Continued coincidences! In the personal column of this issue: "Walter Bain, who has been quite ill, is improving." p3c2

Land transfer: "J H Murphy and wife to Louis Straus, lot and improvements at Sulphur Well, $2,000." p3c3

Local feud: The Best brothers, Will and Humphrey, have been feuding with John Campbell. One day Campbell walked into the store at Paint Lick, and the younger Best spoke to him. Campbell merely nodded and sit down. Best took offense at this supposed slight and reached for his pistol. Campbell also drew his gun, and both began firing. Humphrey Best was killed, Campbell was shot in the right lung, and may live. One bystander was killed by stray shots, and another was hit in the shoulder. Humphrey Best was said to be under the influence of whisky. This was a violent family. The father, Ebenezer Best, has killed four men in his lifetime. p3c8

September 9, 1892

Howard Murphy is in the East buying his fall and winter stock of clothing.

September 16, 1892

Kentucky Congressman McCreary is a member of the Foreign Relations Committee. He is promoting stronger relations with the Latin American countries, seeking to substitute US trade for France, Germany, and England. McCreary feels that there should also be an intercontinental rail line in addition to the steam lines now available. Delegates of the Pan American Congress are scheduled to visit various cities in the US, including Lexington. p1c6

"The Democratic Convention at Winchester Thursday of last week was the scene of one of the most remarkable specimens of political dishonesty ever witnessed." p3c4 The District Chairman of the convention refused to accept the credentials of the delegation from Madison, which were being contested, and also refused to give the floor to anyone who wished to protest. This precluded the Madison delegation from voting on the officers, and in organizing the committees.

September 23, 1892

"Born to the wife of Mr E J Aldrich (nee Miss Sybelle Wilds), On Tuesday, Sept. 20th, a fine daughter--Elizabeth Madeline." p3c6

Murphy & Horine are offering the merchandise they purchased from Levy at a bargain. They say they plan to make young men's suits, overcoats, hats and shoes their specialty.

September 30, 1892

"Miss Scottie Hendren, of Nicholasville, who formerly attended the Capital City Business College, and Miss Lettie Brown, a charming young lady of Knoxville, Tenn., have been visiting Mrs W H Van Winkle." p3c2

There is a major flap over the Commonwealth Attorneyship in Madison County. The State Central Committee recommends that the matter be settled by a primary election.

Frankel is trying to increase his market share of the Nicholasville clothing business. He will occupy the new store room adjoining the old one.

Water pipes, 13,500 feet of them, are being laid all over Nicholasville, with 2,500 feet more to go. About forty fire plugs have already been set. p3c1

Kindergarten will begin next Spring. I suppose for the first time in Nicholasville. p3c3

October 7, 1892

"Dr J C Miller, Logana, attended Richmond County Court Monday. He reports a very large number of mule colts on the market, but low prices and slow sales." p3c1

October 14, 1892

"New skirts for the street clear the ground, although the bell shape is retained, with a longer or shorter demi-train, for indoors." p1c6 The mostly frequently seen wraps are those in "triple style, the lowest reaching a little below the waist." p1c6

"The failure of grass, due to the drought, is causing farmers everywhere to sell off surplus stock." p2c2 Harrodsburg reported, on Court Day, that there was an over-supply of stock, few buyers, and lower prices.p2c2

From Hanly: Diphtheria is raging among the children.p3c5

October 21, 1892

What's going on in the world? "Poet, Tennyson is dead." "The Homestead Riot cost Pennsylvania $400,000." "The greatest day's run for a steamship so far has been 515 miles."p1c3

From Pink: "There is little said here in regard to the election. Every one seems to think Cleveland will be elected unless the Republicans use too much `fat' that they fry out of the manufacturers." p3c4 Pink also reports "a good crop of Jennet apples this year". p3c4 I remember a few trees were still left in Sulphur Well when I was a youngster. Lucien

Foster had most of them in an old orchard across from where Arthur West (the old Murphy residence) lived. They were mostly small and knotty, often insect bitten, but I have remembered them all my life as being wonderful! Recently, I discovered that George Ware obtained grafts of trees from several old orchards that are now essentially obsolete.

From Nicholasville: "Miss Scottie Hendren is clerking at Duncan & Son." p3c2

October 28, 1892

At long last! A report from the *Sulphur Well Correspondent*:

*Andrew Sageser has returned from Texas.*
*Mr Jas. Sageser is very ill.*
*Mrs Mattie Bishop, of Illinois, is visiting her parents and other relatives here.*
*Mr Geo. Watters and two sons, Simon and Willie, and Mr Holly Easley, were all in Lexington this week.*
*Miss Carrie Woodward has been quite sick with fever.*
*Clayton Miller has about recovered from diphtheria. p2c3*

The Correspondent gave no reason for his absence. James Sageser is Andrew's father, and Andrew may have returned from Texas on that account. Andrew's wife, Rose, died in 1890.

From Little Hickman: "The school at Oak Hill is progressing nicely, with Miss Susie Hendren as teacher." p2c3 These two people, Susie and Andrew, will soon meet.

November 4, 1892

Enough to make you change your politics! J.L. Jones, tin merchant at Cynthiana and a life-long Republican, is for the whole Democratic ticket. He cannot stand the tariff on tin. "The all-absorbing topic just now is the election...."p1c5 "The campaign which closes this week, leaves the situation extremely hopeful for the Democrats." p2c1

November 11, 1892

"Grover Cleveland has defeated Benjamin Harrison for President" by a decisive vote. p2c1 The "Solid South" furnished big majorities for the Democrat's tariff reform. "Tuesday was the day Protection went down before the banner of Tariff Reform". p2c2

November 18, 1892

The Journal editor sums up the reasons for the Democrats success: He believes the most important issue was the tariff. "But while it was distinctly a victory for Democratic principles, we do not believe that any other Democrat in the land would have been so readily and unanimously trusted as Mr Cleveland." p2c1

November 25, 1892

There is a controversy over "sun time" and standard time. The court house clock is on sun time and the railroad runs on standard time. "We only need one time, and let us use that which brings us into accord with the world." p3c1

December 2, 1892

Some people have bad timing. B D Spears is tearing down the frame building on Main Street and is preparing to put up a brick stable. I wonder how long it was before it was converted? p3c1

Seems to be a fair amount of meanness around. James Walker is charged with putting a railroad tie on the track near Highbridge. p3c1

"Miss Linnie Spruce, step-daughter of J W Baker, of Sulphur Well was taken ill with diphtheria Sunday, followed by bronchial pneumonia." Linnie's mother is Miranda Spruce, who once ran a store in Sulphur Well. She remarried J W Baker, whose farm is next to the Miller farm.

December 9, 1892

Jay Gould died last week. "Though the richest man in the world, like the rest of mortals, he needs and gets but six feet of earth for his final sleep." p2c1

December 16, 1892

Jay Gould bequeathed all, every cent, of his estate to his relatives, none to charity. p2c2

From Spears: "Brack Hill has moved to the neighborhood, having rented Dr Miller's place." p2c3

December 23, 1892

Secretary of State Blaine is in critical condition, and not expected to live. p2c1 A new postage stamp commemorating the 400th anniversary of the discovery of America will be issued January 1, 1893. The portrait of Columbus appears on the stamps. p3c2

December 30, 1892

It is predicted that trolleys will soon connect all the towns in Central Kentucky, enabling people living in the country and small towns to participate in the business and social life of Lexington. Quite a way to end the year! p1c5

There has been only one short article from the Sulphur Well correspondent this year. It revealed nothing to me about the writer and is likely a continuation of the unsigned articles written in 1888, 1889, and 1891. There were enough references in the paper to my family for me to work in quite a bit of family history, particularly Scottie Hendren and her family. It was also possible to let the reader know a little bit about what was going on in the state and in the world.

## FINANCIAL PANIC - 1893

Times have been hard all along, but a shortage of money, and closing of banks, makes this year particularly bad economically. However, this is a really good year for family news.

### January 6, 1893

The correspondent from Glass' Mills says that "dances, pound parties and socials are quite numerous in this community." p2c2 The weather for Christmas was ideal. The deepest snow of the winter so far is on the ground, and those with sleighs are using them.

### January 13, 1893

"One of the most delightful events during the holidays, was an 'old fashioned dress' party...." The young people wore costumes of their ancesters. Dr Miller's son, Rice, attended. p2c2

The merchants of Nicholasville say that the past six months have been the best in history, and they expect the next six months to be unusually good also. p2c1 The new water works in Nicholasville was tested, and the whole town turned out! It worked in general, but several plugs needed repairs, so the town council didn't approve the job. p3c7

Farm prices are mixed. Hog prices continue to rise, with top hogs bringing $7.85. However, the tobacco market continues to be weak. p2c3

### January 20, 1893

"S.M.D.", Samuel McAfee Duncan, the resident historian that has submitted many articles over the years is himself featured. His work in history was recognized by being made an honorary member of the Filson Club in Louisville. He was born in Pulaski County on September 11, 1830. He is described as of medium height, but so emaciated from asthma that he weights only 120 pounds. McAfee was "often prejudicial and always uncompromising, loving and praising ideal and heroic manhood, while denouncing deceit and cowardice." p1c2

### January 27, 1893

There is considerable furor over the senatorial contest. Governor Brown removed himself from consideration, leaving Representative McCreary and others still in contention. Some think that McCreary will get the seat and are lining up for his job. A Democratic caucus will be held in early February. p2c1

Jessamine claims to be ahead of most of the other counties in road building, with nearly every main road being macadamized. p2c1

"Mrs J L Wilds ... went to Lancaster Friday to visit Miss Lena Bright, who has been quite ill." p3c2

Mrs Baker (Spruce) was called to Louisville because of the illness of her daughter (Mrs Joe Woodward).

## February 3, 1893

The Kentucky River, which has been frozen over for several weeks, broke through at last. Logs are expected to be released upstream so the saw mills can begin operation. p2c3 Union Mills reports that "the mud now is as deep as the snow was!" p2c3 The Spears correspondent says that "Dr Miller has 750 shocks of corn to shuck!" p2c3 The farmers are complaining that they are behind in hemp-breaking because of the weather.

Mrs Susan Sageser Watts died at the age of 92. She was the eldest child of Frederick Sageser. Frederick, the son of David Sageser, was born in 1778 in Maryland. The Sagesers were an old German family. Frederick married Catherine Bruner, daughter of Christian Bruner, on October 3, 1790. Susan married John Watts in 1820. Celia Sageser, who married Merriman Miller, is a sister. p3c3

Adam Adcock is still a member of the City Council. A report to the Council stated that several of the fire plugs were still not working.

## February 17, 1893

Sageser-Hendren."At the residence of Elder J M Bailey, on Wednesday, Feb. 15th, at 5pm, Mr Andrew Sageser, of Sulphur Well neighborhood, was married to Miss Susie Hendren, a popular and successful school teacher, and sister of Mrs A K Adcock, of this place. Elder Bailey performed the ceremony." p3c5 "Mrs W D Richardson, of Irvine, is visiting relatives in the county." p3c2 Mrs Richardson's sister, Rose Miller, was Andrew Sageser's first wife. It's likely that Mrs Richardson attended the wedding. There is no mention of Forest or Scottie at the wedding.

## February 24, 1893

"Mr J H Murphy's clothing store is being repapered and other wise improved." p3c1 The Council accepted the water works, but held up payment until certain improvements are made.p3c1

Rice Miller, Dr Miller's oldest son, is listed as a teacher at the Graded School in Nicholasville. p3c6

March 10, 1893

"Thieves bored the lock off the back door of Mr James Miller's store at Sulphur Well, Wednesday night. Only a few dollars worth of coffee was missed. The post-office is in Mr Miller's store, but none of Uncle Sam's stamps were stolen." p3c1

Dr George M Hendren, who recently moved from Sulphur Well to Edenton, is in serious condition. His "horse fell with him, trampling on and badly bruising his left leg between the knee and ankle, also bruising his foot." Gangrene has set in that leg. While his condition is serious Dr Mann feels that he will recover. p3c4

March 17, 1893

"Councilman A K Adcock is building a large refrigerator in his place of business on Harrodsburg Street. The waterworks company is also making connections for running water into his building." p3c1

March 24, 1893

"The large increase in business over the RNI&B railroad during the last six months is almost an absolute guarantee that the road will be completed to Beattyville this summer." p3c6

March 31, 1893

Perhaps, finally, the Civil War is winding down. "General E Kirby Smith, the last of the full generals of the Confederacy, died at Sewanee, Tennessee, Tuesday. "One by one the old veterans are passing away, and soon there will be nothing but a memory of the dread visitation of civil war." p2c1

From the Lancaster Record: "Dr J C Miller and son, of Jessamine, are visiting at Wm. Burton's." p3c3 "Dr J C Miller bought of Robert Burton, Garrard County, a three-year-old jack for $500." p2c2 For readers who may be "city-folk", a jack is a male ass used for breeding, especially with female horses, to produce mules.

"Mr A K Adcock has had an improved hydraulic air pump placed in his large ice cooler, which has the effect of keeping beer at the same temperature for several days." p3c1

Harrison Dean died at his home of pneumonia at the age of 82. He was born in Mercer County, but moved to Jessamine in 1835. He married Nancy Owens in 1839. They moved to Illinois, but returned to Kentucky and lived at Sulphur Well for four years, before moving on to Little Hickman. Nancy died a year before Harrison. Their sons included Clint, Harvey and Melvin Dean. p3c6 The "Miller" farm winds up in the hands of Melvin's decendents, after passing through the Snowdens. I visited the "Dean Cemetery" at Little

Hickman last week. It's on the crest of a very high hill, not far from his original log house. The house is larger because of additions, but the log portion is still there.

The Spears correspondent inquires "What has become of Pomp?"

However, the *Sulphur Well Correspondent* returns this week:

*Arch Stotts, one of our merchants, has moved to Little Hickman. We wish him success.*
*J H Murphy is refilling his store to its full capacity.*
*Andrew Sageser is having his house newly covered.*
*The little son of Johnnie Brumfield has been very low with pneumonia, (but he is) better at present.*
*W R Miller is sick in bed with pneumonia.*
*J H Easley has been in bed for several days from the effect of a broken tooth.* p3c3

April 7, 1893

The Tax Supervisors revised the valuation of dozens of pieces of property in the county. Dr Miller's land was raised, while Elizabeth Miller's land was lowered. Harrison Dean's (deceased) land was raised. Other land-owners whose property valuation were raised were J H Easley (above article) and G M Hendren (now living in Madison County). p1c5-6

Pomp responds to the query as to what became of Pomp. p2c1

The new Spears Livery Stable is about to open. It has two entrances on Main Street, each 18 feet wide so buggies and wagons can come in one door and circle out the other. There is room on each side for several buggies to be parked. The stalls are in the center. There is a hydrant at each end of the stable to water horses or wash buggies. And, there is a waiting room for the lady customers! An elegant building just before technology makes it obsolete! p2c3

James Whitcomb Riley is in town for a performance, and is staying at Hotel Nicholas. He is pictured in an advertisement with his hair parted in the middle and plastered down. He wears nose glasses with a cord. He has on a stiff collar, with a tie (not a bow). His jacket lapels look quite contempary. p3c6

Adam Adcock was reelected to the City Council for another term.

April 14, 1893

A list of the "well to do" was published again, showing those who reported intangible assets of $10,000 or more. Dr Miller made the list again. J P Turner, of Sulphur Well, also made the list. Mrs Elizabeth Jane Miller did not. p1c5

"The Rev. T J Anthony and family have removed to Sulphur Well." p3c2

The *Sulphur Well Correspondent* writes:

*The late rains have thrown the farmers back planting corn.*
*There will be preaching at the Christian Church at this place, Saturday night, Sunday and Sunday night, by Bro. Carter.*
*Personals-Rev. T J Anthony has moved to the house vacated by Mr Stotts....Miss Ella Woodward was at home spending a few days with her parents this week. p3c4*

This isn't quite the style of our usual correspondent.

## April 21, 1893

A heavy frost fell this past Saturday and Sunday. People are returning home from Florida-- Lucy Scott and her grandmother Naomi Bailey, Mrs Alliband, and Bettie Dorman.

## April 28, 1893

There was a thunder, wind, and rain storm that did considerable damage Monday night. Mrs Pendleton Cobb was struck and killed by lightning near Hunter's Ferry. A report of a death by lightning at Sulphur Well proved to be untrue.

Adcock's liquor licence was again renewed.

## May 5, 1893

The Riney B has been extended several hundred feet in Irvine for the convenience of it patrons. p3c4 I couldn't quite picture what they meant from the article.

## May 12, 1893

Rice Miller graduated from Central University in Richmond last June and is now employed by the Nicholasville Graded School.

The firm of Denman and Spears is dissolving. Robert Duncan Sr purchased a brick house on North Main Street that will be occupied by Spears and Robert Duncan Jr. The firm will sell dry goods, notions and shoes. p3c3

## May 19, 1893

"The adoption by a large majority of a resolution in favor of Woman's Suffrage is perhaps the most remarkable act of the big Republican gathering in Louisville last week."p2c1
The editor goes on to say that it is unpopular in Kentucky not only because it is new and untried, but also because "certain political elements" want to selfishly keep their position. However, he feels that it is inevitable because two states already permit it fully, and almost every state allows female suffrage to some extent.

"The past week or ten days has been remarkable for the large number of business failures. More than forty banks failed in two days last week in this country." p3c2

"Mrs J E Nave, of Danville, visited friends here recently." This Susan Miller Nave, daughter of Merriman Miller. p3c2

May 26, 1893

A special committee of the Fayette County Court passed the following resolution: "Resolved - That the County of Fayette accept and maintain free of toll to the traveling public any turnpike road in Fayette County." p1c3

A strong article was written by S S Deering on observing Sunday as a day of rest. You can sympathize with a merchant that needs a day off, but the inconsistency of blue-laws and their enforcement obscures the rights of the patrons.

June 2, 1893

Every since Cleveland was elected the paper has been full of articles about job-seekers, for post-offices and such. The *Sulphur Well Correspondent* articles have been infrequent, but we are fortunate to have another this week:

*Mr W D Richardson and wife, of Irvine, spent a few days with Mrs Frank Miller.*
*James W Miller is in Estill County, on business this week.*
*Walter Hendren is home from Edenton, Madison County, on a little vacation.*
*Fishing is in full blast at Diamond Lake; some good ones are being caught. Ike Taylor caught one that weighted 7 lbs.*
*Geo. S Williams, of Red House, returned home after several days visit with his sister, Mrs Frank Miller. He is in very bad health.* p2c6

This is the first reference I've seen to any of Elizabeth Williams Miller's relatives. Redhouse is between Boonesboro and Richmond. Three of the five items above pertain to the Millers. It appears that someone close to the family is authoring these reports. Diamond Lake was on property owned by the George Diamond family, that was located across the little road from the church.

June 9, 1893

Nearly every bank in Chicago had heavy runs Monday and Tuesday, and there were some failures on the first day. It appears that the Panic of 1893 is underway. This is the second reference to banking woes.

"Miss Lizzie Miller entertains this evening at the residence of Mrs W H Hoover." p3c2
This is the daughter of Dr Miller. She was born in 1875, and would be about eighteen years old.

Nancy Baker sold a house and lot to J P Turner at Sulphur Well for $500. p3c4

J W Overstreet, the correspondent from Little Hickman, "Pomp", is pictured in the paper this week, together with his profile. He is not as large as I thought he might be. He was born in 1849, became deaf in 1862 as a result of typhoid fever, and was educated at the Kentucky Institute for the Deaf at Danville. He is a merchant, and the postmaster at Little Hickman. Pomp claims to have ridden every road in the state on his bicycle. p3c5

There is a sawmill down on the river near Spears owned by (D) Miller and Soper.

### June 16, 1893

From the Estill Eagle. "Stephen Snowden, of Sulphur Well, Jessamine County, is visiting his brothers, Arch and Wm Snowden." p3c2

### June 23, 1893

The farmers are getting in their hay, and getting ready to harvest wheat.

Many Nicholasville families are attending the World's Fair in Chicago, including the Duncans, Bells, Hoovers, Barnes, and Woods families.

### June 30, 1893

Kentucky's agriculture display at the World's Fair consists of tobacco, hemp, some grasses, and wheat. There was no mention of bourbon.

"It's the semi-annual settling up time. Time to pay your bills. Seven merchants have gone on the cash system, and others are considering taking such a step."

"Mrs Van Winkle, of Frankfort, is visiting her sister, Mrs Adam Adcock." p3c2

The High Bridge Camp Meeting is announced, with Sam Jones to preach, as usual.

### July 7, 1893

From Logana comes the word that Hugh Miller, son of Dr Miller, will teach in the public school there. The term begins July 10th. p3c5 This is the second son of Dr Miller.

The wheat harvest is over at Troy, but the price of wheat is "discouragingly low", only 50 to 52 cents per bushel. p3c6

July 14, 1893

The July heat has made linen suits a fashionable part of the wardrobes of ladies that are visiting the Fair. A skirt and jacket, with a vest that opens over a white linen front and tie, is the style.

Mrs Stanford said, when thanked for establishing the university at Palo Alto, "Do not call it a kindness on our part; we should not be thanked, for the reason that we had to sacrifice nothing." p1c6

The thirtieth anniversary of the Battle of Gettysburg was celebrated. General Sickles advocated the purchase of the battle ground by the government and making it a national park.

July 21, 1893

"Lieutenant Peary is already far on his way into the remote and frozen north...." p1c4

Abraham Lincoln is reported to have said "Die when I may, I want it said of me by those who know me best, that I always plucked the thistle and planted a flower...." p1c5

John A Chappell, a candidate in Lincoln County, is running on the issue of "free turnpikes".

Elbert Masters, mentioned several times earlier, has returned to Huntington, W. Va. We also have the *Sulphur Well Correspondent* with us:

*Miss Mary Anderson, of Lancaster, is visiting the family of T J Horine.*
*Mrs Bass and daughter, Miss Fannie Haskins, of Campbellsville, have been visiting friends and relatives for the past two weeks.*
*Misses Mary and Etta Grey, of Lexington, have returned home after a week's visit to Mrs Geo. Diamond.*
*There will be preaching at the Christian Church next Saturday and Sunday night. The appointment has been changed from the 3rd to (the) 4th week for this month only.* p3c6

Mary and Etta Gray, are Texie and Ida's little sisters. Note that the correspondent has misspelled their name.

July 28, 1893

Sally and Tom Wilds, children of Dr Wilds, are visiting in Lancaster.

Five banks in Louisville have suspended business because of runs on the banks. All are deemed solvent and are expected to re-open. p2c1 The Nicholasville banks are continuing operations, and believed in good condition. p2c1 The State Treasurer has stopped accepting checks in payments due the state, indicating his view of Kentucky banks in general.p2c1 The Valley View correspondent says that "the financial stringency doesn't seem to cripple the prosperity of our thriving little city any". p2c5

### August 4, 1893

The Comptroller of the Currency announced that 105 National Banks have suspended operations in the present panic, but that 14 have resumed operation. p3c4

It has been a very dry summer. However, rain and wind did considerable damage to the northern part of the county, blowing down trees, flattening corn fields, and taking the roof off a barn.

This year's Camp Meeting at High Bridge has not gone as well as usual. There were several complains of disorder off the grounds, mostly unlawful sale of liquor. However, there was a conflict involving several men at the depot, that resulted in one man being killed. p3c2

### August 11, 1893

The Camp Meeting didn't do very well for the sponsor either. Prof. Bristow came up short financially. p2c3

Dr Wilds is improving his property in Nicholasville. "He has had a plank walk laid at the Baker place, and a nice wire fence around the Evans place." p3c1

From Lexington: "Dr E B Johnson was called to Sulphur Well, Jessamine County, last Saturday to do some surgical work." p3c2 I saw no mention for whom it was to be performed.

### August 18, 1893

The S M Snowden family visited friends and relatives in Georgetown. Steve runs the family farm now.

A Frenchman took subscriptions for a Society of Aviation. He also took money for flying machines that he didn't deliver, for which he was arrested. There have been several claims, from London, and elsewhere of flights, but according to the article there was "always one wheel on the ground". p4c5

### August 25, 1893

The wheat buyers say there is more unsold wheat in the county than ever before! p2c3

J Pink Overstreet is the executor of the Harrison Dean estate.

A Nicholasville businessman says that he is seeing more currency that normally. He thinks the problem with the banks is due to people holding money, instead of putting it in banks and checking on it.

September 1, 1893

The businessman apparently was right. Secretary Carlisle said that the amount of currency outside the Treasury was $70 million greater than in the previous year.

The *Sulphur Well Correspondent* writes:

*The farmers are all busy ploughing for wheat.*
*There has been a great deal of sickness in this neighborhood. Those on the sick list are: Mrs Dinah Moore, Mrs Hunter and Mr Frank Horine.*
*Mr Forest Mills (sic) has returned from a visit to Irvine.*
*Mr Will Masters and two charming young daughters are here from Bloomington, Ill., visiting friends.*
*Will and Walter Hendren left Monday for the "Windy City".*
*Tobacco cutting is now in full blast, and the crops are looking exceedingly well.*
*Easley & Sageser have purchased a new clover huller and have been busy hulling for the two past weeks. They report the crop as yielding more than expected.*
*Our school is progressing very nicely with Mr Rice Harris as teacher.*
*Born--To the wife of J H Easley, a son. p2c7*

This is Forest Miller back from Irvine. The Hendrens are evidently going to the World's Fair in Chicago.

Susan Nave's husband died. She is the daughter of Merriman and Celia Miller, and sister of John C Miller, Mann Miller, Kitty Barkley, and Sarah Miller Overstreet.

A telegram received here last Friday announced the sudden death in Chicago of the well-known veterinarian, Dr J E Nave. The Doctor and Mrs Nave were in Chicago attending the World's Fair. Heart disease, from which he had been troubled for the past three or four years, caused the Doctor's death. His demise occurred about 12 o'clock on the night of the 24th inst., and in the 65th year of his age. He retired that night seemingly in his usual health, but awoke Mrs Nave in the night asking for water, and before the water could be handed him (he) expired. Dr Nave was the youngest son of the late Dr Peter Nave, and was a native of this county, but about eight years ago removed to Danville, where he continued to practice his profession. Dr Nave was married twice, and by his first wife leaves one child, a daughter, the wife of Capt. Jas. M White, now a resident of Florida. His second wife, who survives him, is the daughter of the late Merriman Miller. Dr Nave had many friends in this county, where he spent the most of his life in the practice of his profession and in handling trotting horses. Among some of the valuable horses he owned or handled were Buckskin, 2:23, and Grafter, 2:16 1/2. Funeral services were held at the residence of his kinsman, Mr Lem Ender, by Rev. Morrisey, of the

Methodist Church, Chicago, Friday, the 25th inst., when his remains were shipped to this place, arriving Saturday at noon, and the interment took place in Maple Grove Cemetery (on) Sunday. p3c4

From Logana: "Mr W M Miller (sic), of Irvine, spent Sunday and Monday with his brother, Dr J C Miller." p3c7 This is a printing error. It should be M M Miller, who is Mann Miller. Also from Logana: "Rice Miller, of Nicholasville Graded School, is teaching for his brother Hugh, who is in Chicago attending the World's Fair." p3c7 "Miss Lizzie Miller, of Jessamine County, is visiting relatives at Irvine." p3c2 Rice, Hugh, and Lizzie are the children of Dr Miller.

## September 8, 1893

The dry summer is continuing. Nicholasville is running out of water, and what is left is of poor quality. The farmers in lower Garrard are selling off their hogs because the corn crop is so bad.

Hugh Miller is visiting friends in Edenton. p2c7 Edenton is on Poosey Ridge in Madison County, just a short way from the river.

## September 15, 1893

"The Harrison Dean Executor completed the sale of the farm land, livestock, and personal property." This is J Pink Overstreet. p2c4

Texie is back! "Mrs Tom Cooley and daughter, of Omaha, Neb., are visiting friends and relatives in the town and county." p3c2

Dr Miller was visiting in Richmond this week. p3c2

## September 22, 1893

All the local gentry that hadn't been to the World's Fair are now going! However, few merchants are going to New York this year because of the "money panic".

From Glass' Mill: In the base ball game with Sulphur Well, the home team won 19 to 9. p3c7

## September 29, 1893

There have been numerous bank closings. "During the present year 560 State and private banks in the United States have failed, and 72 of them have resumed. The number of national banks closed during the same time is 155, of which 70 have resumed." p1c6 This is the panic of '93.

October 6, 1893

Johanna (Sittie) Fritzlen married George W Bell, a Presbyterian minister from Las Animas, Colorado, in Nicholasville at a small private wedding. p3c3 She had taught at an Indian school in Taos, New Mexico before teaching in Colorado. She wrote back interesting and informative letters about her experiences.

October 13, 1893

The Blue Front is having a closing out sale for the purpose of dissolving the partnership involving Joseph Frankel. p2c7-8 Murphy and Horine's ad shows three styles of hats: top hats; flat, summer straw hats; and bowlers. p4c1-2

October 20, 1893

Not only old soldiers, but old slaves, also still live. Jackson Hardin was born in 1825, the property of Joseph Morris. Morris was a kind "master" and took his servants to church with his own family, so Hardin has been a member of the M E Church for 62 years. p1c3

October 27, 1893

The *Sulphur Well Correspondent* writes:

*Mrs Frank Miller returned from Irvine Monday.*
*Miss Eudora Murphy is visiting friends and relatives in Lexington.*
*Master Charlie Terhune, of Braxton, Mercer County, was visiting friends here last week.*
*Mr Henry Poston, telegraph operator at Valley View, was the guest of Millard F Davis, Sunday.*
*C T Taylor, of Lexington, was here last Friday.*
*J P Turner and wife, spent Sunday with Giles Sanders, at Paint Lick.*
*Mr and Mrs James Turner returned from Chicago last Saturday.*
*Elbert Walker had a nice fat steer to die last week, caused by drinking too much water.*
*Tom Horine lost a fine yearling colt recently from diphtheria.*
*J Howard Murphy is having a substantial string of stone fence built on his farm. Milton Price, of Hokeyville, the well-known contractor, is doing the work.*
*Miss Viola Davis is on the sick list this week. Millard F Davis is teaching her school during her illness.*
*S M Duncan was down last week hunting new sorghum molasses.* p2c2

> Mrs J E Nave, of Danville, Ky., aunt of Charlie Miller, of this place, gave him a fine yearling colt sired by Gambetta Wilkes, full brother to the King that sold for $20,000. The season for this colt cost $300. Name of colt, Gov. Owsley; standard and registered. From the Estill Eagle. p2c3

This is Charles Wallace Miller, son of M M (Mann) Miller. Charles was born April 1, 1876 in Irvine and died May 10, 1963 at Lexington, Ky. He was a graduate of Centre College in Danville. He also graduated from Yale in 1896 as the president of his class. He then obtained a law degree from the University of Virginia in 1898. Charles went on to become United States Attorney for the West, and later United States Attorney of the District of Eastern Oklahoma, serving directly under the Attorney General. He retired in 1941 and returned Lexington. This is from the <u>Sageser Genealogy</u>.

November 3, 1893

"Mrs Nave, since the death of her husband, Dr J E Nave, has removed from Danville to this city, and is occupying the J L Sageser residence, on West Street." p3c2

November 10, 1893

There were "sweeping" victories for the Republicans in the elections last Tuesday. Republicans captured everthing but Virginia, Maryland, and Kentucky. In Kentucky the Democrats increased their majority in both houses of the legislature. p2c2 Another indication, if one is needed, how "Democratic" that Kentucky really is!

"Prof Rice Miller is in Richmond. His sister, Miss Lizzie, is teaching in the graded school in his absence." p3c2

Adam Adcock was not reelected to the City Council. There was great surprise at the organized opposition that ousted every old member "except E R Sparks" from the Council. p3c3 There never was an indication as to the reason.

> On the afternoon of Wednesday, Nov. 8th, at the Christian Church, Sulphur Well, Mr Walter S Hendren and Miss Linnie M Spruce were married, Elder J M Bailey officiating. The attendants were Mr Walter Bain, of Nicholasville, and Miss Addie Hendren, of Madison. The bridegroom is a son of Mr William Hendren, of this county, and resides at Edenton, Madison County, where for several years he has been engaged in the mercantile business. The bride is a step-daughter of Mr J W Baker, of Sulphur Well. p3c3

November 17, 1893

There is a very good history of Nicholasville and Jessamine County written by W J Lampton in the <u>Courier Journal</u>, and reprinted in the <u>Jessamine Journal</u>.

November 24, 1893

Congress is considering an income tax, perhaps 2 percent on salaries over $3,500 or $4,000.

At Thanksgiving time the *Sulphur Well Correspondent* writes:

*Miss Lila Taylor, of Lexington, is visiting her grandmother, Mrs Marguerite Horine.*
*Miss Ida Nave and brother, Moses, spent Sunday with Misses Betsy and Nancy Hare.*
*Misses Lizzie Robinson and Ida Clark, two of Logana's prettiest girls, spent from Friday until Monday with Miss Viola Davis.*
*E D Vincent, of Lexington, was the guest of M F Davis last week.*
*Chas. Weber, of Kirklevington, has moved to this place and is engaged in blacksmithing.*
*N D Davis shipped a car load of hogs last Thursday.*
*The meeting held at the Christian Church by Rev. Jos. Ballou, closed Sunday night with no additions.*
*We are glad to report Miss Viola Davis able to resume her school. p2c4*

December 1, 1893

J W Overstreet, Pomp, was written up in the Southern Wheelman. When asked to list hotels or restaurants in his city, he replied that there were none, but that his wife was the best cook in the country, and that he would be insulted if any wheelman passed through without stopping for lunch or dinner. p1c5

Apple brandy is scarce this year because of the failure of the apple crop. A K Adcock, whose saloon is on Harrodsburg Street, says he sent an agent to the brandy districts of the mountains, but found none.

"Uncle" Billy Hendren, who has been in feeble health for some time, is reported quite ill at his home near Sulphur Well. p3c2 His son Walter just married Linnie Spruce.

December 8, 1893

The new City Council still refuses to pay the water company its third installment because of failure to comply with the contract.

Thanksgiving was quietly observed in Nicholasville with a union service at the Baptist Church. Pomp says that only one turkey was served in Little Hickman. I suppose they had ham!

"A J Sageser has sold his farm, containing 90 acres adjoining the village of Sulphur Well to F M Horine, for $4,500, and bought of J H Easley, 84 acres, Pink neighborhood, at $2,600." p2c3

December 15, 1893

The flu, better known as "la grippe", has been incapacitating many during this month. There are several marriages planned at this time of the year, and some have had to be called off due to illness. The merchants are advertising their Christmas merchandise.

Land transfer: "J H Murphy &c to Andrew Sageser, 1 1/2 acres of land near Sulphur Well, $100." p3c5

Helen Keller, at this time a little girl, writes about what she "saw" at the World's Fair. She was allowed to hold the Tiffany diamond, and to feel laces, marble, and wood carvings.

### December 22, 1893

Holiday excursions are advertised. The merchants are much smarter this year. They are advertising candy, fruits, dolls, clothing and jewelry for Christmas. Some people are going to Lexington to see the decorations. There are also closing exercises for the school in Logana taught by Hugh Miller at 6:30pm Friday evening. "They will consist of recitations, singing, dialogues, and the presentation of prizes." Patrons and friends are invited. p2c4

On the eve of Christmas the *Sulphur Well Correspondent* writes:

*Mr E D Vincent, of Lexington, is the guest of Mr N D Davis this week.*
*Mrs C T Taylor and her two daughters, Misses May and Lila, returned to their home in Lexington after several days visit to Mrs Margaret Horine.*
*Miss Fannie Hoskins, of Campbellsville, is visiting Mrs J P Turner.*
*Rev. H G Turner was with his parents for a few days this week.*
*Messrs. Manfred Murphy, George Snowden and Forest Miller were in Lexington this week.*
*Elder Jesse Walden preached at the Christian Church last Saturday, Sunday and Sunday night, also Tuesday night.*
*Last Saturday, Wilson Masters happened to a very painful and serious accident in getting out of his spring wagon, at the public pump. His foot slipped and he fell on a rock, breaking his leg just above the ankle. He was taken home immediately, a doctor was summoned and set the broken bones. He is getting along very nicely at present, and it is thought he will be out before many days.* p2c5

I see that Horace Turner has become a minister. According to Bernard Moynahan, his grand-nephew, he attending a divinity school in Boston. He held pastorates in the Methodist church of Nicholasville and other places. He later left the ministery, was for one term a county judge, and later formed the insurance firm of Turner and Bishop. His brother Jimmy married Elma Grinstead, daughter of a Methodist minister.

### December 29, 1893

"Mrs Van Winkle and Master Leo. Hendren, of Frankfort, are visiting Mrs A K Adcock." p3c2 This is the first reference I've seen to Leo Hendren. He is the younger brother of Scottie and the others.

Fortunately, an end-of-the-year article from the *Sulphur Well Correspondent*:

*Rev. T J Anthony has the grippe.*
*Died, the infant son of Richard Fain.*
*Will and Marshall Davis are in Harrodsburg this week.*
*Clayton West, Miss Viola and Millard Davis are visiting friends and relatives in Henry County.*
*Miss Lizzie Butler, of Portwood, Madison County, is visiting Miss Myrtie Snowden this week.*
*Mr and Mrs Jas. Turner spent a few days with her parents, Rev. W S Grinstead and wife, at Millersburg. p3c6*

The Myrtie Snowden above will marry Melvin Dean, and one of their children, will be Dr M L Dean, whose widow now owns the family farm.

The last item is about Jim Turner, who married Elma Grinstead. Bernard Moynahan lives "upon the hill" in Sulphur Well where his grandfather lived before him.

There have only been a few articles from Sulphur Well this year, a total of nine. There have been no indications to me who the correspondent is, or may be. I have noted that over the years the correspondents write mostly about the people they know, and this correspondent writes frequently about the Millers, and the Hendrens. None of the correspondents, except Pomp, sign their articles any more.

## MODERN TIMES - 1894

Times are changing for the better--telephone, electricity, transportation. All are becoming more widespread. Free turnpikes are near at hand.

### January 19, 1894

In the list of "wealthy" citizens of Jessamine County there is included: Matilda Miller and Forest Miller, both of whom are under trusteeship of F W Noland. p1c5 This is evidently their share of the Merriman/Frank Miller estates, over $5,000 for each. Perhaps this is where Forest gets his money to invest in the Murphy & Horine Clothing Store. This issue is badly damaged, and parts are missing.

### January 26, 1894

> Mr Forest F Miller, of Ambrose, an energetic and promising young man, has purchased Mr Horine's interest in the clothing firm of Murphy and Horine, and in the future the firm will be Murphy and Miller. The new firm is composed of men who thoroughly understand their business and they will no doubt meet with the success their efforts deserve. p3c1

Forest Miller is a nephew of Dr John C Miller and my maternal grandfather. The store, by the way, is located on Main Street, directly across from the courthouse. The firm's first advertisement also appears in this issue:

> The clothing business of Murphy & Horine will be conducted hereafter under the firm name of Murphy & Miller, Mr F F Miller having bought a half interest in the business. The goods were invoiced very low, some of them far below cost, even as low as 50c on the dollar, and the new firm now proposes, for the next thirty days, to make room for spring goods, which they are now buying in large quantities, to sell at invoiced prices. Now is your time to buy goods cheap, especially neckwear, underwear, gloves, hats, caps, boots, shoes, overcoats, and clothing; in fact everything in our line will go, regardless of cost. Do not fail to see our cheap line of clothing, &c (at) 25c on the dollar. Murphy & Miller. p3c5

You can see that the merchants in Nicholasville are having a hard time. They are having drastic sales - 25% off, cost, one says he will "cut, slash, and butcher" every article at a bankrupt sale.p2c7-8 Reedy's Racket Store owner says he has "lost sight of not only the profit, but also the cost in closing out my stock." p2c6 The sale of George Diamond's personal property, which was to have been held at Sulphur Well was postponed because of weather.

February 2, 1894

"Dr John C Miller purchased of Mr Wm Burton, of Garrard County, one of the finest Denmark saddle stallions in Kentucky for $500. Fine saddle horses are now on top. Dr Miller sold to Mr Burton, for $380, his fine-bred 3-year-old trotting stallion, Whitmore.... Dr Miller also sold Mr Burton three extra fine yearling Holstein-Friesian heifers, delivered, for $120. This is very fine stock." p2c2 The way I add this up, it looks like a trade to me, but maybe they wanted to establish prices for the stock.

"There was a large crowd at Geo. S Diamond's sale, at Sulphur Well, last Tuesday, and everything brought all they were worth." Things that were sold included farming implements, a buck board and a wagon, some colts, horses, steers and a milk cow. p2c3

Deed transfers: "Andrew Sageser &c to F M Horine, two tracts of land near Sulphur Well, $4,250." p1c6

Excursion rates to California: Every Thursday evening a train leaves Cincinnati, enroute to New Orleans and San Francisco, at a cost of $51.50. A berth in a sleeping car is only $4. p1c6

Joseph Altsheier writes to the Louisville Star saying that Honolulu is about the size of Lexington, and reminds him very much of it. He says that although the climate is delightful, that it becomes monotonous!

"Politics is red hot in the Blue-Grass metropolis just now. Sixty-two candidates have declared for office in Fayette County...."p2c2 In Jessamine: "Candidates are hustling around as if their lives depended on electioneering." p3c1

February 9, 1894

The Journal published the history of Bethel Academy in Jessamine County. The site chosen for the academy was one hundred acres located "about fifteen miles from Lexington and eight miles west of Nicholasville. In Jessamine County great numbers of the first Methodists, including local and traveling preachers, settled. All these circumstances were in favor of making that the location of Bethel Academy." p1c3-5 This was in 1790.

February 16, 1894

"Miller-Hendren.-At Edenton, Madison County, Wednesday, Feb. 14th, Mr Hugh Miller and Miss Addie Hendren were united in marriage, Rev. R L Prunty officiating." p3c3 Hugh is Dr Miller's son. Addie is the daughter of Dr and Mrs George M Hendren of Sulphur Well. The Salem Christian Church is in this area, but there is no mention where the ceremony was held. As I said before, Edenton is on Poosey Ridge Road in Madison County.

February 23, 1894

It is not quite clear to me what is going on, but the guardianships of Forest and Matilda Miller are still involved in the County Court process, and the word "settlements" was used. p3c4

March 2, 1894

From the Irvine Sentinal: "S N Snowden, of Jessamine County, has sold his Drowning Creek farm to W S Witt, our Superintendent of Schools. Price, $2,900. Possession given immediately." p2c3 I don't know the location of this farm, or who W S Witt is. However, Victor Witt married Anna Miller, a niece of Lucy Miller who is married to Steve Snowden. By coincidence, or the way family history plays out, Tom Bonney, Jr., grandson of Anna Miller, now owns the Frank Miller homeplace in Wisemantown, and is also the Superintendent of Estill Schools!

March 9, 1894

"Mr Franklin Foster, of Sulphur Well, is a prospective candidate for coroner."p3c1

Groom Taylor died at Hanley on Tuesday, March 6th. He was a farmer, but at one time was also a storekeeper at the Gray Distillery at Sulphur Well, and other locations as well.p3c4

March 16, 1894

Murphy and Miller are still running the same advertisement that they began with.

March 23, 1894

The clothing prices as advertised for Murphy & Miller are very low, men's suits from $5-$12.

"Miss Ola Davis will attend school at Detroit, Mich., this summer." p3c2

March 30, 1897

"The mercury here Monday morning registered 16 degrees below freezing .... Nearly all the fruit is killed...." p3c3

April 6, 1894

Coxey's "army of tramps", on the way to Washington, are making "less progress than they anticipated; bad weather, bad food, bad traveling facilities...." p2c1

April 13, 1894

From the Irvine Sentinal: "Steve Snowden, of Ambrose, Jessamine County, accompanied by his son George, is making a short visit in Estill." p3c2

April 20, 1894

The primary election will be May 3rd. Congressman Breckenridge has lost his legal battle with a young woman over the parentage of her child. In his defense, he claimed that she was permiscuous, and had seduced him. In any case, she was awarded $15,000. It is widely expected that he will "pay again at the polls for his immorality." p2c1 The Vanceburg Sun proposed legislation to prevent this problem from happening again:
> Be it enacted by the General Assembly of this Commonwealth: Sec.1. That it shall be unlawful for any school girl between the ages of 15 and 20 years, by artifice, promise of marriage, threat, intimidation, or fear, to seduce any Congressman in the Commonwealth while said Congressman is at the seat of Government in line of duty, or on board of cars going to or from the Capitol.... p1c4

April 27, 1894

Deaths: "Woodward-Johnny, the five year-old son of Mr and Mrs Joseph Woodward, of Sulphur Well, died at the home of his parents Monday, of tonsilitis. The burial took place in Maple Grove Cemetary, Nicholasville, Tuesday." Lulu Spruce is the mother.

May 4, 1894

Samuel McAfee Duncan is featured by the Journal this week. It called him "the most remarkable man in Kentucky today." The editor says:
> His historic contributions to the local press show a wonderful depth of research, as well as power of thought and expression. He is a veritable encyclopedia, and is esteemed as trustworthy authority upon all mooted questions. Mr Duncan is a hale, hearty man, of unassuming manners, and is especially gifted in historic narration. p1c4

The accompanying picture shows a man with a full beard and a rather stern appearance. It was said about him in an earlier article that he was humorless, and took everything seriously.

May 11, 1894

"Mr Hamilton Dozier, of Lexington, was in town Wednesday." p3c2 He was one of the "dudes" that used to come to Sulphur Well back in the late eighties.

May 18, 1894

The opposition to Breckenridge's candidacy met at the Opera House in Lexington, "a great protest led by clergy, women and chuch people...." p2c1

May 25, 1894

The Irvine Sentinel reports:"Miss Myrtie Snowden, one of Jessamine County's fairest belles, formerly of Estill, is visiting her many friends near Winston." p3c2 This is M L Dean's mother. "George, the son of S D Snowden, of Ambrose, Jessamine County, has been visiting his many friends in this locality, writes Capt. S F Rock, in the Irvine Sentinel."

> We did not know that Steve had a son so nearly grown. The sulphur water and pure air about Sulphur Well, in Jessanine County, is certainly fine, to produce such results in so short a time. Our last remembrance of George was some four years ago at the foot of Drowning Creek Hill; he was then breaking a yoke of calves or some work of that nature. We also cherish a memory of a little sprightly maiden skipping about like a sunbeam. Wonder if she has grown so tall as to necessitate the doffing of our hats to her on the streets? p3c2

June 1, 1894

Sam Duncan (SMD) visited Sulphur Well this week. He finds it to be a beautiful and restful place because of "...the birdnotes, the leaves, the blossoms, the quiet paths among the trees, cool valleys watered by rippling brooks, the pale blue canopy with its fleecy vapors, the soft sighing many voiced wind, the perpetual incense of earth to heaven from flower chalices...." He arrived in time for lunch at L B Taylor's. Duncan says he is reminded of his visits here with Taylor and Newton Davis thirty-five years ago as a young man. He says "as I walked near an old field on a gentle hill, and could see many names on the plain head stones which I remembered and with which were associated the pleasantest scenes of boyhood." Many, he says, died young. He notes that the "farmers are not getting rich here very fast. Some are growing poor, many are discouraged, and say that farming doesn't pay." p1c6 This is quite a contrast in moods, isn't it? First, he is struck by the beauty of the setting; then, upon reflection he sees hard work with little recompense, and short lives.

On account of business depression, about 200 employees on the Cincinnati Southern have been laid off. p3c1

Murphy & Miller advertises a $12 suit and a watch, and declares that no one will undersell them.

June 8, 1894

"The reception given by the 'Posmala Club' Wednesday evening at the home of Miss Mary Holloway, was one of the most delightful in the social history of Nicholasville." Miss Holloway "received" in a white organdy dress "trimmed with narrow bands of white ribbon." The house was decorated with ferns and roses. "The lawn was softly lighted by a number of Japanese lanterns and the delightful music furnished by Anderson's Orchestra.... At eleven o'clock most delicious refreshments were served in charming style." p2c3 Among those attending this social occasion were Dora Murphy and Forest Miller of Sulphur Well.

The E J Curley Distillery at Camp Nelson was a substantial producer of whisky. Thirteen hundred barrels, with a value of $104,000, were shipped to Baltimore for export. p3c1

> Dr J L Wilds was prostrated Tuesday by a slight attack of congestion of the brain, which rendered him unconscious for several hours. The physicians of the town gave him every attention, and now report that he will soon be entirely well. Exaggerated reports of the Doctors's condition spread over the county, and the interest manifested, if it did nothing else, demonstrated his wide popularity. p3c1

Hard times: "The many friends of Mr W G Moseley, the popular dealer in agricultural implements, buggies, etc., will regret to learn that he has made an assignment of his property for the benefit of his creditors." p3c4

June 15, 1894

"Prof Rice Miller is at Harrodsburg, where he is taking a summer normal course." p3c2

The next three items are reprinted from the <u>Estill Sentinel</u>. Rice's younger brother Meade is in Irvine. "Meade Miller, of Jessamine County, is visiting his cousin, C W Miller." p3c2 C W is Charles Wallace Miller, son of Mann Miller, who was given the horse a few months ago. But, there is more: "Miss Maude Miller left this morning to make a visit to her cousin, Miss Lizzie Miller, of Jessamine." p3c2 Maude is the daughter of Mann Miller, and Lizzie is the daughter of Dr Miller.

Frank, Dr John C., and Mann Miller were brothers. Frank's widow is also out visiting: "Mrs E J Miller, of Jessamine County, is visiting her son, Jno. P Miller, and family, at Wisemantown. She had the pleasure of eating her first mess of green beans with them on Wednesday." p3c2 John Pink Miller is her son, and is operating the store that was run by his father, Frank, before his retirement or death in 1885.

Two Wisemanton boys also visited George Snowden in Sulphur Well. George is a grandson of Elizabeth Jane Miller. p3c2

The Riney B Railroad, which has been in receivership, has been ordered sold at public auction, with a reserve price of $550,000. p3c3 It is my recollection that the road was constructed from Shelbyville to Beattyville, but evidently the part being sold is from Versailles to Beattyville.

Deeds recorded: "Malinda Masters to Geo. M Hendren, 3 1/2 acres of land and improvements near Sulphur Well, $1,500." p3c3 Dr Hendren formerly lived in Sulphur Well, moved to Edenton, Madison County, but now appears to be moving back to Sulphur Well.

From Camp Nelson: "The warehousemen are mourning the loss of 'Old Net', a favorite mule. She was 18 years old, and had worked in the warehouse for 15 years, often working without a driver." p3c4

June 22, 1894

"The many friends of Dr J L Wilds will be glad to know that he is rapidly improving in health, and out of danger. An internal abcess that had formed on the left side, broke Monday, giving him immediate relief." p3c2

June 29, 1894

The affair of Congressman Breckenridge continues, with Miss Pollard giving "vapid detail of confidential gush, wormed out of a shameless, conceited and bold woman..." and spread over the Sunday papers. p2c1 During a recent serenade of Congressman Breckenridge in Frankfort the band played, "He never cared to wander from his own fireside." p2c1

"Lizzie Miller entertained several young people at the home of Dr Miller from Saturday until Monday." p3c2

There hasn't been a single report from the Sulphur Well correspondent this year. Fortunately, there has been a lot information on the Miller family from other sources, and some other things of interest as well.

July 6, 1894

A short, unfortunate marriage between Andrew Crow, of Nicholasville, and a young girl from Lexington has ended in a suit for divorce. p2c5

A "young daughter of Samuel C Barkley died at the home of her parents on the Harrodsburg pike, Monday, after only a week's illness from typhoid fever, aged five years." p2c3 She was buried in "the old Barkley burying ground, on the R N I & B railroad, near Nealton." p2c3 I may look this place up some day.

A fire that began in the stable area of Curley's Distillery inflicted a serious loss, particularly of mules, but also one of the warehouses caught fire, and several barrels of whisky were lost. p2c4

### July 13, 1894

The resort, Estill Springs, is shaded by Sweet Lick Mountain.

"Mrs A K Adcock and family leave Tuesday for a two weeks' visit to Mr Adcock's father at Thorne Grove, Tenn." p3c2

### July 20, 1894

"Mr Charles W Miller, of Irvine, is visiting relatives in the county." p3c2

"Mrs W H Van Winkle, of Frankfort has returned home after a visit to her sister, Mrs Adam Adcock." p3c2 This is Lizzie and Addie, sisters of Scottie and Susie Hendren.

"Miss Lena Bright, with her charming little niece and nephew, Laura and Lee Doty, of Lancaster, are visiting Mrs A M Askins, of Ambrose." p3c2

### July 27, 1894

Dr Jas. L Wilds. Sad death of a Nicholasville physican. Seldom is a community so startled as was Nicholasville last Friday morning when it was learned that Dr Jas. L Wilds had been found dead in his stable loft, hanging by a rope from a rafter. The doctor had been in very bad health since the first of last June, suffering from cerebral indigestion, and about three weeks ago came near dying from an attack. p3c4

Dr Wilds was the second son of B F Wilds and Eliza Dismukes, and was born October 11, 1851 in Garrard County. He was in the mercantile business in Lancaster until 1874, then in Buena Vista until 1877 when he came to Nicholasville. He married Lizzie Welch, daughter of Dr J C Welch, in 1874. Dr Wilds began studying medicine in 1883 and passed his State Medical Board examination in 1884. He began his practice of medicine in Sulphur Well. He is survived by his wife, and six children. p3c4

The Masons have terminated Congressman Breckenridge's membership. The editor cites the fable of the crow seizing a snake for prey, but itself being mortally wounded. It then exclaimed in agony "O unhappy me! who have found in that which I deemed a happy windfall, the source of my destruction." p2c1

Dick Tate, the absconding State Treasurer, has never been found, and many think he is dead. Yet, stories of him keep coming up. An ensign of the US Navy, who was recently in Frankfort, says that he not only saw him in Japan, but visited him at his home. p2c1

August 3, 1894

"Miss Viola Davis, of Ambrose, has begun her school at Oak Hill." p2c4

It's another hot, dry summer, and the Kentucky River is very low.

Has all been forgiven? "About fifty persons from this place, accompanied by the Jessamine Brass Band, will attend the Breckinridge barbeque at Nonesuch, tomorrow." p3c5

"Mr Adam K Adcock and family have returned from a two week's visit to relatives in Tennessee." p3c2 Scottie Hendren went with them, but extended her stay. She was working for Duncan and Spears at the time, and according to her autobiography "Mr Spears gave her permission". She wrote Forest that it had "rained one of the previous weeks and that she wanted to stay longer to see all the points of interest." She also told him that she and Lettie Brown were having a photograph made the following day. I still have one of them. Scottie also wrote in her autobiography that Lettie had a brother named Charlie. "We liked one another real well, and I've afterwards said 'if I weren't already engaged to Forest, I would have married him, as he asked me'." Charlie and Lettie make one more trip to Kentucky in August, 1895.

August 10, 1894

"Miss Scottie Hendren returned Monday from a visit to friends at Knoxville, Tenn." p3c2

The New York Herald says that "the McKinley Tariff is the chief obstacle in the way of agricultural prosperity" because it forces up the price of virtually everything that the farmer has to buy. p1c5 At the same time increasing wheat production in Argentina, and good harvests in Europe, have decreased the markets for US wheat, and drastically lowered prices. p1c5 The price of No 2 wheat was selling for 50.5 cents per bushel in Chicago. p2c3

The fifth annual Jessamine County fair was proclaimed a success. The exhibits were good, the attendance was good, and it was a financial success.

August 17, 1894

"Mr Forest Miller is taking in the sights at Niagara Falls." p3c2 It's possible that he was on this excursion. "On August 14, a Second Grand Excursion from points in Kentucky and Tennessee to Niagara Falls....Unusually low rates have been put in for the excursion. An unusually good chance to get away to the cool and pleasant summer resorts of the North." p3c6

August 24, 1894

Breckinridge has a worthy opponent. Thirty thousand people attended a barbeque in Lexington for W C Owens. p2c2 I believe that I would interpret this number in biblical terms, not necessarily a head-count.

"Hugh Miller, a Jessamine County farmer, will locate near Richmond. He is an excellent farmer and a good citizen." This is reprinted from the Richmond Climax. p3c2 Hugh is Dr Miller's son, and I would guess that he is farming the land owned by Dr Miller in Madison County.

The will of Dr Wilds was offered in probate court. It was in his own handwriting, dated June 22, 1894, giving all his property to his wife, Lizzie Welch, and making her executor of the estate. p3c4

August 31, 1894

The income tax law becomes effective January 1, 1895. It is a two percent tax on incomes over $4,000.

September 7, 1894

Lizzie Wilds renounced her right to qualify as executor, and requested that T R Welch be appointed. This is probably her brother.

"Miss Bertha Hendren left Monday for Frankfort, where she will attend school." p3c2 Another of Scottie's sisters.

"Miss Lizzie Miller, of Ambrose, Jessamine County, is visiting the family of her uncle, M M Miller...."p3c2

September 14, 1894

"In forty-eight hours the most heated, political campaign ever known in Kentucky will have ended." p2c1 This refers to the Breckinridge vs Owens race. It is said to be the first time in the history of the state when women were taking a part in politics.

September 21, 1894

Owens won the primary, but only by 200 votes. It's tough to beat an incumbent! Madeline Pollard, the Lolita who brought down Breckinridge, is now with a theatrical group.

Hughes & Adcock's horse, Judith, won a $500 purse race at Latonia on September 12th. p2c4

September 28, 1894

"Mr and Mrs Adcock spent Tuesday and Wednesday in Cincinnati and Covington." p3c2

The Democrats are planning the biggest barbeque ever, in Jessamine, as they are hosting the next congressional district meeting.

October 5, 1894

"Elbert Bourne, son of Mr and Mrs Everett E Bourne, Sulphur Well, died from the effects of fever at age fifteen. Interment took place in the Harris family burying ground, which is one and one-half miles west of Sulphur Well." p3c6 I was at this little cemetery today (September 19, 1996), but didn't see his stone. It's grown up pretty badly as most family sites are. But, it's always easier to find something when you know it's there. It is purely coincidental that I am proofing this the same day.

October 12, 1894

There have been no Murphy and Miller ads for several weeks.

October 19, 1894

Having leased my farm for a term of years, I will on Saturday, October 27, 1894, at my farm about one mile west of Sulphur Well, sell to the highest and best bidder 4 work mules, 2 work horses, 4 head of cattle, and my entire outfit of farming implements, consisting of 1 wagon, binder, mower, plows, gear, &c. Terms: A credit of 6 months will be given on all sums of ten dollars and over; under that amount, cash. Elizabeth J Miller. p2c5

The weather for the Democratic barbecue was very nice. "At 10:30am the special train from Richmond arrived and a few minutes later the Richmond Silver Band marched up Main Street...." The band was followed by carriages with the speakers and 600 Madison Democrats. "The procession proceeded on to the fairgrounds, followed by a vast throng (of people)." At the grounds there were 1,000 gallons of burgoo for lunch! Congressmen McCreary told the crowd that farm prices had decreased 13 percent in the decade of the eighties. p3c4

October 26, 1894

"The ladies of the Acme Club have effected their winter's organization and with the addition of some four or five new members are ready for their work. French history and literature are to be the studies, and a very complete program has been arranged...."p1c3

The first article this year from the *Sulphur Well Correspondent*:

*Born, to the wife of Mr James Turner, a daughter.*
*Mr C T Taylor contemplates moving to Lexington soon.*
*Corn is selling at $2 per barrel, delivered.*
*A little son of Robert Wiley was severely scalded by falling into a kettle of boiling water.*
*Mr Andrew Sageser is building a new residence upon the site of the one recently destroyed by fire.*
*Dr Phil. Roberts, Republican nominee for Congress, visited Dr Hendren, Wednesday and Thursday.*
*While shoeing a horse Mr A M Askins had his foot severely crushed by the horse stepping upon it.*
*Moses Reynolds is confined to his bed, suffering from a complication of diseases.*
*The temperance lecturer, Mr Crit Hughes, has been to see us and gave the usual lecture on the sins of intemperance.*

You might think that the leading item would be an explanation for not writing since last December! It appears that Dr Hendren has returned to Sulphur Well to live. The Correspondent seems underwhelmed by the temperance lecture. Do you remember the strong feeling that "B T" had about that subject a few years ago?

The public sale announcement of Mrs Miller was repeated this week.

"Mr A K Adcock, Jr, of Thorn Grove, Tenn., while on his way to Northern Ohio to become pastor of the Church of Christ at Fields, Loraine County, stopped off at Nicholasville to spend a few days with his uncle, A K Adcock, Sr." p3c2 I believe that it would be correct for the younger Adcock to be "the second" rather than junior.

Z T Chrisman has for several years been breeding trotting horses on the Chrisman Mill Road. He has had to make an assignment of assets because he purchased broodmares at $2,000 that are now worth $200, and paid stallion fees of as much as $400 to get the best stallions available for his mares. The decline in prices, and the scarcity of money is the cause of the assignment. Samuel B Muir and his son have also made assignments. The Muirs had a 734 acre farm and many investments. The failures are related. Chrisman owes the Muirs $8,000, both had their farms mortgaged. p3c3

The families of two large landowners on the Sulphur Well Road were joined with the marriage of Strashley Price Berryman and Mildred Lee Hemphill. p3c4

According to the editor the young people are trying to enjoy themselves in spite of the hard times. Miss Lulie Myers, of Spears, entertained a number of friends at her home, with an eleven o'clock supper. Clayton West of Sulphur Well attended. p3c5

November 2, 1894

The general election is next Tuesday.

Dr Chalmers is credited with saying: "A house-going pastor makes a church-going people". p3c4

Pomp reports from Little Hickman that "the gentle rain which fell Monday night and Tuesday was a great blessing to the wheat." p2c3

G W Lyne reports a small crowd at Mrs Elizabeth Miller's sale last Friday, and that "everything offered brought fair prices. Farm implements sold for all they were worth; horses and mules brought from $5 to $35." p2c3 I'd say the sale was a bust! The auctioneer, Lyne, couldn't draw a crowd and wanted to put the best face on the sale to protect his reputation. Times are very tough! In this paper alone their are three public sales of farms and farm propery, plus an Assignee's sale of the farm and trotting track of Z T Chrisman.

Mr F P Taylor, who has moved his furniture and undertaking business to Lexington, "has sold his residence on North Main Street to A K Adcock for $4,000, possession on December 1st." p3c1

November 9, 1894

The Democrats lose Congress. "They were routed in almost all sections of the Union, including Kentucky and the South. The solid South is no more." p2c1 Not even Kentucky stood against the tide. Instead of one Republican congressman, at least five were elected, and possibly six. However, Jessamine and the Eighth District remained Democratic.

Hughs and Adcock have a horse named "Judith" that has won again. They also have a "Tom Elmore" that came in second and third in two races in Nashville.

Chrisman's farm, known as the Jessamine Stock Farm, was said to be the largest in the county. This in the one that was recently assigned.

The station agent says he has never seen so many tramps as there has been the past ten days. He had to call the police to evict them from the waiting room when he closed one evening.

From the Irvine Sentinel: "Mrs Groom Taylor, of Hanly, Jessamine County, and Miss Myrtie Snowden, of Ambrose, are visiting the family of A D Snowden." p3c2

Quite a number of Nicholasville and Jessamine County ladies attended the Chrysanthemum show in Lexington.

November 16, 1894

Do you remember Clell Johnston, the "dashing young lawyer" that visited Sulphur Well so often in the late eighties? From Garrard County: "The friends of Letcher Owsley, who was only defeated by fifteen votes for county attorney by W McC Johnston, are urging him to contest the election." p2c2

November 23, 1894

"Free turnpikes are in sight in Fayette County. Several pikes are already open now and nearly all of them will be free in a year or two." p2c1 The method is for the County to buy the stock, and then maintain the road through taxes.

"Mr A K Adcock and family will move Monday to their new home on North Main Street." p3c2

From the *Sulphur Well Correspondent*:

*E J Curley is buying quite a quantity of corn at this place.*
*A J Hendren and son, of Kansas, are visiting Mr James Hendren.*
*A M Askins' mare, "Old Kate", died last week. Alex says she snagged herself.*
*John Miller, of Irvine, was on a short visit to his mother, Mrs Elizabeth Miller, last week.*
*Ambrose has been a very lively business point for a month or so past. It may arise out of its ashes yet. Quien sabe?*
*A daughter of Mr Thompson Reeder died of consumption last Friday and was buried at Pleasant Hill on Saturday.*
*There is some talk of constructing a telephone line from this place to Nicholasville. It is one of the "long-felt wants."*
*Miss Mary E Goforth, who lives below here and was married to James Humes, last week is said to be only twelve years of age.*
*A good many hogs have changed hands here recently at from $3.85 to $4. Turkeys on foot sell at 6c and cattle at various prices.*
*J H Hendren, of Madison, formerly in the revenue service at Curley's distillery, accompanied by his family, is visiting friends in this vicinity.*
*Jessamine County courts are very popular with Garrard and Madison citizens. A large crowd from the borders of these two counties passed here Monday on their way to our court; also a considerable quantity of stock passed through for the same point.* p3c6

November 30, 1894

"Mr and Mrs A K Adcock's little daughter, Russie, has been quite ill for several days of fever." p3c2

The Knights of Labor are holding their convention in New Orleans this year, and they have voted against admitting lawyers or barkeepers. The Ashland News editor says he can understand their excluding the lawyers "but why the hard working barkeeper should be thus ostracized passes comprehension." p2c1

December 7, 1894

"One hundred thousand pounds of turkeys were shipped November 28th from Paris, Winchester, and Richmond to Boston. The entire shipment was carried on one train over the L & N." p2c3

December 14, 1894

The wheat crop is quite low, some estimating it at only one-half the usual crop. It appears that the corn crop will average 28 bushels per acre.p1c5 Court Days in the city are changing. In the past the farmer brought his produce, his cattle, or horses to town, and they were auctioned on the spot. He could then use the proceeds to pay his bills and to shop for needed merchandise. It has now become more practical to get the cattle to the railroad and ship them to a market such as Cincinnati. So, there are fewer farmers in town, and the volume of retail sales is also down. (This appears to be on page one, but I believe that it is p2c3) Court Days are the ideal time for the politicians. They circulate among the people, and after dinner they go to the courthouse and speak for two or three hours, or until the crowd thins out.

December 21, 1894

"Mrs W H Van Winkle, Frankfort, is visiting her sister, Mrs Adam Adcock." p3c2

The *Sulphur Well Correspondent* reports:

*Mr Charles Hudson has been on a visit to relatives here.*
*Mr Charles Saunders, of Madison, was visiting Miss Rhoda Peel last Sunday.*
*Mr Holly Easley's youngest child dislocated its shoulder by a fall Thursday of last week.*
*That which speaks well for our community is the good attendance at our church every Sunday.*
*Our public school which has been closed for sometime, is again in session with full attendance.*
*Mr C T Taylor, having rented his place to Cyrus Davis, will move to Lexington soon.*
*Mr Reece, of Hopkinsville; Mr Will H Davis, Miss Beulah Davis and Miss Bertie Funk, of Nicholasville, visited Miss May Taylor, Sunday. p3c5*

It appears that above article was supposed to have been in the previous week's paper because this following article of the *Sulphur Well Correspondent* seems to refer to C T Taylor:

*Mr Wilson Baker was prostrated by sickness on last Sunday.*
*Typhoid fever is prevalent in the Mt Lebanon neighborhood.*
*The "Well" is quite a resort for the youngsters on Sunday. The people of this village are glad to see them.*
*We would like for our people, renowned for their hospitality, to show their liberality by fixing up the public pump.*

*Our genial friend, Ewald Schneider, was visiting the neighborhood of Sulphur Well last Sunday, the guest of Mr M P Horine and family.*

*It is said that the gentleman we spoke of last week as moving to town will move to Valley View, but we can't say whether this is correct or not.*

*People are afraid to leave their dwellings now for a social visit for fear of fire. If there is a "fire bug" in this community he ought to be treated to a dose of "bug juice".*

*The old dilapidated pump at the "Well", once time-honored and time-tried, has been pumped by the town and country as well, until the old thing is about pumped out.*

*A dwelling house owned by Mr Jas. Grimes, of Lexington, burned to the ground Thursday night, Dec. 6th. The house had not been occupied for some months, and was supposed to have been set on fire. The dwelling was insured for $500, but it could not be rebuilt for near that money.*

*Mr John T West, residing about one mile from this place, had a narrow escape from losing his residence Saturday night. A hen house in the yard close to the dwelling caught on fire early in the night and burned down. It is supposed to have ignited from some wood ashes that had been left in it during the day. The dwelling also caught fire from sparks, but the flames were extinguished...(The remainder of the article is destroyed). p2c4*

The Correspondent seems to be greatly perturbed at the incidence of fires in the neighborhood in recent days. Those frame houses, with kitchen stoves, grease and other flammable materials close by, made it almost inevitable that they would burn. The vacant house fire could well have been set, but others were probably accidental. It appears that even in cold weather that the young people gathered in Sulphur Well. They always have in the summertime. I also noted that the pump is in bad condition. That, too, was almost always the case. While everyone used the pump, no one seemed to feel any responsibility for maintaining it. When I was a youngster, Joe Breiner was the person who kept it in repair.

December 28, 1894

This issue of the Journal is missing, and the past three issues have been fragmentary. It seems rather strange that the Sulphur Well correspondent has written so few articles in 1893 and 1894, and most of those in the month of December. I have sensed a growing modernity in the past decade, and the change from 1877 has been notable. I am gratified to have found as many references to the Miller and Hendren families as I have. I am confident that when I finish that we will have a much better knowledge of the generations covered by Merriman Miller, my great, great grandfather; his children, Dr John C Miller, Frank Miller, and Mann Miller; and their families. On the Hendren side we have discovered a lot about Will D and Levisa Hendren, my great grandparents, and their children. It fills the void in much of my family history.

MARRIAGE - 1895

My grandparents, Scottie Hendren and Forest Miller, were married at Christmas time in 1895. There is a lot going on in the community, and the Correspondent is prolific this year.

January 4, 1895

An assignee's sale of a brick store room fronting on Main Street is advertised. First came the "money stringency", now the business fallout. The <u>Journal</u> is advising businessmen to begin the year on the cash basis, because credit is one of the principal causes of failure. The <u>Journal</u> also carried an article written by someone who had recently been in China. He said that New Year's day is the national payday. If you can't pay you are declared bankrupt. Locally, custom has payments due twice a year--January 1 and July 1. Even state government is affected. "The State Treasury, which has been in such hard times for several months past, relapsed into a state of practical suspension today...." p2c1

H G (Horace) Turner is attending school in Boston. He was home visiting his parents in the county and "preached a most excellent sermon at M E Church, South, Sunday morning".p3c2

Dr Welch, administrator of Dr Wilds' estate, is offering property on Mulberry Street for sale.

Susan B Anthony will speak in the college chapel in Wilmore on Jan. 11th at 7pm.

So, the *Sulphur Well Correspondent* writes:

*The principle (sic) amusement now is sleighing--to those who are fortunate enough to be able to buy, beg, or borrow a sleigh.*
*It is said that the roads of Poosey, Madison County are so crooked that one in going anywhere is liable to meet himself coming back.*
            *Christmas holidays with all its joys,*
            *Was delightful to the girls and boys.*
*A great deal of ice has been gathered here during the past two days.*
*Mr William Snowden, of Estill County, is visiting his brother, S N Snowden.*
*Mr Ben Spears and wife were visiting Mr Hare's family last Sunday.*
*Mr William Richardson and wife, of Irvine, who has been visiting Mrs Miller for the past week, returned home yesterday.*
*Mrs Viola Million, of Richmond; Miss Bertie Funk and Miss Beulah Davis, accompanied by Messrs. James Gordon, Robert Webb and Brown Anderson, of Nicholasville, visited Miss May Taylor and Miss Eudora Murphy Sunday.*
*Miss Lulu Scott, a twelve year-old girl who lives with Wm Walker, of this place, fell from a hen house, dislocating her wrist and also fracturing the scaphoid bone. The dislocation was reduced and the fracture set by Dr Hendren, and Miss Scott is now rapidly recovering from her fall.*

*Now is the time to form good resolutions, not rash promises or make determinations that nobody, yourself included, believes will be lived up to, but resolutions that could be and ought to be followed faithfully. Even if one fails he is all the better for having followed them however short the time. No one refuses to get up when he falls for fear of falling again. So no one should fail to resolve to live better lives, beginning with the new year because he has time and again fallen by the wayside in the past, but make good resolutions and make a heroic effort to keep them.*
p3c6

The Correspondent does not just report the news, but waxes philosophical as well. He even bursts out in rhyme at one point in the report. The Snowdens and the Richardsons married daughters of Elizabeth J Miller. Poosey Ridge Road, in Madison County, runs from Hunter's Ferry to Kirksville. Edenton, a small community on the Poosey Road, was once the home of Dr Hendren.

January 11, 1895

A large hacienda in Mexico with 45,000 acres has been purchased by a group including John B Embry, Z T Chrisman, and D V Miles of Kentucky. They expect to apply American agricultural practices to the property. p3c5 Z T Chrisman is the trotting horse breeder on the Chrisman Mill Pike that went bankrupt in October, 1994. I don't know how he has the assets to engage in this purchase.

> Snowden-Taylor.--Mr George T Snowden and Miss Nora W Taylor, daughter of the late Groom Taylor, were married at the home of Mrs Elizabeth J Miller, Sulphur Well, on the 9th inst. Mrs Miller is the grandmother of the bridegroom.
> p3c4

From the *Sulphur Well Correspondent*:

> *The ice-houses are full.*
> *The jinglet has left the sleigh bell.*
> *Elder Finley will occupy the pulpit of the Christian Church Sunday.*
> *The rain Saturday night melting the snow has greatly swollen the streams.*
> *Calvin Bruner bought several head of fine cattle in this locality last week.*
> *C T Taylor will move to Lexington Tuesday. Cyrus Davis will move into Mr Taylor's residence.*
> *F M Horine and W L Hendren have been spending a few days at Lexington attending the Exposition.*
> *Is the hog meet(?) or the goose bone responsible for all this variegated weather, or has the weather clerk dumped it all on to us at once and taken a holiday.*
> *Mr Knowit wants to know, "yeh know," how the jinglet got into the sleigh-bell. So? well--*
> *Which was first, the egg or the hen,*
> *Mr Knowit, tell me then--*
> *Then with pleasure I will tell,*
> *How came the jinglet in the bell.*

*On the Kirksville and Kentucky River turnpike road there are toll gates at nearly every house, yet it is said tollgatherers with poles on their shoulders patrol the roads between gates for fear some poor devil will escape down some hollow.*

*Brer Rabbit had a hard road to travel during the snow. Twelve hundred of them passed through here at one time on the way to market, all having been caught in the same locality. Why not have a rabbit law as well as a quail law. This is not Australia--the timid animal can be exterminated here, and soon will be at the present rate of wanton destruction. Why not turn your shot against the little English miscreant? It is said they make a good pie, and a sparrow pie ought to be as good as rabbit hash any day. p2c4*

The Sulphur Well correspondent has shown a definite propensity to editoralize as well as report the news. In this report he rails against the toll-roads, which indeed have become unpopular everywhere. He also takes a stand against a few hunters or trappers that are decimating the rabbit population, which are apparently unprotected by law, at least by possession limits. I must say that over the years the hunters have shown a willingness to kill anything that moves. At least every year someone is written up in the paper as killing something that has become very rare, just to kill it. Then they carry it to town to show it off. Here is a perfect example: "Mr A P Mitchell, Union Mills, killed a hen hawk last Friday that measured four feet four inches from tip to tip of wings". p3c1

January 18, 1895

The *Sulphur Well Correspondent* reports:

*Our public school closed its session last Friday.*
*The bicycle club is not so popular here as it once was. Now for the sa--racyle, then.*
*A vacant house in the country is said to be used for balls at night.*
*Is our projected telephone gone to "Hello"?*
*Miss Scott is visiting at Mr Easley's.*
*An infant of S N Underwood has been seriously sick with convulsions.*
*James Grimes says he will rebuild. Glad to hear it.*
*Mr Mich. Masters has again located on his farm in this county.*
*The stirring music of tin pans, tin horns, cow horns, etc., suddenly broke the stillness of the night hours Thursday, Jan. 10. The boys were serenading the new bride and groom in true charivari fashion.*
*We would like to say something more about the weather, but as we cannot do it justice without using words that wouldn't sound well in a meeting house, we will only remark, en passant, that Bro. Finley, who occupied the pulpit Sunday, didn't have a very large audience to hear him.*

*Where, old winter, are you drifting,*
*Every day;*
*Why this constant changing, shifting,*
*Every way;*
*Are mortals now who only fret you,*
*Living only to forget you;*
*Are fewer growing to regret you,*
*Every day?*
*Yes, the time is drawing nigher*
*When you'll die;*
*For the sun is climbing higher*
*In the sky;*
*Then your grasp on us gets slighter,*
*And your burden will be lighter*
*When the days grow warmer, brighter-*
*In July!  p2c4*

The Correspondent now uses Latin phrases, and expresses himself in rhyme. Some of you, including myself, may wonder what the term "*charivari*" means. It is the same as chivaree, with which we are more familiar.

January 25, 1895

One of Nicholasville's most interesting citizens is leaving town. H C Rodenbaugh has been in the mercantile business, postmaster, U S gauger, proprietor of Hotel Nicholas, and a member of the City Council. He also has raced a string of horses, primarily at Hawthorne Park in Chicago.

February 1, 1895

The Little Hickman correspondent (Pomp) says most of the farmers there have finished stripping, but have found no market for their tobacco.

The *Sulphur Well Correspondent* reports:

*Mrs Diana Moore has been very sick.*
*John Fain is very sick with breast trouble.*
*Thomas Hughes is crippled up with sciatica.*
*There is an abundance of the beautiful again.*
*Sheep-killing dogs are said to be on the warpath.*
*Butler Cobb is seriously sick with a lung affection.*
*Thompson Reeder, aged 70, died Wednesday at 6 am.*
*Miss Carrie West, of Garrard, who is visiting her uncle, Jno. T West, has been quite sick.*
*James Grimes, of Lexington, is visiting Alex. Askins this week. He has collected his insurance and talks of rebuilding. p2c4*

February 8, 1895

Dan V Miles writes back about his first trip to Mexico. He went by rail, his route taking him throught St Louis, and on to Mexico City, then to Vera Cruz. He boarded a steamer at Vera Cruz bound for Coatzacoaloos. He said that the ranch is fifteen miles from the Gulf and six miles from the mountains, and that while the weather is pleasant, that a coat is comfortable all the time. p1c3-4

Other citizens opting for warmer climes: "Mr Alex Willis left last Friday night for St Petersburg, Fla., where he goes to engage in the orange business." p3c2 "E E Denman left Tuesday for Florida on a prospecting trip. He will probably locate at Orlando...."p3c2 Denman is a sign painter.

The *Sulphur Well Correspondent* reports:

*Mr Joe Durham, ex-magistrate, is on the sick list.*
*Mr J M Long, of Madison County, was in Sulphur Well Friday on business.*
*I notice that there is more work done around the store stoves in winter than is done in the fields in summer.*
*There is a dearth of news just now, so we just sit around the fire and talk of the weather, which surely needs all the abuse it receives.*
*It is reported that Joseph Deboe, formerly of this county, has been missing for two weeks. It is thought by some that he was drowned in Paint Lick Creek.* p3c5

February 15, 1895

Another wanderer reporting in: W A Logan, writes from the Black Hills area. It's not clear whether he is mining or farming, maybe some of both. He claims the weather in South Dakota is better than in Kentucky. He also says that county politics is unknown there. p1c3 And, still one more: Ed Guerrant, a minister, writes from Umatilla, Fla. saying that a blizzard, and 14 degree temperatures, has ruined the groves in that section. He said it had been sixty years since that temperature had been so low. p1c3

Nicholasville lost two of its citizens. An old rag-picker entered an Old Soldiers Home in Dayton, and a demented woman who was a house-to-house begger moved to Lawrenceburg. This is part of the fabric of the times. The weather was so severe the past month (Hanly reports 17 below zero) that it exceeded the means of "the ladies, who are foremost in acts of charity...." The mayor and the county judge each donated $50 from city and county funds for the "relief of the destitute and suffering." The Mayor asked the churches to take up a collection Sunday to add to the fund. Volunteers have been visiting homes and distributing orders for coal, food, and clothing. p3c2 The Sheriff of Garrard County advertises that the property of 290 delinquent owners will be offered for sale. p2c2 These items reflect the hard times and suffering of the old and poor, and the limited resources to care for them.

There may be even more competition in the Nicholasville clothing business. Harry Klein, from Louisville is taking over J Frankel's Blue Front Store and says he will have a large stock and sell at "city" prices. p3c1

There seems to have been a shift in referring to Sulphur Well by its post-office name Ambrose. Fortunately, after the post office was gone, it has been referred to as Sulphur Well. In times past the little community of Canton, near Little Hickman, was called Pink after its postoffice. Now that the store and the postoffice are gone, it is hard to find someone who now recognizes it by either name.

### February 22, 1895

From "Ambrose", the *Sulphur Well Correspondent* reports:

*Mrs Elizabeth Miller is on the sick list this week.*
*Mrs Squire Miller has been quite sick for some days.*
*Charles Bronson is recovering from an attack of pneumonia.*
*Mr E E Bourne has been quite ill for some time.*
*Wm Hendren, who has been an invalid for three years, is worse than usual.*
*There is considerable sickness in this community, mostly from exposure to the inclement weather.*
*Mrs Fanny D Jasper, of near Hanly, is visiting her daughter, Mrs M E Hendren this week.*
*Mr Jack Hendren, of Iowa Point, Kansas, returned home Tuesday.*
*Mr Joseph Durham, who has been quite ill some time, is thought to be in a dangerous condition.*
*The lowest temperature recorded here during the late frigidity was 12 degrees below.*
*Mrs Geo M Hendren is visiting her daughter, Mrs Hugh Miller, Richmond.*
*Hon. C M Davis has returned from a visit to friends and acquaintances in Louisville and vicinity.*
*Mr Butler Cobb, who is low with lung and heart trouble, was baptized in the church at Mt Pleasant by Rev Absolom Reynolds a few days ago.* p2c5

It seems pretty evident that this was a memorable winter. It takes a toll on the weak and elderly. You couldn't just hunker down and wait for the weather to improve. You had to keep fires burning, and stock fed and watered. Everything about living in the country in primative conditions is miserable. Currier and Ives never lived on a farm!

### March 1, 1895

J W Overstreet (Pomp) wrote a letter to the paper advocating free turnpikes and forcing politicians to state their position of the matter.

We have the first advertisment for Murphy and Miller in several months. I don't see how they can make money this way. They say that they auctioned off all their old stock last fall, replenished with winter merchandise that they are selling at cost or below cost to make room for their new spring merchandise. They will sell any suit or overcoat in the house for $10.00. p4c1-2

From the *Sulphur Well Correspondent*:

*Born to the wife of Newton Brumfield. Feb. 19th, a daughter.*

*Mr Ben Grimes, of Lexington, was visiting here Sunday.*

*C M Davis has about recovered from his late indisposition.*

*Mr John Masters and wife, of Valley View, were visiting Wm Walker's family Sunday.*

*Mr N D Davis shipped 22 head of 1250 lb. steers to Cincinnati Monday, together with a lot of hogs.*

*The extreme cold weather has greatly decreased the spring lamb crop in this section.*

*Miss Lizzie Burton, of Portwood, Madison County, who has been visiting Miss Myrtle Snowden, returned home Saturday.*

*We think there will be some more weddings, accompanied by the sweet peals of the marriage bells and the harmonious strains of the charivari, in the near future.*

*We have in our town a mimic of no mean pretensions. "Cap" Masters can imitate the pecularities of the human voice to perfection as well as that of birds and animals so closely as to deceive the animals themselves.*

*Hemp breaking has been progressing rapidly during the few warm days we have lately enjoyed. The extensive hemp growing done in this section in former years, has, owing to low prices, been almost suspended of late; tobacco taking its place largely. Apropos of this, many think that hemp could yet be used in the "suspension" business greatly to the advantage of the country.*

*F M Horine had quite an exciting sleigh ride recently. While driving down a steep descent on a slide, the horse became frightened at the slide running upon him and ran away, and although Frank was unaccustomed to fast sleighing, he is so well pleased with the ride he is talking of buying a sleigh in anticipation of the next snow fall. It is to be hoped that he will not need one.*

*A young mare that Mr Newt Davis had been driving to a buggy for only a day or two was left hitched in a pasture for a few moments, when she reared up and fell, breaking a shaft and then concluded to run away without her driver. After running, turning and falling for some time without further damage, she came to a standstill, but a dog, evidently liking to see the sport, nipped her heels, causing her to run again, this time completely demolishing the buggy. p3c5*

The Correspondence has enlarged his role of reporting on comings and goings around Sulphur Well. He has become a storyteller as well. And, he seems to be letting his sense of humor come through.

March 8, 1895

George S Diamond, an eighteen year veteran clothing salesman, quit "his position with Murphy and Miller" about a month ago with the intent of entering another business. However, he has decided to take a sales position with B L Cook. "Walter S Hendren has taken Mr Diamond's place as salesman at Murphy and Miller's." p3c1 Walter is a brother of Dr Hendren.

The *Sulphur Well Correspondent* reports again:

> Mrs Elizabeth Miller is quite ill from the effects of a burn.
> Prof. C M Davis opens a subscription school here next Monday.
> Mr Joseph Durham has about recovered from a protracted spell of illness.
> Mr and Mrs George Snowden were visiting Mrs Miller last Sunday.
> Colds and la grippe are very prevalent since the recent thaw.
> Pike repairing all along the line makes it dangerous traveling at present.
> Mrs Meda Reynolds has been very low with pneumonia and a complication of diseases.
> Farmers are very generally having their corn crushed for feed, to the great advantage of the stock.
> Dirt roads are almost impassable from an abundance of mud. Give us pikes, and free pikes at that.
> Willard Davis has returned from Cincinnati, where he had been with a car load of cattle and hogs.
> With very few exceptions, I think, the people of this district, and in fact the whole county, is in favor of free pikes.
> Mr Archie Whittaker and Miss Eliza Tudor, both of Madison County, were married last Tuesday.
> Mr John M Burton, of Madison, was here Monday, having recently returned from Indiana, to locate in Madison again. He thinks Kentucky good enough for anybody. p2c5

The Correspondent is taking a strong position on free turnpikes. He also reports the widespread sickness in the community. George Snowden visited his grandmother, Mrs Miller this week, sporting his new wife, Nora Taylor. Willard Davis' farm is about a mile from Sulphur Well, near Black Bridge. I don't know Eliza Tudor, but Scottie Hendren's mother was Levisa Tudor also from Madison. The Correspondent seems to be reporting the doings of the Madison people pretty regularly.

March 15, 1895

Hughes & Adcock's trotter "Tom Elmore" has started three times in the past two weeks and won all of them. p2c3

The *Sulphur Well Correspondent* writes:

*Mrs Hurt, wife of Michael Hurt, is quite ill from symptoms of fever.*
*Mr Wm V Warren is very low with typhoid fever.*
*Whooping cough is prevalent in portions of this section.*
*The vogue now is to dehorn young milch cows. It's a sensible fashion.*
*The river being in boating order, numbers of valuable logs are going down.*
*The old time corn shucking with its fun and frolic having passed away, the fete champetre has taken its place.*
*According to prognostications of weather prophets and the goose bone, we will have one or two more snows yet.*
*Mr and Mrs Hugh Miller, of Richmond, were visiting Dr G M Hendren Saturday and Sunday.*
*Young Brother Adcock, of Tennessee, preached here, at Elm Fork and Little Hickman last Sunday. He will continue his meetings nightly at Elm Fork during this week.*
*Dr Fount J Dickerson, brother-in-law of Dr J C Miller, died at Richmond Friday. He was a very successful physician for many years, and a polished gentleman.*
*Mr Ruce Small and Ina English, daughter of Levi English, eloped last Saturday night. This is the third elopement very recently and the fourth one attempted, but failed.*
*Some extra quality tobacco grown in this county is being hauled through...(paper torn and missing).* p3c4

I don't understand how Dr Dickerson could be a brother-in-law of Dr Miller. I suspect an error. His first wife was Nanie Rice of Madison County, and his second wife was Emma Crain Reynolds. One sister married an Overstreet, one a Nave, another a Barkley. However, this is from the obituary: "Dickerson-Dr Fountain J Dickerson, who died in Richmond on the 7th inst., was a brother-in-law of Dr J C Miller and Mr Jas M Nave, of Jessamine County. He was also related to the Dickerson and Welch families of this place, and at one time was associated with the late Dr J C Welch in the practice of medicine." p3c3 I had to look up "*fete champetre*". It's literal meaning is rural holiday. I don't know what holiday has taken the place of corn-shucking!

March 22, 1895

Adcock purchased a two-year old colt by Julien, out of Blue Bonnie by True Blue for $120.00. p2c3

The *Sulphur Well Correspondent* reports:

*Miss Mary Taylor is visiting Mrs J W Cobb this week.*
*Miss Iva Scott is visiting at Mr J H Easley's.*
*Mansfield Gibony and Rutherford B Hendren are preparing to go to Kansas within a few days.*
*The question of prohibition will be voted upon in Poosey district, Madison County, soon.*
*Wild geese flying northward would seem to indicate that old winter has finally lost his grip.*
*Elder Finley did not preach at the church Saturday and Sunday as was expected, thereby disappointing a large audience.*
*It was Reece Sewell and Ina English, daughter of Leroy English, who eloped and not as misprinted in our last letter.*
*Is whisky getting high, or people less dry, that fewer go swaying and yelling home from court days?*
*Morris Dean sold four head of good cattle to Wm Scott at from 3 to 3 1/2cts. Also J H Easley sold one head to same party for 3 1/2 cents.*
*Squire Yarnell, living on Charles Hemphill's place, had the misfortune of splitting his foot open with an axe Monday, making an ugly wound.*
*Our farmers, becoming restless from long inactivity, are beginning to plow before the soil is fairly dry enough in some localities.*
*Sore throat seems to be very prevalent in this section. Dr Hendren has been seriously ill and confined to his room several days with an attack of acute pharyngitis.*
*There will certainly be no peach crop this year, in this latitude at least, as all of that fruit is killed and a large portion of the trees, especially the younger ones.*
*Everywhere there is fencing being done in this portion of country I notice it is of the slat and wire pattern. It seems to be the best and cheapest to make and a favorite with the farmers generally.*
*A horse hitched to a carriage and belonging to W L Buford, did some high cavorting on the street Friday, during which he turned completely in the shafts, falling with his head under the vehicle without doing much damage.*
*Some new houses are going up in this neighborhood and in the hills. They all seem to be of the box style of architecture and many of them iron roofed. This is quite and improvement on the "little old log cabin in the lane", variety. p3c4*

The Correspondent is concerned in this letter with sickness, religion, prohibition, the weather, new residential construction, visiting, and farming--plowing and fencing. That's some range of topics for one week.

Camp Nelson reported that Mrs House, of Sulphur Well, was the guest of Mrs Will Burton last week. They are sisters-in-law.

March 29, 1895

Free roads: "The act provides that, on petition of 25 percent of the qualified voters of any county, the Fiscal Court shall order an election on the question, and, if a majority of the voters favor the plan, the court shall then have the power to levy a tax, not 'to exceed 10 cents on $100 in any one year'...." These funds are to be used to acquire and maintain the roads." p1c3

From Keene: "Prof Rice Miller was the guest of W F Cleveland from Saturday 'till Monday." p2c1

From Glass' Mills: "Mr J H Murphy, the clever and hustling manager of the Glass Milling Company, will make a trip to Tennessee in April, in the company's interest." p2c4 Murphy also has the general store in Sulphur Well, and half interest in the Murphy and Miller clothing store in Nicholasville. I assume this means that Forest Miller was managing the store in Nicholasville.

The editor says that "with the silver question, free turnpikes, legislative race, locating the Confederate soldiers' monument, closing the postoffice on Sunday, &c, our local 'agitators' have not been at a loss for something to 'agitate'." p3c1

The *Sulphur Well Correspondent* writes:

*Wm D Warren, Madison County, died Wednesday of typhoid fever.*
*Neighboring farmers, generally, were having their dairy cows dehorned last Wednesday.*
*La grippe is becoming quite prevalent in this place, and in the neighborhood.*
*Our school seems to be in a flourishing condition and the patrons well pleased.*
*One of our enterprising young batchelors, at last, thinks of committing matrimony.*
*Hemp breaking is about over and considerable of that article is going to market.*
*Born, to the wife of Frank Hudson, Tuesday, March 26th, a daughter.*
*Mr Jerry Comley and son have established a store at Miles' ferry across the river.*
*Mr Luther Saunders and Park Ferrell were visiting at Valley View last Sunday.*
 *There is more talk of small-pox. We hear of it now and then, but such talk seems to be simply all "bosh".*
*Mr Vince Collins, Madison County, had a child burned to death last Tuesday.*
*Mr Elzy Million's little child was seriously burned Tuesday, having its clothes caught from a stove.*
 *At Hunter's Ferry on Saturday evening at 5, Mr Mack Brock was married to Miss Lee Annie Sewell, daughter of Geo. W Sewell, by Absolem Reynolds, D.D.*
 *Many persons wish to be vaccinated; but is not a physician liable to indictment if he vaccinates without registering?*
 *We have a letter from Dr F O Young, Lexington, saying they have the small-pox under complete control, not having had a new case since the 12th inst.*
 *Now that the tariff question is an old issue, our K N K Club (kickers of the nail keg) is discussing the financial problem. The club meets every day and night.*
 *H P Cobb, who has been on a visit to Lexington for some days, finds that on his return his friends are all shy of him.*

*Mr M S Reynolds, who has been on a visit to Ambrose and the county generally, authorizes us to state that he was empowered by his nephew, Mr Luther Saunders, to purchase a licence for him while in Nicholasville. p3c5-6*

The Correspondent seems to be oriented toward the eastern part of Sulphur Well, the part that goes from the pump on the Elm Fork Road, through West's Lane, toward Mt Lebanon, Hunter's Ferry, and Southern Madison County. I think that accounts for what is essentially a new set of names in the weekly items. Is the correspondent implying that someone is vacinating people without a medical licence? And, is the letter from Dr Young, one doctor to another? By the end of the winter, the correspondent appears to be sick and tired of the loafers around the stove from early morning until closing time. The items are a curious mixture of medicine and merchandising.

## April 5, 1895

A number of announced candidates for the legislature are running on the free turnpike question.

Johannah " Sittie" Bell of Las Animas, Colorado has a little daughter.

The *Sulphur Well Correspondent* has this report:

*Sam Askins was visiting the Well Sunday.*
*Mrs Belle Rice has been on a visit to N D Davis this week.*
*Mrs Mede Reynolds is slowly recovering from a protracted illness.*
*Preaching last Sunday at Elm Fork by Eld. Adcock.*
*Mr Elbert Walker is on a visit to friends in Fayette.*
*Dr Geo. M Hendren made a visit to Richmond Monday.*
*Bro. Fenley preached at Sulphur Well Saturday and Sunday.*
*Our fine fish pond is at present a Mecca for piscatorial anglers.*
*Mr Jas. M Grimes is thinking of building soon on his vacant lot.*
*Esquire J Mettemiren, a merchant of Brassfield, was here this week.*
*La grippe has prostrated a considerable portion of our colored population.*
*Sulphur Well, with a small outlay, could be made a famous health resort.*
*Mr J P Turner is losing many of his sheep by worthless curs and disease.*
*A daughter of Mr Perry Myers has been severly ill for the past few days.*
*The pleasant showers Monday were a great advantage to the grass and wheat crops.*
*A protracted meeting is in progress at Wesley's Chapel near Little Hickman.*
*Simpson Warren and family, of Madison, were visiting Jno Reynolds, Sunday.*
*The doctors of both Jessamine and Madison counties are busy with la grippe.*
*Jackson Ware sold to A C Miles 11 head of hogs at 3 3/4c and one heifer, weight 700 at 2 3/4c.*
*Mr Lucien Holmes, of Louisville, paid a flying visit to Jessamine and Madison counties this week.*
*Robt. Reagan, of Edenton, recently visited friends in Jessamine on his way to Cincinnati.*
*Mr Jas W Miller, our urbane and efficient postmaster, has increased his stock of goods.*
*Some of our prominent men want to form a gas company. There is no doubt of gas being near the earth's surface here.*

*Last Friday about 11 o'clock the residence of T J Horine caught fire on the roof of the rear portion, and came near burning down. Only the prompt and energetic attention of the neighbors and family saved it. A large portion of the roof was destroyed. No insurance. p3c4*

This article contains one of the few mentions of Jim Miller, brother of Forest Miller, my grandfather. The language in this article is reminiscent of that used in the very early articles, eg, "urbane and efficient". He also mentions the presence of natural gas, as he has done much earlier.

### April 12, 1895

From New York: "Fayetta silk is in great demand for graduating dresses and lovely gowns intended for spring and summer fetes." p1c5 The reporter says that Fayetta silk "has more body, and is dressier than India silk, the soft shimmer on its surface, rendering it more refined than taffeta, and (it has)... unusal draping qualities...."p1c5

From Hanly: "Miss Emma Reynolds, of Ambrose, visited H B Land and family, this week." p2c4

### April 19, 1895

Sam Jones, the evangelist, said that a "fellow who has more religion than he has sense is a fool; when ... (he) has more sense than religion, he's a rascal." But, he says, "when a fellow that has a good level head gets his will consecrated to God, he will be a power anywhere." p1c6

A good article on the history of Camp Nelson is in this issue of the Journal. p4

### April 26, 1895

The new income tax collector for the Eighth District reports that he has received 257 returns; 102 personal and 155 corporate. You only needed to file a return if your income exceeded $4,000 annually.

From the *Sulphur Well Correspondent*:

*Butler Cobb died last week of consumption.*
*Our school house will very soon have a new fence around it.*
*Mr E Walker sold two fat cows to Smith Bros., Monday.*
*The churches were pretty well attended on Easter Sunday.*
*J M Horine sold a cow to Mr W L Scott at 3 3/4c., Monday.*
*Mr Jeff Hibbard, Madison County, was over on business, Monday.*
*New fences are going up all around, but not before they were needed.*
*Mr Simpson Warren, Madison County, was visiting here last Sunday.*
*The grippe seems to have the proper name, for it is determined to not let go.*
*Several head of fat cattle have been sold around here within the last few days at 3 3/4cts.*
*There seems to be an unusual amount of sickness at the present time, mostly influenza.*

    *J N Hendren, Madison County, sold some fine cattle at 5 1/4 cts., and a lot of hogs at 4 1/2 cts.*

    *Citizens of the village are making complaints of having their horses and mules ridden at night.*

    *Mrs James Turner, (nee Grinstead), left Monday for a ten days visit to her parents at Millersburg.*

    *Mr T J Horine, E Walker, C W Horine and several others are complaining of symptoms of la grippe.*

    *Bro. Finley will hereafter preach at the church on second Sundays and Saturday nights preceeding.*

    *A larger area of hemp than usual is being sown this year, and about the usual acreage of tobacco will be planted.*

    *Mr John P Miller, Estill County, was on a visit to his mother here, Monday, on his way to Cincinnati to purchase goods.*

    *This fine weather the farmers are all very busy and the village stores look lonesome and deserted and the nail keg club is almost annihilated.*

    *Mrs Miller is improving her place considerably by fencing, white washing, etc. That improvement is needed on every hand is but too apparent.*

    *Roving, depredating stock is a source of great annoyance to many people, and is productive of much ill feeling among neighbors as well as no little profanity.*

    *We have but little talk of politics in this corner of the county, but the unforgotten voter and ever present floater will be "thar" when the primary comes around.*

    *Among the many apparently paradoxical reasons many men offer for drinking is one that it stimulates their dormant mental faculties; but isn't it a good idea to be sure of the possession of the requisite quality of mental substances before they commence an experiment?*

    *Mr Stephen Sallee, of McAfee, Mercer County, was on a visit last Sunday to his mother, Mrs Hannah Sallee, of Madison County, who is in feeble health and is 92 years old. Mr Sallee's father, William Sallee, was 91 years of age when he died, fourteen years ago. Mrs Sallee resides in the same house on the farm her husband purchased and moved into soon after their marriage, more than seventy years ago, and where they lived their long and uneventful lives continuously until he died. The Sallees were a long lived people, several of them living beyond 90 years. p3c5*

I see that Sulphur Well has undergone some changes in recent years that are not for the better. Do you remember S M Duncan's visit to Sulphur Well last year? He said that farmers were getting poorer. This letter clearly shows that fences and property have deteriorated. Livestock is roaming the neighborhood unattended and unobstructed by fencing. The Correspondent notes that this has created some ill feeling among neighbors. The saying that "good fences make good neighbors" is probably true. I also see more low class people in the neighborhood that the Correspondent refers to as floaters. I gather that Sulphur Well has had an increase in shiftless families who sell their votes; and, they, or others, as well, are drinking excessively. It was evident to me all my life in Sulphur Well, that certain landlords rented their shacks to families that made life miserable for everyone one else but the landlords. They trespassed on everybody's land, but the landlords. Note that horses and mules were being ridden at night. This doesn't count their half-starved dogs that ranged the neighborhood at all times.

### May 3, 1895

"Mrs Wm Van Winkle, Frankfort, has been visiting her sister, Mrs A K Adcock." p3c2 Adcock is refurnishing his place of business. "The new set of bar furniture bought by Mr A K Adcock ... is the handsomest saloon furniture ever brought to Nicholasville. The fixtures are all of oak .... The mirror to the sideboard is ten feet in length, five in height and is of the finest French plate glass." p3c4

From the *Sulphur Well Correspondent*:

*Mrs Miller is having her house and veranda repaired.*
*Miss Hattie Jones, of Buckeye, was visiting Miss Viola Davis and Miss Emma Spruce, Monday.*
*Mr J P Turner sold a work horse to Henry Graves last week for $80.*
*Mr Wm Hendren after a long and serious illness, was visiting the Well Monday.*
*Mr A M Askins is having a nice plank fence built along the pike in front of his place.*
*Mr J W Baker is in bed with the all prevailing disease, the la grippe.*
*Tilford Watts was thrown from a young horse he was breaking Sunday on the Danville pike and had his leg broken above the ankle and his ankle dislocated.*
*Miss Lilly Bourne, Messrs Ike Dunn, Robt. Jennings and Wm Scott, of Bryantsville, were visiting Miss Emma Spruce on last Sunday.*
*Mr Wm Burton, of Buckeye, Garrard County, was visiting the capital of Jessamine on Saturday last.*
*Mr James Turner sold a nice beef heifer to Mr Tutt for 3 1/2 cts, Monday.*
*Corn planting and hemp sowing is about finished in this locality.*
*Our school house is dressed up in a new spring coat or two of paint. It needs an overcoat still, although the weather is pleasant. p3c4*

It appears that Emma Spruce, third daughter of Miranda Spruce Baker, has come of age! She appears to be the only young lady on the scene at present.

### May 10, 1895

There is a really tough race for the Democratic senatorial nomination coming up involving the incumbent, a congressman, the current governor, and two ex-governors. One issue continues to be the free coinage of silver versus "stable" currency backed by gold.

The United States Circuit Court held that the Riney B has to be sold to pay its debts. It gave preference to the contractors, who have claims of $600,000 plus $100,000 in interest. The bondholders were subordinated to the contractors, which means they will get nothing. The road is to be sold no later than October 1st.

### May 17, 1895

From Keene: "Miss Lizzie Miller, the lovely daughter of Dr J C Miller, of Nicholasville, who has been visiting Miss Irene Lyne, returned home Tuesday." p2c4

May 24, 1895

The income tax has been declared unconstitutional and said to be laid to rest! Don't they wish!

The *Sulphur Well Correspondent* wrote:

*Mrs Media Reynolds is again quite sick.*
*Mrs Emily Peel is on the sick list this week.*
*Mrs Elizabeth Miller has been very ill for several days, from an attack of typho-malarial fever.*
*We have had "blackberry winter" but will not have the fruit thereof.*
*Cut worms are still ravaging the country, but some green things have escaped their notice.*
*Gardens to a great extent will have to be replanted, as none escaped the late frosts and freezes.*
*Some nice fish were caught out of the pond last Saturday. T J Horine landed some newlights weighing two pounds.*
*Mr John Waller was thrown from a young horse last Sunday and somewhat bruised.*
*Morton Stinnett is very sick from gastric irritation.*
*There was a large crowd in attendance at the meeting at Elm Fork, Sunday.*
*Corn fields since the freeze and blighting frosts, look rather scorched and yellow.*
*N D Davis having leased some lands to a mining company, there will probably be commenced very soon mining operations for zinc and lead ore.*
*It would undoubtedly pay some enterprizing company to bore for natural gas that exists at a shallow depth in this locality.*
*A man down at Needsmore has never heard of Trilby! Happy man.*
*At Cottonsburg, Madison County, Mr Ed Cotton died a few days ago, of alcoholism, aged 28 years.*
*Mr Milton Reynolds, of Silver Creek, Madison County, passed through town Monday with nine hogsheads of tobacco for Cincinnati.*
*Born, to the wife of Hugh Miller, Richmond, on the 20th inst., a daughter.*
*Madam Rumor says there will be a wedding at Sulphur Well on next Thursday if nothing happens to prevent.*
*We would venture to suggest as an addition to the famous receipe of "how to cook a husband" --that you first catch your husband, etc.*
*The gold bugs and silver insects are not disturbing the calm serenity of the people in this neighborhood, but the cut worms receive their undivided attention. p2c2*

The last item is a clear indication that the people are more concerned about local than national issues. Cutworms are easy to understand and affect you directly. The free coinage of silver issue is complex, and has indeterminate effects. Trivia: In case you wondered what the man from Needsmore didn't know about Trilby, it's a soft felt hat, with a deeply creased crown, very British. The "wife of Hugh Miller" is Addie Hendren, daughter of Dr and Mrs George M Hendren of Sulphur Well. Their little daughter's name was Alma. According to Sageser Genelogy she retired as a school teacher, died about 1974 without ever marrying. There has been a lot of sickness in the community this year, Mrs Miller among many others.

May 31, 1895

There is quite a good article concerning toll roads, the law, rates, etc. For example, the toll was two cents per head of cattle, ten cents for each vehicle drawn by one horse. p1c3-5

The *Sulphur Well Correspondent* writes:

*Dr J H Perkins, of Edenton, was on a visit to the Well this week.*
*A good deal of tobacco is being shipped to market at 4c.*
*An election will be held Saturday to raise school funds and to select a trustee.*
*The wheat crop is not in as bad condition as it was supposed to be a few days ago.*
*Mrs Miller, who has been sick for some time, is slowly improving.*
*Mr Alex Dean sold to A C Miles 15 head of hogs averaging about 200 pounds at 4c.*
*Mr Geo. W Lowry, who lives near Mr Lebanon, about three weeks ago found what is supposed to be a mad stone; on the farm of Dr Jno. C Miller. The stone is light grayish in color, under a magnifying glass, extremely porous and light in weight; less than 1/2 ounce, and is 3/4 inches thick, 1 7/8 wide, and 1 3/4 long. It is doubtless a valuable find, if a genuine madstone. I understand he has had several tempting offers for it already.*
*Mr Pat Co-----ter, visited his parents here for several days last week.*
*Mr Adolph Kaufman has gone to Cincinnati to spend a few days with his parents.*
*Will Corrigan sold a horse last Saturday to Frank Schuler, Lexington, for $95.*
*Miss Maggie Lane is visiting the Misses Hunter, Nicholasville, this week.*
*Mr Sam Preston, Louisville, is visiting friends and relatives here this week.*
*Mr L Stull has completed his new residence at this place and moved in Saturday.*
*Poor & Embry sold 600 cattle to Nelson Morris, Chicago, and will ship 300 of them the latter part of this week.*
*Distillery No 3 will close down June 15. No 15 will run until about the first of July.*
*Born, to the wife of Humphrey Walters, on the 18th inst., a daughter.*
*Mr John Rolan, Mrs Sallie Kaufman and Miss Alta Boner attended the meeting at Wilmore Sunday.*
*The cut worm has about dried up and what they did not kill the frost ruined.*
*Richard Temple caught twenty-five pounds of very nice fish at this place Thursday.*
*Fred Knight is making a race for school trustee and his platform is low tariff and the free and unlimited coinage of silver. Mr Louis Clark is also a candidate and in favor of free turnpikes.*
*Miss Addie Martin's school closed last week with a very entertaining program. The songs and recitations by the pupils received high praise from those present, and all the patrons expressed themselves well pleased with Miss Martin and predict for her a bright future.*
p2c2-3

The Correspondent seems to be poking fun at the candidates for the school board. The tariff and silver questions are national issues, and free turnpikes a state and county issue. It could be Dumb and Dumber in the race. I was also interested in his description of the madstone. Over the years I have read how it was used. My recollection is that the stone is placed over the wound made by a hydrophobic animal. If it adhers then the "poison" is drawn from the wound, and there would be no ill effects. I will try to do some research on this. I must say that the Correspondent is naming names of people an families than I have never heard of ever being in Sulphur Well. Just for example, in this letter, Adolph Kaufman, Will Corrigan, Maggie Lane, L Stull, John Rolan, Sallie Kaufman, Alta Boner, and Richard Temple certainly didn't leave any footprints, or decendants either!

June 7, 1895

Rev W C Taylor's baccalaureate sermon at the Jessamine Institute: "Paul's life was often painful and sad, but he rejoiced in it because he felt that God was using him for great purposes of grace and was daily writing out lessons in his life that the world would read and in reading understand eternal truth better...." p1c3

"The scholars in Prof Rice Miller's room were given an outing at Brooklyn Saturday. The lads and lassies had a gala day of it." p3c1

June 14, 1895

From New York: "Thin dresses are usually made over a drop skirt sewn in with the material and in the most expensive, it is of tafeta silk." p1c5

June 21, 1895

Another of several recent articles about free turnpikes: The writer argues for toll roads. He said that no more roads would be built if they were free, and present roads would not be maintained. p1c3

A few Kentuckians are getting in the spirit of the silver question. They proposed a resolution that said that it was the "sense of the Bell County Democrats" that the Federal Government "open a silver mine in every county in the State of Kentucky, not more than two miles from the county seat, and handy to wood and water." p2c1

Childhood diseases sometimes struck families hard: "Mrs Martha Eaves has buried within five months, three children." p3c1

The *Sulphur Well Correspondent* writes:

*The light rain last Saturday only intensified the dryness.*
*Mrs Sudie Richardson, of Irvine, is visiting her mother, Mrs Miller.*
*Mrs Fanny Bundle, of Harrodsburg, is visiting her sister, Mrs N D Davis.*
*Mrs Alex M Askins was quite sick last week of pneumonia.*
*Mrs Hugh Miller, of Richmond, is visiting her father, Dr G M Hendren, this week.*
*Circuit Court has raised the price of pills, and also raised the doctors in their own estimation.*
*Sam Askins has bought the lot on which the school house was burned last year.*
*Hay harvest is in full blast this week. Wheat harvest will soon be on.*
*J H Murphy now drives around in a brand new buggy.*
*W McClellan Johnston, of Lancaster, is on a visit to Mr J H Hare.*
*Mrs Wilson Masters, a few days ago fell in the cellar and severely injured herself.*

*Mr G S Watkins, of Mercer, visited friends in Jessamine. p3c4*

I don't think the property Sam Askins bought was the school property. I would guess it was the Grimes house that burned earlier. It is just up from the general store, near the first turn going to Nicholasville. He had his carpentry shop down on the road, and his house near the crest of the hill. His garden and orchard were behind the house. I'd say there was about three acres in the lot. The "new" school, the one my parents attended, was next to the Christian Church. It is now a residence. The old log school was behind the new one.

Note that the following date is 1995. Compare the humor in this story with that of 1895. This story is from the Greensville, Ky. Leader-News, June 21, 1995:

> Paul Jarvis usually raises a good crop of potatoes, and I usually buy a bushel or two from him when the price is right. However, this year I may get my 'taters elsewhere.
>
> You see, last year I was running short and I stopped by Paul's place to inquire about the price of his spuds.
>
> "Five bucks a bushel", he said without even looking up.
>
> "Five dollars!?" I echoed, "why, I can get them from your neighbor for $3 a bushel", I protested.
>
> "Well", Paul came back, "why don't you go over there and get your 'taters then? That's a good price."
>
> He had me dead to rights--and he knew it.
>
> "Can't Paul", I told him, "he ain't got none left."
>
> "Ain't got none left, and he's getting three bucks a bushel," Paul shot back with a little grin.
>
> "He's robbing you. Why, man, when I ain't got none left, I just get $2 a bushel for 'em".

June 28, 1895

State Democrats are split on the silver and gold question.

The High Bridge Camp grounds have been improved, and three new cottages added. The railroad has offered an excursion rate for July 4th, of fifty cents for a round trip from Nicholasville. You can get "the best dinner in the country" there for 25 cents. p3c3

> Miller-Reynolds.--Married in Lexington, Tuesday afternoon, June 25, Dr J C Miller and Miss Emma Reynolds, Rev C F Oney officiating. The bridegroom is one of Jessamine's most prominent physicians and citizens, and commands the respect of everyone. The bride is the sister of Mrs T J Horine, Ambrose, and a lady of excellent character. Dr Miller and bride returned Tuesday evening and were driven to his home in the country. p3c3

Evidently, Miss Emma wasn't any "spring chicken". According to <u>Sageser Genealogy</u> (59) she was born in 1850, making her 45 at the time of marriage. The couple had no children. It is said she attended Science Hill School, at Shelbyville, a very exclusive school for girls. She died in 1940 and was buried on the O P Reynolds' lot in Maple Grove Cemetery.

The paper is again in tatters, and the letter is not complete, but the *Sulphur Well Correspondent* writes:

*The abundance of rain in the last few days was a God-send to the farmers.*
*Mrs Hugh Miller, of near Richmond, who has been on a visit to her parents here, returned home Saturday.*
*Wheat harvest is in full blast and the crop throughout this section will be far better than anticipated. p2c4*

Fortunately, we have had many long, and complete letters from the Correspondent so far this year, and have a very good picture of Sulphur Well in 1895.

July 5, 1895

The turnpike issue is joined again this week. This writer is for free roads. He says that it costs about two cents per mile to travel by tollroad. p1c3

Gen Watt Hardin is the Democratic nominee for governor. The old military men sure know how to squeeze the lemon! Governor Brown has withdrawn his name from the senatorial race. The State Democratic Platform: Applauds the repeal of the McKinley tariff; condemns the effort to create a distinction between people of different faiths; supports the national party; proclaims that under Democratic rule, the state has lowered bonded indebtedness, doubled support for charitable institutions, decreased the rate of taxation, increased support for common schools, and more. p2c1

Victor Bloomfield has purchased the clothing business of B L Cook. His headquarters are in Cincinnati, and he has interests in stores in Winchester and Midway. H W Rose is closing out his stock of clothing in the next thirty days. The Lexington clothiers advertise in the <u>Journal</u> every week. The competition was fierce! My grandfather was in this dog eat dog arena in the firm of Murphy and Miller.

Quite a social occasion! Col Bennett H Young, a successful Jessamine countian and railroad official who was often mentioned for governor, married Miss Eliza Sharp in Bardstown. He took about seventy of his friends from Jessamine on a private car. After the ceremony they came back to Nicholasville, and the next morning the couple proceeded on to New York on a private car furnished by the president of the B & O Railroad. "On July 6th they set sail for Europe to remain until fall." p3c2

The High Bridge Camp Meeting runs from July 12th to the 29th, covering three Sundays.

July 12, 1895

Sheep-killing dogs are so bad in Madison County that farmers have to set up nights with shotguns to guard their flocks. p2c4

July 19, 1895

Interest has revived in the old vineyard that I described several years ago. It is placed on the right bank of the Kentucky River about five miles above the mouth of Hickman Creek, on the farm now owned by George McQuerry. They say that portions of the old stone wall surrounding the vineyard can still be seen (in 1895). Grapes and vines drifted down the river two or three miles and transplanted themselves in loam soil on the opposite bank and are still producing excellent fruit (in 1895). p2c4

A poll of editors around the state on the money issue: for free silver, Democrats 13, Republicans 1, Independents 9; for the gold standard, Democrats 34, Republicans 8, Independents 18. It appears that the preponderance of Kentuckians of all political persuasion are opposed to free silver. p2c1 The *Journal* has contended for some time that the question has no business in state politics.

The *Sulphur Well Correspondent* writes:

*The rains came just when needed the most.*
*The growing corn crop looks remarkably well in this locality.*
*Prof Joseph Deboe has been teaching in the neighborhood of Sanders.*
*Some fine fish are being caught in Kentucky River.*
*Mr Giles Saunders, of Garrard, is complaining from an aggravated case of eczema.*
*Threshing is temporarily suspended on account of the rains.*
*Mr Warner and Miss Hill, of Garrard, were on a visit to N D Davis last Sunday.*
*C M Davis will teach the Sulphur Well school, commencing after the Teachers' Institute. Mr Thompson, of Wilmore, will teach the Sageser district school.*
*Mr Jason Tudor, of Cottonburg, has been visiting relatives in this section.*
*The hay crop is short and hay will undoubtedly be very scarce and high.*
*Mr Warner, of Buckeye, was on a visit to friends here last week.*
*Mrs Mahala Miller, who is 93 years old, is very ill with heart trouble.*
*Mrs T J Horine, who has been on the sick list, is out again.*
*Mr Andrew J Smith and family, of Huntington, W. Va., are visiting relatives here.*
*Bro. Finley, who preaches here once a month, goes on a visit to his old home in Alabama this week.*
*About all the tobacco raised in this vicinity has been sold at a low price.*
*There are no free silverites in this community, for every one has to work for all the silver he gets.*
*Miss Mattie Shearer is visiting friends and relatives in Lewisburg, Tenn. She will be gone a month or so.*
*Our little village puts on a hustling appearance at this season of the year as we have enough machines to thresh all the wheat in the county.*

*The preparation of the mining company for extending their mining operations goes rapidly forward and it is to be hoped that they will meet with the full measure of success that they undoubtedly deserve.*

*Mr J Howard Murphy is extensively improving his residence here, and when completed, will present a handsome appearance.*

*Tobacco raisers in this section, which by the way raises considerable of the weed, are putting forth every exertion to have a good crop, and it is to be hoped that they will succeed.*

*Last Sunday morning a gang of negro men, women and children created pandemonium for several hours in the village by singing and yelling as they went down the public highways. -------- appeared to think that the white people have no right to peace and quietude,-------- they were bound to, in any way respect. It was altogether --------- and inexcusable tumult which should not be repeated "very often".*

*The greatest present need of Sulphur Well is the improvement of the well. Its present condition is a shame and disgrace to the people of this place, and they should have pride enough in their pretty village and famous watering place to at least put the pump in a presentable and respectable appearance.*

*Mr Franklin M Hudson, who ten days ago fell into a sixteen foot well he was digging at his residence on Hickman Creek and injured himself severely on the head, after lingering in a precarious, and most of the time in an unconscious condition, is in a fair way to recovery, should no unfavorable symptoms arise which his physician thinks is now not likely to occur.*
*p2c2-3*

This last item is a "German" sentence, full of clauses. The Correspondent also returns to his call for repair of the pump and appeals to community pride. It is not clear who the negroes were, or where they were bound. I am unaware of any racial problems in Sulphur Well. George Ware told me that the improvements to Murphy's house involved building a new front, adding the long veranda on the north-east side, and moving a part of the old structure to a new site further back on the farm. He said that plumbing was installed and a system of cisterns and gutters added to the barn and house so as to supply the water.

Here is another article penned by the *Sulphur Well Correspondent*. The paper is in such disarray that the date is indeterminant, but could be July 19th. In any case the item pertaining to F M Hudson follows an item in the previous article:

*Mr W Walker has painted his dwelling a beautiful red color.*
*Miss Duncan, of Nicholasville, was visiting at J T West's this week.*
*F M Hudson is rapidly recovering from his dangerous fall into a well.*
*Miss Mollie Burton, of Buckeye, is visiting Dr G M Hendren, this week.*
*Our postmaster is selling 13 two-cent postage stamps for a cent and a quarter.*
*Mr Forest Stapp, of Garrard, was visiting here last Saturday and Sunday.*
*A son of S N Underwood is down with typhoid fever, but improving slowly.*
*A large crowd from this place attended High Bridge camp meeting, Sunday.*
*Miss Hattie Jones and Miss Lilly Bourne of Garrard, are visiting friends here this week.*
*The urbane advertising manager of The Argonaut, Lexington, Mr Louis Pilcher, called on us last Saturday.*
*Mr Forest Stapp and Miss Mollie Burton, together with quite a party of Garrard and Jessamine youngsters, drove through from here to camp meeting Sunday.*

*There are a few chicken thieves and all-around rogues in this community who ought to be exterminated. They are well-known and the people have put up with them long enough.*
*When a man starts down hill every one seems ready to accelerate his downward course, but let him start upward and every hand is stretched forth to pull him back.*
*The picnic at Chalybeate Springs, Saturday, was a grand success, some (one) thousand people from surrounding counties attending. Bros. Snively, Adcock and others addressed the Sunday School children. p2c6*

The Correspondent is clearly fed up with the petty thievery and general nuisance of some low-down people in the neighborhood. In something of a contradiction he seems to be somewhat cynical about the people's willingness to help others when they are down. There must have been quite a turnout of people from this area at the Camp Meeting and at the picnic at the springs near Little Hickman. Think about the stamps and see if you get the joke. Answer in a few weeks!

July 26, 1895

The paper continues to be in tatters, and the way it has been photographed makes it difficult to even tell for sure which page you are on. Nevertheless, the *Sulphur Well Correspondent* writes:

*(The first part is missing)*
*Miss Mary Hendren, of this place, is on a visit for a couple of weeks to her sister, Mrs Miller, of Richmond.*
*Those who have been holding their tobacco for a raise, sold too soon at last, as 6c tobacco two months ago is now worth 12 to 15c.*
*Mrs Elizabeth Miller, of this place, who has been quite seriously sick for some weeks with typho-malarial fever, is well enough to make a visit to her children at Irvine this week.*
*Dr G M Hendren, who has been quite sick for some time and an invalid for a month, is again able to be out, but not as yet able to attend to his practice. He will go to Estill this week.*
*Notwithstanding the backwardness of the season, the following dry weather and the unprecedented army of cut worms this season, the good price of tobacco that has for some weeks prevailed, has stimulated tobacco growers to their utmost to put in a good crop and to work against adverse circumstances in doing so.*
*There can be no better indication of the enterprise and progressiveness of our citizens than the preparations for improvements now going on upon every hand. Each property owner seems to try to make his place the nicest in town. p2c4*

This last item seem to be summarizing improvements he has mentioned previously. I suppose if he could get the pump fixed he would be happy. Mary Hendren is the daughter of Dr G M Hendren. She is visiting her sister that married Hugh Miller. Dr Hendren is probably convalescing at Estill Springs. It appears that the price of tobacco has stimulated the farmers and given the Correspondent a more optimistic outlook.

August 2, 1895

"Prof Rice Miller has been appointed principal of the Campbellville High School at a nice salary. He is one of Jessamine's most worthy young men and a splendid teacher." p3c1

"Mr Chas. Brown and sister, Miss Lettie, are visiting the family of A K Adcock." p3c2 The Browns are from Knoxville. This is the Lettie Brown whom Scottie Hendren visited in 1894 and the Chas Brown who asked her to marry him.

The *Sulphur Well Correspondent* writes:

*Mr John Saunders, of Garrard, was visiting friends here this week.*
*An infant of Mr John Fathergill died from bowel affection last Sunday.*
*Mrs Miller is improving her place very much by having it painted white.*
*Miss Flemming and Miss Haydon, Lexington, are visiting Mr J H Easley.*
*Mr D Switzer has been very ill for some days with a complicated bronchial trouble.*
*The recent heavy rains have damaged, by washing out, the pikes and dirt roads considerably.*
*Miller Hawkins, an educated and respectable young colored man, having died of tuberculosis, was buried here Tuesday.*
*The Peel boys have rented the farm now occupied by J H Easley and will remove to it and cultivate the land next year.*
*Married on the 25th ult., at the residence of the bride's parents, Miss Mary Jane Stinnett and Mr Alexander Campbell Reynolds.*
*James Wood discovered swimming leisurely around in his pond, a large fish, about (?) feet long. It has also been seen at other times by different ones.*
*All growing crops look exceedingly well since the wet spell set in. The corn crop will doubtless be exceptionally heavy, if the favorable weather continues a few weeks longer.*
*Mr Ricketts Baker, son of Mr J Wilson Baker, in cleaning a loaded pistol the other day, accidently shot himself in the region of the left knee joint, making a bad wound. The ball which was imbeded deeply in the tissues and tendons of the knee cap was extracted by Drs Mann and Hendren. p2c2*

August 9, 1895

"Immigration becoming alarming. From July 1, 1894 to April 1 of the present year ... 140,980 immigrants came into this country." p1c5 The writer compared the influx to the Gauls sweeping down on Rome. It also sounds like the contempory "invasion" of the illegals into the US right now!

Hughes & Adcock's "Judith" has developed into quite a sprinter. She won at Oakley last Friday, doing three quarters of a mile in 1:14 3/4. p2c3

H C Rodenbaugh, horseman and hotelier, was fatally shot by a drunken guest at the Hotel Woodford. His only son was shot and killed also during the same argument. p3c3

August 16, 1895

Texie still lives! "Mrs Tom Cooley returned to her home at Omaha, Neb., Monday, after several weeks visit to her parents and other relatives." p3c3

Here is another tragic-comic story typifying life. Miss Mary Tate, described as a petite blond, about 20, who lives in Lexington, has been visiting her uncle who lives in Logana. For the past week or more, Monroe Faddis, aged 18, has been visiting Mary. They fell in love, and the girl, knowing her father would object, decided to elope. The Faddis family accompanied the two to the county clerk's office to get the licence. They presented the clerk with a note ostensibly signed by her father giving his permission. Unfortunately, it was not witnessed, so the clerk refused to accept it. Mary then gave an affidavit that she was 21, and the licence was issued. The party then proceeded to Judge Phillips to perform the ceremony. In the meantime, the uncle grew suspicious, and sent word to the father that "something was up". He immediately jumped in his buggy and flew toward Logana. He met the wedding party two miles out of Nicholasville on the Sulphur Well Road. "Halting the party, he wasted no words, but drew his pistol...", and ordered Mary into his buggy. She complied, and he warned "young Faddis that under no circumstances should his daughter ever live with him." Tate then drove back to Lexington, and Faddis returned to Nicholasville and swore out a warrant for Tate's arrest for carrying a concealed weapon, and breach of peace. An officer was then sent to Lexington to arrest Tate, which was done, and returned him to Nicholasville. Tate later came before Judge Phillips, who fined him $25 and sentenced him to ten days in jail for carrying a concealed weapon, and $25 for breach of peace. Both will be appealed. Tate is threatening that he will sue Faddis for forging his name to the note. p3c3 This probably isn't the end of this sad story, but it is all we will ever know about it.

There seems to be an epidemic of typhoid fever. There are six deaths in this week's paper, and four of them listed the cause of death as typhoid fever. One, a young girl of fifteen, Dora Tipton, died without any visitation by anyone in the community, and "no one was present but the undertaker to lay out the body." p3c3-4

August 23, 1895

The opening debate between Gen Hardin and Col Bradley occurred in Louisville last Monday night. Hardin embarrassed the Democrats by not standing on the party platform pertaining to the silver question, instead making his "own personal construction of it." p2c1 The editor again says it's not a state issue, so everyone should stand with the party. One of the debates between the candidates is to be held in Nicholasville on September 8th.

The *Sulphur Well Correspondent* writes:

*Mrs Williams and little son, of Richmond, are visiting Mr Geo W Turpin.*
*An infant of Isaac Taylor, colored, died Tuesday, of whooping-cough and pneumonia.*
*Mr W B Walker was taken suddenly ill early Friday morning with cholera morbus.*
*Mr F M Hudson, who had apparently recovered from his fall into a well and suffered a relapse from exposure to the hot sun, is improving.*
*The little son of S N Underwood, who has been down with typhoid fever for several weeks is still very low, but hopes are entertained for his recovery.*
*Mrs Anna Fain was taken suddenly ill Sunday morning and is still very sick.*
*The meetings at Mt Pleasant Church are still in progress, with considerable interest manifested.*
*A protracted meeting has commenced at the Elm Fork Christian Church, conducted by Elder Adcock.*
*Mr W L Neal is visiting his uncle, Louis Neal, of this vicinity.*
*Our preacher, Bro. Finley, being away on a visit to his home in Alabama, his place was supplied last Sunday by Bro. Payne, of Athens.*
*With paint and white-wash, Sulphur Well presents a cleaner appearance than it has hitherto for many a day. It now begins to look like some new western village.* p2c3

I wonder why the Correspondent compared the newly renovated area to "some new western village". I don't believe that Sulphur Well ever looked anything like any village west of the Mississippi. Sulphur Well is a valley or perhaps two converging valleys with a meandering stream, and roads forming a "T" intersection. Most of the houses sit somewhere on the surrounding hills, and a very few buildings are in the valley itself. The theme of the Correspondent in recent letters has been the prevalence of illness, the importance of religion, visitations, and property improvements.

August 30, 1895

The changing technology has affected the market for mules. During the eighties, many farmers were breeding mules very profitably, and selling them for around $100. At Cynthiana on Monday mule colts sold at $5 to $25. p2c3

The Hendren family was visiting: "Mrs W H VanWinkle has returned to her home at Frankfort, after spending a few weeks with her sister, Mrs A K Adcock." p3c2 "Miss Lettie Brown, of Knoxville, Tenn., after a visit of several weeks to her friend, Miss Scottie Hendren, has returned home." p3c2 I feel sure that Scottie is still living with the Adcocks in Nicholasville, so I guess that she, her sister Lizzie VanWinkle, and Lettie Brown were all together with sister Addie Adcock.

The Millers were equally, or more, active: "Mr Chas. W. Miller, of Irvine, who graduated at Centre last June, will leave for Harvard College early in September, to take a post-graduate course, after which he will enter the profession of law or medicine." p3c3 This is Mann Miller's son, Charles Wallace Miller, who chose law as his profession.

Prof Rice Miller left Wednesday for Campbellsville to assume the principalship of the graded school at that place. Prof Miller is one of the best qualified teachers that has ever taught in the city school at Nicholasville, holding a first-class certificate and being well adapted to his profession. The <u>Journal</u> can highly commend him to the people of Campbellsville, not only as a good educator but a gentleman of excellent moral character. p3c3

Charles Wallace Miller and Rice Miller are first cousins, their respective fathers, Mann Miller and Dr John C Miller, being sons of Merriman and Celia Miller.

Before Rice went away he enjoyed a social outing which was also attended by his sister, Lizzie. "The Misses Holloway and Mrs Ida Shaw entertained with a house party from Thursday until Monday...." There was music and dancing every evening, and "many visitors added to the enjoyment." p3c3

The following appeared under the heading of "Matrimonial":

To Wed.-Rumor has it one of our society young men living near this city, will soon wed a very pretty young lady visitor, and that the pair will live in a southern Kentucky town. The young lady in question, resides in one of Kentucky's most important cities, and the young man leaves Nicholasville the first of September to take charge of an institution that he is especially fitted by education to assume the care of. p3c4

This couldn't fit any one but Rice Miller. There is no indication who the young lady may be, although she must be from Lexington.

The *Sulphur Well Correspondent* writes:

*Rev. J A Sawyer was visiting Mrs Elizabeth Miller here on last Monday.*
*Mrs Milton Price is very ill from a complication of troubles.*
*Mr and Mrs Walter Brumfield were visiting friends and relatives here on last Sunday.*
*Mrs Harry True of Mt Lebanon neighborhood, is seriously ill from puerperal septicema.*
*Mr J Howard Murphy, being indisposed, will visit Linietta Springs this week.*
*Mr Moses Reynolds, who has been confined to his bed for a year with tuberculosis of the lungs, is some better this week.*
*Miss May Taylor, Lexington, who has been visiting Miss Dora Murphy, returned home yesterday.*
*Miss Edna Grinstead, of Millersburg, is visiting her sister, Mrs James S Saunders.*
*Mrs Wm Hudson, of the Little Hickman Creek neighborhood, is on the sick list.*
*There is an abundance of sickness in this section and the surrounding country.*
*Mr J Holly Easley has rented the old Carter farm and will move to it some time this fall.*
*Bros Adcock and Smith are conducting a very successful meeting at the Christian Church at Little Hickman.*
*Mr S N Underwood's son, Arthur, who has been extremely ill with typhoid fever, complicated with heart trouble for nine weeks, is convalescing.*

*Married, on Thursday, August 29th, at the home of the bride's mother, Mr Sam Taylor and Miss Bertha Harris, all of Jessamine County. Congratulations my young friends, and may your pathway through life be strewn with flowers.*

*Come my friends of Sulphur Well and repair your public well, and don't let it be a shame and reproach any longer. The citizens are a liberal, generous and kind hearted people, and should show their enterprise. p2c3*

The litany of illness continues! Mrs True is suffering from complications of childbirth. Infectuous and communicable diseases such as typhoid and tuberculosis were serious problems for the medical profession of that day. The Correspondent uses medical terms with ease.

September 6, 1895

According to the <u>Interior Journal</u> of Stanford there has been 48 murders committed in the state since January 1st. The editor says that it is no wonder that there has been so much grief because their loved ones were felled "by murderer's bullet." He goes on to say that the laws are in place if only they were followed: "...quit bribing your judges and juries, and see the law carried out fairly...." p1c6

The Jessamine Institute has the best of music teachers. Their previous teacher returned to Switzerland to work on his doctorate. His replacement is from Germany. She is Miss Martha Burnmeister, a native of Hamburg. "She performs with ease, and artistic skill, the most difficult pieces of the old masters as well as of modern composers." p3c2

The debate between Hardin and Bradley was called off, but Hardin spoke at the court house anyway.

J Wilson Baker, who five years ago married Miranda Spruce, died at the age of 61 at his home near Sulphur Well. The funeral took place at the residence and he was buried in the cemetery on the home place. p3c5-6 The home place is next to the Miller farm on the Hoover Pike.

The *Sulphur Well Correspondent* writes:

*Mrs Wm Lee Fain is down with fever.*
*Mrs Geo W Diamond is visiting at Mr J P Turner's this week.*
*Mrs Geo W Gray, Lexington, is visiting at Mr Jno T West's.*
*Mr Richard Burton, of Buckeye, was visiting Jessamine, Tuesday.*
*Mr W H Hare's son, Willie, is said to be still in a very critical condition.*
*Stock water and cisterns are getting very low and the grass is burning up for want of rain.*
*Miss Emma Spruce has returned from a several days visit with friends in Garrard.*
*A daughter of Mr McKey Peel is visiting her grandmother, Mrs Emily Peel.*
*It is reported that another one of W H Hare's family, Miss Annie, is down with typhoid fever.*
*The thresher of Walker & Cobb broke down in the middle of the pike Monday and was only removed after borrowing another axle and considerable delay.*

*Several persons have called on our postmaster for thirteen two cent stamps for one cent and a quarter. They were disappointed and chagrined to find that the quarter was 25c.*

*The melon-colic days have come,*
*The saddest of the year,*
*And old C Morbus' lurking 'round*
*The country too, we hear.* p2c3

The Correspondent is pretty happy at his wit in catching people on the stamps. He has returned to rhyme to express himself. In the third line of the rhyme the "C" stands for cholera, and while I don't know the difference between the various terms, I gather he is saying that too many mellons may cause diarrhea. I also note that Mrs Gray, mother of Textie and Ida, is visiting the neighborhood after being aways for several years.

September 13, 1895

"New fall and winter goods are characterized by rough effects in weaving, and close, indistinct mixtures of color." p1c5

September 20, 1895

Another really good article on Camp Nelson and Camp Dick Robinson is in this issue of the Journal. p1

Sittie Bell must be back in town. "The Rev Geo W Bell, Los Animas, Col, preached a fine sermon at Troy Sunday night to a fine congregation." p3c4 I wonder if they are going to get a local church and relocate?

"Rev H G Turner leaves tomorrow for Vanderbilt University, Nashville, Tenn., where he will resume his theological studies." p3c2 This is one of the sons of J P Turner that owns the farm, east of Sulphur Well.

The James Sageser sale was held last Saturday at Sulphur Well. Some horses and mules were sold. p2c3 This is the father of Andrew and Oscar Sageser.

Another sale, the personal property of J Wilson Baker, is being held on September 24th. His farm is located adjacent to the old Miller Farm on what is now called the Hoover Pike. Snowden Lane separates the two farms. It was called the Hanly and Sulphur Well Turnpike then. Being offered in the sale are: "seven head of well bred trotting horses", mules, a bull, several hogs, two milk cows, a surrey, buggy, farming implements, both stored and growing grain and hay, and household and kitchen furniture." p2c4

Miss Viola Million, Richmond, spent Saturday and Sunday at Ambrose, the guest of Miss Dora Murphy. p3c2

"Miss Nannie Hare, daughter of W H Hare, Ambrose, is very ill of typhoid fever, while her sister, Miss Bettie, is also threatened with the same malady." p3c2 Here is an obituary:

Hare.-Willie, son of Mr and Mrs W H Hare, Ambrose, died on the 12th inst., of locked bowels, the result of an attack of flux about seven weeks ago. The deceased was brother of Mrs B D Spears, Nicholasville, and a bright, promising lad. Owning to illness in the family there were no services at home or church. The remains were brought to Nicholasville, Saturday afternoon and interred in Maple Grove Cemetery, after a short prayer at the grave by Elder V W Dorris. p3c4

The *Sulphur Well Correspondent* wrote:

*We are needing rain badly as grass is burning up and water getting scarce.*
*W M Hendren, Speedwell, is visiting friends in the neighborhood.*
*Dr T T Davis, of Marion, Kansas, is visiting relatives and friends here.*
*Mr R B Hendren has returned from a sojourn in Kansas.*
*Quite a crowd of Madison's citizens were over last Monday.*
*The watermelon trade seems to continue quite brisk.*
*Some corn is being cut this week, the hot, dry weather maturing it rapidly.*
*Considerable more intoxicating was observable on the roads from court Monday than usual, but we are glad to say that few of them were Jessaminites.*
*Elder John F Rowe, editor of the Christian Leader, Cincinnati, will preach here next Saturday night and Sunday morning on his return home from a southern trip.*
*The interesting protracted meeting that closed here Sunday night with 25 additions, was conducted by Elders Finley and Smith, two young and vigorous preachers who give much promise of future usefulness in the cause of christianity, and we hope their efforts will be crowned with equal success wherever they may be called to labor.* p2c3

## September 27, 1895

Mr and Mrs A K Adcock spent a few days in Cincinnati this week. p3c2 "Miss Laura Hendren, Atlanta, Ill., is the guest of her cousin, Mrs A K Adcock." p3c2

"Miss Nannie Hare, Sulphur Well, is still quite ill, and great fear is entertained of her recovery." p3c2

Rice Miller is pleased with his new school! He says: "I have a fine school; large, substantial, two-story brick building, campus of thirty-nine acres of woodland and a beautiful location; four teachers now, and shall add another soon." p3c4

## October 4, 1895

"Miss Viola Davis, Ambrose, is visiting Miss Sallie Warner, Louisville." P3c2

October 11, 1895

The Democrats are writhing over Hardin's free silver policy while the party supports "sound money". p1c3 Col Bradley is making that the chief issue in his campaign. p2c1 He spoke in Nicholasville at the court house to a good crowd. p3c4

Pratt Neal writes back to his mother from Jamaica. He went there with a shipment of horses from Kentucky to be used in the construction of a railroad. He describes the terrain and weather, and the abundance of fruit. He says they go bathing in the sea quite frequently. p1c5-6

"Prof Rice Miller, of Campbellsville, spent Friday and Saturday with the `home folks'." p3c2

"Born-To the wife of County Attorney W McC. Johnston, Lancaster, a pretty eight-pound girl who has been christened Mayme Higginbotham." p3c3 The mother was Mayme Hare of Sulphur Well.

October 18, 1895

The ladies of the Acme Club of Nicholasville have chosen to study German history and literature for their winter program. p1c3

"Garrett Davis left for the Queen City Monday and says he will put in a car load of eye-poppers for the boys." Murphy and Miller. p3c1 "Messrs J H Murphy and Garrett Davis have been in Cincinnati this week on business." p3c2

"Mrs W H VanWinkle, of Frankfort, is the guest of Mrs A K Adcock." p3c2

The *Sulphur Well Correspondent*, who has been absent for a few weeks is back again with a long letter, including items about the Millers:

*Mrs Elizabeth Miller has been very ill for several weeks with liver trouble.*
*Mr A M Askins is on the invalid list this week.*
*Elder A M Finley preached here on last Lord's day and at night.*
*Mr Luther Ware is down with a severe attack of typhoid fever.*
*The excessively dry weather is very productive of fever and general diseases.*
*Born, to the wife of Squire Miller, a son.*
*Mrs Eliza West, mother of Mr Jno T West, fell from the porch a few days ago, injuring herself severely.*
*Mrs Mary Taylor has taken up her residence with Mrs Elizabeth Miller.*
*Mr Russell Woodward, an old and respected citizen of Little Hickman, died on the 13th inst.*
*The cool nights and warm days are very prolific of colds and malaria.*
*Mr W H Hare's daughters, who have been sick for some time, are reported better.*
*Mr C M Davis, who was sick for some days with a severe attack of stomatitis, is again able to continue his school.*
*Mr J P Turner has bought a portion of the Chrisman farm from Wm Hendren.*

*It is reported that we will soon have another merchantile establishment at Sulphur Well.*
*Mr John Miller, of Irvine, who has been visiting his mother here, returned home this week.*
*Mrs Sudie Richardson, of Estill County, is visiting her mother, Mrs Frank Miller.*
*Mr John Brock has taken up his residence in the late residence of Elder Benjamin Goggins.*
*Water, water! is the cry, and everything is yet quite dry.*
*Mr John Scott, son of Dr Scott, of Estill County, was visiting in the village recently.*
*Mr Ezekiel Vincent, of Madison, was visiting James Hendren, this week.*
*Dr Hendren is having his residence repaired; we hope others will catch the needed repairing infection.*
*Mr G S Watkins, the Mercer painter, will locate here soon to follow his trade.*
*Mr F M Horine sold a nice bunch of shoats Monday to Nicholasville butchers at 3 1/2cts.*
*The corn crop is splendid throughout this section of the county, but no price has as yet been established.*
*On dit, that there will be a wedding soon here, and a surprise at that, but old "on dit" is very unreliable at all times.*
*As the sulphur water of our beautiful village and handsome pump contains no microbes, it is a good time to drink the water and be healthy.*
*The creeks, branches, springs and almost all sources of water supply are dry as dust; what the people are to do for water if it does not rain soon, is a puzzling question.*
*Elder John F Rowe, editor of the Christian Leader, Cincinnati, will commence a protracted meeting here on the Saturday night before the second Sunday in November. p3c6-7*

There are some related items in the letter above. First, Mrs Elizabeth Miller has been sick, and it appears that Mrs Taylor is going to stay with her, to help out. Mrs Miller's children, John and Sudie, have come to look in on her. Second, Luther Ware, my grandfather, was staying with Alex Askins, and they are both sick, Luther with typhoid fever. The daughters of Mrs Hare, who recently lost her son, are recovering from typhoid fever. The Correspondent blames the cool nights, warm days, and dry weather for illnesses such as fever, colds, and malaria. I don't know whether there is any scientific basis for such an assumption or not. However, the Correspondent also claims that the water from the village well is microbe free. He apparently prevailed upon the locals and got the pump replaced; he now says that it is handsome! The Correspondent uses a French phrase *On dit* in one of the above items, meaning "They say". A little pretentious perhaps. Russell Woodward, age 85, who lived at Pink, was buried in the Harrison Dean Cemetery.

October 25, 1895

The editor hates a turncoat! Cassius M Clay, who the editor says might well have been the nominee for governor himself in four years, has thrown his support to Bradley, the Republican candidate for governor. So the editor asks "how a man who boasted of the Democratic principles that Clay did, can make such an ass out of himself is astonishing. Ring down the curtains and let him be buried with the past." p2c1

Towns are all reporting good crowds on court days at the public speakings, but that the prices on livestock sales are low.

Dr Miller is still holding his annual colt show. However, the show appears to be misnamed, this year at least. All the entries getting prizes were fillies, mostly by the stallions Dr Jackson and Big Jim Wilkes. The dam of one of the prize-winning fillies was by Graftonian, Dr Miller's sire of an earlier year. p2c3

"Lizzie Miller, daughter of Dr Miller, was visiting the Misses Holloway in Troy." p3c4 Lizzie was also in Keene visiting Miss Irene Lyne last week. p3c6 The gals really circulate when they begin to reach marriageable age.

Contrary to last week, the *Sulphur Well Correspondent* has little to say:

*Mr J T Chapman, of Versailles, visited Mr N D Davis Monday night.*
*Mr Charlie M Clubb, a prominent farmer of Henry County visited Miss Viola Davis last week.*
*Miss Emma Spruce, of Nicholasville, visited Miss Viola Davis of Sulphur Well Monday and Tuesday.*
*Mr J L Graves, of Lexington, bought of Mr N D Davis, of Sulphur Well, 27 head of fine cattle.* p2c3

Mr Clubb and Miss Davis hit it off I guess. I went to High School with Margaret Clubb, their granddaughter. Marshall Davis, Viola's brother, will eventually marry Emma Spruce.

November 1, 1895

The Democrats are trying to scare the voters by saying that there will be negro equality in Kentucky if the Republican party comes to power. The article says that during reconstruction that "not a single state" controlled by the Republicans "escaped the full recognition of the negro" and that they were elected to every office. In a debate at Hopkinsville between Hardin and Bradley, the negroes stood up as a group and demanded equality. p1c4

The *Sulphur Well Correspondent* writes:

*Water is being hauled from the Sulphur Well in all directions.*
*Since the light rain of last Sunday the growing wheat looks much better.*
*Mich. Masters is storekeeper at the brandy warehouse.*
*Mr Wm L Hendren has taken up his residence in Cincinnati.*
*Mrs Elizabeth Moore, an aged lady living with Geo Peel, of this vicinity, has been quite ill for some days.*
*The corn crop being so heavy and the price so low, farmers seem to be holding for an advance.*
*Of the two cases of typhoid fever in this vicinity, one is almost well and the other is getting better.*
*The Kentucky River pike is being thoroughly repaired between here and the river by receiving a lot of gravel.*
*A corn mill is being put into the old shop by J W Cobb and others to accommodate the neighborhood.*

*William Collins, of Poosey Ridge, Madison County, died of lung trouble, at an advanced age on last Saturday.*

*Mr Giles Sanders, formerly of this place, who was taken suddenly and dangerously ill with kidney trouble last Saturday, is improving.*

*Mrs Miller, after a long illness from a liver trouble, is slowly recovering her health, and it is hoped will be up again soon.*

*The zinc mine has resumed operation after a bad breakdown of the pumping machinery, and it is now running day and night, working two sets of hands.*

*Mr C T Taylor, of Lexington, paid our village a hasty visit a few days ago, but seemed to be in a big hurry to get away. Probably it was too dry here for him.*

*The river is lower than it has ever been known before by the oldest inhabitants of its borders. They say that they have never known as much water to be hauled away as is being taken for miles back into Garrard, Madison and Jessamine, and that more stock is daily being driven there for water than at any previous time within their knowledge.*

*Mrs Hannah Sallee, of Paint Lick Creek, Madison County, and who was said to be between 90 and 100 years old, died last Saturday. She had resided in the same house she died in for upwards of 70 years. She and her husband, William Sallee, who recently died at an age near the century mark, moved into the residence shortly after their marriage, and lived quiet and uneventful lives, rarely leaving the homestead for even a short visit. p2c4*

"Miss Lizzie Moore, aged 73, died Thursday, Oct. 31st, at her home near Ambrose. The interment will take place today in the Wm Harris' burial ground." p3c4

### November 15, 1895

The Republicans won in a landslide. Judge Hardin, brother of the gubernatorial candidate, gave several reasons, including: "the continuous hard times, without any promise of relief, either present or prospective, which the common people always attribute to the party in power...." p1c6 He declined to assess the importance of the silver question. Despite the shift in state politics, Jessamine stayed firmly Democratic.

The issue of free turnpikes carried six to one in Anderson County. p3c1

### November 22, 1895

This is a hoax, or perhaps an election joke, since "free" silver was one of the issues in the campaign. The Sulphur Well correspondent told us on November 1st that a zinc mining was being worked. This item appeared today in the <u>Journal</u>, not the Correspondent's column:

> Struck it rich.-It will be gratifying news to the many friends of Mr Thomas Downing, the polite clerk at Duncans's dry goods store to learn that he has stepped from a position of $1,500 a year into a wealthy speculator, perhaps worth millions. Several weeks ago he bought some stock in a zinc mine at Sulphur Well, in this county, says the correspondent of a daily paper, and last week instead of striking zinc ore, as they had been for several days, struck what proved to be silver in abundance. p3c3

November 29, 1895

It's merely the aftermath of the election, and some hunting news. Nothing much going on. Thanksgiving has been no big deal with the natives.

December 6, 1895

"Football. Morally, it's more demoralizing than prize fighting." Formerly, a young man was sent to college for a classical education. Now, "college life is rapidly deteriorating from a desire for intellect into the football craze...." p1c3

The horse and mule market in Atlanta is overstocked. This is where some traders from Jessamine sent them by the carload. Apropos, on page one of this issue: "Without horses.- In discussing the horseless carriage Mr Edison said: 'It is only a question of a short time when the carriages and trucks of every large city will be run with motors.'" p1c4 He goes on to say that the expense of keeping horses in big cities such as New York makes their cost prohibitive.

December 13, 1895

Politics and store sales. That's all for this week. Nothing going on at all!

December 20, 1895

"Misses Laura and Scottie Hendren have returned from a visit to Mrs W H Vanwinkle, Frankfort." p3c2 See next week!

December 27, 1895

The *Sulphur Well Correspondent* writes:

*Rev H G Turner delivered a splendid sermon at the church here last Sunday night.*
*Mr C T Taylor has built a good substantial fence around his yard.*
*Mr James Woodward who has been located at Versailles, is visiting his parents for a few days.*
*Mr G S Watkins, the painter, is assisting A M Askins at his shop this week to catch up on work.*
*Miss Mary F Turner, of Wilmore, is visiting the family of Mr L B Taylor.*
*Mr J P Turner, who has been sick for some time, is able to be out again.*
*Mrs Elizabeth Miller, who has been an invalid for some months, is getting much better and is out again.*
*Mr Forrest Stapp and Miss Mollie Burton, both of Garrard County, were married at Danville on the 24th inst., and went on a tour to Atlanta, Ga.*
*Mr James Woodward last week slaughtered a fine lot of hogs.*
*Whooping cough is among the children of the neighborhood.*
*One great improvement of Sulphur Well is the grist mill, but many people complain that they toot their whistle too often.*

> *Mr Allen Teater, of Garrard County, killed himself at home in his room Sunday evening late, with a double barrel shotgun. He told his mother and the children to leave the room as he was going to clean and reload the gun and it might accidentally go off and hurt some of them. They soon after heard the report of the gun, and on returning found him dead, the load having taken effect in the right side of the face and head, tearing the jaws, arteries and skull to pieces. As no cause is known for his committing suicide, it is not known whether it was that or an accident. But most, if not all, his neighbors and friends believe the sad tragedy to have been accidental.*
>
> *Mr Giles Saunders, of Garrard -----(paper creased)------ Tuesday night, December ?? at 9 pm. The funeral took place at 10 am, Thursday, and the remains buried at 1 pm in Maple Grove Cemetery. p2c5*

I would prefer to leave out the gruesome death of Allen Teater, but kept it in so that the Correspondent's writings would be intact. I apologize for the poor taste.

In the interest of keeping family history straight I want to report the marriage of Scottie Hendren and Forest Miller. The Journal is in bad shape and what is left does not contain this article clipped from the Journal that I just received from Edith. The date would be December 27, 1895.

> Double Wedding.-For some time it had been whispered around that Mr Forest Miller and Miss Scottie Hendren were soon to be married, but each date fixed proved untrue. So, to make the contract more binding, on Christmas night at 11 o'clock, the young couple went to the residence of Eld. V W Dorris and were made husband and wife. They were accompanied by Mr John Overaker and Miss Laura Hendren, of McLean County, Ill., who have been here on a visit, who also caught the matrimonial fever and were married at the same time and place, both ceremonies being performed by Elder Dorris. Immediately after the ceremony, Mr Miller and bride took the midnight train for the Atlanta Exposition, while Mr Overaker and bride were driven to Lexington, where after remaining for several days, they will leave for their future home. The best wishes of the Journal are extended to both couples. (unknown page).

According to Scottie's autobiography, they had been "going together" for three years. I have recorded earlier how they had met, which I guess must have been in about 1892. They were married December 25, 1895. When they returned from their wedding trip on December 30th, Mrs Miller held a reception for them. The Sulphur Well correspondent doesn't report this until March 6, 1896, so I suppose he kept a list of events going, and reported as he got around to it. Scottie writes that she and Forest lived with Mrs Miller up until Mrs Miller's death (which is 1904), and they are recorded in the 1900 census as all living together.

This closes another year, a very good year. I have gleaned a lot of family history, and learned a lot about Sulphur Well exactly (as I write today, December 2, 1995) one hundred years ago.

## UNCLE RAY'S BIRTH - 1896

Ray E Miller, son of Scottie and Forest Miller, was born in September. They are living with Elizabeth Jane Miller at the time.

### January 3, 1896

From Hanly: "Miss Jennie Hendren, the charming daughter of Mr and Mrs Levi Hendren, visited Miss Nora Carter and other friends during the holidays, before leaving for her home at Lexington where her father recently moved." p2c5

### January 10, 1896

"George Diamond is now clerking for Murphy & Miller, and will be glad to have his friends call and see him." p3c1

"Miss May Taylor, of Lexington, who has been the guest of Miss Dora Murphy, Sulphur Well, returned home Sunday."p3c2

### January 17, 1896

The *Journal* gives the history of Wilmore and Asbury College in this issue. Wilmore began as a stop on the Cincinnati Southern Railroad in 1876. A postoffice was added, and then a general store. "There was nothing unusual in the advancement of Wilmore until ... Asbury College was erected by Rev J W Hughes." Ground was broken in 1890 and opened with "two teachers and eight pupils." Buildings were added, and enrollment reached 162 students in 1894. p1c3-6

"Mr A J Sageser sold on last Wednesday his farm of 90 acres, one mile from Ambrose, to E C May, Brannon, for $2,500, possession to be given by March 1st." p2c5 This is Susie Hendren Sageser's husband.

The *Sulphur Well Correspondent* writes:

*Mr and Mrs Whitenack, of Mercer, are visiting Mr and Mrs Cobb.*
*Mr A M Askins, who has bought the Taylor property, will move into it this week.*
*Mr J P Turner, after having been confined to his room for some time, is out again.*
*Mrs E J Miller is off on a week's visit to her children at Irvine and Wisemantown, Estill County.*
*The young people of this neighborhood had a turkey walk last Saturday that caused considerable amusement.*
*Bro Finley has again accepted the work for this church and will enter upon the duties of his charge for another year with a flattering prospects of an acceptable ministry and good work for the cause in the future as in the past. p3c6*

January 24, 1896

The work on Lock No 7 on the Kentucky River is about to get under way. It is to be located 700 yards below High Bridge.

"The New York Store" has taken possession of Spears and Duncan's stock of goods and will close them out for less than the manufacturing price in order to make room for the new spring stock. p2c3-4 This is where Scottie Hendren was working in August, 1994 when she vacationed in Knoxville.

From Little Hickman: Pomp's wife evidently doesn't share his love of the bicycle; her's is for sale.

From the *Sulphur Well Correspondent*:

*The trustees of this district have decided to plant shade trees around the school house.*
*Mrs Miller is on a visit to her children in Estill County.*
*A J Sageser has sold his desirable farm on Hickman Creek to D E May.*
*Mr George Moore, of this place, has rented Allen A Dean's farm in Garrard, and will soon move to it.*
*Mr Jno P Turner, who has been confined to his room for several weeks, is able to be out again.*
*Mr J P Turner bought 61 1/2 acres of Mrs Melinda Masters tract of land Monday at $26.50 per acre, and Dr Jno C Miller bought 86 1/2 acres from the same party at $26.78 per acre.*
*Mr A M Askins has decided to locate permanently among us, having bought the Taylor place, and will move to it this week after making some decided improvements. The community is glad that Mr Askins and his family will still be with us.*
*Mr Samuel Askins, it is said, will erect a nice residence on the site of the building burned down more than a year ago.*
*Old Uncle Joseph Myers is reported to be very feeble and needs the constant care of some of the family. Uncle Joe has been a hard working and genial man all his life, and we hope his neighbors and friends will make the evening of his life as pleasant as possible.*
*------ some talk of a revival of ------ Sulphur Well and we see no reason why such should not be the ----, as there is undoubtedly a vast store-house of wealth beneath us, only awaiting the genius and enterprise of some fortunate individual to develop and reap a rich reward.*
*There will be planted in this neighborhood this year a greater acreage of tobacco and hemp than for some years. The Peel brothers will, I understand, plant about twenty-five acres in hemp this spring and about ten or fifteen acres of tobacco. p2c1*

The two tracts of land that were purchased from Masters adjoins the present farms of Turner and Miller. p2c2

January 31, 1896

"Moore.-Died, at her home near Ambrose, on the 26th inst., aged 77 years, Mrs Diana Moore, wife of the late Rainey Moore...." p3c3 She is buried in the family cemetery.

H W Rose is closing out his stock of goods, and will sell the remainder at public auction next court day.

February 7, 1896

Property transfered: "Wilson Masters and wife to W B Walker, 12 acres near Sulphur Well, $160." p1c4

The *Sulphur Well Correspondent* writes:

*Mrs Hugh Miller, of near Richmond, visited her parents at this place last week.*
*Mr A M Askins is making extensive repairs upon the residence he recently purchased from Frank Taylor, Sr.*
*The many friends and acquaintances of the late J N Broaddus, who formerly lived in this county, were shocked and pained at the news of his untimely death at Lancaster on the 25th ult. Mr Broaddus was liked by all who knew him. He leaves a widow and five children to mourn his loss. p2c4*

February 14, 1896

The *Sulphur Well Correspondent* writes:

*----------------Mr Frank M Hud----------seriously sick from an ----------al pneumonia.*
*--------------Hendren, of Kansas, who------------extended visit to his -------------- start for home on ---------.*
*--------------has just returned ----------- of late, protracted -------------. It is said Cu------------------ -------------------grass capital.*
*------------------, formerly -------------- president of Belle-----------------from a trouble ---------of the brain.*
*--------------bought the ---------ders, widow -----------. The price ------------ $2,000. Mrs. ----------- --- week to ---------- which Mr ----------------------tains more--------of the best -----------------------.*
*------------------------days -----------une, --------move to the farm --------------------. Mr Brown has rented the farm to Mr Moore.*
*Miss Carrie Woodward is making up a subscription school at this place.*
*Bro Finley, of Lexington, preached at our church on last Saturday and Sunday to large and appreciative audiences.*
*Mr H G Turner, son of Mr J P Turner of this place, a promising young minister of the gospel, now attending Boston University, was recently honored by being selected from among hundreds of other bright young men in attendance at that renowned seat of learning, as its representative in the Massachusetts State Prohibition Oratorical Contest to be held at Worcester, Mass., this month, the winner being the State representative in the National contest. The selection is an honor worthily bestowed upon one of Jessamine's most promising young men, and one whom his friends are justly proud of. p2c1*

February 21, 1896

Dr Miller sold "two thoroughbred Holstein heifers" for $85 and 14 shoats "at $3.75 cwt." p2c3 His daughter, "Miss Lizzie Miller has returned from a visit to Miss Ella Gregory at Louisville." p3c3

"Ralph Greenbaum, son of the well-known Midway distiller, and Miss Mattie Bowen, of Lexington, daughter of Jas L Bowen, Ambrose were married in Covington, Monday ...." p3c4

February 28, 1896

"A funny trial took place" over at Stanton the other day. "A mountaineer was arrested on a warrant charging him with a misdemeanor, and the case came up in ... court." His attorney demanded a jury trial, so six jurors were summoned. "Five of the six were objected to by the attorneys", but after some discussion they agreed to let the sixth juror decide the case. "The testimony was introduced, the judge gave his instructions to the `jury'..." and told him to retire to the jury room and consider the case. The lone juror was "solemn and dignified" as he took the papers and left the courtroom. "After staying out over a half an hour, the `jury' returned ..." without a verdict, saying that he couldn't reach a decision. p1c5 I made up the end because the paper was torn.

The future as seen by an electrical engineer in 1896: "Transmission of energy for considerable distances has already been achieved." So, "wherever in the future there is a demand for power, it will be delivered. Electricity will displace gas for lighting purposes; coal and stoves for heating; steam (for) ... propulsion; and horses (for) ... locomotion." He envisioned that farmers would have electrical equipment for grinding feed, pumping water, and heating green houses and residences. p1c6 Don't forget. This is 1896!

March 6, 1896

"Much style attaches to duck or pique suits made with short jackets opening over vests...." p1c5

"Spain, it seems, has now gotten on her war paint and is thinking of attacking America." p2c1

Experiments are being conducted using X-rays. Besides skeletal views, digestion of food can be observed. p4c5

"Marshall Davis and sister, Miss Viola, entertained quite a number of friends last evening at the home of their parents, Mr and Mrs Newton Davis, near Sulphur Well." p3c6

The *Sulphur Well Correspondent* writes:

*Mr James Woodward had his left eye injured by the explosion of a rifle shell.*

*Mr Courtney Horine, of Chicago, Ill., has been on a visit in this neighborhood, returned home on Monday.*

*On December 30th, Mr and Mrs F Forest Miller, of this place, having returned from their bridal tour, which included among other interesting points, Atlanta, Ga., and its grand exposition, were given a reception by Mrs Elizabeth Miller, mother of the bride-groom, Monday evening, at her residence here. The bridal couple seemed to have enjoyed their happy wedding journey immensely, and were enthusiastically welcomed by their many friends and relatives. An elegant and sumptuous supper was served at 8:30 o'clock to a delightful gathering of the young people (and to some old ones too), of the neighborhood. Among the invited guests present were: Misses Viola Davis, Eudora Murphy, Mirtie Snowden, Nellie and Mary Hendren, of Sulphur Well; Lizzie Butler, of Richmond; Messrs M. Murphy, Marshall Davis, Johnnie Snowden, Dr and Mrs G M Hendren. It was altogether a delightful affair, and the writer can only hope that similar functions will occur more frequently in this vicinity hereafter. Mr and Mrs Miller were also charivaried in an old fashion style on Tuesday night, and again right royally entertained their serenaders. p3c4*

At least one of the "other interesting points" the couple visited was Lookout Mountain. They had an excellent picture made there that I still have. Nellie and Mary Hendren are children of Dr and Mrs Hendren. Obviously, the only "old people" that were mentioned were Dr and Mrs Hendren. I believe that it would be fair to assume that those attending the wedding reception would be the closest family friends. Thus, Elizabeth Jane Miller and Dr and Mrs Hendren must have been the closest of friends.

March 13, 1896

"It will be a relief to the people of Kentucky when the present legislature adjourns, which will be next Tuesday, and if Gov (William O) Bradley has one inch of genuine back-bone, he will not prolong the session. The whole proceedings from the start has been an disgrace to the State; sixty days gone and nothing done." p2c1 So, what has changed in a hundred years?

The Nicholasville Fairgrounds has been sold, and the new owner is offering to sell the lumber in the present buildings in any quantity to suit the purchaser.

"The Cincinnati base ball club passed through Nicholasville over the Q & C last Tuesday, enroute to New Orleans for spring practice." p3c1

March 20, 1896

"LSF", from Nicholasville, has been wintering in Umatilla, Fl., and writes this week about the wind, the flimsy fences, and the lean hogs. Somewhat philosophically, she speaks of the advantageously early season for planting and harvesting, and says "Truly Florida supplies the country with luxuries but very few of its necessities. She will always be the hot-house of the rich man rather than the garden of the poor." p1c3-4

There was a young widow in Madison County "who put up a costly monument for her late husband" that had inscribed upon it "My grief is so great that I cannot bear it". A year later she remarried, and after some thought, added "alone" to the inscription on the monument. p1c6

### March 27, 1896

Judge Phillips and his family are enjoying a fishing trip in Florida. Mrs Phillips says that oranges are scarce because of a killing frost the prior year. There is quite a contingent from Kentucky. She says "I suppose there are thirty-six now here from Kentucky, some of them doing light housekeeping and a number boarding. You can get good board here very reasonably." p1c3

### April 3, 1896

"Henry Ward Beecher was a great lover of a fine horse." Once he hired a rig at a livery stable, and looked admiringly at the horse. He remarked "That is a fine looking animal. Is he as good as he looks? The owner replied "Mr Beecher, that horse will work in any place you put him, and do all that any horse can do." Mr Beecher looked more admiringly at the horse, and said "I wish to goodness that he was a member of our church." p1c5

The *Sulphur Well Correspondent* writes:

*Measles are epidemic in this section, a great many adults having been taken down.*
*Mrs Elizabeth Miller continues very low from liver trouble.*
*Elder Adcock preached here last Sunday.*
*Heavy rain fell during last Sunday evening. About 1 o'clock there was a tremendous hail storm followed by a cloud burst, and then another hail storm, flooding the country and booming the small streams.*
*In regard to the question of an early or late Democratic primary election for the nomination of candidates for the various county offices, after questioning quite a number of the farmers and others of the party in this vicinity, I am led to believe that the sentiment of the people is pretty evenly divided between the two opinions. But if there is any difference at all, those who desire an early primary are in the majority, and they are certainly more in earnest in declaring for an early settlement of the matter.*
*Mr John Fain, of Mt Pleasant, near this place, died from heart disease Monday night at about 11 o'clock. Mr Fain was a pensioner and was well known in the county as "Keno", in fact many knew him only by that name. He was well advanced in years, having been born in October, 1813, and was consequently in his 83rd year. The deceased had been in bad health for some years.* p2c3

Note the topics: illness and death, weather, religion, and politics. In some respects this particular letter captures the essence of life, and the recurring themes throughout the years. I would gather that the Correspondent is a Democrat, from his interest in the Democratic primary.

April 10, 1896

Summer capes "are of Persian or Dresden silk with varied hue, (that) form a charming contrast to black skirts and harmonize equally well with a black hat trimmed by ribbon...." p1c5

April 17, 1896

A letter from a Kentuckian visiting Arizona says that the air is fresh and invigorating, and is purer than Florida. He compares February weather there to the best days in May in Kentucky. p1c3

April 24, 1896

There was little market in the Bluegrass, so a Kentuckian with a large number of horses on his farm wrote to a friend in Washington to see if he could dispose of some them there. He waited anxiously, and finally, he got this disappointing reply:

The people of Washington ride bicycles, the street cars are run by electricity, and the Government by jackasses. There is no demand for horses. p1c6

Murphy & Miller are advertising their new spring merchandise. Their first for a long time.

The *Sulphur Well Correspondent* writes:

*A woman tramp or gypsy entered the residence of J W Cobb, Thursday of last week and stole a comb and Mrs Cobb's bonnet.*
*Conrad Fain fractured one bone of his left arm last week by having it caught between a wagon wheel and a load of lumber. The arm was also considerably bruised and lacerated.*
*Mrs Hugh Miller and little daughter, of Richmond, are visiting her parents here.*
*Jefferson Reynolds has moved from near the river to town.*
*Measles, which have been so prevalent and virulent here this spring are abating somewhat.*
*The highest temperature reached here last week was 93 degrees in the shade. The oldest inhabitant never felt anything like it in April before.*
*A wedding occurred near here Tuesday. Mrs Nannie Lay, daughter of the late Marany Moore, was married to Ezekiel Hendren. The wedding has been talked of for some time.*
*Considerable excitement was created here late Monday evening by a mad dog scare. A Newfoundland canine belonging to A M Askins went mad and after biting some of his dogs started throught the village, but got away and was next heard from on the Danville pike, where it bit John Wallace's dogs and probably many others. The mad dog was heard in the village again that night, but not seen until Tuesday morning, when it appeared at Newt Underwoods and had a fight with his hounds in the yard, where it was killed by Jim Durham with a shot gun loaded with bird shot. p2c4*

It has become obvious that the Correspondent likes to talk. He takes his time in telling a story. It's not "just the facts, ma'am".

May 1, 1896

I've had days like this! There is the story(paraphrased) of the Scottish farmer who was to deliver a load of hay to a customer. He led his horse out of the barn, but instead of backing it into the shafts of the wagon, he absentmindedly led the animal all the way to Perth. He asked the stableman where he should back it into. The stableman replied "Back what into?"." The hay, you stupid idiot!" he said. "What hay? ye've nae hay!" Turning around the farmer saw that he had left the wagon at home, and in his haste to correct his error, he began trotting back home to get the wagon. He was half way back home before he realized that he had left the horse in Perth! p1c5

May 8, 1896

I don't understand the political interest in Kentucky for "free silver". I don't see how it could possibly benefit Kentucky. Nevertheless, General Hardin, who was recently defeated in the gubernatorial race, is going around the state speaking on the issue. Jessamine County even has a "Free Silver Club". Members from Sulphur Well are: H C Hemphill, Andrew Sageser, Everett Bourne, and Newton Davis. p3c3

May 15, 1896

Not to be outdone, opponents have formed a "Sound Money Club". Its Sulphur Well members are L F English, Henry Mackey, J W Duncan, Sr., J G Scott, Thomas Lear, Wm Hoover, Elbert Walker, and Manifred Gibony. p2c1 This issue has split the Kentucky Democrats right down the middle!

The *Sulphur Well Correspondent* writes:

*Eld. John F Rowe preached here last Sunday, and also Elder Fenley, at night.*
*Mrs Bettie Brooks, while reading last Saturday, fell suddenly from her chair to the floor unconscious. She appeared to be in a critical condition for some time.*
*Mrs Mays, widow of William Mays, died Monday morning of paralysis and debility of old age, being 82 years old.*
*Dr Nelson Mays and family arrived Monday evening in response to a telegram to attend his mother's funeral.*
*Mr E N Wallace, who has been seriously ill since the first of the month from inflammation of the bowels, is slowly improving.*
*Mr Morris Dean's family are down with the measles. That neighborhood seems to be suffering from an epidemic of measles at present.*
*Mr Thos. Bruner had a little child very sick this week from threatened pneumonia, but is better now. p3c6*

Best that I can tell, Mrs Mays lived in the Little Hickman neighborhood. She was buried with her husband. I am almost sure that Morris Dean's family also lived around Little Hickman. It appears that the Sulphur Well Correspondent is reporting all the news that he hears.

May 22, 1896

Sabbath Laws: "No work or business shall be done on the Sabbath day except the ordinary household offices or other work of necessity or charity...." p1c6

There has been a vast change in the school census since I began this chronicle. I remember writing that Sulphur Well had almost as many school children as Nicholasville. Now it is Sulphur Well 67, Nicholasville 354. I won't try to be definitive, but I believe that reflects the shift of people into the cities from the farming areas during the 1877-1896 period.

Fit or "Misfit" leads the Murphy & Miller ad this week.

"Miss Dora Murphy has returned from a visit to Lexington." p3c2 For whatever his reason, the Sulphur Well Correspondent rarely reports her activities.

The Journal reports that Mrs J W Overstreet (Pomp's wife) is in critical condition. p3c2

May 29, 1896

"Miss Bertha Hendren, who has been attending school at Midway has returned home." p3c3 This is Scottie's sister.

"Prof Rice Miller closed his school at Campbellsville, Friday last, which the paper of that place reports as the most successful school taught there in years. Prof Miller left for Poughkeepsie, N Y , Tuesday morning where he will take a commercial course during the summer in the business college there. Prof Miller was given the principalship again of the school at Campbellsville without opposition." p3c3 The commercial course was accounting.

June 5, 1896

The Silverites have won in Jessamine, Shelby, Anderson, and Garrard. It is on its way to becoming the Democratic national position. Look out for the next presidential election! The Republican candidate will be McKinley. The Democratic National Convention is to held in Chicago on July 7th.

June 12, 1896

The Glass' Mill correspondent said: "The money question is all the talk of the people. We think if they will talk less and work more they will prosper by it." p2c5

"Mason County now has free turnpikes, the court of appeals affirming the decision of the circuit court." p3c1 This may be the first county in the state to have free roads.

"Miss Dora Murphy is the guest of Miss Viola Million, Richmond." p3c3

I wonder for whom? "Mrs Walter Hendren (Linnie Spruce), Misses Emma Spruce and Mamie Long attended the commencement exercises at the Kentucky University, Lexington, Tuesday." p3c3

"The prospects are very bright" that Nicholasville will soon get a badly needed telephone system! p3c4

Shakertown Inn has been established and "it is fast becoming a favorite place" to stay in the summer. The hotel is "first-class", rates are reasonable, and the "scenery is beautiful." p3c4

This will hurt the local economy. There is evidently an oversupply of whisky again. Kentucky distillers have agreed to shut down next July, and remain closed until January, 1898. p3c5

The *Sulphur Well Correspondent* writes:

*Cholera among hogs is said to be causing considerable loss to the farmers of this section.*
*John Sanders, of Garrard, was visiting E Walker this week.*
*Mrs Beatty Robinson, of near Boone's Ferry, is seriously ill.*
*Mrs E Miller and Jas W Miller are away for a week's visit to Irvine and vicinity.*
*At the school election last Saturday, W L Buford was elected trustee for one year and Thos J Horine for three years.*
*Mr John McHatton, wife and little daughter, and Mr Luther Hanks, of Port Royal, Ky., and Mrs W H Bright of Lexington, were visiting Mr A M Askins Saturday and Sunday.* p2c5

The Askins and Brights came from Garrard County to Sulphur Well. The Brights moved on to Lexington, and are buried in the Lexington Cemetery. William H died in 1912. His wife, Dovie K, lived until 1938.

The Correspondent doesn't always write about the things that I think he ought to. For example, one of Sulphur Well's leading citizens, J H Murphy, was elected Republican County Chairman and there is no mention of it. The Democrats are talking about nothing else but the silver question, and the Correspondent takes no note.

June 19, 1896

A Confederate monument was unveiled on the Court House lawn. The ceremony was attended by an estimated crowd of some 3,000 persons. The train arrived with Col Bennett Young accompanied by 136 people from Louisville and a brass band. They were met at the station by Confederate soldiers from Jessamine and surrounding counties, and they formed a line and marched to the Court House. "First on the program was Dixie (played) by the band." After songs and addresses, the covering was removed, and the band played Dixie again. "The crowd cheered loud and long...", accompanied by several "rebel yells." p2c1 I don't want this to sound comical. This was a serious occasion. Nicholasville was cleaned up and decked out with bunting. Visitors were very complimentary. There were some bitter-sweet moments. The rendering of "O Lay me away with the Boys in Gray" by a quartet was said to be "soul-stirring". Confederate paraphernalia was on the platform to be viewed, and one old jacket had been worn by R T Haley of Louisville when he lost a leg. He was asked to come forward to let the crowd see a man who had been in battle. He was warmly received.

Madison will vote on free turnpikes at the next regular election.

Murphy & Miller ask you to see their "Kool clothing".

The *Journal* received a letter from Rice Miller from Poughkeepsie, NY where he and Luther Saunders, another Kentuckian, are attending Eastman College. p3c2

### June 26, 1896

At their convention in St Louis, the Republicans nominated McKinley for president.

Pomp's wife: "Mrs J W Overstreet, Little Hickman, is slowly improving, but still very sick." p3c3

"Miss Ola Davis, Sulphur Well, will leave in a few days to visit friends at Albany, Ind." p3c3

"Miss Bertha Hendren, of this place (Nicholasville), is the guest of her cousin, Miss Marie Wheeler, of Cincinnati, O." p3c3 This indicates the relationship between two branches of the Doven Hendren family--through William and granddaughter Marie; and Harrison and grandaughter Bertha.

"Mrs Eliza West, widow of Turpin West, died Friday at the home of her daughter, Mrs N B Long, near Kirksville, aged 82 years." p3c4 Eliza is a daughter of Doven Hendren. She is buried in the Salem Cemetery as is her brother Harrison Hendren. Eliza was born October 20, 1816 and died June 15, 1896. Her husband, Turpin, died in 1882 at the age of sixty-nine.

### July 3, 1896

If you remember, one of the earliest articles in this chronical was about canned goods. That was almost twenty years ago. There is now a new law: After July 1, 1896 it is unlawful to sell "preserved or canned fruits and vegetables of other articles of food ... unless such articles bear a mark to indicate the grade or quality, together with the name and address of such firm, person or corporation that packs the same, or dealer who sells the same." p1c5

The silver question has split the Republicans as well as the Democrats. Five or six western states (silver producers) have bolted the Republican party because of its stand against the free coinage of silver. p1c5 The National Democratic Party has taken a stand in favor of free coinage and the Republicans against. Its obvious that the states that produce silver have a lot to gain. What anybody in Kentucky could possibly gain defies my imagination! Even the Chautauqua has gotten involved. On the 4th of July, the Lexington Chautauqua will feature two national speakers on the issue of free silver (pro and con).

The High Bridge Camp meeting is scheduled to run from July 17th to the 26th. Can the evangelists avoid the burning issue of the day?

"Harriet Beecher Stowe died at her home in Hartford, Conn, on Wednesday last, aged 84 years." p2c1

The *Sulphur Well Correspondent* reports:

*Wednesday a new carrier, Mr James Hagar, commenced to carry the mail from Little Hickman to town.*
*Our postmaster has concluded to sell 13 two cent stamps or 26 one cent stamps for a cent and a quarter. If you don't believe me, ask him.*
*Wheat threshing commenced in earnest Tuesday, both of our threshers starting out the same time. They report the wheat as light straw and heavy grain.*
*Mr John Myers, of Illinois, is on a visit to friends and relatives in the county. He is a son of Joseph Myers, dec'd.*
*Miss Clark, of near Logana, is visiting at N D Davis' this week.*
*L H Hendren fell under and was run over by a heavily loaded wagon Tuesday evening. He has several ribs broken and was otherwise severely injured.*
*Mrs Sallie Cobb, widow of the late John W Cobb, died last Sunday of flux, aged --. She had been sick only a few days but had suffered from bowel trouble for more than a year, and at her advanced age, the disease coming upon her in its most formidable type, she could not withstand its attack. She died at the residence of A A Burton, where she was taken sick while on a visit. The funeral was preached by the Rev Vaughn to a large concourse of people at the late residence, when she was buried by the side of her husband.* p2c3

The Correspondent can't let go of his postage stamp joke. The L H Hendren who was run over by the wagon is the son of William and Eliza Hendren. He was still living at home at the time of the 1900 Census.

July 10, 1896

Paint Lick apparently was being referred to in "Uncle Tom's Cabin" when Stowe wrote "In the quiet little town of P-----" and then described the geographical area around Paint Lick. p1c3

"Miss Dora Murphy is visiting Miss May Taylor at Lexington." p3c3 The Sulphur Well Correspondent seems to ignore her visits.

The minister makes Sulphur Well sound like a resort:

> An enjoyable evening to be spent July 11th from 7 to 9 o'clock at Sulphur Well. A fine supper of ice cream, sherbert and cake. Plenty of sulphur water to drink. Buggy and boat riding and many other sports in which all may engage. All are cordially invited to come and spend a pleasant evening. Supper served at 15c: A P Finley, Minister. p3c3

July 17, 1896

William Jennings Bryan is the Democratic nominee for president, and a leading advocate for the free coinage of silver. I wonder if the term "silver tongued orator" originated as a pun on Bryan's oratorical skills.

The *Sulphur Well Correspondent* writes:

*Miss Hattie James, Buckeye, and Miss Lulu Holman, Nicholasville, were visiting Mr N D Davis, Saturday and Sunday.*

*Mr Ike Thompson and Miss Grimes, Lancaster, were visiting at A M Askins, Saturday and Sunday.*

*Miss Nellie Wagner, Newport, and Miss Emma Spruce were visiting Dr Hendren and family Saturday and Sunday.*

*Mr Baumstark, Waco, was visiting Mr J H Turner, last week.*

*Mr Robert Masters and wife, Louisville, are on a visit to his father, Wilson Masters.*

*Mrs Kitty Knight is visiting at Mrs Elizabeth J Miller's this week.*

*Miss Lila Taylor, Lexington, and Miss Carmen Davis were visiting Mrs Margaret Horine this week.*

*Miss Lucy Saunders was visiting at J H Murphy's Sunday.*

*The public school of this district will commence its session on Monday, July 27, with Mr N D Thompson, teacher.*

*An infant son of Mr Melvin Peel has been quite sick with summer complaint, but is now better.*

*A child of Thomas Peel has for some days been seriously ill from cholera infantum, and its recovery is despaired of.*

*Thomas Peel, Jr son of the late Dr Peel, who has been for some three or ------(paper torn and missing).*

*------------------------r's is*
*---------------.*
*------------------------Mrs Mi-*
*------------------------Mr and*
*------------------------is week.*
*------------------------to take*
*------------------------recklessly*
*------------------------streets at*
*---------------.*
*---------------------ven here last*
*Sa--------------------the manage-*
*ment----------------the Christian*
*church----- success. It is to be*
*hoped----- will soon give another.* p2c3-4

I'm sorry that not much can be made of the last few items. Recent papers have been in poor condition. Please keep Kitty Knight in mind, there will be several references, and finally she will be placed in the family.

July 24, 1896

"Miss Bertha Hendren and her guest, Miss Marie Hendren, spent Saturday and Sunday with Mrs Forest Miller, Sulphur Well." p2c3 Bertha is visiting her sister Scottie. I believe that this is Marie Wheeler. Her mother is a Hendren.

"Dr John C Miller has been confined to his bed for several days." p3c5

August 7, 1896

The *Sulphur Well Correspondent* writes:

*Miss Lizzie Butler, of Richmond, is visiting Miss Mertie Snowden, this week.*
*Miss Anderson and Mrs Martin, of Lancaster, were visiting Mrs T J Horine, last week.*
*Mr and Mrs Hugh Miller, of Richmond, were on a brief visit to their parents last week.*
*Mr G S Watkins has removed temporarily to Pink where he will artistically adorn Mr Pink Overstreet's house.*
*Mr Frank Horine is mistaken about all the darkies about here being for free silver. There is only a solitary one in favor of the white metal.*
*The Compulsory Educational law is bringing out the children of this district handsomely.*
*Hemp cutting has commenced in earnest in this section and there is a promise of an extraordinary crop.*
*The corn crop in this portion of the county never, within the memory of the oldest inhabitants, looked better than at present, and the yield will certainly be enormous.*
*The bluegrass was never finer at any season of the year and all kinds of stock are fat and ready for the market. And there seems to be a lively trade in stock at present not-withstanding the low prices.*
*The tobacco crop which is now just beginning to be cut, promises well for an abundant yield, and there was a large acreage planted.*
*A little son of Mr Melvin Peel died Monday evening after a protracted illness of summer complaint following measles. There has been several deaths in this vicinity lately from the same malady.*
*Thomas Peel, aged 13, son of the late Dr Thomas Peel, died on Monday, after a lingering and painful illness from bowel trouble that was hard to diagnose by his numerous physicians.*
*There is considerable sickness in this section, especially among children, which seems to have followed the measles that was so prevalent during the spring and early summer months.*
*Stock of all kinds appear to be extraordinarily annoyed by the flies this summer, and the fly is doubtless of the swamp variety, distinct from the common house or cattle species in that it has a flat hairy body, small head, and a spear-like bill more than twice the length of its head. This can be readily seen under a good magnifying glass. It is probable that the heavy rainfall and the consequent stagnant swamps and pools tended to breed them in unusually large numbers. We should protect our stock from this terrible annoyance as much as possible.* p2c5

You can't read this article with any degree of thought without seeing the interrelatedness of every single item. It has been a hot, wet spring and summer. It has been good for crops, but bad for people. There was an epidemic of measles in late March and early April. There was heavy, freaky rain and hail in April, with the temperature reaching 93 degrees at one point. Even without any scientific or medical knowledge on my part, its obvious that the conditions for bacterial infections were present in abundance, and that the children paid the highest price. Not even money and the best medical care available could save the young from diarrhetic type diseases. The daughter of Dixie Knight, perhaps the wealthiest person in Jessamine County at that time, died from cholera infantum. p3c4

Some additional family news:
> Quite a pleasant social entertainment was given by Miss Bertha Hendren in honor of her guest, Miss Marie Wheeler, of Cincinnati, and Miss March, of Illinois, at the residence of her sister, Mrs A K Adcock, on Main Street, last Friday evening, the feature of the evening being some beautiful musical selections by Misses Wheeler and March. The pleasure was made complete by a delightul lunch of ices and fruit. p3c3

Murphy & Miller have changed their ads. They now call themselves the "leading clothiers". p3c7-8

And some more neighborhood news: Joseph and Larkin Fain, the two brothers who had a difficulty in the Sulphur Well neighborhood some time ago, when Joe was struck and badly hurt with a rock, were tried before Judge Phillips Monday and fined $25 and $15 each. Both are now on the "chain gang." p3c1 This is not the Larkin Fain who ran the general store in Pollard.

August 14, 1896

Extreme weather. There is now drouth conditions in western Kentucky.

Rev H G Turner preached at a union service in Richmond Sunday night. "He has a good command of language and preached an elegant and instructive sermon." p2c5 This is Horace Turner of Sulphur Well.

"Dr Jno C Miller was in town Wednesday, the first time in six weeks. He is looking much improved, and will soon be himself again." p3c4

August 21, 1896

The Democrats want to "break the backbone of the Wall Street monopolies" with their silver policy. p2c1 They blame the eastern bankers for the money problems, particularly those in 1893, that have depressed the country.

August 28, 1896

New corn is selling in Madison at $1.15 per barrel. p2c2 This is an incredibly low price. At some point I am going to see what the price was 15 to 20 years earlier.

"Miss Bertha Hendren will leave Monday for Midway where she will attend school." p3c3

September 4, 1896

A bit of history about Dix River: "Flowing for many miles between deeply-cut cliffs through the Blue Grass Region of Kentucky is the beautiful Dick's River ...." The river rises "not far from the old Southern summer resort Crab Orchard (in Lincoln County) and empties into the Kentucky River in sight of where the world famed `High Bridge' spans that waterway from towering walls of solid limestone." p1c6

September 11, 1896

A report of two young men from Nicholasville have gone east say that even the Cleveland Democrats in New York are for McKinley.

The *Sulphur Well Correspondent* writes:

*There appears to considerable typhoid fever in the country.*
*Mr Rad Fain, who has been sick for some time, continues very low.*
*Born, to the wife of Forest Miller, Sept 7, a son, Ray Miller.*
*A McKinley Club of 60 members has been organized at this place.*
*Rev H G Turner delivered an address upon the political issues of the day here Wednesday night to a good audience. He is a brilliant young orator. p3c6*

Ray Miller, my uncle and my namesake died in 1918, but when I was youngster in the 1930's, people still called me Ray Miller. I resented it at the time, but now in retrospect I realize that people were still bestowing upon me their affection for Uncle Ray. I know that my mother idolized her older brother.

Even Sulphur Well is now wrapped up in the silver question. You may not realize the import of a McKinley Club in Sulphur Well with sixty members! It was a Democratic village in a Democratic county of a Democratic state. It was still solidly Democratic when I lived there. I only knew one Republican by name.

September 18, 1896

Some of the merchants have gotten into the spirit of the money debate. "Silver or gold is what Denman's wants for his boots and shoes." p3c1

October 2, 1896

Miss Nellie Hendren, the daughter of Tom Hendren, who lives in Nicholasville, won a declamatory contest in Cynthiana. This is a form of dramatic speaking, sometimes a skit, as I understand it. However, Miss Nellie became an accomplished violinist, so a musical instrument may be involved.

October 9, 1896

No report from Sulphur Well. Nothing going on except politics.

October 16, 1896

The *Sulphur Well Correspondent* writes:

*Mr Hugh Miller, wife and daughter, of Madison County, were visiting Dr G M Hendren this week.*
*Mrs Sam Moberly and Mrs James Vincent, of Edenton, were visiting Mr James Hendren Saturday and Sunday last.*
*Mrs Miller is having her residence covered with iron roofing. Its a great improvement.*
*Mr J P Turner sold Monday to J B Hunter, for J B Embry, 57 fat hogs, averaging 322 1/2 lbs. for $2.75.*
*Mr R M Hill, who has been quite sick for some time past, is reported as getting better.*
*The sale of Dan W McQuerry, lately deceased, of Garrard, was well attended Tuesday, and things brought prices corresponding with hard times.*
*The Rev Mr Baird is thinking of moving to this place and of occupying the Dr Mays residence. Would be glad to have him as a neighbor.*
*Mr William Richardson and wife are visiting her mother, Mrs Elizabeth Miller, at this place.*
*Mr Wilson Masters is building a front to his dwelling at Hokeyville, a suburb of this place.*
*At the church Saturday and Sunday, besides the regular preaching of Bro Finley, Bro Clingman also delivered a discouse. These monthly meetings are well attended.* p3c6

October 23, 1896

Wheat is 85 cents per bushel in Chicago. Corn is being delivered for 80 cents per barrel in Jessamine. Hogs are selling for 3 cents per pound. p2c5 Wouldn't you love to be in the business of raising corn and pigs!

The marriage of Rev H G Turner, of Eminence, son of Mr J P Turner, of Ambrose, this county, and Miss Ella West, of Georgetown, is announced to take place in the early winter. p3c3

"From now until Nov 3, the political pots will be set to boiling ...." p2c1

The *Sulphur Well Correspondent* writes:

*Several sales of horses, etc, have been made here payable when Bryan is elected.*
*Mrs Witt, of Estill County, and Mrs McGuire, of Valley View, are visiting Mrs Miller.*
*Born, to the wife of A J Sageser, on the 15th inst., a son.*
*The silverites of this precinct were addressed on the money question a few evenings since by the fluent speaker, G L Watkins.*
*Saturday there will be a public speaking at John Overstreet's store. It is said that there is no end to the making of books and -------(paper torn and missing).*
*-------- those prices, as buyers are confident of purchasing delivered at from 60 to 75 cents when husking begins.*
*The recent cold snap caused a lively hustling around among our negligent neighbors for a load or two of coal.*
*Mr William Hunter, of Logana, died of typhoid fever last Saturday and was buried on Sunday evening.*
*Mrs Green Collins, of Indiana, on a visit to her parents here, is quite sick and has had two physicians called in to see her.*

*It is gold, gold, gold.*
*We daily are told.*
*Is the cause of all our "woes".*
*But silver men say*
*A happier day*
*will dawn with election day's close.*

p3c5-6 I don't know who Mrs Witt is. Victor Witt later marries Anna Miller, Elizabeth's granddaughter, but at this moment she is under ten years old. The son born to Andrew and Susie Sageser was named Hubert. This is their second child. Ada was the first. Ada married Charlie Mann Dean and their children "did well". One son, Robert Mann became a doctor, and the two daughters, Dorothy and Evelyn were super nice people. The oldest was Carl, who I remember, but not very well. Hubert was a nice person, quite heavy. His wife had some emotional problems, and was in a sanitorium, at least for a while. She died quite young, maybe by forty. I suppose Hubert was on some sort of pension, since he was in World War I; at least he didn't work.

It appears that the Correspondent has, as everyone else, gotten caught up in the election craze. Besides making bets, people were also setting two prices on horses, such as $150 if Bryan wins, $50 if McKinley wins. So, in effect, if the horse was worth $100, they were making a $50 bet.

October 30, 1896

The *Sulphur Well Correspondent* writes:

*J P Turner sold Monday to J B Hunter, for Jno B Embry, more than 100 hogs at about 3c.*
*Mrs Miller and daughter, Tee, are on a visit to Mr and Mrs Richardson, at Irvine.*
*There will be two weddings on the 12th of November--William Jesse Miller and Miss Melinda Barnes, and L Lee Davis and Miss Annie Byrnes.*

*Clayton West, while on a visit beyond Lancaster, lost his fine saddle mare. Supposed to have been stolen. Mr Frank Taylor, of Mt Lebanon, also lost a mare last Sunday night.*

*Thieves seem to be plentiful, as they are frequently seen prowling about at unseemly hours of the night, or rather morning, at from midnight to daylight, or when they think they can't possibly be seen to fall down in the fence shadows when out on moonlit nights. A dose or two of buckshot well delivered would be an excellent remedy. p3c6*

Mrs Richardson is Mrs Miller's daughter, Sudie. I see a fair amount of frustration in the Correspondent at the degree of trespassing and petty thievery. It is a sign of society being eroded.

### November 6, 1896

The election is finally over. Both sides still claim victory, but McKinley has the edge. Apparently Jessamine went for Bryan by 83 votes, the state by a little over 200, so this is indeed a close election.

"Miss Emma Spruce has accepted a position in the New York Store in Nicholasville." p3c2

All the merchants in Nicholasville are said to be adopting the cash system on January 1st of the new year. Collections have been difficult for years.

### November 13, 1896

There will be a Republican majority in the state legislature, 70 to 66. Really incredible!

Horace Turner will be married December 2nd in Georgetown.

### November 20, 1896

"Horseless mail wagons are being used in New York, the first in the United States." p2c1

The final vote count in Kentucky is 218,073 for McKinley and 217,829 for Bryan. So, a narrow victory, but Kentucky did go Republican! All the electoral votes but one is for McKinley. p2c2

### November 27, 1896

Some citizens, or vandals, as you may view it, are destroying toll gates. One toll-keeper was told by a mob of about thirty men that if he continued to collect tolls that he would be "severely dealt with". The editor decries this lawless action, and says that while most people favor free roads, that mob action is not the proper course of action. p3c4 Similar problems, which the editor calls "anarchy", are being experienced in Washington and Anderson Counties.

"Miss Dora Murphy has returned from a two week's visit to friends at Louisville." p3c3

The *Sulphur Well Correspondent* writes:

*N D Davis has purchased a new buggy.*
*Hokey Masters has his new residence almost completed.*
*J P Turner has removed his cattle scales to the S n'ers' farm.*
*J H Turner has erected an addition to his residence.*
*Mrs Bettie Murphy has been very sick for some days.*
*Rev Baird will move to our village in a few weeks.*
*R M Hill, after a long illness, is out again.*
*Reuben Stapp is painting the new residence of Wilson Masters.*
*Mrs Meda Reynolds has been on the sick list for some days.*
*Mrs Elizabeth Miller and daughter have returned from a two week's visit to Estill County.*
*Jas W Miller is visiting his brother, John Miller, in Estill County.*
*Conrad Fain, whose wife died some week's ago from typhoid fever and a complication of diseases, will remove to the mountains soon.*
*Born, to the wife Wm D Clark, on the 15th inst., twins, boy and girl. The boy is named Geo M and the girl Mary McKinley. Good Luck!*
*It is said that Mrs Lutz, who ran away some days ago with young Masters, has returned to her husband.*
*At the Barnes' wedding a few days ago, several young men had their hats and overcoats cut to pieces. And this said to be a civilized country.*
*On last Tuesday night a young man by the name of Raymond Davis, while riding along the road near Potts Mill, Madison County, which is on Paint Lick Creek, was fired upon from behind a gate post by one Parker, and his horse was killed and himself slightly wounded. It is said that Parker, seeing the horse fall and supposing that he had killed both horse and rider, told a neighbor of his deed and fled the country.*
*The invitations are out for the marriage of our esteemed fellow citizen and brilliant young orator and divine, Rev Horace G Turner, to Miss Ella Bailey West, of Georgetown, on Dec 2. We extend to them, in advance, our hearty congratulations and best wishes for a bright and happy future and all the felicity this world affords.* p3c4

This past week indicates that economic pressures have destabilized the social structure. Young people, likely girls, cut up the coats and hats of young boys at the wedding. I suppose you could call this a "prank". People are taking the law into their own hands concerning the toll roads. During this year the Correspondent has described poor fences and wandering livestock, people wandering the country-side at night, and thievery. In Nicholasville you have to keep your buildings locked, or they will even steal your coal! Illness and infant mortality have been widespread. You can't read the <u>Jessamine Journal</u> and call this decade the "Gay Nineties".

December 4, 1896

"Bourbon County now owns one hundred miles of its turnpikes and by January 1 will own the remaining two hundred." p2c1

## December 11, 1896

Murphy & Miller have moved their ads from the back page to the front page of the paper.

"The tollgate raiders visited Mercer County Saturday night and destroyed six gates" and threatened the gatekeepers about collecting additional tolls. p1c6

A barn burned down in Sulphur Well belonging to N D Davis. It was referred to as a tobacco warehouse, and contained 45 hogsheads of tobacco that belonged to M F Davis. It was insured for $4,100. p3c6 My math tells me this would be over 40,000 lbs of tobacco. In these days you would have to grow about 40 acres to strip out this much tobacco.

Another fire. "Friday morning about five o'clock, Mr George Snowden, living near Hanly, discovered his two-story brick house to be on fire, which with most of its contents were burned. Mr Snowden thinks it the work of an incendiary and saw a man leaving the premises about the time the fire was discovered. Loss, $3,500; insurance, $1,500." Supplement, p1c1 George's mother is Lucy Miller Snowden, daughter of Mrs Elizabeth Miller.

## December 18, 1896

In looking through the delinquent property tax list, I found J W Miller, 5 acres, adjoining W Masters. p2c3 I am reasonable sure that this is not "Uncle" Jim Miller. I believe he lived with his mother. There was no record of property being disposed after his death in 1898.

"Born to the wife of Walter S Hendren on the 12th, a son." p3c3 They had two sons, Marion and Harold, I believe Marion first.

"Askins-Walters.-Married at the residence of the bride's father, near Sulphur Well, on the 12th inst., Mr Sam Askins of Nicholasville, to Miss Emma Walters." p3c6 Sam recently was building a house where one had burned. He has the reputation of being a good carpenter. He was also stingy, opinionated and stubborn, and thought he knew everything. There are several stories about Sam, but perhaps the best one was about the time he wanted to build a rock wall on his place. Thinking he knew exactly how to build it, he got his rocks and built several layers. When it became obvious that it wasn't going well, he got a stone mason to come by and finish the job for him. The mason looked at the wall, and said "Sam, the worse problem I see, is that you have piled your rocks where you want the wall to be!"

December 25, 1896

The *Sulphur Well Correspondent* writes:

 Mr Sam Askins will, we understand, build a residence on the site of the Grimes' house, lately destroyed by fire.
 Born, to the wife of Robert Wade, on the 15th inst., a daughter.
 There has been considerable sickness in this section for some weeks past.
 Mrs Bettie Murphy is visiting the family of her son, J H Murphy. She has been for some time almost helpless from sciatica, but is now very much improved.
 Rev Baird will, on January 1, move into the Dr Mays' residence here. We welcome the addition of himself and family to our community.
 Cyrus Davis will move out of the C T Taylor residence, which will, we understand, be occupied by a colored family.
 Mr John Adams and wife, (nee Tudor) of Richmond, accompanied by Mr Jason Tudor, have been visiting friends in this neighborhood for some days. We understand that Mr Adams has been negotiating for the purchase of the Watts Mill property, now owned by L H Hendren.
 Prof Sibold is teaching night classes in music at the church. His pupils learn rapidly and are well pleased with ------ advance in the accomplishment.
 Mr W B Walker has been quite indisposed for some days from and old chronic trouble from which he suffers severely at frequent intervals.
 Our pater and mater familias are preparing to greet Chrismas with the usual cherry welcome, not forgetting at the same time the little ones and their stockings which are hung up with so much childish hope, implicit faith and wondering at the welcome Santa Claus. A Merry Christmas to all our friends, with the hope of many happy returns of the same. p2c3

Well, we've enjoyed many articles and a lot of family news this year!

CLOTHING STORE - 1897

Forest Miller purchased the remaining interest of the clothing store in Nicholasville. His advertisements are interesting and revealing of the times in which he lived. He clearly states his business philosophy--honesty in dealing with his customers.

January 8, 1897

George Dozier made an assignment. He only has assets of $500. George has been the proprietor of the Madison Monument Works for some time, and was doing well, but his collections were slow. p2c1

> Three deaths occurred in the family of Mr and Mrs A K Adcock this week, in the loss of their little daughter, Enis, Mrs Adcock's brother Fountain J Hendren, and -- ---------- Mr Allen Tudor, of Madison County. Mr Tudor was buried-------- Hendren on Tuesday ------------ on Wednesday. p2c2

The daughter is probably buried at Maple Grove. Fountain was born on November 25, 1865, the oldest child of Levisa and Will D Hendren. He died on January 8, 1897 at the age of 32, and is buried beside his parents in the Mt Gilead Cemetery in Madison County. My grandmother, Scottie never mentioned her brother, Fount, and never decorated his grave to my knowledge. It appears that Fount lived with the Adcocks, and may have worked in Adcock's saloon. Fount apparently never married. There is no cause of death for any of the three. I assume that Tudor's death was coincidental to the other two. They may have had the same disease.

January 15, 1897

The J W Miller property, with the delinquent taxes, adjoins W Masters. p2c5

January 22, 1897

"Mr and Mrs Adcock take this method of thanking their friends for the many kindnesses shown them during their recent troubles." p3c1

The *Sulphur Well Correspondent* writes:

> *Willie Long, son of John Long, of Edenton, died Saturday night of typhoid fever.*
> *Mr J P Turner is out again after a long spell of sickness.*
> *Mr Joseph Renfree, of Madison County, aged 80 years, died last Saturday from senile decay.*
> *A little party of young folks were pleasantly entertained by Mr and Mrs A M Askins, Tuesday night, with excellent music by Mr M R Harris, with his brother and sister and Mr N D Thompson.* p2c5

The Correspondent reports a lot of Madison County news. Both the Long and Renfree items related to Madison.

January 29, 1897

The *Sulphur Well Correspondent* writes:

*The sad news of the sudden and lamentable death early last Sunday morning of Luther Turner while away from home, came as a terrible shock to his doting parents and family, as well as to the whole community. Luther was universally liked by companions, friends and all who knew him, and was looked upon by all as a sociable, upright and industrious young man, with the prospect of a bright future and a useful life before him. For a beloved son to be stricken down at the very threshold of his young manhood, is calamitous enough to fond parents at any time, but for the blow to come as it did, swiftly and without any warning to that one under the circumstances, and undoubtedly with out attention, away from home and the loving care of the dearest ones on earth to soothe his last moments, is indeed a doubly grievous blow to his inconsolable parents, who have the deepest and heartfelt sympathy of their friends and neighbors. p2c4*

Luther is the youngest son of J P Turner. His older brothers are Jimmy and Horace. I had never heard his name before he was mentioned in a previous article.

According to the obituary (p3c3) Luther was 19 years old. He was sent to Garrard on business for his father. On his way home, he was approached by several parties who asked him to "chip in" on some liquor. He first said "no", but later the liquor was bought. After heavy drinking he was taken unconscious to the home of William Stotts where he died at 2 o'clock Sunday morning. Funeral services were held Tuesday morning at the Turner home in Sulphur Well. He is buried at Maple Grove Cemetery.

"Lizzie and Hattie Warner, the two little daughters of Mrs Nannie Warner, of this place, were taken to the Cleveland Orphan Institution, Versailles, Tuesday." p3c1 I don't believe that there is any doubt that this is the "Miss Hattie" Warner that became the principal of Nicholasville High School. She taught History that was a required subject for graduation, and she was a strict disciplinarian. She terrorized students from my mother's generation to mine. She was a very nice person after you graduated! Her sister Lizzie, who married a Hart, was a ding-a-ling. Both sisters were teachers.

February 5, 1897

A patent has been obtained to cool a residence in summer as well as heat it in winter. p2c1

February 12, 1897

Jessamine has 129 miles of turnpikes, of which 13 miles have been abandoned. The tax valuation of the roads upon which tolls are collected is $21,400. "Very few of the turnpikes pay any dividends to the stockholders." The Sulphur Well and Hanley Turnpike was valued at $100. This is better known as the Hoover Pike. The Nicholasville and Kentucky River Turnpike ran to the river by way of Chrisman Mill. The juncture of the road to Sulphur Well was still known in my day as the "Double Tollgate". It was valued at $2,000. This route and the Union Mill Road were the most direct means to Madison County. p3c3

### February 19, 1897

Willard Davis was badly cut by a thief who stole his valise at Livingston, Ky. p3c4 Willard has the farm on the left before you get to Black Bridge.

Clayton West, son of John West of Sulphur Well, married Lizzie Robinson at the home of the bride's father. p3c5

### February 26, 1897

"The silver and gold Democrats of Madison County will unite in their coming primary and support whoever the nominees may be." p2c1 The editor declares this to be "good sound sense".

### March 5, 1897

"Mrs Sue Nave, widow of the late Dr J E Nave, is reported dangerously ill at her home on West Street." p3c3

### March 12, 1897

Politics has apparently reached a low ebb. A disgruntled voter's letter to the editor is on the front page of the paper entitled "Incompetency of Political Aspirants".p1c6 Then on page two the editor says "the municipal government of Louisville was bad enought when the Democrats were in power, but under Republican administration it is rotten to the core and an open disgrace to the State." p2c1

### March 19, 1897

"Wm McC Johnston, who was nominated for county attorney by the Republicans of Garrard County last Saturday is a brother-in-law of Mrs B D Spears, of this place." p3c1

### March 26, 1897

In a bizarre twist, two murderers, implicated Dr Geo B Wagner, brother-in-law of Dr Geo M Hendren, of Sulphur Well. Dr Hendren prepared a statement that Wagner had been with the family, and the Commercial-Tribune confirmed that the accusation was a hoax. p3c2 There is to be more next week.

April 2, 1897

Dr Wagner, who lives in Bellevue, suffered violent dimentia at the time of, or shortly before, the murder of a young girl in that area, but was in no manner connected to the murder. He was, in fact, in Jessamine County at the residence of his father-in-law, William Hendren, two miles from Nicholasville. Dr Hendren and Walter Hendren are his brother-in-laws; Dr Wagner married their sister Annie. She wrote the family from Bellevue, described his condition, and asked for help. Walter went to Bellevue and brought Dr Wagner home with him. It appears that the murderers read of the doctor's plight and sought to put the blame on him. p1c3

April 9, 1897

According to the Courier Journal, Kentucky exports over 75,000 head of cattle to England each year, at an average value of $65 per head. It is claimed that Kentucky has some of the best breeding stock in the country. p1c3

April 16, 1897

Life is really difficult for those who are trying hard to make a living. Roving dogs kill sheep all the time. Chicken thieves are a constant problem. The East Hickman correspondent says "It is hard to decide which are the most annoying, sheep-killing dogs or poultry stealing men." p2c4

April 23, 1897

George F Snowden and others conveyed 15 acres of land to Samuel F Taylor, for $300. It is adjacent to Vince Brumfield. p2c3

"Rev H G Turner, of Eminence, is visiting his parents at Ambrose." p3c3 Mrs J H Turner, is visiting her parents, the Grinstead's at Stanford. p2c3

"Dr Geo B Wagner is the guest of relatives here where he will remain for some days, with a view of locating in the county. His mind seems to be fully restored." p3c3

A petition for free roads has been presented to the County Judge. He will put the question on the ballot for the November election. p3c4

Lock No 7 is now about twelve feet high. Eight more feet will be added beginning in May. Some 600 men will be employed.

April 30, 1897

L S F, from Wilmore, recently visited Tampa, and declared it somewhat disappointing. He considered its downtown unsubstantial and its residences to lack elegance. It has become an important cigar manufacturing center, primarily because of several thousand Cubans living there. He made very derogatory remarks about them and their mode of life. p1c1-2

Wm J Denboe was elected U S Senator on the 112th ballot of the Legislature. He finally beat Blackburn and two other contenders. p2c2

Dr John C Miller is advertising a breeding season to a saddle stallion for $7. p3c4

May 7, 1897

"Rev H G Turner and wife, of Carrollton, are visiting his parents, Mr and Mrs J P Turner, Ambrose." p2c3

May 14, 1897

It looks like its going to happen in a rush, free roads, that is. All the counties are voting on the question.

The Democratic primary election will be May 25th.

Olive Wilds, daughter of the late Dr Wilds, is graduating from the Jessamine Institute.

The *Sulphur Well Correspondent* writes:

*Miss Ola March has been visiting for several days at Mrs Elizabeth Miller's.*
*Rev Hildebrand, of Lexington, preached here Saturday and Sunday last.*
*A daughter of George Walters, near here, has been sick from typhoid fever for some weeks.*
*Mrs Hattie Davis and daughter, Carmen, were visiting at Dr Hendren's last Sunday.*
*Miss Lulu Holman and Lulu Snyder, of Nicholasville, visited N D Davis last Sunday.*
*Mr Ike Dunn, of Garrard, Luther Saunders and Earnest Duncan visited friends here Sunday.*
*Mr William Masters and son, of Bloomington, Ill., were visiting friends here last week.*
*Several old soldiers, among whom were Allen A Burton, B F Foster and James Hendren, and several plain citizens attended the G A R reunion at Lexington Monday.*
*R M Hill, who died recently of pneumonia, was one of the most respected citizens and energetic business men of this community and had the esteem of all who knew him for his sterling worth and integrity.*
*Mr Henry Woodward, son of James Woodward, of this place, was badly poisoned Friday evening by the fumes of a sheep dip inhaled and absorbed for about one-half day while assisting some other hands in dipping sheep for N D Davis. He was seriously sick from Friday night till Saturday forenoon, but is out again apparently as well as ever. One of the other hands, Jesse Miller, was taken sick before night and had to quit and go home. The dip was composed of lime, tobacco, carbolic acid and some other ingredients unknown to your correspondent. p2c4*

I remember when Guy Stacy used to have a sheep dip pen in one corner of the crossroad. It seems that they always started early in the morning, and I can still hear the baa's of the sheep as they were driven into the pen, and then run single file though the trough that held the dip. Someone stood beside the trough with a crook, to push the sheep under, as they passed by. This dipping occurred right after the sheep were sheared. They were quite a pathetic sight after being sheared and dipped.

May 21, 1897

The Fayette County Court House was totally destroyed by fire, all the records too.

May 28, 1897

Home grown strawberries are selling for 10 cents a quart, and spring chickens are selling at 20 and 25 cents each.

"George Snowden visited friends at Winston, Estill County, last week." p3c2

"Dr Jno C Miller spent from Friday until Monday with his son, Prof Rice Miller, at Campbellsville, where school closes next week and the trustees and patrons are unanimous in their expression for Prof Miller's return next year." p3c2

June 4, 1897

The turnpikes pro and con are front page news.

June 11, 1897

The *Sulphur Well Correspondent* writes:

*Rev Walter S Smith, of Indiana, preached here Monday night.*
*Miss Ora Masters is visiting Mr James Woodward's family.*
*Mr Hugh Miller and family were visiting Dr Hendren last week.*
*W L Buford was elected trustee in this school district last Saturday.*
*George Snowden will rebuild soon his residence that burned down some time ago.*
*Mr Wilson Masters is out again after the accident of breaking his arm and dislocating the wrist.*
*Although it greatly increases the labor of the trustees of a school district, the new rule of taking the school census is evidently a good one and the results justify the fore-sight of the present Superintendent of Public Instruction in promulgating it.*
*The school funds will now be more equitably distributed. The country districts, from whence fairly honest lists were sent in, suffered from the padded censuses of the crowded city districts, as witness the falling off of 1,500 children in the city of Lexington this year.*
*Some amusing things are often interposed with the more serious happenings of life. For instance, the directors of the Kirksville & Kentucky River Turnpike last Thursday concluded to remove their toll-gate, throwing open the road to free travel. But the raiders that night restored one of the gates in as good order as it was before. The gate-keeper was in a quandary what to*

*do and appealed to the president of the road who ordered her to destroy it with an axe, which was done with the remark: "There, I guess the rascals won't put it up again." p2c7*

June 18, 1897

A good man.-Prof Rice Miller, of Nicholasville, is one of the applicants for Principal of the High School, and has been here this week stating his claims to the board. Prof Miller is a graduate of Central University, and is not only a fine scholar and excellent instructor, but a polished and popular gentleman, as well. For the past two years he has had charge of the Campbellsville public school. We do not know whether the Board intends to retain Prof Hough or not, but we do know that it will make no mistake if, in its wisdom, it selects Prof Miller to be Principal for the next scholastic year. This is reprinted from the Richmond Register. Jessamine Journal. p3c2

More about Rice:
It is rumored around that the handsome applicant for the Caldwell High School principalship, Mr Rice Miller, of Nicholasville, will about the first of September take unto himself a wife. The young lady's name could not be learned, but we have been told that her home was in the neighborhood of the Pond Meeting House on the Barnes' Mill Pike." From the Richmond Climax. Reprinted in the Jessamine Journal p3c3

A former resident of Sulphur Well dies. Mrs George Diamond, age 37, died after a long illness. She was born and raised in Sulphur Well; her first name was Arkie; her first husband was Melvin Davis; no indication of her maiden name. She is buried in Maple Grove Cemetery. p3c4

June 25, 1897

"Mrs James Turner is visiting relatives at Stanford." p3c3

A heavy hailstorm passed over Nicholasville at 3pm Sunday.

July 2, 1897

Union Mills is featured in this issue of the Journal. "Union Mills ... is situated about four miles east of Nicholasville, on Hickman Creek...." A long dam "rises eight or ten feet above the creek bed." The area is described as extremely beautiful with wild flowers, shrubs and trees, in a natural setting. p1c5 After reading this description, I went out to take a look at it. Such is no longer the case. An abandoned steel bridge is an eyesore. The distillery buildings that were located there have now been torn down, and no evidence remains that they were ever there.

July 9, 1897

Trusts and monopolistic combinations that strangle competition, together with a monetary system that is unable to expand the money supply when needed, is blamed for causing the economic contractions, often called "panics".

High Bridge reports that blackberries are ripe and plentiful. p2c5

"Prof Rice Miller went to Campbellsville Monday." p3c3 He and two other professors applied for the Richmond principalship. Prof Clark, who had the position two years ago was reelected. p3c4

July 16, 1897

L M P writes the following description of the Sulphur Well neighborhood:

Between the Danville pike and Sulphur Well, on a good road, and about three-quarters of a mile from the village you pass the home of Mr W H Hoover, Sr. I say pass, but many do not, but stop, for it is an open home, and many are the guests who are welcomed. All through Jessamine County are men, women and children who are eager to testify to this home as one of the most pleasing among the hospitable homes of Kentucky to visit, and to verify the fact that Mr and Mrs Hoover are a model host and hostess. The family is a well known one, two of our prominent men being the only children of this home--E B Hoover, our present county attorney, and an able lawyer, and Mr W H Hoover, Jr, a prominent farmer and horseman. The Hoover home is a pretty one; the house, a large, two-story frame, situated a slight distance from the pike, being surrounded with pleasing grounds. Mr Hoover owns a good farm, well cultivated, and it produces well this year. Mr and Mrs Hoover command the love and respect of their many acquaintances, and much more in praise could be said of them was there space here for it. Just a little further down the road is situated the house of Mr Newton D Davis. This is also a hospitable home, and Mr and Mrs Davis are held highly by the good people of Ambrose and many others. They have among their possessions, a number of agreeable children, and the Davis household altogether is one deserving of worthy mention. In the village of Ambrose is the pretty residence of Mr J Howard Murphy, the lawn of which is fronted by a beautiful hedge, and made all the prettier by a honeysuckle that twines its fragrant blossoms with the green of the hedge. Mr Murphy is a well-known business man, and a most agreeable acquaintance. He is the proprietor of the store at Ambrose. And then there is the Horine family with the two pleasing bachelors, one of whom was a candidate for representative, but withdrew before the day for nomination. And down near the Well lives Mr Tom Horine in his home on a commanding hill. It is from this same Ambrose that much of the best bread of Nicholasville is buttered. Mr Alex Askins, the dairy-man, makes the finest of butter which is duly appreciated by his patrons. (I don't understand this. He is a blacksmith) The home of Mrs James Peel, whose husband was an own cousin to E R Sparks, is situated back of a very pretty although equally as small lake. This lake is in proportion to Ambrose as Lake Mingo is to Nicholasville. The home of James Cobb is centrally placed in the village, and everyone knows Mr Cobb too well for anything further to be said by me. Beyond the village lives Dr J C Miller whose home is well-known by the many friends of the family, and on the other side of the Well you find the beginning of the long avenue that leads to the home of Mr J P Turner. Farther up you find the Hare residence." p1c6

I omitted the beginning and the end of this very long article since it did not pertain directly to Sulphur Well. I was born in the Jim Cobb house that is mentioned. Forest and Scottie Miller purchased the house in a later year that I will have to look up. I also lived on the Hoover farm. It was purchased by Luther Ware in a later year, and my father Frank Ware was the tenant for several years, during the thirties. I think that we moved from the farm about 1940, and moved in with Forest and Scottie Miller. I lived in Sulphur Well until I married in 1961, and my mother lived there until after she retired from teaching and moved to Lexington, perhaps about 1980. Forest Miller also purchased the Murphy Store that is mentioned, and operated it for approximately forty years. Forest retired from the store and my father operated it for perhaps two years thereafter. We rented the store to Guy Stacy and Joe Breiner for several years, then sold it to them. We didn't sell the house until after my mother moved. It is quite a coincidence that in this one article that I have these close ties. George Ware inherited the Hoover farm, and still lives there. I am a little surprised that the writer mentions Dr Miller, whose farm is miles away, and neglected to mention Mrs Elizabeth Miller's house, which was a large house between those of Alex Askins and Tom Horine, both of whom are mentioned. I also wonder why he failed to identify Dr Hendren's house, which is next to the store, and worthy of mention. The Peel house, above the pond, is where Luther Ware later purchased and lived. What incredible coincidences!

I guess you could call this pre-flight. "C H Lamson ascended to a height of 50 feet near Falmouth, Me., the other day on one of his big kites." p4c5 Undoubedly, the construction of these "kites" was similar to the ones that the Wright brothers attached bicycles.

The High Bridge Camp Meeting runs from July 23 to August 1.

July 23, 1897

Old ties: "Miss Emma Spruce is visiting Miss Hattie Jones, Buckeye, Garrard County." p3c3

July 30, 1897

Here are some farm prices for comparison with past years. Wheat is $0.63 per bushel; steers 4 cents per pound; and one crop of tobacco averaged 9 cents per pound. p2c3 These prices are about the same, or lower than they were in 1877, twenty years ago.

August 6, 1897

Nicholasville will soon have a telephone exchange.

Japan has agreed to arbitrate the Hawaiian matter.

J H Turner lost his certificate for his ten shares of the Farmers Bank stock, and applied for a duplicate.

"Miss Annie Wagers and Mr Charles Miller, of Irvine, have been the guests since Friday of Dr Jno C Miller and family, returning home today." p3c3 This is Charles Wallace Miller, the attorney and son of Mann Miller who is the brother of Dr Miller.

The *Sulphur Well Correspondent* writes:

*Mr William Hendren has recovered his old family horse that was stolen some nights ago.*
*The three children of Tip Broaddus, who were taken with fever a few days ago, are better.*
*Mrs Wash Brock was seriously ill last week.*
*Mrs G M Hendren returned from a visit to Richmond.*
*George Fain's little son was so unfortunate a few days since as to fall and dislocate his wrist.*
*The eclipse was an object of general curiosity in this vicinity.*
*J P Turner lost a very valuable 1,600 lb steer by its falling into a walled up spring last week.*
*Little Mamie Turner, daughter of J H Turner, was quite sick a few days since, but is better now.*
*A great deal of stock is collected at this point by the various buyers.*
*There is considerable fever among the colored population of this neighborhood.*
*Mr Ray Miller has been quite sick, but has about recovered.*
*The public school was opened here Monday with a good attendance.*
*The thermometer was only 98 degrees here on Monday.*
*The storm Sunday did very little damage except tearing the trees somewhat and blowing down some corn.*
*A good sized delegation from here visited camp meeting Sunday and missed the storm.*
*The hemp crop as well as the corn crop will simply be immense in this section.*
*Melvin Dean and others delivered a nice lot of shoats here for A C Miles, Tuesday, at $3.25 per hundred.*
*We had a show here a few days ago, it was grand--the grandest fraud since the "perfessor" of figgers was with us.*
*A protracted meeting will commence here Saturday night before the second Sunday of this month.*
*Tuesday was one of our hottest days, the mercury climbing rapidly to the 100 mark and remaining there or thereabouts the rest of the day.*
*Monday night some enterprising or desperate burglar tried to force his way into A M Askins' house by way of a rear door at about 11 pm, but made too much noise and awoke Luther Ware who aroused Mr Askins, when with guns they looked for the thief who had by this time gone around the house. On getting sight of him, Mr Askins fired, but it is not supposed the man was touched, by the rapidity of his movements in seeking another locality more congenial to his feelings and health, by way of the garden gate and out through the palings to safety.*

*During the heavy storm Sunday evening, William Sallee, who resided on Silver Creek, Madison County, was struck by lightning while standing in the door and almost instantly killed, as he only made a few gasps and died in about a minute. He was a son of John Sallee, a good citizen and leaves a young family. It is also reported that in Garrard County, lightning on Sunday evening instantly killed William Sadler, an old soldier, just as he was closing the door to keep the storm out. There are also other reports of lighting destroying barns and other buildings, stock and hay and wheat stacks in that county, and playing havoc generally. p3c6*

August 13, 1897

T R D (Roland Dean), of Little Hickman, writes about the possibility of gas or oil in that area. He points to the abundance of sulphur or chalybeate springs. He also says that there are commercial quantities of sand. p1c3

August 20, 1897

"George S Diamond leaves next Monday for New York City, where he has accepted a position in a hat house." p3c3 His wife died earlier, and the house in which he was living just burned.

Several people are visiting. Oscar Sageser has just returned from a six month visit in Virden, Illinois. Hamlet Dozier, Lexington, visited his sister, Mrs G W Horine last week. This is the "Ham" Dozier that frequently visited Sulphur Well with Elbert Masters and Walter Bain. They were all Nicholasville boys. Mr E J Curley, distillery owner at Camp Nelson, is cruising aboard a yacht at Bar Harbor, Maine. p3c3

"Masters-James.-Married, at the home of John Lear, Nicholasville, Gabriel Masters, Ambrose, and Miss Ella James, daughter of Eli James, dec'd, Rev Russell Baird officiating." p3c4 They had a son, Gilbert, and a daughter Josephine. Gilbert and his wife were friends of my parents, and their children, Harold and Mildred, were friends of mine. I believe they wound up in Mississippi. Gabe and Ella lived on the hill in the curve to the left, going toward Nicholasville.

I am reasonably sure that this is "White Cloud". G M Berry, "the handsomest man traveling from Lexington", is still with Louis Stix & Co., Cincinnati. Berry looks "much younger with his hat on than with it off." He dresses well and is in a good humor all the time. p3c3 If you go back to September, 1887 you will see when the Windom correspondent twitted the Sulphur Well correspondent that the only reason that he wouldn't get Gray was because he was bald. By that time the Gray family had moved to Lexington. Ida and Texie Gray visited Sulphur Well, and a week or two later George M Berry visited Lexington. Then in February of 1888, came the news that Ida Gray had married George M Berry, who traveled for a Cincinnati house. The last article written by the person who identified himself as White Cloud was September 23, 1887. The next article was December 9, 1887 and was identified as being written by Joy, then Ivy. Berry was a contemporary of Johnston, Dozier, Walker, Woodward, and other young men of the late eighties. George and Ida are buried in the Lexington Cemetery. He was born in 1854, and died in 1928; she was born in 1868 and died in 1923. Both sisters, Ida and Texie had relatively short lives.

The *Sulphur Well Correspondent* writes:

*Miss Viola Davis is off on a visit to Pleasureville.*
*Two young Garrard County gentlemen, Messrs Jones and Hendren, were visiting here Sunday.*
*Pensioners are just now being made happy by the getting their checks from their "Uncle".*
*Squire Hendren and wife, of Madison County, are visiting his father, James Hendren.*
*Miss Emma Soper is visiting Mrs Clayton West this week.*
*Mrs Egbert and children, of Lexington, are guests of Mrs Margaret Horine for a few days.*
*Mrs S N Snowden and daughter, Myrtie, are visiting at Mt Sterling.*
*There is considerable sickness in this vicinity, but none in the village to speak of. This is a healthy town.*
*Mrs Ezekiel Hendren has been quite sick for some days, but is now better.*
*This being Institute week the schools are all closed.*
*F M Horine has bought the C T Taylor place.*
*Jerry Bennett, a colored pensioner, died on the 10th inst., just before the arrival of his check.* p3c5

August 27, 1897

The Teachers Institute of Jessamine County convened in Nicholasville on August 16th. It lasted a week, and the schedule indicates that they had a visiting consultant who listened to a selected group of teachers describe their method of teaching a particular subject. He, then, offered suggestions for improvement. Each day began with a devotional and the singing of "America" or other patriotic songs. p1c3-4

"J S Hill sold Tuesday to J H Turner 143 acres of land near Sulphur Well." p2c3

"Dr J C Miller had 21 acres of wheat in Jessamine to average over 40 bushels to the acre. Another tract of 31 acres averaged about 30, and a third containing 26 acres, 27 bushels. One hundred acres on his Madison County farm yielded about 2,000 bushels." p2c3

Buffalo Bill's Wild West show came to Lexington. About 50,000 people attended the parade; 16,000 bought tickets that afternoon; and 9,000 more that night. Many people expressed their disappointment in the show, saying that it didn't live up to their expectations.

Some visiting going on. "Miss Dora Murphy is the guest of Miss May Taylor at Lexington." p3c3 Dora's father is the proprietor of the general store in Sulphur Well. "Miss Bertha Hendren is visiting her friend and schoolmate, Miss Beatrice Wells, Junction City." p3c3 Bertha is Scottie's sister. "Misses Mattie and Ella Woodward, of Jessamine County, are the guests of Mr and Mrs G M Berry, 87 South Spring Street, for a few days." p3c3 This is George and Ida Berry popping up again.

The *Sulphur Well Correspondent* writes:

*Mr Jas W Miller has returned from a visit to friends at Irvine.*
*Mr Hugh Miller and family, of Richmond, are visiting Dr G M Hendren this week.*
*E G Walker and Mr Hall visited Versailles this week.*
*Mr F F Miller has acted as postmaster this week in the absence of our genial Jim.*
*Mr Clayton West has moved to Mr Allen Robinson's, his father-in-law, near Logana.*
*Mr J H Turner will shortly move back to his home here.*
*Mr and Mrs James Woodward, Jr were visiting relatives here Saturday and Sunday.*
*Mr Hamlet Foster was visiting his father, B Frank Foster, last Sunday.*
*Mr Sam Askins is painting his new house a beautiful straw color.*
*Thursday night, Aug 10, the "boys" gave Gabriel Masters, the young married son of Wilson Masters, a charivari in good old-fashioned style.*
*The old darkey, Jerry Bennett, who died here a few days ago, had been married ten times. Two wives were sold south and eight others died. It is said he was thinking of marrying again when death come to him instead.*
*Mr Frank Bishop and family, of Virden, Ill, who are visiting his father-in-law, Mr James T Sageser, was taken suddenly and violently ill Thursday evening of last week with heart trouble and it was some time before his physician thought him to be sufficienly recovered to be pronounced out of immediate danger.* p2c1

September 3, 1897

"Prof Rice Miller left Wednesday to assume the principalship of the Hardin Collegiate Institute, at Elizabethtown. Prof Miller is a fine instructor and the citizens of that place can feel assured that their institution of learning will be safe in his hands." p3c3

The *Sulphur Well Correspondent* writes:

*Hemp growers are paying $2.25 per acre for having it cut.*
*The Peel brothers, it is said, will soon move to the old Peel farm.*
*Napoleon B Long, of Madison County, has rented the W H Hoover, Jr, farm and moved to it.*
*F M Horine sold seven head of cattle to Christian & McDaniels, of Chilesburg, at $20 per head.*
*N D Davis has purchased the interest of Geo S Diamond in (the) Hunter homestead here, now occupied by Mrs Emily Peel.*
*J P Turner sold a nice lot of sheep to J B Embry last week. Mr Turner also sold to Fayette County parties 38 head of cattle at 4 1/2c per pound.*
*Our citizens as a rule, are for free pikes, and it is broadly hinted at everywhere that there will be trouble if they are not voted.*
*Jas H Turner has moved back to his residence here lately occupied (by) Clayton West. He purchased the R M ---- farm ------------- $4,000 cash.*
*(The last item is unreadable)* p2c2

J H Turner purchased the J S Hill farm containing 143 acres.

September 10, 1897

"The paper collar industry which at one time reached $1,750,000 a year is now fast vanishing." p2c1

"Mule colts are selling at from $25 to $60." p2c3 "J B Embry shipped two car loads of sheep to Cincinnati this week for which he paid $3 per head." p2c3

It appears that Forest Miller has purchased the interest of J Howard Murphy in their clothing store. There was no other announcement. This is his first advertisement that spreads across the lower three inches of the entire front page:

> FEAST OF FALL FASHIONS! A great temptation is placed before the men and boys of Nicholasville and Jessamine County in the magnificent display of our NEW FALL GOODS. This temptation is not altogether our fault. The makers must answer for the stylish and extreme low prices of our showings. We have simply brought to Nicholasville the BEST and CHEAPEST line of CLOTHING, SHOES, HATS, FURNISHING GOODS, etc., ever seen here, and we purchased them to sell and please our customers. Call and inspect them this week. No trouble to show goods. F FOREST MILLER, Clothier and Furnisher. p1c1-8

The store was located directly across from the Court House. The First National Bank was located there when I was a teenager. It now houses a radio station.

September 17, 1897

H W Rose is auctioning off his stock of clothing, hats, caps, and furnishings. p1c7-8

Property transfer. "Geo S Diamond to N D Davis, interest in 70 acres of land, $350." p2c3

It's been a dry summer. The High Bridge correspondent says "the river has been drained and the springs have almost dried up." p2c4

The *Sulphur Well Correspondent* writes a long letter:

> *Mr F M Hudson has been on the sick list for some days.*
> *Mr Forest Miller has returned from a brief visit to Cincinnati.*
> *Lee Davis was married to Miss Annie Barnes Thursday.*
> *Mrs Sudie Richardson, of Irvine, was visiting her mother here last week.*
> *There is considerable sickness along Hickman Creek; mostly malarial trouble from low water.*
> *Mrs George Snowden has been very sick for some days with the prevailing fever.*
> *Mr William Hendren and wife are visiting for a few days at Buckeye, Garrard County.*
> *The Rev Absolom Reynolds will preach at the church here next Sunday.*
> *John Durham was married to Miss Anderson, daughter of Eli Anderson, Thursday, Sept 9, at 3 pm.*
> *Mr William Turner and bride, of Bowling Green, have been on a visit to his brother, Mr J P Turner.*

Miss Lulu, daughter of Wilson Masters, fell from a wagon last Monday and dislocated her right wrist.

Mr S N Underwood has two children very sick from remittent fever and a mild form of scarlet fever.

James Woodward, Sr, who has been very sick from fever for some days, is getting better, and will be out in a few days.

Our old friend, Edward Murphy, we are glad to say is now one of Uncle Sam's pensioners.

There has been several cases of mild scarlatina among the children in the Little Hickman neighborhood.

Mr J E Gott, of Madison County, has rented the Arkie Diamond farm for next year for $350.

Mr Ambrose Cobb, of Peel's Branch, has some children sick with malarial fever.

Mr James Hendren and his brother, Jack, and family, have just returned from a visit to Madison County.

Mr James Richardson, of Irvine, Estill County, is on a visit to friends and relatives in this section.

Robert Grant, son of our merchant, J William Grant, will wed Miss Luella, the handsome daughter of Mr S N Underwood, this week.

John Underwood will this week wed the belle of Mt Lebanon, the daughter of Mr Jerry Comley.

Mr William Hall, of Woodford County, is visiting his brother, Henry Hall, this week.

The Republicans held a precinct meeting here Saturday and selected delegates to the convention that meets in town on (the) 8th inst.

Mr Elbert G Walker, our enterprising stockman, sold a bunch of yearling cattle to Leroy Hisle, of Spearsville, at 3 1/2c and one calf alone brought him $26. He asks, "if this isn't prosperity, what is it?"

Franklin Bishop, of Virden, Ill., a coal miner, who is on a visit to his father-in-law, Jas T Sageser, has had several very serious attacks of heart failure.

It is said that Mr Ernest Duncan and Miss Vena, eldest daughter of Mr Wm Henry Cobb, will be married this week.

Mrs Kittie Knight is on a visit of several days to Mrs Elizabeth Miller.

The watermelon crop in this section is fine, and melons are, notwithstanding the enormous crop, selling at good figures.

Col T B Demaree, and William Lowens, candidate for county judge on the Prohibition ticket, spoke here Wednesday night, Sept 8.

Water is in great demand in this section and enormous quantities of it are hauled from the public pump daily. p2c4

Mrs Miller has her daughter and son-in-law visit her this week. Her son Forest has gone to Cincinnati, probably for merchandise. Then, she is visited by Kitty Knight.

## September 24, 1897

"N D Davis shipped to Cincinnati, Tuesday 200 sheep for which he paid from $2.25 to $4." p2c3 "Half the wheat in Mercer County is yet unsold, and is being held for $1.25." p2c3

October 1, 1897

The new lock and dam will be ready for use October 15th.

The extreme dry spell has not been surpassed in years, probably since 1881. The railroad has been busy putting out fires in pastures beside the tracks. About 30 acres of grass was destroyed by sparks from a fire in a cooking stove used by workhands that were camping out while cutting corn. p3c2

Technology. "The wonderful veriscope, presenting pictures of the Corbett-Fitzsimmons fight at Carson City, will be seen at the Lexington Opera House this (Friday) afternoon and tonight, also tomorrow afternoon and night." p3c2 A really expensive telephone conversation took place last week when John Embry, the cattle buyer held a five minute conversation with his employer in Chicago. It cost Mr Embry $3.75. p3c2 Mrs Embry was equally extravagant. She entertained all the children on Wagner Avenue last Saturday afternoon by giving them a picnic at Duncan Heights. p3c3

According to the Richmond Register a bunch of New York capitalist are going to buy the Riney B and extend the line on to Beattyville. They have been over the line several times recently. p3c3

The *Sulphur Well Correspondent* returns this week:

*There seems to be considerable fever still of the malarial order.*
*Mrs J H Turner, who has been quite ill from fever, is better.*
*Elder R G Frank will preach at the Christian Church next Sunday evening.*
*Mr N B Long's infant child has been very sick with pneumonia for several days.*
*Mr Jno P Miller, of Wisemantown, was on a few days visit to his mother here last week.*
*Mrs Emorine Crow is visiting relatives at Winchester this week.*
*Vince Brumfield sold a lot of shoats to Willard Davis at $3.65. J P Turner sold a lot of lambs to Nath Hughes at good prices.*
*The old village pump is in a fair way to be repaired at last. Water for all purposes is very scarce and all vegetation is as dry as tinder.* p2c5

"At a recent meeting of the law class of the University of Virginia" Charles W Miller was elected President. "Mr Miller is the son of M M Miller, of Irvine, Ky and a nephew of Dr John C Miller, of this county." He is a graduate of Centre College and Yale University. A fellow classmate from Centre, Brutus Clay of Paris, Ky, made the nominating speech. "He was Centre's representative in the intercollegiate oratorical contest in 1894, and (his nominating speech) won the admiration and applause of all...." p3c6

Granddad Miller sure has some tough competion. Vic Bloomfield & Co is advertising 24 styles of all wool suits for seven dollars. p3c7-8 Kaufman-Wilson (clothiers) in Lexington is in receivership.

Steve Snowden was an election officer at the Sulphur Well precinct. p4c6

October 8, 1897

The Jessamine Journal for the next several weeks is publishing old marriage records. The very first one was the marriage of Frederick Sageser to Catherine (Kitty) Bruner, Oct 3, 1799. p1c5 These are the parents of Celia Sageser who married Merriman F Miller. Both Merriman and Celia are buried in the family cemetery on the Miller farm.

The drouth has had its effect on stock prices. Feeder cattle were selling for 2 1/2 to 3 3/4 cents per pound at Richmond's Court Day. Horses and mules could scarcely be sold at any price. p2c3 The Pinckard Correspondent says several carloads of cattle had been shipped from there recently. p2c4 The Union Mills correspondent says that Hickman Creek is dry, and that dead fish are everywhere. p2c4

Mrs Mahala Miller, who died at Ambrose, was perhaps one of the oldest persons in Jessamine County. This is her obituary. "Mrs Mahala Miller, widow of the late William Miller, of Ambrose, died Tuesday morning at 1 am., of heart disease, at the residence of Jefferson W Miller, at the advance age of 94 years." p3c5 Her husband, William, was a son of Francis M Miller, and a brother of Merriman Miller. Jefferson W Miller is Mahala's son. He married Mary E Blakeman. Their children included Frank Miller and Nettie Miller.

Voter registration was this past Tuesday and both parties were active in getting voters registered. The editor says that people who have never before been interested in politics are urging others to register. p3c2

Rev H G Turner and his wife are visiting J P Turner. p3c3

October 15, 1897

The October issue of the Ladies Home Journal begins a series of articles "Inside of a Hundred Homes" picturing "interiors of the most artistically furnished houses in America." p1c5 I'll bet that stimulated a lot interior decorating around the county!

The latest New York fashions feature Russian blouses. The correspondent says that "the craze is phenomenal ... since ingenuity could hardly devise more unsightly outlines than a bagging at the waist line." p1c6

Times are indeed hard. The Nicholasville Fiscal Court reduced the salaries of county officials--the judge, the county attorney, and the school superintendent. p2c1

William Jennings Bryan still draws hugh crowds to hear him speak.

The *Sulphur Well Correspondent* writes:

*Mr James Snowden, of Irvine, Estill county, is visiting friends here.*

*Some few sales of clover seed have been made in this section at $3 per bushel.*

*Stock sales of hogs, sheep and cattle were never more numerous in this neighborhood than at present.*

*J P Turner sold 200 sheep to the Davis boys at $2.65 per cwt. They were shipped to Cincinnati.*

*Tobacco growers are very hopeful, and with good cause owing to the advanced prices in the "weed".*

*Mrs Martha Whittaker, of Garrard County, has been on a visit of several days to her sister, Mrs N B Long.*

*Sulphur Well as a stock yard is almost equal to Union Stock Yards in Cincinnati as a buying and shipping point.*

*Candidates on the hand-shake are in evidence now wherever you go, and are very solicitous as to yours and your family's health.*

*Mr Roy Whittaker and wife, of Madison County, have returned home from a visit to his father-in-law, Mr Napoleon Long, of this neighborhood.*

*Young fruit and shade trees set out last fall and this spring seem to be dead or dying from the drouth and in fact some old forest trees are apparently dead from the same cause.*

*Mr Franklin M Hudson has returned from a visit to his brother, Charles W Hudson, at Richmond, where he is the efficient agent of the Singer Sewing Machine Company.*

*Mr Charlie Clubb, of Pleasureville, Henry County, recently visited friends at this place, and it is supposed that one of our most charming young ladies is the attraction.* p2c3

I suppose that it is an exageration that Sulphur Well is equal to Cincinnati as a shipping point, but there is no doubt that several local dealers made Sulphur Well a center of trading activity. The charming young lady being visited by Charlie Clubb was Viola Davis. Some rain fell on Monday, but was not considered enough to break the drouth.

The "New York Capitalists" didn't buy the Riney B after all! It was purchased by the lien-holders, the chief of whom was the prime contractor, Shanahan. p3c2

October 22, 1897

Forest Miller changed his advertisement as follows:
READ THIS, CLOTHING BUYERS! We will offer for sale, beginning SATURDAY, OCT. 23, the largest, cheapest and best selected line of Men's suits and Overcoats ever brought to the Nicholasville market. Boy's and children's suits and overcoats a specialty. Knee Pants in Casimers and Corduroys. Double-breasted Reefers for children. Men's fine shoes consisting of Box Calf, Patt. Leather, Patt. Leather Tans and Enameled calf shoes---will give lowest prices. Special prices on Overcoats and Suits for SATURDAY, OCT. 23. p1c1-8

"Died, after a severe attack of fever of three week's duration, Mrs Amy Dean, wife of Mr M L Dean, passed quietly away on October 15." p2c4

"Miss Ida Friend, of Paris, was the guest last week of Miss Lizzie Miller (Dr Miller's daughter)." p3c4

October 29, 1897

The *Sulphur Well Correspondent* writes:

*A son of J C Lutes is sick with indications of pneumonia.*
*Mr E Hendren is very low with some form of convulsions.*
*Mr E Vincent, of Edenton, Madison County, is visiting here for a few days.*
*Mr Addison Hendren, of Iowa Point, Kansas, is here on a visit to relatives.*
*Mr Hugh Miller and family, of Richmond, have been visiting here this week.*
*Mr N D Davis has built another large barn on his farm for tobacco purposes.*
*Mr S J Brown, of this place, is reported very sick at his brandy distillery in Garrard County.*
*Mr Jas T Sayer has secured a pension from Uncle Sam of $6 per month and back pay for several years.*
*A chessnutting party composed of Walter S Hendren and wife and Hugh Miller and family will start from here tomorrow for the mountains to be gone several days.*
*The long needed repairs on our portion of the pike are at last on the eve of commencing and we hope soon to have better roads, as the toll remains the same if the roads are good, bad or worse.* p2c3

Dr E O Guerrant will preach in the afternoon at 3 o'clock at Sulphur Well. p3c6

November 5, 1897

The election was Tuesday, November 2nd, and the Democrats prevailed. p2c1 The Lancaster Register said Monday was a failure so far as business was concerned. "A small crowd stood about the streets, talked politics, complained of the drouth and went home none the wiser or richer than when they came in." p2c3 After three months of drouth, the rains finally came to Jessamine County, so that the ground is in condition for sowing wheat.

The *Sulphur Well Correspondent* writes:

*Rev E O Guerrant preached here to a good sized congregation Sunday evening.*
*Harry P Hendren, of Edenton, Madison County, is visiting at A J Sageser's.*
*V P Brumfield has sold his farm to George Snowden for $3,000, and purchased Calvin Blakeman's farm at Pink for $3,400.*
*Mrs Richard Fain is quite sick from a severe attack of tonsilitis.*
*A young unbroken horse that Hunter Peel and his brother were driving to a cart became frightened and tried to kick things to pieces, but gave up the job and whirling spilled the occupants out, who under the circumstances, were probably not unwilling to vacate, and jumping the fence, cart and all, into Mr Turner's field, ran several times around it but finally halted without doing much damage.* p2c3

This is "Pat" Hendren. His name is Harry P Hendren, and he is visiting his sister Susie Sageser. The item indicates that he is living in Edenton, probably with relatives. He spent the latter part of his life living in Lexington. I don't know when he married; however, he and his wife, Hattie Foster, are buried in the Lexington Cemetery. She died in 1973, he on April 26 1976 at the age of 93. According to his obituary he was a member of the Woodland Christian Church; and was a retired restaurant operator, having been employed by the Lafayette Hotel and by Keeneland Race Course.

Other family notes: A K Adcock has been reelected to the city council. p3c3 "Meade Miller, son of Dr J C Miller, went to Elizabethtown Tuesday to attend Hardin Collegiate Institute." p3c4 His brother, "Prof Rice Miller, principal of Hardin Collegiate Institute, Elizabethtown, came over Saturday to visit his father, Dr J C Miller, and cast his vote." p3c4

Vic Bloomfield & Co., Clothier's are going to quit business and liquidate their stock.

November 12, 1897

Nicholasville will be one hundred years old next year, and is beginning to think about its Centennial celebration.

> Double wedding.--Two very interesting marriages took place in the parlors of the Phoenix Hotel, Lexington, Tuesday morning last. The contracting parties were Miss Olie Davis, of Sulphur Well, this county, and Mr Charles Clubb, of Pleasureville; Miss Lulie Holman, of Nicholasville, and Mr W W Davis, of Sulphur Well. p3c5

This is a brother and sister, Willard and Viola Davis who are marrying their respective partners. I knew Willard and remember his wife vaguely, but can't remember her being called Lulie. I think her name was Myrtle.

November 19, 1897

N D Davis' half-brother, "M F Davis, of Ambrose, shipped a car load of hogs to Cincinnati last week, also one car of choice hay...."p2c3

When the water rises sufficiently high behind Lock 7, Hickman Creek can be used as a shipping outlet. Curley Distillery is building an elevator to the River at Camp Nelson, and intends to ship all its freight on the river. This means a discontinuance of the hauling wagons from Nicholasville to the river.

Other transportation. Raiders are tearing down tollgates over the county, including the one near Sulphur Well.

November 26, 1897

Forest Miller has a new ad:

> PROSPERITY! Prosperity has surely come, or at least it makes us feel that it has when we think of the big sale of last Saturday and Monday. Why is it when our competitors are advertising to close out regardless of cost here and in Lexington? We can tell you why our sales are so large: People have confidence in our house. We sell only good goods. We keep what they want. We advertise nothing but what we carry out. Our prices are always the lowest." p1c1-8

The turnpikes are about to be leased by the county. The county will then be divided into districts headed by magistrates responsible for maintaining the roads in that district. All the gates are now open.

The *Sulphur Well Correspondent* writes:

> *Mr J P Turner talks of erecting some dwellings on Main Street in the near future.*
> *Mr F M Horine intends to make some extensive alternations in his recently acquired property.*
> *Well, we have plenty of travel now, and probably will have until we get used to free pikes.*
> *Mr Jas W Miller has gone on a visit to his children in West Virginia. Forest Miller will act as postmaster during his absence.*
> *Mr "Buster" Locker and Miss Ina Agee were married at the home of the bride last Sunday, Rev Henry Masters officiating.*
> *William Cobb, while riding along the river road on the Garrard County side Monday night in the intense darkness, pulled his horse over the embankment, thinking it was the road, but doing little damage to horse or man, except a good shaking up and a fright.*
> *Monday evening as Thomas Perkins, who lives at Saunder's Ferry, was riding across the river, his horse became frightened and threw him, his feet becoming entangled in the wagon harness as he fell and the horse commenced to kick him viciously as he dragged him along in his mad career. Before Perkins had become free of the harness he sustained many painful and some serious wounds. His knee cap was fractured and his left leg also broken just below the knee; besides it is feared by his physician, Dr Hendren, that he has sustained internal injuries as well, but hopes for his ultimate recovery.* p3c6

December 3, 1897

The Riney B was sold to Adolph Segal, a wealthy brewer from Philadelphia, for $250,000. Shanahan and the other lien holders got 27 cents on the dollar. The road was originally capitalized for $4,800,000. p2c1 I'm sure the promoters of the road took care of themselves financially in the initial stock offering. Nevertheless, there is a considerable difference in the cost of building the road, and the "going concern" value of the road, based upon earnings potential. It indicates that many railroads of that day were economically unjustifiable.

S J Greenbaum, the distiller, died at his home in Louisville. He purchased the distillery property at Sulphur Well from George Gray, and operated it for five years, until it was destroyed by fire. p3c3

The *Sulphur Well Correspondent* writes:

*Mr Jeff Hibbard, of Madison County, was here recently.*
*Mr Jas W Miller has returned from a visit to Point Pleasant, W Va.*
*Mr Chas M Hendren and wife, of Richmond, are visiting relatives here.*
*Mr Henry Hall has moved to the Elkhorn neighborhood.*
*Mr Mich Masters has completed and moved into his new residence.*
*Mr F M Hudson is building a new barn.*
*Mr J W Cobb has returned from a visit to Harrisburg.*
*Mr E Walker is home from a hunting trip to the mountains.*
*Mr John Fathergill has some sickness in his family.*
*Mr William Rice is doing some brick work for Mr AM Askins.*
*The colored folks enjoy the free pike riding immensely.*
*Mr Frank Bishop and family, who have been visiting here for some time at Mr J T Sageser's, returned to Illinois this week.*
*Mrs Emily Peel has rented the Mays residence and will move to it in January.*
*Our mail carrier was off the route one day this week on account of the death of a grand child. Thomas Hughes supplied his place.*
*Mr Thomas Perkins, who had his left leg broken below the knee from the kicks of a horse, also had his left thigh broken.*
*Mr Allen A Burton was assigned to duty and left for his post at Silver Creek distillery, Madison County, Tuesday.*
*Mr J P Turner sold and delivered to A C Miles on Tuesday 200 hogs averaging about 220 lbs., at $3 per cwt.* p3c6

December 10, 1897

Illness often ran through a family with tragic results. In East Hickman, a Kellar family has had three children die from diphtheria in the past ten days, and have another child sick. p2c4

A phonograph has been placed in George Crutcher's store for the benefit of his customers. He has songs, recitals and instrumental music to play on it. The editor says that an hour spent listening is very interesting. p3c2

December 17, 1897

The *Sulphur Well Correspondent* writes:

*A M Askins has moved into his new shop.*
*N D Thompson's school will be out this week.*
*The bridge over Hickman Creek is again open for travel.*
*Thomas Perkins, who had his leg badly broken by a horse's kick, is recovering.*
*We understand that Thos B Walker has bought the Dr Mays residence.*
*W R Harris and N D Thompson were visiting at Dr Hendren's a few evenings since.*
*Mr John Williams and family have moved to Elkhorn neighborhood.*
*Joseph Durham and John Urton have moved into the old shop to reside.*
*Melvin Peel will move to town January 1. He has built a cottage on Duncan Heights.*
*Geo E Fathergill, son of John Fathergill, is very low and not expected to recover with typhoid pneumonia and other complications.*
*Elijah Lowry's son, John, who had his hip joint out of place for nearly three weeks and had it reset by Drs Hendren and Welch, assisted by Dr Vanarsdall, is recovering very slowly.* p2c4

Two former residents of Sulphur Well are still on the move. The Little Hickman correspondent says that "Arch Stotts has moved to his farm near Buckeye." And, "Dr Mays, of Paint Lick, was in the vicinity last Sunday." p2c3 Note that Tom Walker just purchased Dr Mays' former residence in Sulphur Well.

December 24, 1897

Forest Miller's ad proclaims:

> THERE IS A PREVAILING IDEA with some people that honesty and business are two widely different things. But a true business can not exist without honest value, there is no better example to be given than the B., S. & Co's. garments. They contain style, quality and honest workmanship. We do not hesitate to guarantee such suits, and the prices are reasonable, too. We have a large and well-selected line of soft and stiff hats, also a big line of winter underwear, corduroy and jeans pants, duck brand mackintoshes. Sole agent for Smith & Stoughton shoes." p1c1-8

"H L Hersperger, bookkeeper for Forest Miller, will locate in Kansas City, Mo., early in January." p3c3

"Prof Rice Miller is home from Elizabethtown until after the holidays. His brother, Meade, who is taking a course in bookkeeping there, is also at home." p3c3

The *Sulphur Well Correspondent* writes:

*Mrs Emily Peel will move to the Mays' residence about January 1.*
*Mr James Hagar was very sick last Thursday but is better now.*
*Will Hutchison died last Monday from pneumonia. He had been sick over two weeks.*
*D Boone Tudor and family skipped out between two days for Illinois last week.*
*What little corn there is on the market is selling at $1.50 per barrel.*
*F M Horine is removing a portion of that old Sulphur Well landmark, the old Henry Alverson shop.*
*A party of youngsters thoroughly enjoyed themselves at Mr L B Taylor's last Thursday night. Mrs Taylor knows how to entertain and gave a nice supper to her young guests who enjoyed her kind hospitality till long past midnight.*
*George Edward Fathergill, son of Mr John Fathergill, died Wednesday morning at 2 o'clock after a lingering illness of some weeks, of typhoid fever, pneumonia and scrofula. He had been in bad health for several months.* p2c1

December 31, 1897

"Charlie Glass, of Camp Nelson, has purchased 15 acres at the mouth of Hickman Creek. He plans to build a warehouse, coal elevator, and saw mill, and will also deal in country produce." p3c2 The Kentucky River is "now navigable for boats drawing up to six feet", for a distance of four miles upstream from Lock 7." p3c3

"A K Adcock and daughter, Bessie, are visiting relatives at Knoxville, Tenn. Mr Adcock will also visit his father at Thorn Grove, who is very feeble." p3c4

This ends twenty years of history as seen throught the eyes Sulphur Well correspondent of the Jessamine Journal. The Journal, itself, is twenty-five years old, but the early copies are not in existence. This last issue is so badly tattered, that I don't know for sure whether the Sulphur Well correspondent reported or not.

# THE WAR - 1898

There really are two themes in this year's reports. The war was of over-riding interest and occupied the most time. However, the blooming of Dr Hendren as a poet was significant at Sulphur Well.

## January 7, 1898

The Kentucky Legislature is in session, and William Goebel is President pro tem of the Senate. The Governor presented his message the General Assembly on Wednesday. He called the toll-gate raiders "knights of the road," and further says:

> They have undertaken to regulate the quantity of tobacco the farmer should cultivate, destroying his plants if he dared to disobey; having notified the miller that he should charge no more for flour than the price fixed by them; threatened with the shotgun and the torch farmers who had posted their lands, if the boards were not taken down and they allowed to hunt without hindrance; and, notwithstanding all this high-handed conduct not one of the ruffians has been punished. p2c1

Governor Bradley seems to be describing anarchic conditions in the state at this time. It is a bit strange that he called them "knights of the road", a title more suited to "good guys".

The *Sulphur Well Correspondent* writes:

> *Mr and Mrs Whitenack, of Mercer County, were visiting J W Cobb last week.*
> *Mr and Mrs Charles Clubb, of Pleasureville are visiting N D Davis.*
> *Mr C T Taylor and family, of Lexington, were visiting Margaret Horine a few days last week.*
> *Mr S E Gott, Madison County, has moved to the Davis residence.*
> *Mr J H Turner, who has been quite sick, has about recovered.*
> *Rev H G Turner and wife, of Carrollton, are visiting his parents, Mr and Mrs J P Turner.*
> *Mr David English and wife are on the sick list.*
> *Mr B Ray, of Buckeye, was in this vicinity last Monday.*
> *A new residence will take the place of the old Alverson shop which was recently partly demolished.*
> *Mr Larkin Fain was married to Miss Amelia Masters, of Garrard County, last week.*
> *Mr William Cobb and Miss Mary L Cobb, daughter of Henry Cobb, were married on the 30th ult.*
> *Mr Andrew J Sageser has moved to his farm near N D Davis.*
> *Mr James Woodward and wife, of Harrodsburg, visited his parents during the holidays.*
> *Miss Nellie G Hendren has been sick for several days.*
> *Mr F Forest Miller, the clothier, moved to Nicholasville this week.*
> *Numerous witnesses have been summoned to appear Friday in the trial of Ezekiel Hendren's family troubles. p2c4*

Ezekiel Hendren recently married the widow, Mrs Lay. I don't know the nature of the trouble, but they remained married up to the time of Ezekiel's death. Bronston Ray has resurfaced after more than a decade. He was a good friend of "White Cloud" as was his sister, Mary.

"Forest Miller has moved to Nicholasville, occupying the residence of Mrs Lucy Hersperger on Wagner Avenue." p3c1 His usual advertisement is not in this issue of the paper.

The Richmond Register reports: "Prof Rice Miller, Principal of Hardin Collegiate Institute, Elizabethtown, looking portlier and handsomer than ever, was here last week visiting friends." p3c4 This gives some indication of Rice's physical characteristics, if not made tongue in cheek.

Charles Miller was also home for Christmas, and is returning to Law School at the University of Virginia. p3c4

Charles' sister, Maude Anderson Miller, is also on Christmas break. She is visiting her uncle, Dr J C Miller in Nicholasville. Maude is a "student of Hardin Collegiate Institute, Elizabethtown, where she will graduate next June, and of which her cousin, Prof Rice Miller, of this county, is principal." p3c4 Maude was born in Harris City, Indiana on February 6, 1878 (so, she is almost twenty at this time) and died December 26, 1959 in California. She was two years old when her parents returned to Irvine. There she joined the Methodist Church, and never changed her membership. According to the Sageser Genealogy, she also attended Central University in Richmond, and majored in Mathematics. Her father, Merriman (Mann) Miller, was going to send her to Dental School, but she eloped with James Metcalfe Ross on August 28, 1906. They were interesting people. They toured the south for a year on their honeymoon, and came back with $1,000 and all expenses paid! By this time the families had recovered from shock, and the Millers were quite pleased with James Ross. He became an insurance agent in Lexington, and since Maude liked farming, they purchased a farm at Greendale. They, and their daughter, Betsy, moved to California in 1919 where James was the manager of Speed, a magazine for Western Air Express. Later, he published a Masonic magazine in Southern California. He died of angina on March 13, 1931, and Maude continued the publication until the beginning of World War II. All this is from Sageser Genealogy.

January 14, 1898

"Among New Year gowns, velvet has a conspicuous position... that if black, or in a dark color or gray, it is suitable for street or carriage wear...." Streetwear means for carriage or short promenades in genteel surroundings, not in crowded thoroughfares! p1c5

I have noticed that candidates for governor in Kentucky rarely have a second life. Politicians were pulling their hair because Watt Harding, the defeated Democratic candidate, was considering another race. The editor expressed his sentiments about this very succinctly. He said "Mr Hardin stands no chance whatever for the nomination, as his strength, like Jno B Thompson's, has been tested once." p2c1

The toll roads are now being surrendered to the Fiscal Court. A few miles were surrendered without cost to the county, but the remainder will have to be valued, and leased from their owners. p2c2

January 21, 1898

The *Sulphur Well Correspondent* writes:

Mrs J C Lutes is also upon the sick list.
Mr Malear, aged 86, is sick at the home of Mrs Perry Walters.
There seems to be considerable sickness at present, mostly from colds.
Out of our sight he still is gone, that good man, Wright, who went all wrong.
Mrs Emily Peel lost a fine cow Tuesday night, probably from eating sorghum seed.
John Taylor, formerly of this place, but now of Texas, was visiting relatives here for several days.
Your Ambrose correspondent was the first correspondent of the Journal when it was first established by Capt Parrish 25 years ago.
The pike roads are getting into a very bad, not to say dangerous, condition, but nobody seems to be responsible for that condition.
This little town and vicinity is overrun by worthless curs. One can hardly get into a store or even into his own premises without climbing over a pack of the dirty mongrels. It's a dog-gone nuisance.
Luther Silverburg, an aged slavery time darkey, died Monday of senile decay, it is supposed, as he must have been between 80 and 90 years old. He was a quiet, inoffensive old time darkey (of) whom but few remain.
Mr B Frank Foster fell from his hay loft Friday evening, dislocating his left shoulder badly. Under chloroform the dislocation was reduced by Dr Hendren, assisted by Dr Van Arsdall. He is getting along very well now and resting easy. p3c6

We will accept as accurate the Correspondent's statement that he was the Journal's first correspondent. However, I am positive he has not written "all" the articles that I have passed along to you. I believe that the first series of articles in 1887 were submitted by George M Berry. I suspect Joy/Ivy was Mrs Spruce (later Baker), who wrote in early 1888. "She" was followed by Alaric later in 1888, of whom I haven't a clue. "He" was followed in 1889 by W H Bright, a merchant of Sulphur Well. I would attribute all the unsigned articles since that time to the present correspondent.

January 28, 1898

News from outside the state: "President McKinley put on his war clothes this week and ordered the war ship Maine to Havana." p2c1 A bill has been introduced in the Ohio Legislature for women's suffrage. p2c1

The *Sulphur Well Correspondent* writes:

*Thomas Hunter has moved to Lexington. William Hunter will buy his residence.*
*John T West sold last Monday 5 shoats to Wm H Hare at 3c.*
*N D Davis is receiving ---- quantity of tobacco at his barns.*
*Two children of A M Askins, have been quite sick from severe attacks of tonsilitis.*
*The health of the community ----- to be quite good, not-withstanding the unfavorable weather.*
*Miss Gott is soliciting subscribers for a school at this place. I understand she is a good teacher and hope she will meet with success.*
*E E Bourne last Sunday drove off Hickman Creek below the iron bridge and came near being drowned before he could get out.*
*Rev Mr Simpson, of Lexington Bible College, will preach here next Sunday morning and night.*
*Burglars entered the postoffice and store of W Miller Monday night, ---- it is thought that they secured only a small amount of goods. Some candy and other small articles thus far being missed.*
*Some of our readers are just a little irritated at our dog tale of last week. I didn't mean that all dogs are nuisances, not at all, and wouldn't curtail the rights of any respectable dog, but referred only to those that had nothing to do but loaf around stores and shops to the exclusion of the biped species, and whimper with currish insistence of the dogged hard times and the demnition bow wows the country was coming to, with hardly a mutton in sight to feast upon and make merry over as in the good old dog days when they were the pampered pets and dog stars of the howling four hundred.  p2c4*

It's hard to tell whether the Correspondent is backing up a little on his criticism of dogs, or whether he is now including their owners in his criticism. I gather that as the winter goes on he becomes increasingly tired of the people, and dogs, loafing around the store. W Miller is James William Miller. I guess someone left out the J.

A union service will be conducted Sunday at 7 pm on behalf of the Cuban sufferers. The Meeting is held in response to a call of the President and Governor of the State. The object is purely charitable and all who are interested (in) suffering and starving humanity are urged to be present. p3c2

February 4, 1898

The *Sulphur Well Correspondent* writes:

*Napoleon Long sold to John A Baker, Monday, five 100-lb shoats at $3 per cwt.*
*Mr Frank M Horine sold a nice Jersey milch cow and calf at her side for $20, this week.*
*There seems to be some special--or is it the irresistable magnetic influence of a pair of sparkling eyes that so attracts the footsteps of a certain Willmorian toward our attractive little burg? Quien sabe?*
*Chicken thieves, besides being very numerous are becoming quite bold at their predatory meanderings. They are not chicken-hearted, either, for they have sand enough in their craven craws to walk out at your front gate at an early hour loaded down with your best poultry as they did, or at least as one did at J P Turner's a few nights ago.*
*At the meeting at the church Sunday night about $20 were raised for the starving Cubans. Starving men, women, and children for the cause of liberty at our very doors, and we have but to lift a hand to free them from a worse than English oppression that caused the colonies to revolt and our forefathers to fight for seven long years; to freely lay down their lives in that holy cause of liberty that we, their children, profess to love, while we let fire and sword, rapine and murder run riot over the loved home of a brave people to satiate Spanish lust and greed, while we throw them an occasional crumb and advise them to wait. Wait for what? For their children to starve, their fathers to be murdered, their wives to meet a worse fate than death, until comes death itself. Is this liberty loving America? Or are we degenerate sons of patriotic sires? p3c6*

It appears to me that over time the Correspondent is becoming as much an editor as reporter. He took a very strong position on Cuba in this article.

February 11, 1898

Dr G M Hendren, the *Sulphur Well Correspondent*, submitted the following article, and poem to the Journal:

*Who now in the prime of life cannot well remember when he went across fields, down hill and branches to the old log school house and sat on the benches, resting his slate and books upon his knees, or keeping them under the benches or in the cracks during the school hours. He can remember the time when the rooms were heated by the great wide fire places, if at all, and cooled by the long chinks between the logs, and the general openness of the venerable old log pen. Thought the facilities were very crude and very limited, still from those rough school buildings walked the men and women, who are the backbone of the country, of its institutions today, and who regret to see the passing of the old log affairs which were surrounded by so many memories, to them, of the happy days of the bygone that have drifted into the gathered dust of the forever past, and of those who now dwell where the eternal stars glimmer on a shadowless land.*

## THE OLD LOG SCHOOL-HOUSE

O, the little log school-house
At the bottom of the hill,
The school-master and the scholars,
I remember them all still,
Where the hours were long and weary,
And the days went trooping by
Like they now are sadly fleeting
As the evening shades draw nigh.

How my memory lingers 'round it,
Standing lonely neath the hill,
With its rooms of spelling classes,
I can hear their voices still,
As the teacher with his speller,
Back is answered with a shout,
As those eager little faces
Are all waiting to turn out.

Though other scenes may fade away;
Gone the people we have met,
And voices we so loved to hear
Soon their melodies to forget;
But like dreams that haunt us still,
Spread those scenes of life about
The silent walls of memory
Until time shall blot them out.p1c3

This is a somewhat melancholy recollection of bygone days, which comes with age; Dr Hendren is about fifty-two at this time. He is Scottie's father's first cousin. He lived in the same neighborhood as Scottie, attended her wedding dinner, and may well have been her physician, yet I never heard her mention his name.

Flourishing.-The Hardin Collegiate Institute, Prof Rice Miller princpal, has more students now than ever before in its history and the school is giving entire satisfaction to the patrons. It is in the hands of a thoroughly competent and cultivated corps of teachers. The course of the study is the highest of any school in the county and its graduates can enter the junior class of any of our Universities.

This was reprinted from the Elizabethtown News. p3c3 I had been wondering if it was more than a high school. It is a junior college.

Our cup is really running over this week. The *Sulphur Well Correspondent* writes:

> Mrs E O Barkley, of Middlesboro, state agent for a New York publishing house, was visiting her brother, A M Askins, a few days last week.
> Good clover hay has been selling at $8 per ton, delivered, from this neighborhood.
> Mr L D Hendren, an employee of Cincinnati's Consolidated Street Railway Company, was on his way to Madison County to visit relatives there Monday.
> The little "spell" of open weather is taken advantage of by the hemp raisers and the hemp breaks are very busy.
> Mrs Eliza Reynolds, wife of Jefferson Reynolds, is almost totally blind from an eye affection.
> The ground, already thoroughly saturated with water, causes the dirt roads to be almost impassible from the frequent freezes and thaws.
> There will be an oyster supper given by the matrons of this place for India Missionary purposes, at the residence of Mr J E Gott, this Friday night. The young people, and the old as well, are invited to attend and requested to not forget to bring along some change to assist the good cause of saving the starving thousands of that country. p3c6

Sulphur Well seems to have become interested in outreach of late.

## February 18, 1898

The battle ship Maine exploded in the harbor at Havana, Tuesday night. Two hundred and fifty three crew members are missing. "The supposition is that it was an accident...." p2c1

The *Sulphur Well Correspondent* writes:

> Mr J Tandy Ellis, of the Louisville Dispatch, was down to see us last week.
> Mr and Mrs J W Cobb has gone on a visit to Harrodsburg for a few days.
> Mr E E Bourne made a short visit to Mr J H Woodward at Harrodsburg last Friday.
> Mr J H Campbell, of Wilmore, was around on a business trip last Friday.
> Mr J W Perkins, who was so badly injured by a horse some time ago, is out again.
> J P Turner sold to A C Miles, 13 head of shoats averaging 125 lbs, at $3.20 per cwt.
> Miss Dora Murphy has gone on a two weeks visit to friends at Pleasantville.
> Mr Addison Hendren, who has been visiting here for some months past, started for his home at Iowa Point, Kansas, Tuesday morning.
> A shoe drummer upset his wagon and trunks of samples into a deep hole of water and sand on the Kentucky River banks Tuesday of last week without doing any great damage, however.
> Buky Reynolds was arrested by Constable Mulkey last Friday night, but as they came out to get upon their horses to start for town, Buky bounded like a kangaroo out into the darkness and escaped. The two shots fired by the Constable only hastened his flight.
> The oyster supper last Friday night given by the ladies for the benefit of Indian Missions was a successful and a thoroughly enjoyable affair. The attendance, which, notwithstanding the very unfavorable weather was large, was pleasantly entertained by Mr and Mrs J E Gott and family till a late hour and highly appreciated their kindness and hospitality. The young folks especially enjoyed the occasion to the fullest extent with music and song and converse until they reluctantly departed for their several homes. The receipts were about $13. p2c4

February 25, 1898

"There is a universal opinion prevailing all over this country that the butchery going on in Cuba should be stopped and that President McKinley and Congress should take steps to that effect." p2c1   The Captain of the battleship Maine wired Washington to "suspend judgment until further investigation" of the explosion aboard ship. p2c1

The *Sulphur Well Correspondent* writes:

*Some hogs have been sold at this place for $3.25 per cwt.*
*Raymond Burchill is down with a bad case of pneumonia.*
*There are some few cases of "malicious" fever down on Possum Row.*
*J P Turner has had two patent gates put up on the driveway to his residence.*
*Mr James Luttrell, of Madison County, passed through here on a business trip to Illinois, Monday.*
*The youngest patient ever sent to Eastern Kentucky Lunatic Asylum passed through here on his way home last week. He is the 8-year old son of Wolford Tudor, of Madison County.*
*The floating saw mill recently located at Saunders' Ferry, passed on down the river last week after sawing all the available logs in that vicinity into lumber.*
*Mr Archibald Whittaker, of Garrard County, shot some one in his hen house a few nights ago, but the thief, though evidently body wounded, succeeded in making his escape.*
*Wednesday evening Mr J A Dean fortunately escaped what might have been a serious accident. His buggy became uncoupled as he was driving along the pike near Woodward's shop, throwing him out. The young horse he was driving started to run, but he held to the lines and was dragged along some distance. Mr Dean was unhurt and no great damage was done to the buggy.*
*There are a few young sports of budding criminality, too lazy to work, who practice their thieving propensities wherever and whenever honest folks are so unfortunate as to be disgraced by their presence, and opportunity offers for their petty pilfering. Even the sanctity of the church is not exempt from this thieving, and it would be well to nip it in time.* p2c4

March 4, 1898

The Jessamine Fiscal Court has agreed to a purchase price for approximately forty miles of toll roads, including the one to Sulphur Well. The cost is $19,400. The state roads are not included in the purchase. p3c2

"The Goebel Bill. The bill provides for the appointment of a State Board of Election Commissioners, which body shall in turn appoint county boards. The county boards shall appoint all officers of elections and have full charge of matters thereto pertaining." p1c3 A bill paid for with his life!

March 11, 1898

"Is war with Spain justifiable? The question of war with Spain is troubling the hearts and minds of all our American people." p1c3-4

After several weeks without an advertisement, Forest Miller placed a smaller notice that he was agent for Edward E Strauss & Co clothing. p1c7-8

"The *Journal* is glad to note that Dr Jno C Miller and family will move to Nicholasville." p3c4

"Rev H G Turner, of Carrollton, came in Wednesday to spend a few days with his parents at Ambrose." p3c4

The *Sulphur Well Correspondent* writes:

*Mr S J Brown has moved from the George Moore place to the toll-house on the Watts Mill pike.*
*Mr and Mrs Hugh Miller, Richmond, having visited here several days, returned home Tuesday.*
*An infant of Mr Roy Whittaker, at N B Long's, is very sick.*
*Mr Jesse Miller has moved into the Moore residence on "Possum Row."*
*There are indications of a large increase in the tobacco crop this year, but it is not likely that the good prices will cause an over production.*
*Every dog has its day, but the coons have their nights in this neck of the woods, and fights, fracases and fandangos are the order of the day, or rather of the night. Saturday night there was a hurrah and a hubbub of the underside of "society" here, lasting well into the small hours of the otherwise peaceful Sunday morning. The fight having originated in town late Saturday evening, over a white man who "ran off wid a coon," transferred its base of operation to this strategic point, in consequence of one side remembering, "all to onct," that discretion was the better part of valor, and it raged on nearly all night. Six or seven warriors have been gathered in from various points by the officers of the law and will be tried today. We hope the nuisance will be abandoned before something more serious occurs than an all-night row that would put the "Tenderloin" or "Bucktown" precincts to the blush.* p2c4

It seems that Sulphur Well is going through a pretty rough time. A bad element seems to be in the neighborhood--dogs and no-goods.

March 18, 1898

Forest Miller is back with a new advertisement across the lower portion of the front page.

SOMETHING NEW AND STYLISH. Our Spring Styles in Men's and Boy's Clothing, Hats, Furnishings, Etc., defy competition. SATURDAY, MAR. 26, we place on sale 100 ALL WOOL SUITS AT HALF PRICE. Come early and make your selection. These are great bargains. p1c1-8

"The Cuban rebellion began on Feb 24, 1898 that Jose Marti raised the standard of Cuba Libre in Camaguey." The revolution commenced at Baire and the Spanish immediately "suspended constitutional guarantees by proclamation ...." p1c5

The *Sulphur Well Correspondent* writes:

*Born, to the wife of E E Bourne, on the 10th inst., a daughter, Mayme.*
*There appears to be an epidemic resembling grippe prevailing in this section.*
*Mr James Hendren and wife have returned from a visit to Madison County.*
*Mr N D Davis and son, Marshall, are home from a few days visit to Pleasureville.*
*Mr John Malear, aged 86, is again quite ill at Mrs Perry Walters.*
*Rev H G Turner, of Carrollton, who has been visiting his parents, Mr and Mrs J P Turner, returned home last Saturday.*
*The fine spring-like weather is being utilized to its fullest extent by the hemp breakers.*
*Mr Charles Haynes has moved into a house on J P Turner's place.*
*The young folks had a little social party at N D Davis' Thursday night of last week.*
*A little child of James Watts was severely burned a few days ago.*
*Mrs Louise Gibony has moved to Nicholasville.*
*Mr Ed Carrier, an old Madisonian, passed through here from Boone County this week.* p3c6

March 25, 1898

"Dr Jno C Miller had a fine two-year old filly killed last week by lighting." p2c4

April 1, 1898

The editor of the Journal thinks President McKinley has delayed action against Spain for too long. p2c1 The High Bridge correspondent thinks that the loafers have talked the Spanish situation into oblivion. p2c4

The *Sulphur Well Correspondent* writes:

*William Rue died at his residence here Wednesday March 23, at the advance age of 89 years. He was ill but a day or two.*
*Mr John Malear, at Mr John Burchells, continues quite ill. He is 87 years old.*
*Mrs Marion Johns is very low from a serious lung trouble. She has been down for about a year.*
*It is reported that Taylor Saunders, of Silver Creek, Madison County has small pox.*
*Mr Porter Wesren, of Garrard County, visited Mrs Emily Peel a few days last week.*
*Mrs Charles Peel was visiting here last week on her way to Illinois.*
*A case of small pox is said to be at Paint Lick, Garrard County only a short distance from Lancaster and Kirksville.*
*Edward Ware, son of Jack Ware, who has been critically ill from neuralgia of the stomach for some days is much better.*
*John Mays and a party of friends went coon hunting a few days ago and were lucky enough to bag four of the --ly varmints. John says that they had some beautiful battles.*
*F M Horine is fixing up his new cottage in fine shape and it is quite an ornament to the town.*
*Walter Harris stood the civil service examination at Danville last Saturday. He thinks he is all right this time.*

*Elijah Harris, who was tried in Justice Fain's court before a jury for alleged burning of fence rails, was discharged as the evidence was not conclusive enough to convict.*

*Edgar Layton, of Madison County, near Hunter's Ferry, is down with a case of small pox, and it is also reported that there are two cases of the disease at Ruthton, in the same vicinity.*

*A party of seven trampish looking fellows passed through this burg late last Sunday evening. As they were a suspicious looking lot and were headed toward the toll gate, it is supposed by some that they were raiders. p3c5*

The Correspondent is reporting rumors of small pox. The Correspondent is a paradox. He at times seems well educated for the times, using French, Latin, and Spanish phrases on occasion. He writes rhyme, even poetry. At other times, his writing is pretty pedestrian. His reporting has also gotten pretty far afield. The William Rue in his first item lives in Little Hickman. The correspondent there says Mr Rue had been married three times, and fathered fourteen children. His last wife and three children outlived him!

April 8, 1898

Dr George M Hendren, of Sulphur Well, is becoming a published poet. He has another one this week:

### TOGETHER

A little hand in mine,
The one I can not live without;
My anchor in the sea of doubt-
It I can not resign.
Are sweeter days in store
Here, or only when life is done;
That hand then lead me gently on
Into the evermore.
And though I can not say
Fit words for such a fond request,
My head will speak with thine the rest,
In its mysterious way.
Blest be that faithful hand,
Which saves me while it holds me fast,
And leads me onward to at last,
Life's tempests to withstand.
Dear little hand in mine,
The one I can not live without;
My anchor and my hope in doubt,
Lead me and make me thine. p1c3

At first I thought it referred to the hand of a child. But, even with the adjective "little" it appears to be the hand of God.

Spain is willing to "make every concession demanded by the United States", but the pressure to go to war is intense throughout the country. p2c2

The *Sulphur Well Correspondent* writes:

*Mr William Harris is on the sick list from an attack of la grippe.*
*Miss Rowena Gott, who is attending school at Wilmore, was made sick by vaccination and had to return home.*
*Mrs Fannie Jasper is visiting her daughter, Mrs G M Hendren, this week.*
*The hemp in this section has been about all broken out and a pretty large acreage will be sown this year.*
*The Methodist meeting that was to have met at Mrs Millers, has been postponed to some futher date.*
*After a long forsaking of friends at Sulphur Well, the genial Mr Thomas Hughes was visiting friends here this week.*
*There will be an effort made to extend our mail line to the post office at Stone, Garrard County, at the mouth of Sugar Creek and near the located government lock.*
*The war is all the talk now. Any of our warlike Kentucky "colonels" could easily raise a splendid regiment here in no time and become a colonel ipso facto.*
*Our former school teacher, Mr N D Thompson, of Wilmore, was visiting his many friends around here a few days since.*
*Many unknown movers and travelers pass through and about here almost daily, but as the war excitement absorbs all, they receive scant attention.* p2c2

Dr Miller is advertising "Senator Blackburn", a combined saddle stallion, $8 per season for a live foal. p4c6

### April 15, 1898

The editor says that whether or not there is war with Spain, one thing is evident: "every city and hamlet of America is thoroughly aroused." p2c1

"Miss Bertha Hendren, who has been in Lexington for several weeks having her eyes treated, has returned home much benefitted by the treatment received." p3c3

### April 22, 1898

Turn-pike superintendents have been appointed for each district. Their duties are to inspect the condition of the roads, estimate the cost of needed repairs, and report to the Fiscal Court. p1c3

"Cuba must be free!" So proclaimed a congressional resolution. p2c1 "No north, no south, but all will march under one flag and the battle cry will be, `Remember the Maine'. That would enthuse every American heart." p2c1

The *Sulphur Well correspondent* writes:

*Eld Rob't G Frank will preach here the fourth Sunday.*
*Rev E C Savage, of Wilmore, preached at the residence of Mrs Elizabeth Miller last Friday night to a good audience.*
*Mr John P Miller, a prominent merchant of Wisemantown, Estill County, on his way to Louisville, stopped over to see his mother here Saturday and Sunday.*
*Since the Danville pike has been made free our road is having a much needed rest.*
*Miss Ella Carter, who has been critically ill with pneumonia, had a partial relapse Saturday but is improving and will be up in a few days.*
*Elijah Lowry, disgusted with his attempt to square the circle of Syl Overstreet's round head with a two-foot iron rule, has departed for parts unknown.*
*Mr Richard Fain gave a birthday party to his son, Dillard, Saturday night. After the splendid supper the thirty-two guests enjoyed themselves with music, etc. and were very pleasantly entertained till a late hour.* p2c1

"Turner.-To the wife of Rev H G Turner, at Georgetown, on the 21st inst., a son." p3c2

From Pink: "Mrs Kittie Knight paid a visit to friends at this place recently." p3c6

## April 29, 1898

"The first naval engagement between the United States and Spain took place at Matanzas, when three of American ships ... were fired upon from the forts on the island Wednesday." p2c1

County Attorney J W Mitchell was in the process of organizing a company of men from Jessamine. However, the Adjutant General of Kentucky informed him that the call was for only three regiments and that the state militia would have first preference. p2c1

Mr Simon Weil, the Lexington cattle buyer, says that he was engaged in buying cattle for export for a firm in Baltimore. Owing to the near prospect of war he received instructions to make to no more contracts. p2c3

## May 6, 1898

The War: "The problem of equipping a great army of volunteer recruits is taxing the utmost energies of the War Department...."p1c3 However, indications are that George Dewey is already in possession of Manila.p2c1 On the local front: "The young ladies of Jessamine Institute...," wishing to show their support of Kentucky soldiers who might see service against Spain, wanted to present a silk flag to the nearest military company. Friday morning, thirty-two members of the company came to Nicholasville from Lexington to receive the flag. They came by special car, and were entertained by the young ladies. At 3 o'clock that afternoon, the soldiers, "headed by the Nicholasville drum corps, marched to the Institute grounds and lined up in front of the platform that had been erected for the occasion, being viewed by at least 2,000 persons. Miss Lena, daughter of Judge W H Phillips, ..." made the presentation. After the company commander's response, the troop marched to the campus of the Graded School, where they gave an exhibition of their military tactics. In passing the Institute, on their way back to the depot, "the soldiers stopped and sang `The Soldier's Farewell'. The young ladies responded with ... `God Be With You Till We Meet Again', to which the soldiers sang `Nearer My God To Thee,'... as they marched away the girls sang `My Old Kentucky Home'." It was said that no general of the U S Army ever "looked more like a war general than did Capt Wilson on this occasion." p3c3 This is indicative of the patriotic support given the troops in the time of war, and the role played by the young women of the nation. Lena Phillips went on to become a national figure as founder and leader of the Business and Professional Women's organization.

The horse market has been quite lively. The U S Government agents have been buying several hundred head of calvary horses, with prices ranging upward to $135 per head. However, B F Stafford, a farmer in the Mt Lebanon neighborhood was not so fortunate. He had two tobacco beds containing enough plants for fifty acres of tobacco destroyed Saturday night. A note was left stating that he would be allowed to grow five acres of tobacco, but that if he went beyond that his barns would be burned. p3c1

May 13, 1898

"The latest bulletin from Washington states that all preparations have been made to invade Cuba on Monday." p2c1

Just to put things into prospective, a DeWitts Hazel Salve advertisment states:

> The Cuban question and political issues sink into insignificance for the man who suffers from piles. p1c2

Property transfer: "Tinie Deboe to Meade Miller, her interest, right and title in 100 acres of land on (the) Chrisman Mill Pike, $100." p2c4 Meade is Dr Miller's youngest son. This must have been just to clear the title, as it was only $1 per acre.

May 20, 1898

Dr Thomas P Welch, Nicholasville, has completed his internship in St Louis, and "has been commissioned a surgeon in the U S Army and assigned to the Second Missouri Regiment, with the rank of lieutenant." The position "pays $2,000 per year, besides allowing him two assistants and two horses." p3c2

The market for hemp has been active since Dewey took Manila. Since Manila was the hemp producing capital of the world, and its rope used extensively on ships, the demand for locally grown hemp has grown markedly. p3c4

"Miss Bertha Hendren has been visiting her aunt, Mrs Mary E Woolfolk, Merino Street, Lexington." p3c3

No one could survive the competive clothing business. Competition comes from Lexington as well as Nicholasville. Louis and Gus Straus are overstocked, and are selling "500 men's suits of Cassimeres, Worsteds, and Cheviots for $4.00." p2c1-8

The *Sulphur Well Correspondent* writes:

*Mr E Vinsant, of Madison County, visited Mr James Hendren last Sunday.*
*Mr Griggs, of Madison, was visiting Mr J E Gott a few days ago.*
*Mr Charles Clubb and wife, Pleasureville, were guests of Mr and Mrs N D Davis a few days last week.*
*Miss Georgie Hunter, of Nicholasville, was visiting Miss Irene Bourne last week.*
*Mrs Evaline Laws, of Madison County, was visiting Mr J W Miller for a few days last week.*
*Rutherford Fain, of this neighborhood, has joined the U S Army.*
*Our mail line has been extended to Stone in Garrard County.*
*Cinda Jackson, an old colored woman, dropped dead from heart failure last week.*
*Cyclers from town are frequent visitors here these beautiful spring evenings.*
*Fishing in the pond is good, but catching the finny tribe is quite another thing.*
*Pal Davis enlisted in the army, but failing to pass a final examination he returned home disgusted.*
*Rev E C Savage preached at the residence of Mrs Miller last Friday night.*
*Mr Edgar Layton, of Madison County, who has just been released from the small pox hospital at Richmond, passed through here Monday for Lexington to join the army.*
*Our little town has improved more in the last year than it did in twenty years before. It didn't improve any in the twenty years. Our pump still remains in a state of desuetude. Let it rest in peace.*
*Mr William Snowden is visiting his brother, Mr Stephen Nolan Snowden.*
*In addition to the complimentary notices of the press, and the Journal in particular, of the "Old Log School House", all of which is highly gratifying to the writer, appends the following:*
*Rev E C Savage and H G Turner will conduct religious worship at Mrs Elizabeth Miller's residence on Friday night, June 17. The neighbors should all turn out to hear them, and expecially our eloquent young divine and former townsman, Mr Turner.*
*Three men supposed to be deserters from the army were prowling around here last Sunday evening and at night, and their peculiar and suspicious actions caused some excitement as it was not known what they were after and they would give no account of themselves.* p2c3

The writer of this letter identifies himself as Dr G M Hendren, for it was he who wrote the "Old Log School House".

## May 27, 1898

The Spanish fleet is bottled up in Santiago harbor, and U S troops are on the north coast of Cuba preparing to attack Havana. p2c1 Sombrero hats have become a fad with the girls this spring. They "come in cream color, gray, black and dun shades", and are trimmed with "a leather strap and one feather". p3c1

"The <u>Journal</u> acknowledges receipt of an invitation from President Rice Miller, of Hardin Collegiate Institute, Elizabethtown, to be present at the closing exercises of the school, May 29-June 1, 1898." p3c1

The *Sulphur Well Correspondent* writes:

*Mr A J Hendren started for his home at Iowa Point, Kansas, last week.*
*Mrs Bettie Murphy has a severe attack of sciatica.*
*Mr Crayt Turpin's little child fell from a horse last Monday upon some sharp rocks cutting himself severely just below the left eye.*
*Mrs Frank Hendren has been dangerously ill.*
*The health of the community is at present exceptionally good.*
*Miss Dora Murphy is visiting at Lexington.*
*Nicholasville, Ky., Feb. 11, '98*
*My Dear Sir: I have just read the "Old Log School-House", in the <u>Jessamine Journal</u>. It is a little poem of such true merit that I am prompted spontaneously to compliment you, the author. It reminds me of schoolboy days spent in the old log school-house. It awakens memories of the past in a natural and most touching manner, and you address the heart as well as the mind. I congratulate you upon the success of this effort. Yours friend, Geo R Pryor.* p2c6

The above letter was incorporated into the column, presumably by the Correspondent or the editor.

June 3, 1898

Our Correspondent, Dr George M Hendren, has now written a patriotic and heroic poem entitled "Manila"; however, I chose not to copy it. p1c4

The residence of A K Adcock was entered Tuesday night and $10 was stolen. p3c2

June 10, 1898

It's graduation time at JFI, and one lass who came home "finished" moved her pa to write a poem. The first stanza went like this:

> Our Mollie's home, an' fixin' up for her Commencement week;
> She pets the cat in Latin an' axes grace in Greek;
> An' she's wearin' gold-rim spectacles
> to hid her eyes so bright;
> But she's all we've got--God bless her--an'
> I reckon that she right!    p1c5

June 17, 1898

The U S is deploying more troops, and the final battle seems to be close. p2c1 If you "ask a Spaniard what an island is, he will reply: `A body of land surrounded by United States soldiers'." p2c3

The *Sulphur Well Correspondent* writes:

*Miss Nellie Bourne, of Garrard County, was visiting at E E Bourne's this week.*
*Miss Burris, of Vanceburg, is visiting Mr S E Gott.*
*Miss China Johns was visiting N D Davis, last week.*
*Mrs E Miller and Mrs F F Miller are visiting at Irvine and vicinity. Master Ray was also of the party.*
*Mrs J H Turner has returned from a visit to her parents at Stanford.*
*Mr James Hendren and wife have returned from a week's visit in Madison County.*
*Miss Mary Tudor, of Madison County, is visiting her grandmother, Mrs Mildred Hendren, here this week.*
*Born to the wife of Mr Samuel Askins, Tuesday, a son.*
*The stone platform top of the Sulphur Well is at last complete, and we will soon have a more sightly watering place.*
*Elder Jenkins preached to large audiences here last Saturday and Sunday.*
*Mr W H Teater, of Madison County, was visiting this county, this week.*
*Mr J M Burton of Madison County, was over to see us this week.*
*Rev Horace G Turner, wife and little son, of Carrollton, are visiting his parents, Mr and Mrs J P Turner, here this week.*
*A serenading party discoursed sweet music, both vocal and instrumental, at several residences here Saturday night.*
*Mr John Malear, an old soldier and pensioner, died at the residence of Mrs Belle Walters, Saturday, aged 86. He had been quite feeble for some months and his death was not unexpected as he had been slowly breaking down from old age.*
*The earthquake shock and appalling rumble accompanying it was distinctly felt and heard here by your correspondent. It continued for perhaps 15 or 20 seconds, making windows and doors fairly hum. It was awfully startling while it lasted, and it is reported that it demolished worm fences in several places in this neighborhood. There is no use denying the fact that it caused cold chills to chase each other up and down the spinal column with extreme rapidity.* p2c4

The links with 1898 still live! The son born to the Askins was named Julius, nicknamed "Mousey", that's all any one, except possibly his parents ever called him. He was a barber by trade, and never stopped talking. I suppose he plied his trade in Nicholasville for forty or fifty years, and sometime thereafter moved to Florida. Just a year or so ago Nicholasville had a "Mousey Askins Day". He came back for the celebration. He was about 95 at that time, and as far as I know is still living.

June 24, 1898

Governor Bradley has asked each community where there are volunteers for military service to organize clubs to provide assistance for their family members. p2c1

July 1, 1898

There is a Commissioner's Sale of the property of Julia A Myers ordered to satisfy a debt to Wm Hendren. The property consists of 17 acres, and is described as being near Sulphur Well bounded as follows: "On the north by lands of Charles Beasley, on the east by the Paint Lick Road, and on the south and west by lands of Lewis Taylor." p2c5

Vic Bloomfield & Co is quitting business in Nicholasville.

The Fourth of July is to be celebrated with a parade this year. Participants will be the various fraternal organizations, businessmen, the fire department, horsemen, and wheelmen. They will be led by a brass band. p2c2 As I have indicated before, there generally has been very little celebration of the holiday. I suppose it's the patriotic fervor of the current war.

"Carl Hendren and sister, Miss Nellie, are visiting at Speedwell." p3c3

The *Sulphur Well Correspondent* writes:

*Heavy showers and Hickman Creek is raging.*
*Farmers are about through wheat harvest. The wheat is said to be fine.*
*Tobacco looks well and there seems to have been a fair acreage planted in this section.*
*The pike roads begin to look as though they need looking after.*
*Mr C T Taylor, of Lexington, was down visiting friends last week.*
*Squire William Harvey, of Newby, Madison County, was visiting Mr J W Cobb a few days since.*
*Mrs James Hendren has been quite sick for several days.*
*Mrs Kit Knight is visiting her old friends at the Well.*
*Rev E C Savage preached at the residence of Mrs Miller Friday night.*
*Rev H G Turner, of Carrollton, preached to a good audience at Mrs Elizabeth Waller's residence Sunday night.*
*Julius Dow Askins is the name of a small edition of a prospective voter in our precinct.*
*Joseph Lynn Turner is the name of a young gentleman visiting his grandparents here for the first time recently.*
*A horse ridden by Mrs Zach Taylor, Monday, took sick here and died in a short time after she had dismounted.*
*Dr Hunter, a graduate of a Baltimore medical college, the son of Henry Hunter, formerly of this county, was around looking for a location to practice last week.* p3c5

July 8, 1898

The newly formed Business Club of Nicholasville was proud of its successful organizing of the Fourth of July parade, and has called a special meeting to begin planning for the Centennial in September.

The *Sulphur Well Correspondent* writes:

*Miss Kate Grinstead, Stanford, is visiting her sister, Mrs J H Turner.*
*Mrs Leslie Whitenack, of Mercer, is visiting Mr J W Cobb.*
*Mr and Mrs Hugh Miller, of Richmond, were visiting Dr G M Hendren this week.*
*Mr Rice Harris and Miss Nellie Hendren attended the Chautauqua at Lexington Monday.*
*Born, to the wife of Mr Louis Neal, twin girls on the 30th of June. This makes the fourteenth child.*
*Miss Lulu Taylor, of Frankfort, returned home from a visit to J W Miller this week.*
*Wilburn H Bright and family, of Lexington, were visiting Mr A M Askins last week.*
*Mr N D Davis is building two large tobacco barns on his farm.*
*Mr N D Thompson, of Wilmore, was around visiting friends last week. He will take the school here, commencing August 1.*
*Mr Gabriel Masters has bought the Henry Alverson place from F M Horine. The price was about $300.*
*Henry Myers is quite sick from some type of fever, probably malarial.*
*Threshing has commenced in full blast and will be on hand for some time.*
*The blackberry venders have commenced to reap the crop, which promises to be large.*
*A little social party of youngsters enjoyed themselves at L H Hendren's last Thursday night.*
*Our military critics should be consulted in regard to the conduct of the war. The government is certaily making a serious mistake in not doing so, and disastrous results may be the consequence of its unfortunate neglect in this important matter.* p2c4

Items 3 and 4 pertain to the Correspondent's daughters. I feel sure that the printer made a mistake and meant William H Bright rather than Wilburn. Wm Bright was one of the grocers a few years ago, and submitted some of the Sulphur Well articles. The Askins and Brights were family friends.

July 15, 1898

The war is on people's minds in various ways. Sailor hats have become popular, particularly when trimmed with a bow at the back. They have "a jaunty look when worn with pique or wool yachting dresses." p1c6

War or not, the political process has to go on! The Democratic Convention to nominate a candidate for the Eighth District was held last Tuesday. p2c1

The Glass' Mill correspondent says that most of the men and boys in that area have gone with the thresher instead of going to Cuba. p2c4

Not related to the war, Rice Miller has been visiting his parents. He has returned to Elizabethtown and is "working in the interest of the College and other matters." p3c3

The *Sulphur Well Correspondent* writes:

*Mrs S N Underwood is quite sick with bilious fever.*
*James W Miller visited Lexington Monday.*
*Our mail carrier had a run away and smash up Monday.*
*The wheat crop will probably average 20 bushels to the acre in this section.*
*The tobacco crop looks well and will probably be above average.*
*Mrs L H Hendren has been quite sick for some days.*
*The three-year old son of Roy Whittaker died sunday morning from whooping cough and summer complaint.*
*Miss Mary Woolfolk, of Lexington, is visiting her sister, Mrs Levi Hendren.*
*It has been suggested to Spain that the famous seaman, Mr McGinty, would make them a first-class admiral.* p3c8

July 22, 1898

The Sulphur Well correspondent closed last week with a reference to the war. This week the <u>Journal</u> reports that plans to attack Havana have been deferred, but that troops have been ordered to Puerto Rico. p2c1

Small pox has appeared in several mountain counties. p2c4

"Miss Bessie Adcock is the guest of Miss Annie Lee Woolfolk, Lexington." p3c3

The *Sulphur Well Correspondent* writes:

*Mrs Bettie Murphy is again on the sick list.*
*There seems to be considerable malaria in the section at present.*
*Quite a large number of Madison County citizens were over last Monday.*
*Mr Cyrus T Taylor, of Lexington, was visiting our village again this week.*
*Mr Thos. H Walker has purchased the Mays residence for $700 and will move to it January next.*
*A yellow catfish caught near Boone's ferry and weighting 14 pounds, was sold here last week.*
*The heavy rains have stopped all threshing and made the dirt roads very disagreeable traveling.*
*Eld R G Frank preached at the Christian Church Sunday night to a large congregation.*
*Mr William Askins, Misses Lizzie and Mary Askins, of Buena Vista, Garrard County, visited relatives here Saturday and Sunday.*
*Several fellows whose "jags" got too heavy for them on their way home from town Saturday night retired in rest on the pike and didn't awake till late Sunday morning.*
*Our little town with the best water in the state and the healthiest people, needs just more adjunct. A little more push and energy. Although it has improved more this year than for 20 years past, there is still room for more improvement.*
*There was an egg found here by one of our citizens in his hen house last week that is certainly a great curiosity. It is two well formed eggs joined together by a stem making the whole look like a dumb-bell. The egg (or eggs) is 3 1/2 inches long; the stem joining them 3/4 of an inch long and 1/4 of an inch in diameter.* p3c6

July 29, 1898

Despite peace overtures from Spain, McKinley has ordered troops to hurry on to Puerto Rico and plant the flag. p2c1 Once set in motion war has a life of its own, a kind of inevitability.

The *Sulphur Well Correspondent* writes:

*The infant son of A J Sageser has summer complaint and spasms.*
*A M Askins is on the invalid list and his infant daughter has euterocolitis.*
*The pike in places is almost ruined from the heavy rain last week.*
*A great deal of sickness prevails in this section, especially among children.*
*Miss Mary Hendren has returned from a visit to Miss Nellie Bourne, of Bourne.*
*It is hoped that parents will send their children to school promptly on the opening day, Monday next.*
*Mastin Fain, while on his way home from Lexington, was seriously injured by his horse running away with him.*
*Park Ferrell, who lived at Mt Lebanon and carried on a blacksmith shop there for several years, died at the home of his sister, Mrs Speed Taylor, in Mercer County, last week, from dropsy.*
*The continued rain has interfered with threshing, but not with the luxuriant growth of the weed crop. And, by the way, it wouldn't be amiss for some gardens in this place to be mowed.* p2c3

"Miss Emma Hendren of Speedwell, Madison County, who has been visiting her cousin, Miss Nellie Hendren, returned home Wednesday." p3c3

A number of people are camping at the Kentucky Palisades, and attending lectures on the grounds. p3c4

August 5, 1898

The war appears to be drawing to a close. p2c1

The Jessamine County Teachers Association met this week. They have five days of intensive training. p1c3-6

August 12, 1898

At Saratoga, "for a morning stroll to the springs, street dresses of white poplin, Irish linen, pique, duck or satin cloth" are quite appropriate. p1c6

Dr Miller is having a dispersal. He announced a public sale to be held on September 1st, in which he is offering 40 horses of all ages, 13 mules, and 13 cows and calves. p2c7-8

"Miss Maude Miller, of Irvine, is the guest of her cousin, Miss Lizzie Miller." p3c3

The *Sulphur Well Correspondent* writes:

*Mrs Susie Ellis, of Lexington, is visiting at Mr J P Turner's.*
*Mrs Julia Myers is on the sick list.*
*Mr J W Cobb visited Harrodsburg Saturday and Sunday.*
*Mrs Suda Richardson and little Miss Leah Stacy, of Irvine, are visiting Mrs Elizabeth Miller.*
*Thos J Horine now rides in a new buggy.*
*Mrs Mary E Wheeler and daughter, Mary, of Cincinnati, are visiting relative in this section.*
*Elder Stafford is conducting a protracted meeting at Elm Fork.*
*Mrs Bettie Reynolds, of Alvin, Texas, widow of the late Rev M D Reynolds, formerly of this place, is visiting at Mr T J Horine's.*
*Mr Clell Johnston and son, Bradley, who recently visited Chattanooga, are both down with typhoid fever at Mr Henry Harris.*
*A daughter of William Wright, who formerly lived in this vicinity, was killed by a train near Beattyville a few days ago.*
*A son of Henry Reynolds, who lived just across the river in Madison County, had an arm cut off by a shell at the battle of Santiago.* p2c1

Mrs Miller is being visited by her daughter and grand daughter. "Aunt" Sudie raised Leah when her mother died. The Richardsons had no children of their own.

August 19, 1898

The war with Spain is over. My search shows no reports of any charge up San Juan Hill in the Journal. However, later it reports Roosevelt's heroism in that battle.

"Marshall Davis, of Ambrose, and Miss Emma Spruce, of Nicholasville, and Miss Wheeler, of Cincinnati, were the guests of Miss Hattie Jones, Buckeye, the first of the week." p3c3

The *Sulphur Well Correspondent* writes:

*Mrs J Wilkes Miller is on the sick list.*
*Mrs S N Underwood, who has been very low for some weeks, is slightly better.*
*Rev H G Turner was visiting his parents, Mr and Mrs J P Turner, a few days last week.*
*There have been several additions to the church at Elm Fork.*
*Mrs Myra Turner, who has been sick for some time, is better.*
*F M Horine is building a large stock and tobacco barn on his place.*
*Watermellons are very cheap and plentiful.*
*J Newton Hendren, of Edenton, Madison County, was visiting in this section a few days this week.*
*A J Sageser has presented to himself a brand new carriage.*
*N D Davis is building two large additional tobacco barns.*
*Kentucky River has been on quite a tear, carrying down a large quantity of logs, etc.*
*S J Brown, who was arrested for technical violation of the revenue laws, has been released on bond.*
*Irvin Peel sold to Houston Woodward three acres of tobacco in the patch for $125.* p3c5

August 26, 1898

As a result of his celebrity status in the war, Teddy Roosevelt is being "boomed" for president. p2c1

September 2, 1898

"The big stock sale of Dr Jno C Miller yesterday was one of the most successfully conducted that has ever taken place in Jessamine. A large crowd was in attendance, bidding spirited, and good prices realized on every head of stock sold. G W Lyne acted as auctioneer and Rice Miller as clerk." p2c3

September 9, 1898

The *Sulphur Well Correspondent* writes:

*Mrs James Hagar has been quite sick for some weeks.*
*Miss Fina, daughter of Mr Leroy Taylor, is ill of typhoid fever.*
*Mr Henry Nichols, who has been on the sick list, is out again.*
*Miss Nell Johnston, of Garrard, is visiting at Mr Henry Hare's.*
*Mr Wm McC Johnston, who has typhoid fever, is better.*
*Mr William Walters, of Virden, Ill., is visiting his parents here, Mr and Mrs George Walters.*
*Mrs Elizabeth Miller sold to J B Hunter a fine cow for $3.05 per cwt.*
*Mrs Thomas Clark, an old pensioner, is very low with heart trouble.*
*The clover hullers report that the crop averages about one-half bushel per acre.*
*Misses Grace and Linnie Grinstead, of Stanford, are visiting Mrs J H Turner.*
*Mrs Elma Turner visited her parents at Stanford last week.*
*Several old sailers passed through here Monday en route to the GAR reunion at Cincinnati.*
*Mr and Mrs Hugh Miller, of Richmond, have returned home after a visit of several days in the neighborhood.*
*Mr Courtney Horine and wife, of Chicago, who have been visiting Mrs Margaret Horine for some days, returned home Tuesday.*
*Carl Price, colored, son of Mit Price, and one of our best and most industrious colored citizens, was arrested by officers of the law last Saturday for alleged hog stealing. I learn that he has confessed to stealing at different times eight hogs, and driving them to town at night, where they were sold for a small sum each.* p2c5

September 16, 1898

The Nicholasville Centennial Celebration is underway.

There are two clothing stores remaining in Nicholasville at the time of the Centennial. p1c3 Forest Miller's advertisement follows a military theme:

THE ROUGH RIDERS; The Rough Riders always win in their battles; so does F Forest Miller. He has been waging war on high prices ever since he first engaged in business and has succeeded in giving the people the best Clothing, Hats, Furnishings, and Shoes for the least money. p1c1-8

The *Sulphur Well Correspondent* writes:

*Miss Nell Bourne, of Bourne, Garrard County, is visiting at Mr E E Bourne.*
*Miss Fina Taylor, who has been very low with typhoid fever, is considerably better.*
*Wm R Davis and Arthur West were baptized Tuesday.*
*Mr and Mrs John Teater, of Buckeye, were visiting here last week.*
*Mr Burton Roberts and Miss Susie Long, of Madison County, were visiting here Sunday last.*
*There were seven additions to the church here during the progress of the meeting just closed.*
*Mr William Burton, Buckeye, and Miss Myrtie Hendren, of Cottonburg, were visiting here last week.*
*The protracted meeting conducted by Elder McGarvey, of Lexington, closed Tuesday. He lectured Tuesday night on the Holy Land and illustrated his interesting lecture with stereoscopic views of the scenery and places in that country, and also some fine pictures of our famous war ships, guns, etc. p2c4*

This is absolutely the first mention of Authur West, who later will marry Dora Murphy. There has never been any mention of his schooling, coming home on holidays, etc. Yet, he used to pontificate at the store, around the stove, on the porch. I'll never forget his usual preamble to new things: "I hadn't heard of this, and I know you haven't". Late in his life he had the most beautiful, and best preserved, LaSalle touring car you'll ever see. It was deep maroon in color, with black trim, and probably had been driven no more than 5,000 miles. Somewhere between 1948 and 1951, when I was nineteen or twenty, he asked me to go with him when he traded it in for a new Pontiac. I can't remember why he wanted or needed me to go with him, and I can't remember if I drove either car. My father, Frank Ware, was a salesman at Garland Holcomb's Garage, and that may have had something to do with it. I do remember how my grandfather, Luther Ware, got his new International Truck. Dad thought he needed a new one, and he did, so he had me drive a new truck out to Inky and leave it with him.

The Pink correspondent says some much needed repairs are being made to the Sulphur Well and Paint Lick turnpike. p2c5 Note that they are still being called turnpikes, even thought they are free.

A footnote on the Centennial:

Sulphur Well, or Ambrose, as its post office is named, is also a little village, about two and one-half miles distant on the Sulphur Well pike, chiefly noted for its never-failing well of good, strong, sulphur water, in combination with some other minerals. A large number of our best known county families are located near here. p4c4

Both observations are true: it was noted for its unfailing water, and there were at least three entrepreneurial families that were prominent in the county.

Also, some more about Union Mills. I didn't know that it was "the birthplace of the Lexington Club Distillery, whose brands of whiskies are known all over the country." p4c4

September 23, 1898

The following notice reminds me of some of my talks with clients getting divorces--the wives get the assets, they get the liabilities. A blacksmith at Kirksville announced a change in his business as follows:
> Notis-De copartnership heretofore resisting between me and Mose Skinner is hereby resolved. Dem what owes de firm will settle wid me, and dem what the firm owes will settle wid Mose. p1c5

The *Sulphur Well Correspondent* writes:

> *Mr Charles Peel, of Leroy, Ill., is on a visit here to relatives.*
> *Mr D Hendren and sister, of Kirksville, were visiting here this week.*
> *Miss Susie Long, of Cottonburg, was visiting friends here last week.*
> *Mr James Vincent, of Edenton has been very low with typhoid fever for some time.*
> *Mr Sam Moberly, of Edenton, was visiting here last week.*
> *Mr and Mrs James Prather, of Madison County, were recent visitors in this neighborhood.*
> *Dr Phil Roberts, of Richmond, was over last week looking as hale and hearty as ever.*
> *Mrs Barnette, of Lancaster, is visiting Mr A M Askins, this week.*
> *Mr Bryant and wife of Stanford, are visiting Mr J H Turner.*
> *Mr Richard Burton and Miss Myrtie Hendren, of Edenton, were visiting friends in this vicinity during the Centennial.*
> *Miss Etta Cotton and Ada Roberts, accompanied by Mr Lester Cotton, of Cottonsburg, were visiting here Friday and Saturday last.*
> *Lieut Johnson of the 4th Ky Regiment, U.S.V., is out on a furlough visiting his brother's family at Mr Henry Hare's. p2c4*

I notice that the Sulphur Well correspondent has been spelling the name "Johnson" rather than "Johnston". This is the brother of Wm McC Johnston who married Mayme Hare. This letter is almost entirely about Madison County people visiting Sulphur Well this week, with only a passing mention of the Centennial. The celebration must have underwhelmed the villagers, as a young lady in East Hickman said she was glad that the Centennial only came every one hundred years. p2c4 The editor of the <u>Jessamine Journal</u>, on the other hand, said that it was witnessed by ten thousand and would be "a delightful remembrance of all". p3c3

September 30, 1898

"Col Roosevelt, commander of the Rough Riders, was nominated for governor of New York by the Republicans Wednesday." p2c1

October 7, 1898

"Roosevelt made himself famous by his bold charges at Santiago as the leader of the 'Rough Riders', but in his race for governor of New York, he will go down before Van Wyck ...." p2c1 But, he didn't!

Levi Hendren is now living at Hanly. His son, Oscar, is visiting him from Kansas. p2c3

The *Sulphur Well Correspondent* writes:

*B Ray, of Buckeye, was over last week.*
*Mr and Mrs John Lutes have malarial fever.*
*Charles Peel returned home to Leroy, Ill., last week.*
*Mrs Myra Turner, who has been on the sick list, is better.*
*Mr and Mrs B F Foster were visiting in Louisville last week.*
*Frank Broaddus, who had a bad attack of typhoid fever, is out again.*
*Quite a crowd took advantage of the low rates to Louisville last week.*
*J H Turner shipped a nice lot of fat cattle to Cincinnati Monday.*
*Mr and Mrs T H Walker will be a welcome addition to our little burg Jan 7.*
*W L Hendren sold his fine black harness horse, to Jewell & Patterson for $100.*
*Miss Ethel Hendren is down with something like malarial fever. There is plenty of marlaria in the county.*
*Our postmaster who has been on the sick list for some time was well enough to visit Richmond Monday, court day.*
*Our pike will soon have its much needed coat of metal. Its old coat was getting quite threadbare and shabby.*
*A C Miles has bought several small lots of cattle from different parties during the last week at good prices.*
*S N Snowden and family were out on an extended visit to Estill and adjoining counties recently.*
*Messrs Beatty and Allen Vincent, Edenton, were over to witness the Sowder-Tudor wedding.*
*Mr and Mrs Parker, of Stanford, who have been visiting Mr and Mrs J H Turner, have returned home.*
*Rev H G Turner, wife and little son, of Carrollton, returned home Saturday from a visit to his parents here. He has been transferred by Conference to the Scott Street Church, Covington.*
*A protracted meeting already of several days duration is in progress at Mt Pleasant Church conducted by the Rev Cannon.*
*At the trustees election, Saturday, N D Davis was elected for three years and Jeff M Miller for two years in place of W L Buford, who resigned.*
*A prolonged protracted colored meeting is still in progress at the Black Bridge near here. The longer their meeting are protracted the better they like it.*
*B F Foster sold a nice steer to A C Miles this week for 3 1/2c per pound.*
*The protracted meeting that has been in progress at Little Hickman for several days closed Sunday night with six additions. The converts were all baptized just below the Black Bridge Sunday in the presence of an immense crowd of spectators.* p2c4

W L Hendren is the son of William Hendren, who is the son of Doven Hendren of Madison County. William married Elizabeth J Reynolds. Their children who were still at home according to the 1900 census were: William L and Levi H and wife Louisa, their daughters Ethel (also mentioned above), and Jennie. My line of decent is by way of Doven's son Harrison, a brother of William. The Jeff Miller mentioned above is the son of William and Mahala Miller. I am reasonably sure that I have swum at the place where the people were baptized. If so, it was called the Belle Walters Hole. I remember one sloping, gravelly, side to enter the pool, which was perhaps three or four feet deep in some places.

October 14, 1898

After many twists and turns the Riney B has been purchased by a syndicate headed by Bennett Young. The group is expected to extend the road to Beattyville as originally planned. p3c3

October 21, 1898

Forest Miller is continuing his war theme.

LESSONS OF WAR: The lessons of the late war are many. Not the least of them is that the American is invincible. Just as Uncle Sam is without a peer in the sombre theatre of war as F FOREST MILLER is without a rival in the field of CLOTHING, HATS, FURNISHINGS, GOODS, SHOES, ETC. He sells nothing but the best at the least prices. p1c1-8

It does appear that he has outlasted his competition. The only other competitor for men's clothing is R J Duncan, but there are several shoe stores. He is clearly feeling his oats!

October 28, 1898

The sale of the Riney B has been overturned by the US Court in Louisville because the judge ruled that certain buyers had been excluded. p3c4

The *Sulphur Well Correspondent* writes:

*N B Long is reported on the sick list.*
*Considerable malaria still exists in this part of the county.*
*Mrs Robert Davis, of Pink, is seriously sick with malarial fever.*
*Mrs Elizabeth Miller and Mrs Sue Nave are visiting relatives at Irvine.*
*W B Ray and wife, of Buckeye, were visiting on this side (of the river) this week.*
*It is said that the fly is considerably injuring the wheat that was sown early.*
*Mrs Emarine Crow has returned from a lengthy visit to friends in Clark county.*
*Mrs William Merrill, of Elm Fork neighborhood, fell dead Friday night as she was walking across the floor.*
*Mr Ezekiel Vincent, of Edenton, has taken board and lodging in our village for the winter.*
*Mrs Mary E Cobb has returned from a week's visit to Mr and Mrs Whitenack's, near Harrodsburg.*
*Dr G M Hendren has been confined to his room for three weeks with an aggravated case of sciatica.*

*A serenading party visited us Monday night and discoursed sweet music at several residences.*

*A good deal of stock--hogs and cattle--have changed hands at fair prices here within the last week and some hogs were shipped to Cincinnati markets.*

*A son of one of our citizens has become so incorrigible that his father, it is said, made a present of him to some of his friends to bring him in the way he should go, as he could do nothing with him.*

*Mr Charlton Alverson, who died from a paralytic stroke Friday was the last of three sons of Mr Jesse Alverson, of Madison County, who was well on toward a century in age when he died recently. Only two sisters remain, one of whom is the wife of Dr Evans, and the other the wife of Mr W A Clark, of Helene, Mont., the millionaire mine and ranch owner, and who was mentioned by the press as a possible candidate for the vice presidency with Hon W J Bryant.p2c1*

November 4, 1898

The Sageser Genealogy was wrong! Rice Miller did get married:

Miller-Payne.-Prof Rice Miller, principal of the Hardin County Presbyterian Institute, Elizabethtown, was married Wednesday evening (Nov 2) at 8:30 o'clock in the First Presbyterian Church to Miss Julia Blackburn Payne. Dr L H Blanton, Chancellor of Central University at Richmond, officiated. The church and the handsome residence of Col and Mrs Jas B Payne, parents of the bride, were beautifully decorated in red and white in representation of the colors of Central University, where the groom was graduated several years ago. After the ceremony the bride and groom returned to the home of Mr and Mrs Jas B Payne, followed by nearly all who were at the church. The bride was dressed in white satin, with point lace, and carried white flowers. Her sister, Miss Lena Payne, the maid of honor, was attired in pink organdie over --- and carried flowers of a corresponding hue. The groom's best man was his brother, Mr Meade Miller, of Nicholasville, and the ushers were Mr Samuel T Payne, of Elizabethtown; Mr C W Miller, of Irvine; G W Welsh, of Danville, and J B Arnett, of Nicholasville. Courier Journal. Mr and Mrs Miller will arrive today on a visit to relatives here." p3c6

Among those from Nicholasville and vicinity who attended the Miller-Payne wedding at Elizabethtown Wednesday were: Dr Jno C Miller, Miss Elizabeth Miller, Meade Miller, W T Cleveland and J B Arnett. p3c3 Wonder why his grandmother, Elizabeth Jane Miller, wasn't mentioned.

November 11, 1898

Teddy Roosevelt won the gubernatorial election in New York. p2c1 Jessamine County voted to issue bonds to pay for the toll roads. p3c3

Forest Miller proclaims:

> VICTOR AND VANQUISHED. There never was the slightest doubt as who would be the `victor' and who the `vanquished' in the `late unpleasantness' between the United States and Spain. Just so in the city of Nicholasville in the contest for the favor of the public F Forest Miller is universally victorious. See our fall lines. The best goods at the lowest prices. p1c1-8

Unfortunately, pride does often go before the fall.

Dr G M Hendren again publishes a poem on the front page, entitled "Rich and Poor". Basically it says that whether you are rich or poor, you are made of clay, and that life is a brief interval. p1c5

"Mr and Mrs J T Hendren, of Kirksville, and Mrs Miller and daughter, of Richmond, have been the guests of Mr and Mrs Walter Hendren." p3c3 This is Mrs Hugh Miller, daughter of Dr Hendren. Walter is the brother of Dr Hendren. Over to meet Rice's new wife, I suppose.

The *Sulphur Well Correspondent* writes:

> *The election passed off as quietly as a Sunday School meeting.*
> *Mrs Kittie Hudson is on the sick list.*
> *Mr Newt Wallace, of Little Hickman, is seriously sick.*
> *A child of James Peel died Saturday of diphtheria. This dreadful scourge of childhood is prevalent along Hickman Creek.*
> *Mrs Ophelia Berkley, of Texas, is visiting Mr A M Askins.*
> *Elder Hildebrand preached here and at Little Hickman Sunday.*
> *The novel sight of a drove of about 100 geese being driven to market through here recently.*
> *Prof Rice Miller and bride, of Elizabethtown, arrived at his father's, Dr J C Miller, Thursday evening, Nov 3rd.*
> *Mr and Mrs Hugh Miller, of Richmond, were visiting her parents, Dr and Mrs G M Hendren, for a few days last week.*
> *Mr and Mrs J P Turner recently visited their son, Rev H G Turner, at Covington.*
> *David Hunter, of Garrard County, will shortly move to Jessamine and occupy a residence J P Turner is building for him on his farm. Mr Hunter and his amiable wife will be welcome accessions to our county.* p3c4

## November 18, 1898

The Adcocks have another child, a son born on the 12th. p3c4 I don't know which, Byron or Adam, Jr.

From Pink: "Mrs Kittie Knight has moved to the village of Pink." p2c6

Farm prices are still depressed. However, Kentucky farm produce enters foreign markets. John Embry purchased 150 cattle for export for $4.50-$4.65 per hundred. The U S exported 12,547,155 bushels of corn last month. p2c3 Tobacco growers are having a continuing problem and are holding an organizational meeting to oppose "the combination of tobacco manufacturers". p2c3

The *Sulphur Well Correspondent* writes:

*Corn is selling at 25c per bushel delivered.*
*Uncle Sam has again remembered his numerous nephews.*
*J W Grant has a little child sick with pneumonia.*
*Geo Peel, Sr, removed last Tuesday to Russell Cross Roads.*
*Hogs are selling at $2.80 (per cwt) at this market.*
*Newton Wallace is recovering from a severe attack of bowel trouble.*
*Mountain wagons retail chestnuts at 25c per gallon.*
*Cattle are said to be dull sale at present, but good demand for milk cows.*
*Mrs Henry Cobb, a life-long invalid, died a few days since after a very short illness.*
*Rev E C Savage, held a meeting here last Friday night at a private residence.*
*Rev Collins, of the Methodist Church, after preaching at several of the neighboring churches, closed his series of meetings at Wesley Chapel last Sunday.*
*Mrs William Hudson died Tuesday evening from asthma and heart trouble from which she has been a long sufferer. She was buried at the family residence, Thursday, at 11 am. Funeral services conducted by Rev F W Noland.* p2c4

November 25, 1898

There is a public sale of Mrs Hudson's stock, household and kitchen furniture to be held next Tuesday. She left one good family mare, a milk cow, a young heifer, some hogs, a buggy, a spring wagon, some harness, and some farming implements. p3c7 (this issue is microfilmed after the December 2 issue)

This is Forest Miller's latest advertisement.

> HOW CAPTURED CITIES ARE HELD. Cities captured by force of arms are held by force of arms. The favor of a people captured by a merchant's fair dealing and attractive prices can only be held by a continuation of those methods. We have won the support of the people of Nicholasville and Jessamine County on those lines and we shall endeavor to hold them similarly. Our motto is: The Best Goods for the Least Money! p1c1-8

Meade Miller may be associated with Forest Miller's store. His ad reads: "Bale your Hay. Having bought a new hay press I am prepared to bale hay and straw. Will bale for cash or on shares." p3c1 He then gives his address as being at F F Miller's clothing store. Also connected: "The firm of Roberts and Hendren is being dissolved. Roberts will continue the jewelry business, and W S Hendren will be connected with the firm of F F Miller, Clothier." p3c4 W S (Walter) is Dr Hendren's brother.

G M Hendren has become a prolific poet. He is not on page one this issue, as Thanksgiving has taken the forefront, but he has written "What They Seem". It's about an old woman who falls asleep just after Thanksgiving dinner, and dreams that she has found a place on earth where things are exactly what they seem. His themes are somewhat melancholy, and introspective. I believe he is feeling his own mortality. p2c1

The *Sulphur Well Correspondent* writes:

*Miss Irene Bourne is sick with fever.*
*There was meeting at the Chapel Sunday morning and night.*
*Mr A M Askins sold a lot of shoats to A C Miles last week at $2.75 per cwt.*
*Louis Fain, private of Fourth Kentucky Regiment, stationed at Anniston, Ala., was home on furlough last week.*
*Davis Bros have bought several crops of tobacco in Madison and Garrard County.*
*Mr Cooley, of the river vicinity, had his home destroyed by fire a (few) days since. Insured in Hurst Home.*
*Mrs William Hendren badly injured her arm from a fall off a porch a few days ago.* p2c5

The last item pertains to the correspondent's mother.

## December 2, 1898

The *Sulphur Well Correspondent* writes:

*Mr and Mrs James W Cobb have returned from a visit to Mr John Whitenack's in Mercer County.*
*Mrs Ellen Taylor, Lexington, visited her mother, Mrs Horine, Thanksgiving day.*
*The Peel brothers have rented and will move to the F M Hudson farm on Hickman Creek soon.*
*Mrs Green B Willis, daughter of William Hudson, who was visiting her parents, returned to her home in Indiana last week.*
*Mr Gabriel Masters has moved into the old Henry Alverson residence purchased recently from F M Horine.*
*Several of our citizens attended Thanksgiving services at Nicholasville. Services here were slimly attended, as our people were perhaps too busy to attend.* p2c1

## December 9, 1898

"Mr and Mrs W S Hendren entertained Saturday evening in honor of Mr and Mrs Wade Cardwell, of Shelbyville." p3c3

A K Adcock's father died in Thorn Grove, Tenn. on Nov 25th, after a long illness, at the age of 70. "He was twice married and leaves nine children." p3c5

The *Sulphur Well Correspondent* writes, beginning in verse:

*Whom first we love we seldom wed,*
*A single poet's song hath said;*
*His silent lay, when married, read*
*We seldom love whom first we wed.*

   Sam Taylor's house, near here, burned down about 10 am Tuesday. It was insured for $350.
   The attendance at the Wm Hudson sale was good and prices fair.
   William Peel, formerly of Nicholasville, has moved to the James Hagar house on Hickman Creek.
   Hugh Peel, of Boyle County, bought the Lear toll house on Danville Pike for $600, and will move to it soon.
   Rev Jno P Lowry, of Little Rock, Ark., and Prof and Mrs Fogg, of Covington, were the guests of Mr and Mrs J P Turner last Wednesday.
   Mrs E C Miller has returned from a two months stay at her brother's home in Kansas City, Mo., where her niece, Miss Lilly Reynolds, after a long illness, died from an attack of sycoma.
   The sick list of this suburb this week includes Irvine B Peel, Jas W Cobb and others. Everybody is afflicted with the "worst" cold of their lives.
   Geo N Snowden sold to A C Miles eleven head of cattle at 3 cents. p2c5

The Correspondent is consumed by verse! The couplet may be more meaningful if you define "lay" as a ballad or song. I don't know who E C Miller is, but it isn't Elizabeth J Miller.

### December 16, 1898

Forest Miller dropped the war theme and got in the spirit of Christmas.

> CHRISTMAS PRESENTS. For a handsome XMAS GIFT there is nothing more welcome to man or boy than a nice stylish SHIRT, handsome TIE, warm MUFFLER, nobby HAT, dressy SHOES, good UNDERWEAR, nice CANE, handy UMBRELLA, etc. Your boy would appreciate a nice SUIT or OVERCOAT. See my line. p1c1-8

G M Hendren has penned another poem, "A Deserted Church". In it he walks pensively around the old church while images of bygone days fill his mind. No sounds disturb the silence, and no worshipers throng the church, for, he says, they now walk in a different place. Their hearts are stilled, and they are laid in narrow cells of the campground for the dead. p1c5

The *Sulphur Well Correspondent* writes:

*J P Turner is on the sick list this week.*
*Miss Irene Bourne is improving.*
*S E Gott is confined to his room with an attack of sciatica.*
*Thomas Walker has moved into the Dr Mays' residence.*
*Mrs Emily Peel moved to the F M Hudson farm on Hickman Creek last week.* p2c4
December 23, 1898

"Prof Rice Miller and wife, of Elizabethtown, will arrive today to spend the holidays with his father, near town." p3c4

From Pink: "Oscar Hendren, who has been in Kansas for the past seven years, is visiting his parents here." p3c5

"Died. Mrs Cynthia Hendren (wife of Harrison Hendren) died at her home near Edenton, Madison County, Wednesday (Dec 21), aged 86. The deceased was an aunt of Mrs A K Adcock, Nicholasville, and also related to the Hendren family of this county." p3c6 Damn, it's frustrating getting the family in order! According to the information that I just received from the Historical Society in Frankfort, she is the mother of Will D Hendren, and so should be Mrs Adcock's grand-mother, not her aunt. Wouldn't you think she'd know?

Property transfer: "W S Hendren and wife to W L Hendren, undivided one-third interest in lot known as Sullivan's addition, near C S depot, Nicholasville, $700." p3c3

The editor wrote to the correspondents as follows: "One of the great factors in the success and popularity of a country paper is its country correspondents." p4c4 Then he went on to tell them that all births, deaths, marriages, sales, serious illnesses, visitors from a distance, religious or school items, etc constitute proper items for their reports.

The *Sulphur Well Correspondent* writes:

*Edward Chandler, Edenton, was a guest of James Hendren, Wednesday last.*
*Mrs Ophella Barkley, of Texas, was visiting her brothers, Messrs Sam and Alex Askins, last week.*
*Mr N P Cobb, of Madison County, was visiting his brother, J W Cobb this week.*
*Miss Essa Hockaday, of Richmond, and Miss May Taylor, Lexington, are guests of Miss Dora Murphy.*
*T F Walker and bride paid his father's family a short visit this week.*
*S N Underwood has about recovered from his severe fall a few days ago.*
*Norman Simpson, private of 1st Ky Vols., is home on a sixty day's furlough from Puerto Rico, USA.*
*Arthur Hardison and family, of Nashville, Tenn., were visiting Mrs Margaret Horine last week.*
*James Watts has moved into his residence lately purchased from F M Horine.*
*Messrs E G Walker and James Woodward have returned from a hunting trip to the knobs.*

*The running ice in Kentucky River has interferred considerably with the Garrard County mail on this line.*

*Last Tuesday the thermometer registered 6 degrees below zero; this Tuesday it stands 56 above.*

*Joe Durham, Esq., late of our village, has moved to the mountains.*

*Our public school closed Tuesday evening. Mr N D Thompson is a capable and efficient teacher and has taught us successful schools for three years. p3c4*

December 30, 1898

Dr Hendren again writes a poem. This one is "The Vacant Chair". As the family sits around the fire in the evening, the poet asks if there is someone missing and remembered only by a vacant chair. He asks if his name is ever spoken, if there still isn't someone who loves him, whispers his name, or sheds a tear. He wonders if there isn't someone who would welcome him back to the vacant chair? p1c5 This is the same theme as was in the obituary of Rose Miller Sageser, signed by B T.

## STORE CLOSING - 1899

Forest Miller was forced to close his clothing store because of his inability to service a bank loan. He and his family moved back to Sulphur Well. This was a dramatic change for Forest and Scottie.

### January 6, 1899

We begin another year, and the weather is inclement as usual in January in Kentucky. The papers must have been bundled by year, because the first and last issues are almost always in tatters.

The *Sulphur Well Correspondent* writes:

*W B Walker, who has been on the sick list, is out again.*
*Mr John Williams and wife, of Richmond, are visiting M---- D Turpin.*
*Jessie Miller has moved from the George Moore place to M------rry.*
*W H Hoover, Jr has bought 150 acres of land from T-----Butler.*
*Mr William Montgomery of the 1st Ky Vols was visiting ---- B Taylor last week.*
*Rev Hildebrand preached this Saturday and Sunday, but the ------ weather prevented the usual good attendance.*
*Rev H G Turner, Covington, visited his parents, Mr and Mrs J P Turner, for a few days this week.*
*Mr and Mrs Alex Askins entertained a few young people Wednesday night in honor of Miss Mollie Berkley from Lexington.*
*The young man, ---atty Vincent, of Madison County, who was accidentally shot during a frolic near Pinckard by an irate husband who was attempting to slay another man dancing with his wife against his protest, was brought home last Friday. He is not seriously injured.*
*A horse and buggy that were driven by a soldier escaped from Salem Church, Madison County, Sunday night and wandered to the river at Miles Ferry, four miles distance, plunging over a steep bank into deep water. The horse's struggles attracted the attention of several persons, but before they could reach him, both horse and buggy had disappeared. p3c4*

### January 13, 1899

"Princess gowns are the natural outcome of sheath-like skirts..." that are worn for evening and formal occasions. p1c6

The *Sulphur Well Correspondent* writes:

*James Green bought a nice beef of F M Horine, Tuesday.*
*Miss Rhoda Peel has opened a small subscription school in the village.*
*Mr Charles Hudson, of Lexington, was visiting his father Monday and Tuesday.*
*James H Turner's little daughter had a light attack of la grippe last Monday.*
*Mr Albert House, of Sanders' Ferry, and Miss Layton, of Hunter's Ferry, were married last Friday. The bride is a daughter of William Layton, who recently lost a son by accidental shooting.*
*Mr Geo W Sewell lost a horse last Wednesday probably from over-driving as he had been driven to the mail wagon on the previous day.*
*Monsieur La Grippe, as the French so aptly named the very unwelcomed foreigner, is taking a stroll through this section of the country.*
*Kentucky River has been on a tear and got too big for its banks. It carried off a quantity of corn, fodder, etc.*
*Mr James Hager, our mail driver, is recovering from a severe attack of grippe. Geo Sewell, who was driving in his stead, was also taken down with it.*
*S E Gott will move to the neighborhood of Jack's Creek about March 1, and Mr Clubb, son-in-law of N D Davis, will occupy the residence.*
*Thieves paid the Hon. N D Miles a visit some time last Saturday night and carried off his poultry, but not satisfied with that haul, they went into the kitchen and took a lot of flour and a dressed chicken and departed leaving their tracks in the snow which were soon lost among others along the pike toward Chrisman's Mill.*
*The old year goes with time's revolutions*
*And leaves us resolving the same.*
*The new year but finds our good resolutions*
*Broken all to pieces again. p2c4*

January 20, 1899

Dr Hendren writes a poem "His Audience". It's about a preacher's sermon and not very good. p1c6

Drunkenness is still a problem. Lancaster has no night policeman and the correspondent there says that the town is in the hands of a drunken crowd every night. p2c2

"Miss Bertha Hendren returned Sunday from a visit to Bryantsville." p3c4

"W S Hendren, J H Murphy, and Rev George Bealer attended the State Association of the the poultry show at Louisville Wednesday and Thursday." p3c4

January 27, 1899

The *Sulphur Well Correspondent* writes:

Green B Hill was considerably injured last Thursday by his horse falling with him.
Miss T Miller left last Thursday for a month's visit among friends in Estill County.
Mr Alex Askins has been on the sick list for several days.
Mr Samuel Peel's little son, thirteen months old, has been seriously ill of grip and pneumonia for two weeks, is improving rapidly.
John, son of L B Taylor, has been quite sick of the prevailing grip.
Allen A Burton, stationed at Ripey's distillery, Tyrone, is home on a few ------------------.
Frank Hendron's little daughter has been quite sick of grip.
Mr Sam Askins gave to the young people of the village Thursday night, Jan 19, a nice little social party.
The idea of repairing the Paint Lick Pike by giving it a coat of Hickman Creek mud was a peculiar ------- anyone who splashes along through the sea of black mud will be ready to admit. p2c4

February 3, 1899

The *Sulphur Well Correspondent* writes:

Mr Thomas H Walker has been on the sick list for some days.
Mr Charles Clubb and wife, of Pleasureville, have moved to this place where they will reside this year.
Mr and Mrs Charles Hudson and wife, of Lexington, returned home Thursday from a visit to his father.
J P Turner sold to James Green two beeves averaging 2,450 pounds, at 3 and 3 1/4c.
Tuesday night the mercury fell to 4 degrees below zero at midnight and was at 6 degrees below Wednesday morning.
Clarence Peel, having been discharged from his regiment, has returned home. He expects to re-enlist.
Mr Robert Burton, of Edenton, was visiting here a few days last week.
Mr Creed Gott, of Fayette County, was here to see old friends last week.
Mr Green S Watkins, who has recently returned from Florida, has returned to Jessamine and taken lodging at Mr James Teater's.
Mr Justin Burgin lost a daughter by death Monday and has another one very low from the same disease, which is said to be a mysterious affection. p3c6

February 10, 1899

Dr Hendren has become the bard of Sulphur Well. He has another poem this week. This one is a commentary on how people lead their lives, some accomplishing so little that they leave only a mound of dirt to record their passing. This is only the first verse. p1c6

"THE TRAIL"
Of all who tread along this vale,
How few are they that leave a trail,
So light their foot-prints lie;
Upon the pathway where they fell,
There's scarce a track left there to tell
That they have just gone by.

"Pat Hendren, brother of Mrs A K Adcock, who has been very ill of pleurisy, is some better." p3c3

February 17, 1899

During the extreme cold snap a Madison County farmer lost twenty head of cattle, and hundreds of lambs froze in the county. p2c3 The snow was 18 inches deep in Nicholasville. p3c1 The ice on the river is three to five feet thick.p3c6 The coal dealers have a limited supply of coal and are rationing the amount to each customer.

The winter has been severe, and it shows as the *Sulphur Well Correspondent* writes:

*"Was it cold enough for you?" deserves a frigid reply, but if anyone has seen worse weather, don't mention it.*
*Miss Rosa Stinnett was visiting her aunt, Mrs N D Davis, last week.*
*The scarcity of coal during the artic weather did make some old moss-backs hustle after all.*
*On Wednesday morning of last week the mercury stood 2 degrees below zero here. Thursday morning it was 14 degrees below, Friday and Monday 24 degrees below. p2c2*

February 24, 1899

The *Sulphur Well Correspondent* writes:

*James W Watts has moved to a farm near Logana.*
*Wm B Walker, who has been confined to the house for three or four weeks by illness, is out again.*
*Prof Jason Tudor, of Cottonburg, closed his mathemathical school at Sageser's school house last Friday.*
*John Green, of Little Hickman neighborhood, has rented the Watts residence and moved to it.*
*It looks as if there would be more acres of tobacco planted this year than last, and tobacco barns are in demand at good figures.*
*The late cold spell seems to have been too much for the festive la grippe bacillus, the health of the community being considerably better.*

*Rev F S Haskell, the blind missionary Baptist minister, of New York, preached here last Saturday and Sunday and left Tuesday to fill an appointment at Roberts Chapel that night.*

*The cold weather killed about fifty head of cattle near Edenton, Madison County. Mr Nat Cotton lost 27 head and Ben Cotton 14. These were the largest individual losses, but several of the neighbors lost smaller lots. The cattle were in good condition but insufficient shelter was responsible mainly for the losses.*

*Several prominent traders from Madison County came over to Jessamine last Monday notwithstanding the terribly wild small-pox stories they heard on the way and that frightened back scores of visitors. Among them were: N C Cobb, Simpson Warren, Capt Hill, Capt Vincent, Edward Chandler, Elisha Warren and others. p2c5*

The small-pox scare has been real in some areas. There is one new case in Nicholasville, but he, and all those who came in contact with him, are in quarantine.

March 3, 1899

"Mr William Hendren, one of Jessamine's oldest citizens, has been quite feeble for several days. Mr Hendren has been married over sixty years." p3c3

I have know for years that a sizable number of people from Lexington and Central Kentucky wintered in Santibel, but didn't know the custom went this far back! "Mrs Jacob Troutman and Miss Florence Troutman are expected home this week from ... Santibel Island." p3c3

The *Sulphur Well Correspondent* writes:

*Mr Alvin A Burton came home Tuesday from Tyrone, on a visit.*
*Hillery Overstreet will move into the brick grainery at Watts Mill.*
*"Babe" Sageser moved into the toll-house property on the Sugar Creek Pike Tuesday.*
*Mrs Jessie Miller is at the home of her father-in-law, W R Miller, sick.*
*Mr John W Fathergill has moved into the George Moore residence.*
*Mr M F Bybee, representing W F Baumstook, Waco, Madison County, was here Thursday.*
*Miss Annie Taylor, who has been sick for some time, is getting better.*
*Mr Sam H Taylor, whose house burned down last fall is building a new residence on the site of the one destroyed.*
*Messrs Oscar and Charlie Hendren, William Kates and Eugene Carter, all young men, started Tuesday for Bloomington, Ill., to try their fortunes there.*
*Mrs Kitty Knight has taken boarding with Jas T Sageser's family for a few weeks.*
*Jim Watts did not move to the Logana farm as reported, but to Hunter's Ferry in Madison County instead. p3c7*

There are already some Hendrens living in Bloomington.

March 10, 1899

Dr Hendren returns with his latest poem "Love and Law". This is a considerable change of pace! Its about a young man who wants to propose to his ladylove, and feels that if he were in a court of law that he could present his case quite well, but feels himself a poor advocate in a court of love. She responds in this manner in the final verse:

> But, William, I'd be more contented,
> A grand juryman's place to now fill;
> From evidence you have presented,
> Already I've found my true Bill. p1c5

The *Sulphur Well Correspondent* writes:

*Louis Peel has rented and moved to a residence on Geo B Peel's place.*
*Lee Davis has moved to the toll-house lately occupied by John Fathergill.*
*Geo M Berry, of Lexington, was down last week on business.*
*Miss T Miller returned home Friday from a pleasant visit to friends and relatives in Estill County.*
*George Moore has built an addition to his residence near the iron bridge.*
*James Hendren has been quite sick for several days.*
*Mrs Sudie Richardson and Miss Leah Belle Stacy, of Irvine, are visiting Mrs Elizabeth Miller.*
*The river has been very high from the heavy rains, rising eight feet last Friday night.*
*The thermometer made quite a descent Monday night from 32 degrees to 2 degrees above zero.*
*Hon N D Miles has sold a portion of his Hunter's Ferry farm to Mr Cassidy, who, it is said, will erect warehouses, etc., on it, and provide shipping facilities in readiness for slackwater. It will make a good shipping point for that locality.* p2c5

I should mention that the owners of the turnpikes are selling off the houses that the toll collectors lived in. This accounts for Fathergill's move. And, isn't it nice that George Berry keeps popping up periodically, our correspondent for a short time. The reference to shipping facilities at Hunter's Ferry between Mt Lebanon in Jessamine County and Edenton in Madison County. The new dam, under construction at Lock 8 just below the mouth of Hickman Creek, will raise the level sufficiently for more commercial shipping.

March 17, 1899

"New sailor suits are made chiefly in three styles - tight fitting with fly front jacket, with short reefer jacket, and with short half fitting jacket...." p1c6 I suppose this still reflects the recent war.

March 24, 1899

Pollard, between Elm Fork and Paint Lick, has just been established as a postoffice.

The *Sulphur Well Correspondent* writes:

*Born, to the wife of Joseph Gill, a fine son.*
*An infant of Lee Davis' died last week of croup.*
*The indications are for a larger tobacco crop than any previous year for some time.*
*Prof Tudor seems to have been very successful in teaching another class during the winter.*
*L H Hendren is contemplating selling off a portion of the Watts Mill tract.*
*Several colored men of the neighborhood have enlisted in the U S Army at Lexington.*
*Jno P Miller, of Wisemantown, Estill County, was visiting relatives here last Friday and Saturday.*
*Mrs Elizabeth Miller gave a musical to a few young folks Thursday night of last week.*
*Mrs Sudie Richardson and Miss Stacy, who were visiting Mrs Miller, have returned home.*
*Elder Hildebrand's meetings were well attended, notwithstanding the unfavorable weather.*
*Very little plowing has been done by the farmers so far and they are necessarily very much behind with farm work.*
*The pike roads are fast becoming dirt roads or worse. Holes and deep ruts make them unpleasant and unsafe.*
*Miss Mary Taylor, of Lexington, and Miss Stella Duncan, of Richmond, were visiting Mrs Horine last week.*
*Mr Ezekiel Vincent, who has been boarding here this winter, returned to his home in Madison County, Sunday.p2c5*

The transition from toll roads to free roads is being difficult. However, I suspect that by March of any year, after a severe winter, the roads are really bad. This letter has some family visitation.

March 31, 1899

This is an unflattering description of William Goebel, probably by an editor that opposes him:

Mr Goebel was never a pleasing personality. In his veins coursed Ohio artesian water instead of warm Kentucky blood. But his very coldness, his immobile face, his silence, all helped to make a politician of him. p1c6

Forest Miller is advertising his "spring clothing--honest quality, lowest prices, latest styles." p1c1-8 Miss Elizabeth Miller, of Nicholasville, is visiting Mr and Mrs Hugh Miller.p3c3

The *Sulphur Well Correspondent* writes:

*Whooping cough is spreading in this neighborhood, three of William Clark's children being afflicted with it.*
*Alex M Askins's youngest daughter has been quite sick with catarrhal pneumonia.*
*A little son of Jas W Grant has been sick for several days, threatened with pneumonia.*
*Several children of C A Tatman, who recently moved here from South Elkhorn, are sick with the prevailing catarrhal congestion of the lungs.*
*J W Grant will auction off his goods and move to his recently purchased residence on Duncan Heights, Nicholasville, in a few days.*
*The thermometer went from 54 degrees to 24 degrees Wednesday and the blizzard was terrific for a time during the evening.*
*An infant of Joseph Gill's has been seriously sick since last Saturday.*
*All water courses have been higher since the recent rain storms than at any time during the winter, and a good deal of sickness prevails in consequence, expecially among children. p2c3*

Absolutely freakish weather has prevailed! Torrential rain, blizzards, and rapid shifts of temperature have occurred as fronts moved through. Dr Hendren thinks the sickness has resulted from the high water, and he might be correct. Privies were usually in places where waste was carried off by the water, and wells could be contaminated by seepage. Cattle lots, pig pens, and stables undoubedly contributed in the same way.

Alex Askins youngest daughter was named Mattie, who married a Stultz. They had a daughter, Ann, and son, Bobbie. Mattie later married Chess Woodard. Bobbie and I were good friends as kids, even though he was four or five years older. He taught me to play Monopoly. He married Roberta Wilhoit, a beautiful girl. They are both still living, and have made their home in Lexington, for at least the last forty years. They never had any children.

April 7, 1899

The much vaunted "horseless carriage" doesn't seem to be exactly "safe for a lady to drive."p1c4 A lady's car in Nice, France got out of control and did some damage.

Forest Miller has his usual advertisement on the front page. But, on page three he has this announcement:

> TO QUIT BUSINESS. Great in-season Clearance Sale of Clothing, Furnishings Goods, Hats, Shoes and Notions. The F Forest Miller Clothing House, Nicholasville, to sacrifice the big, new stock with a view to a change of firm. Every article is to go at prime first cost. Much new Spring Clothing for men and boys just arrived and now on sale. All profits are wiped out. Many articles to be closed out at less than cost and all old and out-of-date stock will be sacrificed at one-half price. This is the time to buy with the ready money. It will be the very time for the people to supply themselves with new and stylish clothing, hats, shoes, and all other stock at wholesale prices. This will do away all talk of hard times, as all profits are lost sight of. This is a bona fide reduction sale to make a change in business as I am determined to retire and the reduction sale is in order to close out the whole stock after a few weeks to another party. I have never faked the good people and they will be sure to find that I intend to do as I represent. Tell your neighbors and friends about it and take advantage of the sale to supply yourself, which begins Saturday, April 8 and when you come to the house you will find every garment and article marked in plain figures--for the cash. p3c1

"The clothing store of F Forest Miller will be closed today (Friday) so as to have all goods marked down for the great clearance sale which begins tomorrow." p3c2

The *Sulphur Well Correspondent* writes:

> *An infant of Joe Gill's was quite sick for a time last week.*
> *H C Tatman's little daughter was seriously ill last week with catarrhal pneumonia.*
> *J W Grant moved his family to Nicholasville Monday where he will reside in the future.*
> *The creek and branch roads were so torn up by the heavy rains that they are in a "rocky" condition.*
> *Mrs Myra Turner visited Rev H G Turner, her son, at Covington, last Thursday, returning home Saturday.*
> *Elder Hildebrand preached an interesting Easter sermon on the resurrection last Sunday.*
> *Mrs James O Tudor, of Madison County, while visiting her parents here was taken violently ill with congestive asthma and was quite sick for several days.*
> *Daisy Fain accidentally cut her hand with an ax the other day so severely that a blood vessel that had been severed had to be ligated by Dr Hendren, before the profuse hemmorhage could be stopped.* p2c2

April 14, 1899

Forest Miller's front page ad is gone this week. Also here is the reason for his sale:
> A great surprise.--The assignment of F Forest Miller, the clothier, to B M Arnett, of Farmers' Exchange Bank, Monday morning, was a great surprise in business circles. The indebtedness amounts to about $5,000 and if Mr Miller had been given time, would have paid dollar for dollar, but being forced to close his doors, will pay about fifty cents on the dollar. p3c2

The *Sulphur Well Correspondent* writes:

*E E Bourne is building a front to his residence.*
*An infant of Newt Peel has been quite sick.*
*William A Harmon, of Madison County, visited friends here Monday.*
*Mr Jno C Hendren, of Edenton, was over last Tuesday.*
*Mr J Tudor is canvassing for subscriptions to an arithmetic school.*
*Mr C E Hudson, of Lexington, is visiting his brother, Frank.*
*B F Foster is erecting a nice front to his residence near here.*
*Ed Ware accidently cut an artery in his horses leg just above the hoof, and the animal came near bleeding to death.*
*A telephone line from Nicholasville to Sulphur Well and probably connecting with the one at Buckeye for Lancaster, is being built, the poles having been delivered along the line to this point. p3c4*

Well, Forest is about twenty-five years old at this time, and has a wife and young son. He has lived in Nicholasville for the past year. I suppose that he over-extended himself with his spring merchandise. We will never know how much of his own money that he invested when he first acquired his one-half interest with J H Murphy, or again when he later acquired Murphy's interest. It's possible that his bank debt goes back to these events. I think that his mother, Elizabeth, or his older brother in Wisemantown, John, could have bailed him out, if they had chosen, or if he had asked. George Ware has said that his father, Luther, always maintained that Murphy had somehow taken advantage of Forest. We will never know if Forest paid too high a price for his interest or not, but he was in a position to know the value of the stock before he acquired Murphy's interest, and we can't blame Murphy for asking as much as he could get.

April 21, 1899

Assignee's sale of Clothing, Furnishings, Hats, Shoes and Notions. The large stock of goods of F Forest Miller, assigned to me, will be closed out as rapidly as possible at great bargains. In the stock will be found no shoddy goods, but all up-to-date brands. This will be an opportunity of a life time to get bargains. B M Arnett, Assignee. p2c7-8

"Mr J H Murphy has been in Cincinnati this week on business." p3c3

The *Sulphur Well Correspondent* writes:

*Miss Maggie Gott and Miss Tuttle, of Spears, visited Mr S N Snowden Monday.*
*Mrs John Waller is on the sick list, threatened with pnuemonia.*
*Quite a crowd of Madison County farmers were out on Monday.*
*Mr Sam Askins lost a fine calf Sunday from a peculiar affection, probably black leg.*
*A magic lantern exhibition of Spanish war scenes, etc., was given at the school house last Saturday night, but it was slimly attended.*
*Morton Teater, of Buckeye, died at his home, Thursday, April 13. aged 38.*

*Thomas J Horine visited his daughter Mrs Andy Smith in Louisville Wednesday.*
*Stephen N Snowden has been very sick for several days.*
*Mr Bailey Richardson has broken up house keeping, the neighbors taking his children to keep.*
*Tom Horine plowed up an old Spanish coin of the date of 1812 on his place a few days ago.*
*Mr and Mrs Hugh G Miller, of Richmond, returned home after a several days visit with Dr Hendren, accompanied by Miss Mary Hendren, for a few weeks stay in Madison.*
*Edward Ware came near losing a horse by bleeding to death Tuesday. He incautiously cut into the foot above the hoof to remove a spavin and cut an artery.*
*A great deal of hemp passes through here from the borders of Garrard and Madison Counties for shipment or sale at Nicholasville. Locking and damming the Kentucky will be a great convenience to the farmers of that section of the country.*
*Russell, the 6 year-old son of S N Snowden, was thrown from a horse Wednesday, April 12, and (was) found soon after in an unconscious condition, remaining so till next day. He is apparently none the worse from his fall at this time. p2c3*

April 28, 1899

The *Sulphur Well Correspondent* writes:

*Meade Miller intends to go to Oklahoma about May 1 to engage in farming.*
*J P Turner went on a visit to his son, Rev H G Turner, at Covington, Friday last.*
*Thos B Walker, is building a new veranda to his dwelling.*
*Hogs are selling at $3.25 per cwt in this locality.*
*Rev W S Grinstead, of Millersburg, was visiting his daughter, Mrs Jas H Turner, last week.*
*The school census for this district is completed with 78 children of school age.*
*A good many calves are dying of black leg in this locality. p2c5*

Meade did go, and he stayed in Oklahoma. While he will visit several times, this may be a good place to give some of the information about his family that is in the <u>Sageser Genealogy</u>: He married Mae Benjamin and they had three children; Nancy, Laura, and John C. Miller (II). Nancy was living in Oklahoma City when the <u>Genealogy</u> was written (1978). John C moved on to Phoenix, Arizona. Meade lived until 1968.

May 5, 1899

Forest Miller's stock is still being advertised by the Assignee.

May 12, 1899

Andrew Carnegie sold his interest in the Carnegie Steel Co to Rockefeller and others for $150,000,000. p2c1 "The trusts of the country are raising the price of almost every branch of trade, but the wages of the working man still remain stationary." p2c1

The *Sulphur Well Correspondent* writes:

*The health of the community is good.*
*The mercury went up to 92 degrees here last week.*
*H C Tatman is sick with malarial fever.*
*J W Cobb has returned from a visit to Harrodsburg.*
*The white blossom has about taken the meadows.*
*F F Miller has moved in with his mother, Mrs Elizabeth Miller.*
*Rev H G Turner and wife, of Covington, are visiting his parents, Mr and Mrs J P Turner, this week.*
*Eld Hildebrand preached to a small audience, on account of the bad weather, last Sunday. Eld Elliott also preached on foreign missions.*
*F M Horine, our hustling trader sold to A C Miles 20 head of hogs at 200 pounds each for 3 1/2 cts (per pound). Also to other parties 11 tons of hay at $8.50 per ton, and some fat cattle to James Green at 3 3/4 cents and has lots of stuff on hand yet.*
*Some miscreants one night last week castrated a young bull of N D Davis' and mutilated him so badly that he was found dead in the pasture the next morning.*
*The hands at work on the telephone line under E Walker struck for shorter hours of labor and all work is at a standstill for a time.*
*Mrs James Hagar has about recovered from a long spell of sickness.*
*Mrs Eliza A Hendren, who has been seriously ill with inflammatory rheumatism, is better.*
*The old William Hunter residence, now the property of A L Rice, is being repaired.*
*Wednesday night, May 3, while Walter May was visiting at Geo Walton's, someone turned his horse loose on the pike. When found some distance away the animal had stripped himself of the harness, demolished one wheel and otherwise damaged the buggy.* p2c4

It seems like their are some really mean people living in Sulphur Well at this time.

Mrs Eliza Hendren is the wife of William Hendren, son of Doven Hendren.

I have a great deal of empathy for Forest Miller. I'm sure he felt like a failure at this moment, and it must have been difficult to come back to Sulphur Well.

May 19, 1899

"The Democratic candidates for governor continue in their abuse of each other ...." p2c1
The Democrats are still fighting the silver battle.

"Miss Bertha Hendren is visiting Miss Nellie Bourne at Bryantsville." p3c3

The *Sulphur Well Correspondent* writes:

*Rev H G Turner and wife, who have been visiting relatives here, returned home Friday.*
*William Askins, wife and son, of Garrard County, were visiting A M Askins here last week.*
*Mrs Susan Taylor, quite an aged lady, is seriously ill.*
*Mrs James Hendren was seriously attacked with lumbago Monday and cannot walk.*
*Mrs Lena Smith and step-daughter are visiting her father, T J Horine.*
*A daughter of Wm R Miller is down with fever.*
*Miss Eudora Murphy returned Monday from a visit to Lexington.*
*William Hendren, Sr., who has been quite ill this week, is better.*
*F M Horine bought of Joe Peel two head of cattle weighting 800 lbs for $55. Also two cows from James Adams for $24 each. p2c3*

May 26, 1899

Dr Hendren has composed another poem. This one is "Things I've noticed". He has noticed that there is a wide difference in what people say and do. p1c4

"The white clover crop is an immense one and bee keepers are jubliant over the honey prospects." p2c3

The *Sulphur Well Correspondent* writes:

*Sam Askins lost a fine young Jersey cow Thursday by hydrophobia.*
*Miss Rhoda Peel has been sick for a few days.*
*Aunt Kit Knight was so unfortunate as to dislocate her arm while on a visit to Little Hickman.*
*Mrs Margaret Horine, who is quite an aged lady, is afflicted with a persistent eye trouble.*
*Miss Mary Miller has about recovered from an attack of billious fever.*
*Mrs F M Hudson, who has been sick for some time, was taken suddenly worse Wednesday and her symptoms were quite alarming for several hours.*
*Thomas Bruner handled a large quantity of tobacco through here this week for delivery in Lexington.*
*Rev W M Zeigler, who has been canvasing this neighborhood with bibles (an article not found in every household) has gone to Little Hickman. p2c2*

June 2, 1899

The gubernatorial race is still running strong, Hardin vs Goebel for the Democrats.

June 9, 1899

"Mr L H Hendren and little daughter, Ethel, of Ambrose, are spending a few days in ------------- with his -(sister)-, Mrs Mary E Wheeler." p3c3 As I look at the 1900 Census L H and his wife Louisa, and their two children, Jennie and Ethel are living with his parents in Sulphur Well.

"Bessie Adcock is entertaining friends on her 13th birthday." p3c3

"Mr and Mrs Rice Miller will leave Saturday for their home in Jessamine County. Mr Miller has purchased one of the finest blue grass farms in that section and expects to devote himself to farming. He has been the principal of the Hardin Collegiate Institute for the past two years." p3c3

The *Sulphur Well Correspondent* writes:

> Mrs C H Tatham was quite sick for a few days last week.
> Miss Dora Fain, daughter of Richard Fain, died of typhoid fever last Friday, June 2.
> The strawberry supper given by the ladies of the Christian Church last Friday night was largely attended and was a success, as they took in more than $20, which is to be used for the benefit of the church.
> Miss Mary Hendren returned Sunday from a lengthy visit in Madison County.
> Mr and Mrs Hugh Miller and two children were visiting Dr Hendren this week.
> A little colored boy was kicked by a mule last Sunday and badly mutilated, having his lower lip cut in two down to the chin and losing nearly all his teeth on the right side of both jaws.
> Dr Jno C Miller started for Oklahoma last Tuesday, where he will probably invest in real estate. p2c2

Dr Miller's son, Meade, just moved to Oklahoma a few weeks ago. His son Hugh is mentioned above as visiting Dr Hendren, and his son Rice has just purchased a farm. Mary is Dr Hendren's daughter.

## June 16, 1899

From Logana comes the word that "Prof Rice Miller and his wife have moved to the farm of his father, Dr Jno C Miller." p2c5

The *Sulphur Well Correspondent* writes:

> A N Rice is building a large barn on his premises.
> F M Horine sold to Marshal Smith last Monday a good beef cow at $3.35 per cwt.
> Mrs Alice Hendren was quite sick for a while Sunday night.
> Measles have broken out among the colored people here.
> Joseph Woodward was taken suddenly with acute gastritis Sunday at his father's house, and was critically ill for some time.
> Miss Nannie Hare is visiting relatives in Lancaster this week.
> Mrs W S Grinstead, son and daughter, of Millersburg, are visiting her daughter, Mrs Jas H Turner.
> Miss Nellie Johnson, of Lancaster, returned home Monday from a few days visit to W H Hare.
> Mrs John Burchell, while visiting at John C Lutes Sunday, was very suddenly attacked with neuralgia of the stomach, and was seriously ill for several hours.
> Mrs A M Askins and daughters returned home Sunday from a week's visit with friends in Lexington. p2c5

The Askins are probably visiting the Grays, who are former residents of Sulphur Well. Nellie Johnston is W H Hare's granddaughter. Her father is Wm McC Johnston.

### June 23, 1899

At the Democratic County Convention, delegates were chosen for the State Convention coming up. The delegates were instructed to vote for Wat Hardin for governor. p2c1

Dr John C Miller, writes to a friend about what he is seeing in Oklahoma. He says the good land around Oklahoma City sells for $25 to $50 per acre (about the same as in Kentucky). At this time Oklahoma City has a population of 12,000, and is growing. p2c3

"Thomas Welch Downing, of New York, writes friends here that he will visit Nicholasville about the first of next month and spend two weeks in the Bluegrass Region." p3c3 This is the future husband of Elizabeth Miller, Dr Miller's daughter.

Property transfer: "James Hendren and wife to J H Turner, lot at Sulphur Well, $75." p3c4

The *Sulphur Well Correspondent* writes:

*W B Ray, of Garrard County, was over on a visit last Wednesday.*
*C E Hudson and wife, of Lexington, are with relatives here for a week's visit.*
*Mr William Burton, of Buckeye, was over Monday.*
*Mr Newt Wallace was temporarily on the mail route route last week on account of the sudden illness of Mr Hagar's wife.*
*Mrs Elizabeth Miller returned home Thursday from a two weeks' visiting at Irvine and in Estill County.*
*Mrs C H Tatman returned home Monday from a visit to her mother near Lexington.*
*Rev H G Turner, wife and son, of Covington, are visiting his parents, Mr and Mrs J P Turner here, this week.* p2c5

I suppose that "W B" is Bronson Ray, but I'm not sure.

### June 30, 1899

"The long contest for the Democratic nomination for Governor ended with Wm Goebel" being named the nominee "on the 26th ballot." p2c1

"Dr Jno C Miller has moved from the country to the Beasley residence on Noland Street." p3c3

The *Sulphur Well Correspondent* writes:

*Miss Nannie Hare returned home Tuesday from a visit to Garrard County.*
*A horse driven by Mr Edgar Thompson, Sunday, became unmanageable and kicked the buggy to pieces. He and Miss Bertha Askins, who was with him, escaped unhurt.*
*Mrs Mamie Johnston, of Lancaster, is visiting her parents, Mr and Mrs W H Hare.*
*Mrs Emerine Crow left Wednesday on a visit to her sister in Clark County.*
*Mr Newt Wallace's little daughter was quite sick last week.*
*A little son of Mr Crayton Turpin was viciously attacked by a Jersey cow Tuesday and only the fact of her being dehorned saved the little fellow's life. He was considerably bruised before he could be rescued.*
*Dr Joseph Myers, wife and two children, Byron Myers, of Clinton, Ill., and William Simpson and family, of Teatersville, Garrard County, were visiting Julia Myers from Sunday till Monday when Dr Myers returned home, where he conducts a large drug store in connection with his practice. He is a son of Jordon Myers of this county.*
*Thieves seem to be on the rampage in this neighborhood. They are very industrious as well as quite hungry. They visited Mrs Elizabeth Miller's garden and picked her beans, also her hen house and gathered in her chickens. They also visited the garden of J H Turner for beans, peas and beets, winding up their gardening expedition at T J Horine's for more beans, peas, etc. The other neighbors will have to look out when they get another hungry spell on.* p2c4

July 7, 1899

"Thos W Downing, of New York, is in town mingling with his old friends." p3c3

The bard of Sulphur Well composed "The Inner Man". The first verse goes like this:

> T'would be a most marvelous thing
> If man could for inspection bring
> His inner self to outward view,
> Where he could for himself pursue
> The wide divergencies in the plan
> Of outer and of inner man.

This is reminiscent of his poem "Things I've Noticed" back in May whose theme was that that people varied in what they said and what they did. I gather that hypocracy bothered him a great deal, and that he saw a lot of it. p1c5

The *Sulphur Well Correspondent* writes:

*Samuel Hill sold to A C Miles, 14 fat hogs at 3 1/4c.*
*F M Horine reports having 25 acres of wheat that threshed out 26 bushels to the acre.*
*John Perkins is rebuilding his residence lately burned down.*
*Frank Miller, Wisemantown, Estill County, is visiting his grandmother, Mrs Elizabeth Miller.*
*Mrs J H Turner has been quite sick for several days with a severe attack of tonsilitis.*
*The glorious fourth passed off unnoticed by our unpatriotic citizens.*

*Mr William Askins and the Misses Mary and Elizabeth Askins, of Buena Vista, were visiting at A M Askins' this week.*

*It is so extremely dry in this section that the grass is dry as tinder and gardens are about dried up. Corn is undoubtedly seriously injured.*

*There was a large attendance at church last Sunday, it being Elder Hildebrand's regular monthly meeting. He is a bright young minister and shows a wonderful knowledge of the scripture for one so young in the cause. p2c3*

Frank P Miller, the oldest child of John P Miller and Flora Scott, became a doctor and married Fannie Kimbrough. That's all the Sageser Genealogy has on him. Maybe one of the Wisemantown decendents of John P Miller has more information.

July 14, 1899

Dr Hendren composed the following poem:

### "THE HOUSE WHERE I WAS BORN"

O, the homestead of my boyhood
Off among the grassy hills,
Mid the fragrance of their meadows,
And the purling of their rills;
Where the long and happy hours
Of my childhood's early morn,
Were but dreams of youthful pleasure
In the house where I was born.

O, the home that I remember--
Still for it my heart will yearn;
And those days of childish pleasure
That will never more return,
O, I never can forget it,
For those cherished dreams will throng,
Even through the years of manhood,
Of the house where I was born.

But that homestead of my childhood--
It is changed, as well as I,
By those unrelenting fingers
Of the years that drifted by,
In my dreams I see it standing,
But so changed and tempest-torn
That it seems, in slumber, haunted--
The old house where I was born.

> For it's silent and deserted
> In the visions that I see,
> As it all had now departed
> Who once trod its walks with me,
> And I feel as one forsaken
> On the old play-ground forelorn,
> In the dreams that haunt my vision
> Of the house where I was born. p1c5

"Miss Bertha Hendren is visiting at Bryantsville." "Miss Emma Spruce is visiting friends at Shelbyville." "Mrs A K Adcock and children left yesterday to spend several days at Estill Springs." p3c3

The Camp Meeting at High Bridge begins July 21st and goes on for ten days. Sam Jones and others will speak. p3c4 The people of Jessamine are also being treated to an excursion, at a cost of only $1.50 roundtrip, to Natural Bridge next Wednesday. p3c4 These excursions really gave people an opportunity travel at reasonable expense.

### July 21, 1899

The Republicans nominated W S Taylor to be their party nominee. p1c6 He is a farmer, self-educated, and has been circuit clerk, and county judge of Butler County. Taylor is married and has seven children.

Notice: "All persons indebted to F F Milller are requested to call on Jno H Welch and settle at once and avoid cost.   B M Arnett". p2c6

Nicholasville's "Street Fair" begins at 7:30 am next Thursday. They think bringing people to Main Street will help the merchants more than races, and other attractions at the fair grounds.

"There is more wheat being shipped along the river than two boats can handle for several months." p3c3

"Meade Miller, son of Dr Jno C Miller, left Monday for Oklahoma Territory to make it his future home, and where he will be joined by his father in about three months." p3c3

"Mr George Berry, the popular drummer, was in Nicholasville Monday after being confined to his room for the past three weeks from a painful operation." p3c3

From the <u>Lebanon Enterprise</u>: "Thomas W Downing, of New York, with his two brothers, John and Nathan, are visiting their aunt, Mrs H S Clair Cox. These gentlemen occupy places of profit and trust, and they are examples of what push and energy will do." p3c3 They really were outstanding young men. John was in banking, and highly respected.

July 28, 1899

The crowd for the Street Fair was large, and exceeded expectations. They showed their horses and traps, had a mule race, foot races, pie-eating contests, selected the prettiest girl and ugliest man, showed fruits and vegetables, gave prizes for the largest family, oldest couple, etc. p3c4

August 4, 1899

Dan P Hemphill, a state champion wheeler, has purchased an interest in a Nicholasville drug store. p2c2

James Miller died. This is his obituary:

> Miller.-Jas W Miller died at his home in Ambrose, Friday, July 21, of locked bowels, aged 46. Mr Miller was a native of Estill County, where he resided until 10 years ago, when he moved to Ambrose, this county, engaging in the general merchandise business. At the time of his death Mr Miller was postmaster at Ambrose, a position he had occupied for a number of years. The deceased was a son of Mrs Frank Miller, of Ambrose, and a brother of Mr F F Miller, formerly of Nicholasville. Funeral took place Saturday, and the remains interred in the old Miller burying ground, Rev T W Watts conducting the services at the grave." p3c3

James Miller was born August 31, 1854 in Wisemantown, the second child of Francis S Miller and Elizabeth Jane Williams. He married Maggie Edwards on September 18, 1879. I don't know if she died, or they separated or divorced. He once visted his children in West Virgina. I will try to pull together all the information I have about him in one place. In any case, he has had no family with him in the ten years that he lived in Sulphur Well. I have never been able to determine conclusively whether or not he lived with his mother during that time.

The *Sulphur Well Correspondent* writes:

> *Frank Rettig, of Louisville, visited J H Murphy last week.*
> *An infant of Mr M Willis is very sick with congestion of the lungs.*
> *Mr James Clark, of Louisville, is visiting his parents here.*
> *The public school opened Monday with Miss May Taylor as teacher.*
> *Mrs Lizzie Greenstreet, of Kansas, is visiting her father, Frank Taylor, Sr.*
> *Mr and Mrs John Whitenack, of Harrodsburg, were the guests of J W Cobb last week.*
> *Miss Emma West was taken suddenly and seriously ill last Sunday evening on returning home after attending church.*
> *Mr and Mrs William Hendren have been very sick for several days with dysentery. Mrs Hendren is still seriously ill.* p2c4

Mr and Mrs William Hendren are Dr Hendren's parents.

August 11, 1899

"Wm McC Johnson is building a handsome residence on Danville Street, Lancaster." p2c2

From Pink: "Mrs Kitty Knight is reported to be very sick." p2c4

August 18, 1899

The platforms of the Republicans and Democrats are laid side by side on the front page. It would be difficult to do each side justice by summarizing them in a few words. They both seem to be against trusts and restrains on trade. They each address the problems of the cost of text books for the public schools, and improved transportation and freight rates. The anti-Goebel Democrats have nominated their own slate of candidates, headed by former Governor John Y Brown. I suppose they have to run as Independents.

The *Sulphur Well Correspondent* writes:

*Miss Emma West, who has been quite sick, is out again.*
*Mr J P Turner has been sick for several days.*
*Elder Hildebrand has been spending several days visiting among his congregation.*
*Mrs W H Cobb is on the sick list, with a malarial trouble.*
*Mr Hugh Miller and wife will visit Oklahoma Territory soon with a view of locating there.*
*J P and J H Turner sold last Friday 82 head of hogs, averaging 220 lbs., to Cron Coy, of Madison County, for Lexington parties, at 4c.*
*Miss Bettie, daughter of Wilson Masters, who has been down with fever, is much improved.*
*Miss Annie Taylor is very low with consumption of the bowels.*
*David Switzer, an old Mexican pensioner, is very low and not expected to recover.*
*Many of our citizens paid a pleasant visit to the fair at Lexington Thursday and Friday of last week.*
*Mr A M Askins' little daughter has been very sick from the prevailing summer disease.*
*Mr M Willis' little daughter, who has beeen quite low, is improving.* p2c4

Isn't it strange that the villagers had a nice time at the Lexington Fair, but no mention of the Nicholasville Fair?

August 25, 1899

The Democrats who bolted the party put as the first plank in their platform that:
> We declare that during the recent convention of the Democrats of Kentucky, in Louisville, by reason of the autocratic, unlawful and unprecedented ruling of its Chairman, aided by the intervention of armed police, and the fraud, deception and trickery of the person who dictated and dominated the proceedings of said convention, one-third of the Democrats of Kentucky were disfranchised .... p1c4

I seem to recall a biblical expression, something to the effect: "As you sow, so shall you reap!"

From Pink: "Mrs Kitty Knight, who has been very sick, is able to be out again." p2c5

September 1, 1899

Dr Miller has written a very long letter to the <u>Jessamine Journal</u>, extolling the virtues of agriculture in Oklahoma. He describes the geography of three counties in the area. I want to exerpt one paragraph to reveal his personality:

> Cleveland County, west of Oklahoma (City) -- Norman, (the) county seat, has 3,000 inhabitants.... These three counties lie on the north side of the South Canadian River, which is about one mile wide, and whose bottom is quick sand, ready to submerge the beast that stops in the river. The Chickasaw Nation lies south. The Nations have numerous white farmers and cattlemen. My son, Meade Miller, is now on his farm, 1 1/2 miles south of Oklahoma City.

Dr Miller then concludes as he ends his letter:

> A man can buy the land on time and pay for it in two years. But must have money sufficient to buy four work horses, a gang plow, binder, harrow, drill, seed wheat, harness, and provisions. A man without any money should not go to Oklahoma. p1c5

W S Hendren won a prize at a Shelbyville poultry show for his Buff Pekin Bantams. p2c3

"Harry P Hendren is visiting his uncle, Mr Robert Reagan, in Madison County." p3c3

The Deans had a reunion: The reunion of the Dean family was held at the home of Melvin L Dean--the old homestead--near Pink, last Saturday. The morning was devoted mostly to photographing various groups of the family. They had quite a dinner, then all adjourned to Chalybeate Springs where there was singing by a young choir, and several speeches. p3c2 This is the father of Dr M L Dean who reassembled most of the Miller farm that contains the family cemetery. More family history is given.

> The late Harrison Dean, who was born in Mercer County, Ky., was the fifth son of James and Keziah (Greene) Dean. In 1832 he came to Jessamine County to live and in 1835 married Nancy Owens, daughter of Fleming and Annie (Tombs) Owens, both of whom were born in Halifax, Virginia.

They had eight sons and two daughters. Melvin Lowery was the youngest son, being born January 16, 1860. Both Harrison and Nancy are buried in the cemetery on the farm.

The *Sulphur Well Correspondent* writes:

*A little daughter of Ben Wheeler has been very sick with cholera infantum for some days.*
*Miss Mattie Berkeley, of Lexington, is visiting A M Askins.*
*Born, to the wife of Jno W Underwood, on the 23rd inst, a daughter.*
*Several additions to the Little Hickman Church were baptized near the iron bridge last week.*
*The remnant of the stock of goods of the late J W Miller was auctioned off last Saturday.*
*The neighbors and friends had a delightful fish dinner near Sanders' Ferry last Friday.*
*Elder Neal closed his protracted meeting at Little Hickman Church Thursday night, Aug 24, with several additions.*
*Mrs Emerine Crow has returned from a long visit to friends in Clark County.*
*Mrs Geo M Hendren left Tuesday for a few days visit to her daughter, Mrs Hugh Miller, Richmond.*
*J P Turner sold last week to Mr Ford, of Stamping Ground, a car load of nice heifers at 3 3/4 cents per pound. p2c5*

I see that they auctioned off the last of "Uncle" Jim's goods out of the general store that he ran. The only thing that we have left of his worldly goods is his bible. We recently had that rebound, and it is now in good condition. It is owned by Alice Kirk who lives in Knoxville. There is no indication that he was survived by children or other family. Neither was there any mention that they attended his funeral, or shared in his estate.

Hugh Miller is still out in Oklahoma with his father looking at land.

September 8, 1899

Labor Day was observed only by the banks and the postoffice. p3c1

"Miss Emma Hendren, of Richmond, is the guest of Miss Nellie Hendren." p3c3

"A K Adcock is adding two rooms to his house on North Main Street." p3c4

September 15, 1899

"New millinery is marked by great apparent heaviness." Large birds or breast feathers with massive appearance are placed on brims, and felt is used by the yard. p1c6

"Cornelius Vanderbilt ... died very suddenly Tuesday." p2c1

"J H Murphy & Co's new warehouse, corner Main and Depot streets, is rapidly approaching completion, and when finished will be the largest building in town (Nicholasville)." p3c1

The *Sulphur Well Correspondent* writes:

*Creed Gott was over from Richmond Sunday to see his best girl.*
*Elder Latimer and wife, of Wilmore, are visiting J W Cobb.*
*Rev W S Grinstead, of Taylorsville, was visiting J H Turner last week.*
*The protracted meeting will close Thursday night.*
*W B Walker fell unconscious from an attack of vertigo in front of the blacksmith shop, Tuesday evening.*
*George Walters sold two fat cows to W C Tutt for $55.*
*Emmet Million and J T Rice, of Richmond, are visiting at J H Murphy's.*
*John Waller is building a residence and will move here as soon as it is completed.*
*F M Horine sold to Jas W Carroll last week 12 head of cattle at 4c to be delivered next week.*
*W F Carter's loss by fire on dwelling and household goods was adjusted by the Hurst Home Company last Friday at $535.*
*Elders Coyle and Hildebrand's meetings here have been well attended. They are two fine speakers and earnest christian young men. There have been several additions, four of whom were baptized Tuesday evening.* p2c4

September 22, 1899

A party of about twenty from Nicholasville and Richmond are going to Oklahoma to "inspect the country with the view to locating there." p3c3

September 29, 1899

"Dr Jno C Miller offers for sale October 14, a lot of stock and some land. p2c3 He is offering, at public sale, at his homeplace on Kentucky River turnpike, four miles east of Nicholasville, 83 acres of hemp land lying between the farm of J T West, J P Turner, and

Rice Miller, which will be offered in parcels and as a whole." He is also offering some cattle, horses and goats. p2c6

"Mr and Mrs Adcock spent Monday in Louisville." p3c4

The *Sulphur Well Correspondent* writes:

> *William Hendren is visiting in Indiana for a few weeks.*
> *Mr E Doty was the guest of A M Askins a day or so last week.*
> *J M Long and William Burris, prominent farmers of Madison County, were over last week.*
> *Geo W Warner, of Edenton, was shaking hands with friends Monday on this side.*
> *Lieut John T M Hill, of Madison County, was over on one of his infrequent visits Monday.*
> *Mrs Speed Taylor and daughter, Hattie, of Newby, were visiting J W Cobb, Saturday and Sunday.*
> *Rev H G Turner, of Richmond, was visiting his father, J P Turner, a few days last week.*
> *W H Hoover, sold to A C Miles, 20 head of hogs at $3.25 per cwt.*
> *A little daughter of W D Harris has been quite sick for some days.*
> *F M Horine bought of James Teater two head of steers at $45.*
> *Miss Mollie Berkley, Louisville, is the guest of her uncle, A M Askins.*
> *N D Thompson, Wilmore, was the guest of Dr Hendren Tuesday.*
> *James Clark, Louisville, accompanied by Fred P Kern, are visiting their friends in this section.*
> *Dr G M Hendren is very low with heart trouble.* p2c4

Dr Hendren is, I presume, self-diagnosing his problem.

## October 6, 1899

Rice Miller may have intended to join the troop to Oklahoma: "All those who desire to go to Oklahoma, Tuesday, Oct 17, should see Rice Miller between this and Monday, as general agents will be to see him on that day and make lowest rates." p3c1 However, it was not to be.

The Lexington Herald reports: "The well-known traveling man, Geo M Berry and his wife, of 67 Spring Street, are receiving the congratulations of their friends over the arrival of a 10-pound boy at their home last Sunday morning." p3c3 Good old George and Ida. George must have had the best personality of anyone on the road.

## October 13, 1899

I hope that our good doctor, and correspondent, is well. This has been no report since he said he was ill.

October 20, 1899

This issue of the Journal is devoted almost exclusively to the detailing the businesses located in Nicholasville and their proprietors. It's very good history. However, there is no report on the Miller sale of land and livestock.

October 27, 1899

The work on the locks and dams is progressing very rapidly. They are finishing the paving and other work on Lock No 7. They have purchased the site and are beginning work on Lock No 8, and surveying possible locations for Locks No 9 and No 10. p2c1

Our former wheelman and now pharmacist, Dan Hemphill, spent Saturday and Sunday in Lancaster with his friend Miss Ada Dickerson. p3c3

November 3, 1899

The front page of the Journal is missing. The election is next Tuesday, and there is a lot of promotion. Electric lights for Nicholasville is on the ballot.

The editor is wondering who will be the first owner of a "horseless carriage." Progress is coming quickly now.

Fortunately, the *Sulphur Well Correspondent* is back, and writes:

*Mrs Elizabeth Miller has returned from a visit to friends at Irvine.*
*J H Turner sold a car load of hay to parties (in) Chattanooga, Tenn.*
*John Broomfield sold this week 15 hogs to A C Miles at $3.25.*
*John Waller has about completed his residence and will move into it this week.*
*The new post-office building and store of F F Miller is completed and the office moved into it.*
*F M Horine lost a fine filly by some mysterious affection last week. She was apparently well 20 minutes before she was found dead in the lot. p2c3*

I believe that the location of the new post-office and store was in the intersection near or next to Mrs Miller's, and across from the Cobb house, that Forest later purchased.

It is Dr Hendren who continues to write "Broomfield" rather than "Brumfield". I will review earlier articles, to see which he may have written.

November 10, 1899

Early election results: It appears now, before all precincts have reported, that the Democrat, Goebel, will win the governor's chair. p2c1 There is a lot more to come about this! Locally, the question of electic lights carried easily, together with the bonds to finance them. p3c4

The wife of one of A K Adcock's bartenders became jealous, and when she discovered her husband in the house of Mrs Betts, she began firing. Two of her bullets struck Mrs Betts, but not fatally. The husband jumped through a window on the first shot, and although he was "closely pursued" by his wife, she was unable to catch him. p3c2

"Meade Miller, Oklahoma City, Okl., is visiting relatives in the county. He is much pleased with his new home and thinks it the Chicago of the new west." p3c3

November 17, 1899

The early attempt to grow grapes in Kentucky is being revisited. The place chosen for the vineyard was a hill slope on the Kentucky River just below the mouth of Sugar Creek, which was one and one-half miles above Lock No 8. The site of the old vineyard is owned (in 1899) by George McQuerry. The only signs still left are parts of a stone wall built to enclose the ground, and the walls and cellars of the house. The article is written by T R Dean, and he gives references as to where photographs and maps can be found. p1c3

The election results are still not official. While Goebel has a plurality of the uncontested votes, Taylor, the Republican, has a plurality of the contested ones. p2c1

A K Adcock was elected to the County Board of Education.p2c1 He was active in community affairs, having served also on the city council.

"Dr John C Miller will sell Tuesday, 10 am, Nov 28, his fine farm 24 acres, fine residence, 10 rooms, 2 halls on Barnes Mill Pike, two miles from Richmond, Ky." p2c5 The farm actually has 294 acres. A printing error occurred.

The *Sulphur Well Correspondent* writes:

*Rev H G Turner, of Richmond, was over on a short visit last week.*
*J T Floyd and wife, of Kansas City, Mo., were visiting A M Askins last week.*
*Mr and Mrs Hugh Miller, of Madison County, were visiting Dr Hendren last week for several days.*
*Corn is selling in this locality at $1.75 per barrel.*
*Forest Miller has laid in a small stock of groceries in connection with the post-office.*
*Miss Druey Quinn, of Madison County, is visiting at J W Cobb's.*
*N D Davis sold four fine steers to Dr Alexander, of Fayette County, at 4 1/2 cts.*
*Caused a Panic.-A wild panic and stampede was caused by Lee Humphrey during religious worship at Pleasant Hill last Friday night. It seems that Humphrey, who has been crazy, and was for a time in an asylum, took it into his head to make an exhibition of himself, and his wild and wooliness during services. He drew his pistol, marched up the aisle and flourished the weapon in the ministr's face. Of course there was a wild scene, but fortunately no one was seriously hurt in the scramble for egress. After creating this scene, Humphrey took his seat as calmly as if nothing unusual had happened. p2c4*

November 24, 1899

"Meade Miller returned to Oklahoma, Tuesday." p3c3

The *Sulphur Well Correspondent* writes:

> Mr and Mrs A C Miles left Friday for a visit to friends in Garrard County.
> Sam Askins is improving his premises by erecting outbuildings.
> Mr James Luttrell, of Garrard County, was over Tuesday on his way to Lexington.
> The genial drummer, Geo M Berry, was here Tuesday bragging about another boy who is "visiting" him--named Carl Walden Berry.
> J H Turner is building a large barn on the Rufus Hill farm.
> N D Davis sold to W C Tutt, the butcher, some nice butcher stuff, at 3 1/4c.
> Four thousand and sixty pounds of tobacco were raised on a little more than two acres of land on the Horine farm.
> A great deal of tobacco is being delivered to Davis Bros. at from 7 1/4 to 8 1/2c.
> Several hundred barrels of corn have been sold and delivered in this section at $1.75 per barrel.
> The "Leonids" failed to exhibit their unrivaled attraction of steller firewords as advertised, on account it is said of a year's mistake in the calculations of our "scientific" astonomers. Well, we can wait till they get the comets tail and science more in accord on the date of the proposed performance of the falling bodies. p2c4

December 1, 1899

"Prof Rice Miller has been confined to his bed for several days with typhoid fever, but is convalescing." p3c3

December 8, 1899

Geo F Snowden sold 27 acres of land to J C Lutes for $426. p2c4

The *Sulphur Well Correspondent* writes:

> Mrs Hugh Miller and children are visiting her parents here in route to Oklahoma Territory, their future home.
> A M Askins has rented a shop in Nicholasville and will move there with his family Jan 1st.
> William Harris sold two hogs Wednesday weighing 550 pounds at 3 1/2 cents.
> T J Horine sold a milk cow Monday for $25.
> Some days ago, J H Murphy lost a valuable work mare from hemorrhage.
> The funeral procession of Mrs Betsy Jennings, an old resident of this neighborhood, and who died at Wilmore, passed throught here Monday.
> Mrs F M Hudson was quite sick from stomach and bowel trouble Sunday night.
> Mrs Emily Peel will arrive home this week from an extended visit to relatives in Kansas and Illinois. p2c3

Hugh Miller and family do settle in Oklahoma, but eventually wind up in Arkansas.

December 15, 1899

This is a real shock to me. Rice Miller has died suddenly. He's only been married a few months. This is his obituary:

Miller.-Rice Miller died at his home on the Chrisman Mill Pike, 4 1/2 miles east of Nicholasville, Tuesday morning, Dec 12, after a month's illness of typhoid fever. He was the eldest son of Dr Jno C Miller, of Nicholasville, and was born in this county, Aug 14, 1869. He attended the common schools of Jessamine until 1888, when he went to a preparatory school for one year at Irvine. In September, '89, the deceased entered Kentucky University, Lexington, where he remained two years, going thence to Central University, Richmond, from which institution he graduated in June, '92, in the classical course, taking the degree of Bachelor of Arts. A few weeks before graduation he was elected to the position of assistant principal of the Nicholasville Graded School, where he taught three years, at the expiration of which time he accepted the principalship of Campbellsville High School, and held that position until a year later, when he resigned to accept the presidency of Hardin Collegiate Institute, Elizabethtown, a branch of Central University. During the vacation of 1896 Prof Miller attended Eastman National Business College, Poughkeepsie, N Y, and graduated from same with the highest honors of this class, having the degree of Master of Accounts conferred upon him. While engaged in his educational work at Elizabethtown, Prof Miller was married to Miss Julia Payne, daughter of Col and Mrs Jas B Payne, the marriage taking place at Elizabethtown, Nov 2, 1898. Soon after his marriage Prof Miller returned to Jessamine County and purchased a farm in the neighborhood where he was born and reared, and where he resided when stricken with the disease that ended his life. Only those who knew Rice Miller intimately could appreciate his worth, for he was of a quiet and retiring disposition that seldom revealed his true self to the world. Upon his devoted wife, his father, brothers and sister, he lavished the wealth of his love, and no task was too heavy, no sacrifice too great, if their happiness and comfort were involved. Conscientious and careful to a fault, if such can be, he went about his daily duties with a just appreciation of all obligations, and with a personal interest that manifested itself in the smallest details, finding his highest reward in the excellence of his work and its appreciation by others. To those whose eyes are suffused with tears and whose hearts are torn and bleeding, the Journal extends its sympathy, and for consolation commends them to Him who knoweth and doeth all things well. The funeral took place yesterday (Thursday) morning from the home place at 9 o'clock, services being conducted by Rev Dr L H Blanton, Chancellor of Central University, assisted by Rev R E Douglas and F W Noland, after which the remains were taken to Richmond and interred in the cemetery of that city. p3c4

He is probably buried where his mother is buried, Dr Miller's first wife. It appears that he had no child from his year of marriage. I must tell you that I have seen a lot of city fathers buried with much less extolling of their virtues. The editor really thought highly of him.

"Mr Walter Hendren has severed his connection as clerk with the clothing department of W C Denman." p3c3

"A M Askins, of Ambrose, and C L Pates, of Nicholasville, will exchange blacksmith shops Jan 1, Mr Askins moving here and Mr Pates going to Ambrose." p3c2 It didn't happen.

"Wm S Taylor (Republican) was inaugurated Governor of Kentucky Tuesday in the presence of several thousand persons." p2c1 While the other constitutional officers took the oath of office, they were served with notices that their elections were being contested. The Hanly correspondent said that several of their citizens attended the inauguration, but the *Sulphur Well Correspondent* did not comment. He writes:

*Tom Willis, who has been sick for some time, is out again.*
*Capt Hill, of Edenton, is visiting friends here.*
*William Walters, of Illinois, is home on a visit to his parents.*
*The Christian Church has been painted a beautiful white.*
*W Kates and R R Hendren, of Illinois and Kansas, respectively, are home on a Christmas visit.*
*Mrs Pencelar Murphy, an aged pensioner, died from the effects of a fall of about 10 feet from a back door last week in Madison County.*
*Jas O Tudor, of Edenton, died last week from a severe attack of typhoid fever, after only a few days illness.*
*Oscar Hendren, of Ruthton, Madison County, who was severely stabbed just below the nipple with a six inch blade by young Connie Whittaker, is out again.* p2c4

I would say that there is an interesting story behind this last little gem. Oscar is Dr Hendren's nephew. If I live a long time, I will read the Richmond paper, and see if I can get more about it.

### December 22, 1899

There was a violent flurry in the New York Stock Exchange that required vigorous intervention by the Treasury Department. Stock dropped precipitiously, and a large New York bank failed. Speculators had their loans called, and the Clearinghouse banks had to come to the rescue. p2c1

As if there weren't enough trouble over the contested election! The legislature meets Monday week. p2c1

"Mrs Hugh Miller, of Madison County, spent Monday with Mrs W S Hendren, enroute to Oklahoma." p3c3

"Mr Meade Miller arrived from Oklahoma last week threatened with fever and is at his father's home." p3c3

"Mrs Rice Miller accompanied her father, Col J B Payne, last Saturday to Elizabethtown, where she will spend the winter." p3c3

December 29, 1899

When the General Assembly meets the Senate will select three of its members by lot, the House will select eight. From the eleven, seven will be drawn by lot, and constitute a board to try the contested election and determine the winner. p2c1

Merchants are pleased with the Christmas trade. p3c1

The *Sulphur Well Correspondent* writes:

*Mr Cyrus T Taylor, wife and daughter, of Richmond, are visiting Mrs M Horine.*
*Mrs Hugh Miller and children, who started for Oklahoma City last Tuesday, arrived there Wednesday evening.*
*Mr and Mrs Clubb entertained a few friends at dinner yesterday.*
*Rev H G Turner, of Richmond, is over on a visit to his parents.*
*Will Askins and brother, of Buena Vista, and Miss Doty, of Brannon, are visiting A M Askins.*
*William Richardson and wife, Irvine, are visiting Mrs Elizabeth Miller.*
*Dr G M Hendren has been confined to his room for several days with a severe attack of sciatica.*
*James Watts, who has been living on N D Miles' farm in Madison County, will move back to his residence here soon.*
*Mr William Blakeman has a little child very sick and not expected to recover from a complication of diseases.*
*Mr N D Davis was taken quite suddenly ill Tuesday evening while at Murphy's store and it was some time before he was able to be removed home.*
*Mr Richard Runyan, who had made arrangements to succeed A M Atkins in the blacksmith business here, has declined the idea and we understand Willard Davis, of Nicholasville, will occupy the residence and furnish a smith to run the shop. We are sorry to lose Mr Askins and his family.*
*The entertainment ---------------------- school children on Friday night was a successful and enjoyable affair and was well attended, the church being crowded to its fullest capacity. (the paper is torn) p2c4*

This ends another year. There is a lot this year about Dr Miller's family, and about Dr Hendren's family.

## SUSAN NAVE - 1900

Susan Miller Nave, sister of Dr Miller, died after a long illness. She is buried in the Miller Family Cemetery.

### January 5, 1900

Preparations are being made to take the census.

### January 12, 1900

There was a large Court Day crowd in Lexington, and considerable stock on the market.

### January 19, 1900

"Skirts are now made with a double box pleat at the back, very few being plain." p1c4

"At Frankfort Tuesday at noon in the lobby of the Capital Hotel, Col D G Colson, of Middlesboro, shot and killed Lieut Etherlbert D Scott of Somerset...." Two others were killed by stray bullets. The two "renewed a quarrel" from last year. p2c1 Conflicts were frequently settled with guns. It definitely didn't pay to be an innocent bystander!

Dr Miller is the administrator of the Rice Miller estate. He is offering all the farm equipment, horses and livestock at public sale on January 30th. He is also offering for sale privately two tracts of land. p2c7 I imagine that Dr Miller took a large note when he sold Rice the farm. It appears that the two tracts of land that he is selling privately are his own. I didn't see any land transfers the previous year.

Property transfers: "J C Miller to Levi Francis 6 3/5 acres on Hickman Creek, $270." p3c5

The *Sulphur Well Correspondent* writes:

*Phillip Foster is building a residence on his father's farm.*
*Beverly Dean, son of Morris Dean, is quite sick with rheumatic fever.*
*F M Horine sold to W H Hare 11 fine shoats at a good price.*
*B F Foster is an applicant for census enumerator for this district.*
*S N Snowden sold to A C Miles 15 head of hogs at $3.60 per cwt.*
*Wm West, of Speedwell, has been visiting his brother, J T West, for several days.*
*There is considerable sickness in this section at present.*
*Henry Woodward has moved to Harrodsburg, where he has secured a position with the laundry there.*
*James Waits has moved back to his property here, occupied by Mr Green.*
*The mail route from Little Hickman to Stone, in Garrard County, has been discontinued. Stone is now supplied from Buckeye. p2c3*

January 26, 1900

"Married in Richmond, Charles Hendren, of Speedwell, and Miss Belle Harris." p2c2

"Mr Harry Hendren is attending the Hospital College of Medicine at Louisville. He will make a successful practitioner, we predict, from the fact that he has the education and ability and is a practical chemist." p3c4 This is not Pat, Scottie's brother.

The *Sulphur Well Correspondent* writes:

*Mrs J O Tudor left Thursday for Illinois to make it her future home.*
*Mike Yates and wife left Monday for Cincinnati, their future home.*
*James Hendren, who has been confined to his room by illness for several weeks, is out again.*
*A M Askins has rented out his shop in Nicholasville and moved back to his stand here this week.*
*John Green has rented rooms from Jas T Sageser and moved into them last Monday.*
*Lee Davis bought a lot from F M Horine for $200, on which he will build at once a residence opposite A M Askins' place.*
*Tommy Masters, who lives down on Hickman Creek, last week, swore out a warrant for several fast young men, and some not so slow, older ones too, for disturbing the peace and quietude of his rural home--breach of the peace, or rather of the "pieces", as they fractured all his table ware in the last course.* p2c4

February 2, 1900

State Senator Goebel was shot as he approached the State Capitol. "A few minutes after the shooting, Holland Whittaker, of Butler County, was arrested on suspicion, and when searched three pistols and a dirk knife were found on his person." Governor Taylor issued a state of insurrection and had troops keep the legislature from meeting either in the Capitol building or in the court house. p2c1 The Legislature then met in the hotel and declared Senator Goebel the elected governor. The Chief Justice then administered the oath of office. p2c2 What they did was swear in a man on his death bed, so a Democratic lieutenant governor would succeed him.

Cold weather reduced the crowd that attended the sale of Rice Miller's property. It doesn't appear that the prices were very good. p2c4

The *Sulphur Well Correspondent* writes:

*Born, to the wife of Conrad Cobb, Sunday, Jan 28, a son.*
*Charles Peel and family, of Leroy, Ill., are visiting friends in the neighborhood.*
*Little Miss Mayme Turner who is on the sick list, is better.*
*There is considerable sickness in this neighborhood, principally pneumonia. As many as two or three cases occurring at the same time in one family.*
*James Woodward has moved to a farm near Wilmore.* p3c7

February 9, 1900

Goebel died from his wounds, and Lt Gov John Beckham has been sworn in as Governor of Kentucky. p2c1 and p1c3

So, Dr Hendren wrote a poem rather than a letter this week.

### THE MAN WITH THE GUN
The man with a plow or the man with a hoe,
We readily acknowledge, is grand--
But here in Kentucky he hasn't a show
With the man with a gun in his hand.

This is the first verse, and probably has something to do with the Goebel slaying, or any one of the weekly shootings recorded in the Journal. p1c6

February 16, 1900

Taylor has filed suit for an injunction to prevent Beckham from assuming office. p2c1

"Dr Jno C Miller, sold this week to L S Cassity, of Logana, 66 3/4 acres of land on the Chrisman Mill Pike at $58.86 per acre." p2c2

Elbert Walker is still single. He and some other "young" people are visiting in Bryantsville.

February 23, 1900

"Rev H G Turner, pastor of the Methodist Church, Richmond, delivered an address at Berea College, yesterday, Washington's birth anniversary. The subject of his address was 'Twentieth Century Citizenship'." p3c1

The *Sulphur Well Correspondent* writes:

*A child of Jeff W Miller died of pneumonia Thursday, Feb 15.*
*L McL Reynolds, of Stanford, Ill., who has been visiting here for some time, returned home Friday.*
*Miss Rhoda Peel is teaching a private school at the district school house, and has quite a fine school.*
*Oscar Sageser left for Illinois last Monday to be gone about a year.*
*Walter Brumfield and Miss Pollard, daughter of Thos Pollard, of Logana, were married yesterday.*
*Mr and Mrs William Walters left for Illinois last week to make that their future home. p2c1*

March 2, 1900

Dr Hendren writes another poem:

### AGAINST THE WALL
The friends that flatter in the morning
When the sun is shining clear,
Soonest foresake you in the dawning,
When cloudy days appear
\*\*\*
And when your summer's sun's not shining,
Flatterers, both great and small
Will leave you to your own repining
When you're up against the wall.p1c6

This is the first and third verses of the poem. I wonder if the theme was suggested by the troubles of Republican Governor Taylor, who the Cincinnati Post says is financially bankrupt. "He has an invalid wife and six daughters.... He does not have a law practice to return to, as all his old clients were lost when he became Attorney General four years ago. At that time he was "worth $20,000." The contested election has "consumed the last dollar". p1c4

John C Miller received $3,900 for the 66 acres of land he sold to L S Cassidy. p2c3

The *Sulphur Well Correspondent* reports:

*A good deal of sickness in this neighborhood.*
*It seems that the wedding reported last week was a mistake. (Walter Brumfield and Miss Pollard)*
*Samuel Lear has moved into the house opposite W B Walker's residence.*
*Our pike having recently been heavily coated with rock is a "rocky road to travel."*
*William Wylie sold 18 hogs to A C Miles last week.*
*Hay is in very good demand as corn is very scarce.*
*Mrs Kate Knight has taken boarding with Mrs Elizabeth Miller.*
*Some farmers here are buying corn in Indiana and having it shipped at a cost of about $2 per barrel.*
*Samuel Switzer was taken suddenly with cramps last Tuesday and is seriously sick.*
*Roy Whittaker and family moved to Illinois to reside, last Tuesday.*
*F M Hendren was taken with a slight attack of pneumonia last Friday night, but is improving. (Probably G M Hendren)*
*John Quimby is said to be very low with diabetes. p3c7*

Here is Kate Knight, usually called Kittie Knight, now staying with Mrs Miller.

March 9, 1900

The John Quimby above, aged about 47, died March 3 of appendicitis in Little Hickman. He was buried in the family burying ground. p2c1 As I've said before, Dr Hendren, perhaps because of his medical practice reports on people out of the Sulphur Well neighborhood.

"F P Taylor, of Lexington, and W S Hendren, of Nicholasville, yesterday bought out the undertaking and furniture business of Sisco & Co, and will take charge of same March 15." p2c1 W S Hendren resigned his position with a clothing store a few weeks ago.

The *Sulphur Well Correspondent* writes:

*W C Wylie, Edenton, was over last week a short time.*
*The health of the community is pretty good at this time.*
*Will Peel sold a lot of hogs to J P Turner at $3.75 per cwt.*
*F M Horine sold some hogs to Sam Askins at 4c.*
*"Aunt" Kit Knight was very sick last Saturday with dysentery.*
*Elder Hildebrand preached at the church last Sunday morning and night to good congregations.*
*F M Horine bought a nice horse from Wm Peel for $75 and sold one to Marshall Davis at $70.*
*Mrs Taylor, wife of Ike Taylor, living on J P Turner's farm, died Saturday night from consumption.*
*Messrs Sageser and Peel, who had the contract for repairing the pike road, have completed the work and have put on 71 rods of rock.*
*Revs Dills and McNeal, of Wilmore College, preached at the residence of Mrs Elizabeth Miller last Friday night.*
*Rev E C Savage will preach at Mrs Miller's every Friday night before the first Sunday in each month.*
*There will be preaching at the church by Revs Dill and McNeal, of Asbury College the second and fourth Sundays.*
p2c2

Arnett, the assignee of Forest Miller, is still settling his business affairs. p2c8 "Meade Miller left Wednesday for Oklahoma City, OT." p3c3 "Mrs Sue Nave, widow of the late Dr Joe Nave, has been lying at the point of death for several days at her home in Nicholasville." p3c3

> A juicy plum.-Chas W Miller, of Lexington, son of M M Miller, of Irvine, and nephew of Dr Jno C Miller, of Nicholasville, has been appointed Auditor's Agent at Lexington by Auditor Coulter. The office is said to be worth from $2,000 to $2,500. Young Miller was the Democratic nominee for (the) legislature in the Estill-Powell district last fall, and an original Goebel man." p3c4

I'm glad someone benefitted from this affair.

March 11, 1900

This week Dr Hendren composed the following poem. I am including three of the four verses. p1c4

ACROSS THE LINES
Into the boundless space beyond
A swift procession passes on
Toward the setting sun;
And through the ages it has trod
With weary feet the beaten sod
Until the race is run.

And when both you and I are gone,
Those we leave will follow on
With just as swift a tread;
And they will leave behind them here
Those who will hold them just as dear
And mourn as long their dead.

Yet through the mists of coming years
The living will forget the tears
They shed above the bier,
For it is but the common lot
To step aside and be forgot
By those that tarry here.

The Elizabethtown News says that "The lust for office is the greatest curse of Kentucky and it is responsible for all our troubles at the present." p2c1 It is my best judgment from reading the Journal that Goebel's election law, and its application to the contested votes in the close election, gave the Republicans considerable justification in feeling that the election was stolen by the Democrats. This led to Goebel's assassination, and the continued action by the courts.

Some of the good old boys of bygone days in Sulphur Well are still popping up. "Mr and Mrs Ham Dozier are rejoicing in the coming of an interesting visitor to their home--Miss Kathleen Elizabeth Dozier." p3c5

March 23, 1900

Dr Hendren's latest poem seems to signal the end of an era. However, I don't think this is the Sulphur Well church to which he is referring, more likely to the one he attended in Edenton, Madison County as a youngster growing up.

## THE OLD COUNTRY CHURCH

As my mem'ry wanders backward
To the years of long ago,
I remember by the roadside
The old church I used to know,
And the shadows seem to vanish
As the scene returns to me,
And I see the ancient building
Standing as it used to be.

I can see the friends and neighbors,
As they slowly wend their way,
To that humble place of worship
On a pleasant Sabbath day.
I can hear the anthems rising
As the congregation there,
Sends their voices up to heaven
On the wings of love and prayer.

There are still the pleasant faces
Of the crowds about the door,
That on Sunday morning gathered
In the days that are no more.
Then their joy banished all sorrow,
As their paeans upward roll
That re-echoed only gladness
In the language of the soul.

And it seems that Heaven was nearer,
As they all arose to sing
These songs of old that shook the wall,
And that made the rafters ring.
The old church now has passed away,
Its walls in ruins lie,
Where prayers and praise from many hearts
Went up to Him on high.

Of those who often worshipped here,
Alas, how few remain!
The congregation's scattered now
To never meet again.
Where songs arose, now silence reigns--
The meetings here are o're,
The many feet that trod those aisles
Now tread another shore. p3c3

L H Hendren sold his Watt's Mill property for $1,600 to S N Bishop, of Wilmore. p3c4
L H is Levi, brother of Dr Hendren.

March 30, 1900

Susan Nave died. Her obiturary follows:

> Mrs Sue Miller Nave, after an illness of several weeks, and of patient suffering, died Friday, March 23, at her home in Nicholasville, aged 68 years. The deceased was the widow of the late Dr Joseph Nave and was born in Jessamine County. She leaves two sisters and two brothers, Mrs J P Overstreet, Mrs Kate Barkley, Dr Jno C Miller, of this county, and M M Miller, of Irvine. The long suffering through which Mrs Nave passed made her long for a release and while death was gathering about her she expressed a willingness to go. The funeral was conducted from the M E Church, South, Saturday by Rev Thos W Watts, assisted by Rev F W Noland. The interment took place at the old family burying ground in the Hanly neighborhood." p3c4

There were seven children of Merriman and Celia Miller as I knew there were. The *Sageser Genealogy* is in error by not including Susan Nave. It is also in error by stating that Kate (Kitty) never married. She married Samuel Barkley on January 2, 1879 at the age of 37. The Miller Cemetery is located on what is now Snowden Lane, just off the Hoover Pike, and several miles from Hanly.

The *Sulphur Well Correspondent* writes:

> Mrs Susan Taylor, aged 77, died of senile decay at her home on Hickman Creek, Sunday, March 25.
> Mr and Mrs John A Dean, of Stone, were visiting relatives in this neighborhood this week.
> A child of Wesley Davis is quite sick with the prevailing grippe and complications.
> Calvin, son of the late Fount Peel, was very ill with grippe and lung congestion several days this week.
> F M Horine sold to James Green, Tuesday, four head of cattle at $3.60 per cwt. He also sold to different parties bunches of fat cattle at the same figures. p2c3

April 6, 1900

Dr Hendren pens "Ups and Downs" in a totally different mood. It's about Billy Brown who loves to drink until he gets the lowest down, then he gets the hardest up. p1c4

John D Rockefeller has given $2 million to the University of Chicago. p2c1

The *Sulphur Well Correspondent* writes:

*Miss May Taylor, Richmond, is visiting Mrs Margaret Horine, her grandmother.*
*Jas H Woodward and wife were visiting relatives here Sunday.*
*A son of Mrs Elizabeth Peel, who has been quite sick with pneumonia, is reported out of danger.*
*Sam Switzer, who has been very low, is improving.*
*Jas Watts is walking on a crutch from abscesses on the leg.*
*J P Turner will put 175 acres in hemp on his hill farms this season.*
*Hamlet Foster moved from near Lexington, to his new residence on the Watts Mill road.*
*William Hudson was taken very ill Sunday night, but is improving.*
*Corn is unobtainable in this section of the country.*
*A good deal of hemp is being hauled to town from Madison and Garrard Counties.*
*John Green will move to N D Miles' farm soon, where he will reside for a time before moving to the mountains.*
*Rev E T Savage and son were the guests of Mrs Lizzie Miller, Friday night, where Brother Savage held religious worship with a fair sized congregation.*
*Gardening is now in full blast as the season has been so long unfavorable.*
*Green S Watkins has applied for an increase in pension and should have it without delay, as he is undoubtedly entitled to it. He is a worthy citizen and was an efficient soldier.*
*Eld Hildebrand had a good audience out to hear him Sunday. He will remain with the church here another year preaching the first Sunday of each month. Services at 11 am, and 7 pm.*
*Rev R D Bivins came near having a serious mishap in crossing the branch on the road leading to J P Turner's residence. His horse slipped and fell on the slick rocks and it was some time before he could be disentangled from harness and shafts. However no serious damage was done to buggy or horse.* p2c1

April 13, 1900

The Kentucky Court of Appeals upheld the election of Goebel, the Democratic candidate, and his successor Lt Gov Beckham, but the two Republican members of the Court stated "that they believed the Legislature had decided wrongly and denounced the election law." They had to decide on the basis of the Legislature's right to select, not their manner of selecting, the winner. p1c4

The sudden popularity of the Eton jacket "is a surprise of the season." p1c6

Dr Miller's youngest son, Meade has taken a bride:

> Meade Miller, son of Dr Jno C Miller, Nicholasville, and Miss Mary Benjamin were married at the residence of Mr Harvey Riddell, brother-in-law of the bride, in Denver, Col., Wednesday, April 4. The bridgegroom is well-known in Jessamine where he was reared and resided until his removal to Oklahoma about a year ago. The bride is a niece of Judge Robert Riddell, of Irvine, and has visited in Kentucky where Mr Miller first met her. She is said to be quite a pretty and accomplished young lady. Mr and Mrs Miller will reside at Oklahoma City, OT. p3c3

April 20, 1900

The *Sulphur Well Correspondent* writes:

*James Durham is reported quite sick.*
*"Aunt" Kitty Knight will move shortly to (the) Pink neighborhood.*
*John Turner, of Bowling Green, is visiting his uncle, J P Turner, for a few days.*
*Dr Bryant and wife, of Stanford, were visiting his brother-in-law, Jas H Turner, last week. Dr Bryant is a druggist and will go into business at Versailles.*
*Sam Askins lost his fine Jersey cow last week. This is the second one he has lost recently, besides four calves from some mysterious affection.*
*This is a hay producing section of the country as hundreds of tons of baled hay are shipped north and south annually form here. Prices rule from $10 to $12 per ton.*
*A successful experiment of making "buckle and tongue meet" was tried by a little colored boy last Thursday, and while the experiment worked to a charm it was far from satisfactory to the experimenter. He passed a double buckle over his tongue and the buckle tongue fastened into his tongue. In the absence of a doctor some neighbors relieved his distress by using a pair of wire pliers and a hand-saw file. Probably his tongue will remain unbuckled hereafter as well as unbridled. p2c2*

April 27, 1900

The Miller boys are doing well in Oklahoma. Here is an exerpt from a letter from Hugh to his father: "Meade has recently moved into his elegant new residence on 320 acres of the best and most desirable land in the Mustang country, 6 1/2 miles southwest of Oklahoma City. He has 205 acres of growing wheat ... and about 50 acres of oats." He added "I have 320 acres, and my new residence is about 3 1/2 miles southwest of Oklahoma City in the best country I ever saw for farming." p1c3 He goes on to tell about the property.

"Mrs Julia Ware, aged 75 years, died at her home in Lincoln County, April 23, leaving a family of seven children, of whom A J Ware, of near Ambrose, this county, is a son." p3c5

The *Sulphur Well Correspondent* writes:

*Miss Rhoda Peel's school closed last Friday.*
*Mrs Elizabeth Miller left Saturday for a visit to friends at Irvine and vicinity.*
*Wheat never looked better and the prospect for a heavy crop is fine.*
*Gardening is somewhat delayed in this section by the continued wet weather.*
*Hogs, especially sows and pigs, are in demand, almost any old thing brings $20 or more.*
*Allen Teater, of Garrard, is out again after an eight weeks siege of typhoid fever.*
*There seems to be some remnants of la grippe left in the neighborhood yet.*
*J W Cobb sold a 150-lb sow and seven pigs to J W Carroll for $20.*
*G S Watkins is out again after a somewhat protracted indisposition.*
*There is some talk of rural mail delivery and ruralites would be real glad of its realization.*
*N D Davis was taken seriously ill Sunday morning with stomach trouble, but is now some better.*
*J W Green bought of N D Davis Saturday a fat cow for beef that weighed 825 lbs at $3.60 per cwt.*

*John Murphy, of Buckeye, was a guest of J W Cobb Sunday night en route to Richmond for a week's visit among old friends.*

*F M Horine sold last Saturday to Nathan Hughes a fat cow weighing 820 lbs for butchering at $4 per cwt. Also one to A C Miles weighing 830 lbs at the same price.*

*Hay is scarce as well as corn, hay dealers saying they could sell scores of tons even now did they have it on hand to fill the numerous orders.* p2c5

May 4, 1900

Delegates are being selected for the upcoming district convention.

May 11, 1900

The editor says "it is difficult to tell which is the harder problem to solve, whether the Boers will be whipped by the British first, or the Fillipinos defeated by the Americans."p2c1

"Dr Jno C Miller was in Cincinnati Tuesday on business." p3c3

The *Sulphur Well Correspondent* writes:

*Mrs H G Turner and little son, of Richmond, returned home Monday after a few days visiting at J P Turner's.*

*Wm Sallee, of Garrard, is visiting friends in this neighborhood.*

*Captain Vincent went to Richmond Monday for the purpose of purchasing a bunch of grazing cattle.*

*Capt Hill and B Whittaker, of Madison County, were over on a visit last week.*

*N D Davis is out again after a pretty severe illness from stomach and liver trouble.*

*A post office has been established at Sanders' Ferry, on Kentucky River, on the Garrard side.*

*Mrs F D Jasper is visiting at Dr Hendren's this week.*

*Mrs Elizabeth Miller returned home Thursday from Irvine, Estill County, after a pleasant visit of several days.*

*Eld Hildebrand, of Lexington, preached to fair sized audiences Sunday morning and night, notwithstanding the disagreeable weather.*

*The dogs have almost taken possession of this town and make night hideous with bow-wowing. It's a dog-gone shame.*

*Mr James Scott lost some calves last week from hydrophobia. They took the disease from licking in a trough where a mad dog had been seen to have a fit a few days previous.*

*Arch Stotts, of Garrard County, about 66 years of age, died Wednesday, May 2, after having had his leg taken off to stop the ravages of gangrene that had set up in his foot. He formerly lived in this county and was for several years a merchant and a magistrate here.*

*The 14 year-old daughter of Moses Simpson, of Little Hickman, ran away from home last week, but her father overtook her at Lexington and brought her back home.* p3c5

Stotts left Sulphur Well several years ago, and W H Bright purchased his house. He may have purchased his store also. Bright wrote the Sulphur Well column for a while.

May 18, 1900

"Melvin Dean, a well-known farmer of Pink neighborhood, and Miss Myrtle Snowden, daughter of S N Snowden, of the same locality, were married at the home of the officiating minister, Rev G W Neal, in Winchester, Wednesday, May 16." p3c5 I can't imagine why they would go to Winchester to get married. I would assume that Myrtie was living on the farm on Snowden Lane.

The *Sulphur Well Correspondent* writes:

*Mrs Elizabeth Miller was on the sick list Tuesday.*
*Miss Nellie Hendren is very much better.*
*Leslie Teater has a severe eye trouble.*
*Messrs Manfred Murphy, F Horine, and Wm L Hendren paid a flying visit to Richmond Monday.*
*A daughter of William Sanders, Madison County, is very sick.*
*Mrs M E Cobb is visiting in Mercer County.*
*A J Smith and wife, of Indianapolis, Ind., were visiting her father, T J Horine, Sunday.*
*Caperton Vincent bought 17 head of cattle in Richmond Monday at about $17 per head.*
*F M Hudson sold last Monday to A C Miles, one fat cow of 1070 lbs at $3.75 per cwt. F M Horine also sold to same party one cow of 1,000 lbs at $3.60 per cwt.*
*Last week a dog belonging to Thos Barker went mad and ran amuck among the dogs of the neighborhood mutilating a score or more of them before he disappeared. A general slaughter of the canines was the result.*
*Dr William Peel last Monday presented the writer with the third volume of the Medical History of the War of the Rebellion. It is a valuable acquisition to any one's library, as it is a library within itself, and the doctor has our thanks for the same.* p2c1

May 25, 1900

The *Sulphur Well Correspondent* writes:

*W B Ray, of Buckeye, was over on a short visit last Thursday.*
*Wash Farthergill, who has been sick some time, died at Carvess Ferry last Friday.*
*The wife of Harrison Smith died rather suddenly last Friday near Watts Mill.*
*James Watts sold to E Walker, Saturday one milk cow and calf at $52.50, and purchased one at $45.*
*W H Hare in sinking two wells on farm struck water in one at 30 feet.*
*W L Hendren, Manfred Murphy and C W Horine paid a flying visit to Madison County last week.*
*Jno Teater, of Buckeye, lost a fine cow last week, dying suddenly from mysterious cause.*
*Jas W Cobb lost his only cow, a fine Jersey, last week, from eating clover.*
*Edward Chandler and E Warren, of Madison County, were over on Monday.*
*William Johns, G W Peel and Fayette Brooks delivered to G W Strode, of East Hickman, Monday, 41 head of hogs at $4.25 per hundred.*
*William Whittaker, of Stone, Garrard County, has secured the contract for carrying the mail daily for four years from that point to Nicholasville by way of Little Hickman, Pink and this place.* p2c3

June 8, 1900

F M Horine sold a lot in Ambrose to J H Murphy for $700. p2c3

The *Sulphur Well Correspondent* writes:

*The little son of Sam Askins was quite sick last week.*
*Jas H Turner, wife and daughter visited Dr Bryant, Versailles, Saturday and Sunday.*
*Ike Dunn, of Garrard County, was over Sunday visiting some of the young ladies.*
*John B Bourne and daughter, Nellie, of Garrard County, were the guests of E E Bourne, Sunday.*
*Mrs M E Wheeler and daughter, Ida, of Cincinnati, are visiting at Wm Hendren's for a few days.*
*Jason Tudor has been allowed a pension and considerable back pay.*
*Thursday evening, June 7 pm, at the residence of J P Turner, the nuptials of Mr Creed Gott and Miss Ruth Johns were solemnized, Rev H G Turner, of Richmond, officiating.*
*A horse hitched to a buggy got away from some parties Sunday night as church broke up and went on a tear, coming near running over several. No serious damage was done, however.* p3c5

June 15, 1900

"Harry P Hendren is visiting his uncle, Robert Reagan, at Edenton, Madison County." p3c4

"Messrs J D Hughes and A K Adcock have been in New York City this week attending the big horse sales where several Jessamine County yearlings were sold." p3c4

The *Sulphur Well Correspondent* writes:

*James W Cobb visited Harrodsburg Thursday and Friday.*
*Mrs G M Hendren was quite sick Monday night, but is some better now.*
*Forest Miller, wife and son have gone for a week's visit to relatives in Estill County.*
*Mr and Mrs Jno Whitenack, of Harrodsburg, are visiting Mr and Mrs J W Cobb.*
*W B Walker, who has been quite ill for some days, is said to be no better.* p2c1

June 22, 1900

"The attack of the Chinese upon foreign missionaries at Pekin has caused troops to be sent there from the United States, Germany and Austria...." This became known as the Boxer Rebellion. p2c1

"Gov Roosevelt, of New York, was nominated by acclamation yesterday at Philadelphia, for the vice presidency as a running mate to McKinley." p2c1

From Little Hickman: "Wheat cutting is in full blast. Murphy & Horine sold two Plano binders in this neighborhood last week." p2c5

The *Sulphur Well Correspondent* writes:

*W B Walker is improving slowly.*
*William Smith, of Edenton, was over Wednesday.*
*John Waller is acting P M in the absence of Postmaster Miller.*
*E C May sold to M F Davis this week, 1500 pounds of tobacco at 6c.*
*F M Horine sold to Martin & Green 6 shoats, weight 685 lbs, at 4 1/4c.*
*Cobb & Walker sold their thresher and huller complete, to Melvin Ware, for $150.*
*Some very fine poplar logs from Garrard has passed through here in the last week. Such lumber is extremely scarce.*
*Miss Vessie Hockaday and Miss May Taylor, also Earl Smith, of Richmond, are visiting at J H Murphy's.*
*Mrs Cyrus T Taylor and daughter, Lils, of Richmond, are visiting at Mrs Margaret Horine's.*
*Mr and Mrs O T Wallace, Point Leavell, Garrard County, were the guests of Mrs Margaret Horine, Saturday and Sunday. Mr Wallace was the former nominee for governor on the Prohibition ticket. He was over for the purpose of attending a Prohibition convention at Nicholasville, Monday.* p2c5

June 29, 1900

The Kentucky Chautaugua will be held in Lexington at Woodland Park from June 29 through July 4. "There will be music with humor, science, and philosophy. (The) greatest lecturers in the country will speak on leading questions." p1c5

Even though William Jennings Bryan will not be at the Kansas City convention, "he will receive the Democratic nomination by acclamation." p2c1

Work on the lock and dam at Valley View will begin in August. p2c2

Pomp has given up his bicycle in favor of a buggy, saying the roads are in such bad condition that it is dangerous to ride. p3c2 Maybe Pomp is just getting old!

"Dr Jno C Miller received a nice box of peaches and plums this week from his son, Meade, who is farming in Oklahoma. The Doctor favored the <u>Journal</u> with a few samples which were large, well formed and delicious eating." p3c4

The *Sulphur Well Correspondent* writes:

> C T Taylor, of Richmond, was visiting at Mrs Margaret Horine's from Saturday till Sunday.
> Rev H G Turner, of Richmond, spent Tuesday and Wednesday with his father, J P Turner.
> Franklin M Hudson delivered 17 nice lambs to H B Campbell Wednesday at 5 cents.
> John C Dean sold 7 head of hogs to A C Miles at $4.25 per cwt.
> N D Davis sold to Nathan Hughes 75 head of lambs this week at 5 cents per pound.
> F M Horine sold to Martin & Green one nice cow, weighing 700 lbs.
> Oscar Sageser, who has been in Illinois for several months, returned home last week.
> Wheat is turning out well; better than most farmers expected.
> William Richardson, of Irvine, was in town Tuesday. p2c5

July 6, 1900

Nicholasville will have its second annual street fair on August 2 and 3. The first one was surprisingly successful. p3c2

July 13, 1900

The Democrats nominated William Jennings Bryan for president as expected.

The *Sulphur Well Correspondent* writes:

> James Watts is digging a cistern on his premises.
> Mr John Brown and sister, of Rockcastle County, are visiting Miss Carrie Woodward this week.
> John C Hendren, of Edenton, Madison County, was visiting relatives in town Tuesday.
> James Scott sold Tuesday to A C Miles 13 head of hogs weighing 1,925 lbs at $4.40 per cwt.
> Hundreds of bushels of wheat have sold in this locality during the past week at 73 to 75c per bushel.
> Threshing is in full blast this week and wheat is turning out remarkably well.
> George Sewell is carrying the mail for William Whittaker who has had the contract for the ensuing four years.
> Rain is needed very badly in this locality at present, as gardens and grass are beginning to suffer considerably.
> William Easly, of near Giles post-office, who has been very low for some time is reported better.
> All the young men are buying new buggies. Look out for more weddings soon.
> Judging from the length of the doctors' faces the health of the community must be very good indeed.
> Miss T Miller returned this week from a two weeks visit with her brother, John P Miller, at Wisemantown, Estill County.
> Rev Owen J Young of Madison County, a forcible and popular preacher, occupied the pupit at the Christian Church Sunday morning and night. p2c5

July 20, 1900

Dr Hendren has written a rather long poem this week, entitled "The Procession". He thought that if everyone in the world could pass in review, each onlooker could see through his eyes all the vices of the others. Yet, he says, only God can weigh our weaknesses in the scales of justice. p1c4

The Democratic State Convention nominated Beckham for governor by acclamation. p2c1

The *Sulphur Well Correspondent* writes:

*John Teater and wife, of Buckeye, were the guests of Wm Hendren, Monday.*
*Shirley Land, of Edenton, had his leg broken by a horse falling on him Sunday night.*
*Jas W Cobb was taken quite sick Friday, but is able to be about.*
*Dr Bascom Johns and mother, of Lexington, were visiting at N D Davis' last week.*
*Lightning struck and destroyed a wheat stack of Geo D Turpin's farm during the thunder storm Thursday of last week.*
*Capt Irwin F Willis and wife, of Shelbyville, were the guests of James W Cobb last Friday.*
*Mrs Ben Wheeler, who was so severely hurt in a runaway last Saturday, is improving.*
*There was a good attendance of the older members of the Christian Church last Sunday, and they had an old fashion meeting among themselves later at the residence of Dr G M Hendren.*
*Lightning struck a barn of N D Davis' Thursday evening, July 12, in which some men were unloading hay from a wagon, and one of the hands, Elder Graves, a colored man, was knocked headlong from the wagon apparently dead, and remained unconscious for some hours. It is a miracle that the others in the barn and on the wagon were not killed or seriously injured, as they probably would have been had not a lot of bailing wire that hung among the rafters scattered the electric current, thus diminishing its force. Dr Hendren attended the injured man and finally revived him sufficiently to be sent home where he is slowly recovering from the effects of the shock.*
*The peaceful midnight slumbers of the villagers were rudely aroused Saturday night by a wordy war of oaths and imprecations around the public pump. It seems that Richard Young, of unsavory notoriety, and a white man named Joseph Dunn, became involved in a drunken quarrel and proceeded a la Jeffries-Corbett to settle their fancied differences. It is said they tried for two hours to cut maps of the Sulu Islands on each other's physiognomy and during the intermissions hurled beautifully but true epithets at each other. But finally Dunn proceeded to stave in Young's breast bone with a ten pound stone. After the fight there was a foot race with Dunn in the lead, but as he was too fleet footed for Dick the latter soon gave over the unprofitable pursuit, and coming to the conclusion that he was about "Dunn" up, sent for a surgeon to repair his damaged carcass. p2c3*

Susan Nave's will was probated in the county court Monday bequeathing "all of her property, personal, real and mixed--to her nephew, Chas W Miller, and nieces, Maude and May Miller, children of M M Miller, of Irvine, with the request that they provide for her sister, Katherine Barclay (Kitty Barkley), during her life." The will is dated May 15, 1897, and names M M Miller as executor. p3c4 I wonder how that came out for everyone financially. Kitty lived until 1923.

July 27, 1900

There is a long letter about the Indian Territory, around South McAlester, Oklahoma from T R Dean. p1c3-5 His relatives live in Little Hickman.

August 3, 1900

The *Sulphur Well Correspondent* writes:

*F B Long is on the sick list with rheumatism.*
*W M Short and family, of Madison, were over visiting friends last week.*
*Creed Gott and wife moved to Richmond last week to make that city their home.*
*Smith Turpin was taken seriously ill last Friday, but is now improving and will soon be out again.*
*Mrs Myrtie Dean went on a visit to Estill County last week to be gone a few days.*
*John Whitenack and wife, of Harrodsburg, are the guests of Mr and Mrs J W Cobb this week.*
*Hans Stacy, of Irvine, is visiting in the county and attending the camp meeting at High Bridge.*
*Rev H G Turner, of Richmond, is visiting his parents, Mr and Mrs J P Turner.*
*Quite a crowd from this place have been attending the Wilmore camp meeting.*
*William Richardson and wife, of Irvine, were visiting Mrs E Miller several days this week.*
*John Miller and family, of Wisemantown, were visiting his mother, Mrs Elizabeth Miller, this week.*
*James W Cobb, who has been on the sick list for some time, is out again.*
*Mrs Mary E Wheeler, Cincinnati, is visiting relatives and friends in the town and county.*
p2c3

The Miller family is quite active this week. Myrtie is Mrs Miller's granddaughter. Hans Stacy is the widower of Belle Miller. They had five children, and all were farmed out. He apparently took no responsibility for them. Susan Richardson is Mrs Miller's daughter. John Miller is her son, who is also visiting. Mary Wheeler is Dr Hendren's sister.

August 10, 1900

Fourteen thousand attended the Nicholasville Street Fair and it has been proclaimed a success by the editor. p3c3

"Harry Hendren left yesterday for St Louis, Mo., where he has accepted a position with Simmons Hardware Co. `Pat's' friends wish him much success." p3c3 Pat is Scottie's brother.

August 17, 1900

The State Legislature is being called into a special session by the governor to consider modifications to the Goebel election law. p2c1

George Snowden sold three-quarters of an acre near Ambrose, for $100 and other considerations. p2c5

August 24, 1900

Julia M Spears, the eldest daughter of Mr and Mrs W H Hare, died. She is buried in Maple Grove Cemetary. She is the mother of Bob Spears, Ray Miller's best friend. You will read more about them in the Epilogue. p3c4

The *Sulphur Well Correspondent* writes:

*There is a prospect for an immense corn crop in this section.*
*Geo B Peel last Friday sold to Calvin Bruner a lot of cattle at 3 1/2c.*
*The runaway horse of A J Sageser last week did but little damage.*
*Creed Gott and wife have moved to Richmond to make it their future home.*
*Misses Allie and Bettie Anderson, of Garrard, are the guests of Mr and Mrs T J Horine.*
*Nat Hendren, of Mercer County, was visiting relatives in this section, Saturday and Sunday.*
*A protracted meeting will be held here commencing the first Sunday in September, by Elder Hilderbrand, assisted by Eld Campbell.*
*Mrs Elma Turner and daughter, Mayme, left for Slate Lick Springs, Wednesday to be gone two weeks.*
*Mr and Mrs J P Turner returned from a two weeks' outing at Slate Lick last week.*
*The Christian Church has added some needed improvements in the way of fencing and a gateway into the yard instead of the old time and obsolete stiles to climb over.*
*Last Sunday morning, Sam Brown, while on a visit to Levi Turner's, was accidentally shot with a double-barrel shot gun in the hands of the latter. The load, consisting of shot and a heavy oak ramrod, took effect in Brown's left leg. Pieces of the ramrod from two to four inches long and almost one-half inch in diameter were cut out of the leg by Dr Hendren. The wounded man is doing well.* p2c5

The Journal has been microfilmed out of sequence for the issues on August 24 and August 31, 1900.

August 31, 1900

A great deal of tobacco has been cut and housed already.

The *Sulphur Well Correspondent* writes:

*J H Turner left this week for Slate Lick Springs to be gone several days.*
*Mrs Julia Myers was taken quite suddenly and seriously ill Sunday night with cholera morbus.*
*Rev H G Turner, Richmond, was over and spent several days last week.*
*Wm Short, of Madison, has rented a residence near the old Greenbaum distillery and will move over soon.*
*N B Howard, Madison County, was over a day or two last week.*
*J P Turner shipped 100 head of hogs to Cincinnati Monday.*
*F M Horine sold Monday to Nathan Hughes one cow weighing 1,200 lbs at 3 1/2c.*
*N D Davis sold a few days ago 38 lambs to Nathan Hughes at 5c.*
*A son of Milton Price, five or six years old, living near here, fell a distance of 20 or 25 feet from a peach tree, the limb which he was on breaking. His left wrist was badly dislocated and his right arm broken near the wrist. Dr Hendren attended to his injuries. p3c4*

The Correspondent has begun weaving himself into the stories.

September 7, 1900

The *Sulphur Well Correspondent* writes:

*J P Turner, after having been very sick for several days, is up again.*
*Mr David Owens Hunter has been on the sick list for some days.*
*Mr Emmett Million, of Richmond, is visiting at J H Murphy's.*
*Jas H Turner has returned from a few days stay at Slate Lick Springs.*
*Mrs David Hunter was taken quite sick Friday morning, but is able to be out again.*
*Oliver Vincent, of Edenton, Madison County, has rented a residence in town and will move to it in a week or so.*
*Roy Hendren, of Madison, who has been in Oklahoma City for about a year, returned home last week.*
*Mit Price's little son, who fell from a tree, fracturing one arm and dislocating the other, threw his arm out of place again and it had to be reset Saturday.*
*Misses Bertha and Blanche Askins gave an enjoyable little birthday party Tuesday to their young friends. They were both 16 years old that day. p2c1*

September 14, 1900

A tidal wave hit Galveston Saturday night, "leaving the city in ruins, and killing about 3,000 persons." p2c1

The wheat market is still unsatisfactory, and experts disagree on the future outlook. p2c3

The *Sulphur Well Correspondent* writes:

*School has opened with a fair attendance of pupils.*
*Born, to the wife of Elijah Lowry, on the 9th inst., a son.*
*Charles Cobb is quite sick with something like fever.*
*Mrs J H Turner and daughter, Mayme, have returned from a long stay at Slate Lick.*
*Rain is badly needed in this section as water is getting scarce and grass is drying up.*
*Mrs Emerine Crow, of Estill County, has returned to Mrs E Miller's where she will make her home.*
*The protracted meeting conducted here by Elds Hildebrand and Campbell closed Sunday night with two additions by letter. p2c1*

Poor Granny! I'm sure it was difficult enough having to live with Mrs Miller, but to have to put up with boarders too!

September 21, 1900

Fresh oysters are now available from Baltimore, and can be bought in any quantity. p3c1

"Misses Emma Spruce, Dora Murphy and May Taylor are visiting at Bryantsville." p3c3

The *Sulphur Well Correspondent* writes:

*Perry West has returned to his home near Lancaster.*
*J A Dean and wife, of Stone, were over Monday.*
*Miss House, daughter of Ben House, is quite ill with heart trouble.*
*Mrs William Grimes, of New York, is visiting her relatives, Mr and Mr A M Askins.*
*John Warren, of Madison, has rented the Rufus Hill farm and will move to it soon.*
*Andrew Bogie, of Buckeye, was over Monday swapping stories with old school mates.*
*Wm Burris, Captain Hill, Edward Chandler, Jno A Hammon, a prominent merchant of Edenton, and several other Madisonians were over last Monday.*
*The little daughter of Alex Askins came near fatally poisoning herself with carbolic acid a few days ago. All that saved her was there was not enough of the acid in the bottle she accidently found to swallow, but just enough to burn her mouth quite severely. p2c5*

This last item is about Mattie, who later married a Woodard.

September 28, 1900

Glass' Mill reports that sorghum making is in full swing. J H Murphy lost a good mare, caused by getting her hoof cut on barbed wire. And, Mrs Walker, from Sulphur Well, was down visiting her son. p2c3

October 5, 1900

J P Turner appears to be dispersing his livestock at public auction on the 17th. He is offering Polled Angus cattle, cows and calves, and three bulls; mules; horses; boars, sows and pigs; sheep; and farming implements. p2c6 I believe he is about ready to retire and move to Nicholasville.

Partridges are said to be plentiful this year.

"Mrs Julia Miller, of Elizabethtown, is visiting Dr John C Miller and family." p3c3 This is Rice Miller's widow.

October 12, 1900

The High Bridge correspondent says that the last few nights and early mornings has been a reminder that fall is here.

"Mr and Mrs A K Adcock are home from Chicago." p3c3

The *Sulphur Well Correspondent* writes:

*W B Walker sold to Lambert Dietrich a fine cow and calf for $75.*
*E G Walker bought a sow and pigs from B F Foster at $15.*
*A M Askins was elected school trustee for this district Saturday.*
*Jno P Miller and family were visiting his mother, Mrs Elizabeth Miller, a few days ago.*
*Mrs E Lowry has been on the sick list for some time.*
*Born, to the wife of Frank Miller, (nee Reynolds) Oct 1, a son.*
*Mrs H Underwood is reported quite ill at her home near Elm Fork.*
*Mrs Dr Bryant has returned to her home at Versailles after a lengthy visit with her sister, Mrs J H Turner.*
*Born, to the wife of Robert Grant, October 6, a daughter.*
*A son of David O Hunter was taken sick very suddenly Saturday night.*
*N D Thompson paid us a pleasant visit last Saturday night.*
*C T Taylor, of Richmond, was visiting Mrs Margaret Horine Tuesday and Wednesday of this week.*
*W H Hare sold a lot of fat hogs to A C Miles Tuesday at $4.75 per cwt. Also Al Baker sold to same party 7 head of hogs at $4.75. p2c3*

### October 19, 1900

A number of Hanly citizens went to Lexington Monday to hear Teddy Roosevelt's speech. p3c4

There is an excursion to Estill Springs on Thursday, Oct 25th. p2c1

### October 26, 1900

I am again frustrated by not being able to follow up certain stories. There is nothing on the J P Turner dispersal sale to be found, and the Sulphur Well correspondent doesn't even mention it.

The *Sulphur Well Correspondent* writes:

*Several lots of fat hogs have been sold recently at this place at $4.75.*
*J W Cobb visited at Harrodsburg this week.*
*Rev H G Turner, of Richmond, spent several days with his parents here last week.*
*Several from here took advantage of the excursion yesterday to Estill Springs.*
*F M Horine sold to A C Miles 5 yearling steers at 3 1/2c.*
*N D Davis bought one steer weighing 800 lbs from John Carr at 3 1/4c.*
*While Thomas House, of Saunders Ferry, was at Lexington attending his son's trial, some unknown parties visited his place Friday night and killed a number of fat hogs, shot his house full of holes and did other devilry. It seems that a number of persons loaf along the river in shanty boats and otherwise and sell whisky and are a great disturbance to the peaceful citizens who say they are very tired of it.* p2c1

### November 2, 1900

Nimrod H Easley, who runs a shanty boat on the Kentucky River on the Jessamine side, went to Lexington Saturday night with Mary Jones and tried to get a marriage licence. The clerk refused because the girl was only fifteen. A warrant was served on Easley, and he was charged with disorderly conduct. p3c2

The farmers have begun stripping tobacco at Glass' Mill.

The election is next Tuesday and the activity is pretty intense.

### November 9, 1900

McKinley wins nationally, but Bryan carried Kentucky. Beckham, the Democratic nominee, won the Kentucky governor's race. p2c1

November 16, 1900

Corn is being delivered at $2 per barrel at Glass' Mill. They say not as much tobacco has been stripped at Brannon this time of year as usual because of the unusually dry weather. Tobacco has to come into "case", i.e., absorb moisture from the air, otherwise it can't be handled because it would crumble. Wheat is being shipped from Camp Nelson by packets running "down" the Kentucky River to Carrollton, and then on the Ohio River to Louisville.

The *Sulphur Well Correspondent* writes:

*Stock water as well as wells and cisterns are exhausted.*
*There is more corn being hauled and delivered to different parties this year than usual. It appears to be the only traffic at present and is in good demand at $2 per barrel delivered.*
*Mr James Vincent, of Madison County, was over this week looking for a location.*
*J H Turner sold Tuesday to N Davis six head of fat hogs at 4 cents.*
*Corn is worth only $1.50 in lower Madison and Garrard Counties.*
*There are no visits to report. People seem to be staying at home and attending to their own business since the election. p2c4*

November 23, 1900

The results of the 1900 Census are in, and Nicholasville has a population of 2,923, a gain of 201; the county's population is 11,925, for a gain of 325. This small increase indicates that Jessamine is not sharing the nation's growth. p1c3

I reviewed the Sulphur Well data to see who was living around the neighborhood at this time. I found that Andrew J Sageser had a new family. He married Susie Hendren, Scottie's sister, and they had two children, Ada and Hubert. A brother in law, W D Hendren, and a sister in law, Jennie, were living with them also. Neither of these two people were brother or sister to Susie, so I can't explain the entry.

Elizabeth Miller had in her household Matilda (Aunt T), Forest, Scottie, and Ray.

Steve Snowden, who leased the family farm from Elizabeth Miller, had in his household Lucy (Miller), his wife, and four children: John, Russell, Virgil, and Bessie.

G. M. Hendren was also in Sulphur Well. His wife, Mary E (Jasper), and two children Nellie and Mary made up the household. Their oldest daughter, Addie, married Hugh Miller, and was no longer at home.

There was James Hendren and his wife Mildred.

And, there was William Hendren and wife Eliza: sons William L (Jr), and Levi H and Levi's wife Louisa (Tudor),and their children Jennie and Ethel. William Hendren's farm was close to the Chrisman Mill fork in the road.

Alex Askins was listed along with his wife Sally, children Bertha, Blanche, and Mattie. Luther Ware was living with them at the time and was either an apprentice or journeyman in Askins' blacksmith shop.

Andrew J Ware and his wife Sallie had in their household Melvin and Edward, who are Luther Ware's brothers.

J H Murphy and wife Mary (who was a Horine) had two children C Manford and Dora, and two servants in their household.

There was also a Taylor family, Ike the father, and children: William, Dera, Dela, Jamie, Julie, and Sally.

William B Walker, his wife Elizabeth, and son Elbert, were living a short way out the Elm Fork Road.

Then there was Tom Horine and wife Eliza, on the hill above the pump.

There was also James Sageser, with his wife Martha, and son Oscar in his household.

Belle Walters, whose farm lays between Watts Mill Road and Black Bridge, had only her son, William Perry Walters, at home.

N D Davis, his wife Belle, their sons Marshall and Walter, daughter in law, Mary, and half-brother Millard made up this household.

John Myers had only his two sons, Charles and Henry, at home. During my youth, Henry lived in their homeplace, at the edge of what I consider Sulphur Well, on the road to Elm Fork.

Wilson Masters, his wife Josephine, and daughters Mattie, Alma, Lulu, Bettie, and Kate were still at home. His son Gabe was already married.

Charles Clubb and his wife Viola Davis were living in the Diamond house, on the hill above the church.

N B Long, his wife, Allace, and children were somewhere in the neighborhood.

Ezekiel Hendren and his wife Nannie also lived somewhere in the neighborhood, but I'm don't know where.

Henry Alverson, a blacksmith, now 83, his wife Emla, and an unmarried 42 year old daughter, Luella were in Sulphur Well.

S N Bishop, a miller by trade, now 67, lived with his wife Charity in the neighborhood, possibly on or near the Watts Mill Road.

Walter D Harris, only 36 at this time, and his wife Myrtie Overstreet, daughter of John P Overstreet, and Sarah Miller lived on the Watts Mill Road. Walter's parents were William P Harris and Frances Woodward. Their farm "backs up" to the Miller Farm.

George Snowden and his wife Nora are in this same area.

Benjamin Foster, his wife Eliza, sons Egbert, Jesse, Phillip, and daughter in law Manerva were also living on the Watts Mill Road.

Frank Hudson and his wife Allace, were farming in the area.

Everett E Bourne, his wife Malinda, daughters Irene and Mamie, and sons William, Morris, Edwin E, are still at home.

James Woodward, Sr, now 74, his wife Caroline, son Houston, and daughter Carrie make up a household. It is not clear to me how the Woodward's and Harris' were sharing the farm. James is elderly by this time, and both he and Caroline are buried in the family cemetery on the farm. However, Walter D Harris does wind up with the farm, and the cemetery is know now as the Harris Cemetery.

I must confess to being something less than methodical in this census listing because I didn't list everyone, and I haven't provided the same level of information about ages, relationships, occupations, for all. I selected familiar names that I thought would help the reader know what constituted Sulphur Well at the turn of the century. The reader should see the Family section that appears at the end of the story for more information.

While at Maple Grove Cemetery I saw the grave site of Elizabeth Miller, daughter of Dr John C Miller, who married Thomas Welch Downing. She lived from 1875 to 1957, yet I never met her. Dr John C Miller's second wife, Emma Crain Reynolds (1850-1940) is also buried in Maple Grove, in the O P Reynolds lot.

"Miss Maude Miller, the accomplished daughter of Mr and Mrs M M Miller, of Irvine, met with a painful accident recently. A horse she was driving ran away throwing her out, cutting a gash in her forehead, breaking her left leg and dislocating her foot." This is reprinted from the Richmond Register. The editor goes on to say that she is the niece of Dr Miller, and has relatives in Oklahoma. p3c2

"Mr Marshall Davis, of Ambrose, and Miss Emma Spruce, of Nicholasville, will be married at the residence of her sister, Mrs W S Hendren, next Wednesday, Nov 28, at 8 pm." p3c3 Mrs Spruce once operated a store at Sulphur Well. She had three daughters-- Lula (Lulie), who married Joe Woodward; Linnie who married W S Hendren, Dr Hendren's brother; and Emma. Marshall Davis is the son of N D Davis, farmer, cattle dealer, tobacco broker, etc. that appears regularly in the Sulphur Well reports.(The marriage is reported in the <u>Journal</u>, Nov 30 p3c4)

John C Hendren, of Poosey, has been appointed one of the tax supervisors in Madison County. p2c2 He is the son of Tom Hendren of Nicholasville.

Little Hickman says that the long-wished for rain was a welcome visitor Tuesday. Union Mills reports that Hickman Creek has more water that it's had for a long time. p2c3

The *Sulphur Well Correspondent* writes:

> F M Horine bought of John Guy one cow at 2 1/2c.
> W G Jones and son, of Buckeye, and Oscar Hendren, of Edenton, were over Monday.
> Four fat hogs lost by Wm Hendren, Sr, and supposed to have been stolen, were inadvertently shipped to Cincinnati by A C Miles.
> John March, formerly of Madison County, but now of Illinois, is visiting for a short time friends in this county.
> W H Hare is reported on the sick list.
> Luther Ware has been sick for some days.
> Corn is still selling for $2, delivered.
> The sound of the hunter's gun is heard in the land. Poor little Bob White.
> Andrew Higgs has been quite sick for some days.
> The infant son of Frank Miller, who has been quite sick, is better.
> L H Hendren, who recently sold the Watts Mill property and moved to Normal, Ill, has moved on to Oklahoma.
> E Vincent, of Edenton, is boarding with his brother, Caperton.
> Tom Bruner bought a nice lot of 100 lb shoats at $3.40 last week and sold to Lexington parties at $4.
> W B Walker has been quite indisposed for several days.
> There seems to be a good demand for hogs in this section.
> J P Turner has bought several hundred barrels of corn at from $1.85 on the ground to $2, delivered.
> Thomas Bruner sold to N D Miles seven steers averaging 900 lbs at 3 3/4c. Robt Waide sold to same party 7 fat hogs at 4c; J H Turner to same 12 hogs at same price; (and) Mrs Fountain Peel to same 12 head at 4c.
> Mr E G Walker, who four years ago, was for his well-known golden propensity, ousted as the Democratic precinct committeeman, and succeeded by Mr Elzie Sageser, was on Saturday last re-elected to his former position on the committee over his old competitor by a vote of about 30 to 10. p2c7

Elbert Walker apparently supported "sound money" rather than "free silver", and was ousted for his sins. After the free silverites, under Bryan, were defeated in two national elections, his sins apparently were considered forgivable.

I have noted that the Correspondent has been reporting quite a few livestock sales the past few weeks.

November 30, 1900

Elbert Masters (this is Masters, not Elbert Walker above), one of the Nicholasville "dudes" that visited the girls at Sulphur Well in the eighties, was finally married In Bloomington, Ill, and is making that his home. p3c4

"Mr John Snowden, of Ambrose, and Miss Sarah Butler, of Waco, Madison County, eloped to Jeffersonville, Thursday, Nov 22, and were married." They returned to Richmond Friday, "where they were entertained by Misses Bessie and Mary Coyle, cousins of the bride." After a short visit with the Butlers, the couple will reside in Jessamine County. p3c4 This is a grandson of Mrs Elizabeth Miller. I remember John and Sally quite well.

The *Sulphur Well Correspondent* writes:

*Jno T West sold to Jesse Bryant 12 head of 90-lb shoats at $4.25.*
*John H Warfield died of consumption, Saturday, Nov 24.*
*Jas W Cobb has returned from a trip through Mercer and Garrard counties.*
*A son of Samuel Hill, on Hickman Creek, is quite sick with typhoid fever.*
*A child of John Fathergill is quite sick with symptoms of scarlatina.*
*W S Hamon, of Edenton, was visiting here this week.*
*Mrs Robert Davis, Garrard County, died last Thursday with typhoid fever.*
*Mr and Mrs J P Turner returned Monday from a few days visit with their son, Rev H G Turner, at Richmond.*
*The Hurst Home Insurance Co sent Inspector Kennedy around last week examining property and especially insecure flues.*
*John Perkins, who has been afflicted for some months with partial paralysis, was completely paralyzed last week and died on the 23rd inst., without regaining consciousness. He was buried at Pleasant Hill Church.* p2c3

Scarlatina is a mild form of scarlet fever. Just look at the deaths reported this week!

December 7, 1900

Dr Hendren composed "Day Dreams" this week. Even when fortune is smiling upon us, we dream of things unattainable, and don't appreciate the pleasures we have. p1c6

Dr Hendren's mother died.

Mrs Eliza A Hendren, wife of Wm Hendren, Sr, died at her home near Ambrose, Friday, Nov 30, of paralysis and abscess of the liver, aged 78. She was the daughter of Levi and Henrietta Reynolds, of Madison County. She was married March 8, 1838, and is survived by her husband and nine children.

Dr Hendren and William Hendren, Jr live in Ambrose. W S Hendren lives in Nicholasville. Mrs Hendren was a member of the Chrisian Church. The funeral was held on December 1 at the Hendren residence, and she was buried in Maple Grove Cemetery. p2c1

The *Sulphur Well Correspondent* writes:

*F M Horine bought of James Booker one fat cow at 2 1/2c.*
*Miss Grace Grinstead, of Taylorsville, is visiting her sister, Mrs J H Turner.*
*Mrs Ella Taylor and daughter, Lila, of Richmond, are visiting Mrs Margaret Horine.*
*Richard Burton, Buckeye, visited Dr Hendren, Saturday and Sunday.*
*F M Horine bought from Samuel Hill five head of cattle at fair prices.*
*The attendance at church Sunday to hear Elder Hildebrand's last sermon of the year was very large.*
*In Lower Garrard corn is selling at $1.50 and hogs are in brisk demand at $4.50 to $4.75.*
*Mrs Levi Davis died in Garrard County, Thursday, Nov 29. The day previous her infant child died also.*
*E Hendren sold 17 head of shoats Monday at $3.75; also a few were sold at $4 per hundred. Some hogs have brought $4.50 recently.*
*Married, at the residence of the bride on Hickman Creek, Thursday, Nov 29, Mr Edgar Ware and Miss Minnie Lee Reynolds, daughter of John Reynolds.*
*Mr and Mrs John Teater and Mrs William Burton and son, Dick, of Garrard attended the funeral of their sister, Mrs Eliza A Hendren, on Saturday last.*
*Two Morman missionaries of Utah have arrived in the neighborhood of Mr Pleasant Church, and it is said are anxious to persuade the curious to hear their pernicious doctrine. They will probably not be allowed to try to delude the people from the pulpit of the church, as many of the members and some of the officers are not willing for them to pollute the sacred precincts of their house of worship. p2c3*

This letter makes it clear that the Correspondent records items in diary-fashion. His lead item is about the sale of a cow. Only one of his items is dated, the marriage of Ed Ware, on the 29th. Then, his mother died on the 30th, but his only reference to her death was that of her sisters attending her funeral the previous Saturday. His last item would have to be early in the week, because the letter had to be posted and arrive in time to be printed that same week.

Reference to the item above about the relative prices of corn and pigs: The farmers are practicing good economics. The price of corn is so low, that they might as well feed it to the hogs. Some are taking the opportunity to sell their young pigs (shoats) on the good market.

## December 14, 1900

"Dr Jno C Miller and wife will leave in a few days for Oklahoma City, OT, where they will spend the winter." p3c4 "F P Taylor will occupy the residence on Noland Street that the Millers vacated." p2c4 The price received was $1,400.

The *Sulphur Well Correspondent* writes:

*Ben House moved Monday from his farm near Pink to his residence in town.*
*Simon Walters, who has been several months in Illinois, returned home Monday.*
*F M Horine sold and delivered several hogsheads of tobacco to the Continental Tobacco Company, Lexington, at $5.50.*
*James Ward, aged about 90 years, died at his home at Buckeye, last week. He had lived there nearly all his life.*
*Levi Reynolds and wife, of near Buckeye, died within a few hours of each other last week.*
*Several hundred bushels of millet seed were sent to parties in Lexington, Tuesday by farmers of this place.* p2c3

I believe that the item concerning the deaths of Mr and Mrs Levi Reynolds, would be the mother and father of Mrs Eliza Reynolds Hendren, who just died a week ago. Her parents were located in Madison County in the obituary, but near Buckeye in this item. The county line between Madison and Garrard is Paint Lick Creek, and is "near Buckeye".

December 21, 1900

Dr Hendren writes a poem, taking a rather populist view of the difference between the wealthy and those who must work for a living. p1c6 One of the middle verses is as follows:

THE TOILERS
By a chance of birth he follows the plow,
And tills the earth by the sweat of his brow,
That out of his toil the rich should be fed,
And idleness eat of his hard-earned bread;
By pitiless fate foredoomed to drudge
For the paltry pay that wealth would begrudge.

You can celebrate the holidays with goodies from Waide's--candies, fire works, nuts, bananas, and grapes. Or, you can take the Queen and Cresent to Florida for the holidays!

December 28, 1900

"Fire destroyed the store-house and office of Dr Geo M Hendren, at Ambrose, Tuesday night at 8 o'clock. The fire originated in a mysterious manner, probably from some Christmas explosion. There was insurance of $200 on the building and $100 on books, medicines, etc., which does not cover the loss." p3c1

Thus ends another year in Sulphur Well. The Correspondent has had a lot going on this year, writing both poems and letters to the editor. In December, he lost his mother, and around Christmas-time had this fire.

## MILLERS SETTLE IN OKLAHOMA - 1901

Dr Miller's sons and their families settle in the area around Oklahoma City. Dr Miller spends part of the year visiting with them. Daughter Lizzie marries Tom Downing in Nicholasville, and moves to New York.

### January 4, 1901

Samuel McAfee Duncan, Jessamine County's resident historian, died at age 70 in St Joseph Hospital on Monday night. He had an encyclopedic memory, collected information, and contributed enumerable papers, that "showed a wonderful depth of research, as well as power of thought and expression." Although he was a cabinet maker by trade, his consuming interest was in history. He was asthmatic, and two weeks ago had a severe heart attack. He is buried in Maple Grove Cemetery. p3c4 He wrote many articles for the Journal, and I reported two pertaining to Sulphur Well.

The *Sulphur Well Correspondent* writes:

> *A child of Josh Warfield died Wednesday from loss of ------. It was only a few days old.*
> *Miss T Miller left Saturday for several week's visit at Wisemantown, Estill County.*
> *Ray Miller, the little son of Mr and Mrs F F Miller has been quite sick.*
> *Squire Hendren and wife, of Cottonburg, were visiting James Hendren Chrismas week.*
> *Green B Willis and daughter, of Edinburg, Ind., who were paying Wm Hudson a short visit, returned home Monday.*
> *William Richardson and wife, and Leah Stacy, of Irvine, were visiting Mrs E Miller Christmas week.*
> *James Hurt, Dry Ridge, died very suddenly last Saturday. He was 80 years old on Friday before he died. Heart trouble is supposed to have been the cause of death as he was subject to rheumatism.*
> *Mail carrier George Sewell had a narrow escape from serious injury on Friday of last week. On the hill descending to the iron bridge across Hickman Creek his horse ran off. He ran for about a mile kicking and finally dashed throught a plank fence over the embankment, buggy and all, throwing out Sewell and Jack Long, a passenger, who escaped unhurt, though Sewell was kicked in the breast.*
> *Pulaski County's boast of 20 weddings in one week can almost be duplicated by Madison County in one day, and in one neighborhood. At Edenton, eight couples married on the same day and it wasn't a good day for weddings either. Several weddings are said to have occurred of which my informant had forgotten to secure the names, and several other weddings are announced to come off soon. The eight couples were: James Warner and Miss Anna Warren, Walter Sanders and Lizzie Masters, Louis Dillon and Minnie Hendren, Abe Burton and Barbara Howard, Arthur Taylor and Callie Long, Elisha Foster and Janie Short, Nat Coy and Miss Melinda Hendren. p2c1*

Lizzie Miller got married without her family, all of whom are in Oklahoma:

> The society gossipers of Nicholasville were never more taken by surprise than on Monday moring last when it became known that Thos W Downing, of New York

City, would wed Miss Lizzie Miller, only daughter of Dr Jno C Miller. Several months ago it was surmised that this wedding would take place, but as Mr Downing, who was then visiting here, returned without a bride, nothing more was thought of it. The marriage, which was a very quiet one, took place at the country residence of Mrs W H Hoover, Jr., at high noon, Rev E G B Mann officiating, the ceremony being a most beautiful one. There were only a few ... immediate friends present.... The bride, who was a picture of beauty, wore a brown cloth tailor-made suit with hat to match, carrying in her hand a bunch of American Beauty roses. The bridegroom, who never looked handsomer, wore the conventional black. As the two young people looked into the eyes of each other, the happiness of one reflected upon the face of the other. p3c4

Downing has been employed by a large store in New York City for the past three years. After the wedding, they went on to Lexington, and had dinner with the Downings, and then on to New York by train.

### January 11, 1901

Velvet is extremely fashionable for matrons, and the "brocades and other rich silken goods" for the season are designed just for them. p1c7

### January 18, 1901

The Jessamine Fishing Club left for New Smyrna, Florida on January 2. They seem to be having fun. They write back weekly to the <u>Journal</u> to report their goings on. They've done this for years.

The *Sulphur Well Correspondent* writes:

*Nearly everybody herebouts has the grip.*
*Joe Woodward was on the sick list last Tuesday.*
*Miss Irene Bourne is visiting relatives in Garrard County.*
*Ernest Duncan and wife are both sick in bed.*
*Miss T Miller returned from a visit to Estill County last week.*
*F M Hurst, general manager of Hurst Home Insurance Co., was here last week on business.*
*Luther Ware was quite sick Monday, but is again able to be out.*
*Mrs A M Askins was taken suddenly Tuesday night with pleurisy.*
*Ernest Bourne, of Bourne, Ky., was --------- Bourne last week.*          p2c1

### February 1, 1901

W S Hendren carried off several premiums at the Louisville Chicken Show with his Buff Pekin Bantams. p2c1

February 8, 1901

There is an extremely long letter from Dr John C Miller on the front page about Oklahoma. It is essentially an economic geography of the area around Oklahoma City. He concludes by saying, "Don't come here unless you have cash money." p1c3-5

February 15, 1901

Temperance clubs are being organized all over the country in honor of Mrs Carrie Nation. Their emblem is a hatchet. p1c5

"A K Adcock is in New Orleans attending the Marti Gras." p3c3 "Miss Dora Murphy is visiting the Misses Taylor, Richmond, this week."p3c3 Marshall Davis has bought half interest in the Kirkpatrick Meat Store. p3c4

The *Sulphur Well Correspondent* writes:

*Nearly every one has had the grippe and pneumonia seems to be following in its wake.*
*Cyrus Teater's infant son has been very sick for some days.*
*Edward Chandler, of Edenton, was visiting this vicinity a few days since.*
*Ezekiel Vincent has applied to his Uncle Sam for an increase of pension.*
*J T West, who has recently been confined to his bed with kidney trouble, is out again.*
*Miss Irene Bourne has returned home from a lenghty visit with friends in Garrard County.*
*A child of Sid Smith is expected to die as it has pneumonia.*
*Thomas Bruner left Wednesday on a business trip to the mountains.*
*Ernest Duncan, who has been sick for quite awhile, and has recently had a slight attack of pneumonia in addition, is improving.*
*Mr and Mrs Clubb, invited a few of the young people of the village to an informal reception Tuesday night to meet Mr Ellery Clubb, of Pleasureville, Henry County, who is visiting them for a few days. They had a pleasant time.* p2c1

February 22, 1901

There has now been two young Jessamine County men killed in the fighting in the Philippines.

Well, a generation is passing. George W Gray died at his residence in Lexington, Friday, Feb 15, at age 62. Although born in North Carolina, he moved to Jessamine at an early age. He married Margaret Hunter on June 15, 1865. They had six children--Texie, who married Tom Cooley and went to Omaha; Ida, who married George M. Berry and lives in Lexington; a son George also lives in Lexington; and others. He was engaged in the distillery business in Sulphur Well until about fourteen years ago when he moved his family to Lexington. He is buried in the Lexington Cemetery. p3c4

The *Sulphur Well Correspondent* writes:

*Dr Wm Ray, of Buckeye, was over Monday.*
*Mrs Cyrus Teater was quite sick for several days last week.*
*Mrs T J Horine, who has been on the sick list for some time, is better.*
*Born, to the wife of John Waller, on the 14th inst., a daughter.*
*Mrs Meda Reynolds is down with a severe attack of la grippe.*
*Jno A Ham, of Edenton, was over last Monday.*
*Edgar Ware has built a house on his father's place and will move into it this week.*
*J Irvine Short, of Edenton, was in town last Friday.*
*A little daughter of Elbert Chatman who has been very low with pneumonia, is better.*
*Miss Viola Hendren, of Edenton, was taken to the hospital at Lexington last Saturday for eye treatment. She has already lost the sight of one eye.*
*Pneumonia seems to be very prevalent among the colored population, in some families as many as two or three at a time being down with it.*
*In a letter of a recent date from Oklahoma, Dr Miller with grim humor declares, that thought the news from Kentucky is that he was starved to death, the contrary is nearer the truth for he says he eats so much that it makes him sick, but he is still in the land of the living.* p2c3

March 1, 1901

Dr Hendren has composed "The Old Calendar". This one must have been written in December, as leaves are torn off as each month passes, and he says it hangs on the wall, a single leaf remaining. It tells him that he's growing old; his life, like the leaves have flown. He wonders where the years have gone, but his memory is filled with the treasures of the past, that become richer to him every year. p1c4

The *Sulphur Well Correspondent* writes:

*Ben Wheeler's little daughter, who was crippled by a fall some time ago, is in a precarious condition.*
*Wesley Davis' infant son has been seriously ill for some days with lung trouble*
*John Sanders, of Buckeye, was visiting here a few days this week.*
*Perry Shropshire has moved from the toll house at the forks of the pike to the Union Mills pike.*
*Henry C Masters, of Madison County, was over last week.*
*The youngest daughter of Alex Askins has been quite sick with an attack of acute gastritis.*
*Mrs James Hagar, of Mt Lebanon, who has been very sick, is improving.*
*Edward Chandler, of Edenton, was over for a few days visiting friends last week.*
*Miss Dora Evans, of Junction City, is visiting Mrs W H Hoover, Sr, this week.*
*The wife of Milton Price died at Lexington hospital, Sunday.*
*W H Moore, of East Hickman, bought of Frank Horine, two calves at $44.*
*N D Davis bought of F M Horine 18 head of hogs averaging about 175 pounds, at 5c, this week.*
*Some unknown parties left the skinned carcass of a horse on the pike near W H Hoover's Monday night. The horse had been seen there during the day, but it is not known who slaughtered him.*

*Mrs A M Askins was taken seriously ill Monday evening from having taken too much of one of those humbug secret nostrums. As the poisonous principle of May apple root enters largely with its composition she had a narrow escape. p2c4*

March 8, 1901

The *Sulphur Well Correspondent* writes:

*John Bourne, of Bourne, Garrard County, visited EE Bourne a few days last week.*
*Ben House moved from Nicholasville to his farm near Pink, Monday.*
*Miss Mattie Woodward is home from a visit to Lexington.*
*Elder Martin, of Lexington, will preach here next Sunday.*
*Miss Dora Murphy is visiting Miss Mary Taylor, Richmond.*
*Elbert Walker and Houston Woodward were visiting friends in Garrard Saturday and Sunday.*
*Alexander Ray, of Cottonburg, Madison County, paid Jessamine a short visit Friday last.*
*J P Turner returned Monday from a visit to his son Rev H G Turner, Richmond.*
*Miss Emma West was severely scalded by steam Monday.*
*Mrs Emma Askins, Misses Minnie Walters, and Carrie Woodward were visiting the family of J Holley Easley near Buena Vista, Garrard County, Saturday and Sunday, last.*

*During the high and incessant winds last Sunday, a large pine tree standing in Mrs Lizzie Miller's yard was uprooted and blown across the pike, obstructing travel for a time. Other timber throughout the neighborhood was destroyed; hay and straw stacks and fodder shocks were sent whirling throught the air and scattered over the country broadcast, and many roofs were more or less damaged.*

*This whole section is overrun by worthless curs that go in packs like wolves, making night hideous with their howls and yelping. They have become so vicious as to attack stock in broad daylight, as they did J P Turner's last week, in plain view of the pike, when they downed a yearling steer and would have destroyed it had they not been driven off. Every man and boy, white and black, has from three to six of these mongrels trotting at his heels. For what purpose, is a mystery. And, the more worthless the cur the more favor he seems to receive from his master. A law taxing these nuisances would be a most beneficient measure in morals, manners, money, and Morpheus. p2c5*

March 15, 1901

Dr Miller writes about his trip from Oklahoma City to Galveston. It appears that he made the trip to survey the damage done by the tidal wave. p1c3-4

Some of the members of the "Fishing Club" have returned to Jessamine from their trip to Florida. They stopped for the day in St Augustine. They stayed over a couple of days in Jacksonville, and proceeded by train on to Chattanooga. They toured the battlegrounds at Chickamauga, and went upon Mission Ridge. Then on to Lookout Mountain, and finally home. p1c6

Former President Benjamin Harrison died at his home in Indianapolis, Wednesday. p2c1

The *Sulphur Well Correspondent* writes:

*Charles Cobb, Sr, is said to be very low with dropsy of the heart.*

*Mrs John Durham has been quite sick for several days.*

*William House, of Mr Lebanon, has been down for several days with a low type of remittant fever.*

*A little child of James Watts had an alarming attack of spasmodic croup Tuesday night.*

*Elder Williams, of Bethany College, Va, preached at the Christian Church Sunday morning and at night.*

*A little son of W J Brumfield, who has been very low with a severe attack of pneumonia, is considerably better, and his physician considers him out of danger.*

*Shirly Cotton, of Cottonburg, Madison County, and Emmett Taylor, of Ruthton, were visiting friends in this section last week.*

*F M Hurst, of Millersburg, the General Manager of Hurst Home Insurance, was around Monday, adjusting losses occasioned by the recent storm. The company suffered forty losses from that little Sunday breeze, within the sphere of it operations, two being at this place.* p2c3

March 22, 1901

Dr Hendren has written another poem. No matter how long or how hard you have strived, the goal (light) that you seek is always in the distance before you. p1c6 The last verse is as follows:

### THE LIGHT THAT WILL NOT FADE

So transient are prospects--deceptively near,
The beautiful mirages lay,
That the dreamer--he dreams on forever--
The toiler--he works while it's day.

The *Sulphur Well Correspondent* writes:

*L D Hendren, of Cincinnati, is visiting relatives in Madison and the county.*

*J Irvine Short, Edenton, was over Friday and Saturday.*

*Mrs Justin Burgin, Mt Lebanon, has been suffering severely for some weeks with a complication of diseases.*

*A son of John Cobb, Mt Lebanon, had a slight attack of pneumonia last week, but soon recovered.*

*Wm Gill, of Chrisman's Mill, is down with a severe attack of pleurisy.*

*Idalia is the pretty and euphonistic name of the new post-office just established at Miles Ferry.*

*Born, to the wife of Tilford Baker, on the 14th inst, a son.*

*Miss Sudie Pardee, of Colesburg, is visiting EE Bourne, this week.*

*Mrs Elizabeth Miller left Tuesday for a ten day's visit to relatives in Irvine and Estill County.*

*Otis, the six year old son of William Brumfield, who had about recovered from a severe attack of pneumonia of the left lung was taken suddenly with the dread disease in his right lung Tuesday last and for a time his reovery was very doubtful, but he is again on the road to recovery, after his second severe struggle for life.* p2c2

March 29, 1901

Quick thinking: A man was stealing a ride on the trucks of a train, when the train ran into a mule. (A truck is a swiveling frame with wheels at each end of the railroad car or locomotive.) The train stopped, and the crew looked around to survey the damage and spied the man. "What are you doing here", they asked. "Why", he replied "I wuz ridin' dat mule". p1c6

E C May, near Ambrose, sold his farm of 90 acres to H M DeWitt for $2,550, giving immediate possession. p2c4

Nicholasville is about to get concrete walks this spring.

April 5, 1901

It didn't get served! A bachelor over around Valley View, who is also a deputy sheriff, was given an attachment to serve on a young widow in that area. He called on her and said "Madam, I have an attachment for you". She blushed, and replied "that his attachment was mutual". He said "You don't understand, you must proceed to court". "I prefer you do the courting" she replied. He grew impatient and told her not to trifle, that the Justice was waiting. "The Justice", she said, "Why, I prefer a minister!" p1c6

Carrie Nation came to Kentucky on a speaking tour. However, her audiences in Cincinnati and Lexington were very small. It is said she is not having as much success on the platform as she had with her hatchet! p2c1

April 12, 1901

"E P May, of Ambrose, bought James King's 100 acre farm near Bryantsville for $2,000." p3c2

Dr Hendren's father has died:

> William Hendren passed away at his home two miles east of Nicholasville, April 5, at the advanced age of 82 years. He was a native of Madison County, where he was born March 12, 1819, near Salem Church. His ancesters on his grandfather Taylor's side (his father, Doven, married Jane Taylor) were descendants of Swedish-Lutherans, who settled in Virginia and Pennsylvania in 1726; his grandmother was the daughter of a native Swede, Charles Frederick Bartleson. Elder Wm Hendren was married to Eliza Ann Reynolds, March 8, 1837, in Madison County, who preceded him in death four months ago, eight living children being the result of the union: Levi H, Wichita, Kan; Mrs Louisa Gibony, of this county; Mrs Mary E Wheeler, Cincinnati; Dr Geo M, Ambrose; Mrs S E Davis, Nicholasville; Mrs G B Wagner, Bellevue; Wm. L., Mrs John Baskett and W S Hendren, of Nicholasville. (W S is Walter Scott) Two brothers survive him,

Messrs Thomas Hendren, Nicholasville, and Talton Hendren, located in Indiana. The deceased, who had been a very religious man from his early boyhood, united with the church in 1835 in his native county, at a meeting being held near Silver Creek. Mr Hendren had been an elder in the Christian Church for nearly 40 years and was ever loyal to his vows. At all times and under all circumstances he could be found upon the side of moral questions, being a very strong advocate of the Prohibition question. The funeral services were conducted from the Christian Church at Ambrose, Sunday afternoon, by Elders Hilerbrand and Vernon, and the body laid to rest in Maple Grove Cemetery. p3c3

He and his wife Eliza are buried in Section A along with other members of the family: Ida Hendren who married John A Baskett; Walter S Hendren who married Linnie Spruce; and Dr and Mrs Hendren. Actually, nine children were living at this time.

The *Sulphur Well Correspondent* writes:

*Wm Smith, of Edenton, was over last week.*
*Jessie Newby, of Newby, Madison County, was over Friday of last week.*
*James Woodward, Sr, has been quite sick for several days.*
*Mrs Harry Hagar, of Hunter's Ferry, has been quite sick for some time.*
*Mrs Wm Huddleston who was stricken with paralysis some days ago, is better.*
*Born, to the wife of Sam House, Jr, on the 27th ult, a son. Also to the wife of Lee Davis on the 4th inst, a son.*
*Dr G M Hendren was taken with a severe chill and fever Wednesday night, the precursors of a short sharp attack of pneumonia that followed.*
*Mrs A M Askins is again quite sick. Mrs W B Walker is also on the sick list.*
*Askins and Ware are fixing to improve their shop extensively.*
*Mrs Bettie Reynolds, of Texarkana, Texas, who has been visiting relatives in this and Madison Counties for some time, has returned home.*
*Elder W F Neal preached at the church on the first Sunday morning and night.*
*Elder Hilderbrand preached an able and effective funeral discourse over the remains of Wm Hendren, Sunday. The funeral was largely attended, notwithstanding the inclemency of the weather a very large number following the remains to the burial place, Maple Grove Cemetery, where was laid to rest as faithful a soldier of the Lord as ever girded on the armor of the right and heard the welcome plaudit, "Well done thou good and faithful servant".* p3c6

The Correspondent has had a difficult time the past few months, losing both his parents, and having some health problems as well.

April 19, 1901

"D B Miller died at his home near Valley View, Wednesday, April 10, aged 79. The deceased was the father of Mrs Ora Soper, of this county, and formerly owned and operated a saw and grist mill on the site where Mr Soper's mill is now located. Several children survive the deceased." p3c4

"Mrs Mary Wheeler, of Cincinnati, and Mrs Annie Wagner, of Newport, attended the funeral of their father, Elder Wm Hendren, last week." p2c5

"W L and W S Hendren qualified as executors of the estate of Wm Hendren, deceased." p2c5

April 26, 1901

"Rev H G Turner, of Richmond, will deliver an address before the graduating class of Millersburg Military Institute at their Commencement, June 4." p3c2

Heavy rains have caused a rise in the Ohio and Kentucky Rivers. The river rose fifteen feet at High Bridge. p3c3

May 3, 1901

The Cincinnati market for cattle seems to be pretty good. Fair to good steers, $4.65 to $5.10; choice $5.15 to $5.25. p2c4

May 10, 1901

A K Adcock's "Whitefield" won in a race at Louisville Monday and ran second one day last week. p2c3

More about Oklahoma from Dr Miller, who has returned to Kentucky:
> Dr John C Miller and wife returned home Thursday of last week after an absence of four months in the southwest. Most of their time was spent in Oklahoma with the Doctor's two sons, Hugh and Meade, who live 3 1/2 and 6 1/2 miles respectively, south of the territory's capital, Oklahoma City. The Miller boys each own 320 acres of the finest rolling prairie land, lying between the North and South Canadian rivers. They cultivate each about 200 acres of wheat and 80 acres of oats, and cut the meadows and bale the hay from the mower as soon as cut. Their farms cost about $14,500 and they have refused $7,000 profit. Both are satisfied and happy and are popular with their neighbors. While gone, Dr Miller visited Nevada, Mo, the home of osteopathy, and took a course in magnetic healing and osteopathy, receiving diplomas in both branches. En route home Dr and Mrs Miller spent three weeks in Kansas City, which they pronounce a great city, full of happy and prosperous people. In conversation with the _Journal_ the Doctor said that notwithstanding the newspaper and other reports, he experienced no trouble of any kind during his absence, never had better health, and greatly enjoyed the trip which was full of comfort and pleasure. At some future date Dr Miller will favor the _Journal_ readers with another one of his interesting letters in which he will endeavor to show up in true color the various pathies of medicines, also giving a description of the country between Kansas and Galveston, with notices about ex-Kentuckians whom he saw in the west. p3c3

Bertha Hendren, Scottie's sister, has just married Alford Bennett. They were quietly married at Bloomington on Wednesday. The ceremony was performed by the pastor of the Christian Church. "The bride hansomely was attired in a traveling suit of venetian cloth and looked very pretty. She is the orphaned niece of Mesdames John March and James Millin, with whom she has been visiting since last October. Her home was with her sister, Mrs A K Adcock, at Nicholasville, Kentucky. She has won many friends here. The groom is a prosperous young business man, of Canton, Ill., where he is held in high esteem. Mr and Mrs Bennett will go to housekeeping at once in a neat new cottage home already prepared for them in Canton." p3c6 I don't know if her aunts were Hendrens or Tudors.

The *Sulphur Well Correspondent* writes:

*The little son of Frank Miller was quite sick a few days ago.*
*Askins & Ware have about completed extensive improvements to their shop.*
*Since the siege of sickness experienced in this section, there seems to be but little sickness.*
*Little Ray Miller fell from a wagon a few days ago and severely bruised his face, besides running a narrow risk of a broken neck.*
*Dr J C Miller and wife returned from their western trip and are the guests of Mr and Mrs T J Horine.*
*Mrs Mary E Wheeler, of Cincinnati, returned home Sunday after a visit of several days.*
*George Snowden's barn burned last Friday at about 2 pm. It contained considerable hay and farming equipment, all of which were destroyed. It was fully insured.* p2c3

The Askins & Ware blacksmith shop is across from where Dr Hendren lived, and still stands today.

May 17, 1901

The executors of the Wm Hendren estate are advertising a sale at public auction his farm of 50 acres located two miles east of Nicholasville on the Sulphur Well road. There is a seven room, two story house on the property. Farming implements and household and kitchen furniture will also be sold. He apparently only had two horses and a milk cow. p2c3

May 24, 1901

The *Sulphur Well Correspondent* writes:

*Oscar Hendren, Abe Burton and several other Madisonians were over from Edenton last Monday.*
*Mrs Gabriel Masters was taken suddenly and seriously ill last week, but is able to be out again.*
*Mrs Elizabeth Peel, of Pink, was taken down with an attack of pnuemonia last week, but it was only of short duration, being of mild form.*
*Luther Ware visited Lexington one day last week.*

Elbert Brumfield's son, who has been sick for some weeks, is improving and it is hoped will soon be out again.

Bert Easley and family, of Bowling Green, are visiting his father, Wm Easley, of Pink, and will remain for some time. Mr Easley has resided in Bowling Green for about nine years.

Elder Crabtree preached at the church Sunday morning and at night. The church has now no regular pastor since Elder Hildebrand left.

The heavy rains Saturday did considerable damage to growing crops and to plowed land along the border of the river in this and Garrard counties. Some fields seem to be literally washed away. In places fences were submerged in mud or entirely torn away by the force of accumulated mud and water. It was without doubt a cloudburst, and a tremendous one at that.

Carl Price, a colored man, who has been in trouble before, was arrested by George Snowden and Houston Woodward early Wednesday morning and taken to town for the alleged theft of a buggy rug belonging to Mr Snowden, which was taken from his buggy standing near the postoffice Tuesday night and thrown over a hedge fence near W B Walker's residence. It is said Price does not deny throwing the rug over the fence, but that another fellow had it and he hid it to "devil" him. p2c4

May 31, 1901

Asbury College is having its eleventh commencement exercises.

June 7, 1901

Charles Hemphill purchased the Wm Hendren farm for $97.25 per acre. He "bought the farm for his son-in-law, Mr S T Berryman, of Versailles, who will move here shortly and superintend Mr Hemphill's farm. Farming implements, household and kitchen furniture brought good prices." p2c5 This farm lies between the farm known as the Woods farm, when I was young, and the Chrisman Mill intersection.

"Dr Miller was seen mingling with the Court Day crowd in Richmond on Monday." p3c4

The *Sulphur Well Correspondent* writes:

Mrs Jas T West, who has been ailing for quite a while, is improving.

A spirit of improvement seems to have taken possession of our citizens and the town is on a boom.

Mr Louis Pilcher, of the Lexington Observer, was a guest of Dr Hendren's last Tuesday and Wednesday.

Miss Daisy Switzer, of Harrodsburg, was the guest of Mr and Mrs J W Cobb Thursday and Friday of last week.

Mr and Mrs J Reynolds have moved into the residence of Gabriel Masters to make it their home.

Mr Alex M Askins has been on the sick list for several days. Also Mrs A M Askins has been quite sick for some time.

Edward Chandler, of Edenton, was married to Mrs Morton Teater, of Buckeye, Garrard County, last Tuesday, at the home of the bride.

A new pike is prospected from Geo B Peel's place to Milford Fain's store, on the Nicholasville and Hunter's Ferry pike--and it will be a road long needed.

*There seems to be an epidemic of thievery in our little village. At least it seems that the thieves selected this point as a field of operation for a general raid this week. Monday night they visited the residence of J H Murphy, and entering through a window, stole his watch and pants containing about $1.50 in money and decamped, leaving the trousers in the front yard. They also visited the residence of Dr Hendren and attempted to affect an entrance through the rear hall, but made so much noise that the Doctor was awakened and scared the thieves off by getting up before they had gotten into his house. p2c3*

June 14, 1901

There has been a burglary "ring" with headquarters in Cincinnati, that has been operating in the area. They have been taking the stolen goods, particularly watches, back to Cincinnati for sale. The thieves also hit the Miles residence on the Sulphur Well Pike, and took dresses, pocket books, watches, and a small sum of money. p3c2-3

There is an excursion to Cincinnati on June 16th for the baseball game between Cincinnati and Pittsburg. "Coney Island, Chester Park, the Zoo, and all summer resorts are open." The round trip fare is only $1.25 p1c6

"Miss Mary Anderson Miller, youngest daughter of M M Miller, of Irvine, and neice of Dr John C Miller, received the highest honor of her class at Sayre Institute, Lexington, and as a result she will be given a scholarship for next session. p3c2 Seventy-five years later, my son, Steven Douglas Ware, went to Sayre and received similar scholarships almost every year that he was in high school.

Following the unfortunate death of a young man playing baseball on Sunday in Richmond, "the Rev H G Turner, pastor of the Methodist Church there took his text on Sabbath desecration, and in a vigorous sermon, scored the mayor and city council for permitting ball playing on Sunday. The church people there have become aroused on the subject and it is said that the mayor will be petitioned to issue an order prohibiting ball playing on the Sabbath." p3c6 I have always hated "blue" laws, and find it offensive that a minister would use the death of a youngster in a self- serving manner to stop something he didn't want anyway.

June 21, 1901

"There will be a gospel and temperance meeting in the court house yard Sunday afternoon at 4 o'clock. The exercises will consist of singing, preaching, etc." p3c2

The Rev R D Biven, who has been pastor of the Main Street Methodist Church in Nicholasville for the past two years was brought into court last Saturday and fined $5 and costs for assaulting one of the members of the church. It seems that a rumor has been circulating about the minister that reflected poorly on his character, and a committee from the church went to ask him about the matter. He became very angry and kicked one them down the stairs. One of the officers of the church says his resignation will be asked for at once. p3c2

June 28, 1901

"Mrs Julia Miller, of Elizabethtown, is visiting her sister, Mrs J H Marriott." p3c4 This is Rice's widow. I wonder how her relationship is with Dr and Mrs Miller. There has been no evidence that she received any property, or settlement. Several young people are "tenting" at the Chautauqua in Lexington (p3c3), and several others are spending ten days at Niagara Falls and other "points of interest". p3c4

July 5, 1901

Independence Day seems to have been ignored. You remember that everyone was very patriotic during the Spanish-American War.

July 12, 1901

J W Overstreet, better known as Pomp, the Little Hickman correspondent, has been one of the foremost advocates of good roads in the county. He says that when there were turnpikes that at least there were some good stretchs of road, and now that the roads are free that they have deterioriated. They are so bad in Jessamine, he says, that he has given up riding his bicycle. p1c3

"Oscar Hendren and Edna Prather of Edenton, were married in Richmond, on July 3." p2c2

"Miss Emma Hendren, of Richmond, and Mrs Alford Bennett (nee Hendren) of Canton, Ill, are visiting Mrs A K Adcock." p3c3

"Mr and Mrs A K Adcock will leave next week for St Louis to visit Mrs Adcock's sister, Mrs W C Crosley and brother, Pat Hendren, who has a splendid position with Simmons & Co hardware." p3c4 Lizzie Hendren Van Winkle, of Frankfort, was last heard from Dec 20, 1895. It appears that Lizzie has remarried a Crosley and moved to St Louis.

The *Sulphur Well Correspondent* writes:

*Miss Emma West is visiting Miss Ada Roberts, of Ruthton, Madison County.*
*Mrs Alice Owens, of Newport, is visiting Mrs Lon J Gibony.*
*Miss Mary Taylor, Lexington, is visiting her grandmother, Mrs Margaret Horine.*
*Ernest Grimes, of Lexington, is the guest of Misses Bertha and Blanche Askins.*
*Chas. W Horine and Miss Dora Murphy visited relatives at Lexington Sunday.*
*Talton Hendren, of Louisville, visited James Hendren Saturday and Sunday of last week.*
*Larry Bolan has been busily engaged for a week or so in piking the driveway from the pike to the residence of J P Turner.*
*Threshing has begun in full blast with a prospect of about one-half a crop.*
*Dillard Hunter lost a valuable horse from overheat last week, during the heated term.*
*W B Walker is able to be out again attending to business, after a six months absence in town.*

*Harry DeWitt has been appointed a store keeper guager and assigned to Old Lexington Club distillery.*

*Mrs Bertha Bennett (nee Hendren) of Canton, Ill, is visiting relatives and friends here.*

*The farmers are all hale, hearty, hopeful and happy as the prospects for fine crops of corn, hemp, and tobacco are cheering.*

*There are only two steam attraction threshers located at this place but the boys expect to "fan out" a golden harvest of sheckels in competion with 20 or 30 other machines of the county as long as the thing lasts. Hope they will succeed as competion is the life of trade even in threshing.*

*Dr G M Hendren has completed painting his "castle" a beautiful white, red, green, gray and several other colors, and is highly complimented on the improvement he has made. Hope it will prove contagious and that others will be attacked by the same spirit of much needed improvement in our once beautiful village. A slight expenditure of muscle and means would soon regain its lost prestige. p2c4*

Dr Hendren hasn't mentioned it, but the Spears correspondent brags that "their beautiful little village is now connected with the different counties by telephone." p2c5

July 19, 1901

"W S and W L Hendren, as executors of the estate of Wm Hendren, dec'd sold publicly Monday ten shares of National Bank stock...." p3c3 The price was about $130 per share.

"Dr Geo M Hendren, of Ambrose, left Wednesday on a prospecting trip through Oklahoma and Indian Territory." p3c4 One of his daughters married Hugh Miller, who is now living in Oklahoma.

July 26, 1901

Dr Hendren's prospecting trip may be related to the situation paraphrased in this article:

> The Kiowa, Comanche, and Apache reservations, located in the southern part of Oklahoma, are being opened for settlement. The area is roughly bounded on the south by Texas, on the west by Greer County, on the north by Washita County and the Washita Indian Reservation. The latter is also being opened for settlement. Four new counties are to be created out of the reservations, each with a county seat. Lots are to be sold by auction, each bidder being limited to one business and one residential lot. Most of the land to be opened is prairie land, which is arable, up to the Washita Mountain range. The railroads are competing to secure choice routes, and an army of settlers are on the borders waiting for the opening.

The writer of the article (source unnamed) says that "there are vast possibilities of undreamed of wealth." p1c3-4 This was a powerful magnet for farmers who were still getting the same prices for their crops that they got a generation earlier, and caused many to leave Kentucky.

Dr Hendren offers another poem before leaving that he titled "My First Sweetheart". p1c5

I believe that one of the early subjects of the Sulphur Well correspondent just passed away at the age of 51. He is Robert (Bob) Mosely who suffered from Bright's disease. It doesn't appear that he ever married. He was for several years a U S storekeeper, and may have been assigned to the Gray distillery near Sulphur Well at one time. p3c4

August 2, 1901

Dr Hendren has sent back two letters to the <u>Journal</u> from Oklahoma, one dated July 21 from Oklahoma City and the second dated July 24 from El Reno. He says that "Of all the hot trips discontented mortals take to an imaginary quest for a land that is `fairer than this'... we experienced the hotest...." He says that he went through Tennessee, Alabama, Mississippi, Arkansas, Indian Territory and Oklahoma to get to his distination. The crops he saw were very poor, and showed the effects of the heat and lack of water. Dr Hendren said that there were a few fields along the bottoms of the South Canadian River that might make a barrel of corn to the acre. He noted:

> The high temperature and want of rain has made this country at present a district of dryness and dust, the mercury ranging all the way from 104 degrees to 110 degrees in the shade. No one attempts to wear a coat or vest, but lays open his collar, rolls up his sleeves.... Dust is everywhere. A ride of one hundred yards covers you with red dust. Your clothes are red; the fields, fences, and farmhouses are red....

Despite this rather harsh description of the area he says that everyone is astonished at the "surprising progress and prosperity of a city still not in her teens by several years" p1c3

Dr Hendren has gotten himself in the middle of a land rush in the middle of a hot summer, and he's not happy. He says there are over 100,000 people, a cross-section of humanity, trying to get land! He, Meade and Hugh Miller, joined 6,000 other people on the train to El Reno, that was packed "from floor to ceiling", with people even riding the top of the cars. When they arrived, they joined a long, double line of people waiting to register for the government lottery of the lands. After what seemed an eternity to Dr Hendren, they returned to the train to find a spot anywhere they could, "or lay down and die--nobody cares which you do." He say that registration closes July 26th, then the drawing begins for farm land. He thinks that the chance of drawing a farm is nil, since he expects so many people to register. The sale of lots in the new county seats begins on August 6. Lawton is considered the best location. He thinks that he, Hugh, and Meade will go there to invest in a lot or two. He closes by saying he will write to the <u>Journal</u> "from Lawton if I go there." p1c3-4

Wheat prices in Kentucky are the pits. The Pinckard correspondent says that the highest price paid for wheat in that neighborhoods has been 65 cents per bushel. p2c1

August 9, 1901

"England is preparing for the most magnificent spectacle in its history, the coronation of Edward VII." p2c1

August 16, 1901

We didn't get Dr Hendren's letter from Lawton. There is however, a note from Luther Spears who has been with a threshing outfit in Oklahoma. He was in El Reno during the drawing, and says that thousands of acres of the lands are almost worthless and that within a short time the homesteads can be bought "for a song". p3c6

August 23, 1901

Now we get Dr Hendren's letter, one that I wish I could reproduce in its entirety. In it he recounts his travel by wagon and horseback from Oklahoma City to Chickasaw. His party had a scary crossing of the South Canadian River, ran a gauntlet of robbers and cut-throats, and encountered inhospitable land with little water. From there they went on to Lawton which was crawling with lawless people, "at least 50,000 people in tents, camped around an oblong square of 160 acres of ground." As you can imagine, it took a while to sell all the lots in a town. The prices ranged from $65 to $475 for lots outside the center of town. He expected the center lots to bring several thousand dollars, and must have decided not to bid, because he then set out for Anadarko, another county seat. Lots there were selling for $60 to $1,100, but he didn't like the town; it had too many Indians and renegade whites to suit him. His party boarded the train for El Reno. Although he was appalled by the barbarity of the land, he concludes in this manner:
> But one thing is certain--and time will prove the truth of my assertion--and that is that whoever comes to this country, either into old Oklahoma or into this new country just opened up and sticks a few years will not regret it. He has no chance back East but here the world is before him and a good one it is. p1c3-4

August 30, 1901

"Dr John C Miller will sell on Saturday, Sept. 14 to the highest bidder, his Madison farm on Barnes' Mill Pike two miles from Richmond, containing 294 acres with fine improvements." p3c1

September 6, 1901

"Charles Hendren, son of Postmaster J H Hendren, will shortly move to Winchester where he has secured a position with the Adams Express." p2c2

With no hint that he has been away the *Sulphur Well Correspondent* writes:

> Jas P Prather, of Edenton, was over last week.
> W B Barton, Buckeye, was over last week.
> Rev Crabtree preached here last Saturday and Sunday nights.
> Allen A Vincent, of Cottonburg, was visiting this section last Tuesday.
> Lieut Hill, of Poosey, was visiting this vicinity recently.
> John Taylor, who has been very ill, is reported better.
> Ezekiel Vincent has returned from a week's visit to relatives in Madison County.
> A lodge of the Woodmen of the World will be organized here shortly.
> William Warner, of Madison County, was over Monday among his many friends.
> C T Taylor, of Lexington, was down last Thursday on a visit to his relations.
> Talton Hendren, of Lexington, was here on a visit to relatives last Saturday.
> F M Hudson was on a visit to Fayette County last Tuesday.
> Louis Pilcher, of the Lexington Morning Democrat, was here last Friday.
> Thomas Masters, who has been seriously ill with typhoid fever, is a great deal better.
> Samuel Switzer, who has had a second attack of appendicitis, is able to be out again.
> Mrza S K Neveeya, who lectured here last Sunday on Persia and her customs, religion, etc.

lectured at the Christian Church again Wednesday night at 7:30 pm on the same subject. p2c3

September 13, 1901

"When the news flashed over the wires Friday afternoon that President McKinley had been shot at the exposition grounds in Buffalo, during a public reception, very few at first believed it." p2c1 The attempted assassin's name is Leon Czolgosz. The editor blames the tradegy on the immigration of a lawless class of anarchists called the Mafia. p2c1

> President McKinley is rapidly recovering and will soon be able to take up his duties at Washington, if unlooked for complications do not come up. p2c1

From the <u>Estill Leader</u>: "Mr M M Miller and family are making preparations for moving to Lexington where they will go in a short time." p3c4

The *Sulphur Well Correspondent* writes:

> William Cornelison, formerly of this place, but now of Louisville, visited John Carr last Monday.
> Caperton Vincent sold his place near the iron bridge to Milton Peel for $150. He will move back to his old home in Madison County.
> C T Taylor, of Lexington, is visiting here for a few days.
> J H Turner bought five head of cattle from Andrew J Cobb at 3c.
> F M Horine sold to Luke Shearer 15 head of hogs averaging about 120 lbs at $5.20 per cwt.
> Old corn is selling at from 60 to 65c per bushel.
> Mrs Bettie Murphy is the guest of her son, J Howard Murphy, for a few days.
> Caryton Turpin sold a lot of hogs to A C Miles for 5c per pound.
> J P Turner sold a load of corn to Ben Spears at $3.25 per barrel; also a lot of hogs to J Carroll at 5c. p2c2

September 20, 1901

"President McKinley had a sudden change for the worst", and died Saturday morning at 2:15am. p2c1 A memorial service was held at the M E Church, South, Sunday night. A very large crowd attended the service. p3c3

September 27, 1901

Dr John C Miller took down his farm, near Richmond, which was offered for sale Saturday, there not being any bidders present. p2c2 That's strange!

The *Sulphur Well Correspondent* writes:

*An epidemic of bad colds is prevalent in this vicinity.*
*Eld Clark held services at the church Sunday and Sunday night.*
*Mr Bennett, of Canton, Ill., is visiting relatives here. He will return to Illinois in about two weeks.*
*Mrs Theresa Tudor, of Bloomington, Ill, is visiting her father, James Hendren.*
*Mrs Hugh Miller and two children, of Oklahoma City, OT, who have been visiting her parents, Dr and Mrs G M Hendren, for some weeks, returned home Tuesday by way of Memphis, Tenn.*
*Some gentlemen from Madison County were over Sunday looking for a well-know thief who had stole a horse in that county. In the same neighborhood he appropriated a saddle to his own use, as well as some wagon lines, probably with a view of having them ready when he stole a wagon and team. Then to see if he had time to steal the whole neighborhood, he stole a schoolhouse clock. Then (he) broke into Milton Colton's store and took some loose change. Coming over to this coutny he put himself on the invalid list after his hard and arduous task of theft and sent for a doctor. No doubt but what he thought while the Doc was feeling his pulse he could go through his pockets, as doctors are alwasys known to be loaded down with "easy" earned cash. Yet before he recovered he got wind that someone was after him and skipped out by the light of the moon. p2c5*

October 4, 1901

The twenty-ninth annual meeting of the the Kentucky Trotting Horse Breeders Association begins on October 3. p2c3

October 11, 1901

The *Sulphur Well Correspondent* writes:

*Ezekial Hendren sold Monday to J H Hare 26 shoats averaging 30 lbs at 5c.*
*Mrs Elizabeth Miller left Monday for Irvine and vicinity for a three week's visit.*
*Elder Simpson preached at the church last Sunday and will hold services again on the fourth Sunday.*
*There seems to be a big demand for old corn and there will be for new, but land owners have less and less corn planted each year.*

> *This could be very appropriately called dog town; but what a howl it would raise were it proposed to exterminate the useless canines.*
>
> *A few nights ago Houston Woodward fired two shots at a suppositionist horse, or some other kind of a thief, but without any known results.*
>
> *John P Miller and children, of Irvine, stopped over on their way home from Conference, Saturday and Sunday, with his mother, Mrs E Miller.*
>
> *Alfred Bennett and wife, of Canton, Ill., who have been visiting here for some weeks, returned home Friday. p2c1*

Dogs and thieves seem to be making life in Sulphur Well miserable for Dr Hendren.

October 18, 1901

The *Sulphur Well Correspondent* writes:

> *James Clark, of Frankfort, is visiting his mother, Mrs Harriet Clark, this week.*
>
> *William Masters, of Bloomington, Ill., is visiting his many friends and relatives in this neighborhood.*
>
> *Sam Allen, of Indiana, was summoned home to Garrard County, near Sugar Creek, by the critical illness of his mother and brother, Ras Allen.*
>
> *John S Masters and wife, of Lebanon, Ind., are visiting friends here after an absence of several years, he having gone away in 1851. He has only paid one short visit since that time in 1857, to his native home. p2c3*

October 25, 1901

Meade Miller sent the Journal a picture post card showing a business block at Oklahoma City. p3c3

November 1, 1901

Nicholasville was visited last Friday by a "representative of Northern capitalists" in the interest of the Blue Grass Interurban Railway that would connect the towns of the region with electric lines. They also proposed supplying the town with electricity. p3c3

The Secretary of the State Board of Health advises that all valuable dogs be muzzled and that all worthless dogs be killed because rabies has become such a problem. p3c3

"Levi Hendren, who moved from Jessamine County to Clearwater, Kan, two years ago, arrived Saturday with a view of locating here again." p3c4

November 8, 1901

The result of the election was to increase the Democratic majority in the State Legislature. p2c1 The Democrats also swept all the city and county offices. p3c4

"Mrs Bertha Bennett, who has been spending several weeks with relatives here, has returned to her home at Canton, Ill." p3c4 Her brother "Harry Hendren who has been in St Louis for the past year, has returned to his home here on account of bad health, where he will spend the winter." p3c4

November 15, 1901

"Clayton West will shortly move from Dr Miller's place to A W Robinson's farm, in Logana neighborhood, Marshall Davis has rented the Miller farm for the ensuing year." p2c1

The *Sulphur Well Correspondent* writes:

*M T Whitaker, of Garrard County, was over Monday.*
*Mrs Caperton Vincent is down with malarial fever, but is improving.*
*J H Turner is having extensive additions made to his residence.*
*The telephone line is now complete to Teater's store at Pink.*
*Elbert Walker left Tuesday for a week's hunting in the mountains.*
*J H Turner sold two head of fat cattle to W C Tutt at 3 1/2c.*
*George Moore sold his place Tuesday to Wm Walters for $550.*
*Caperton Vincent will move back to his farm in Madison County, Dec 1.*
*William Hill, of Madison County, was visiting in the county last week for several days.*
*Mr and Mrs J P Turner visited Rev H G Turner, at Richmond, lask week.*
*F M Horine sold 10 head of 1,000 pound cattle to Elbert Walker for Simon Weil, of Lexington, at 3 1/2c.*
*John Tudor, formerly of Madison County, but for the past 17 years a resident of Illinois, is visiting friends in the county.*
*Speed Taylor, after a residence of six years in Texas, has returned to make Kentucky his home again.*
*Smiley Reynolds, who has been living in Illinois for 25 years, is on a visit to friends and relatives in the county.*
*Mrs Sam Moberly and wife of Edenton, Madison County, were visiting James Hendren Saturday and Sunday.*
*A M Askins, Thomas Walker and Dr Hendren had telephones put into their residences last week.*
*Corn is selling at $2.50, and $3 is talked of delivered. Many a poor old cow's hide will go to the tanyard before this winter is near over.*
*Hogs are selling at $4.50 to $5 and some 20 head were sold by J H Hare at $6.50 to W C Tutt, the butcher.*
*James Woodward, Sr, who has been confined to his room for some time, was out again during the recent pleasant weather.*
*N P Cobb, of near Mt Lebanon, has bought the farm of J N Hendren near Edenton. Mr Hendren recently purchased the farm of Nat Cotton near Cottonburg, for $10,000.*
*Col Richard Young, a well-known character of this section, has moved to Madison to make that county his future stamping ground.* p2c1

You can see civilization coming! Electric lights in Nicholasville, telephones in Sulphur Well. We had one of the few telephones at the Well, and people came to our house all the time to use it. I remember going to get people when other people called for them at our house.

### November 22, 1901

This is Wm Herman Jesse's parents: "Miss Helen Wolfe, second daughter of Mr and Mrs B(ernard) Wolfe, and Mr Watson Jesse, of Woodford County, were married in Lexington, Wednesday afternoon at the residence of Mrs Mary R Young, with Esq Ben D Bell officiating. Mr Jesse is a brother of Prof Madison Jesse, principal of the graded school in Versailles. He is engaged in farming. After the ceremony Mr and Mrs Jesse drove to the newly furnished home where an elegant supper was in waiting. Miss Dora Wolfe accompanied her sister to Lexington." p3c4

### November 29, 1901

Hugh and Meade Miller are partners, and the managers of the farm department of the Jas Mechan & Co. (Realtors). Their ad: "Do you want Oklahoma land cheap? If you do, address people you know." p2c4

The cars are coming! "Henry Fournier, of Paris, France, champion automobilist of the world, went three miles on Oakley track at Cincinnati Saturday in 3:50 and the track was very heavy at that." p3c2

The *Sulphur Well Correspondent* writes:

*N D Davis sold to James Carroll 30 shoats at 4 1/2c.*
*Roberts & Winkle sold this week to Willard Davis 110 bushels of hemp seed at $2.25 per bushel.*
*A M Askins, Luther Ware and others have been hunting and fishing in Garrard County, near Buena Vista.*
*The church here has decided by unanimous vote to employ for the ensuing year, as its pastor, Elder Hildebrand, who has preached here for some time with entire satisfaction.*
*Elbert Walker, Clint and James Woodward have returned from a hunting trip in Adair County. They had a pleasant time and killed about 300 quail. p2c4*

### December 6, 1901

"Messrs Frank Buford, Joe Smither and Miss Nellie Hendren, of Nicholasville and Mr and Mrs R L French, of Richmond, spent Thanksgiving with Miss Emma Hendren at Speedwell." p3c4

Something that I may not have mentioned in all the years so far because it had not struck me before, is the prevalence of fraternal orders in Jessamine County. I knew that my great grandfather Francis S Miller was a Mason, but there are now five orders published in the paper each week--Masonic, IOOF, Knights of Pythias, AOUW, and the Knights of Maccabees. As a former member of Rotary, I know how these organizations bind members together. I just didn't realize the extent of "exclusionary" organizations there were a hundred years ago. You may recall that I have mentioned other organizations as well, when I once remarked that someone in Davis County that wasn't a Democrat and a Baptist must have felt lonely. I guess what I'm saying is that the spirit of community is hindered more than helped by these organizations, regardless of how much good each one does individually.

December 13, 1901

The Atlanta mule market is at a standstill. The traders there are merely buying to maintain stock. You remember in the "good old days" that carloads of mules were assembled in Jessamine for the Atlanta market. p1c3

So many fires are started by Christmas trees that insurance men are talking of prohibiting them or excluding losses caused by them. p2c3

Mrs Sutherland's is definitely a Christmas kind of a place! You should place your orders for oysters and celery with her. She also has all kinds of nuts, confections, fine candies, crystalized fruits, chocolates, and bon-bons. p3c2 There is no comparion with advertisements in today's paper and twenty years ago. The merchants are featuring the items that would make good gifts, as opposed to just their names and "notions" of past years.

Times are definitely changing. Hagan's, in Winchester, advertises gasoline engines, portable and stationary. p3c6 However, no cars are yet owned in Nicholasville.

Story paraphrased: A visitor dropped into a back pew of the church, and whispered to a parishioner "How long has he been preaching?". The parishioner thought for a moment and replied "About thirty or forty years, I reckon". "Well" said the stranger "I guess I'll stay then. He must be nearly done." p3c1

The Jessamine Institute has established a new department--business--that offers bookkeeping, stenography, typewriting and telegraphy. p3c2 Notice that it is no longer called the "Female" Institute.

December 20, 1901

J M Hendren is the postmaster at Speedwell. p2c2

December 27, 1901

A year-ending letter from the *Sulphur Well Correspondent*:

*N C Cobb, of Cottonsburg, was visiting friends in the county, Monday.*
*Small-pox is reported at Silver Creek and Kirksville, Madison County.*
*Born to the wife of Bailey Richardson on the 18th inst, a daughter.*
*Elisha and Simpson Warren, of Edenton, were visiting in the county, Tuesday.*
*Howard King and Mrs Wm King were visiting N D Davis a few days last week.*
*Thomas Peel, who has been located at Pontiac, Ill, arrived home last Saturday.*
*John Taylor, Louisville, who had his skull cracked by the police, was visiting his relatives here a few days last week.*
*Eld Geo W Hildebrand will preach here the third Lord's Day in January, which is the beginning of his pastorate of the church the ensuing year. p2c1*

Much change, much news. Another year has passed. I see them kaleidoscopically.

## DR HENDREN IN OKLAHOMA - 1902

Dr Hendren, caught up in the speculative movement, travels extensively in Oklahoma. In the process of writing letters about his travels he becomes a raconteur of the times.

### January 3, 1902

The *Journal* reports that there were the usual dances, receptions, dinners, and house parties during the holidays. p3c4

There have been 11,279 cases of small-pox in Kentucky in the past two years, scattered throughout 108 of the 119 counties. However, there were only 184 deaths. There were 382,280 persons vaccinated. p1c3

### January 10, 1902

"Miss Hare, of Ambrose, is visiting her sister, Mrs McClellan Johnston, Lancaster." p3c4

The *Sulphur Well Correspondent* writes:

*W H Hare sold 15 head of hogs to James Carroll, Saturday, at 5 3/4c.*
*Milton Fain residing at Pink, went to town Monday and then notified his family that he had left them indefinitely.*
*Cap Hill, of Madison County, was on a visit to friends in the county last Monday.*
*N B Coy and Wm Prewitt, both of near Kirksville, and prominent citizens, are said to have small-pox, and Miss Bessie Prather, of Edenton, also is reported to have the dread disease.*
*Steve N Snowden sold Saturday to James Carroll eleven head of hogs averaging 271 lbs, at 5 3/4c.* p3c6

### January 17, 1902

Good old boys to the fore. "Ham Dozier.-Mr J H Dozier, who has for the last three years been with the firm of Hawkins & Sweeney, and for nine years previous to that with the firm of Cassell & Price, has accepted a position with Chinn & Todd.... Mr Dozier is a young man of ability, and has a great many friends, all of whom wish him the best of success in his new position." p1c3 Several of the young men of the eighties that were friends have become salesmen or drummers.

The *Sulphur Well Correspondent* writes:

*The infant son of John Snowden died Tuesday night.*
*Corn is selling at $3 per barrel delivered and hay at $12 in the rick.*
*Born to the wife of Albert Turner on the 12th inst, a son.*
*Rain is needed for the wheat and stock water is becoming scarce in places.*
*Next Sunday Eld Geo W Hildebrand will preach at the Christian Church.*
*The caw of the crow that used to be so familiar in our boyhood days, but has of late years become almost silent in the land, was again heard in this section Monday as several*

*thousand of the knowing birds held a big "cawcus" on the big branch for some purpose known only to crowdom. In a short time only they had departed and not a caw has been heard there since.*

*Runaway Accident.-Last Saturday night three young men, two of them sons of Charles Cobb and one a son of Zach Taylor, as they were driving home from town happened to a dangerous accident. The horse they were driving, being somewhat vicious, ran off after kicking out the dashboard and seat of the buggy. The accident occurred coming down the hill near N D Miles' place. Young Taylor was thrown over the fence into Miles' field, but sustained no great injury. Young James A Cobb, more unlucky than the rest, was run over by the buggy receiving severe injuries. The right leg was broken above the ankle and his right ankle dislocated, and besides other bruises, the left knee cap received a partial fracture. The badly smashed-up young man was brought on by his companions to the residence of Dr Hendren where his wounds were attended to and he was sent on to his home near Pleasant Hill. His wounded limbs have been placed in plaster and he is doing well under the circumstances. The other young Cobb, who has only recently returned from the Philippines, received no injuries whatever. p2c2*

January 24, 1902

"Meade Miller, representing the James Meecham & Co, Real Estate Agents at Oklahoma City, O T, will arrive in Nicholasville, Jan 27, and will be prepared to give all who visit this rapidly growing section low rates of transportation as well as to look after their comfort, etc. Mr Miller will return to Oklahoma, Feb 4." p2c3

The *Sulphur Well Correspondent* writes:

*Miss Irene Bourne, of State College, Lexington, was home visiting her parents Sunday.*
*Eld Geo W Hildebrand, of Wilmore, preached his first sermon for the year to a large audience Sunday.*
*James Allen Cobb, who was so badly mangled in a runaway a week ago is improving rapidly.*
*Caperton Vincent, formerly a resident of this county was over Monday on a visit to his old neighbors and friends.*
*Mrs Geo W Davis, of Madison County, is not expected to live and her demise is hourly expected.*
*Elisha Warren and son Simpson, of Edenton, substantial farmers of Madison County, were over last Monday.*
*George W Warren, of Idalia, were visiting here among his many friends yesterday.*
*Meade Miller, of Oklahoma City, will arrive here on the 27th inst, and leave for the Territory on Feb 4th. He hopes to get up a good crowd to accompany him to the "land of promise" and will be prepared to furnish the lowest transportation possible.* p2c4

January 31, 1902

"The Board of Council met last night for the purpose of granting the Blue Grass Traction Company a franchise to construct and operate an electric railroad through Nicholasville." p3c6

"The heavy rains of Sunday night, Monday, Tuesday and Tuesday night, lasting through Wednesday, resulted in a sleet, the like of which has not been experienced in this section for years." p3c3

The *Sulphur Well Correspondent* writes:

*Dr John C Miller sold to Jas H Turner 40 acres of the Mrs Melinda Masters' tract at $35 per acre.*
*Mrs N B Long left Thursday for a visit to her children in Decatur, Ill.*
*Thomas Peel started for Pontiac, Ill, Wednesday, where he has a good position at $49 per month.*
*Richard Fain sold to James Foster his place of four acres and residence --------------lower toll-house last week for ------.*
*Meade Miller, of Oklahoma City, O T arrived Monday and will remain till Feb 4th. Anyone visiting the "Land of Promise" can get very low rates going with the party.*
*The heavy sleet, the worst we have had since -------- 1892, has greatly damaged the timber, fruit and shade trees, as well as completely crippled the telephone lines. p2c1*

In case you read the above letter without noticing, please note now that "a good position" pays $49 per month!

February 7, 1902

The Kentucky River is gradually being made navigable as the locks, located about every twenty miles, are being built. Lock No 9 is now under construction at Valley View. p1c4

"Miss Russie Adcock entertained about thirty of her friends January 30, in honor of her fourteenth birthday and a most pleasant time was reported by the misses and lassies, each wishing Miss Russie many more such occasions." p3c5

February 14, 1902

"Mrs J P Overstreet who has been dangerously ill of pneumonia and heart trouble is improving." p2c2 This is Sarah Miller.

I don't know if things are going well, or poorly, but Meade Miller is staying in Kentucky until the 18th rather than leaving on the 4th as first intended. p2c3

February 21, 1902

"The Journal would like to get an expression from the farmers of Jessamine why our court days are getting to be such a failure. If it is because the stock has been ordered kept off the streets, then let the council take some action in the matter. The crowds are large, but business as a general thing with the merchants is not what it used to be." p2c5

An "Old Time Fiddler" contest will be held in Nicholasville on March 17th. Each contestant must play a 5 to 7 minute piece, twice, not repeating his first program. All contestants then must play "Yankee Doodle" and "Dixie" just before the prizes are awarded. p3c3

Valentine parties were numerous this year, and they were not only for kids and youth people either.

## February 28, 1902

Dr Hendren, our Correspondent, writes the Journal from Oklahoma City. It seems that he, W L Hendren and Morris Dean, along with several other Kentuckians accompanied Meade Miller back to Oklahoma. He says his next letter will be from Lawton where he is next headed. p1c3 There is also an article about the good doctor in the Daily Times Journal of Oklahoma City:

> Dr Geo M Hendren, an eminent physician, who combines literary talent with his practice, is in the city for a few days from Nicholasville, visiting his daughter, Mrs Hugh Miller, who resides near Oklahoma City. Dr Hendren is the author of many pretty and tender poems of tender sentiment, among them 'The Little Old Log School House on the Hill', 'My Mother's Chair', 'The Wayside Mill', and others of popularity. The poetical doctor combines shrewd business acumen with his other gifts and left Kentucky for the West several times to invest and last August he was in the Lawton push where he bought some town lots which he hasn't seen since. If things are as represented over there he will add some improvements. Col William Hendren, the doctor's handsome brother, accompanied him. 'Doc' Dean, of Pink, came out with the Hendrens and is over at South McAlister, where he has a son. p3c3

## March 7, 1902

N B Long, of Sulphur Well, is selling his stock and farming implements at public sale on Wednesday, March 19 at the farm of W H Hoover, Jr. p2c6

"The storehouse of Mr J H Turner, of Ambrose, was destroyed by fire Thursday night of last week about 8 o'clock. It contained 20,000 pounds of hemp and 800 pounds of flour. Loss over $1,800, with no insurance. The origin of the fire is unknown." p3c2

## March 14, 1902

Dr Hendren writes again from Oklahoma, but not Lawton, as he had promised. He is still in Oklahoma City, and this letter concerns climate and crops, and the various business enterprises of Oklahoma City. p1c3

Home from Oklahoma.-Dr Geo M Hendren and his brother, W L Hendren, who have been on a visit of several weeks to the cities of Lawton and Oklahoma City, O T, returned home yesterday morning. They expressed themselves as being well pleased with their trip to the progressive West, so much that they both have now an interest in that country. They report the climate as all that could be desired as a summer resort. The other gentlemen who accompanied them are well pleased with the prospects of the country, expecially Mr Morris Dean and Louis Pilcher who have located at South McAlister, I T." p3c3

The cold, bad weather has played havoc with the lamb crop. p2c2 Dogs have taken a terrible toll on sheep this winter. Many farmers report losing fifteen to twenty after an attack.

March 21, 1902

Dr Hendren's Lawton letter arrived at the <u>Journal</u>. He described their attendance at one of the war dances that the Indians put on--for money--these days. He said:
> They form a circle of squaws and papooses and dance to the so-called music of a sort of drum beaten by three or four bucks at the same time chanting a montonous, dolorous chant that is more of a discordant howl than anything else imaginable, and is anything but agreeable to the nerves of a white man ....

Dr Hendren said that he and Will stood it about as long as possible and then slipped out.
> I don't know how Will felt when we slipped out throught the flap in the tent, I had that vague feeling a child feels at night when telling ghost stories--an apprehension of something about to grab us from behind.

He says that in less than a year that Lawton already has a population of seven or eight thousand inhabitants, and that all types of business are well represented there. p1c3-4

The fiddler's contest was successful, even though the weather turned bitterly cold, and there was only one stove in the building. p3c4

March 28, 1902

"Miss Dora Murphy has returned from a trip to Louisville." p3c4

"Harry Hendren, brother of Mrs A K Adcock, leaves Saturday for St Louis, Mo., to resume his position with the Simmons Hardware Co., for whom he formerly worked." p3c4

April 4, 1902

Still another letter from Dr Hendren about his trip to Indian Territory. He begins by telling how comfortable it is to go by rail from Memphis to Oklahoma City, with reclining seats, etc. A few miles from Oklahoma City he came upon McLoud, with "great wheat fields" flourishing around it. Next was Shawnee, a city of 8,000, "with car shops, foundries, manufactories, large mercantile establishments, enterprising people with a good farming country around it." Tecumseh, the county seat of Pottawotomie County, "is another good live town, but is on a branch of the main line a few miles away to the south of Shawnee." Finally, there is South McAlister 120 miles from Oklahoma City. It has 6,000 people and "is quite a railroad center, but above all is a coal mining town." He speaks of other Oklahoma towns, and their growth, because of new rail lines, coal, and the influx of people, and says that growth is "not a matter of centuries ..., but of months." He concludes his journey back through Arkansas into Little Rock, and across the Mississippi "into Memphis, the terminus of the Choctaw Route." p1c3-4

Tom Hendren's daughter: "The pupils of Miss Nellie Hendren's music class had intended to give a recital April 7, but on account of Miss Hendren's recent illness, has been postponed until April 14." p3c1

Rice Miller's widow is remarrying: "The engagement is announced of Mrs Julia Payne Miller, of Elizabethtown, Ky, and Prof David Spencer Hill, of the faculty of Smith Academy, Washington University, St Louis, Mo., and a son of Dr Felix R Hill, pastor of the Broadway Methodist Church of this city (Louisville)." The bride-elect "is known and loved in a wide circle in Kentucky for her charming and gracious personality." The date of the wedding has not been set, but is expected to be in June. p3c4

The *Sulphur Well Correspondent* writes:

*"Ricks" Baker left last week for Illinois.*
*Ben House sold to J H Turner a load of corn at 65c per bushel.*
*William Bourne left last week for an indefinite visit at Decatur, Ill.*
*Eld Geo W Hildebrand preached to a good audience and his sermon was well received and appreciated.*
*Hemp breaking seems to be a slow process as the weather continues damp.*
*Thomas Tudor, of Edenton, Madison County, is over visiting friends on his way to the west.*
*N B Long and his family left last week for Decatur, Ill., to make that place their future home.*
*Rev H G Turner, Richmond, visited his parents, Mr and Mrs J P Turner, a few days last week.*
*Oscar Sageser will leave Tuesday for Amarillo, Texas, to be gone at least three weeks. If he likes he may stay longer. Enroute he will stop at Oklahoma City.*
*Jno W Taylor, of Irvine, has gone to Oklahoma City. Immediately on his arrival there he secured a job of carpentering at 35 cents an hour.*
*M F Davis is thinking of going to Oklahoma City or some other live town of the Territory to go into business. J B Smither will accompany him.*
*Messrs J P and J H Turner contemplate taking a trip out west, taking in the Indian and Oklahoma Territories. They will probably go early in April and may be gone some weeks.* p2c3

Well, the Millers and the Hendrens have sure stirred up the natives! It's easy to see why people are excited about an area that is growing and developing before their very eyes. Whereas the population of Jessamine has remained approximately the same through the past two decades, the Oklahoma towns have reached populations twice that of Nicholasville in a matter of months, or at most a few years. They want to leave a stagnant economy for a growing economy. You can see from the price of corn or the price of cattle, sheep, and hogs that prices haven't changed in the past twenty years.

## April 11, 1902

"Cecil Rhodes left $10 million for Anglo-American scholarships in Oxford College. The will provides two scholarships for each state and territory in the United States, tenable for three years." p2c1

"Dr Jno C Miller will erect a handsome residence on the lot purchased of County Clerk N R Dickerson." p3c1

The *Sulphur Well Correspondent* writes:

*Mr and Mrs Crossley, of St Louis, Mo., were visiting for some days last week relatives in this neighborhood. They have many relatives in the county, as Mrs Crossley is a sister to Mrs A K Adcock.*
*The snow Tuesday morning was quite a surprise, as everybody had been gardening in the warm sunshine of Monday. The fall of temperature in one night from about 70 degrees to down into the 20's was enough to make a Greenlander's spinal column shiver.*
*Mr Joseph Walton, a tobacco farmer, of Georgetown, with his family, has moved into the old Alverson house, lately vacated by Gabriel Masters who has moved in with his wife's mother, Mrs James.*
*Died, on the 2nd inst, of consumption, Maud, daughter of James Masters at his residence near Pink.*
*M F Davis returned Sunday evening from a short business trip to Cincinnati, and will leave Wednesday for a trip to Louisville.*
*Dillard Fain has moved into the house opposite A M Askins residence recently vacated by R Lee Davis.*
*A letter from Oscar Sageser says that he has arrived at Oklahoma City, but was delayed for some time at Chattanooga by high water.*
*Wm G Jones, a prosperous merchant of Buckeye, accompanied by his son, William, were visiting N D Davis last Sunday.*
*Gardening is somewhat late on account of the frequent rains, snows and boreal blasts.*
*McClellan Johnston and family, of Lancaster, were visiting Mr and Mrs W H Hare several days this and last week.*
*Morris Dean, near Pink, gave a pleasant little social party to the young folks Tuesday night. They enjoyed themselves till a late hour before the entertainment broke up.*
*At the sale of Evan Fain, deceased, last Wednesday a large crowd was in attendance and the personalty brought fair prices.*
*This place is quite a tobacco market and a good many thousands pounds are annually sold here and, after prizing, shipped to Louisville and Cincinnati. It brings this season all the way, according to grade, from 4 1/2 to 8 cts per lb.*
*Hon N D Miles remodeled the old tollgate house at the forks of Chrisman Mills and Sulphur Well pike roads into a more modern like dwelling and otherwise improved the place; also he has erected a commodious blacksmith and repair shop on the lot. He will have a neat little tenement house when completed.* p2c2

I may have to give up with Gabe Masters's residence. As I understand it, he lived in the little house across from Askins. That is the house my mother was born in. Gabe and Ella were living beside Sam Askins on the curve toward Nicholasville during the time I knew them.

These tobacco prices are ridiculous. If anybody knows how much work goes into raising the damned stuff, to even think of selling it for 4 1/2 cents per pound would make you sick, even a hundred years ago. Prizing must mean pressing, but in my day, this was done in all the stripping rooms. They couldn't dry the tobacco, so I don't know what else was done to it.

April 18, 1902

"Miss Hendren's pupils' recital.-A large crowd of friends filled the Institute chapel Monday night to hear the program prepared by Miss Nellie Hendren's music class. It is composed largely of little folks, who entered into their performances with great zeal, and having done their best, elicited much applause. Miss Eula Jackson, of Lexington, added two recitations to the evenings pleasure which were enthusiastically received. Miss Hendren played two violin selections most charmingly." p3c4 This is Tom's daughter.

The *Sulphur Well Correspondent* writes:

A child of Albert Hagler was quite sick Saturday night.
W B Walker, who has been confined to his bed for some time, is reported as improving.
Mr F M Hudson had a severe attack of neuralgia Sunday night, but is better.
W G Jones, accompanied by his son, William, of Buckeye, were over on a short visit Thursday of last week.
William Sallee, of Edenton, who has been visiting James Hendren, returned home Monday.
J H Tatman sold to William Cobb his place on Peel's branch near Pleasant Hill Church for $175.
James Hendren, who has been confined to his room for several days with a severe throat trouble, is out again.
F M Horine, one of our most energetic farmers-traders, is the first afield, so far as heard from, in corn planting. He planted two acres last Friday.
Next Sunday is the regular monthly meeting day at the Christian Church. Come out and hear Elder Hildebrand, morning and night.
Harry DeWitt sold his farm near Black Bridge, on Hickman Creek, containing 80 acres or more, to Melvin Peel for $3,000 and paid his tenant $100 for possession. p2c4

April 25, 1902

The *Sulphur Well Correspondent* writes:

*J A Dean, Stone, was visiting in this section Monday.*
*N B Howard, of Baldwin, was over Monday.*
*James Blakeman, Buena Vista, was visiting friends here Sunday last.*
*James West, of Edenton, died after a short illness Saturday last, of ----- consumption.*
*John W Cobb, of Mt Lebanon, has a little son very ill with pneumonia.*
*Wylie Burton, and William Wylie, of Giles, were over on this side Monday.*
*Lafayette Howard and Caperton Vincent, of Edenton, were mixing with the crowd Monday.*
*Sam Baldwin, formerly of this county, now of Red House (in) Madison County, was visiting in the county Monday.*
*There will be preaching the first Sunday in May at the Christian Church by Eld Hilderbrand.*
*Mrs Ellen Cloyd Hicks, of Middlesburg, Casey County, was visiting her nieces, Mrs Maria Dean and Mrs Dr G M Hendren, this week.*
*Marion Simpson, Dock Simpson and W G Jones, of Buckeye, were over Monday visiting friends and attending court.*
*Jno B Bourne and wife of Bourne, Garrard County were visiting E E Bourne here Sunday. J Holly Easley and wife, of same place, were the guests of E E Bourne at the same time.*
*A mad dog was killed near Edenton, a few days ago after biting three or four people and several head of stock. John Long, its owner, and his son were bitten and a neighbor's son; some cattle and horses in the neighborhood were also included in its wild foray before being caught up with and slaughtered. The madstone failed to stick and bitten ones are supposed to be out of all danger of hydrophobia.*
*Luther Ware, of this place, came into possession recently of an ancient curiosity in the shape of a razor. It resembles a fr-e more than it does a modern razor. It is attached to a substantial wooden handle, and in appearance, and size, must have been made for some giant of legendary days. It would, no doubt, delight an Ethiopian to have it included in his armament at one of their "festivals", when they get their savage interests worked up to the point of fury and commence their bloody assaults with the "razzor". p2c1*

I wish I knew the modern medical view of a madstone. The good doctor seems to give it some credence, but it sounds more like witchcraft to me.

May 2, 1902

Mrs Thomas Hendren died Tuesday morning, April 29. She and Tom were married September 11, 1877. They had four children- Nellie, Carl, Clyde and Emmett. Her funeral services were in the chapel at Lexington Cemetery, so I guess she is buried there. p3c4 Emmett is the father of E W Hendren, a high school friend who still runs the wallpaper and furniture store in Nicholasville.

The *Sulphur Well Correspondent* writes:

*Born, on the 22d ult, to the wife of Ernest Fain, a son.*
*The fine rains were greatly needed as the earth was getting very dry.*
*J H Murphy is having an addition built to the tenement house near his store.*
*Dr Vincent, of Edenton, formerly of this county, was visiting here Monday.*
*Several fine, large catfish have been caught out of Woodward-Rice pond in the last few days.*
*John C Hendren, a prominent farmer of Edenton, Madison County, was visiting in the county last Saturday.*
*From preparations to plant, there will undoubtedly be a very large acreage of tobacco this year.*
*The Journal is greatly appreciated by its many readers here, and is eagerly scanned each week for its county items.*
*The eight-year-old son of Wesley Davis, Mt Lebanon, has been quite sick for several days with malarial fever.*
*Mrs Ellen Hicks and Mrs Maria Dean paid a visit to Mrs Nannie Mitchell, Tuesday and Wednesday.*
*Don't forget next Sunday morning and evening the sermons of Eld Hilderbrand at the Christian Church here.*
*Rev B F Jenkins, president of the Kentucky University, was the guest of Mr and Mrs J P Turner at tea, Sunday evening.*
*Mrs Ellen Hicks left Saturday morning for a short visit to friends at Lawrenceburg, on her way to her home at Middleburg, Casey County.*
*Hubert, the 2-year-old son of Jno W Cobb, of Mt Lebanon, who has been critically ill with double pneumonia, is now out of danger.* p2c2

May 9, 1902

The *Sulphur Well Correspondent* writes:

*Newton Chandler, of Edenton, has been critically ill with pneumonia.*
*Dock Simpson, of Buckeye was over Friday.*
*A C Miles, of Buckeye, was over on a business trip last Friday.*
*W B Giboney was calling on some of his old friends and acquaintances here last Thursday.*
*Frank M Horine lost a fine heifer Sunday night from eating too much clover while the dew was on.*
*John C Hendren, of Edenton, was over last Wednesday attending the funeral of his stepmother, Mrs Thomas Hendren.* p2c3

May 16, 1902

Martinique has had a volcanic eruption that has wiped out St Pierre. Thirty thousand are estimated dead, and 50,000 homeless. Relief is pouring in from all over the world. p3c3

The crop outlook: "the hemp acreage surpasses anything in the past 15 years"; wheat "will not exceed 65 percent of an average crop"; oats has been planted more extensively than previously in Kentucky; tobacco will be about average; "lambs are good and nearly all sold at good prices." p3c3

The *Sulphur Well Correspondent* writes:

*The shower Monday was welcomed as it was much needed.*

*Miss T Miller returned Monday from a two weeks visit with friends at Irvine.*

*A German carp weighing 12 pounds was caught out of the Kentucky River recently near Lock 8.*

*Houston Woodward lost last week a good work mule from blood poisoning caused by a bruised heel.*

*Cut-worms are not only damaging the gardens greatly, but are destroying the young hemp to an alarming extent.*

*Dr and Mrs Miller, F F Miller, Andrew Sageser and Mrs A M Askins and daughter Bertha, visited Lexington, Monday.*

*Quite a little crowd from this place took advantage of the cheap rates to visit the Queen City, Sunday. Among them were E E Bourne and sons, M F Davis, Hamlet Foster, Guy Stacy and others.*

*Found--on the Hickman Creek Road, near the Hunter Bridge, by a son of Charles Cobb, a gold rimmed pair of spectacles, which the owner can have by proving property and paying for the notice.*

*On the Whitenack farm, in Mercer County, J W Cobb stumbled upon an ancient relic in the shape of an old home made ax. In appearance it must have been made and used by some one of the first settlers of the wilds of Kentucky. It is quite a curiosity.* p2c2

May 23, 1902

It has become apparent from the visitations from both Madison and Garrard counties that Dr Hendren has become the "Oracle" of Sulphur Well, and that his knowledge of the West is being sought by everyone with dreams of riches. A sensitive reader should also be cognizant that racism was widespread, and that people sometimes used words that are now considered offensive. The *Sulphur Well Correspondent* writes:

*Wm Smith and Edgar Layton, of Idalia, were over Saturday.*

*Mrs J H Turner was visiting Mrs Dr Bryant at Versailles last week.*

*William Sallee, Silver Creek, was visiting friends here Tuesday.*

*N P Cobb, Cap Hill, Allen Vincent and Oscar Hendren were visiting in the county Monday.*

*Miss Minnie Walters was visiting Mrs Claud Herron, Lexington, last week.*

*Lieut John F M Hill, of Idalia, paid a brief visit to the county last Tuesday.*

*Forrest Stapp, William Fain and Wm Jones, of Buckeye, were visitors Monday.*

*Mrs J Milton Cotton, of Edenton, died after a short attack of stomach trouble Sunday last, and was buried at Salem Church, Monday.*

*Rev H G Turner, wife and son, of Richmond, were visiting his parents, Mr and Mrs J P Turner, here this week.*

*People were feeling so well after the fine rains that (they could be said) to be "distressingly" healthy.*

*Austin Smith, Daniel Simpson, Elisha Warren, Allen Vincent, Ezekiel Vincent and Samuel Moberly, of Edenton, were among the many visitors Monday.*

*E Walker's spring wagon hauling slop from Old Lexington Club Distillery, at Union Mills, had a bad smashup on the road Monday and nearly drowned the little black coon who was driving, before he could extricate himself from the fremescence.*

> *Copies of The Creek Chieftain and The Capitol News of Okmulgee, Indian Territory, were recently received by us. They contained letters written by a "Kentucky Coyote" which is evidently a strange animal as none of that breed were ever known to snap and snarl in the "wilds" of Kentucky. The Creek Nation is only a part of the Indian Territory and is governed by a council composed of the house of Kings and the house of Warriors; a principal chief, Pleasant Parter, and a second chief named, perhaps appropriately, Monty Tiger. There is also a Creek Indian chief called Crazy Snake. This council meets only once a year, in October, to attend to their tribal affairs. p2c3*

Dr Hendren now writes novelettes! He has a three column letter "The Human Tiger", in which he offers a sketch of Geronimo, then an encounter of "Eastern girls" with a Native American. He starts by saying that the settlement of Oklahoma occured so rapidly that they didn't have time to import lumber for their dwellings, that a majority of the homesteaders made their homes in tepees. The 320 acres comprising Lawton, which contained 40,000 people, became a town of tents. He describes the tepee as being constructed of thick yellow cloth, with a hole in the center for a stovepipe in winter. Beds are spread around the perimeter of the tepee encircling benches and a table. Near the flap is the "parlor" where the squaws sit and gossip, or spin yarns of bygone days. He tells how tribes arrange their tepees in different ways--the Comanches pitch their tepees in a circle leaving room in the center for councils and dances; the Apaches huddle their's as close together as possible; while other tribes pitch their camps in long rows along streams. He says that Geronimo lives in a tepee near Ft Sill, where he is nominally a prisoner of war, drawing $35 per month as a government scout. (I don't know whether this is historically correct or not.) "His relatives have pitched their tepees around his, making a considerable settlement." At this time Geronimo is around eighty years old and considered docile. He and 289 other Apaches are about to be released. Dr Hendren glories in Geronimo's endurance and escapades saying "he rode once, on horseback 500 miles without rest. On another occasion he ran 40 miles, one day....In the height of his power his face wore a demoniacal expression of ferocity."

Dr Hendren says that the Indians now living around Lawton own the best farms, horses, and cattle, and have plenty of money. "They seem to be contented and friendly." Some of the Indians had become educated and professionals--doctors and lawyers. He recounts the story of Dr P-, a dentist, whom he had met in the Keegan House, as having given up the tomahawk and "had established himself in this flourishing town...." Dr Hendren was accompanied by Dr P to the depot to board the train for Oklahoma City. "`Ah', he said animatedly, `I have learned that in this great country that to be venturesome is to be happy'."

Just then some Eastern girls gathered "around three or four dirty, blanketed, unpicturesque Indians reclining listlessly in the sand with their backs against the depot walls. One of them, evidently a high school girl from way back East, and unused to the substratum of humanity was just saying:
    `Oh, girls, let's do go and speak to them. Aren't they some of our fellow creatures whom we have pledged ourselves to uplift?'

'Oh, I'm afraid of the horrid creatures,' said another, 'They are so exceeding vile and dirty looking. They don't, one bit, resemble those lovely pictures one sees of them at home. They must be inferior specimens of their race.'

'Well, I'll have to admit that they are not very prepossessing,' assented the first speaker as she eyed the Indians leaning against the walls, stolidly looking at nothing in particular, But I never saw a real live, wild Indian before, and I'm going to speak to them; besides I think it's my duty to talk to them and help lift them from their terribly ignorant, and certainly miserable condition, to a higher plane of civilization.'

'Oh won't that be just grand to tell of when we get back home?' said another girl from way back East. And they then solemnly, hesitatingly drew the circle of undaunted femininity nearer the trio of bloody scalp snatchers. They introduced themselves as members of the 'National Indian Rights Society,' or something similar, and extended their small white aristocratic hands which were immediately grabbed by two big, ugly red hands that were thrust out with a 'How!' while the third simply touched his hat politely.

'We' stammered the first girl,'we--you know--we girls of the Society would like to talk to you--to real live Indians, you know.'

'Me big Indian. Me real live thing.' broke in a big buck, smiling at the girls--a real expansive smile--who were all a-tremble with excitement at their own rashness, but bravely determined to carry it through.

'Please Mr Indian man', said another, 'tell us your name, won't you?'

'Me big chief. Me got big, long name,' and here he rolled in his gutteral language, something that sounded somewhat like 'Ocheemagoocheelaho', and folded his arms in solemn majesty across his broad chest.

'Oh, my goodness! exclaimed the girls in chorus, 'How will we ever, ever remember all that? What does it mean? Can't you tell us Mr Indian, please what it means in English?'

'Me United States?' he asked, 'United States me Peter Pug' he said with lofty dignity, patting himself below the belt and looking with the solemnity of an owl off into the blue etheral infinity of space, as the girls nearly collapsed at the unexpectedness of this rendition into 'United States'. But, they had grown accustomed to those uncouth 'Wards of the Nation' and persisted in their further search for Indian lore."

This goes on much longer, but this shows the degree to which Dr Hendren has become a raconteur, and has become recognized as such. p4c3-5

May 30, 1902

Dr Hendren must have stopped practicing medicine and become a full-time poet and writer. This poem is "Local Liars". It's a pretty good description of what goes on in the country stores in villages such as Sulphur Well. It still continued unchanged during the time I grew up there. My grandfather endured it for the forty years that he ran a country store. I've chosen only the fifth of the six verses, which goes like this: p1c4

LOCAL LIARS
In the line of agriculture
Our equivocators shine,
And they show a touch of talent
That approaches the sublime;
For they raise hemp and tobacco
By the million pounds or more,
When they start to winter farming
On the nail-keg at the store.

The *Sulphur Well Correspondent* writes:

*Mrs Bettie Murphy is down with sciatica again.*
*Mr Walton's little son was quite sick Sunday night.*
*Mrs Mastin Fain, an aged lady, is reported seriously ill.*
*Askins & Ware have added an improvement to their shop in the way of stocks.*
*It is rather a long fall from up in the 90's down to the 40's; but we should not be surprised at anything but the fall of "bug juice".*
*They said are you friz?*
*And I said, yes, I iz; But we don't call this cold in Kentucky.*
*The heavy rain, wind and thunder storm here Monday was of the proportions of a waterspout in some sections and did considerable damage to ploughed fields and growing hemp and corn. The small spring branches became raging torrents and were impassible for some time. No destruction to life or property has been reported, though the wind and lightning was severe for a time.* p2c2

"Miss Emma Hendren, of Richmond, is visiting Miss Nellie Hendren." p3c4

June 6, 1902

According to the <u>Journal</u> editor, the moral condition of the town's youth is deplorable. He says that "it is a common occurrence to see a boy between the ages of 15 and 19 years, drunk." He concludes that if the churches of the city don't recognize the problem, they will "reap a bitter harvest". p2c1

Dr Hendren has composed a very short poem this week "In Sleep". He says that we stride across the stage (of life), then lie down in sleep. And, whether we drudge or drawl, we lie down in sleep. After we have gotten our little store, we get no more than dreamless sleep. Whether we smile or frown, in the end we lay our cares down in endless sleep. p1c5

J P Turner has purchased 127 acres of unimproved land, south of Nicholasville, running from the Danville Pike to the Sulphur Well Pike, at $70 per acre from John Brown. Mr Turner will erect a handsome residence on the property, facing the Danville Pike, and will move to same as soon as finished." p2c8 It still stands at the edge of town.

The *Sulphur Well Correspondent* writes:

*Mrs John Burchell was taken quite suddenly Tuesday night with a severe attack of neuralgia of the stomach.*
*Born, on the 30th ult, to the wife of Dillard Fain, a son.*
*J H Murphy is improving his residence and store by a thorough painting.*
*It is said that a child was recently born in this neighborhood with two tongues. Strange--and it is said to be a boy.*
*A narrow path made by the deer, in early days, going to and from a salt lick, was finally widened and deepened by the rains into a narrow, deep valley in which the pure, sparkling waters of Chalybeate Springs burst out to the view of the early settlers of the neighborhood of that region now known as Pink, but formerly (as) Canton. There is also a sulphur spring near, and the place has gradually become quite a resort for invalids.*
*The severe wind, rain and thunder storm Tuesday evening did some damage to trees, telephones, etc., being at one time almost a hurricane in its violence. Several trees were blown down in the writer's yard and the woodland pastures show the storm's effects. In some places the roads were obstructed by uprooted trees.* p2c7

June 13, 1902

I remarked some years ago about the importance of distilleries in the farming economy. Besides selling the corn, "during the distilling season just closed in Anderson County, there were 2,345 cattle and 1,560 hogs slopped".p2c4

The inter-urban railway to Lexington is almost complete, and trolley parties are being planned for its opening. p3c1

"Eugene Monyhan is laying the foundation for Dr Jno C Miller's new residence on North Main Street. It is likely the carpenters will begin work next week. It is to be a two-story frame dwelling." p3c4

Dr Hendren has composed "Did You Ever?". p1c5 The first four lines go this way:

DID YOU EVER?
You grumble at fate, and your burdens deplore,
And sigh for relief from your foes;
But brother, dear brother, didst ever before
Get struck in the dark by a half open door?

The *Sulphur Well Correspondent* writes:

> George Peel sold to Chas Hisle nine head of hogs at 6 cents.
> J P an J H Turner visited Lexington last Tuesday.
> The physicians say that the country is distressingly--etc.
> Mrs Lulu Whitenack, of Harrodsburg, was visiting J W Cobb from Saturday till Monday.
> A. Jackson Ware sold to Phillip Foster a nine year old harness mare for $75.
> W H Hare sold Monday to L M Jackson one 875 lb steer at 3 3/4 cts, and one fat cow, 1065 lbs at 3 1/2 cents.
> Friday the little son of Mrs Whitenack fell from the doorstep and painfully injured his right arm.
> W R Bryant sold to R A Dodd forty head of 70 lb lambs at 5 1/2 cents and fifteen head of 100 lb old sheep at 5 cents.
> Mr and Mrs Gilbert Grinstead, B Letcher Grinstead and Miss Bybee, of Richmond, were visiting Mr and Mrs James H Turner Sunday.
> The heaviest rain storm that has fallen for years flooded this section of country last Saturday. In a few moments dry streamlets were raging torrents. The lightning also did some damage to telephones, etc. p2c2

The weather is apparently very unsettled. This is the second storm reported recently.

June 20, 1902

"Miss Emma Hendren, Lexington, is the guest of Miss Nellie Hendren." p3c3

Mrs Julia Payne Miller was married Saturday, June 14th to Prof Spencer Hill of St Louis. He is "connected to one of the leading medical colleges in St Louis." p3c5

The *Sulphur Well Correspondent* writes:

> Sam Askins has been on the sick list for a few days.
> Miss Arkie Hunter, Lancaster, was visiting Jno T West, Sunday.
> Mrs F F Miller and son, are visiting friends at Irvine.
> N B Howard, of Baldwin, Madison County, was over Monday.
> Hay and wheat harvesting commenced in earnest Monday.
> Miss Lizzie Grimes and Ike Thompson were guests of A M Askins this week.
> Elder Hildebrand preached to a good sized audience Sunday morning and night.
> J H Murphy, is spending a few days at Tatham Springs in Anderson County.
> Revs H G Turner and C H Eversole, of Richmond were the guests of J P Turner Thursday evening.
> A son of John Baskett fell from a high porch one day last week and fractured his arm.
> Several farmers have lost some young calves recently from an unknown, but quickly fatal malady.
> William Sanders, of Edenton, was over Monday among his many friends.
> Taylor Sanders, of Stone, Garrard County, was in this section on a trading expedition Monday.
> J P Turner sold and finished delivering Saturday to Lexington parties, 130,000 pounds of hemp. He realized the neat little sum of $6,000. p2c3

June 27, 1902

Dr Hendren has composed "Aquarium" this week. p1c6 I am in a quandry as to what to do about these poems. They certainly tell something about the composer, but how much is enough? My primary interest is in the Correspondent telling about Sulphur Well, so will limit his poems.

The *Sulphur Well Correspondent* writes:

*Miss Sue Ellis, Lexington, is visiting Mrs J P Turner this week.*
*J H Murphy has returned from Tatham Springs.*
*Caperton Vincent, Edenton, was on this side Saturday.*
*Mrs Lizzie Miller is visiting at Irvine.*
*It is said that Miss Lilly Ross and a Mr Riddel of Irvine will wed next Saturday.*
*William Hill, of Cottonburg, was visiting here Saturday and Sunday.*
*Mrs Jas H Turner is visiting her sister, Mrs Catherine Beasley, at Stanford, this week.*
*Master Ray Miller was quite sick Saturday night. Houston Woodward was also on the "complaining" list the same night.*
*Mrs Bettie Reynolds of Alva, Texas, widow of the late Rev M D Reynolds, formerly of this place, was visiting Mrs T J Horine.*
*Dr G M Hendren this week sold through a real estate agent, his Lawton, O T property, bought ten months ago from the Government, at a very handsome profit. p2c4*

I suppose the good doctor, after advising so many people, would want them all to know that he did well, and they could too, if they followed his advice. There is probably a little one-up-manship with the other local entrepreneurs such as J P Turner, J H Murphy, Newt Davis, and Dr Miller. There were some pretty substantial people around the Well at this time.

July 4, 1902

"Mr L H Hendren went to Clearwater, Kas, Tuesday with the view of disposing of his interests there and returning with his family to Nicholasville, where they will reside permanently." p3c3 This is Dr Hendren's brother.

Dr Hendren wrote "There Are Others" this week. p4c6

July 11, 1902

From Madison: "J Harry Hendren, of Edenton, was among a class of sixty-five who were awarded diplomas by the Hospital College of Medicine, Louisville. p2c2 This isn't "Uncle Pat". Family names get recycled so often. I don't know who his parents are.

From Little Hickman: Pomp is back! "After a long vacation we greet you again." p2c3

The *Sulphur Well Correspondent* writes:

*Houston Woodward is visiting in one of the adjoining counties.*
*Frank Miller moved last Wednesday to Thomas Mackey's.*
*E Hendren sold to W H Hare 30 shoats averaging 51 lbs at 6 cents.*
*J T West sold to L M Jackson two head of cattle at 3 1/4c.*
*A little son of Wesley Davis was quite sick with fever this week.*
*A colored girl at Mr Turner's fell and dislocated her arm last week.*
*Mrs Jas H Turner has returned from her visit to Stanford.*
*Frank Stacy, of Irvine, is visiting Mrs Lizzie Miller.*
*Mrs John Burchell had another severe attack of gastritis last week.*
*Mrs Elizabeth Miller has returned from a two weeks visit to Estill County.*
*J H Turner sold 21 head of shoats at 6 cents to H B Campbell. They averaged 80 lbs.*
*J P Turner sold two cows to Lexington parties at $90. N D Davis sold two cows to the same parties at $123.*
*A J Sageser lost his buggy mare last week by being cut by barbed wire. Chas Clubb also lost a horse recently from the same cause.*
*Morris Dean received Saturday by express from his son, Jasper Dean, of South McAlister, I T, a little spotted fawn. It stood its thousand mile trip in good condition.*
*Hugh Miller, of Oklahoma City, O T, will be in Kentucky in a few weeks for a short visit in Jessamine County. p2c4*

Frank Stacy is one of the five children of Belle Miller Stacy, deceased.

July 18, 1902

The *Sulphur Well Correspondent* writes:

*William Isbill, of Silver Creek, was visiting in the county Tuesday.*
*Several days last week the mercury went above 96 degrees.*
*Squire Walters will teach the public school here this year.*
*Bailey Richardson has gone to Lexington to reside.*
*Quite a crowd attended Wilmore camp meeting from here, Sunday.*
*Dry weather has begun to effect the crops seriously.*
*Rev H G Turner, of Richmond, was visiting his parents, Mr and Mrs J P Turner, this week.*
*Davis Bros have bought in Woodford County about 20,000 lbs of tobacco at an average price of 6 1/4 cents.*
*Mrs Elizabeth Miller, who has been indisposed for several days had a severe cramping attack.*
*Wheat threshing is about over and the crop is considerably below the average.*
*Sunday seems to have degenerated into hoodlum day around the village pump, for idlers and loafers from the country round about collect there and create as much noise as if it was the 4th of July they were celebrating instead of the Lord's Day. It is a disgraceful nuisance and should be stopped forthwith. There most certainly is enough howling and yelping every day of the week to test to its fullest capacity the most powerful lung-tester ever invented--enough noise to satisfy the craziest Comanche that ever went out on a raid, and for God's sake give us a rest, a little rest, on Sunday. p2c3*

I'd say the good doctor has just about had his fill of Sulphur Well. I think the end is near.

## July 25, 1902

The public sale of J P Turner will take place on August 20th. p2c5 The announcement states that he has decided to quit farming, and will sell his farm 3 1/2 miles east of Nicholasville on Wednesday. Turner will also sell livestock, farming implements, household and kitchen furniture. He plans to sell privately 225 stock ewes. p2c5 Either the farm didn't sell, or J H Turner, his son, purchased it.

"Mr Walter Davis and Miss Mary Hendren, of Ambrose, surprised their many friends July 11, by hieing away to Lexington and being joined together as man and wife. The bridegroom is a son of Mr N D Davis, and a young man of industrious qualifications, while the bride, is a daughter of Dr G M Hendren." p3c6 One of his other daughters, Nellie, married Dr Miller's son Hugh, so this ties three strong families together.

The *Sulphur Well Correspondent* writes:

*Squire Yarnell moved to the J P Turner place last Tuesday.*
*Plowing has commenced for fall seeding in this section.*
*Mrs W S Hendren and children were visiting here Tuesday.*
*Charles Hemphill lost a work horse by choking to death.*
*Two children of John Waller were very sick Sunday from cramps.*
*Temperature was only 100 degrees Thursday of last week and 54 degrees Saturday morning.*
*A protracted meeting will commence at the Christian Church (the) second Sunday in August.*
*Wm G Jones, of Buckeye, Garrard County, was visiting here Monday.*
*Mrs Annie Wagner and daughter of Newport, were the guests of Dr Geo M Hendren last Tuesday.*
*Lee Bryant sold last Tuesday to R A Dodd, 46 lambs, averaging 72 lbs at 6 1/4 cts.*
*The storm Saturday caused a commotion at Little Hickman camp grounds.*
*The little daughter of Albert Hagler was seized with convulsions last week and was for a time alarmingly ill.*
*Mrs William B Walker while alighting from her horse, slipped and fell, hurting herself quite severely.*
*Miss Mary Smiley, of Lexington, was the guest of Miss Irene Bourne this week.*
*Miss Etta Gray, Lexington, was the guest of Mrs Jas T Sageser this week.*
*George Walters lost a good work horse last Thursday by breaking his neck. He became entangled in a rope by which he was tied around the neck and was dead when found.*
*William S Sallee, James Vincent and Dr Watkins, of Edenton, were over among their friends last Monday.*
*There is a fine prospect for all kinds of crops since the splendid rains of last week. Tobacco and hemp are expecially looking fine, and corn will undoubtedly make a good crop.*
*J P Turner will have a public sale of his stock, farming implements, household and kitchen furniture, Aug 20.p2c5*

## August 1, 1902

"Mrs A K Adcock and children left Wednesday for Slate Lick Springs, they will stay about ten days." p3c3

August 8, 1902

"Chalybeate Springs is located on the old Harrison Dean homestead farm, now owned by Melvin L Dean (Dr M L Dean's father)." The Dean family is having a reunion there on August 22nd. p3c3

August 15, 1902

The *Sulphur Well Correspondent* writes:

*A J Sagerser sold to M F Davis 16 shoats at $6.25.*
*M F Horine sold some corn to N D Davis at $3.50 per bbl.*
*Geo W Gray, of Lexington, is visiting John T West.*
*Jas H Turner sold to James Carroll 71 lambs at $4 per head.*
*Our public school opened with Squire Walters as teacher.*
*Simon Walters and sister, Minnie, are visiting at Mt Pulaski, Ill.*
*J P Turner sold to James Carroll 157 lambs at $3.50 per head.*
*J H Turner sold to Pat Foster 27 head of 800 lb heifers.*
*Andrew Hemphill sold to W D Davis eleven head of 180 lb hogs at $6.60 per cwt.*
*Mrs Scottie Miller has returned from a visit to Slate Lick Springs.*
*Charles Manfred Murphy and Ike Dunn went to Mammoth Cave last week.*
*Rev Horace Turner and wife visited his parents, Mr and Mrs J P Turner last week.*
*Misses Myrtle Hendren, of Kirksville, and Lelia Hendren, of Edenton, were recent visitors at John T West's.*
*Misses Bertie May and Helene Bright, who have been visiting here for some weeks, have returned to their home in Lexington.*
*Frank Stacy, who has been visiting his Grandmother Miller for several weeks, returned home last week.*
*William Richardson and wife, of Irvine, stopped over here a short time, on their way to Hot Springs, Ark., where Mrs Richardson goes for her health.*
*Mrs Thomas House, of Sanders' Ferry, died at her residence Wednesday, Aug 6th, after a long illness, aged about 45 years, and was buried at White's Station Thursday afternoon. Mrs House was a sincere Christian woman, being a devout member of the Baptist Church. She was a loving wife and mother, devoted to her home, her husband and children, eight of whom she leaves behind to mourn her irretreivable loss. She bore with Christian fortitude her long days of suffering, but was resigned to the call into that mystery beyond which we all must sometime know.* p2c4

Perhaps the eulogy above inspired Dr Hendren to write a poem: "Life's Limited. Aboard The Through Life Limited, We travel day and night, Toward the station just ahead, That's veiled from human sight." p3c6

August 22, 1902

Maybe this answers my question about the madstone! "Dr A D Price, of Shelbyville, says that the madstone is a myth, and never, since the beginning of time, has the application of a stone cured a case of hydrophobia." He adds "that any light porous stone will adhere to a wound," and that is no indication that the person will not contact rabies. He says that as soon as it is determined that the animal is diseased, go immediately to a Pasteur Institute. p1c6

Quite a crowd attended the sale of J P Turner, and "very fair prices" were received on the stock and farming implements." p2c3 Nothing is said about the farm.

From Wilmore: "Two unknown gentlemen passed through our village Tuesday evening with an automobile which attracted a great deal of attention, as it was the first seen in our village." p2c4

"Rev G W Hilderbrand, assisted by Rev H K Berry, is conducting a very successful meeting at Sulphur Well. There were seven additions to the church Sunday. The meeting will continue for several days." p2c4

"Mrs Meade Miller, of Oklahoma City, Okla, is visiting friends in Jessamine and Estill County." p3c4

## August 29, 1902

The Dean reunion was held very successfully. A picture of Harrison Dean and his wife, Nancy Owens, and another picture of their seven children still living, was reproduced in the paper. p1c3-4

The *Sulphur Well Correspondent* writes:

*Miss Cordie Taylor, of Harrodsburg is visiting Mrs J W Cobb.*
*John Catlett, of Mercer County, was visiting Mrs Julia Myers last week.*
*Wm Snyder, Oscar Hendren, and Allen Vincent, of Edenton, were over last week.*
*F M Horine left last Wednesday for London to attend the fair.*
*Mrs Clarence Ecbert and children, of Lexington, are visiting Mrs Margaret Horine this week.*
*Al Baker sold last week to John Baker seven head of steers, average weight 800 lbs at 4cts.*
*Andrew Hemphill sold to N D Davis this week eleven head of 200 lb hogs at $6.60.*
*L B Taylor sold one steer, weight 1,110 lbs, at 5 1/4 cents, to Wm Steele; Ben Wheeler sold to same party one steer at 4 cts.*
*Mrs Meade Miller and little daughter, of Oklahoma City, who have been visiting Dr J C Miller, have gone to Irvine to visit friends there.*
*The protracted meeting conducted by Eld G W Hilderbrand and Bro Berry, of Owenton, closed Friday night with 19 additions to the church. The meeting was a successful one and was very largely attended at night, and the best of order prevailed, eliciting the most flattering compliments and praise from Bro Berry for this section of the country.* p2c4

## September 5, 1902

The Eighth Congressional District meeting of Republicans was well attended, and W L Summerall was nominated as representative. p2c1

September 12, 1902

From Little Hickman: They came in a variety of ways, but they came! "The meeting closed last Sunday night with 48 additions to the church--one from the Methodist, two restored, two by letter, eight by statement, and 36 by confession and baptism." p2c4

"Mr J P Turner bought yesterday from G A Roby the latter's two story frame residence on North Main Street for $4,000." p3c5

The Richmond Climax reports that Rev H G Turner will continue as pastor of the Methodist Church in Richmond. "He returned Tuesday from London, bringing the news that Conference has sent him back for another year." p3c5

September 19, 1902

T Roland Dean, an attorney in South McAlester, I T, came in for the Dean family reunion, and was the master of ceremonies. p4c5

"Miss Hare of Nicholasville is visiting her sister, Mrs McClellan Johnston." p3c4 Her parents live in Sulphur Well.

September 26, 1902

"Miss Hare, the efficient book-keeper and stenographer of the school, is with the Institute again this year, much to the gratification of those who met with her last year." p1c3

> Meade Miller, of Oklahoma City, O T, arrived here last Monday, looking unusually well, and wearing an air of prosperity and contentment. He says that all crops in the territory, except wheat, were very good, and he never before saw such fine fruit of all kinds. He thinks it a great country for the young man with limited capital. p3c4

October 3, 1902

The *Sulphur Well Correspondent* writes:

> *Ike Thompson, of Buena Vista, was a guest of Alex Askins recently.*
> *W H Bright, of Lexington, was visiting A M Askins recently.*
> *Wm Sanders, of Idalia, Madison County, was visiting in the county Thursday.*
> *Samuel Moberly, of Edenton, Madison County, was over last Sunday.*
> *Mrs Theresa Tudor left Sunday for a two weeks visit in Madison County.*
> *Mrs Meade Miller and little daughter are visiting at Irvine, Estill County.*
> *Hugh Miller, of Oklahoma City, will shortly arrive in this county for a brief visit.*
> *N B Howard of Newby, Madison County, was over a few days since for a short visit.*
> *John A Ham and Mrs Sue Reagan of Edenton, have returned from a visit to Bloomington, Ill.*

W B Ray, and daughter, of Buckeye, were visiting Dr Hendren Thursday of last week.

Wm Wylie, of near Giles, Garrard County, was over Wednesday last.

Mrs D O Hunter who has been seriously sick for some days is very much better.

Mrs Scottie Miller is recovering from a severe attack of malarial fever.

Jno P Miller, of Wisemantown, Estill County was visiting his mother here a few days recently.

Several persons attended the big show at Lexington Saturday.

Dr G M Hendren and wife were visiting Robt Reagan, of Edenton, last Monday.

Caperton, Ezekiel and Beatty Vincent, of Paint Lick Creek, were over last Tuesday.

Mrs Ida Cobb who was reported seriously ill Tuesday, is improving.

Dr G M Hendren was called by telephone last week to see a case of scarlatina in Madison County, where that disease is epidemic.

There was quite a reunion of the old-time friends of Maston Hunter, who has been in Iowa for 32 years, at Mrs Maria Hunter's last Tuesday.

Scarlatina is very prevalent in Madison, the public schools are being dismissed in consequence. Several fatalities having occured among the children.

B Frank Foster killed last Thursday, near the residence of William Hudson, a monster snake of the cowsucker species. When he discovered it, the reptile had wound itself into an enormous coil ready to strike. It was 8 feet long and about 10 inches in circumference. Its broad track had been seen in that locality for several days. p2c4

October 10, 1902

"James Hendren sold to T M Toomey, of Clark County, 100 acres of land on Silver Creek at $16.50 per acre." p2c4

The *Sulphur Well Correspondent* writes:

George William Wylie, of Edenton, was visiting here, Wednesday.

A C Miles, of Buckeye, was over Tuesday.

Austin Smith, of Madison County, was paying his friends a visit here Tuesday.

Jas H Turner will move to the residence of his father, J P Turner, in a few days.

William Wylie was among his friends here last Tuesday.

Mrs Emaline Peel has rented and will remove to J H Turner's place shortly.

Henry Wiley, of Bloomington, Ill, who has been visiting his father's home, returned to Illinois, Tuesday.

Mrs Theresa Tudor returned from a week's visit among friends in Madison County, Sunday.

J P Turner will move to the residence he bought in Nicholasville, shortly.

Chills and fever are very prevalent along the river since it has been locked and damned. In some localities whole families are down.

Mrs Meade Miller, of Oklahoma City, who has been visiting here for some weeks, returned home last week, stopping with relatives at Little Rock, Ark, on the way. p2c6

October 17, 1902

George Marion Hendren composed "The Old Country Store". p1c5 Let me pick a verse or two, because it demonstrates so well that the country store was much more than a place to buy merchandise.

### THE OLD COUNTRY STORE

'Twas here the neighbors oftimes met
On idle days, or when too wet
To be about their farming;
When sometimes on affairs of State,
They'd wax so wrothy in debate,
That it seemed quite alarming.

Here would the country gossips come,
To tattle with a nimble tongue,
Of all things in creation;
They knew all scandal to be found,
And retailed it for miles around
With many a variation.

I think this is one of Dr Hendren's best efforts, in so far as it so vividly portrays the life and times in small, relatively isolated, farming communities.

The *Sulphur Well Correspondent* writes:

*Meade Miller visited Georgetown Saturday, returning Monday.*
*F F Miller has bought the store and stock of goods of J H Murphy.*
*F M Horine sold to L M Jackson two fat heifers averaging 800 pounds at 3 cents.*
*Thomas Barker has sold his farm and is contemplating visiting Oklahoma soon.*
*The heavy rains Saturday and Monday were much welcomed, for stock water was getting scarce.*
*Ben House sold to E Walker one fat steer weighing 985 lbs at $4.35 per cwt.*
*Mr and Mrs Clubb are spending the week among friends in Henry County.*
*R L Bogie, of Edneyburg, Madison County, was over Thursday looking for a location.*
*Elijah Cromby has bought out the Ingram store and will run it in connection with his store at Pollard.*
*William Warner, a prominent farmer of Edenton, Madison County, was over on business Thursday.*
*L H Hendren has sold out in Kansas and will return to Kentucky again in ten or twelve days.*
*M F Davis bought of Charles Overstreet four steers averaging 980 lbs at 4 3/4c per pound; from Henry Harris seven head averaging 970 lbs, at 4 and 4 1/2c; from William Teater, of Stone, three head averaging 980 lbs, at 4 3/4c.* p2c1

I have some documents relating to the purchase of the store by Forest Miller. He executed three notes for a total of $1,000 for the store. I have the checks paying off the notes. He also executed four notes for $50 each which I assume to be for the stock, or counters. This is another sign of generational passage--both J P Turner and J H Murphy were great entrepreneurs of their day. I think that N D Davis, another tycoon of Sulphur Well, is nearly through also.

October 24, 1902

Nicholasville now has electric lights and the editor says that "after nightfall it has the appearance of a town of some enterprise." p3c2

I have tried my best to give the flavor of the times as we go along, but periodically something attracts my attention to the fact that I have left something out. There were a lot more accomodations than you might expect for people that were transient, such as drummers, people passing through or visiting, students, and people who sold their property and were seeking other houses, or building a residence. There were hotels in places where they no longer exist, such as in Nicholasville, High Bridge, Keene, Paint Lick, etc. And, there were boarding houses and "rooms" in private residences. I suppose sometimes there was competiveness, or close relationships. A doctor was just shot at Paint Lick by the hotel manager, because he left the hotel for a boarding house, and then invited a drummer to have dinner with him at the boarding house. p3c3

The *Sulphur Well Correspondent* writes:

*W B Ray and daughter, Lelie, of Buckeye, were visiting Mrs D O Hunter, Monday.*
*John Ramsey, of Lincoln County, while on a visit to a relative, Lindsey Ray, of Buckeye, died of consumption, Sunday night.*
*Squire Hughes, of Buckeye, formerly of Jessamine, was a visitor from Saturday till Monday.*
*Dr Geo M Hendren went on a business trip to Edenton last week.*
*Corn sold at a sale across the river last week at from $1.27 to $1.40 per barrel.*
*The wife of Willard Whittaker, of Edenton, died last Sunday of typhoid fever.*
*Willard and James Stapp, of Newby, were over Monday.*
*Woodson Million, of Madison County, was the guest of his father-in-law, John Stapp, this week.*
*Meade Miller, of Oklahoma City, returned home Monday after several weeks visit.*
*Willard Wilson, of Buena Vista, was here this week.*
*Mrs Mary Woolfolk, of Lexington, was a visitor here last week.*
*John A Ham, one of the most prominent merchants of Madison County, was here Monday.*
*Edgar Layton, a popular young farmer of Idalia, was among the Madison visitors Monday last.*
*Geo W Million, of Million, Madison County, was among the visitors Monday.*
*N B Howard, one of the prominent and prosperous farmers of Newby, was among his many friends in Jessamine, Monday.*
*Among the numerous visitors here from Buckeye were: W B Ray, W F Burton, W A Stotts, and others. The Buckeye people are peaceable, prosperous and hospitable--in a word, they are good people.*
*Among the visitors from Madison were: William Warner, Samuel Moberly, Capt Hill, Wm Wylie, James Witt, James, Oliver, Caperton and E Vincent and William Barnes, all prominent citizens of Edenton neighborhood. p2c1*

I not sure whether Dr Hendren is listing all his patient visits or what. It is either that, or they are considering investments in Oklahoma.

October 31, 1902

The election is next Tuesday.

November 7, 1902

Ten Democratic congressmen out of eleven were elected.

The *Sulphur Well Correspondent* writes:

*Mrs Geo D Turpin was quite sick last Tuesday.*
*The little son of CC Cobb is quite sick with lung trouble.*
*Ernest Duncan, who was on the sick list, is, we're glad to say, out again.*
*W B Ray and daughter, Miss Lelia, of Buckeye, were on a short visit to Dr Hendren last week.*
*Corn is selling here at $1.75 delivered and at $1.50 at the heap. Hogs 6 to 6 1/2 cents.*
*Jno T Colling, Edward Murphy, Wm Short and others of Edenton were over last week.*
*Mrs James T Sageser was taken suddenly and seriously ill one day last week, but is much better now.*
*Mr and Mrs Creed Gott, of Richmond, formerly of this place, were visiting friends in this county last week.*
*Maston Hunter, of Iowa, who left here 32 years ago, was visiting here among his old friends last week. He returns home this week.*
*The election here last Tuesday passed off as quietly as a Sunday School picnic, if not more so. A very light vote was polled.*
*The beautiful, balmy, summer-like weather, of the past few weeks has induced the lilacs to bloom again, the second time this year. It looks strange and rather awesome to see the beautiful blue flowers in November. p2c1*

The Correspondent's mention of the lilacs reminds me of the immense row of lilacs on either side of our house in Sulphur Well. They were really old; their trunks several inches in thickness, and they bushed up and outward ten to twelve feet. I have always regretted that I took them all out because they had become so scrubby, and were so suseptible to frost, that they were no longer pretty. However, I should have saved at least one.

November 14, 1902

"Chiffon, lace crepe de chine, or soft finished satin, are used preferably for bridal gowns, the latter preceptibly different from the thick, stately material of former days." p4c3

November 21, 1902

"Dr Jno C Miller has moved into his handsome residence on Main Street. Mr J P Turner has also moved from Ambrose to his newly purchased home in Nicholasville...." p3c4

The *Sulphur Well Correspondent* writes:

*Samuel Moberly, of Edenton, was over last Monday.*
*Edgar Layton, of Idalia, is very low with typhoid fever at the residence of his father.*
*Mrs Taylor Sanders, of Stone, Garrard County, died of typhoid fever last week.*
*William Wilson, of Buena Vista, was over among his Jessamine friends Monday.*
*Clayton Turpin, wife and son, left Friday for Union City, for a few days visiting.*
*Thompson Hill and Miss Lelia Ray of Buckeye, were visiting Dr G M Hendren last Sunday.*
*Miss Nellie Hendren is spending the week with the family of Wm B Ray, at Buckeye.*
*W F Burton, of Giles, was on the sick list last week with the "shakes".*
*James W Cobb and wife are visiting Mr and Mrs John Whitenack, near Harrodsburg.*
*Messrs Ike Dunn and Richard Moore, of Bourne, Garrard County, were visiting their son, Charles Clubb, at this place. (It appears that the printer combined two items into one, this is obviously wrong).*
*J H Turner has moved to his father's residence, which he (the father) vacated recently to reside at his residence in Nicholasville.*
*Mitch Masters sold his farm near Pink last week to Geo Peel for $1,000. The farm consists of 55 acres. Masters bought the old Montague Carter place.*
*Frank Hubbard, L D Hendren and Rutherford Hendren, of Cincinnati, were visiting Robert Reagan at Edenton last week.*
*Dr Hendren spent Monday and Tuesday of last week with Robt Reagan at Edenton. Mr Reagan several days ago had a slight attack of paralysis, but is rapidly recovering.* p2c1

November 28, 1902

It's Thanksgiving and Dr Hendren has composed "Modern Maud Mullers". p4c7

December 5, 1902

From Little Hickman: "Mrs J P Overstreet was seriously sick last week, but is now improving." p2c4

The *Sulphur Well Correspondent* writes:

*Stephen Hill, of Buckeye, was visiting Dr Hendren, Sunday.*
*Irvine Peel arrived home from Decatur, Ill, last week.*
*Austin Smith, of Edenton, was visiting here Monday.*
*Miss Nellie Hendren returned home Sunday from a two weeks visit in Garrard County.*
*Mrs Emaline Peel moved, Wednesday to the J H Turner residence.*
*A good many hogs have changed hands here this week at 5 1/2 cts per pound.*
*J W Teater, of Edenton, was over on business Wednesday.*
*Oscar Sageser returned Thursday from a long Western trip to Oklahoma, Texas and Illinois.* p2c4

Oscar Sageser, who is the son of James Sageser, passed through Verdin, Illinois on his way back from a trip to Indian Territory. p3c4

December 12, 1902

Hugh Miller seems to have made a good investment with his farm which is now located only one mile from the Oklahoma City limits. He says that some of the land cost him less than $40 per acre, but that he could now sell it for $75. He says he has been offered $100 per acre for ten acre lots, unimproved. p2c1 Don't know when, yet, but eventually the "price was right", because he winds up in Fayetteville, Arkansas. Meade's farm is further out, and some of his decendants stayed around Oklahoma.

The *Sulphur Well Correspondent* writes:

*Austin Smith, of Edenton, Madison County, was over Monday.*
*Mr James Cobb has lost his dog "Dump," and it is a great loss to him.*
*John Mack, a 12 year old colored boy, was fooling with a loaded pistol, Friday night and it went off--those pistols always do that are not loaded--and the ball went through the middle finger, of his left hand. Dr Hendren had to amputate the finger. p2c4*

December 19, 1902

No report from Sulphur Well, and Christmas is a-coming.

December 26, 1902

The merchants are all reporting a better trade this year than at the same time last year. As I have indicated, they are advertising more effectively that they used to, and perhaps 1902 was better economically. Another year has come to a close.

## PASSING OF A LANDMARK - 1903

The old log school at Sulphur Well, made famous by Elder Jesse Walden, was torn down. Many of Sulphur Well's most illustrious citizens attended this school.

### January 2, 1903

The *Sulphur Well Correspondent* now has the soul of a poet. He begins and ends his report in verse:

*There are some who go in for work,*
*And some who go in for fun,*
*And others that around you lurk*
*Whose work is always "dun".*
*A M Askins is on the sick list.*
*J C Walton has moved his family to town.*
*Steve Hill, of Garrard County, was over last week.*
*Gabe Masters has moved back to his former residence at this place.*
*Jasper Wiley, of Madison County, was on this side one day last week.*
*J A Ham and Samuel Moberly, of Edenton, were over Sunday of last week.*
*F M Horine sold Monday four fat cattle to Mr Weisbach of Lexington at $3.60.*
*There died in Madison County last week, Elisha Warren, colored. Believing that he was poisoned, there will be an investigation.*
*Thompson Hill and Miss Minnie Broaddus, of Stone, Garrard County, were visiting Miss Nellie Hendren last Sunday.*
*Caperton Vincent, Geo Teater, Elisha Warren and Simpson Warren, of Edenton, were over a few days ago.*
*Woodson Murphy, an old soldier of Wolford's Cavalry, and who was captured and shot through the head with a carbine and left for dead, died Friday after a short illness from pnuemonia at his home near Edenton, Madison County.*
*O, where shall we go*
*As the beautiful snow,*
*Like coal bills amounting still higher;*
*While we shiver and shake*
*By an empty old grate,*
*Not a cent up can rake*
*To again replenish the fire.* p2c3

### January 16, 1903

Statehood is being proposed for a merged Oklahoma and Indian Territory. p1c

### January 23, 1903

"Kentucky needs two things above all else--good roads and good schools." p1c4 (only the front page is microfilmed)

January 30, 1903

The Secretary of the Interior is planning to auction off certain mineral and timber lands in Indian Territory. It is presently being surveyed and will be open for bids in March.

The Democrats plan to hold a primary to nominate candidates for the state offices. p2c1

The *Sulphur Well Correspondent* writes:

*John Woolfolk, of Lexington, was a visitor here this week.*
*Jno A Stapp, merchant and postmaster at Newby, was over for a day last week.*
*Woodson Murphy, who recently died of pneumonia, received an increase of pension to $30 per month on the day of his death.*
*A M Askins is still on the sick list, unable to run his shop.*
*There seems to be no bottom to the mud roads in this vicinity.*
*John Durham and family have moved to Woodford County.*
*Mrs Fanny Bundle, of Harrodsburg, is visiting Mrs N D Davis, her sister.*
*Mrs Jennie Wheeler, of Lexington, and Mrs Wm King and daughter, Madelle, of Buena Vista, were the guests of Mrs Belle Davis this week.*
*Thomas Warren has bought out the Miles Ferry and farm on the river and will run them himself in the future.*
*James Watts has rented and will soon move to a residence on J P Turner's farm here.*
*N D Davis sold to D C Terhune of Harrodsburg, Monday 25 head of young mules at $105 per head.*
*Geo S Warner, of Idalia, was over on a short visit Saturday.*
*N D Davis was in Lexington last Monday on a business trip.*
*It is said the world has a place for everybody. The trouble is that there's generally somebody else in it.* p3c6 *(There is no front page to this issue.)*

February 6, 1903

Klein's Department Store has a special sale on "Gent's" hats for 98 cents. p3c7-8

February 13, 1903

"There is a greater demand for good mules all over the State than for years and they are bringing good prices." p2c4

The *Sulphur Well Correspondent* writes:

*Colds and la grippe are quite prevalent at this time.*
*Born, to the wife of CC Cobb, a fine daughter.*
*Mrs Theresa Tudor left for a visit in Madison County, Monday.*
*John Andrew Ham, of Edenton, was visiting here Monday.*
*Oscar Sageser bought last week of Matthew Masters a fine pair of work mules for $300.*
*Alvin Howard, a prominent farmer of Madison County was over last Monday on a visit.*
*"Fabe" Peel has been quite sick for some days with nervous prostration.*
*Mrs Mildred Hendren is slowly improving from a serious attack of sciatica. (James Hendren's wife)*
*Miss Blanche Askins was seriously ill for several days this week with tonsilitis.*
*Arch Whittaker, Lerny, Ill, was here recently to see his sister, who was not then expected to live.*
*William Wylie, of near Giles, and a prominent farmer, visits his Jessamine friends quite frequently.*
*The time of holding the monthly meeting at the church here has been changed from the third Lord's Day to the second Lord's Day.*
*Napoleon Howard, W S Sanders and George Warner, all prominent farmers of Idalia, Madison County, were among the visitors this week.*
*A M Askins who has been sick for quite a while, is able to be out again we are glad to state.*
*Hamlet Foster, who will soon be a citizen of our village bought out James Watts, who will move to a residence on J H Turner's place.*
*Thursday evening of last week Oscar Sageser and Mrs Irene Bourne, daughter of Ed E Bourne, slipped off slyly to Lexington accompanied by Mr and Mrs Walter Davis and were quietly married all "unbeknownest" to the "old 'uns". They returned the same night to his father's house where a bountiful feast and a few invited guests awaited the happy pair and all enjoyed themselves till a late hour. The young couple, who have just embarked together upon life's tempestous sea, have the best wishes of the writer and a host of friends who cannot but hope for them a long prosperous and a happy journey down life's road hand in hand together.* p2c3

Dr Hendren's daughter is Mrs Walter Davis, so I feel sure he was one of the guests at the wedding feast. It sure is hard to picture Mr Oscar and Miss Irene running off to get married. I suppose my first recollection of them would be in the nineteen thirties, when they would have been in their fifties. They, as was everyone else their age, were old and "stogy". Even Edith, who goes back one more generation than I, can only remember Jim Cobb sitting on his front porch. I knew many of the people that I am now writing about, because they lived into the forties, fifties, and sixties. As a matter of fact, I was a pall bearer for several of them from the mid-fifties onward.

February 20, 1903

From Little Hickman: "Mrs J P Overstreet bought a family horse from Calvin Bruner for $90." p2c2

February 27, 1903

The *Sulphur Well Correspondent* writes:

*La grippe is quite prevalent and severe in this neighborhood.*
*Snow drifted in places from 4 to 6 feet deep.*
*Mrs Theresa Tudor returned Sunday from a lengthy visit in Madison County.*
*Millard F Davis is having a seige of la grippe.*
*Dr G M Hendren is out again after a very severe attack of illness.*
*Morris Bourne left Tuesday for Decatur, Ill, where he will remain several months.*
*Mrs W B Walker, who has been sick for some time, remains quite poorly.*
*Mrs Walter Davis is recovering from an acute attack of influenza.*
*Mrs G M Hendren is down with a severe attack of the prevailing disease, la grippe.*
*Mr and Mrs J W Cobb returned home Saturday from a lengthy visit to Mercer County.*
*Hemp breaking has been getting on of late rather slowly on account of the very backward weather.*
*Miss Lelia Ray, of Buckeye, and Thompson Hill, of McCreary, Garrard County, will be the guests of Miss Nellie G Hendren, Saturday and Sunday.* p2c2

The deep snow could sure put a crimp in traveling on country roads. I remember stories of how in the "old days" that groups of men would shovel out the drifted areas. Dr Hendren didn't mention that here. Four of this week's items pertained to Dr Hendren, his wife, and two daughters.

March 6, 1903

"A Missouri farmer gave his son eighty acres of land saying 'My son, I believe I am a better father to you by giving you eighty acres of Missouri land than by sending you to college to learn how to smoke cigarettes and play football.'" p2c3

March 13, 1903

This has been a hard winter on cattle, and many farmers have suffered heavy losses. p2c4

March 20, 1903

From Madison: "The Grady residence near Kirksville, owned by Wm Hendren, was destroyed by fire...." p2c4

The *Sulphur Well Correspondent* writes:

*For some weeks the old Kentucky (River) has been on a rampage.*
*Mrs Lee Davis was quite sick last Tuesday, but is now better.*
*W B Ray, of Buckeye, was over on a visit last week. He likes Jessamine County people.*
*W F Burton, of Giles, who has been quite sick with pneumonia, is out again.*
*Miss Lila Ray and Miss Beatrice Ray, of Buckeye, were visiting Dr G M Hendren this week.*
*Mrs J H Turner is visiting her father, Rev Grinstead, at Flemingsburg.*

*Elder Geo W Hildebrand, of Wilmore, will preach at the church here on the second Lord's Day in each month.*

*The fourth Lord's Day in each month at Little Hickman will be occupied by Eld G W Hildebrand.*

*The bottom has about fallen out of the pike and the yellow clay is showing.*

*A M Askins is about again, after a lengthy illness. He has not been able to return to his shop for three or four weeks.*

*Mr Jno A Ham will return to the state of Illinois soon, he thinks of going into business at Bloomington.*

*Dr G M Hendren bought a fine mare at the sale of John A Hammon, last Saturday, at a fair price. He also bought a half-Jersey cow for $50.*

*Mr Fletcher Tudor, of Madison County, who is 89 years old, is as spry as a young man one half his age and is going about wherever he wants to go. p2c4*

April 3, 1903

"King-Hendren.-A very pretty wedding took place at the home of H H Lowry. Sunday afternoon, the contracting parties being Mr Howard King, eldest son of Mr W T King, of Polly's Bend, Garrard County and Miss Nellie Hendren, the pretty daughter of Dr Geo M Hendren, of Ambrose, Rev D B Cooper, officiating." p2c2

April 10, 1902

According to the editor "Lexington will have four hangings in May. If it could have about four a day for a while, perhaps then some of the guilty ones would not longer go unpunished." p2c1

April 17, 1903

The *Sulphur Well Correspondent* writes:

*Thomas Walker is suffering severely from the effects of "poison oak".*
*N B Howard, of Baldwin, Madison County, has been here the greatest part of the week.*
*D H Tudor and family of Bloomington, Ill, have moved in with James Hendren.*
*Mrs Jas H Turner returned from visiting her parents at Flemingsburg Tuesday.*
*Wm Wylie, of Giles, was visiting this section last Wednesday.*
*Jack Hendren, of Kansas, is visiting his brother, James Hendren.*
*E Vincent, of Edenton, was visiting friends here the latter part of last week.*
*John Andrew Ham, lately a merchant at Edenton, has sold out to Mr Fuller of Valley View and moved to Bloomington to go into business.*
*Some dogs that had been among N D Davis sheep met with just deserts Wednesday morning. Its a great pity that more of the worthless curs that overrun this neighborhood don't merit the same fate. p2c3*

I don't know what the attraction is in Bloomington. It is evident that a colony of Tudors and Hendrens live there. Scottie's sister Bertha met Alfred Bennett while visiting that area.

May 1, 1903

The Little Hickman correspondent reports that J C Ferrell has leased over 2,000 acres of land for oil and gas exploration as agent for a Pennsylvania company. p2c4

"Born--To the wife of Mr Charles Clubb, at Ambrose, April 16, a son--Newton D." p3c6 This is the grandson of Newt Davis, the stock-man, trader, and farmer.

The *Sulphur Well Correspondent* writes:

*There is an epidemic of mumps in this vicinity.*
*There is likely to be an exodus to Indian Territory this fall.*
*A J Sageser sold last week his black buggy horse for $100.*
*Hamlet Foster sold a good work horse last week for $150.*
*John Taylor, son of Leroy Taylor, who has been seriously sick for a week or more, is improving.*
*Miss Sallie Grimes of Lexington, was visiting friends here several days last week.*
*D B Tudor and family are visiting among friends in Madison this week.*
*Gardening has scarcely commenced here owing to the continued wet and wintry weather.*
*William Short, an old soldier, died of a complications of diseases, at his home at Edenton, Monday.*
*Mrs E E Bourne was taken Tuesday night with a severe attack of acute indigestion, and for some time was quite ill.*
*Mr and Mrs Howard King, Buena Vista, were visiting Dr and Mrs G M Hendren, Saturday and Sunday of this week.*
*William King left last Tuesday for the Indian Territory and Oklahoma. He expects to make an extensive tour of the two territories.*
*F M Hudson and wife met with what nearly proved a serious accident Monday. Their teams collided with another driven by two young men. The horse became unmanageable and commenced to kick. Mr Hudson was kicked down and his wife also narrowly excaped the heels of the vicious animals. There was some damage done to Hudson's vehicle. p2c5*

I guess that Dr Hendren has stirred the imagination of the natives and that several are considering relocation. His daughter just married Howard King, and William King is about to tour the territories.

May 15, 1903

The first automobile in Jessamine County is owned by J S Stratton. He paid $925 for it, and it was "pronounced by those who saw it as being the finest automobile that has been in Nicholasville." p3c4

May 22, 1903

The Chicago Automobile Club is passing through Nicholasville on its way to Mammoth Cave on July 1 and 2. p4c3

May 29, 1903

"Chas W Miller, city solicitor of Lexington, and one of the most popular young Democrats in the Blue grass Metropolis, was here last Sturday for a few hours. He is a son of M M Miller, a native of Jessamine County, formerly a prominent merchant of Irvine, but now living in Lexington." p3c3

The *Sulphur Well Correspondent* writes:

*Thomas Warren, of Edenton, Madison County, was visiting among his Jessamine friends, Tuesday.*
*An old landmark of the village is being torn away--the old school house where Eld Jesse Waldrop taught pupils from many states before the war.*
*Alexander Shoat, formerly of this county, and son in law of William Walker, of near Sanders' Ferry, was killed at Kokomo, Ind, Monday morning. No particulars were given in the dispatch. Alexander should be quite well remembered by many people with whom he has dealings in the produce line.*
*The store and post office at Edenton, Madison County, was broken into last Friday and some loose change, clothing, knives and other articles were taken. James Durham was captured in Nicholasville with the goods on him. He was doing quite a thriving trade with the dwellers of Hervy-town and selling goods at ridiculously low prices even for a "cheap John". Jim was jugged and acknowledged the stolen goods, but wants Uncle Sam to try him this time. He has already served two terms and is now subject to the habitual criminal law which would land him for life. Jim is smart for one of his age. p2c1*

June 5, 1903

Just as I suspected. Dr G M Hendren, (his brother) W L Hendren, and F M Horine started Tuesday for the Indian and Oklahoma Territories. They will arrive first in South McAlister, continue on to Muscogee and Oemulgee, and then to Oklahoma City. They expect to be gone several weeks, and promise to keep the readers of the Journal informed about their trip. p3c4-5

June 12, 1903

Another son for George M Berry, who for a time was the Sulphur Well correspondent. He weights nine pounds, and his father says that he is a "drummer and a Democrat." p3c5

June 19, 1903

Dr Hendren has written two lengthy letters to the Journal--three columns long. The first is dated June 9, and postmarked Oklahoma City. It describes the beautiful country he sees on the trip out. The next letter is dated June 11, datelined Muscogee. This letter is devoted mostly to describing the procedure to buy or lease Indian lands. p1c3-5

June 26, 1903

Cars on the Inter-urban from Nicholasville to Lexington are expected to be running by September 1st. p3c6

July 3, 1903

Dr Hendren writes from Oklahoma City, which he says is without a doubt "the coming metropolis of the great Southwest." Its population is now 25,000, more than double that when Dr Miller first visited. He calls the country beautiful and fertile; and its climate mild and healthy. Dr Hendren describes the business establishments, schools, and churches. He tells of the agricultural products, and transportation. He concludes by saying that there are still opportunities for investment. p4c1

July 10, 1903

The 4th of July was extremely quiet this year, broken only, says the editor, by an occasional fire-cracker. However, people showed their patriotism by "decorating their residences with the stars and stripes." p3c1

"The fight among the Kentucky Republicans over the nomination for governor promises to be a lively one...." p2c1

"Mrs T W Downing, of New York, who has not been in good health of late, will spend the summer in the Catskill Mountains, and not in Kentucky as many friends here hoped she would." p3c3 This is Elizabeth Miller, daughter of Dr Miller.

July 17, 1903

Dr Hendren writes again from Oklahoma. He says the prosperity of Oklahoma City is based upon the prosperity of the homesteaders. This is how he describes the countryside:
> (He sees)...the orchards and vineyards, the fields of grain and vegetables, the beautiful fields of cotton, white for the pickers, the magnificent pastures with herds of fine grade cattle, and crowning the eminances, the comfortable farm houses and capacious barns. And when he remembers that only 12 years have elapsed since this was all unbroken prairie, without an inhabitant save the cowboys...he is filled with admiration for the hardy pioneers.... p1c5-6

Dr Hendren didn't live to see that same country become a "dust-bowl" and the flood of "Okies" to California, or anywhere and everywhere in the thirties. I wonder how many were Kentuckians by birth!

"Dr G M Hendren returned last Saturday from a trip through Oklahoma and Indian Territories." p3c3

"Harry Hendren, better known as 'Pat' in Nicholasville, who has been with the Simmons Hardware Co, of St Louis for four years, has had his salary increased each year, which speaks well for the young man." p3c3

### July 24, 1903

"...Cassius M Clay died at his home in Madison County Wednesday night, aged 93 years". p2c1 He was the "Lion of White Hall" most of his life, but a pussycat toward the end. Everyone knows that he married a teenager when he was in his eighties. She was totally unschooled and he tried to teach her to be a lady, much like Eliza Doolittle. But, in the end, she ran off with a young fellow and lived in the vicinity of Versailles. He bought a house for them to live in, then later they came to live with him at the mansion. But, that didn't work out either. A sad ending.

Pope Leo XIII "not only recogized by the world as a great prelate, but (also) a great statesman" died Monday in Rome." p2c1

"There will be no camp meeting at High Bridge this summer." p3c1 No explanation was given, but probably because there is a Wilmore Camp Meeting beginning next Tuesday. p3c1

Dr Hendren's daughter Nellie has been hurt in accident at Polly's Bend.

> Mrs Howard King, daughter of Dr Geo M Hendren, of Ambrose, was seriously hurt at her home at Polly's Bend in Garrard County, Tuesday. Mrs King had started to ride from the barn, when her head struck the top of the doorway, knocking her from the horse, badly injuring her left hip and otherwise bruising her. The extent of the injuries can not yet be known. p3c4

### July 31, 1903

Baseball teams are being organized in all the villages. Many people are camping at various sites on the river, fishing and having fish-frys. Imagine the heat and humidity on the river banks in those valleys!

### August 7, 1903

Pope Pius X has been elected "Supreme Pontiff of the Roman Catholic Church". p2c1

Drought has ruined the hemp crop. An auctioneer who travels the area says that not 25 percent of the crop will be broken (fiber removed). p3c2

### August 14, 1903

"Eld Adam Adcock and family of Newport, are visiting Mr and Mrs A K Adcock." p3c3

"Mrs Elizabeth Wheeler and daughters, Misses Ida and Mary, of Cincinnati, are guests of Mrs W S Hendren." p3c3 Elizabeth Wheeler is Mary E(lizabeth), and the sister of Dr Hendren and W S Hendren.

Should you happen to be in the Saratoga or Newport area, you should note that "afternoon gowns at both these resorts, are often quite as dressy as those seen in the evening". The main difference is in the sleeves, arms being bare in the afternoon (except for gloves). p4c1

August 21, 1903

"Mr and Mrs Howard King spent Sunday with relatives in Danville." p3c3

The *Sulphur Well Correspondent* writes:

*A very fine rain last Wednesday.*
*J W Cobb and wife are visiting at Harrodsburg this week.*
*James Walls moved to the W H Hoover place last Tuesday.*
*Jno A Ham has returned from Bloomington, Ill, and bought out the store at Edenton, Madison County.*
*Mrs Mary E Wheeler and daughter, of Cincinnati, were visiting here Wednesday.*
*James Woodward's child, who was quite seriously hurt by a window sash falling on his hand last Sunday, is improving.*
*Mr and Mrs James T Sageser left on Wednesday for a two months visit to their children at Virden, Ill.*
*Mr Drummond McMurtry returned Monday from a visit to Oklahoma and Indian Territories.*
*N B Howard, W A Sanders, Jno A Ham, and several other Madison men were visitors last Monday.*
*Mr Richard Burton, a prominent horse and mule buyer of Garrard County, was over Monday.*
*Walter K Davis has bought and soon will move to the residence of Dr G M Hendren, who is going to Oklahoma City.*
*Messrs Milliard T and Willard W Davis are preparing to go to Oklahoma and the Indian Territories about Sept 15.*
*Dr Hendren and wife who will start for Oklahoma City on Sept 15th, will have a sale of their household goods etc., on Aug 29.*
*Mrs Nellie King, who was recently quite seriously hurt by being thrown from a horse, is slowly improving.*
*John Hendren, who has been visiting his brother, James, for some months, left for his home at Iowa Point, Kans, last Monday.*
*Mr Houston Woodward, who has bought the old homestead, is greatly improving the same. T J Horine is also improving the old Reynolds homestead which he now owns.* p2c3

Although this looks like the end, it isn't. The notice of his public sale shows that he is offering: a horse and buggy, some hogs, a milk cow, another buggy and harness, two suites of furniture, two dressers with French plate glass mirrors, one folding lock bed, two folding couches, and other articles of household and kitchen furniture. p2c7

August 28, 1903

The Nicholasville baseball team played the Bourbon Stars this past Tuesday at home, winning 7 to 2. p2c4

September 4, 1903

Approximately 250 people took the Chattanooga excursion from Lexington this past week. About 50 from Nicholasville, and 80 from Wilmore made the trip. The train departed at 9am and arrived in Chattanooga at 5:30pm. They toured the city that evening, and spent the next morning at Chickamauga. Then, it was on to Lookout Mountain for the afternoon, where they also lodged for the night. The next day they took a trolley to Missionary Ridge and started back home after lunch. The passengers said that it ended "one of the (most) enjoyable outings of a lifetime". p1c5

September 11, 1903

"Mr and Mrs J H Turner, of Ambrose, attended Conference at Cynthiana." Also "Mr J H Murphy returned Monday from a ten days' stay at Spring City, Tenn." And "Mrs W S Hendren is visiting relatives in Cincinnati and attending the Fall Festival." p3c3

September 18, 1903

Dr and Mrs G M Hendren, of Ambrose; Mr and Mrs Howard King, of Buena Vista; --------- Holman, and J Hunt McMurtry of Nicholasville left Tuesday for Oklahoma. Dr Hendren and Mr King will locate at Oklahoma City, and Mr Holman will go to Muskogee, I T, where he has two daughters. Mr McMurtry is making a prospecting trip and will return the latter part of this month. p3c3

October 2, 1903

Kentucky wiped out its state debt when it collected over one million dollars owed it by the Federal Government for claims of the Civil and Spanish American Wars. p1c3

October 9, 1903

Carrie Nation visted her brother at Bryantsville, and later spoke to a packed house at the courthouse in Lancaster. p2c1

October 23, 1903

Several people from Pink, including Melvin Dean, and Mrs Morris Dean, and the Davis brothers from Sulphur Well, have gone to Oklahoma on a prospecting trip. p2c3

November 13, 1903

Tom Hendren, known as "Uncle Tommy", brother of William Hendren, father of Nellie and others, has retired. He has run a grocery and produce store on South Main Street.p3c2

November 27, 1903

Mrs Kittie Knight died at her home in the Watts' Mill neighborhood, Saturday morning, aged 80. She was the mother of James Knight of Camp Nelson. Funeral Services were held at Roberts' Chapel, Sunday, Rev C M Humphry officiating. The remains were interred in the Sageser burying ground. p2c2

Kittie is the daughter of John C and Susan Sageser Watts. She married Aquilla Knight, known as "Quiller". Susan Sageser and Celia Sageser, who married Merriman F Miller, were sisters. One of Celia's sons was named John C Miller; another son was Francis S Miller who married Elizabeth Jane Williams. Kittie Knight and Francis S Miller were first cousins. I assume this is why Kittie and Elizabeth were friends, and maybe considered themselves related, and why Kittie stayed for a while with Elizabeth. I have pieced this together from pp 14 and 27 of the Sageser Genealogy. The tip was Kittie's being buried in the Sageser Cemetery.

December 4, 1903

"The sad news comes from New York City that Mrs Thos R Downing is in failing health and has been sent South for the winter. She is the daughter of Dr Jno C Miller, of Nicholasville, and a most lovable woman." p3c3 Her health problem must have been overcome, because she lived for more than fifty years longer.

December 25, 1903

"Mr and Mrs Alfred Bennett, of Canton, Ill, and Miss Emma Hendren, Speedwell, are visiting Mrs A K Adcock." p3c3

Dr (J) Harry Hendren left Monday for Louisville where he has accepted a position as lecturer in the College Hospital of Medicine. Dr Hendren is one of Madison's brightest young men and all his friends predict great success for him in his profession.
(The preceeding was from the Richmond Pantagraph) The Journal adds:
Dr Hendren spent Monday night with his cousin, Mr W S Hendren, in Nicholasville. p3c3
(The paper is tattered and torn, and the microfilmer layered it beyond recogition. This is the final page of the year.) This ends the thirtieth year of the Journal. Dr Hendren said he began writing his correspondence at the beginning, so he too was in his thirtieth year when he left for Oklahoma. He will be back.

# EARLY HISTORY - 1904

Dr Hendren writes about the early history of Sulphur Well. The name comes from the presence of an ever-flowing stream of sulphur water, pumped from a well, located in the center of the community. This is also the year that Elizabeth Jane Miller dies.

### Jan 1, 1904

From Pink: "Mrs Kate Barkley is very ill at the home of her sister, Mrs J P Overstreet." p2c3

### Jan 22, 1904

The Legislature is in session, and a bill was introduced "to regulate the running of automobiles upon the public highways ..." p2c1 The bill prohibits speeds greater than 15 miles per hour. When meeting a horseman or carriage, the motorist is supposed to stop until they are safely past.

### Jan 29, 1904

From Pink: "Mrs J P Overstreet has been quite sick for several days." p2c4

### Feb 5, 1904

Wheat in Chicago hit 93 cents per bushel this past Wednesday. The extremely cold weather is believed to have hurt the Jessamine crop, and the editor is predicting the price will rise to more than a dollar a bushel. p2c3

### Feb 12, 1904

After spending four months in Oklahoma City, Dr Hendren writes about life there. He started out glowing about the scenic route, and points of interest along the way; but, when he begins to describe the situation in Oklahoma, back home quickly becomes "God's Country" in comparison. The reason is that the influx of people seeking their fortunes, has resulted in high prices for food and shelter. The weather is cold, the people can't find jobs, and they are disgruntled. He describes his search for a house to rent, and the high price of even the most humble of dwelling.

> You move on to the next and the next, and make the weary, hopeless grind only to return to your cheerless cot at night to weep over the memory of the old folks at home, a homesick, houseless stranger in the `greatest city in the world' for its age. I did start out to tell something of the best advertised and the most overdone city in America ..., but I seem to have been led astray .... p1c3-4

Feb 26, 1904

The Panama Canal treaty has been ratified by the U S Senate this past week. Construction will begin as soon as the treaty is signed by both governments. p2c1

March 4, 1904

The Legislature has appropriated $1 million for the construction of a new capitol building, but many in Frankfort are unhappy at the site chosen. p1c3

March 11, 1904

Dr Hendren had some feedback on his last letter, and said that his negative comments pertained only to the pricing of merchants and landlords, and not to the opportunities of the the state as a whole. He points out the good aspects of Oklahoma in this letter. p1c3-4

This could be the continuation of the sad ending of the Dr Wilds story. His wife Lizzie is selling their cottage at the court house door on March 21st. p2c5

March 18, 1904

Meade Miller is convelescing at Hot Springs, Arkansas. p3c3 See the April 1st item.

March 25, 1904

St Louis is making its final preparations for the World's Fair that will open on April 30th. There will be "palaces of Varied Industries, Machinery, Manufacture, Mines and Metallurgy, Education and Electricity." p4c3

April 1, 1904

Hugh Miller's letter to his father is published here. He says that the small towns one hundred miles to the southwest are in great distress. Prairie fires have wiped out many farmers, and left them destitute. He said that his situation is quite different; that his farm is located only one mile from the Oklahoma City limit, and 240 acres of it could be sold for over $19 thousand. He has 80 more acres that he says will be worth at least $10 thousand within four or five years. He closes with a report that Meade has muscular rheumatism. p1c3

April 8, 1904

Dr Edward O Guerrant, an evangelist, formerly from Wilmore, but now a resident of Umatilla, Florida writes the Journal periodically with news about himself and Kentuckians in the area. He says that over fifty Kentuckians have wintered there this year. p1c3

April 22, 1904

"Mr John D Rockefellow (sic), Jr., before his Bible class in the Fifth-avenue Baptist Church, took 'Humility and Contentment' as the subject for his discourse." p1c5

May 6, 1904

Dr Hendren writes again from Oklahoma. This letter concerns mostly one of the early settlers of Oklahoma, a man by the name of David L Payne. Dr Hendren says that he knew him when both lived in Wichita, Kansas. p1c4-5

"Mrs Thos W Downing (Lizzie Miller), of New York ... is with her father, Dr Jno C Miller...." Her health has improved, and she will return to New York after her visit to Kentucky, and expects to "spend the summer in the Catskill Mountains". p3c3

May 20, 1904

"S N Snowden had an attack of paralysis last week but is at present improving." p3c1 I assume that this means that he had a stroke.

June 3, 1904

"The Jessamine County Sunday School Association, representing all denominations, will hold it first meeting for this year at Ambrose Sunday next...." It is an all-day meeting and people are asked to bring "well-filled baskets." p2c2

June 17, 1904

"The eighteenth annual session of the Kentucky Chautauqua will be held at its old home at Woodland Park, Lexington, June 28 to July 8..." A good program is planned and a large attendance is expected. p1c4

June 24, 1904

"Each season has its own peculiar fad, and this summer linen is the rage." Linen dresses are cool and serviceable and this year "free from flounces and furbelows". p1c6

July 15, 1904

"Dr Geo M Hendren is home from Oklahoma." p3c3

"Mrs M L Dean has returned from a trip to Estill County." p3c7 This is Myrtie Snowden.

July 29, 1904

Dr Hendren writes a letter to the Journal based upon his living in Oklahoma for the past ten months. He says that despite the nation-wide depression that Oklahoma continues to grow. He sees statehood in the future as soon as politics permits. p1c5

August 19, 1904

Dr Hendren writes a poem which he dedicated to his wife:

### A HUNDRED YEARS

A hundred years from now, my dear,
A hundred years from now,
No trace of sorrow or of care
Will sit upon the brow,
The summer days that we have known
Then past beyond recall;
The grassy lawn then overgrown
Where now the rose leaves fall. p1c5

The poem goes on for three more verses. It's more poignant than happy. In one verse he speaks of a life of grief, strife, turmoil, and pain they "shall not know again". And, he writes, that in a hundred years they'll both be forgotten, "with none to drop a silent tear, in dearest memory." p1c5 Perhaps he's wrong about that. Ninety-two years later I've done a lot to revive his memory.

"Miss Bess Adcock is visiting her aunt, Mrs (John) Woolfolk, on West Maxwell, Lexington." p3c3 Someday I'd like to learn more about the Woolfolks. Relationships remain confused. To be Bessie's aunt, Mrs Woolfolk would have to be her mother's, Addie Hendren, sister.

August 26, 1904

"Mr Thomas Hendren had a very serious attack of cholera morbus ... but is now out of danger." p3c3

The World's Fair in St Louis is attracting nearly 100,000 visitors a day, and 7 million thus far. p4c3

September 9, 1904

Dr Hendren writes this week about the early history of Sulphur Well. p1c3 He says that it had no particular founder, it "just growed". See the following narrative:

The first recollection any one has of that beginning was a little log tavern kept by Dick Reynolds, way back in the thirties.... That tavern, which some of the older people can remember, stood where the dwelling of Mrs Elizabeth Miller now stands. Jonathan Jones also ran a little grocery store and saloon along in the '40's that stood in the corner of the yard where T J Horine now resides and was demolished several years ago, as has also passed away every vestige of the more recent and more pretentious dram shop in the little but once upon a time, more boisterous village ....

In about the fifties the town also boasted the possession of a tannery and a carding factory, the former run, I think by the McCabes; the latter by Moses Masters, both just back of Miller's store. The church property, where the Christian Church now stands, was deeded to the old Baptist Liberty Society in 1821. The present church house was built in 1886. An academy was built by Elder Jesse Waldrop about 1859, and flourished for several years under his capable management, drawing many students from the surrounding counties and from eight or ten different states.

The sulphur well, from which the village takes its name, and from whose pure and healthful waters the villagers derive almost uninterrupted health the year around-- for it is unsurpassed for these qualities by any waters anywhere--was dug, or rather dug and bored, at least 120 years ago. It is 80 feet deep, 20 feet dug, and 60 bored, and has been a never failing source of happiness and health to the community ever since. At first, it is said by old timers, to have been a deerlick .... This deerlick induced some men to dig for a salt well. When solid rock was reached then boring was substituted and sulphur water was struck instead of salt water. Boring further was stopped by the auger breaking shear off far down the hole.

But sulphur water is by no means the only deep earth product of the place as there is a zinc mine, not now in operation, and a barytes mine, also now unworked, which was used as substitute for white lead, as well as every indication of vast quantities of natural gas close to the surface. It has blown up through the rock formation with a violence sufficient to grind the hard, flinty limestone rock into a powder. The first authentic record of these terrific explosions that have frequently taken place since that time, one of which was witnessed by the writer when huge stones were blown as high as the tall forest oak trees, and others ground into dust by the mighty underground force, occurred while some Irish laborers were excavating stone for the county jail, built about 1869.

Dr Hendren goes on to say that these explosions could only be attributed to natural gas. He added that the "upheavals of gas occur generally near to or in the bed of the little stream that winds through the village, and sometimes, after an explosion, oil has been seen floating on the water." p1c3

The above history is very concise, and I hope accurate. I haven't tried to verify any of it. I am amazed at his certainty of natural gas in the area. It was never mentioned during my life there. I have walked an awfully lot of the branch that flows through Sulphur Well, without ever seeing evidence of such a violent explosion, or of the quarrying that he refers to by Irish workers. The mines that he mentioned are well known, of course.

"Mr Emmett Hendren left Tuesday morning for Minneapolis, Minn., where he has secured a position in the wholesale dry goods firm of his brother W G Hendren. Emmett is a good boy and his many friends here hope he will meet with the success he deserves." p3c3
Emmett came back to Nicholasville, and lived his life there running a paint and wallpaper store.

September 16, 1904

"Dr G M Hendren is in Oklahoma City, OT, on business." p3c3

Mrs Margaret Horine, wife of Joshua Horine who died in 1881, died at her home at age 86 on Sept 9th. She has eight living children: "Mrs J H Murphy, Mrs Mattie J Shearer, Mrs Ella C Taylor, Lexington, Messrs T J, M P, J F, F M, and C W. Horine." p3c6

September 23, 1904

He sounds like a solid citizen, but we have no known family ties.

> The Democrats of Madison County did the right thing when they renominated Hon R W Miller for the legislature. Possessed of a brilliant mind, a charming personality, and an eloquent voice, his future in Kentucky politics is secure. Mr Miller is the chairman of the Democratic Party of Madison County, a member of the State Central Committee... and the Representative from his county. p1c5

The *Sulphur Well Correspondent* writes:

> *Guy Stacy bought of Sam Taylor a fine colt for $65.*
> *Mrs Forest Miller has been confined to her bed for the past week with an attack of fever, but is now able to be out again.*
> *Quite a crowd left Tuesday morning to visit the St Louis Exposition. Among them were E E Bourne, L J Ware, M F Murphy, A O Brooks, Miss Maggie Harris, Sam Taylor and family.*
> *Mr and Mrs John Brooks and little daughter, Margaret, of Lexington, are visiting his sister, Mrs John Wood.*
> *Mrs A M Askins, who has been confined to her bed for some time, is improving slowly.*
> *A young student from Lexington filled the pulpit at this place Sunday morning and night.*

*Mrs Henry Woodward and little daughter returned to their home at Dayton, Ohio, Sunday, after a two weeks visit to his parents, Mr and Mrs James Woodward.*
*The infant son of Mr and Mrs Marshall Davis has been quite sick this week.*
*Jesse Foster purchased the residence of Will Underwood for $450.  p2c2*

September 30, 1904

"Miss Dora Murphy is visiting Miss May Taylor, at Lexington." p3c4 Besides being friends, they are first cousins, the mothers were Horines.

"Mr and Mrs W C Crosley, of St Louis, are the guests of Mr and Mrs A K Adcock." p3c4

October 7, 1904

"The next legislature will be asked to pass a law requiring all nominations of all political parties to be made by primary instead of convention...." p1c5

October 14, 1904

"Mr Meade Miller, of Oklahoma City, O T , is spending a few days with his father, Dr J C Miller. Meade says land is rapidly advancing in Oklahoma Territory and in some sections has doubled in value in the past twelve months." p3c3

November 4, 1904

The *Sulphur Well Correspondent* writes:

*Sam Hill sold a lot of fat hogs Monday at 4 and 4 1/2 cts.*
*Miss T Miller has returned from a visit with relatives in Estill County.*
*Mr and Mrs James Hendren are visiting relatives in Madison County.*
*Mrs A M Askins, who has been sick for some time, continues very low.*
*Mr Allen Vincent, of Edneyville, Madison County, was over on business, Monday.*
*Mrs Jas H Turner and little daughter, Mamie, returned from a visit to the World's Fair, Saturday.*
*Brutus C Sanders, of Madison County, returned from a visit to the west last Monday.*
*Wm Hudson, who has been down with dysentery for some weeks, is still quite ill.*
*Water is being hauled from the well here for miles around as far as (the) Kentucky River.*
*p2c4*

> Mrs Elizabeth Miller died at her home at Sulphur Well, Thursday morning, Nov 3. She had not been well for some time. A few days ago (she) became seriously ill, and continued to grow worse until death came. The deceased was the widow of Frank Miller, and leaves five children, Mrs S N Snowden (Lucy), Miss T Miller, Sulphur Well; Mrs Wm Richardson, Wisemantown; and John and Forest Miller." p3c5

This is the family matriarch, and for some time I considered making her the heroine of this story. The family bible begins with her and Francis S Miller in 1851, and my line of decent is throught Forest, their youngest son. However, as my research broadened, I began to realize that the families of the other children of Merriman and Celia Miller were too important to leave out. Then, to my surprise, I discovered a whole new family of Hendrens, particularly Dr Hendren who turned out to be "the" Sulphur Well correspondent, to whom I am related. So, the story became about Sulphur Well, and the family history of the Millers and Hendrens within that community.

November 11, 1904

Roosevelt was elected by "record-breaking majorities--solid south left alone for the Democrats." p2c1 Despite Teddy Roosevelt's victory Jessamine County Democrats won "by a good majority". p3c4

Lock 10 at Ford, Ky has been completed and is now open for boat traffic. Work on Lock 11 "at Irvine, is being pushed forward at a brisk rate." p3c2 They are gradually working their way up the river toward Beattyville.

The *Sulphur Well Correspondent* writes:

*Miss Nancy Hare is visiting her sister, Mrs Johnston, of Lancaster.*
*The election of this place passed off so quietly we hardly realized we had one.*
*Miss Emma West, after a pleasant visit of several weeks to relatives in Illinois, returned home Saturday.*
*Mrs Will Richardson, who was called home by the death of her mother, Mrs Elizabeth Miller, has returned to her home at Irvine.*
*Messrs Zeke Herndon and Ed Ware, have bought out the grocery of Mr Reynolds at the Black Bridge and will continue to run a store and butcher shop combined. p2c4*

November 18, 1904

"Miss Maude Miller, of Lexington, is visiting Dr J C Miller." p3c4 This is Dr Miller's neice.

The *Sulphur Well Correspondent* writes:

*A J Sageser will move to the place he bought recently from Dr N Sageser, near Hanly about Dec 1.*
*The sale of stock and household goods of Mrs Elizabeth Miller, deceased, will be sold Friday, Nov 25th.*
*A M Askins has installed a hot blast heater in his shop to keep the loafers warm while waiting.*
*The fields were full of Nimrods Tuesday, after the bunnies and Bob Whites.*
*Andrew J Sageser bought at the Sageser sale Saturday, 110 shocks of corn and fodder at $1.20 per shock.*
*Hog killing is in full blast and you ought to "spare" your editor a spare rib at least.*

*F F Miller will administer on the Sulphur Well property of the late Mrs Miller and Jno P Miller, on the old homestead estate.*

*Mrs Sam Royce and Howard Walters started to Mattson, Ill, Tuesday, on a visit to relatives, to be gone several weeks.*

*Mr and Mrs George Barnett and daughter, of Buena Vista, were visiting Mr A M Askins Saturday and Sunday last.*

*Rev Staley will preach at the church on Thanksgiving day and each day thereafter at the usual hour till Sunday night. p2c2*

"Forest Miller, administrator of Mrs Elizabeth Miller, dec'd will on Friday, Nov 25, at Sulphur Well, at 10am, offer for sale some stock, household and kitchen furniture." p2c3

"Administrator's sale. As administrator of Mrs Elizabeth J Miller, dec'd I will at Sulphur Well, Friday Nov 25, 1904, dispose of the following property, 8 hogs, sow and 11 pigs, horse, Jersey cow, surrey and set of harness, household and kitchen furniture. Forest Miller, Adm'r." p3c6

December 2, 1904

Dr Hendren writes another poem, this one titled "Find their level". It's about people with inflated egos. In the third verse he says "Folks air jest like runnin' worter--finds thar level furder on...." p1c4

The *Sulphur Well Correspondent* writes:

*Mrs James Vincent, of Edenton, was visiting her parents Mr and Mrs James Hendren.*
*Mr Hugh Askins and Miss Mary Askins, of Buena Vista, have been visiting A M Askins.*
*James Woodward, of Dayton, O., is visiting his parents, Mr and Mrs James Woodward.*
*Wm D Sanders, of Idalia, was over last week.*
*Walter K Davis, Elbert Walker, James Woodward, Jr., and Clint Woodward last week were in Knox County on a hunting trip. They bagged 75 birds the first day out.*
*At the sale of Mrs Elizabeth Miller, deceased, there was a large crowd in attendance and the bidding was lively. The household goods brought astonishing prices considering the cost of new furniture. Many things going far beyond the retail price of new up-to-date furniture. One 2-year old horse brought $132; one sow and 11 pigs $26.70; eight fat hogs averaging 280 lbs, $76. p2c3*

It appears that Mrs Miller had antiques, or at least "good stuff".

December 9, 1904

With the holiday season under way in New York the fashion is for "evening dresses of plain Brussels net ... (that) are charming for their simplicity, and so much more in keeping with youth and freshness, than elaborate costumes...."p1c5

The *Sulphur Well Correspondent* writes:

*Mrs A M Askins is reported as improving.*
*Elder Calhoun will preach here next Sunday.*
*Mr Morris Bourne is on a visit to relatives at Danville, Ill.*
*Elder Bryson preached at the Christian Church last Sunday.*
*J H Woodward is visiting Lee Terhune in Mercer County this week.*
*Mr Stoker, of Watts Mills, who has been sick for some months, is improving.*
*A J Sageser moved last Friday to the Dr N Sageser place near Hanly, which he purchased some time ago.*
*J T Suger has moved to the old Maraney Moore residence lately occupied by A J Sageser.*
*Josh H Woodward returned Sunday from St Louis where he has been employed during the World's Fair.*
*Miss Bertha Askins was taken suddenly ill Tuesday night with nervous convulsions but recovered in a few hours.*
*The hunting party consisting of Messrs M K Davis, Elbert Walker and James and Clint Woodward, report great success in bagging birds in Knox County, but say that they found a majority of the mountaineers there unaccountably and unreasonably (unfriendly?) to blue grass hunters.* p2c6

December 16, 1904

"The firm of Taylor and Hendren has been dissolved. W S Hendren will continue in the furniture, carpet and wallpaper trade, at the present business location, while Mr F P Taylor will assume control of the undertaking business." p3c1

December 23, 1904

Several Jessamine folks are already in Florida, and writing back about the nice weather, but complaining about the poor fishing thus far. p4c1

There is nothing particularly noteworthy to close the year, and no report from our correspondent since early December.

CORRESPONDENCE ENDS - 1905

The Sulphur Well Correspondent writes his final report this year. He moves on to another community, and there is no record of his returning to Sulphur Well again.

January 6, 1905

"Gov Beckham has issued a call for the General Assembly of Kentucky to convene in extraordinary session on January 12 for the sole purpose of considering a change in the site of the new state capitol building." p2c1

The *Sulphur Well Correspondent* writes:

*Born, to the wife of Wm Scott Jan 2, a fine girl.*

*Mrs Lena Smith, nee Horine, is visiting her parents here this week.*

*Jno B Bourne, of Stone, Garrard County, accompanied by his daughter, Alene, were visiting relatives here this week.*

*Mr and Mrs A F Wheeler, of Lexington, were visiting Mr and Mrs Marshall Davis this week.*

*There has been dinings, dinings galore in our village for the past two weeks. Alas! we couldn't attend them all.*

*Mrs Eckler, with Miss Mary Sue Thompson, of Paris, were visiting Mr and Mrs Marshall Davis this week.*

*Mrs James H Turner had an acute attack of tonsilitis last Tuesday, but is greatly improved now.*

*Messrs I. Will Teater, James Teater, Alvin Howard, Capt Hill and others from Edenton, were over on business recently.*

*Mrs Frank M Hudson was quite ill from an attack of laryngitis and stomach trouble Sunday last.*

*Elder Zachary, of Lexington, preached at the Christian Church Sunday evening.*

*Lee Reynolds who moved to Kansas City, Mo., twenty years ago, is visiting his sister, Mrs T J Horine. This is his first visit back to the old homestead.*

*Married, at Lexington, on the 4th inst., by Elder Finley of the Christian Church, Mr Arthur Brooks and Miss Lena Miller.*

*Mr and Mrs A J Sageser, of Hanley, entertained some young people at a "social" given Tuesday night.*

*Willard Davis is visiting his grandma, Mrs Catherine Johns, at Pleasureville, Henry County, this week.*

*N D Davis lost one of his fattening hogs from his pen one night last week. It was doubtless stolen by some hungry hoodlum.*

*Mr and Mrs Chas. M Dean, of Bryantsville, were visiting Mr and Mrs N D Davis last week.*

*Mr J Harvey Dean has moved to his farm at Camp Dick Robinson, Garrard County. Sorry to lose one of our best citizens.*

*William Underwood moved from this neighborhood to Logana last Monday.*

*Mrs Sam Askins, who was taken seriously sick last Friday night and continued so for several days is very much improved.*

*Mr and Mrs James Woodward, aged 89 and 72 respectively, and about the oldest couple around here were married fifty years ago last Dec. Mrs Woodward, a few days after her wedding, cooked her first dinner of married life when three persons were present—herself, her husband and another. Last Saturday a week ago, her birthday, and fifty long, but happy years of wedded life, after raising a large family, she cooked another dinner when again only three persons were present--herself, her husband and Houston, their youngest child. May their days still be long upon the earth and full of happiness. p3c6*

January 13, 1905

Another poem from Dr Hendren: "Weather Advice". "Stop yer grumblin' 'bout the weather! Thar's no use'n fussin whether it's a suiting ye er not ...." p1c6 He has started composing in dialect. I suppose it's the result of his being in Oklahoma.

January 20, 1905

"Court day in Nicholasville was a very dull one in the stock market the weather being so disagreeable that the fire was the most congenial `companion'." p2c2

Hemphill's Drug Store offers a "One Minute Cough Cure. Clears the phlegm, draws out inflamation and heals and sooths the affected parts, strengthens the lungs, wards off pneumonia." p3c6 Sounds great! I wonder what happened to it?

The *Sulphur Well Correspondent* writes:

*Mrs Minda Romans, who was quite ill with laryngitis at F M Hudson's last week is much better.*
*Miss T Miller and Guy Stacy are visiting relatives in Irvine.*
*Mrs Mida Reynolds, who was taken last week with a severe attack of pnuemonia and with fever as a complication, is improving.*
*Mrs T J Horine and Lee Reynolds visited friends in Garrard County last week.*
*F M Horine was taken ill last week with symptoms of pnuemonia, but is out again.*
*N D Davis sold Tuesday to the Continental Tobacco Co., 7,000 lbs tobacco at 9 cents.*
*L M Jackson bought of S N Snowden, Tuesday, three heifers averaging 800 lbs at 3 1/4 cts.*
*M F Davis visited Lexington, Cynthiana, Paris, Winchester and Maysville this week on business.*
*Wm Noel, of Garrard County, J Will Teater, Geo W Warner and Wiley Burton, Madison County, were among the visitors last Monday.*
*The Ladies Aid Society will hold a bazaar, Saturday, the 28th, at about 2 pm, at Miller's store and dispose of some beautiful articles, for the benefit of the Christian Church. p3c6*

January 27, 1905

It's always better to know where you are going. "`The Difference Between Theology and Religion' will be Mr Timberlake's theme at the Baptist Church on Sunday morning. All who are desirous of having the way of life made plain to them, are cordially asked to come and hear him." p3c6

The *Sulphur Well Correspondent* writes:

*Elder Whitehead preached at the church last Sunday at 10 am, and at night.*
*Dell Hunter has rented the Wm Hudson farm for this year and will move to it soon.*
*N D Davis sold to Pat Foster, of Lexington, 6 head of young steers, weight about 800 each, at 3 1/4c.*
*Geo Snowden is on the sick list with la grippe.*
*F M Hudson, manager of the Singer Company's office in Nicholasville, will move to that city soon.*
*Mr Chas P Thompson, of Buckeye, Garrard County, whose wife has been ill for some months, was over Friday to consult our village medico.*
*Mrs Marshall Davis and little son were both on the sick list Saturday night and Sunday.*
*Roy, the infant son of Ernest Taylor, who has been quite sick for several days is improving.*
*Elder McClelland will preach at the church next Lord's day morning at 11 and at night.*
*Mr Thomas Stoker, who has been seriously ill for nearly a year with dropsy and heart aflection, is greatly improved.*
*Mrs Meda Reynolds, who has been with pneumonia and fever, is so much improved as to be able to sit up.*
*Mr and Mrs W K Davis are visiting Mr and Mrs Chas M Dean, and Mr and Mrs B G King in Garrard County this week.*
*Mr Arthur Brooks and wife left for Decatur, Ill., Monday last to make the sucker state their future home. Sorry to lose good citizens.* p2c5

February 3, 1905

It took the Legislature a while, but they finally did choose the site for the new state capitol building, referred to here as "the Hunt property". p2c1 Having done that, the editor is now ready for the legislators to go home!

February 10, 1905

"If the Jessamanites, who have gone to Florida, could just take a peep at old Jessamine just now, they would see one of the most beautiful sights they have ever beheld--ice several inches thick on the ground, icicles hanging from the houses a foot long ...." p3c2 The railroads are advertising the ease by which snowbirds can get to Florida via their routes. Drawing rooms, observation cars, Pullman sleepers, leaving daily, are "on sale at low rates". p4c7-8

February 17, 1905

From Pink: "Mrs Sallie Overstreet is still on the sick list." p2c2

Farm for sale! Feb 24, at 2 pm, the farm of the late Elizabeth J Miller, know as the Merriman Miller farm, situated near Sulphur Well, and containing 205 acres, now occupied by Stephen N Snowden, will sell at highest bidder. This is one of the best farms in the county. Jno P Miller, Ex'r. p2c2

The *Sulphur Well Correspondent* writes:

*Mr Wilmot Peel is sick with the grippe.*
*E Walker visited Lexington, Tuesday.*
*Mr Billy Price, of Buckeye, was over on a visit last Saturday.*
*Justin Burgin's daughter has been quite sick.*
*Dr Ammons, of Buckeye, has moved to Lancaster.*
*Geo Snowden, who has been sick for some weeks is no better.*
*Thomas Barker is able to walk about the room for the first time since last October.*
*N D Davis has been on the sick list for some days.*
*Mr S N Bishop is able to be about again after an acute attack of lobar pneumonia.*
*Tuesday, Fahrenheit went down below Cairo on a voyage of discovery of the North Pole.*
*Last week Paint Lick brought down an ice gorge that blocked the ferry at Sanders's and stopped travel from the three counties for several days.*
*He sat in a trice, right down on the ice, and with a bad grace contemplated his case--his medicine case, which was beyond hope of recovery, was the doctor's discovery.*
*On Friday, February 24, the old, well known homestead of late Merriman Miller will be sold to the highest bidder. There are about 205 acres in the farm, of good land and anyone will fortunate in getting it. It lies about one mile south-west of this place.* p2c2

March 3, 1905

The *Sulphur Well Correspondent* writes:

*Mr Elmore Stoker, of Watts Mill, was taken quite sick last Tuesday.*
*Jno P Miller, of Irvine, was visiting Forest Miller last Week.*
*Mr Buckles has moved his saw mill from Giles to Heidleburg, Lee County.*
*It has been difficult to ferry at (the) mouth of Paint Lick for several days on account of floating ice and logs.*
*Mr and Mrs James Woodward, who have both been very sick are improving rapidly.*
*Mrs A M Askins, who has been quite low for months, is slightly improved.*
*Little Miss Edna May, youngest daughter of Mr and Mrs Jas H Turner, was quite sick Tuesday.*
*Mrs Lee J Terhune, and son, Jimmie, of Mercer County, are visiting Mr and Mrs James Woodward.*
*Mr and Mrs Howard G King, of Buena Vista, who were visiting Dr and Mrs G M Hendren for several days, returned home Tuesday.*
*Mrs Wiley F Burton, of Sanders Ferry, who has been so dangerously ill for several days that her recovery was despaired of, is somewhat improved.* p2c1

March 10, 1905

Brutus Clay, son of General Cassius Clay, has been appointed ambassador to Switzerland by President Roosevelt. p1c6 His father was ambassador to Russia before him.

James Woodward Sr, of Sulphur Well, died on March 6 at age 80. He is survived by a wife and nine children, and is buried in the "Harris burying ground". p3c5 The Harris Cemetery is close to the Miller Cemetery, and I walked over to see it the other day. It is still in pretty good condition, but gives no evidence of family care. I saw James Woodward's stone, and that of his wife, Caroline. She died in 1908, and appears to be the last of the family buried there. The cemetery apparently was used as early as 1836, and has ten people buried there.

March 17, 1905

From Pink: "J C Ferrell, who died at his home at Little Hickman last Saturday afternoon, will be greatly missed by all." p2c1

W S Hendren's furniture stores advertises "easy rockers" at prices ranging from $1.25 to $15. p1c7-8

March 24, 1905

"The Russians have reached a terrible state of affairs. Whom the Japs do not kill, it looks as though the anarchists will." p2c1

From Pink: "Mr and Mrs Walter Harris spent Sunday with her parents, Mr and Mrs J P Overstreet." p2c2 The daughter is Myrtie Oversteet.

March 31, 1905

Withers Library recently purchased several new books. Among them were: Decent of Man-Darwin; Destiny of Man-Fisk; The Mill Mystery; Aesthetics-Hegel; Complete Poems-Jackson H H; Sea Wolf-London; and others. p1c3

"A large audience filled the Institute Chapel Monday evening to hear the music presented by the piano pupils of Miss Nellie Hendren ...." p3c3

"Mrs J T West of Ambrose is reported quite ill." p3c4

May 12, 1905

The *Sulphur Well Correspondent* writes:

*Mattie, the little daughter of A M Askins, has been quite sick for several days.*
*Mr Jno Sewell, of Buckeye, Garrard County, was over for a short visit last Sunday.*
*Messrs Austin Smith and Sam Hunter, of Edenton, Madison County, were visiting here Saturday and Sunday last.*
*Mr Sam Moberley and wife were visiting Mr and Mrs James Hendren Saturday and Sunday.*
*Justin Burgin's daughter was quite sick last week.*
*Mr Chas Cobb's son, Dave, was quite ill with pneumonia last week.*
*Mr D Fathergill, of Georgetown, was visiting his father here Sunday.*
*Mr Jas Baumgartner has rented a residence from Mr Forest Miller and moved to it this week.*
*Mr and Mrs W K Davis visited Mr and Mrs Charles M Dean, Garrard County last Sunday.*
*Mr Wm King, Jr, of Garrard County, was visiting Mr N D Davis last Tuesday and Wednesday.*
*The writer's thanks are due Mr Wiley F Burton for a nice nine pound string of perch and cat fish.*
*Mrs James H Turner and daughters, Mayme and Edna May, who have been visiting her father, Rev W S Grinstead, at Flemingsburg, returned home this week.*
*Mrs W F Burton, who was so seriously sick for seven or eight weeks, is able to be about her household duties again.*
*In a letter just received from W A Richards, Commissioner of the General Land Office, Washington, D C, in regard to the opening of Indian Reservations, there may be some items of interest to the readers of the Journal. He says in his letter that the Uinta Reservation in Utah will be opened Sept 1st, 1905. In regard to the Crow Reservation he cannot state even approximately when it will be opened, but not in the near future. This also applies to the Flathead Reservation in Wyoming and the Wind River Reservation in Montana. p2c1*

May 26, 1905

The *Sulphur Well Correspondent* writes:

*Born to the wife of Howard G King, Buena Vista, on the 18th inst, a son.*
*W B Walker is again on the sick list with an old chronic trouble.*
*William King, Jr, of Buena Vista was visiting friends here Saturday and Sunday.*
*Tobacco plant thieves are said to be operating in this locality.*
*Masters Paul and Claude Peel, sons of Hugh Peel, of Danville, were visiting their grandma, Mrs Emily Peel Saturday and Sunday.*
*Mrs Dr Hendren was called by phone to Buena Vista, Friday, to the bedside of her daughter, Mrs H G King.*
*Rev G C Calhoun preached to a large and appreciative audience here last Sunday evening.*
*Cut worms are playing havoc with garden stuff and tobacco plants this cool weather. p2c1*

Dr Hendren has a grandson, and his wife was called upon to take care of their daughter.

June 9, 1905

The *Sulphur Well Correspondent* writes:

*Wm B Wylie, of Edenton, Madison County, was visiting on this side Thursday.*
*Mr and Mrs W K Davis and Mr and Mrs Marshall Davis were visiting Mr A F Wheeler, Lexington from Friday till Sunday last.*
*John P Miller, of Irvine, is visiting relatives here this week.*
*Miss Lena Bright, of Lexington, is visiting Mr A M Askins.*
*Mr Sam Moberly, of Edenton, was over visiting Mr James Hendren, Tuesday.*
*Dr Geo M Hendren started Thursday night over the Q & C for Memphis, Wichita and Oklahoma City, to be gone several days, during which time he will visit several points in Indian Territory. He will give his impressions by the way to the many readers of the Journal.*
*It is reported that Wm H Bright, of Lexington, formerly of this place, and who accidentally received a severe knife wound in the lung not long ago, and was taken to the Good Samaritan Hospital, has had a relapse and is in a serious condition.*
*Saturday, Frank M Horine, and probably others of this place, will start from Lexington, over the C & O, for Old Point Comfort and the Chesapeake Bay region--Fortress Monroe, Washington City and other historical points. They will witness the great army and naval maneuvers during this period in which an attempt will be made to capture Washington City and Baltimore and bombard the old fort. It will be an epoch of a lifetime. p2c3*

William Bright survived the knife wound and did not die until 1912.

June 16, 1905

Mr Thomas Hendren and daughter, Miss Nellie, left Wednesday for Minneapolis, Minn., to visit his son. `Uncle Tommy' by which name his familiarly known, will remain at Minneapolis and will be greatly missed in this community. Miss Nellie, we are glad to know, will return to Nicholasville in August. p3c5

Nellie is an accomplished musician and teaches at the Jessamine Institute.

June 23, 1905

A J Sageser vs Jno P Miller, Executor--A very important and an uncommon case was decided by Judge Benton in the circuit court here last Friday. The suit was brought by A J Sageser against Frank Miller's executor to recover the one-eighth of the proceeds of the Miller farm which recently sold for about $15,000. Frank Miller made his will in 1885 and died shortly thereafter. He left at his death eight children among whom was an unmarried daughter, who several years after the death of her father, married the plaintiff, A J Sageser; to this union was born a son. A short time after the birth of this child, the mother and child both died. By the will of Frank Miller he gave his 200-acre farm to his wife for life and after her death provided that it should be sold by her executor and the proceeds divided equally among his children. His widow lived on and conducted the farm until a few months ago. After her death the executor sold the farm for about $15,000. Mr Sageser then brought suit, claiming that he was entitled under the will to his former wife's portion of the proceeds of this farm. The question was novel and created much interest among the legal fraternity here and throughout this judicial district. E B Hoover brought the suit and N L Bronaugh represented the executor. Judge Benton took considerable time on the case and rendered a very able and lengthy opinion, holding that Mr Sageser was entitled to the one-eighth interest that his wife, if living would have received. It is thought the case will be taken to the Court of Appeals. p3c6

I was not able to determine how the suit came out. Perhaps some day I will search the court records.

June 30, 1905

Dr Hendren writes from Wichita, Kansas. He reports that Wichita is thriving. He also decribes his travel by rail. He thoroughly enjoys traveling, and finds no discomfort enroute. p1c4

Mrs Sallie W Askins died at the home of her husband, A M Askins, near Ambrose, Wednesday morning, June 28, of consumption. She is survived by a husband and three daughters. Funeral services were held at the late residence Thursday morning, Elder A P Finley officiating. The remains were interred in Maple Grove Cemetery. p3c6

July 14, 1905

The pay of school teachers is still very, very low. The average of women teachers nationwide is only $40 per month. p1c3

July 28, 1905

The commissioner of the Panama Canal says "that the conditions of the Isthmaus are to be made healthful before the real work of digging the canal begins." p3c6

August 18, 1905

"Misses Ada Sageser and Cecil Adcock are visiting their aunt, Mrs Wm Crossly, in Cincinnati." p3c4

August 25, 1905

The *Sulphur Well Correspondent* writes:

*Mrs T J Horine is on the sick list.*
*The busy time for the farmers is here. Tobacco cutting is in full blast.*
*Mrs David Lear and son, Thomas, are visiting Mrs James Woodward.*
*Miss Mattie Woodward is able to be out after a lingering spell of typhoid fever.*
*Mrs Jas Turner and little daughter, Edna Grace, are on the sick list this week.*
*Mrs Chas Dean, of Bryantsville, is visiting her parents, Mr and Mrs N D Davis.*
*Miss Bettie Masters, of Louisville, is the guest of her brother, Mr Gabe Masters.*
*Forest Miller and F M Horine lost two valuable hogs from being bitten by mad dogs.*
*Mrs James Hendren, who has been sick for the past six weeks, is very little better.*
*Dr Harry Hendren, of New York City, paid our village a flying trip this week.*
*Mrs C T Taylor and daughter, Miss Lola, of Lexington, are visiting their brother, Mr Chas Horine.*
*Mr Edwin Bourne and Miss Carrie Woodward spent from Saturday until Monday in Lexington.*
*Mrs W S Richardson and Miss Leah Stacy, of Irvine, are the guests of Mrs Forest Miller.*
*Dr G M Hendren leaves this week for Garrard County, where he has bought a small farm.*
*Mr Jas H Turner bought from parties in Garrard 21 head of mules from two to five years old.*
*Mrs James Shearer, of Kirksville, Madison County, is visiting her sister, Mrs Mattie Shearer, of this place.*
*Mr J B Bourne, of Bryantsville, attended the funeral of his nephew, Hamlet Foster, Tuesday.*
*F M Horine, is having a large tobacco barn built on the old Davis farm. Frank is a hustling farmer. He expects to leave in two weeks for Indian Territory, to be gone for some time. p2c4*

This is the last letter of Dr George M Hendren, the Sulphur Well correspondent for thirty-two years, to the Jessamine Journal. He left very quitely and unobtrusively, and when Dr Hendren left Sulphur Well, he seems to have left for good. I have at least eighty items pertaining to him and his immediate family between 1905 and 1924, and not one indicates that he ever returned to Sulphur Well. He moved to Buckeye or its environs and remained there for seventeen years until his wife died in March of 1922. He had a sale of all his property, and moved into the household of his daughter, Nellie King, in Bryantsville. Unfortunately, Howard King, his son-in-law, died in August of the same year. King owned a large farm, over six hundred acres, and it was sold after his death. Nellie and her father then moved to Wilmore where he died in 1924. His obituary, as it appeared in the Jessamine Journal, April 25, 1924, p3 follows:

> Dr George M Hendren died at the home of his daughter, Mrs Howard King, in Wilmore, Tuesday, April 18. Dr Hendren was the son of the late William Hendren and Mrs Hendren, pioneer settlers of the Sulphur Well neighborhood. Since his graduation as a physician he has been in constant practice and his reputation as a pneumonia specialist, gained him a wide practice.... He is survived by the following children, Mrs King and Mrs Walter Davis, of Jessamine County; Mrs Hugh Miller of Arkansas; two brothers, William and Walter Hendren of Nicholasville, and a sister Mrs Annie Wagner, of St Petersburg, Fla. The funeral service was held at the grave, Wednesday afternoon at 3:30 o'clock, conducted by the Rev. Rhodes Thompson, pastor of the Christian Church.

The Buckeye correspondent of the Central Record of Lancaster gave a little more information. According to the correspondent Dr Hendren suffered a stroke two years previously and had been in poor health ever since. Mrs Walter Davis (his daughter, Mary) has moved back to Sulphur Well by this time. And, Mrs Hugh Miller (his daughter, Addie) now lives in Fayetteville, Arkansas. The graveside ceremony was at Maple Grove Cemetery in Nicholasville where he is buried beside his wife. Central Record, April 24, 1924, p9.

Just as I kept the Sulphur Well correspondent's diary for him during the early part of this story, I shall have to continue it after his departure from Sulphur Well so that the story can be completed in the Epilogue.

# EPILOGUE

Dr Hendren, the Sulphur Well correspondent, moved away from Sulphur Well and his correspondence with the Journal simply stopped. However, the story of Sulphur Well, my family, and some of Sulphur Well's illustrious citizens was not yet complete. This epilogue, roughly covering the period from 1905 to 1921, continues the essential threads of the story to what I feel is a logical conclusion. Obviously, given a long enough period, everyone dies, and quite a few people do during the epilogue.

There are no issues of the Journal available for 1906. However, there are two items known to me that occurred during that year. My father, Frank Edward Ware was born on May 23, 1906, and my mother, Mary Elizabeth Miller, was born on August 24, 1906. They were married on March 9, 1928. My mother taught in the Jessamine County School System for more than thirty years, most of them at Sulphur Well. My father was basically a farmer/merchant, but did work in a factory in Akron prior to my birth in 1929, and again in Detroit during World War II.

W S Hendren retired from his furniture and wallpaper store on account of poor health. He and his wife then headed for Umatilla, Florida. January 4, 1907 p2c2,3 His brother, W L remained in the store to collect accounts for him. p2c6 He wrote a two column letter about his trip down to Umatilla, and described the village when he arrived. He says that he only weighted 117 pounds at this time. February 1, 1907 p1c5-6 Keep your eye on Walter. After being a virtual non-entity up to this point in his life, he and his family become an active, important part of Nicholasville. He is Dr Hendren's brother.

Dr Hendren will continue to submit poems to the Journal for several years, and I am going to simply note them for the record. He composed "A Midnight Tragedy". March 1, 1907 p1c4

"A K Adcock has purchased a saloon in Lexington on South Limestone Street, but does not intend to move his family at present." March 1, 1907 p3c1

W S Hendren has written a long letter about Umatilla. March 8, 1907 p1c3-5 Umatilla is a few miles northwest of Orlando. Jessamine County folks started going down there because Ed Guerrant, a Wilmore minister, retired there in poor health, but continued to come back in the summer to preach at revivals. I'm sure it was as "out of the way" then as it is now!

Dr Hendren writes "A Lovely Scene". Mar 8, 1907 p1c6

"Miss Ethel Hendren, sister of Mrs Robert Denman, will be married at her home in Wichita, Kansas." March 15, 1907 p3c3 Ethel is the daughter of the late Levi H Hendren, of Sulphur Well, and the neice of Dr Hendren and W S Hendren.

Deeds recorded: "Mary E Cobb and J W Cobb, to F F Miller, lot near Sulphur Well, $800." June 7, 1907 p1c6 Not "near Sulphur Well", it "is Sulphur Well"! It's also the house in which I was born.

"James Hendren, who resided at Sulphur Well for several years, died at Paint Lick on June 15, 1907 at age 81. He leaves two children, Ezekiel Hendren, and Mrs S N Bishop." June 21, 1907 p3c5 This isn't complete. Either Zerelda or Becky married S N Bishop. The other married James Vincent. There is also Theresa who married D Boone Tudor, and another brother, Squire T Hendren of Cottonburg. I have been unable to determine James' parentage, so can't relate him to the decendants of Doven Hendren.

James Hendren was in the Calvary on the Union side during the Civil War, and I obtained a copy of his pension request. In the request he was described as being five feet nine inches tall, dark compexion, black eyes, and black hair. He was born on December 26, 1824 at Edenton. He was an independent cuss who was bedamned if he was going to soldier during January and February. He was listed as AWOL during those months in both 1962 and 1963. In 1963 he must have put out the crops because his status was changed to deserter during March and April of that year. He came back, or was brought back, in May and sent to Tennessee where he was captured in October, 1963, and later imprisoned at Andersonville. He developed a lot of physical problems and was released in a prisoner exchange on December 31, 1864, and mustered out honorably.

Deeds recorded: "John P Miller, executor of F S Miller, to S N Snowden, 205 acres for $14,042.50." July 26, 1907 p1c6 This is the "Miller" farm.

J H Murphy is retiring from the Glass Milling Company. August 23, 1907 p1c4-5

Mrs Meade Miller visited Dr and Mrs J C Miller, then returned to Oklahoma City. September 6, 1907 p3c4

Dr Hendren composes "Tomorrow and Yesterday". September 13, 1907 p1c5

"Adam Adcock is offering for sale his building at Main and Harrodsburg Streets containing store rooms, dwellings, restaurant, and blacksmith shop." September 27, 1907 p2c3

Dr Hendren writes "Just An Ordinary Man". November 1, 1907 p1c4

"Dr John C Miller, who has been sick for several weeks, left Monday for Umatilla, Fla, accompanied by his wife and daughter Lizzie Downing of New York, and son Hugh Miller of Okla City. Meade is looking after business during his father's absence." December 20, 1907 p3c2

Dr Miller died. His picture accompanied the obituary. He has a full beard, and is a very distinguished looking gentlemen. He died in Umatilla last Saturday.

> He had been in failing health for several months, having suffered a stroke a year ago. He was the third son of Merriman F and Celia Miller, and was born in Jessamine on February 10, 1841. He had been retired from farming and the practice of medicine for about ten years. He married Nannie Rice on February 25, 1868, and had four children--Rice, Hugh, Meade, and Lizzie. After her death he married Emma Reynolds in 1895. He is also survived by a brother M M Miller of Lexington, and two sisters, Mrs Kate Barkley, of Nicholasville, and Mrs J P Overstreet of Little Hickman. The funeral services were at the Nicholasville home, conducted by Rev Mann of Lexington. The remains were taken to Richmond for interment. January 10, 1908 p3c4

Dr Miller's will was probated on Monday.

> He bequeaths to his wife, Emma C Miller, household goods, medical accounts, etc., and $30 per month for life, to be paid from rents and proceeds of the home farm of 240 acres devised and entailed to his daughter, Lizzie, during her life, and at whose death reverts to his two sons, Hugh and Meade Miller of Oklahoma City. To his two sons he left 320 acres each, now in their possession, 40 acres south of the home farm and 13 shares of stock of First National Bank.

He divided the remainder of the estate between Hugh and Meade. The will was dated April 25, 1905 and named Hugh as executor. By codicil in 1906 he left the residence on Main Street to his wife for life, and to his two sons upon her death. January 24, 1908 p2c3

Mrs Emma C Miller is unhappy. She petitioned the court to have Hugh removed as administrator of the estate. She alleged that he was a non-resident of the state, that his appointment was not legal; that he had not filed an inventory of personal property, or a sales bill of the proceeds, and had converted the property into money and removed it from the state without legal right to do so; and for the protection of the rights of the widow. April 24, 1908 p3c5 Both Hugh and Meade arrived in Nicholasville the first of the week and hired a lawyer to resist the attempt to remove Hugh as administrator. Hugh has reportedly sold most of his Oklahoma property and is moving back to Kentucky. p3c5 "It is being rumored that Lizzie Downing will contest the will, but no papers have been filed as yet." p3c5

"Mrs Hugh Miller and children of Oklahoma City arrived Wednesday evening." May 1, 1908 p3c5

Judge Phillips declined to remove Hugh since he had returned to Nicholasville, purchased a house, and intended to make it his permanent home. However, Hugh was required to post bond and to provide an inventory of the estate to the court. May 8, 1908 p3c6 Mrs Emma C Miller sued to set aside an alleged prenuptial agreement and to be alloted her distributive share of the estate as a widow. May 1, 1908 p3c5

Lizzie filed suit, but later withdrew the papers, and took no further action. May 1, 1908 p3c5 "Thomas Downing of New York spent several days in town last week on business." May 15, 1908 p3c4 This is Lizzie's husband, who apparently negotiated a settlement for his wife.

"Miss Nellie Hendren, daughter of Tom Hendren, has returned for the summer from Texas, where she has been teaching music, and is staying with the W S Hendren family." June 12, 1908 p3c5

Hugh Miller received a telegram from New York saying that Lizzie had given birth to a son, and was doing well. The son was named Alfred. July 17, 1908 p3c4

W S Hendren has now gone into the real estate business with George Lyne. July 24, 1908 p3c5

A K Adcock sold his house and lot in Nicholasville. December 18, 1908 p1c4

The first Sulphur Well article since Dr Hendren left appears on February 19, 1909 p2c3 The writer is not identified.

"Dr Hendren, of Buckeye, was in Nicholasville Wednesday, and has for a patient Mr Newton D Davis, of Ambrose...." April 16, 1909 p3c3

Mrs George Gray died at the age of 68 in Lexington. She is survived by all six of her children. She is the mother of Texie and Ida. They both are living in Lexington now. Mrs Gray was buried in the Lexington Cemetery. April 16, 1909 p3c5

L P writes that Black Bridge should be called Wareville because the Wares "run the general store, blacksmith shop and woodwork shop, a feed and grist mill and a sawmill." He says that Bourne, Garrard County, was given that name by a "Sulphurwellian" named John Bourne. Bourne is near Bryantsville, just off US 27. April 23, 1909 p1c3-4

Hugh Miller "went back to Oklahoma on business, for an indefinite stay." April 30, 1909 p3c4 He didn't stay very long, he's back already. May 28, 1909 p3c3

Dr Hendren was in Nicholasville treating a patient. He reported that Newt Davis was now up and about. May 7, 1909 p3c3

Dr Hendren is still writing poetry, this time "Hot Enough For You?". July 16, 1909 p1c4

Mr and Mrs Hugh Miller will leave next week for Sulphur, Oklahoma, near the Texas line, where they will be joined by Meade and his wife. They are making a prospecting trip through eastern Oklahoma in company with their cousin, Chas W Miller, formerly of Lexington. July 16, 1909 p3c4 Hugh found that touring the state was too big an undertaking, but did see several new towns. He made no investments on this trip, but expects to return in the fall for the state fair. His wife spent her time at Sulphur Springs. August 20, 1909 p3c5

A K Adcock is now living in Lexington. July 23, 1909 p3c3

I guess that family relations have been restored. Tom and Lizzie Downing and their new son, Alfred, are visiting Hugh. September 17, 1909 p3c3

Newt Davis died at his home in Sulphur Well at the age of 59. He had been a farmer and stock trader all his life. The funeral services were at the Sulphur Well Christian Church, and he was buried at Maple Grove Cemetery. October 1, 1909 p3c3 His brother S E Davis married a sister of Dr Hendren, and his son, Walter, married a daughter of Dr Hendren.

Walter Hendren returned from a trip to Daytona, Florida where he and Dr Kennedy are attempting to buy a hotel on the beach. "Mrs S E Davis (his sister) will manage the dining room if the deal goes through." October 15, 1909 p3c4

"Mrs Geo M Hendren, of Buckeye, spent several days this week with her daughters, Mrs Willard Davis at Ambrose, and Mrs Hugh Miller of Nicholasville." This is a mistake, Mary Hendren married Walter Davis, not Willard Davis. October 22, 1909 p3c4

I guess this is how the family settled their differences: "Hugh Miller and others to Lizzie Miller Downing and Thomas W Downing, 240 acres, $10.00 and other considerations." I also suspect that Hugh is going to leave Nicholasville now. He sold a lot in Nicholasville to J C Guyn for $2,750. November 12, 1909 p4c4 "Mrs Hugh Miller left last week for Oklahoma City to join her husband, who had shipped the household goods earlier. He bought a new home on Park Avenue, and will continue in the real estate business as well as farming." December 10, 1909 p2c3

"Manfred Murphy, son of J H Murphy, died at Sulphur Well after several weeks of illness. Services were held at the Sulphur Well Christian Church, burial at Maple Grove. He was 35 and unmarried." November 19, 1909 p2c3 He and my grandfather Forest Miller were close friends.

The notice of John Dickerson's death appeared in the <u>Journal</u> as follows:

> John M Dickerson died at his home near Buckeye, January 18th after a stroke and a long illness, aged 68. He leaves a wife and five children. He was married late in life to his cousin, Mary Ray. For many years he was a traveling salesman for a Cincinnati hat house, and was well liked. He was born in Sulphur Well and served as a private in the federal army during the Civil War. January 28, 1910 p3c2

Another poem from Dr Hendren, "Down With Meat". February 10, 1910 p1c6

> Dr Hendren barely avoided serious injury when the horse he was riding broke though a culvert pinning him by his right leg. Luckily the horse rolled to his left, and with a surge lifted Dr Hendren from the pit. He said that after it was over, it was the worst scare of his life. February 25, 1910 p3c2

Dr Hendren penned "In Old Kaintuck Again!". March 11, 1910 p1c4

> Nora Snowden, 34, daughter of Groom Taylor, and husband of George Snowden died of peritonitis, after three days illness. She leaves three children. Funeral services were held at the Sulphur Well Christian Church, and she was buried at Maple Grove. April 8, 1910 p3c5

Nora was born March 9, 1876 and died April 3, 1910. George was born March 8, 1874 and lived till April 23, 1932, and is buried beside Nora, although he married Blanche Askins after Nora's death.

W S Hendren has gone to Washington and New York to promote his two recent inventions. One is a mechanical toy. The other is a devise to be used in hotels, restaurants, etc to automatically check hats, coats, and other articles. April 15, 1910 p3c4 His trip was successful and he expects several jobbers to sell his mechanical toy. April 29, 1910 p1c3

J H Murphy and his partners have sold their feed, coal, grain business to the Star Milling Company. April 22, 1910 p2c1 He sold the general store in Sulphur Well to my grandfather in 1902, and his interest in the Glass' Mill in 1907. I believe all he has left is his farm. He was born in 1844, so is now about 66 years old, and may be retiring. His son Manfred recently died.

The Jessamine Institute was sold to satisfy claims of $7,118.62. It was purchased by J P Turner and others for $7,160.00. April 22, 1910 p3c2

"J Pink Overstreet died at his home near Pink, April 14, of pneumonia at age 75. He was buried in Maple Grove. He is survived by his wife, Sarah Miller, and two daughters." April 22, 1910 p3c5 "Mrs Sallie Overstreet is reported to be seriously ill at her home." May 6, 1910 p3c3

Dr Hendren writes "Raise A Pig" this week. April 29, 1910 p1c6

Hugh Miller is back in Nicholasville on a visit. June 24, 1910 p3c4 Another visit by Hugh and his wife. September 22, 1910 p3c3

Dr Hendren is publishing a book, Pneumonia:Its Successful Treatment.

> Dr G M Hendren, well known to the people of Jessamine and surrounding counties, is having published a book under the above title. Dr Hendren during a practice of 36 years has been unusually successful in the treatment of this disease, and his book will undoubtedly have an immense sale among his professional brethern. October 28, 1910, p4c4

Dr Hendren writes "The Way of the World". November 11, 1910 p1c4 This is his last published poem as far as I know.

Edith's birth: "Miller-To the wife of FF Miller, Ambrose, on the 7th inst, a daughter." April 14, 1911 p3c6 Edith just had her eighty-sixth birthday. She has lived in Knoxville for at least forty years, going there when her husband, Wm H Jesse, became the head librarian at the University of Tennessee. Her oldest daughter, Nan, lives in Vermont. Her youngest, Alice, lives in Knoxville. Alice and Donnie Kirk have two sons, and they also have children. So Edith is now a great-grandmother.

"W S Hendren was called to New York on business." July 7, 1911 p3c4

"Hugh Miller spent a week in Nicholasville." July 7, 1911 p3c4

"Miss Tee Miller, of Sulphur Well, has gone to Irvine to visit her brother, J P Miller." September 15, 1911 p3c3

"Nellie Hendren will have charge of the music department of a college in Edinton, Va." September 15, 1911 p3c3

"Mrs Meade Miller is visiting relatives at Sulphur Well." September 29, 1911 p3c3

"Mrs Hugh Miller, of Oklahoma City, after a visit to her kinsmen, Mr and Mrs M M (Mann) Miller, has left for her home. Miss Mary Miller (daughter of Mann Miller) accompanied her cousin to Oklahoma, where she will be her guest for several months." October 20, 1911 p3c3

Mary Ray Dickerson's mother died. Her father was Dr William Ray who died earlier. She was living with her mother. Mary's brother, Bronson, is now a minister in Richmond, Virginia. This is from Lancaster's paper, the Central Record, April 5, 1912 p5

Lena Bright is still around. She was visited by her brother, William. Also in the <u>Central Record</u>.

"Charles W Miller, son of Mann Miller, has wed Mary Talbott, of Paris, in Muskogee, Okla. They will reside in Holdenville, Okla where Mr Miller is practicing law." October 25, 1912 p2c6

"Vernon Stacy, who has been in Detroit, Michigan for the past year, is visiting his brother Guy Stacy in Sulphur Well." October 25, 1912 p3c3 Sons of Belle Miller Stacy.

The Jessamine Institute burned. It had not been used as a school for the past two years, and had been converted to an apartment house. "Over 250 young ladies representing almost every state in the union have graduated from the school since 1885." February 7, 1913 p3c4-6

"Wm McC Johnston has returned from a business trip to Chicago." May 16, 1913 p3c4 Another one of the old-timers!

Hugh and Meade Miller are back in town visiting. May 30, 1913 p3c4

"Dr and Mrs Hendren were in Nicholasville visiting relatives." June 27, 1913 p3c3 His sister, Mrs Baskett died in August of 1913. She is buried in Maple Grove Cemetery in the William Hendren, Sr lot.

"W S Hendren is in Washington, D C on business." August 29, 1913 p3c5 Still pursuing his invention, I suppose.

From Bryantsville: "Mrs Jasper has returned to her home in Nicholasville after a visit to Mrs G M Hendren." October 3, 1913 p4c5 Mrs Jasper is Mrs Hendren's mother.

From Bryantsville: "Mrs Hugh Miller has returned home to Oklahoma after a visit with her parents, Dr and Mrs Hendren." October 17, 1913 p4c4

From Bryantsville: "Mrs Hugh Miller of Oklahoma and Mrs George Hendren of Buckeye, are visiting Mrs Walter Davis." October 31, 1913 p4c5 Mrs Hugh Miller and Mrs Walter Davis are sisters. Mrs George Hendren is their mother.

Marshall Davis visted his brother Walter at Bryantsville last week. October 24, 1913 p3c3

Frank Stacy, Guy's brother, of Middletown, Ohio visited at Sulphur Well last week. October 24, 1913 p3c3

I always wondered where the McDowell's lived in Sulphur Well. They lived in the Turner house on the hill. October 24, 1913 p3c3

"Mr and Mrs Forest Miller entertained in honor of Mrs Miller's sister, Mrs Crossley." January 2, 1914 p2c5

"Meade Miller is in Nicholasville visiting relatives." June 26, 1914 p3c3

From the Oklahoma City Cor. Courier-Journal. July 3, 1914 p3c3 Dr R H Miller is the great-grandson of Mason C Miller, who is the brother of Merriman F Miller, Hugh's grandfather.

> Dr R H Miller, of Mt Vernon, Ky came out a few weeks ago on a visit to his uncle and aunt, Mr and Mrs Hugh Miller, former residents of Nicholasville, Ky, now residing in Oklahoma, and Dr Miller places after his name on the hotel registers, Miami, Okla. Dr Miller looked around and liked it and lost no time in closing a deal for the Red Cross Drug Store, one of the largest and most up-to-date establishments in Miami, Okla. Dr Miller is a graduate of the Louisville School of Pharmacy, and for the past few years has been manager of Rosenthal Drug Company, of Knoxville, Tenn. He takes charge of his new purchase July 1.

"Mr Forest Miller has bought a new automobile." August 14, 1914 p2c3 Edith said it was a Maxwell and was parked in the same shed as the buggy! This is an example of the curious mixture of horse and buggy and the automobile for several years. It would be difficult to say exactly when the former was phased out. Advertisements as to livery stables might be one indication. I happened to see in the Central Record that the five millionth Ford came off the assembly line in 1921, so I suspect that most people had a car by then. However, I also remember that Taylor Silverburg was still using a horse and buggy in the 1930s as his only means of transportation! "Ray Miller motored a crowd of guests to Frankfort recently to see the sights." November 20, 1914 p4c4-7 This was the expression always used, people "motored" to one place or another. They didn't "drive" as we do today.

"Miss Miller, of Wilmore, visited her uncle Forest Miller, Sunday." November 20, 1914 p4c4-7 This would be John P Miller's daughter, I don't know which one, all were educated in Wilmore. This could have been Anna, Cecile, Elizabeth, Scottie, or Ruth. Coralie was too young at this time.

"Mrs Leah Stacy Pullen has returned to her home at Irvine where she has taken rooms for the winter." November 20, 1914 p4c4-7 This is the daughter of Hon Stacy and Belle Miller, and the sister of Guy Stacy.

"Charlie Miller, son of Mann Miller of Lexington, has been appointed Assistant Attorney for the Eastern Oklahoma district, with headquarters at Muskogee. He has been a practicing attorney in Oklahoma for about nine years. He was married three years ago to Mary Talbot, formerly of Paris, Ky." December 25, 1914 p3c3

The residence on the Miller Farm burned. It was located at the end of the lane that is still a gravel road. The level area where the house stood is still visible, but all the foundation stones have been removed or used for the small "tenant" house that was built beside the old residence. Elizabeth W Dean, who now owns the farm tells me that when they prepared a septic field in that area, that many bricks were dug up, and thinks the house may have been brick, or had a brick foundation. She has no pictures of the old dwelling.

> Tuesday night, about nine o'clock, a fire was discovered in the residence of Steve Snowden. It had such a headway that there was no chance to put it out. The cause, or origin of the fire, is unknown. The loss was estimated at $2,000. April 16, 1915 p3c4

"Mrs Sallie Overstreet is reported seriously ill at her home." June 11, 1915 p3c3

"Cecile Adcock married Raymond Randolph, of Lexington. Both are employed at Graves, Cox & Co. They will make their home on Hambrick Avenue in Lexington." July 2, 1915 p3c2

The family assembled for some reason. Tom Downing is in from New York, and Hugh Miller is in from Oklahoma. July 2, 1915 p3c3

My mother's Sunday School class was entertained at Mrs Emma Askins. Lucien and Jouett McDowell were in the group. July 9, 1915 p2c1

Texie died. "Mrs Texie Gray Cooley died in Louisville at the St Joseph Hospital Monday morning of tuberculosis. She was only 49 years old. The funeral services were at St Peter's and interment in the Lexington Cemetery." George Berry, Ida's husband, was one of the pallbearers. July 30, 1915 p3c4

> Sallie Overstreet died Saturday night at her home near Pink after a long illness. She was eighty years old. She was the daughter of Merriman Miller and is survived by two children, one brother Mann Miller of Lexington, and one sister Kate Barkley, of Nicholasville. Funeral services were at her home with interment at Maple Grove Cemetery. August 27, 1915 p3c5

Meade Miller is visiting in Nicholasville. September 17, 1915 p3c3

Sulphur Well School Honor Roll: Named were: Ethel Ware, Lucian Foster, Frank Ware, and Mary Miller. Ethel and Lucian later married, as did Frank and Mary. They were life-long friends. October 8, 1915 p1c5 The teacher was Aliena Hunter. I met her, probably in the forties when she came by the house for a visit. She seemed most interested in seeing Frank who was not in at the time of the visit.

There is a picture of George M Berry in the paper.

> He has been on the road, in the same territory, for twenty-eight years. He has been a member of the Bluegrass Council of the United Commercial Travelers for fifteen years, twelve of which as an officer, and is now Senior Counsellor. He was chosen a member of the executive committee of the Grand Council in 1911, was re-elected in 1913, and again in 1915. He has been chairman of the executive committee for the past three years.

Pomp is still corresponding. March 3, 1916 p2c3

"Ezekiel Hendren, 59 years old, died at his home near Black Bridge, Sunday, July 16. His death was due to paralysis. He is buried in Maple Grove Cemetery." July 21, 1916 p3c2 Ezekiel is the son of James Hendren and Mildred Collins.

Hugh Miller and Tom Downing have become close. They are both visiting in Nicholasville. Hugh is now living in Fayetteville, Ark. Tom is still in New York. August 4, 1916 p3c3

From Sulphur Well: "Mr and Mrs Raymond Randolph visited Mrs Forest Miller." August 4, 1916 p3c6

A M Askins died of tuberculosis at age 63 at his home in Sulphur Well. He was buried in Maple Grove Cemetery. September 6, 1916 p3c4 This is Nancy's grandfather.

Dr Hendren's mother-in-law died.

> Mrs Maria Jasper, 89, died after falling and breaking her hip. She was the wife of Garden E Jasper, and mother of Mrs Morris Dean, and Mrs George Hendren. She is buried in Maple Grove Cemetery." September 22, 1916 p3c4

E E Bourne, oft mentioned in the Sulphur Well reports, died at age 63 at his home last Saturday. He is the father of Mrs Irene Sageser. His funeral was at the Sulphur Well Church, and he was buried in Maple Grove. September 29, 1916 p3c4

Ruth and Scottie Miller, John P's children, visited Mr and Mrs Forest Miller. November 17, 1916 p2c5

"J H Murphy is in Indianapolis getting special medical treatment." December 1, 1916 p3c3 He doesn't die for several years, but in order to improve the flow of my material I need to report his death at this time: "J H Murphy died at his home Saturday night after several months illness." January 14, 1921 p3c3 He had quite a career--surveyor; deputy sheriff; then elected sheriff; barely defeated for county judge; country merchant; storekeeper and later superintendent at Curley's Distillery; operated a feed and implement store in Nicholasville; in the milling business at Glass' Mill; operated a clothing store with my grandfather, F F Miller, who was also one of his active pallbearers; and he was an officer and director of the Farmers' Bank in Nicholasville. He was extremely active in the Sulphur Well Christian Church, as was his daughter Dora who married Arthur West.

Sons of W S Hendren, Marion and Harold, are working for the Goodrich Rubber Co, in Akron. December 29, 1916 p3c4

Mrs Forest Miller (Scottie) is the president of the Sulphur Well Christian Church Loyal Women (L W) Society. February 15, 1918 p1c4

The current papers in 1918 are mostly about the war--draft, questionaires, and physicals. It's strange. There was a lot in the paper about the war when it began in 1914, virtually nothing in 1915 or 1916; 1917 issues are missing. Now in 1918 the war is directly affecting Kentucky and the local people.

Pat Hendren is visiting his sister Scottie Miller. February 22, 1918 p2c3

"Virgil Snowden, who is stationed at Camp Shelby, Hattiesburg, Miss, is on leave with his parents, Mr and Mrs S N Snowden." February 22, 1918 p2c3

"W S Hendren, who volunteered in the YMCA war work and passed the first examination, left this week for Chicago, where he takes the final examination. Mr Hendren has two sons in the U S Army and when he enters the YMCA work every member of his family will be in the service, as Mrs Hendren is an active Red Cross worker and an officer in the Woman's Council of National Defense." July 12, 1918 p2c1 The sons are Marion and Harold Hendren.

Lizzie Miller Downing spent the summer in Nicholasville with the Wm H Hoover's. She is now on her way back to New York. September 20, 1918 p3c5

"Ray E Miller, son of Forest Miller, of Sulphur Well, and Hubert Sageser, son of A J Sageser, of Sulphur Well, will leave Monday morning for Great Lakes, Ill, where they will enter the navy." July 12, 1918 p2c1 They are first cousins.

Prior to entering service, Uncle Ray helped his father in the store "clerking, hauling goods from town, driving horse & spring wagon in coldest weather, attending school in town too." This is from Scottie's autobiography. She goes on to say :

> The sadest of all things during our married life was Ray going off to War in 1918. As First World War was on, all boys had to register when they became 21, and that happened in 1917. The following year in July 1918, he enlisted in the Navy, and was stationed at Great Lakes Naval Training Station.

Ray E Miller went on to Camp Decatur, Great Lakes, Ill. The Journal published a long letter from him to his parents about his first few days in the service. September 20, 1918 p4c1-4

> Ray Miller, aged 21 years died Monday night of pneumonia at Great Lakes Naval Training Station, Chicago, Ill. Besides his parents, Mr and Mrs Forest Miller, of Sulphur Well, he leaves two sisters, Edith and Mary Elizabeth. He enlisted in the navy about two months ago, and was only sick a few days. Mr Miller received a telegram Monday afternoon informing him of the serious illness of his son, and, accompanied by his wife, left immediately for Great Lakes. The lad died before the arrival of his parents. The remains arrived here yesterday afternoon and were taken to the home of the deceased's parents at Sulphur Well. Funeral services will be held at the Sulphur Well Christian Church this (Friday) afternoon at 3 o'clock, Rev H C Bell, of Springfield and Rev R H Wilkerson, of Lexington, officiating, followed by interment in Maple Grove Cemetery." September 27, 1918 p3c5

Scottie writes in her autobiography:

> The great `flu' epidemic broke out in September and Ray lost his life there as lots of other boys did. We received a telegram that he'd been taken to the hospital, seriously ill. We hastened to go, but what good did it do? He died before we arrived. After so long there, we learned he was dead and that his body would not be shipped the same route as we would take and we may as well return home. I can't begin to tell the sorrow and heartache we endured. No one knows only those who have had the same experience. The Bible says `Greater love hath no man, than this, that a man lay down his life for his friend. Also, `He that loseth his life for my sake shall find it'. All of us were members of the Christian Church at Sulphur Well.

On November 9, 1918 Robert Spears wrote to Forest that in Ray's death he had lost the only real brother he ever had, not in blood, but in affection. He said "I can truthfully say that if all boys would have the character and manhood that your boy had, this would be a very different old world."

Scottie wrote to the Naval Station asking if Uncle Ray had left any message for his family. She was informed that he was unconscious before death occurred and had not. The reply was dated December 3, 1918.

Walter S Hendren writes a long letter to the Journal about the services offered by the YMCA at Camp Taylor, near Louisville. October 11, 1918 p1c3

Virgil Snowden, son of Steve Snowden, writes from Camp Mills, N J of the kind treatment he has received from the Red Cross. November 1, 1918 p3c4 It had always been my understanding that his poor health was caused by being gassed in the war, yet within ten days of the Armistice he is in New Jersey!

The Armistice as it was in a small town: Early in the morning the whistles began blowing and the church bells ringing. The flag was displayed from the doors of many of the homes. The mayor asked all businesses to close, and come to the victory celebration that took place at ten o'clock in the morning in the court house yard. They sang patriotic songs, and paid tribute to the servicemen. Many went on to their churches for prayer. At six that evening the lights were turned on for the first time in more than a year. The streets were thronged with people shaking hands and exchanging greetings. November 15, 1918 p1c6

In the first article from Sulphur Well for some time, the news was almost entirely about the people recovering from influenza. The school had just been reopened after being closed for six weeks on account of the epidemic. November 22, 1918 p2c5

Mary Ray also died of pneumonia following influenza. She was born October 18, 1864 and died December 28, 1918. She is buried in Buckeye. This is from the Central Record, January 9, 1919.

W S Hendren has finished his work with the YMCA, and he and his wife will locate in Lexington where he has a position with E L March. February 21, 1919 p5c3-4

"Capt F(rank) P Miller and wife, of Rella, Texas, who have been on a visit to his mother, Mrs J P Miller, of Estill County, stopped off for a visit with his uncle, F F Miller, and family, of Sulphur Well." July 25, 1919 p3c4

Another of Dr Hendren's sisters, Mrs Mary E Wheeler, died. He and his daughters, Mrs King and Mrs Davis, attended the funeral in Nicholasville. Central Record, December 11, 1919.

> Mrs Lucy Miller Snowden died Friday, May 8 (1920), at her home in the Sulphur Well neighborhood. Mrs Snowden was 63 years old, a native of Estill County, the daughter of the late F S Miller. She was married to Stephen N Snowden Jan 23, 1873 and came to this county about 28 years ago. She was a member of the Methodist Church and a good woman whose usefulness in the community in which she lived will be greatly missed. The deceased is survived by her husband, and four sons, George, John, Russell and Virgil, and two daughters, Mrs Melvin Dean and Mrs Raymond Hare, all of this county. Funeral services were held Sunday afternoon at 2:30 o'clock from the late residence, conducted by the Rev J E Moss. Interment in Maple Grove Cemetery. May 14, 1920 p3c6

Steve had diabetes and had a leg amputated. He died in 1934, and is buried next to Lucy in Maple Grove.

The Sulphur Well news has been sporadic for several years, with an article or two a year; nothing of any real interest. Pollard and Little Hickman have been the same way. It now looks like the end is near for Pomp. He says that after forty years that he is now an ex-postmaster, and that because of ill health that he intends to sell his farm and store in the fall. July 30, 1920 p2c3

James W Overstreet (Pomp) sold his farm last week, and will dispose of his personal effects at a public sale in a short time. He says that he expects to visit his son in Colorado, and tour the west for several months. September 10, 1920 p3c3

I wonder if he ever had the chance to see the west? "John Overstreet, now living in Minneapolis, is in Lexington with his father, J W Overstreet who is seriously ill at the home of James Overstreet." February 4, 1921 p3c4

He probably didn't. Since Pomp has been a part of this story since the beginning, I have chosen his last writings to conclude the story of Sulphur Well. The following may be found on page one, of the February 18th, 1921 issue of the Jessamine Journal:

J W Overstreet, (Pomp), died at the age of seventy-one. The following article appeared in the Jessamine Journal:

Gathered around a grave in the Ferrell burying ground at Little Hickman, was a faithful group--a group come to hear a communication from the dead, to hear words of advice from one whose spirit had departed and of whom only the molded clay remained.

They were relatives and friends of J W Overstreet, Sr., and they were there to pay a last tribute to that staunch citizen before they buried the dead. In accordance with his wishes, there was no minister. The eulogy, written by Mr Overstreet several years ago and preserved among his papers, sufficed for the ceremony. The music reflected the home-loving and patriotic spirit of the man for, instead of hymns, the choir sang `Home, Sweet Home' and `America'. That was as it was done. It was a simple ceremony, yet impressive.

He had requested that no flowers grace his coffin, but that he be enveloped in that which stood for his ideals and his convictions--the Star Spangled Banner. This wish, too, was carried out and with his body was buried an American flag, the flag he loved so well. As Mr Overstreet had willed, so it was done.

The address of J W Overstreet now our *Sulphur Well Correspondent* began as follows:

*Ladies and Gentlemen: You are not accustomed to having a man preach his own funeral thru the gifted tongue of another, but this is a precedent.*
*Before you lays all that remains of J W Overstreet, Sr. I was formerly a subject of life. I breathed, perambulated and mixed with my fellow beings. But now my pallid face, expressiveless eyes, stilled tongue, heartless breast and rigid form tells you I am dead--dead to you, dead to the world and dead to all eternity.*
*I have now traveled the oft trod path to the grave, the home of eternal rest, there to rest and sleep in that long, eternal, blissful and dreamless sleep that knows no waking; there no wars,*

*no politics, no religion, no strife, no labor and no worry will ever disturb me in my peaceful slumber.*

*I am bereft of all pain, all feeling; my heart has ceased to beat, my brain has ceased to whirl. I am beyond the slanders of the members of the Ananias Club to do me injury. I was born of poor, but respectable parents, April 8th, 1849. My parents have preceded me to this blissful rest. My mother, the dearest of all beings on earth, was the last to leave me. My whole life was an uphill climb, especially from the age of ten years when I labored at ten cents a day, boarding with my parents.*

*At the age of thirteen years I was stricken with that dreadful disease, typhoid fever, which resulted in the entire loss of my hearing, a benefit of a great boon to manhood. Cut off from an education, handicapped from many valuable pursuits of life, I strove to learn all possible under my own tutorship.*

*My past life from that time proves what I did learn. Humanity! It was part of my study. I learned more about the hypocrisy, deceit and treachery of some of my fellow beings than I care to tell. I once tried to be a Christian, but found the church had so many public praying hypocrites and political bums that I seceded. I met in life and had dealings with many good, true and honest people and many more that were bad and dishonest. I knew them like a book. My books and papers will point out to you who some of them were.*

*I tried all my life to be honest and truthful, but was not immune from both personal and business mistakes, made many and was not alone. Many did so before, many more will do so after me. Honest mistakes are excusable by anyone who has any conscience, a true heart, and is not prejudiced.*

*I had as good a mother as ever lived. I will now sleep as she sleeps in the same City of the Dead. I had as good wife as ever lived. This will be my paradise to sleep eternally by her side, to leave children behind us. We want no better monument to our memory.*

*I lived the best life nature gave me. I could not please everbody, personally and in business, especially the prejudiced. I believed in law and order. I had my own beliefs and disbeliefs, granted me by the Constitution of my State and National Government. I believe in one God and no more.*

The address goes on in similar vein, and closes with:

*If I ever did anyone a wilful injury, I ask his forgiveness. I bid you one and all a last farewell and say `be good and useful, be honest and truthful, you will follow me later on'.*

He asked that his executor get someone gifted in speech to read the above address and the poem that follows:

## WHEN I AM GONE

When I am gone, When I am gone!
It seems so strange that I shall go,
Beyond scenes of my vision's range,
and no more know.

I who so much a part of all in life,
Will cease to feel this beating heart
in joy or strife.

Others will take the work I leave and
bear it on,
In various ways the threads will
weave, when I am gone.

Seasons the same will come and go
with storm and sun,
And rivers with unceasing flow, onward will run.

The busy world with all it's care, will
still speed on.
And flowers will bloom as gay and fair
when I am gone.
But perfect peace and sweetest sleep,
I shall have won,
Naught shall disturb my slumber
deep, When I am gone.

No fitful change, no voice rude, no
night or dawn,
Upon my rest will e're intrude, When
I am gone.

And when sometime, my grassy
mound you look upon.
You'll sense through grace that e'er
is found, to where I am gone?

While I used Pomp to end the correspondence, the reader should know that I now think of myself as also becoming one of the Sulphur Well correspondents. I have so saturated myself in the lives of the people of Sulphur Well, for a period of almost fifty years; longer than anyone else I expect, in that period or any time since. I have come close to achieving the purposes that I had in mind when I began the manuscript. I had my child's memories of the community, and knew many of the people who lived there from the 1930's to the few who live there now in the 1990's. I wanted to begin with the Miller Farm, and the Miller Cemetery, and to follow the family and the community up to the time that I had my first recollections. The reader can now proceed to the next chapter for my personal recollections of the time that follows my birth.

## ABOUT THE COMPILER

I was born May 11, 1929, son of Mary Elizabeth Miller and Frank Edward Ware, in the house at the crossroads at Sulphur Well. The house is adjacent to the public pump and across the road from the old general store run for forty years by my grandfather. My birth is only eight years after the story ends, and I believe that my knowledge of the time, place, and people enables me to make the transition from the past to the present.

My mother was born in a house, now razed, that was on the little road to the church. My father was adopted, but spent his early years at Black Bridge, where his father had a blacksmith shop. This was before the Wares moved to the place upon the hill above the church.

My parents went to school together, and married about the time that my mother finished college. Dad was working in Akron at the time, and Mom went there to live, but came home to give birth in Sulphur Well.

Dad came back home, and became the tenant on Luther Ware's farm on the Hoover Pike. Mom taught school, sometimes at Sulphur Well, sometimes other places. We lived there until about 1940, at which time, I think that Dad and his father had a dispute. My grandfather Miller wanted to retire. George Ware had finished electrical school and had an appliance store, and wired homes for electricity. I guess it all came together, so that Dad took over the general store, George took over the farm, and we moved in with the Millers across from the store where I was born. I was ten or eleven at the time.

My earliest recollections are of growing up on the farm. Even now at the age of sixty-seven I still marvel at my contact with the past. I was born only eight years after my story ends, so knew many of the people who were in the latter part of the story. I lived on a farm in the thirties without electricity, running water, or in-door plumbing! We had kerocene lamps, and coal-fired stoves. We kept food cool with an icebox that was filled once or twice a week by an iceman. We kept a milk cow, and raised our own chickens for eggs and meat. Hogs were butchered every fall or early winter to fill the smokehouse with hams and other meat. I don't believe there was any difference in my early life and the 1890s that I wrote about, except transportation. The cars and roads were pretty good.

The same can be said for the country store. Our store was divided into two rooms. The back room was for storage of bulk products. Flour and meal were back there, chicken feed, the kerocene pump, and a pickle barrel. Crackers came in garbage can sized containers and were sold loose. The selling area was packed with goods. One side contained "dry goods", the other side groceries, with an isle in the middle. In the back of this room was the only stove in the building, which was circled with a bench, and nail kegs for seats. This is where people loafed, sometimes from early morning until closing time, usually around nine o'clock. Horse collars, and other items were hung from the ceiling, and required a long stick with a hook to get down. There were some showcases containing items for display. The candy counter was the most popular. There were "penny" candies, and the choices were delightfully difficult for a kid with only one penny to spend. A nickel could get you a bag full of candy. Christmas was really great! That was when the variety was best.

I went to a two room grade school at Sulphur Well. Each teacher taught four grades. It was a sizable step to move into fifth grade, because some of the boys were fifteen and sixteen years old, and some of the older girls seemed like grown women. All things considered, it was not a bad place to learn. The teachers maintained strict discipline in the classrooms so that I don't remember any difficulty studying even though one class or another was in continuous session. I remember a lot of group projects that all grades participated in, such as drawings and decorations for Halloween, Thanksgiving, and Christmas. We always had a Christmas program that involved everyone in the school. Going out to cut the Christmas tree was really fun, as was decorating it.

Saturday was an exciting day for youngsters. Everyone in the family got their work done, cleaned up and went to "town", meaning Nicholasville. The adults shopped, got haircuts or went to the "beauty parlor". Men "loafed" in various places, poolrooms, liquor establishments, barber shops, filling stations, etc. Women often sought places to park cars where they could sit and talk and watch people coming and going. Kids went to the movies, walked up and down the streets, and hung out at the drug store, or in front of it.

Sunday was church day. The routine in our household was to get as much ready in the morning before church as possible for the biggest meal of the week. Often a chicken was killed and dressed. Ice cream was made in a hand-cranked freezer. Vegetables were gotten in from the garden and prepared. Things such as green beans that were cooked for hours were started. Then everybody somehow got cleaned up again for Sunday School and Church. Everyone took turns inviting the preacher home to dinner, and sometimes friends or relatives were invited. It was a busy time for the womenfolk, usually trying to get "dinner" on the table within an hour or so after church. In those days if the table was too small for all the people, there was a second table, meaning that you had to wait for the first group to finish. Instead of children first, it was children last, and I always felt I would starve before it was time to eat. I can't imagine why anyone thought this was fun, yet it was repeated fifty-two times a year.

When I think of church I think of the people in the community. Not everyone went to church, of course, some gathered at the pump or store to loaf while others were at church. I can't mention everyone's name, but if I pick a period, say around 1940, the families that come to mind are the Wests, Fosters, Hares, Stacys, Sagesers, Millers, Wares, and Walters. There were many others that came to church over the years from my childhood to the time that I left the neighborhood, when I married. I will never forget the support that I got from the church when Sue and I were married. We had a small chapel wedding in Lexington, but invited everyone to the reception afterward. It was a January winter night, but it seemed as though everybody came.

I stressed in the book that Sulphur Well included everyone who went to church there or went to school there, but geographically, I suppose our community stretched along Ky 39 from Pink Dean's house coming from Nicholasville to Oscar Sageser's house as you approach Black Bridge, a distance of a mile or so. Then it would include all those who lived around the intersection of the road near the pump, around the little road to the church and the old schoolhouse, and out the road some distance toward Elm Fork, perhaps where the Meyers lived, and part of West's Lane to where Dan West lived. Other people would probably place other boundaries. In my mind, the people on the "outskirts" were in or out depending upon their involvement in the community.

My mother continued to live in Sulphur Well with her mother in the house across from the store. When my grandmother died at the age of ninety-two, Mom had people stay with her at night, Ethel Foster more than anyone else. I can't remember the complete sequence of events, but eventually, after years of someone having to leave their own house to stay with someone else, the system began to break down. On Mom's Sunday visits with us, she began to recount her woes--how hard it was to get anyone to cut the grass, make minor repairs, leave home on cold winter nights, etc. usually followed by her crying. Finally, Sue and I told her, this has to stop, you have to move to an apartment in Lexington. She moved into the Rolling Ridge Apartments just outside of Gainesway where Sue and I still live. This ended almost two hundred years of our family living in Sulphur Well.

As I grew older, I became interested in the Miller Cemetery on Snowden Lane. I had seen it a time or two over my lifetime, but had no idea who was there, or their relation to me. Dr M L Dean owned the farm, and I asked if I could look it over. It looked like a jungle. You could scarcely get to the stones, that were leaning and broken. I asked if I could clean it up and he agreed. I found two men in Lexington who did the heavy work of cutting the brush and briars. We got the Nicholasville Monument Company to straighten and repair all the monuments. Despite many, many hours of probing with a steel rod, we could never locate two of the monuments, and three of the footstones, although the pedestals still remain. These stones have since been replaced. We continued to clean up the area, and brought in some soil to fill some of the sunken places, and sowed grass. We put up a fence and began to mow on a regular basis. I had known M L, "all my life" so to speak, but we only became friends in the two or three years that we worked together on the cemetery. I had a bad back and was in my sixties. He had more infirmities and was in his seventies. However, our joint efforts restored the cemetery and created a bond that I deeply regretted being broken at his death.

The restoration work stimulated my interest in the family, first, just to find out who these people were. Then, I started reading the <u>Jessamine Journal</u> trying to get additional information on various people. After finding several interesting things about the family, I became serious about putting the family history together in the context of Sulphur Well. That required purchasing microfilm of the <u>Journal</u> from 1877 to 1921, and also purchasing a microfilm reader because I found library research to be very inefficient. I plan to finish the "last" draft of the book this fall and winter, and print a few copies, putting one in the Transy library, one in the Nicholasville library, and a few more for family members. I have two concerns. One, the perpetual care of the cemetery. Second, preservation of enough family records, so that someone doing family research one hundred years from now will find something of value.

Ray M Ware
July 18, 1996

Still more about the Compiler: This part is more personal, and also contains some of the things that I did that I consider worthwhile in my life.

I attended Sulphur Well School, beginning at age five, because my mother taught the first four grades. There was a succession of people taking care for me while she taught, none of whom did well, with one exception. The exception was Mag Smith, a black lady who lived in Nicholasville. She was my "Mammy" and I loved her dearly. I suppose that when she left that Mom thought school was the best alternative. I must say in retrospect that it made life tough for me from grade school all the way through college. I was always one or two years younger than my classmates, and was small for my age too. While I did well academically, I think that my social development would have been better if I had the same maturity level as my classmates. By my entering college at barely seventeen in 1946 along with the returning WW II veterans, I was not only one or two years younger than my peers, but now five or six. I could have benefited by going to a prep school, particularly since Nicholasville High was a pretty poor place to be educated at that time. The school burned during the Christmas Holiday of my freshman year. We had classes in the courthouse and in the Christian Church, the rest of that year. Then all the country kids were sent over to Wilmore, a place that I hated. I transferred back to Nicholasville High, where the city kids went, but they were just a remnant, and were located in an old house. My graduating class had thirteen students, swelled to that number by two returning veterans.

By the time that I finished college in 1950 the draft was reinstituted for the Korean War. No one would hire me with a 1A status so I did some part-time jobs until my father found out that my number was coming up, and was about to be drafted. So, I enlisted in the Air Force, in June of 1951, for a four-year hitch. That's a long time in a young life. The first eighteen months weren't so bad, I did well, had a lot of friends. We were overstaffed, so I had a lot of time to play tennis, golf and bridge, and to come home frequently. The War was winding down, and they started letting people out whose enlistments were nearly up. Psychologically, this tore me up, because I thought that my time would be greatly shortened. It didn't happen. They reached their desired level and stopped the program. Fortunately, by this time I enjoyed my job, which was in Base Finance, and became interested in accounting as a career. I only had the two basic courses in college, didn't do all that well, and had forgotten most of the rest. I began taking the courses over by correspondence, I think we called them USAFI courses. They were virtually free. Just as I was finishing them, the local college, Midwestern University, advertised a summer course in Intermediate Accounting, just when I needed it. I asked to be allowed to attend, and got the approval. I left the Finance Office about mid-morning every day; we had class for a couple of hours, and the instructor and at least some of the students had lunch together. I returned to the Base in the early afternoon. I did well in that course, and was a week or so along in the second course, when I received word that my father had died. They gave me emergency leave, and I spent a week or two at home. By the time I got back the accelerated summer course was beyond my catching up.

My father had committed suicide. I guess we never know what goes through anyone's mind. He was a high school drop-out, and it was a handicap all of his life. Every time he had an opportunity for advancement, his lack of even a high school certificate kept him back. He tried several things. He knew farming, was a storekeeper for a while, was a factory worker before he married, and worked in a defense plant in Detroit during World War II. When he returned home after the war he sold cars. He was a gambler all his life, and it kept him in hot water all the time. I don't know what exactly was going on, no one had seen any particular change, and no one I ever talked to thought he would take his own life. I thought it poignant that he returned to his first home in Black Bridge to do so.

Mom came down and stayed with me in Wichita Falls the next summer, letting me live off base for a while. That was a nice change. Then back to the barracks. However, the Air Force was at it again. You could now get out of the service up to ninety days early if you returned to school. I went to Ohio State in the spring quarter, because that maximized my time off. I continued my work in accounting, and did well. I transferred to UK for the summer term, taking more accounting, continuing to do well. As the fall term approached I was offered a teaching assistantship by Dean Carpenter. That made me want to be a teacher, but I wanted a CPA certificate more at the time. So, after a really good MBA performance, I got a job in public accounting. I worked for a national firm, a regional firm, and two local firms to get my experience requirement, and was totally soured by the experience. It was an apprentice system where you were a flunky until you got your certificate, and they paid you that way; and worked you without compensation for extremely long hours during tax season.

By this time, and for some unknown reason, I decided that I wanted to learn Economics. I returned to UK to work on a doctorate in Economics. Sue and I had a class together while I was working on my MBA and she was an undergraduate. In the fall of 1960 we both returned to school and met again in another class. This time we started dating. We became engaged in a short time, and were married the following January. We really pieced our finances together. I had the GI bill, and a small academic scholarship, and Sue had an equally small scholarship. We found an apartment for $100 per month, and budgeted $10 per week for groceries. A few weeks after we were settled in our apartment, we invited my grandmother Ware for a visit and she brought, I think, about $50 to give us. You have no idea how big that seemed. Surprisingly enough, life was pretty good. Sue had joined the brand-new Tates Creek Country Club before returning to school, and somehow we kept up the membership. That provided the luxury we needed amid the frugality with which we lived.

Sue became pregnant almost immediately, so we were faced with some heavy medical bills when Doug was born. He had a birth defect that the March of Dimes Foundation mostly financed. Fortunately, his problems were correctable, but the medical expenses continued until he was four years old, and now they were our responsibility. I continued my graduate program, and when my classwork was out of the way, I got a job teaching at Transylvania College. I finished the dissertation in two more years, and successfully defended it. The professor who directed my dissertation, Max J Wasserman, and I then collaborated on a book together, in which my dissertation became the historical, and part of the methodological, portion of <u>The Balance of Payments: History, Methodology, and Theory</u>. Then I helped Wasserman and Hultman revise their book, <u>Modern International Economics</u>. Over the years I produced several articles, participated in seminars, and did quite a number of things including helping to found, and becoming the second president of, the Kentucky Economic Association. I was very active on the faculty, serving on almost all of the committees at one time or another over a seventeen year period.

I think that I could have done more if I had better institutional support. Transylvania was going through one of its worst modern slumps. Transy had benefited by the successive presidencies of McLean, and Frank Rose. Irvin Lunger had just taken over when I arrived. I thought he was impressive, and he led the school well for several years. However, by the time the seventies arrived with all its problems with students and finances, he seems incapable of dealing with it and soon retired. The next president was truly incompetent and was in effect fired. During this time of weak presidents, the vice-presidents of Development and Business Affairs were in control, exceeding the influence of the vice-president of Academic Affairs. The officers held their retreats, lived high on Transy credit cards, while blaming the faculy for the difficulty in getting good students. I would guess that the purchasing power of my salary went down every year in the seventies, and Transy was a depressing place to work.

In the summer of 1976 the Assistant State Treasurer left her job, and I was recommended to the Treasurer. I spent the summer there, and was offered the position, but didn't want to give up my tenure at Transy at that time. However, it was a great experience, my only experience in state government and I liked it. A year later I had the opportunity to become a Visting Professor at UK in 1978. By this time Sue had built up our accounting practice, and she had gotten her CPA certificate in 1976, so we decided that it was a good time for me to join her in the full-time practice of accounting.

This was a total change in life for me. I was forty-eight at the time, and every thing I did was different. Instead of teaching, I was doing accounting, and dealing with clients instead of students. I joined Rotary, became active in United Way, and became active in the accounting profession. I became chairman of the Taxation Committee relatively quickly, and there was a lot going on at the time. I got the committee involved, worked with members of the legislature and two cabinet members. I discovered that in at least one large firm that the minutes of our committee meetings were distributed to the staff. This attracted a fair amount of attention, and I was asked to run for the board of the Kentucky Society of CPA's. I did, and received the highest number of votes. They made me Vice-

President the first year of my term. I was Secretary the next year, and was expected to become President-Elect the next year. However, it was customary for members of the Executive Committee to go to a bar after the meetings. I never went because I had to drive back to Lexington from Louisville where the meetings were held. At one of the after-hour meetings, they decided that two others should go before me into the presidency. I really thought that was the end of the line. I perservered, stood for re-election to the board, and again got the most votes. So they really did make me president-elect in my fifth year. My sixth year I was president, and had a full year. This was a time of big changes in the profession, so there was a lot of things coming down from the American Institute, of which I was a Council member, pertaining to ethical and professional standards. That was voted upon by the entire membership, then it was up to the individual state societies to enact the same requirements. This was during my presidential year, and a lot had to be done to implement these things on the state level. By the time the year was over, I felt exhilarated by the accomplishments, and was ready to quit, but had to return to the board as Past-President. What a downer! How anti-climatic! This had been a nine year run, and I was tired!

I had also been active in United Way during this period. I began on the fund-raising campaign side, and got up to Chairman of the Professional Division. Then I switched to Allocations, where the funds are distibuted. I was successively vice chair, then chair of one of the allocation groups, then I became the Chair of the Allocations Cabinet of United Way of the Bluegrass. I was on the Board for six years, and a member of the executive committee for three of those years.

The minister at Crestwood Christian Church, where I am a member, asked if I would be Treasurer for the Church. At that moment I was President of the Ky Society and Chairman of Allocations, so I declined. The next year they asked if I would be a Deacon, and I agreed. The following year they asked me to me Treasurer, and I accepted, and served for three years. I was on the Child Care Council of Crestwood for the same period, and still am at this writing. I then became Finance Chairman for two years, then Elder, and later Chair of the Elders. This essentially brings my life up to date as far as activities go. It is difficult to write about what you've done in life without feeling that someone may think you are bragging. I hope that isn't the case. But in order to give some balance, I need to say that sometimes that I think that I am the luckiest person in the world, and other times I think "My God, why me?" I suppose everyone must feel this way at times. I'm not sure who may ever read this, but I'd like for anyone who happens to be interested, to get to know me. Perhaps it will be a distant relative a hundred years from now who is researching his family, just like I have done for the period 1877 to 1905; with epilogue to 1921. I got to know Dr Hendren and Dr Miller particularly because of their writings and a picture of Dr Miller in the Journal. I got to know Uncle Ray from what Mom and Edith have told me, to some degree through his letter home shortly before his death, and his pictures in the family album. Even my son Doug may, in his old age, find this of interest. We all desire immortality, and in a spiritual way, may find it. But, we also want the family line to be continued, and mine stops with Doug. That is a disappointment that I can do nothing about. It would have been nice if this book were still in a family member's possession in 2096. By putting a copy in the Transy archives, along with all my other professional attainments, perhaps in a hundred years some graduate student will run across this, and gain a glimpse of the past, and feel that I left a trace of my passing.

It seems that my life has been segmented by major events, not of my choosing. I was born into the worse depression in the nation's history. We were just getting out of that decade, when the greatest war in the history of the world was fought. Civilians may escape the horror of the conflict, but not the consequences. It was never out of your thoughts, it affected everything that you purchased and used. We had barely gotten things back to normal when the Korean War broke out. That really affected me personally. Even as I was finishing college, I knew I had no future until I had served my time, which ended in March 1955. Then came the CPA experience and the graduate work. Almost another decade. Also, I have had to live through two never-ending controversies: civil rights and abortion. Things are simple to me. You go through the legislative process. You go through the judicial process. You get an answer and go on with life. For four decades we have people that won't accept the answers, and won't let anyone else go on with their life either. I have been tired of it for thirty years, but I have to go through it bit by bit during every newscast.

Sue and I married in January, 1961 and have already celebrated our thirty-fifth wedding anniversary. We have been a very good team, I think. She has helped me with everything that I have accomplished. We have been practicing accounting together as Ware and Ware, PSC since 1976 as a firm, but we have been doing accounting work since 1962. She became politically active a few years ago, first joining a Republican Women's Club, becoming its president, then District Governor, President of the Kentucky Federated Republican Womens' Club, and a member of the board of the national organization. She is also on the Kentucky Republican Party's Central Committee, and an alternate delegate to the national convention this year (1996).

Over the years the things we seem to have enjoyed most have been our vacations and travels, close and far. We enjoy the state parks as much as anyone, and have visited most all of them, some several times. We like the wild flowers in the spring and the foliage in the fall. We have had some memorable trips, among them three weeks in Mexico, including Acupulco; two or three weeks in Central America and Columbia; and a fishing trip in Canada. We have been to most of the major cities for professional meetings, usually adding a day or two to sight-see, sometimes together, sometimes separately. Our favorite vacation place has been Vero Beach. Sue's parents retired there, and we started making at least one visit per year to see them and to vacation at the same time. They lived inland a few miles, and we wanted to be on the beach and be independent, so we rented places while we were there. About seven years ago we rented a condo in the Kentucky Club, and have every year since during the Christmas holidays, usually from mid-December till the first week in January. It has become a second home, and we love the view of the ocean from the condo.

The Lake Ellerslie Fishing Club has been a major part of my life for the last twenty years. I fish there, of course, but I also canoe, and walk. Its a beautiful lake and a wonderful place to get away for a couple of hours. I not only go there every day, but sometimes twice a day. I've been the Secretary/Treasurer for about eight years. I just remembered that I was also the tennis coach at Transy for five years in the early sixties. I am a member of the tennis club on Redding Road, have played tennis there for fifteen or twenty years, but haven't played in the past two years. Sue and I used to play together, but she developed a bad knee, so we stopped playing. I used to belong to a Wednesday doubles group, but about the time that I hit sixty-five, my partners were in their forties, or early fifties, and those are two different plateaus, so I dropped that. My interest in swimming and canoeing began to exceed tennis anyway, and you can't do everything.

In recent years I have begun to regret not having a larger family, assuming that Sue and I could have. I can see the importance of large families, it increases your probability of carrying on the family name. Harking back to the book, I don't believe that there is a single decendent of Francis S Miller with the Miller name. There were several girls, but no boys in the last generation. Uncle Ray, had he lived, would have been the best bet to carry on. There is also the small number of people available at festive occasions such as Thanksgiving and Christmas, or on anniversaries and birthdays.

These are my thoughts to date. I'm retired, but active, and hope to live at least to my life expectancy, which is about eighty-one at present. If I do, it will be interesting to read this fifteen years from now, to see whether my perspective of life has changed, and if any of this stuff is important to me or not. Barbara Bush said in a commencement address that on your death bed, you will not regret doing one more deal, but how little time you spent with your friends and family. If you read my grandmother's autobiography you will find only the story of her family and church. I fear that when you read mine, you will only find me. Maybe I can change that in the time I have left.

October 8, 1996

I guess I will keep adding on to this until I finally finish it. I really knew that I had a health problem in October 1996, but hadn't quite faced up to it. I was diagnosed with Multiple Myeloma, a cancer that affects your bone marrow, and eventually leads to the disintegration of your bones, not a pleasant prospect. It's never out of my mind, and it is difficult not to be emotional at times. Life may not always be wonderful, but it's hard to give up. At first, I went around the yard, and other places looking at flowers, trees, thinking I'd never see them again in bloom or with their brilliant foliage. There were a lot of places in the world I have never gotten to see, and maybe some things I wish I had done. This went on for some weeks or months, but now, the only regret that I have in life, is that I can't grow old, really old, with Sue. She and I have been soul-mates, having basically the same view of life, and I really thought that we would live a long, long time together. I hate to give up that dream. I am now, perhaps as I have always been, in the hands of God and the medical profession. I pray that with both together my life will be extended as long as possible. April 28, 1997

## THE GEOGRAPHICAL SETTING OF THE STORY

The main north-south corridor through Jessamine County is US Highway 27. It comes south by way of Lexington and forms the main street of Nicholasville. It crosses the river at Camp Nelson, and goes on to Lancaster. The area south and southeast of Nicholasville forms a triangle that includes parts of three counties-Jessamine, Madison, and Garrard.

People crossed the Kentucky River by ferry at several places between those counties, but the two most used by the people I have been writing about were at Paint Lick and Hunters Ferry. People crossed the river at Paint Lick to go from Sulphur Well to Buckeye, Lancaster, or other small villages. They crossed at Hunter's Ferry to go to Edenton, Cottonburg, Ruthton, Kirksville and Richmond. Actually, these two routes are not very far apart, perhaps nine miles at the river, and like spokes of a wheel diverge as the traveler goes to Richmond or Lancaster.

On the south side of the river, Paint Lick Creek divides Madison and Garrard counties, and there is not much much in the way of lateral roads between the spokes because of the ridges in between. The only connecting road between, Cottonburg in Madison, and Buckeye in Garrard, is Dry Branch Road that still requires the traveler to drive across a creek bed. They are also connected several miles further out by Ky 52 between Lancaster and Richmond.

Poosey Ridge, formed by Paint Lick Creek and Silver Creek, is a relatively high ridge that runs for several miles, at least as far as Kirksville. Poosey Ridge Road, like every country road, had stores with post offices every few miles, with names such as Edenton and Cottonburg. As you drive along the road today, you cannot see distinct villages, and have to know the history of the area to know where the post offices were located. I am told that this ridge once was inhabited by many more people that presently live there now, that there was once "a house in ever holler".

Shifting back toward US 27, you cross the Kentucky River at Camp Nelson, site of a military encampment. If you take a side road to the right (going south) you come to Buena Vista. Another crossroad takes you back to US 27 at Bryantsville. Dr Hendren had a daughter living at each place. Camp Dick Robinson is just a little south of Bryantsville. It's not many miles from these villages to Buckeye where Dr Hendren lived after leaving Sulphur Well.

If you take Ky 39 from Nicholasville, you first come to the Chrisman Mill intersection, and then two miles later reach Sulphur Well. Ky 39 goes on to Black Bridge and crosses Hickman Creek. You have another intersection, one road going to Pink and Little Hickman, the other going to the river at Paint Lick.

Returning to the Sulphur Well intersection, the other road goes to Elm Fork, which is between Little Hickman and Pollard. You could continue on that road to Mt Lebanon and complete the circle back to the Chrisman Mill Road.

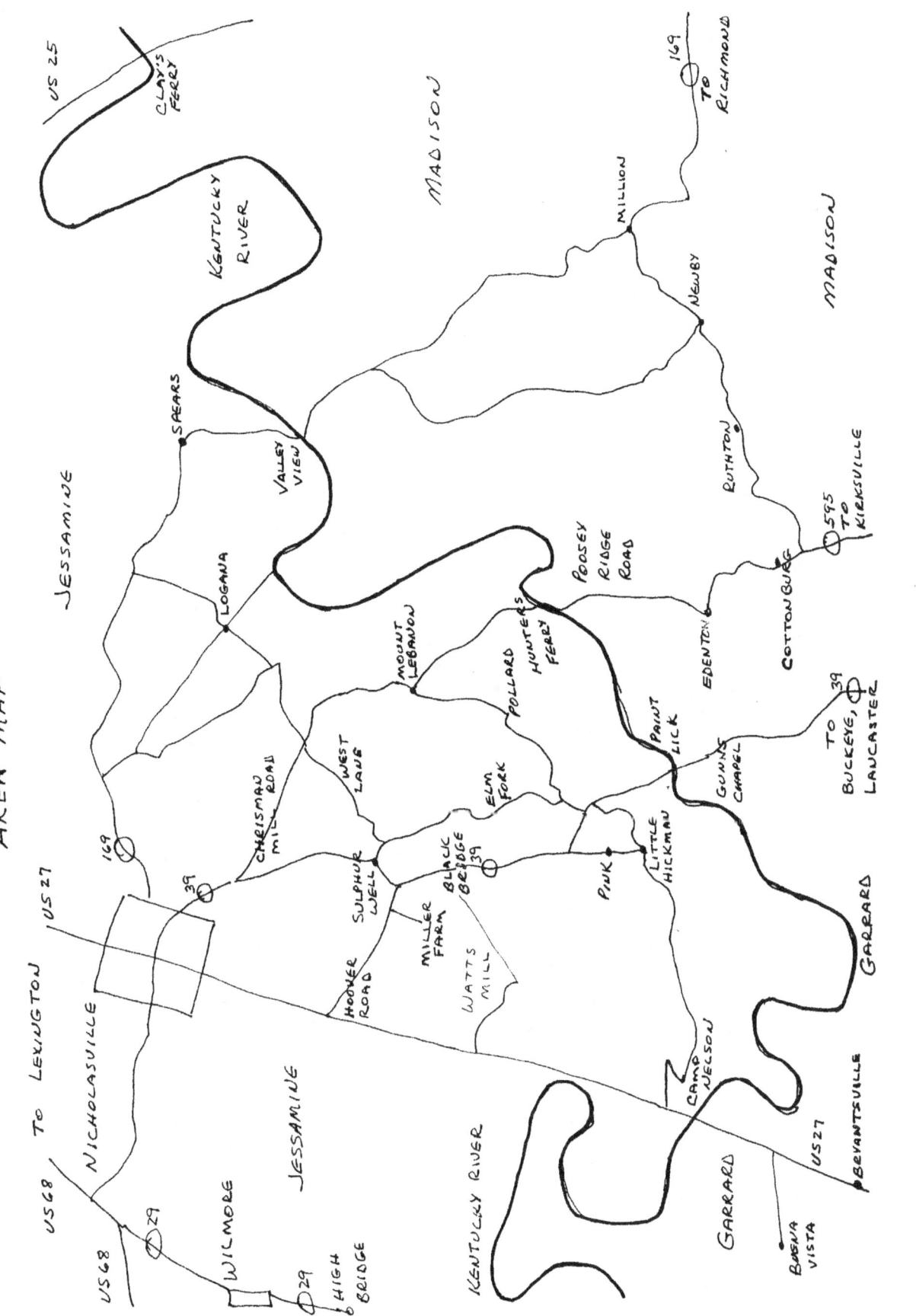

## FAMILIES THAT APPEAR FREQUENTLY IN THE STORY

The families that appear in this summary are not intended to be Sulphur Well's list of "400" or even "40", but a rather arbitrary selection of families that appear to me to have been most active in the era I have selected for study. As I have said before, the correspondent(s) tended to report on the people and events known to them. I hope that this summary of families will help readers better understand the relationships of the people that became part of the story of Sulphur Well. The reader may also see the 1900 Census for more information.

ADCOCK. Adam Adcock, from the Knoxville, Tennessee area, married Addie Hendren, who was born in Madison County, but later lived in Lexington. He was a tavern owner by trade, operated a bar in Nicholasville during most of this story, but eventually moved to Lexington in 1908. Adcock was a horseman, running horses at major tracks in the country. He had a large house on North Main Street in Nicholasville, and helped raise and keep the younger members of his wife's family after their mother died. He served on both the City Council and the School Board in Nicholasville. He is buried in Maple Grove Cemetery in Nicholasville.

ASKINS. Alex M Askins came from Buena Vista in Garrard County in 1887. He was a blacksmith and conducted his business in a shop across the road from the Dr Hendren residence. He and my grandfather, Luther Ware, were associated for several years in that business. He had a brother, Sam Askins a millwright, who came with him to Sulphur Well. Askins acquired the property next to the church for his home. He and his wife, Sally, had three daughters -- twins Bertha and Blanche, and Mattie. Bertha married Guy Stacy. Blanch married George Snowden, and Mattie married Chess Woodard. Sally died in 1905, and Alex died in 1916. Both are buried in Maple Grove Cemetery.

BAKER. The Baker farm is adjacent to the Miller farm, on the Hoover Pike. In 1892
J Wilson Baker married Miranda Spruce, who had three daughters by a former marriage -- Lulu, Linnie, and Emma who thread their way thought the story. Lulu married Joe Woodward. Linnie married Walter Hendren, and Emma married Marshall Davis. Baker had at least one son, Ricketts, from a previous marriage. At this time I cannot relate Tilford, Al, John, or Nancy Baker. Nancy rented her house in Sulphur Well to Dr Hendren in 1889. Baker and J H Murphy operated a threshing machine, and raised cattle together. Baker also had seven trotting horses at the time of his death in 1895. He was 61 years old, and is buried at his homeplace. There is no reference to Miranda after this.

BERRY. George Berry was living in Sulphur Well in 1887, although his roots were apparently in either Madison or Garrard County. I believe him to be the correspondent who wrote the first few articles for the <u>Jessamine Journal</u>. He married Ida Gray in 1888 and they made their home in Lexington. George "traveled" for twenty-eight years for a Cincinnati firm. He was noted for his good humor, and was highly regarded by the tradesmen that he called upon, and by his fellow salemen. He was an officer of the United

Commercial Travelers for several years. George was born in 1854 and died in 1928. Ida was born in 1868 and died in 1923. Both are buried in the Lexington Cemetery.

BISHOP. Frank Bishop, and John March, both of Virden, Illinois, and S N Bishop of Wilmore are related to the Hendrens. Bertha Hendren met her future husband, Alfred Bennett while visiting them. D Boone Tudor and his wife, Theresa Hendren, lived there for a while also. Oscar Sageser, from another branch of the family, spent some time in Virden. Many others from Jessamine and Madison counties drifted to Virden and to Bloomington. These cities were on the rail line between St Louis and Chicago, and I believe that it is, or was, a coal-mining area.

BOURNE. The Bourne family was located just over the river in Garrard County, around the Buena Vista and Polly's Bend areas. Everett was living in Sulphur Well in 1887 and was visited constantly by family members from Garrard. He was a friend of the Bright's before they moved to Lexington. He, Millard Davis, Guy Stacy, and Hamlet Foster went to Cincinnati together in 1902. I belive that Hamlet was a nephew. Everett's daughter, Irene, married Oscar Sageser, and they became a life-long residents of Sulphur Well. They lived in the Moore's former residence, just below the Newt Davis place on the way to Black Bridge. Everett died in 1916, and is buried in Maple Grove Cemetery.

BRIGHT. The Bright's were from Lancaster. They moved to Sulphur Well in 1887 and after a few years in Sulphur Well as a merchant, William H Bright moved on to Lexington. The Bright's were firm friends of the Askins and visited them long after their move. William's sister, Helena, who never married, was a good friend of Lizzie Wilds. The Bright's are connected to the Woolfolk's in some manner, as are the Hendren's. John Woolfolk moved on to Lexington, and their visits continued. Sallie Woolfolk visited in Sulphur Well early, and Mary Woolfork, was once referred to as Bertha Hendren's aunt. William Bright died in 1928 and his wife in 1938. Both are buried in the Lexington Cemetery.

COBB. J W Cobb, known as Jim, lived right in the middle of Sulphur Well. He sold his house to my grandfather, Forest Miller in 1907. The Whitenack's, of Mercer County, were good friends, and they visited each other frequently.

DAVIS. N D Davis' (Newt) farm was located at the intersection of Ky 39 and the Hoover Pike, just south of Sulphur Well. He was a cattle and tobacco dealer and broker, appearing to collect those products from southeast Jessamine and across the river into Garrard County from Buckeye to Buena Vista. His wife was Belle Clay Johns, and their family included Williard W, Walter K, Viola, Marshall, and Grace. Willard, the oldest was born in 1871 and Grace, the youngest, in 1887. Viola and Marshall attended the wedding dinner held for Scottie and Forest Miller, my grandparents. Willard and his uncle, Millard, operated a business similar to Newt's and they were frequently in Cincinnati, a major livestock shipping point in the country. Walter married Dr Hendren's daughter, Mary, in 1902 and they were also a farming family, but not a dealer as were the others. Marshall married Emma Spruce in 1900 and they still lived in my day, but were elderly. I remember

Marshall as a tall, spare man who always wore black suits. He was kind of a Digger O'Dell type in my recollection. I also knew Williard, who was rather portly. The two had absolutely no family resemblance, and I newer knew they were brothers until this research was done. A review of the index will show a slew of Davis' and it would take a family historian to sort them all out, but Margaret Clubb Caywood has helped a lot. Newt died in 1909 at the age of fifty-nine, and is buried in Maple Grove Cemetery.

DEAN. There is also a world of Dean's, and I can barely begin to indentify them. They are really a Little Hickman family. The one's in this story decend from Harrison Dean and Nancy Owens. They had eight sons and two daughters. One of their sons was Morris Dean, who married Maria Jasper. Their daughter, Eunice, married Luther Ware, and they raised my father, Frank Ware. Maria's sister, Mary Jasper, married Dr Hendren. Two other sons of Harrison and Nancy appear in the story. Roland Dean, was an attorney who made his home in Oklahoma. Melvin Dean, married Myrtie Snowden in 1900, and their son Dr M L Dean, reassembled most of the Miller Farm.

DIAMOND. George and Arkie Diamond lived on the hill above the church, on the property with the large pond, often mentioned in the story. The house was purchased by Newt Davis in 1897 and rented to various people - to Mrs Emily Peel in 1897, S E Gott in 1898, and Viola Davis and Charlie Clubb in 1899. It was later purchased by Luther Ware, and he and Eunice lived there the rest of their lives. The Diamond's were close friends of the Grays and they visited frequently. They moved from Sulphur Well, and Arkie died soon thereafter. George worked for the clothing firm of Murphy and Horine, that later became Murphy and Miller. After Arkie died in 1897, and his house burned, George went to New York to live.

DICKERSON. Although frequently mentioned in the story, John Dickerson and wife, Mary Ray, were residents of Buckeye. She and her brother, Bronston, were children of Dr William Ray. John became a traveling salesmen, and died in 1910 after a stroke, and a long illness. Mary then lived with her mother until Mrs Ray died in 1912. Mary, born in 1864, returned to Buckeye where she resided until her death from pneumonia in 1918. She is buried in the Buckeye Cemetery.

EASLEY. J Holley Easley, was probably living in Pink in 1888 when first reported, because he sold his farm in that place to A J Sageser in 1893. He rented a Carter farm for several years, and then moved to Buena Vista in 1901. He continued to return for visits to Sulphur Well, as both the Askins' and Bourne's were close friends.

FOSTER. Benjamin Franklin (B F) Foster was born in 1843, and married Eliza Jane St Clair in 1866. He bought a farm on the Watts Mill road in 1884. Their children were Phillip, Jesse, Lily May, and Hamlet. Phillip built a house on the farm in 1900. Jesse had a home on the Hoover Pike, a mile or so from the Hoover farm. I knew him quite well. Hamlet purchased the James Watts farm in 1903. Hamlet died quite young, but was the father of Garrett and Lucien Foster. Lucien and Ethel lived in the Dr Hendren house in Sulphur Well. Their daughter Jane Kurtz still lives there.

GOTT. J E Gott rented the Diamond farm in late 1897, and lived there during 1898. There was a Rowena Gott attending school in Wilmore in 1898, and a Miss Gott who taught school in Sulphur Well that same year, probably the same person. Creed Gott was living in Lexington in 1899. He married Ruth Johns in 1900 at the J P Turner residence, and they moved to Richmond. I have no indication of family relationships.

GRAY. George Gray, a distiller, was born in North Carolina, and came to Jessamine at an early age. He married Margaret Hunter in 1865, and they had six children that included Texie and Ida. The distillery in which he had an interest was located at what is know as Big Spring on West's Lane. The family bought property in Sulphur Well in 1882, but sold it in 1887 to Andrew Sageser and moved to Lexington. In 1888 Texie married Tom Cooley and moved to Omaha. Ida married George Berry and they made their home in Lexington. George died in 1901 at age sixty-two. His wife Margaret died in 1909. Their oldest daughter Texie died in 1915. All are buried in the Lexington Cemetery. The Gray's had a son also named George, so that the reader should note that all references after 1901 are for the son.

GRIMES. James and Sallie Grimes moved to Lexington at the beginning of the story, but friendship with the Askins, and family ties, brought them frequently back to Sulphur Well. In 1889 Ben Grimes, of Lexington, visits an unidentified brother and sister in Sulphur Well. Delia Grimes, living in Sulphur Well, visits her brother, Ollie Grimes, in Lexington. The Askins are visited in 1900 by Mrs William Grimes; in 1901 by Ernest Grimes; and, in 1902, by Lizzie Grimes. I can't begin to sort them out.

HARE. W H Hare was a farmer with a large family. A daughter, Mayme, married Wm McClellan Johnston, of Lancaster. Another daughter, Julia, married Ben D Spears in 1892, and moved to Nicholasville. They had a son, Robert Spears, who became a best friend of Ray E Miller. Julic died in 1900. Willie Hare had already died quite young in 1895. Both are buried at Maple Grove Cemetery. Two other daughters were Bettie and Nannie (Nancy).

HARRIS. William Harris was born in 1821. He married Frances Woodward, and they had a son, Walter D Harris, who married Myrtie Overstreet in 1886. Myrtie's mother is Sally Miller, daughter of Merriman Miller. The main entrance to the Harris farm is on the Watts Mill Road, but the back entrance is through the Miller farm. The Harris Cemetery is only a hundred yards or so away from the Miller Cemetery. The reader should refer to the Woodwards for more family history.

HEMPHILL. Andrew Hemphill was born in Ireland, but came to Jessamine County in 1820. He married Mildred Tapp, and their children include: Charles, Louis T, and Hugh C Hemphill. Charles married Naomi Wilmore in 1858, and their children were: Kate, Lilly May, and Minnie. Kate married William Woods, and they made their home at the large residence on their 479 acre farm near Sulphur Well. Kate grew flowers in profusion, and generously gave them to our family for Decoration Day. I remember the name Lilly May very well, but can't visualize her. I believe she was a maiden lady. I never heard of Minnie. Louis T Hemphill, born in 1834, married Eliza Price. Their children includes Dan P Hemphill, champion wheeler, later pharmacist. They owned a 170 acre farm. Hugh C Hemphill was born in 1842, and married Ella Oxley in 1873. She died early in this story, leaving young children that included Andrew J and Mildred Hemphill. The Hemphill's owned land that essentially surrounded Sulphur Well in the northeast quadrant. They and J P Turner owned all the land on one side of the road (Ky 39) from about one mile north of Sulphur Well to the intersection of the Elm Fork Road, out to the West Lane, where Big Spring is located on Hemphill propery. I have been told that they had a summer camp or cottage near the spring.

HENDREN. There are at least six branches of the Hendren family in the story, five of whom decend from Doven Hendren of Madison County. His sons are William, Thomas, Talton, and Harrison. He also has a daughter, Eliza, who married Turpin West. William, born in Edenton in 1819, married Eliza A Reynolds in 1838. They had a family of nine children that constitute a major part of this story. Eliza died in 1900, and William in 1901, both are buried in Maple Grove Cemetery. Their son, Dr George M Hendren, is "the" Sulphur Well Correspondent, and his story is so well documented that I only want to give the reader a perspective of his life. He was born in Edenton in 1846, and married Mary E Jasper, of Casey County, in 1870. They had three daughters: Addie married Hugh Miller, Nellie married Howard King, and Mary married Walter Davis. Dr Hendren was practicing medicine in Sulphur Well when my story begins. However, for some reason he moved back to Edenton in 1892, but returned to Sulphur Well in 1894. This accounts for a sizable gap in his reports. He began to write poetry in 1898, and had many of his poems published in the <u>Jessamine Journal</u> over a period of several years. He became interested in the potential of Oklahoma, and his visits there began in 1901. Even as early as 1902, he appears to have become disenchanted with Sulphur Well, and renewed or developed friendships with people in and around Edenton, and Buckeye. In 1903 he sold his home in Sulphur Well, and his household goods, and moved to Oklahoma for several months. He returned in 1904, but never seemed content. Dr Hendren went back to Oklahoma in 1905, returned briefly to Sulphur Well, wrote his last article in August, stating that he was moving to Buckeye. He lived there until his wife died in 1922. He died in Wilmore in 1924, and is buried with other family members in the Maple Grove Cemetery.

Tom Hendren was a merchant in Nicholasville, whose daughter, Nellie was a violinist and music teacher. He also had three sons, Carl, Clyde and Emmett. Talton Hendren, another son of Doven, is mentioned only twice in the story, and I know nothing of his family, if any.

Harrison Hendren had a son named Will D Hendren, who had several children with Levisa Tudor. A daughter, Addie married Adam Adcock, and lived in Nicholasville. At various times she provided a home for almost all the other children, and both her parents died at her house. The boys names were Fount, Pat, and Leo. The daughters were: Addie; Lizzie who married a Van Winkle, then later a Crosley; Scottie who married Forest Miller; Susie who married Andrew Sageser; and Bertha who married Alfred Bennett. This is my branch of the family.

Eliza Hendren, the only daughter of Doven that appears in this story, was born in 1816. She married Turpin West, and they had a daughter that married N B Long, and a son John T West. Both are frequently mentioned in the Sulphur Well reports. Eliza and Turpin are buried in the Salem Cemetery near Edenton.

James Hendren, born in 1824, comes from Madison County, but is not a decendant of Doven. I have been unable to identify his father. He married Mildren Collins, and they have several children mentioned in the story: Ezekiel; Theresa who married a Tudor; Squire T of Cottonburg; Betty and Zerelda, one who married S N Bishop, and the other James Vincent. James Hendren died in 1907.

HOOVER. The Hoover's were a large landholding family along the Hoover Pike. My uncle, George Ware, lives in the old family residence of William H Sr, which is just opposite Snowden Lane where the Miller farm is located. He was born in 1821 and married Sarah Evans of Garrard County in 1857. They had two sons. W H, Jr referred to as a horseman, purchased the Butler farm in 1899, and in 1901 Lizzie Miller married Tom Downing at their home. Lizzie was a frequent visitor on her trips back home from New York, and spent the summer with the Hoover's in 1918. The other son, E B Hoover, was an attorney who represented A J Sageser in his suit against the Miller estate.

HORINE. Joshua (1810-1881) and Margaret Horine (1818-1904) had a large family that included T J (Tom), who along with his wife Eliza Reynolds, lived on the hill above the sulphur well pump, adjacent to Elizabeth Jane Miller. Mrs Miller's house was located on the site of the historic Reynold's tavern. Eliza Reynold's sister, Emma, married Dr John C Miller. Tom (1874-1934) and Eliza were living alone at the time of the 1900 Census, just as they were when I was born in 1929. They improved their home, referred to as the "old Reynold's homestead" in 1903. Frank Horine (1858-1914), another son of Joshua and Margaret, was a storekeeper in the Gray Distillery in 1887, but subsequently made his living as a farmer and stock trader. He purchased 90 acres of land from A J Sageser in 1893. Then he bought the property of C T Taylor, and tore down a portion of the old Henry Alverson blacksmith shop in 1897. He then resold the property to Gabe Masters in 1898. He also sold the lot opposite Alex Askins to Lee Davis, and other property to James Watts in 1898. Frank Horine accompanied Dr Hendren on one his trips to Oklahoma in 1903, and made an extended trip there in 1905. He remained a batchelor throughout the story. Charles, another of the brothers (1860-1923), does not appear to have married either. He is buried in Maple Grove Cemetery. His friends were Walter Hendren, Frank Rettig, Manfred Murphy (a nephew), and McClellan Johnston. Still another brother, J F Horine, (1858-1914) opened a store in Nicholasville in 1892 with his brother-in-law, J H Murphy. That store was known a Murphy and Horine. My grandfather, Forest Miller purchased the interest of Horine in 1894, and the store became known as Murphy and Miller. One of the sisters, Ella (1874-1934), married C T Taylor. It appears that he was a salesman, and must have moved to Lexington as early as 1889, for Ella began "visiting" her mother at that time. He later sold his farm to his brother-in-law, Frank, in 1897.

HUDSON. I don't know the family origin, but Frank M Hudson is often mentioned. In 1895 his residence was on Hickman Creek (toward Elm Fork). He rented that farm to the Peel brothers in 1898, and Emily Peel moved into the house. He was still farming somewhere in 1900, but by 1905 he was the manager of the Singer Sewing Machine office in Nicholasville, and making plans to move there. Frank's brother, Charles W Hudson, left the Sulphur Well area by 1894, was the agent for Singer Sewing Machine in Richmond in 1897, and moved on to Lexington in 1899. William Hudson lived in Little Hickman. His wife died in 1898, and was buried at the family residence. He rented his farm to Dell Hunter in 1905, our last reference.

JASPER. Garden E and Maria (Fannie) were the parents of Mrs George M Hendren and Mrs Morris Dean (Maria). Eunice Dean, daughter of Morris Dean, married Luther Ware and was my adoptive grandmother. Fannie died in 1916 at the age of 89, and is buried in Maple Grove Cemetery.

KING. William T King Sr was a large landholder in the Buena Vista-Polly's Bend area of Garrard County. One of his sons, Howard, married Nellie Hendren, a daughter of Dr Hendren. Another son, William Jr, toured Oklahoma in 1903. William T King, Sr's mother was Newt Davis' step mother.

MASTERS. Wilson Masters is the father of Gabe Masters. Gabe married Ella James, and I knew them well, and their children and my parents were good friends. Gabe and Ella lived on a hill opposite the Turner farm. They purchased the "Henry Alverson" place from Frank Horine. I can't identify all the Masters in the the story, but Bettie and Lulu were sisters of Gabe Masters. A John S Masters left Sulphur Well in 1851, and lived in Lebanon, Indiana. Robert Masters lived in Midway in 1887, and worked in a distillery. James Masters lived in Pink in 1900, and had a daughter named Maud. Mitchell Masters had a farm near Pink, was a storekeeper, who seemed to specialize as a butcher. Most of the references to him were when he purchased beef cattle.

MAYS. Mrs Mays, widow of William Mays, died in 1896 at the age of eighty-two. Dr Nelson Mays, her son, attended her funeral. Tom Walker purchased the Mays' residence in 1897. Dr Hendren "read medicine" with Dr Mays, when Dr Mays lived in Sulphur Well.

MILES. N D (Nathan) Miles was born in Indiana in 1841, raised on a farm where he worked until he was send to various schools, ending in Law School. He practiced law for a while, and in 1871 married Kittie Hemphill, daughter of Andrew Hemphill of Jessamine County. They moved to her family farm one mile south of Nicholasville on the Sulphur Well road.

MILLER. Francis M Miller, born in 1748 in Culpepper County, Virginia, served in the Revolutionary War and received 205 acres in Jessamine County for that service. His farm, that I refer to as the "Miller Farm", is located at the end of Snowden Lane, off the Hoover Pike. He and his wife, Elizabeth Freeman, had several children: Elizabeth, Catherine, Mason, Polly, William, and Merriman. The girls do not appear in the story.

Mason migrated to the Somerset, Mt Vernon area, became prominent in politics, and made his living in merchandising. We pick up one of his decendants briefly, locating in Oklahoma along with Hugh Miller.

William Miller (1803-1874) married Mahala ?Parrent. They had a son named Jefferson W Miller. He married Mary E Blakeman in Fayette County in 1872. Their daughters were Nettie Miller Carter, Louella Miller Easley, Maggie Miller Yarnall, and a son Frank Miller who married a Reynolds. Mahala died at the age of 94 at the residence of Jefferson W Miller. The William Miller property was near Newt Davis on the Black Bridge Road. I still haven't placed Jesse Miller or Squire Miller.

Merriman Miller was born in 1804, and married Celia Sageser in 1829. They had six children, Francis S Miller, Sarah Miller Overstreet, William S Miller, John C Miller, Kitty Miller Barkley, Merriman (Mann) Miller, and Susan Miller Nave. One of the sons, Francis S Miller, married Elizabeth Jane Williams, and though he dies about where the story begins, Elizabeth Jane and her children, continue throughout the narrative. Their children, including the married names of the daughters, that appear in the story are: James W Miller, born in 1854; Lucy Snowden, born in 1856; Matilda (Aunt T), born in 1859 was unmarried; Belle Stacy was born in 1862; John Miller was born in 1864 and he and his family have anchored the Wisemantown branch of the family; Susan Richardson, was born in 1866; Rose Sageser, was born in 1870; and my grandfather, the youngest child, Forest Miller, was born in 1874. Forest and Scottie Hendren married in 1895, and had three children: Ray, Mary, and Edith. My mother was Mary, and I was named for her brother Ray Miller.

Another son of Merriman and Celia was Dr John C Miller, born in 1841, whose family is a very significant part of the story. His children were: Rice, who died in 1899; Hugh (1874-1957), Meade (1876-1968), and Elizabeth (1875-1957). A third son of Merriman and Celia was Merriman (Mann) Miller who became prominent in merchandising, banking, and real estate, living most of the time in Irvine, but later moving to Lexington. The daughters of Merriman and Celia were: Sarah who married Pink Overstreet; Kitty who married Samuel Barkley; and Susan who married a Nave. They wind their way throughout the story also.

MOORE. Moraney and Diana Moore lived on the property adjacent to Newt Davis, on the road to Black Bridge. It was the home of Oscar and Irene Sageser when I was growing up. Moraney died in 1889, and his wife Diana died in 1896 at the age of seventy-seven. Both are buried in the farm cemetery.

MURPHY. J H Murphy was a real entrepreneur. He and Forest Miller owned a clothing store in Nicholasville for several years in the 1890s. He owned the store at Sulphur Well until my grandfather, Forest Miller purchased it from him in 1902. J H was a surveyor who laid out a rail route to Richmond, and various turnpikes. He was a sheriff; a miller owing part of Glass' Mill; a farmer; and operator of a feed and grain store in Nicholasville. He had partners in all his endeavors. His wife, Mary, was the daughter of Joshua and Margaret Horine, another of the large families of Sulphur Well. The Murphy's had a son, Manfred, who was a good friend of Forest Miller; and, a daughter Dora who married Arthur West. Manfred died young, so Dora inherited the farm , and lived there all her life.Their farm is just south of the general store and near the church, along Ky 39. Mr Murphy died in 1921.

OVERSTREET. J W (Pomp) Overstreet was the Little Hickman correspondent to the Jessamine Jounal, a very colorful character. He also ran the general store, and was the postmaster at Little Hickman. He was such an unusual person that I actually end my story with his funeral address and poem. Pomp, the son of Samuel and Martha Overstreet, was born in 1848, and married Lizzie Crutchfield in 1882. It was his second marriage.

John Pink Overstreet was a farmer, merchant, and postmaster at Pink, which is about a mile and a half from Little Hickman. John married Sarah Miller, daughter of Merriman Miller, in 1856. The son of Thomas and Elizabeth Overstreet, he was born in 1835, died in 1910, and is buried in Maple Grove Cemetery. Sarah was was also born in 1835, but lived until 1915.

There was also a Reverent T J Overstreet, but I know nothing of him or his family. I do not know the relationship, if any, of the three families.

PEEL. The Peel family has always been located in and around Elm Fork, and there is a Peel's Branch in that area where many of them lived. Dr Thomas Peel was born in 1835 on a farm south of Nicholasville, and was a farmer until 1856, when he opened a store on Peel's Branch. He also carried on business in Sulphur Well. He began reading medicine with Dr John C Miller in 1867, and later attended Ohio Medical College in Cincinnati, Ohio. After receiving his certificate he began practicing medicine, while continuing to farm. He was married to Armedia Hunter. The couple had eleven children. He is buried in the front yard of the Peel home near Elm Fork Church. One of his sons was named Tom, Jr. There is a Mrs Emily Peel often mentioned in the story that I can't place at this time.

SAGESER. James T Sageser, son of Henry Sageser and Nancy Woodward, was born in 1836, and married Martha Moore. They had six children. One, Andrew J Sageser (1866-1932) whose first wife was Rose Miller, died in childbirth; and, his second wife was Susie Hendren. Another son was Oscar (1878-1975), who married Irene Bourne. The homeplace was just south of Newt Davis' that I have identified as the Moore residence. A daughter, Mattie, married Frank Bishop, and made her home in Illinois.

SAUNDERS. There are several Saunders in the story, and while I am unable to connect all of their family relationships, Perrin's History of Kentucky offers a good start. Giles Saunders was born in Virginia in 1810, but came to Kenucky in 1825. In 1833 he married

Sarah Hockaday of Madison County. Their only living child, Myra, married J P Turner in 1868. The Saunders, Giles and Sallie, were living in Sulphur Well in 1887. They sold their house in Sulphur Well to Elizabeth Jane Miller in 1889. Luther Saunders, of Garrard County, attended Eastman College in New York with Rice Miller in 1896. Lucy Saunders, of Millersburg, visited J H Murphy that year also. A Mrs James Saunders was the sister of Mrs J H Turner. Charles Saunders, of Madison County, visited Sulphur Well. John Saunders, who lived in Buckeye visited Sulphur Well in 1901. Taylor Saunders, of Stone, in Garrard County, visited Sulphur Well in 1902, and died of typhoid fever in the same year. None of these Saunders are in the same family as the Sanders that ran a ferry on the Kentucky River, know as Sander's Ferry.

SNOWDEN. Stephen N Snowden, a son-in-law of Elizabeth Jane Miller, acquired the Miller farm after her death. He and his wife, Lucy Miller had six children -- George, John, Virgil, Russell, Myrtie, and Bessie. The farm was split up among the six children. Bessie's share is still in the hands of her heirs. Mertie married Melvin Dean, and their son, Dr M L Dean, reassembled most of the farm in the 1970s. George Snowden's second wife was Blanche Askins, daughter of A M Askins.

STACY. Guy Stacy, son of J B (Hon) Stacy and Belle Miller, married Bertha Askins, another daughter of A M Askins. Guy was treated like a brother by his uncle, Forest Miller, and lived with Forest and Scottie for a while. He was quite short in stature, but was a very shrewd businessman, and despite being orphaned, succeeded quite well in life. He farmed until he acquired the store that was run for forty years by Forest Miller at Sulpur Well. He and his wife, Bertha, also acquired the property of A M Askins on the hill next to the church, and his daughter, Nancy, lives there today. Blanche Askins lived with them after her husband, George Snowden, died. Nancy, who married Joe Breiner, said she was like a mother to her.

TAYLOR. C T Taylor lived in Lexington, and perhaps for a while in Richmond. He married into the Horine family and is frequently in the story. There is also a John Taylor, of Lexington; a F P Tayor, and a L B Taylor, none of whom I can tie together.

TURNER. Joseph P (J P) Turner was born in 1836 in Garrard County, where he farmed until 1881, when he purchased a large farm in Sulphur Well. The residence sits on a large hill that overlooks the valley where the general store and the sulphur water pump are located. J P married Myra Saunders, daughter of Giles Saunders, of Madison County. They had three children. Horace (H G) was well educated and became a Methodist minister. J H, know to me as Jim or Jimmy, was a farmer and made the "house on the hill' his home after his father retired to Nicholasville. That house is now occupied by a grandson. J H married Elma Grinstead, daughter of Rev Grinstead, and they had two daughters, Mayme and Edna Grace. The youngest son of J P and Myra, Luther, died in his youth.

WALKER. W B Walker lived in a house out the Elm Fork Road from the Sulphur Well intersection less than a quarter of a mile. His son Elbert, also mentioned frequently, lived there until his death. Thomas Walker moved into the neighborhood, but I don't know his relationship to W B Walker.

WALLER. John Waller lived further out the Elm Fork Road, just beyond the intersection with the West Lane.

WALTERS. I don't know the original family, but Perry Walters and Belle lived on the Watts Mill Road, which turns off to the right from the road to Black Bridge. Simon Walters married Fina Taylor, and lived on a small farm on the Black Bridge Road, just below the Moore residence. Emma Walters married Sam Askins, and they lived next to the Dr Hendren residence on the hill opposite the Turner farm. The Belle Walters Hole in Hickman Creek that I mentioned is in Black Bridge.

WARE. The Ware's came to Jessamine from Lincoln County. The original family was that of Andrew Jackson Ware who married Sarah Teater. They had three sons -- Ed, Melvin, and Luther Ware -- who lived in Sulphur Well. The "boys" ran a thresher, and acquired land in and around Sulphur Well. Ed's place was across the road from J H Murphy. Melvin and Luther acquired a farm, that they divided, that included the Dr Hendren residence, all the land west of that residence, including the Diamond residence on the hill above the church, and back to where it had a boundry with the Murphy farm. Mel lived in the Hendren house, Luther in the Diamond residence. Mel never married. Luther married Eunice Dean, of Little Hickman. Mel and Luther also purchased the Hoover farm and divided it between them. George Ware, son of Luther Ware, still lives on his portion of the farm. Luther and Eunice raised my father, Frank Ware.

WELCH. Dr S D Welch lived on a farm just south of Nicholasville on U S 27. I included his biography in the story, so won't repeat it here. He had three sons who became doctors and lawyers, The daughter of Dr J C Welch, Elizabeth, married Dr J L Wilds.

WEST. John T West, a son of Turpin West and Eliza Hendren, was a farmer on West Lane, a road that connects the Chrisman Mill Road, and the Elm Fork Road. His farm was in the vicinity of Dr John C Miller's property. Eliza Hendren was a daughter of Doven Hendren. They are buried in the Gilead cemetery in Madison County. Dan West not mentioned in the story had a farm on West Lane when I was a youngster. Authur West married Dora Murphy, and lived on the Murphy farm. Dan and Arthur are sons of John T West.

WILDS. The Wilds were a Garrard County family. B F Wilds, husband of Eliza Dismukes, came frequently to Sulphur Well. His son, J L Wilds, married Elizabeth Welch, and became a doctor, who practiced first in Sulphur Well, but later in Nicholasville.

WOODWARD. The James Woodward, Sr farm was behind that of the Miller farm. He and his wife, Caroline, are both buried in the Harris Family Cemetery, on what I assume to be his farm. The families were joined when William Harris married Frances Woodward.

VISITORS. There were hundreds of visitors who came to Sulphur Well, some frequently, some perhaps only once. I thought it might be interesting to list the ones who visited most frequently. Someday, I may try to connect them in some way. Most came from Madison County. There was Wiley F Burton of Giles; George Burton, of Kirksville, who taught school at Sulphur Well; and several other Burtons. There were many Cottons, and I have mentioned that there is a place called Cottonburg over in Madison. There was N B Howard of Idalia, N B Long, and other Longs from Edenton. If you go throught the cemetery at Edenton, you will find many Longs resting there. Also from Edenton were: Robert Reagan; J W and William Teater; Caperton and Ezekiel Vincent; Roy and Willard Whittaker; William Wiley; and James, George, William, Elisha, and John Warner. There were also many visitors from Garrard County, particularly Buckeye, but I will only list W B Ray; John Saunders; Allen, John and Morton Teater; and Arch and William Whittaker. You have to keep in mind that nothing separates Madison and Garrard counties, but Paint Lick Creek, and visitors easily crossed the Kentucky River by the numerous ferries. Also, it should be noted, most of the visitors mentioned in the Sulphur Well articles to the Jessamine Journal were written by Dr Hendren, and often they appeared to be drawn to Sulphur Well by him. Others probably were passing through on their way to Nicholasville, or were in the stock trade, such as A C Miles, who made regular trips to Sulphur Well.

I obtained information on several families (Hemphill, Murphy, Miller, Peel, Saunders, and Turner) from a book by W H Perrin, J H Battle, and G C Kniffin. Kentucky. A History of the State. 5th ed. Louisville: F A Battey and Company, 1887, reprinted.

BIBLIOGRAPHY

A History of Gilead Baptist Church. Printed on occasion of the 189th Homecoming 1806-1995, September 24, 1995.

A Story of Four Churches. pp18-23 obtained from Library, Kentucky Historical Society.

Census:
    Jessamine County, Ky, 1880 and 1900
    Madison County, Ky, 1850

Cemetery records and monuments:
    Baker Cemetery, Jessamine County.
    Gilead Baptist Church Cemetery, Madison County.
    Harris Cemetery, Jessamine County.
    Lexington Cemetery. Fayette County.
    Maple Grove Cemetery, Nicholasville, Ky.
    Miller Cemetery, Jessamine County.
    Sageser Cemetery, Jessamine County.
    Salem Christian Church Cemetery, Madison County.

Central Record. Lancaster, Ky. Various issues, 1912-1924.

Department of Interior, Pension Office. Declaration for Pension by James Hendren. May 4, 1898.

Francis Miller. Pension Request. Revolutionary War. Request dated June 7, 1832.

Francis Miller. Last Will and Testament. February 19, 1839.

Francis Miller. Pension Request. By Elizabeth in 1843, after husband's death.

History of Irvine and Estill County, Kentucky. Estill County Historical and Geneological Society. Ravenna, Ky: 1900, reprinted 1984).

History of Jessamine County, Kentucky. Published by the the Jessamine County historical and Genealogical Society, Inc. (Printed in Dallas:Taylor Publishing Company, 1993).

Jessamine Journal. Nicholasville, Ky. Various issues, 1877-1921.

Knouf, Osee and Sageser, John Russell, Jr, Compilers. Sageser Genealogy (Decorah, Iowa: The Annundsen Publishing Company, 1978).

Madison County Kentucky Marriage Records Vol III 1852 - 1876. Compiled by Bill and Kathy Vockery. Privately printed, 1995. Page 31 obtained from Library, Kentucky Historical Society.

Marriages of Jessamine County, Ky 1851 - 1899. Compiled by Bill and Kathy Vockery. Privately printed, 1992. Page obtained from Library, Kentucky Historical Society.

Mahala Miller. Commissioner's Deed. April 21, 1879.

Matilda C Miller. Settlement of Estate. July 27, 1945. Shows all surviving relatives.

Miller Family Bible. Francis S Miller and Elizabeth Jane Williams. December 11, 1851. Entries for their children and some decendents to 1996. Bible in possession of Edith Jesse, Knoxville, Tn.

Nicholasville Democrat. Nicholasville, Ky. September 11, 1891.

Perrin, W H, Battle, J H, and Kniffin, G C. Kentucky. A History of the State. 5th ed (Louisville: F A Battery and Company, 1887) Reprinted by the Southern Historical Press, 1979.

Perrin, W H, Battle, J H, and Kniffin, G C. Kentucky. A History of the State. 8th ed (Lousiville: F A Battery and Company, 1888) Reprinted by the Southern Historical Press, 1979.

Ray E Miller:
- Letter to parents, September 20, 1918 from Great Lakes Naval Training Camp.
- Western Union Telegram. Critically ill.
- Western Union Telegram. Notice of death.
- Letter from Robert Spears to Forest Miller, November 9, 1918.
- Navy Department settlement of accounts, May 13, 1919 and July 19, 1919.
- Obituary, September 27, 1918.
- Contract to purchase cemetery lot, A K Adcock.

Teater, Howard C. Jessamine County Church and Private Cemeteries (Nicholasville, Ky: privately printed, 1992).

Teater, Howard C. Maple Grove Cemetery (Nicholasville, Ky: privately printed, 1990).

Vital Records:
- Frank Edward Ware. Birth Certificate, May 23, 1906.
- Frank Edward Ware. Legal change of name, November 3, 1942.
- Frank Edward Ware and Mary Elizabeth Miller. Marriage Certificate, Mar 9, 1928.
- Mary Elizabeth Miller Ware. Death Certificate, March 20, 1988.
- Frank Forest Miller and Scottie Hendren. Marriage Licence, December 25, 1895.

# INDEX

## —A—

*Adams, Miss*
  *Garrard*, 80
*Adams, Mr and Mrs John*
  of Richmond, 240
Adcock, Adam K, 47, 91, 93, 112, 123, 133, 137, 145, 152, 153, 154, 155, 163, 164, 175, 178, 179, 180, 192, 197, 206, 260, 264, 280, 293, 295, 321, 324, 341, 360, 366, 441, 442, 444, 445, 470
Adcock, Addie Hendren, 18, 19, 39, 47, 54, 55, 62, 64, 71, 82, 86, 93, 95, 116, 133, 135, 138, 142, 145, 152, 157, 165, 174, 181, 197, 208, 212, 213, 233, 297, 316, 367, 370, 385, 387, 399, 420, 470
Adcock, Bessie, 32, 91, 145, 264, 284, 312, 424
Adcock, Enis, 241
Adcock, Mr and Mrs Adam, 32, 90, 91, 142, 177, 212, 241, 322, 349, 370, 417, 427
Adcock, Russie, 145, 180, 383
Adler, Julius, 108
Adler, Mrs Julius, 114
*Agee, Ina*, 261
Aldrich, Elizabeth Madeline, 146
Aldridge, E J, 131
*Alexander, Dr*
  *of Fayette County*, 324
Allen, *Mrs Katie*
  *Franklin, Tenn*, 122
*Allen, Sam*
  of Indiana, 376
Alliband, Mrs, 155
Alliband, W N, 75
Altsheier, Joseph, 168
*Alverson, Henry*, 264, 283, 295, 352
*Alverson, Jesse*
  of Madison County, 292
Alverson, Luella
  Henry's daughter, 352
Alverson, Mrs Hendry
  Emla, 352
*Alverson, Sallie*
  *Hanley*, 28
Alverston, *Charlton*, 292
*Ammons, Dr*
  of Garrard, 434
*Anderson, Allie and Bettie*
  of Garrard, 346
*Anderson, Brown*, 183
Anderson, *Mary*
  *Lancaster*, 158
*Anderson, Miss*
  daughter of Eli Anderson, 254
  of Lancaster, 232
Anthony, Susan B, 183
Arnett, B M, 316, 333
  Farmers' Exchange Bank, 307, 308
Arnett, J B, 292
Arnold, Wm
  Madison, 95
*Askenstedt, Dr Fritz*
  *Cincinnati*, 83
*Askins, A M*, 38, 55, 57, 58, 62, 74, 178, 180, 186, 197, 213, 214, 217, 219, 220, 221, 225, 228, 231, 248, 249, 250, 262, 263, 268, 271, 283, 285, 289, 293, 295, 297, 299, 301, 306, 311, 315, 318, 320, 322, 324, 325, 327, 328, 330, 349, 352, 361, 368, 377, 378, 387, 396, 402, 409, 410, 411, 413, 428, 429, 430, 436, 437, 438, 451, 470
Askins, Emma Walters, 239, 362, 450
*Askins, Hugh*
  of Buena Vista, 429
Askins, Julius (Mousey), 281, 282
*Askins, Lizzie*
  of Buena Vista, 284
*Askins, Mary*
  of Buena Vista, 284, 429
*Askins, Mary and Elizabeth*
  of Buena Vista, 315
*Askins, Mr and Mrs A M*, 348
*Askins, Mr and Mrs William*
  of Garrard County, 311
*Askins, Mrs*
  *Bryantsville*, 28
Askins, Mrs *A M*, 174, 200, 241, 312, 359, 362, 365, 368, 391, 426, 427, 434, 470
  Sallie, 352, 438
*Askins, Sam*, 74, 194, 200, 220, 239, 240, 253, 281, 297, 301, 308, 311, 325, 333, 338, 341, 388, 396, 431, 470
*Askins, William*, 284
  of Buena Vista, 315, 328

## —B—

B T, 105, 106, 178, 298
Bailey, Naomi, 155
Bain, Bertie, 145
Bain, *Walter*, 27, 145, 163, 251
*Baird, John*, 73, 88
  *Camp Nelson*, 62
  *Prof*, 88
*Baird, L E*, 75
*Baird, Mrs John*, 73, 83
Baird, Mrs *L E*, 64, 75
*Baker, Al*, 349, 401
Baker, *Benedict*, 15, 43
*Baker, J Wilson*, 23, 24, 27, 41, 57, 62, 63, 103, 149, 163, 181, 197, 206, 210, 211, 470
*Baker, John A*, 269, 401
*Baker, Miranda Spruce*, 16, 19, 39, 50, 58, 63, 105, 149, 152, 197, 210, 267, 470

*Baker, Mrs Nancy*, 65, 78, 157
*Baker, Mrs Tilford*, 363
*Baker, Ricketts*, 386
   son of Wilson Baker, 206
Baldwin, L D, 34, 38, 41, 44
*Baldwin, Sam*
   *Red House*, 389
*Barclay, J F*, 33
*Barker, Thomas*, 340, 404, 434
Barkley, Kitty Miller, 74, 123, 160, 336, 344, 421, 443, 450
*Barkley, Mrs E O*
   Middlesboro, 271
Barkley, Samuel, 74, 123, 336
Barkley, Samuel C
   Daughter, age 5, Barkley Cemetery, 173
Barkley, Samuel, Sr, 123
Barnes, Dr, 129
Barnes, *Melinda*, 236
Barnes, *William*, 405
*Barnett, Mr and Mrs George*
   and daughter of Buena Vista, 429
*Barnett, Mrs*
   of Lancaster, 289
Bartleson, Charles Frederick, 364
*Barton, W B*
   of Buckeye, 374
Baskett, Ida Hendren, 364, 448
*Baskett, John*
   son, 396
*Bass, Mrs and daughter*
   *Campbellsville*, 158
*Baumgartner, James*, 436
*Baumstark, Mr*
   *of Waco*, 231
Baxter, Amelia, 145
Baxter, Wm C, 145
Beasley, Charles, 282
*Beasley, Mrs Catherine*
   of Stanford, 397
*Beasley, Robert*, 89
Beck, James B, 49, 100, 101
   Senator, 100
Beckham, John
   Gov, 331, 337, 344, 350, 431
Beecher, Henry Ward, 42, 224
Bell, George W, 162
Bell, Henry, 127
Bell, Nettie Bowen, 128
Bell, Sittie Fritzlen, 44, 82, 102, 162, 194, 211
Bennett, Alford
   Canton, Ill, 367, 375
*Bennett, Alfred and Bertha*, 420
   of Canton, Ill, 376
Bennett, Bertha Hendren, 18, 93, 176, 227, 229, 232, 233, 234, 252, 276, 279, 300, 310, 316, 367, 370, 371, 377
*Bennett, Jerry*, 252, 253
Benton, Judge, 438

*Berkley, Mattie*
   of Lexington, 320
*Berkley, Mollie*, 322
   of Lexington, 299
Berkley, *Mrs Ophelia*
   *of Texas*, 74, 293, **297**
*Berry, Carl Walden*, 325
Berry, *George M*, 33, 34, 46, 48, 251, 267, 304, 316, 322, 325, 415, 450, 451, 470
Berry, Ida Gray, 11, 15, 18, 21, 24, 29, 33, 34, 46, 48, 89, 98, 251, 360, 470, 473
*Berry, J T*, 11, 35
Berry, Mr and Mrs George M, 252
*Berry, W Grant*, 17
Berryman, Strashley Price, 178, 368
Best brothers, Will and Humphrey, 146
Best, Ebenezer, 146
Best, William, 66
Betts Mrs
   bartender and jealous wife, 324
*Bishop, Frank*, 262, 471
   of Virden, Ill, 253, 255
Bishop, Mattie Sageser, 478
   Frank
      *Illinois*, 148
Bishop, Mrs S N, 442
   Charity, 353
Bishop, S N, 353, 434, 471
   of Wilmore, 336
Blaine
   Secretary of State, 149
*Blakeman, Calvin*
   of Pink, 259
*Blakeman, James*
   of Buena Vista, 389
*Blakeman, William*, 328
Blanton, Dr L H
   Chancellor, Central University, 292, 326
Bledsoe, Ben, 74
Bloomfield, Victor, 256, 260, 282
   clothier, 202
*Bogie, Andrew*
   of Buckeye, 348
*Bogie, J H*, 41, 62
*Bogie, R L*
   of Madison County, 404
*Bolan, Larry*, 370
*Boner, Alta*, 199
Bonner, Mr, 59
Bonney, Tom Jr, 169
Booker, *James*, 356
*Bourne, Edwin*
   son of Everett E, 439
Bourne, Elbert
   son of Everett E Bourne, 177
*Bourne, Ernest*, 359
*Bourne, Everett E*, 11, 80, 188, 226, 268, 271, 274, 281, 288, 308, 341, 353, 363, 389, 391, 411, 426, 451, 471

father of Irene Sageser, 177
**Bourne, John**
    *Bryantsville*, 341, 362, 431, 439, 444
**Bourne, Lilly**, 197
    of Garrard, 204
**Bourne, Mayme**
    daughter of Everett E, 274
**Bourne, Morris**
    son of Everett E, 412, 430
**Bourne, Mr and Mrs John**
    *Bryantsville*, 11, 389
Bourne, Mrs Betsy, 72
Bourne, Mrs Everett E, 414
    Malinda, 353
**Bourne, Nellie**
    of Garrard County, 281, 285, 288, 310, 341
**Bourne, William**
    son of Everett E, 386
Bowen, James L, 222
Bowen, Mattie
    of Lexington, 222
Bradley, Gov William O, 30, 73, 207, 210, 213, 215, 223, 265, 281
Breckinridge, William C, 171, 173, 174, 175, 176
    Congressman, 170
Breiner, Joe, 182, 249
Breiner, Nancy Stacy, 38
**Brewer, Mamie**
    Danville, 86
Brewer, *Mrs N D*
    *Danville*, 86
**Brewer, Will**
    *Danville*, 86
Bricken, Richard, 76
**Bright, Bertie May**, 80, 108, 400
Bright, Dovie K, 228
**Bright, Helena**, 19, 77, 80, 108, 152, 174, 400, 437, 448, 471
**Bright, J T**, 13, 18
Bright, Mrs *William H*, 19, 28, 33, 108, 228
**Bright, Thomas**, 40
**Bright, William H**, 13, 14, 18, 19, 26, 40, 56, 58, 62, 63, 70, 74, 77, 80, 94, 228, 267, 283, 339, 402, 437, 448
Bristow, Prof, 159
**Broaddus, Frank**, 290
**Broaddus, J N**, 221
**Broaddus, Minnie**
    of Stone, 409
**Broaddus, Tip**, 250
**Brock, John**, 214
**Brock, Mack**, 193
**Brock, Wash**, 250
Bronaugh, J J, 76
Bronaugh, John, 106, 115, 131
Bronaugh, N L, 438
Bronson, *Charles*, 188
Bronston, Ballard

    Richmond, 51
**Brooks, A O**, 426
**Brooks, Arthur**, 431
Brooks, *Bettie*, 226
Brooks, Fayette, 137, 340
**Brooks, Lena Miller**, 431
**Brooks, Mr and Mrs Arthur**, 433
**Brooks, Mr and Mrs John**
    daughter Margaret of Lexington, 426
**Brother Carter**, 155
Brother Mark Collis, 134
Brother Van Pelt, 134
Brother Victor Dorris, 134
Brother, Dr Geo. S, 91
Brown, Charlie, 175, 206
**Brown, John**, 395
**Brown, John and sister**
    of Rockcastle County, 343
Brown, John Young, 114, 118, 123, 125, 151, 202, 318
Brown, Lettie, 147, 175, 206, 208
    Knoxville, 145
**Brown, Miss of Lancaster**, 115
Brown, Mrs Jacob
    Versailles, 31
**Brown, S J**, 259, 273, 286
**Brown, Sam**, 346
**Brumfield, Elbert**
    son, 368
Brumfield, Francis, 50
**Brumfield, J H**, 14, 32, 55, 56, 80, 81, 119
**Brumfield, Joe**, 87
**Brumfield, John**, 323
**Brumfield, Johnnie**, 154
**Brumfield, Mr and Mrs J H**, 62
**Brumfield, Mr and Mrs Walter**, 209
**Brumfield, Mrs J H**, 78
**Brumfield, Newton**, 189
**Brumfield, V P**, 259
Brumfield, Vince, 244, 256
**Brumfield, W J**
    son, 363
**Brumfield, Walter**, 331, 332
**Brumfield, William**
    son, 363
Bruner, *Calvin*, 184, 346, 411
Bruner, Christian, 152
**Bruner, E E**
    *Little Hickman*, 65
**Bruner, Thomas**, 226, 311, 354, 360
Bryan, William Jennings, 231, 237, 257, 292, 342, 343, 350
**Bryant, Dr**
    of Versailles, 341
**Bryant, Dr and Mrs**, 289, 338
**Bryant, Jesse**, 355
**Bryant, Lee**, 399
**Bryant, Mrs**

of Versailles, 349, 391
*Bryant, W R*, 396
*Buckles, Mr*
   of Giles, 434
Buckner, Jessie, 22
Buckner, Simon B, 21, 31, 36, 45
   Governor, 30
Buford, Frank, 378
*Buford, W L*, 192, 228, 246, 290
*Buley, Cory*
   *Louisville*, 27
*Buley, Lena*
   *Louisville*, 27
Bundle, Mrs *Fanny*
   *Harrodsburg*, 200
   of Harrodsburg, 410
*Burchell, John*, 274
Burchell, *Mrs John*, 312, 395, 398
Burchill, *Raymond*, 272
Burdine, George, 123
*Burgin, Justin*
   daughter, 301, 434, 436
*Burgin, Mrs Justin*
   of Mt Lebanon, 363
Burnmeister, Martha
   of Hamburg, Germany, 210
Burnsides, *Willie Belle*, 64
*Burris, William*, 322, 348
Burthon, Mrs Will, 192
*Burton, Abe*, 367
   *Edenton*, 358
*Burton, Allen A*, 230, 245, 262, 301
Burton, *Alvin A*
   *Tyrone*, 303
Burton, *Barbara Howard*
   *Edenton*, 358
*Burton, Fred*
   *Kirksville*, 24
*Burton, J M*
   of Madison County, 281
Burton, *John M*, 190
*Burton, Lizzie*
   of Portwood, Madison County, 189
*Burton, Mollie*
   of Buckeye, 204, 217
*Burton, Mrs W F*
   *of Giles*, 434, 436
*Burton, Mrs William*
   *of Buckeye*, 356
Burton, *Prof George*, 14, 19, 24, 26, 29, 40
   *Kirksville*, 12
Burton, *Richard*, 115, 210, 289, 356, 418
Burton, Robert, 153
   of Edenton, 301
*Burton, W F*
   of Giles, 389, 405, 407, 412, 432, 436
Burton, William, 153, 168
   of Buckeye, 197, 288, 313

Bush, Barbara, 467
*Butler, Lizzie*
   of Richmond, 223, 232
   *Portwood*, 166
*Butler, T*, 299
*Bybee, M F*, 303
*Bybee, Miss*
   of Richmond, 396
*Byrnes, Annie*, 236

—C—

Campbell, Alexander, 134
*Campbell, H B*, 398
*Campbell, J H*
   of Wilmore, 271
Campbell, John, 146
Cannon, R E, 102
Cardwell, Mr and Mrs Wade
   of Shelbyville, 295
Carlisle, John G
   Senator, 100
Carlisle, Secretary, 160
Carnegie, Andrew, 309
Carpenter, Dean, 463
Carr, *John*, 350, 374
*Carrier, Ed*
   old Madisonian, 274
Carroll, *James*, 321, 338, 374, 378, 381, 400
*Carter, Ella*, 277
Carter, *Eugene*, 303
Carter, George, 31
Carter, Mollie, 50
Carter, *Montague*, 407
*Carter, Mr and Mrs Wm*, 62
Carter, Nora, 219
*Carter, W F*, 321
Cassidy, L S, 332
*Cassidy, Mr*, 304
Cassity, L S
   of Logana, 331
*Catlett, John*
   of Mercer County, 401
Chalmers, Dr, 179
*Chandler, Edward*
   of Edenton, 297, 303, 340, 348, 360, 361, 368
*Chandler, Newton*
   *of Edenton*, 390
*Chapman, J T*
   of Versailles, 215
Chappell, John A
   Lincoln County, 158
*Chatman, Elbert*, 361
Chrisman, Z T, 178, 179, 184
   owned Jessamine Stock Farm, 179
*Christopher, Florence*
   *Garrard*, 65
*Clark, Geo M*, 238

*Clark, Harriet*, 376
*Clark, Ida*
   *Logana*, 164
*Clark, James*
   *of Frankfort*, 376
   of Louisville, 317, 322
*Clark, Louis*, 57, 199
*Clark, Mary McKinley*, 238
*Clark, Miss*
   *of Logana*, 230
*Clark, Mrs Thomas*, 287
*Clark, Mrs W A*
   of Helene, Montana, 292
*Clark, Will*, 22
Clark, *William*, 306
Clark, *Wm D*, 238
Clay, Brutus
   of Paris, 256, 435
Clay, Cassius M, 214, 417, 435
Clay, Cassius, Jr, 114
Clay, Henry, 100
Clay, Hume, 117
Cleveland, Grover, 67, 68, 118, 142, 147, 148, 156
Cleveland, W F, 193
Cleveland, W T, 292
*Clubb, Charles*, 215, 258, 260, 265, 279, 300, 301, 352, 398, 407, 414
*Clubb, Ellery*
   of Pleasureville, 360
*Clubb, Mr and Mrs Charles*, 328, 360, 404
Clubb, Newton D, 414
Clubb, *Viola Davis*, 27, 28, 33, 63, 88, 117, 122, 133, 162, 164, 166, 169, 175, 197, 212, 215, 222, 223, 229, 252, 258, 260, 352
*Cobb, Ambrose*
   Peel's Branch, 3, 255
Cobb, *Andrew J*, 374
*Cobb, Butler*, 186, 188, 195
*Cobb, C C*, 406, 411
*Cobb, Charles*, 348, 382, 391, 436
Cobb, *Charles Sr*, 363
Cobb, *Conrad*, 330
*Cobb, Dave*, 436
*Cobb, H P*, 193
Cobb, *Harland*, 40
Cobb, *Henry*, 265
Cobb, *Hubert*, 390
*Cobb, J W*, 55, 62, 88, 121, 215, 225, 249, 262, 265, 282, 283, 286, 296, 297, 310, 317, 321, 322, 324, 338, 339, 340, 341, 344, 345, 350, 355, 391, 396, 408, 411, 471
Cobb, *James Allen*, 382
*Cobb, John W*
   of Mt Lebanon, 230, 389, 390
   son, Mt Lebanon, 363
Cobb, John W, Sr, 109
Cobb, Mary L, 265
*Cobb, Matt*, 15

*Cobb, Mr and Mrs J W*, 219, 271, 295, 341, 345, 368, 407, 412, 418
   Mary E, 442
*Cobb, Mrs Henry*, 294
*Cobb, Mrs Ida*, 403
*Cobb, Mrs J W*, 35, 192, 340, 401
   Mary E, 291
Cobb, Mrs Pendleton, 155
Cobb, *Mrs W H*, 318
*Cobb, N C*
   Madison County, 303, 380
*Cobb, N P*
   near Mt Lebanon, 377
   of Madison County, 297, 391
*Cobb, Sallie*, 230
*Cobb, Vena*, 255
Cobb, *William*, 261, 265, 388
Cobb, *Wm Henry*, 255
Cody, Buffalo Bill, 252
*Colling, John T*, 406
*Collins, Mrs Green*
   of Indiana, 236
*Collins, Vince*
   Madison, 193
*Collins, William*
   of Poosey Ridge, 216
Colson, Col D G
   of Middlesboro, 329
Colton, *Milton*, 375
*Comley, Jerry*, 255
   *Miles Ferry*, 193
Cook, B L, 81
   clothier, 190, 202
*Cook, Mrs Maggie*, 73, 80
   *Keene*, 63
*Cooley, Mr*
   River vicinity, 295
Cooley, *Texie Gray*, 15, 17, 18, 22, 24, 30, 33, 35, 36, 39, 66, 71, 95, 96, 98, 99, 161, 207, 251, 360, 450, 473
Cooley, Thomas, 66
*Cornelison, William*, 374
*Corrigan, Will*, 199
*Cotton, Ben*, 303
*Cotton, Ed*, 198
*Cotton, Etta*
   *of Cottonburg*, 289
*Cotton, Lester*
   of Cottonburg, 289
*Cotton, Mrs J Milton*
   of Edenton, 391
*Cotton, Nat*, 303
   near Cottonburg, 377
*Cotton, Shirly*
   of Cottonburg, 363
Cox, Mrs H S Clair, 316
*Coy, Cron*, 318
*Coy, Melinda Hendren*

*Edenton*, 358
*Coy, N B*, 381
*Coy, Nat*
   *Edenton*, 358
Coyle, Misses Bessie and Mary
   of Richmond, 355
*Crawl, Thomas*, 65
Crittenden, Tom, 22
*Cromby, Elijah*, 404
Crosley, Lizzie Hendren, 387, 427, 438, 449
   first mention See Van Winkle, 370
Crow, Andrew, 173
*Crow, Cal*, 83
Crow, Cordie, 39
Crow, Mrs *Emerine*, 256, 291, 314, 320, 348
Crutcher, George, 262
Curley, E J, 16, 93, 96, 180, 251
Czolgosz, Leon
   McKinley assassin, 374

## —D—

Davis, *Annie Barnes*, 254
Davis, *Beulah*, 181, 183
*Davis, C M*
   Charles, brother of *N D*, 188, 189, 203, 213
   *Prof*, 190
*Davis, Carmen*, 231, 245
*Davis, Cyrus*, 181, 184, 240
Davis, David Newton, 116
Davis, *Dr T T*
   *Marion, Kansas*, 212
Davis, *Edmund*
   *Shelbyville*, 89
Davis, Emma, 77
*Davis, Emma Spruce*, 197, 210, 215, 228, 231, 237, 249, 286, 316, 348, 353, 433, 470
Davis, Garnett, 213
*Davis, Lee*, 236, 254, 304, 330, 365, 387
   infant, 305
Davis, *Marshall*, 64, 135, 166, 222, 223, 274, 286, 333, 352, 353, 360, 377, 448
*Davis, Mary Hendren*, 205, 223, 285, 309, 312, 351, 352, 399, 411, 412, 440, 445, 454
Davis, Melvin K, 430
   brother of N D, 247
*Davis, Millard F*, 89, 105, 162, 164, 166, 239, 260, 342, 352, 386, 387, 391, 400, 404, 412, 418, 432
*Davis, Mr and Mrs Marshall*, 427, 431, 437
*Davis, Mr and Mrs N D*, 222, 279, 431, 439
*Davis, Mr and Mrs Walter*, 411, 433, 436, 437
*Davis, Mrs Geo W*
   of Madison County, 382
Davis, *Mrs Hattie*, 18, 245
*Davis, Mrs Lee*, 412
Davis, *Mrs Levi*, 356
*Davis, Mrs N D*, 26, 27, 52, 63, 65, 77, 133, 200, 302, 352, 410, 471
*Belle)*, 410
Davis, *Mrs Robert*
   of Garrard County, 355
   of Pink, 291
Davis, Mrs S E, 364, 445
*Davis, Mrs Woodie*
   *Kansas City*, 29
*Davis, N D*, 16, 19, 37, 40, 51, 56, 62, 63, 64, 75, 83, 91, 116, 164, 165, 171, 189, 194, 198, 203, 215, 226, 230, 231, 238, 239, 245, 248, 253, 254, 255, 259, 265, 268, 274, 281, 283, 286, 290, 300, 310, 324, 325, 328, 338, 339, 343, 344, 347, 350, 351, 352, 353, 361, 378, 380, 387, 397, 398, 399, 400, 401, 405, 410, 413, 414, 431, 432, 433, 434, 436, 444, 445, 471
*Davis, Pal*, 279
*Davis, Raymond*
   of Paint Lick Creek, 238
Davis, S E, 445
Davis, Walter, 352, 399, 418, 429, 445, 448
*Davis, Wesley*, 398
   and son of Mt Lebanon, 390
   child, 336
   son, 361
Davis, *Will*, 166, 181
Davis, Willard, 67, 89, 190, 243, 256, 260, 328, 378, 418, 431
*Davis, William R*, 288
Dean, Ada Sageser, 351, 438
Dean, *Alex*, 199
*Dean, Allen A*
   farm in Garrard, 220
*Dean, Beverly*, 329
Dean, Carl, 236
Dean, Charlie Mann, 236
Dean, Clint, 153
Dean, Dorothy, 236
Dean, Dr M L, 166, 171, 319, 461, 472
Dean, Evelyn, 236
Dean, Harrison, 153, 154, 159, 161, 319, 401, 472
Dean, Harvey, 120, 153
*Dean, J A*, 272
   of Stone, 389
*Dean, J Harvey*
   of Camp Dick Robinson, 431
*Dean, Jasper*, 398
Dean, *John C*, 343
Dean, Lucy Snowden, 454
Dean, Maria Jasper, 389, 390, 472
   Morris, 451
Dean, Melvin, 153, 166, 250, 319, 340, 400, 419, 472
Dean, *Morris*, 192, 226, 329, 384, 385, 387, 398, 419, 472
*Dean, Mr and Mrs Charles M*, 433, 436
   of Bryantsville, 431
*Dean, Mr and Mrs J A*
   of Stone, 336, 348
*Dean, Mrs Charles M*

of Bryantsville, 439
Dean, *Mrs J Harvey*, 66
Dean, Mrs Melvin (Amy), 258
*Dean, Myrtie Snowden*, 166, 171, 179, 189, 223, 232, 252, 340, 345, 423
Dean, Nancy Owens, 153, 319, 401, 472
Dean, Pink, 461
Dean, Robert Mann, 236
Dean, Roland, 251, 324, 345, 402, 472
Deboe, Prof *Joseph*, 187, 203
Deboe, Tinie, 278
Deering, Chas, 75, 84
Deering, S S, 156
*Deitrich, Mary Hanly*, 62
*Demaree, T B*, 255
Dempsey, 112
Denboe, Wm J
    Senator, 245
Denman, E E, 187
Denman, Mrs Robert
    Jennie Hendren, 441
*Denman, Mrs W J*, 29
Denman, W C, 327
Dewey, Admiral George, 277, 278
DeWitt, Harry, 364, 371, 388
Diamond, Arkie, 30, 50, 89, 103, 158, 210, 247, 255
Diamond, *George*, 16, 62, 86, 105, 110, 137, 145, 167, 168, 190, 219, 251, 253, 254
*Diamond, Mr and Mrs George*, 60, 472
Dickerson, Ada, 323
Dickerson, *Dr Fountain*, 191
    *Madison County*, 41
Dickerson, *John*, 30, 32, 37, 48, 51, 54, 446, 472
Dickerson, *Mary Ray*, 11, 15, 17, 28, 29, 30, 32, 37, 48, 446, 447, 454, 472
Dickerson, N R, 387
*Dietrich, Lambert*, 349
*Dillon, Louis*
    *Edenton*, 358
*Dillon, Minnie Hendren*
    *Edenton*, 358
*Dodd, R A*, 396, 399
Dorman, Bettie, 155
Dorman, Emma, 18, 35, 66, 71
Dorman, Mrs Nannie, 71
Doty, C J, 108
*Doty, E*, 322
Doty, Laura, 174
Doty, Lee, 174
*Doty, Miss*
    of Brannon, 328
Downing, Elizabeth Miller, 156, 161, 163, 172, 173, 176, 197, 209, 215, 222, 259, 285, 292, 305, 353, 359, 416, 420, 423, 443, 444, 445, 452, 477
    son Alfred, 444
Downing, John
    of Georgetown, 316
Downing, Mr and Mrs Tom, 445

Downing, Nathan, 316
Downing, Thomas, 216, 313, 314, 316, 353, 358, 444, 445, 450, 451
Dozier, George, 241
*Dozier, Ham*, 27, 40, 170, 251, 381
Dozier, J H, 381
Dozier, Kathleen Elizabeth, 334
*Dozier, Mr and Mrs Ham*, 334
Dudley, Gilbert, 51
Duncan and Spears, 136
Duncan, A B, 46
Duncan, Ernest, 84, 245, 255, 359, 360, 406
Duncan, J W Sr, 226
*Duncan, Miss*, 204
Duncan, Robert J, 291
Duncan, Robert Jr, 155
Duncan, Robert Sr, 155
Duncan, S M, 43, 71, 120, 151, 162, 170, 171, 196, 358
*Duncan, Stella*
    of Richmond, 305
Dunn, *Ike*, 197
    of Garrard, 245, 341, 400, 407
Dunn, *Joseph*, 344
*Durham, James*, 338, 415
*Durham, Jim*, 225
*Durham, John*, 254, 410
*Durham, Joseph*, 187, 188, 190, 263, 298
Durham, *Mrs John*, 363

—E—

*Easley & Sageser*, 160
*Easley, Bert and family*
    of Bowling Green, 368
Easley, J Holley, 114, 148, 154, 160, 164, 181, 185, 192, 206, 209, 472
    of Buena Vista, 362
Easley, Mr and Mrs J Holly, 61
    of Bourne, 389
Easley, Nimrod H, 350
Easley, *William*, 343
    of Pink, 368
Eaves, Martha, 200
*Ecbert, Mrs Clarence*, 401
*Eckler, Mrs*
    of Paris, 431
Edward VII
    coronation, 373
*Egbert, Mrs*
    of Lexington, 252
*Eld. Geo T Walden*
    *Lexington*, 27
Elder A P Finley, 438
*Elder Adcock*, 105, 178, 191, 194, 205, 208, 209, 224, 417
*Elder Benjamin Goggins*, 214
*Elder Black*, 14, 17
    *Lexington*, 12

Elder *Bronston*, 14
*Elder Bryson*, 430
*Elder Bush*, 105
*Elder Calhoun*, 430
*Elder Campbell*, 346, 348
*Elder Clark*, 375
Elder *Clingman*, 235
*Elder Coyle*, 321
*Elder Crabtree*, 368
Elder *Creighton*, 124
*Elder Cunningham*, 27
Elder Edmonds, 71
*Elder Elliott*, 310
Elder *Ferrell*, 88
*Elder Finley*, 184, 185, 192, 194, 196, 203, 208, 212, 213, 219, 221, 226, 231, 235, 431
*Elder Graves*, 344
*Elder Greenwood*, 32
*Elder Grider*, 21, 24, 31
*Elder J H Perkins*, 50
Elder J M Bailey, 152, 163
Elder J R Hoover, 37
*Elder J S Young*
   *M E Church*, 66
Elder J W Mcgarvey, 132
*Elder Jenkins*, 281
*Elder Jesse Walden*, 33, 91, 165, 409, 415
Elder Jesse Waldrop, 425
*Elder John F Rowe*, 212, 214, 226
*Elder Latimer*
   Wilmore, 321
Elder *Martin*
   of Lexington, 362
Elder Mathews, 66
*Elder McClelland*, 433
*Elder McGarvey*, 288
*Elder Mills*, 124
*Elder Neal*, 14, 320
*Elder O J Young*, 22
*Elder Owen Young*, 50
Elder *Payne*, 208
*Elder R G Frank*, 256, 284
*Elder Redmon*, 105
*Elder Rob't G Frank*, 277
*Elder Simpson*, 375
Elder *Smith*, 209, 212
Elder *Snively*, 205
*Elder Stafford*, 286
*Elder Stanley*, 28
Elder V W Dorris, 212, 218
Elder Vernon, 365
*Elder W F Neal*, 365
*Elder Walden*, 28, 29
Elder *Ward*, 89
   Lexington, 66
*Elder Whitehead*, 433
Elder *Williams*
   of Bethany College, Va, 363

*Elder Wright*, 16
Elder *Zachary*
   of Lexington, 431
*Ellis, J Tandy*
   of the Louisville Dispatch, 271
*Ellis, Sue*
   of Lexington, 286, 397
Embry, John B, 184, 235, 236, 253, 256, 293
Embry, Mrs John, 256
Embry, Talton, 37
Ender, Lem
   Chicago, 160
*English, David*, 265
*English, Ina*, 191, 192
English, L F, 109, 226
*English, Leroy*, 192
*English, Levi*, 191
Evans, Dora
   of Junction City, 361
Evans, E B, 138
*Evans, Mrs*, 292
Eversole, C H
   of Richmond, 396

—F—

Faddis, Monroe, 207
*Fain, Anna*, 208
*Fain, Conrad*, 225, 234, 238
*Fain, Daisy*, 307
*Fain, Dillard*, 277, 387, 395
*Fain, Dora*, 312
Fain, *Ernest*, 390
Fain, *Evan*, 387
*Fain, George*, 250
*Fain, John*, 186
   *Keno*, 224
Fain, Joseph, 233
*Fain, Justice*, 275
Fain, Larkin, 233, 265
*Fain, Louis*, 295
Fain, *Mastin*, 285
*Fain, Milford*, 368
Fain, *Milton*
   *Pink*, 381
*Fain, Mrs Mastin*, 394
*Fain, Mrs Richard*, 259
Fain, *Mrs Wm Lee*, 210
Fain, *Richard*, 166, 277, 312, 383
*Fain, Rutherford*, 279
Fain, Squire, 119
*Fain, William*, 391
*Farthergill, Wash*, 340
*Fathergill, D*
   of Georgetown, 436
*Fathergill, George Edward*, 263, 264
*Fathergill, John*, 206, 262, 263, 264, 303, 304, 355
Fathergill, Lucy, 102

Ferrell, J C, 414, 435
Ferrell, J W, 91, 92
*Ferrell, Park*, 193, 285
Fields, Saint Lue, 31
Fitzsimmons, 112
*Flemming, Miss*
   of Lexington, 206
*Floyd, Mr and Mrs J T*
   *of Kansas City*, 324
*Fogg, Prof and Mrs*
   of Covington, 296
*Ford, Mr*
   of Stamping Ground, 320
*Foster, B Frank*, 245, 253, 267, 290, 308, 329, 349, 353, 403, 472
Foster, Egbert, 353
*Foster, Elisha*
   *Edenton*, 358
Foster, Ethel Ware, 450, 461
Foster, Franklin, 169
Foster, *Hamlet*, 253, 337, 391, 411, 414, 439, 472
Foster, *James*, 383
Foster, *Janie Short*
   *Edenton*, 358
Foster, Jesse, 353, 427, 472
Foster, Lily May
   daughter B F, 472
Foster, Lucien, 148, 450
Foster, *Mahala*, 83
Foster, Manerva
   wife of Jesse, 353
*Foster, Mr and Mrs B Frank*, 290
Foster, Mrs B Frank
   Eliza, 353
   Eliza Jane St Clair, 472
Foster, Mrs David, 90
Foster, *Mrs Sarah*, 73
*Foster, Pat*, 400, 433
*Foster, Phillip*, 329, 353, 396, 472
Fournier, Henry
   of Paris, France, 378
Fox, *Jess*, 57
Fox, *Richard*, 41
Francis, Levi, 329
Frankel, Joseph, 162
   owner of the Blue Front Store, 188
Frazier, M B, 89
French, Mr and Mrs R L
   of Richmond, 378
Friend, Ida
   of Paris, 259
*Fuller, Mr*
   of Valley View, 413
Funk, Beatrice, 76
*Funk, Bertie*, 181, 183
*Funk, Maggie*, 122

—G—

George, Henry, 25
*Giboney, Butler*, 27
*Giboney, W B*, 390
*Gibony, Louisa Hendren*, 274, 364
Gibony, *Mansfield*, 192, 226
*Gibony, Mrs Lon J*, 370
Gill, *Joseph*, 305, 306, 307
*Gill, William*
   of Chrisman Mill, 363
Glass, Charlie
   of Camp Nelson, 264
Glass, J H, 144
Goebel, William, 265, 305, 313, 323, 324, 330, 334, 337
Goforth, *Mary E*, 180
*Gordon, James*, 183
*Gott, Creed*, 341, 345, 346, 473
   of Fayette County, 301
   of Richmond, 321
*Gott, J E*, 271, 279, 473
   of Madison County, 255
*Gott, Maggie*
   of Spears, 308
*Gott, Miss*
   teacher, 268
*Gott, Mr and Mrs Creed*
   of Richmond, 406
*Gott, Mr and Mrs J E*, 271
*Gott, Rowena*, 276
Gott, Ruth Johns
   Creed, 473
*Gott, S E*, 265, 281, 297, 300
Gould, Jay, 20, 149
Grant, *J W*, 255, 294, 306, 307
*Grant, Luella Underwood*, 255
*Grant, Mrs Robert*
   daughter, 349
*Grant, Robert*, 255
Graves, *Henry*, 197
*Graves, J L*
   of Lexington, 215
*Gray, Etta*, 88, 158, 399
Gray, George, 5, 18, 23, 24, 27, 28, 33, 46, 49, 63, 210, 262, 360, 473
*Gray, George Jr*, 400
Gray, Margaret Hunter, 360, 444, 473
*Gray, Mary*, 158
*Gray, Wm*, 23, 32, 56, 60
*Green, James*, 300, 301, 310, 329, 336, 338
Green, *John*, 302, 330, 337
Greenbaum, Ralph
   of Midway, 222
*Greenbaum, S J*, 23, 32, 33, 262
*Greenstreet, Lizzie*
   of Kansas, 317
Gregory, Ella, 222

*Griggs, Mr*
   of Madison County, 279
*Grimes, Ben*, 74, 189
*Grimes, Delia*, 78, 80, 93, 94
*Grimes, Ernest*
   of Lexington, 370
*Grimes, James*, 33, 182, 185, 186, 194
*Grimes, Lizzie*, 396
*Grimes, Miss*
   of Lancaster, 231
Grimes, Mr and Mrs James
   Sally, 473
*Grimes, Mrs William*
   of New York, 348
*Grimes, Ollie*
   Lexington, 78
*Grimes, Sallie*, 29, 32, 35, 56, 83, 93
   of Lexington, 414
*Grinstead, B Letcher*, 396
*Grinstead, Edna*, 209
*Grinstead, Grace*
   of Taylorsville, 356
*Grinstead, Grace and Linnie*
   of Stanford, 287
*Grinstead, Kate*
   of Standford, 283
*Grinstead, Mr and Mrs Gilbert*, 396
*Grinstead, Mrs W S*
   son and daughter, 312
*Grinstead, Rev W S*, 321, 412, 436
*Grow, Fannie*
   *Garrard*, 80
Guerrant, Edward O, 187, 259, 441
   of Umatilla, Florida, 422
*Gulley, of Lancaster*, 115
*Guy, John*, 354
Guyn, J C, 445

—H—

*Hagar, James*, 230, 264, 296, 300
*Hagar, Mrs Harry*
   of Hunter's Ferry, 365
Hagar, *Mrs James*, 287, 310
   of Mt Lebanon, 361
Haggin, Andy, 76
*Hagler, Albert*, 388, 399
Haley, R T
   Confederate veteran from Louisville, 229
*Hall, Henry*, 255, 262
*Hall, Mr*, 253
*Hall, William*
   of Woodford County, 255
Halls, Mrs Selina, 31
*Ham, John A*, 402, 405
   of Edenton, 361, 409, 411, 413, 418
*Hammon, John A*, 413
   of Edenton, 348

*Hamon, W S*
   of Edenton, 355
*Handy, Mr*
   *Casey County*, 62
*Hanks, Luther*
   *Port Royal*, 228
Hardin, Gen Watt, 207, 210, 213, 215, 226
   Democratic nominee for governor, 202
Hardin, Jackson, 162
Hardin, Judge, 216
*Hardin, of Lancaster*, 115
*Hardison, Arthur*
   of Nashville, 297
*Hare, Annie*, 210
Hare, Bessie Snowden, 351, 454
Hare, *Bettie*, 164, 212, 473
*Hare, J H*, 200, 375, 377
Hare, *Mr and Mrs W H*, 15, 78, 314, 387
*Hare, Mrs W H*, 19, 64, 65, 80, 89
Hare, *Nannie*, 15, 19, 164, 212, 312, 314, 428, 473
Hare, *W H*, 52, 62, 65, 74, 77, 80, 136, 183, 210, 212, 213, 268, 312, 329, 340, 346, 349, 354, 381, 396, 398, 473
   *Henry*, 287, 289
*Hare, Willie*, 210, 212
*Harmon, William A*
   of Madison County, 308
Harris & Co, 75
Harris, *Bertha*, 210
Harris, *Elijah*, 275
Harris, Frances Woodward
   William, 473
*Harris, Henry*, 286, 404
Harris, *John D*, 13, 21, 109
*Harris, M R*, 241
*Harris, Maggie*, 426
*Harris, Melvin*
   Lexington, 50
Harris, Mr and Mrs *Walter*, 435
Harris, Myrtie Overstreet, 353, 473
Harris, Myrtie Overstreet., 435
*Harris, Rice*, 160, 283
*Harris, W R*, 263
Harris, Walter D, 37, 71, 108, 274, 322, 353, 473
Harris, *William*, 276, 325, 473
Harrison, Benjamin, 148
   President, 362
Harrison, William Henry, 67
Harvey, Green, 77
*Harvey, Squire William*
   of Newby, 282
Haskins, *Fannie*
   *Campbellsville*, 158
Hatfield and McCoy, 45
*Hawkins, Miller*, 206
*Haydon, Miss*
   of Lexington, 206
*Haynes, Charles*, 274

Hemphill, Andrew
   born in Ireland, 473
**Hemphill, Andrew J**, 400, 401, 474
**Hemphill, Charles**, 78, 80, 81, 192, 368, 399, 473
**Hemphill, Dan P**, 86, 317, 323, 474
**Hemphill, H C**, 15, 55, 73, 80, 109, 226
   Hugh, 473
**Hemphill, L T**, 81
   Lewis, 473
Hemphill, Lilly May, 473
Hemphill, Mildred Lee, 178, 474
Hemphill, Mildred Tapp
   wife of Andrew, 473
**Hemphill, Minnie**, 55, 474
Hemphill, Mrs H C, 11, 12, 474
   Ella, 15
Hemphill, Mrs L T
   Eliza Price, 474
Hemphill, Naomi Wilmore
   Charles, 473
**Hemphill, Virginia**, 86
Hendren, James, 475
Hendren, Mildren Collins, 475
**Hendren, A J (Jack)**, 255, 418
   brother of James Hendren, 180, 188, 280, 413
**Hendren, Addison**
   of Iowa Point, Kansas, 259, 271
Hendren, Belle Harris, 330
Hendren, Carl, 282, 389, 474
**Hendren, Charles**, 303, 373
   of Richmond, 262
   of Speedwell, 330
Hendren, Clyde, 389, 474
Hendren, Cynthia, 297
**Hendren, D and sister**
   of Kirksville, 289
Hendren, Doven, 229, 364, 442, 474
Hendren, Dr and Mrs George M, 223, 375, 414, 418, 419, 434, 448
Hendren, Dr George M, 12, 19, 26, 56, 72, 76, 78, 79, 86, 88, 95, 98, 106, 111, 117, 122, 134, 138, 153, 173, 178, 183, 191, 192, 194, 200, 204, 205, 206, 214, 231, 235, 243, 244, 245, 246, 249, 253, 261, 263, 265, 267, 269, 270, 275, 279, 283, 291, 293, 307, 309, 312, 322, 323, 324, 327, 328, 332, 339, 344, 346, 347, 351, 353, 355, 356, 357, 364, 365, 367, 368, 369, 371, 372, 373, 377, 381, 382, 384, 385, 391, 397, 399, 403, 404, 405, 406, 407, 408, 411, 412, 413, 414, 415, 416, 417, 418, 420, 421, 422, 423, 424, 425, 426, 428, 437, 438, 439, 440, 441, 444, 445, 446, 451, 454, 465, 468, 474
   Article "Eastern Girls", 392
   Article "The Human Tiger", 392
   Book "Pneumonia
      Its Successful Treatment", 447
   Poem "A Deserted Church", 296
   Poem "A Hundred Years", 424
   Poem "A Lovely Scene", 441
   Poem "A Midnight Tragedy", 441
   Poem "Across the Lines", 334
   Poem "Against the Wall", 332
   Poem "Aquarium", 397
   Poem "Day Dreams", 355
   Poem "Did You Ever?", 395
   Poem "Down With Meat", 446
   Poem "Find Their Level", 429
   Poem "His Audience", 300
   Poem "Hot Enough For You?", 445
   Poem "In Old Kaintuck Again", 446
   Poem "In Sleep", 394
   Poem "Just An Ordinary Man", 442
   Poem "Life's Limited", 400
   Poem "Local Liars", 394
   Poem "Love and Law", 304
   Poem "Manila", 280
   Poem "Modern Maud Mullers", 407
   Poem "My First Sweetheart", 372
   Poem "Raise A Pig", 447
   Poem "Rich and Poor", 293
   Poem "The House Where I Was Born", 315
   Poem "The Inner Man", 314
   Poem "The Light That Will Not Fade", 363
   Poem "The Man With The Gun", 331
   Poem "The Old Calendar", 361
   Poem "The Old Country Church", 334
   Poem "The Old Country Store", 404
   Poem "The Old Log School-House", 270
   Poem "The Procession", 344
   Poem "The Toilers", 357
   Poem "The Trail", 302
   Poem "The Vacant Chair", 298
   Poem "The Way of the World", 447
   Poem "There Are Others", 397
   Poem "Things I've Noticed", 311
   Poem "Together", 275
   Poem "Tomorrow and Yesterday", 442
   Poem "Ups and Downs", 336
   Poem "Weather Advice", 432
   Poem "What They Seem", 295
Hendren, Dr Harry, 330, 397, 420, 439
**Hendren, E**, 259, 356, 398
Hendren, E W, 389
Hendren, Edna Prather, 370
**Hendren, Eliza Reynolds**, 15, 52, 230, 290, 295, 351, 355, 356, 364, 440, 474
   wife of William Hendren, 310
Hendren, Emma
   of Speedwell, 285, 321, 370, 378, 394, 396, 420
Hendren, Emmett, 389, 426, 474
**Hendren, Ethel**, 290, 311, 351
   *Wichita, Kansas*, 441
**Hendren, Ezekiel**, 225, 265, 352, 375, 442, 451
Hendren, Fount, 76, 93, 99, 131, 133, 135, 241
**Hendren, Frank M**, 301
Hendren, Harold, 452
Hendren, Harrison, 19, 229, 291, 474
Hendren, Hattie Foster, 260
Hendren, Iva

Richmond, 131
*Hendren, J H*
   Postmaster, 373, 379
   revenue service at Curley's Distillery, 180
*Hendren, J Newton*
   *Madison*, 196
   *of Edenton*, 286, 377
Hendren, J T
   of Kirksville, 293
*Hendren, James*, 180, 214, 235, 245, 252, 255, 274, 279, 281, 297, 304, 311, 313, 330, 351, 358, 370, 375, 377, 388, 403, 411, 413, 429, 437, 439, 442, 451
Hendren, James M
   Speedwell, 135
Hendren, Jane Taylor, 364
Hendren, Jennie, 219, 311, 351
Hendren, John C, 122, 343, 354, 390
   of Edenton, 308
*Hendren, L D*
   of Cincinnati, 271, 363, 407
Hendren, Laura, 135, 217
   of Atlanta, Ill., 212, 218
*Hendren, Lelia*
   of Edenton, 400
Hendren, Leo, 93, 165
*Hendren, Levi H*, 230, 240, 283, 290, 305, 311, 336, 351, 354, 364, 376, 397, 404, 441
Hendren, Levisa Tudor, 19, 39, 93, 241, 474
Hendren, *Linnie Spruce*, 63, 93, 149, 163, 228, 239, 353, 365, 399, 418, 419, 452, 470
*Hendren, Louisa Tudor*, 284, 291, 351
Hendren, Marie, 232
Hendren, Marion, 452
Hendren, Mary Jasper, 16, 74, 351, 474
Hendren, *Mildred Collins*, 281, 282, 351, 411
   James, 451
Hendren, Mr and Mr Levi, 219
*Hendren, Mr and Mrs James*, 427, 436
Hendren, Mr and Mrs *Walter S*, 293, 295
*Hendren, Mr and Mrs William Sr*, 317
Hendren, *Mrs Alice*, 312
*Hendren, Mrs Frank*, 280
*Hendren, Mrs George M*, 87, 188, 250, 276, 320, 341, 389, 412, 436, 445, 448, 451
Hendren, *Mrs Levi H*, 284
Hendren, Mrs Thomas, 389, 390
Hendren, Myrtie, 131
   of Cottonburg, 288, 289
   of Kirksville, 400
*Hendren, Nannie Lay*, 225, 252, 352
*Hendren, Nat*
   of Mercer County, 346
Hendren, Nellie, 282, 389, 437, 474
   musician, 444, 447
   of Nicholasville, 378, 386, 388
Hendren, Oscar, 297, 303
   *of Edenton*, 354
   of Kansas, 290

of Ruthton, Madison County, 327, 367, 370, 391, 401
Hendren, Pat, 93, 259, 302, 319, 341, 345, 370, 385, 417, 452
*Hendren, R R*
   of Kansas, 327
Hendren, Rachel, 101
*Hendren, Roy*
   of Madison, 347
Hendren, *Rutherford B*, 192, 212
   of Cincinnati, 407
*Hendren, Squire T*, 252, 358
   of Cottonburg, 442
Hendren, Talton, 365, 370, 374, 474
Hendren, Tom, 122, 124, 235, 354, 365, 386, 420, 424, 437, 444, 474
*Hendren, Viola*
   of Edenton, 361
Hendren, W G
   Minneapolis, 426
*Hendren, W M*
   of Speedwell, 212
Hendren, *Walter S*, 26, 87, 95, 98, 115, 122, 156, 160, 163, 190, 244, 259, 294, 297, 300, 319, 327, 333, 353, 355, 359, 364, 366, 371, 418, 420, 430, 435, 440, 441, 444, 445, 446, 447, 448, 452, 453, 454
Hendren, Will D, 19, 133, 134, 135, 137, 241, 297, 474
Hendren, *William L Jr*, 17, 19, 32, 43, 95, 98, 133, 160, 184, 215, 290, 297, 340, 351, 355, 364, 366, 371, 384, 385, 415, 440, 441
Hendren, William Sr, 5, 19, 77, 101, 110, 122, 163, 164, 188, 197, 213, 230, 244, 250, 254, 282, 303, 311, 322, 341, 344, 351, 354, 355, 364, 365, 366, 367, 368, 371, 412, 440, 474
*Hendrick, Mr*
   *Cincinnati*, 86
*Herndon, Zeke*, 428
Herron, *Mrs Claud*, 391
Hersperger, H L, 263
Hersperger, *Mrs Julia*, 89
   *Missouri*, 80
Hersperger, Mrs Lucy, 266
*Hibbard, Jeff*, 262
   *Madison*, 195
*Hicks, Mrs Ellen Cloyd*, 390
   of Middlesburg, 389
Higgs, *Andrew*, 354
*Hildebrand, Rev*, 245, 346, 365
   *of Lexington*, 293, 299, 305, 307, 310, 315, 318, 321, 333, 337, 339, 348, 356, 368, 378, 380, 381, 382, 386, 388, 389, 396, 401, 413
Hill, Prof David Spencer
   Washington Univ, St Louis, 386
Hill, Brack, 149
*Hill, Capt*, 348, 381, 391
   of Madison County, 303, 327, 339, 405, 431
Hill, Dr Felix R

Pastor Broadway Methodist Church in Louisville, 386
Hill, General, 45
*Hill, Green B*, 301
Hill, J S, 252
*Hill, Lieut John*, 322
   of Idalia, 391
   of Poosey, 374
*Hill, Miss*
   *Garrard*, 203
Hill, Prof David Spencer, 396
*Hill, R M*, 235, 238, 245
*Hill, Rufus*, 325
*Hill, Samuel*, 314, 355, 356, 427
*Hill, Stephen*
   of Buckeye, 407
   of Garrard County, 409
*Hill, Thompson*
   of Buckeye, 407, 409, 412
*Hill, William*
   of Madison County, 377, 397
Hines, Judge, 56
Hisle, *Chas*, 396
*Hisle, Leroy*
   of Spearsville, 255
*Hockaday, Essa*
   of Richmond, 297
*Hockaday, Vessie*, 342
Hocker, Lizzie, 139
Holloway, Mary, 172
Holloway, Misses, 209
   of Troy, 215
*Holman, Lulu*, 260
   *of Nicholasville*, 231, 245
*Holman, Miss*
   *Harrodsburg*, 87
*Holmes, Lucien*
   of Louisville, 194
Hoover, E B, 438, 475
   county attorney, 248
*Hoover, Mr and Mrs Wm*, 40
Hoover, *Mrs W H*, 65, 156
Hoover, *Mrs W H Jr*, 18
Hoover, *Mrs W H Sr*, 115, 361
*Hoover, W H*, 322, 361, 418
Hoover, W H Jr, 248, 253, 299, 359, 384, 452, 475
Hoover, W H Sr, 248, 475
Hoover, Wm, 226
*Horine, Charles*, 16, 26, 32, 35, 57, 65, 87, 93, 103, 105, 109, 196, 340, 370, 426, 439, 475
*Horine, Courtney*
   of Chicago, 223
*Horine, Frank M*, 16, 21, 63, 81, 93, 103, 105, 133, 160, 164, 168, 184, 189, 214, 232, 252, 253, 261, 264, 269, 274, 283, 286, 295, 297, 300, 310, 311, 312, 314, 321, 322, 323, 329, 330, 333, 336, 339, 340, 341, 342, 343, 347, 350, 354, 356, 357, 361, 374, 377, 388, 390, 400, 401, 404, 409, 415, 426, 432, 437, 439, 475

Horine, J F, 475
   Murphy & Horine, 144
*Horine, J M*, 195
Horine, Joshua, 426, 475
*Horine, M P*, 182
*Horine, Mr and Mrs Courtney*
   of Chicago, 287
*Horine, Mr and Mrs J F*, 17
Horine, Mr and Mrs M P, 122
Milton, 73
*Horine, Mr and Mrs T J*, 86, 96, 367
Horine, Mrs G W, 251
Horine, *Mrs Margaret*, 73, 164, 165, 231, 252, 265, 287, 297, 311, 328, 337, 342, 343, 349, 356, 370, 401, 475
   *wife of Joshua Horine, mother of Mrs J H Murphy; Mrs Ella C Taylor*, 426
*Horine, Mrs T J*, 17, 31, 60, 78, 89, 122, 201, 232, 352, 361, 432, 439
   Eliza Reynolds, 431, 475
*Horine, T J*, 29, 55, 59, 158, 162, 195, 196, 198, 203, 228, 248, 249, 286, 309, 311, 314, 325, 340, 346, 352, 397, 418, 425, 475
*Hoskins, Fannie*, 165
   *Campbellsville*, 86
*House, Albert*
   of Sanders Ferry, 300
*House, Ben*, 357, 362, 386, 404
   daughter, 348
*House, Mrs Thomas*
   *of Saunders Ferry*, 400
House, *Sam Jr*, 365
*House, Thomas*
   of Saunders Ferry, 350
*House, William*
   of Mt Lebanon, 363
*Howard, Alvin*
   of Madison County, 411, 431
*Howard, Lafayette*
   of Edenton, 389
*Howard, N B*, 418
   Idalia, 411
   of Madison, 347, 389, 396, 402, 405, 413
*Hubbard, Frank*
   of Cincinnati, 407
Huddleston, *Mrs Wm*, 365
Huddleston, William, 50
*Hudson, Charles*, 62, 63, 80, 83, 181, 258, 300, 308, 313, 476
Hudson, Frank M, 135, 204, 208, 254, 258, 262, 295, 297, 340, 343, 353, 374, 388, 432, 433, 476
*Hudson, Mr and Mrs Charles*
   *of Lexington*, 301
*Hudson, Mr and Mrs Frank M*, 414
*Hudson, Mrs Frank M*, 193, 311, 325, 431
   Allace, 353
Hudson, *Mrs William*, 209, 294, 296
   Kittie, 293

Hudson, **William**, 337, 358, 403, 427, 433
Hughes & Adcock, 176, 191, 206
**Hughes, Crit**
   temperance lecturer, 178
Hughes, Dr Dimer, 77
Hughes, Francis, 110
Hughes, J D, 341
Hughes, *Miss Ollie V*, 24
*Hughes, Nathan*, 256, 339, 343, 347
*Hughes, Squire*
   of Buckeye, 405
Hughes, *Thomas*, 186, 262, 276
Hughes, Welch, 77, 78
Huls, William, 128
Hultman, Charles, 464
*Humes, James*, 180
*Humphrey, Benj*, 105
*Humphrey, Lee*, 324
Hunt, *Belle*, 31, 39, 40, 42, 43, 65, 68
*Hunt, J C*, 57
   *Lexington*, 56
Hunt, Jane, 17
Hunter, Aliena
   teacher, 450
*Hunter, Arkie*
   of Lancaster, 396
*Hunter, David*, 347, 349
   of Garrard County, 293
*Hunter, Dell*, 433
*Hunter, Dillard*, 370
*Hunter, Dr*
   son of Henry Hunter, 282
*Hunter, Georgie*, 279
*Hunter, J B*, 235, 236, 287
Hunter, J T, 120
Hunter, Kate, 50
Hunter, *Maston*, 403
   of Iowa, 406
*Hunter, Misses*, 199
*Hunter, Mrs*, 160
*Hunter, Mrs D O*, 403, 405
*Hunter, Mrs David*
   *of Garrard County*, 347
*Hunter, Mrs Maria*, 403
*Hunter, Sam*
   of Edenton, 436
*Hunter, Thomas*, 268
*Hunter, William*, 122, 268, 310
   of Loganna, 236
*Hurst, F M*, 359, 363
*Hurt, James*
   of Dry Ridge, 358
*Hurt, Mrs Michael*, 191
*Hutchison, Florence*, 64
*Hutchison, Will*, 264

—I—

*Isbill, William*
   of Silver Creek, 398
*Ison, Fannie*
   *Garrard County*, 32

—J—

*Jackman, Ed*, 27
   *Louisville*, 23
*Jackson, Cinda*, 279
Jackson, Eula
   of Lexington, 388
*Jackson, L M*, 396, 398, 404, 432
James, Eli, 251
*James, Hattie*
   *of Buckeye*, 231
Jarvis, Paul, 201
Jasper, Garden E, 451, 476
   wife Fannie, 74
*Jasper, Mrs Fannie*, 188, 276, 339, 448, 476
   mother of Mrs Morris Dean and Mrs George Hendren, 451
Jennings, Capt. *J P L*, 18
*Jennings, Mrs Betsy*
   of Wilmore, 325
*Jennings, Robert*, 197
Jesse, Edith Miller, 11, 449, 453, 465
   of Knoxville, 447
Jesse, Helen Wolfe, 378
Jesse, Nan
   Vermont, 447
Jesse, Prof Madison, 378
Jesse, Watson, 378
Jesse, William Herman, 378, 447
*Johns, China*, 281
*Johns, Dr Bascom and mother*
   of Lexington, 344
*Johns, Fannie*, 62
*Johns, M L*, 89
*Johns, Mattie*, 26, 77
   *Pleasureville*, 133
*Johns, Mrs Catherine*
   of Pleasureville, 431
*Johns, Mrs Marion*, 274
*Johns, Ruth*, 341
Johns, *William*, 340
Johnson, Dr E B, 159
Johnson, Mary A, 136
*Johnston, Bradley*, 286
*Johnston, Frank*
   *Lancaster*, 87
*Johnston, John*, 75, 78
*Johnston, Lieut*
   4th Ky Regiment, USV, 289
Johnston, Mayme *Hare*, 60, 64, 65, 70, 72, 78, 87, 136, 213, 289, 314, 381, 402, 428, 473

Johnston, Mayme Higginbotham, 213
Johnston, Mr and *Mrs Wm McClellan*, 74, 89
*Johnston, Nellie*, 287
  of Lancaster, 312
*Johnston, Wm McClellan*, 15, 28, 50, 56, 64, 65, 70, 72, 73, 77, 81, 88, 93, 180, 200, 243, 286, 287, 289, 318, 387, 448
  *Lancaster*, 12
Jones, *Dr E B*, 26, 52, 63
  *Danville*, 77
Jones, Hattie, 204
  of Buckeye, 197, 249, 286
Jones, J L
  Cynthiana, 148
Jones, Jonathan, 425
Jones, Mary, 350
Jones, *Mrs Wm.*, 63
*Jones, W G*
  and son of Buckeye, 354, 388
  of Buckeye, 387, 389, 391, 399
Jones, W T, 34
*Jones, William*
  of Buckeye, 387

—K—

Kates, *William*, 303
  of Illinois, 327
*Kaufman, Adolph*, 199
Kaufman, *Mrs Sallie*, 199
Keller, Helen, 165
Kenley, Dr Willis L, 53
Kennedy, Dr, 445
*Kennedy, Inspector*
  Hurst Home Ins, 355
Kenney, *Mrs C A*
  *Princeton, Ind*, 64
*Kern, Fred P*, 322
Kerr, John, 20
Kilvington, Mrs M, 75
King, *Howard*, 380, 413, 414, 439, 476
King, James
  Bryantsville, 364
*King, Mr and Mrs B G*
  of Garrard County, 433
*King, Mr and Mrs Howard*, 414, 418, 419, 434
King, *Mrs William*, 380
  and daughter Madelle of Buena Vista, 410
*King, Nellie Hendren*, 223, 265, 283, 285, 321, 340, 351, 394, 396, 407, 409, 412, 413, 417, 418, 436, 439, 440, 454
  son, 436
King, W T, 476
  of Polly's Bend, 413
King, *William*, 414
*King, William Jr*, 436, 476
Kirk, Alice Jesse, 58, 320
  Knoxville, 447

Kirk, Donnie
  Knoxville, 447
Klein, Harry, 188
Knight, Aquilla (Quiller), 420
Knight, Dixie
  daughter, 233
*Knight, Fred*, 199
Knight, James
  of Camp Nelson, 420
*Knight, Kittie Sageser*, 231, 232, 255, 277, 282, 293, 303, 311, 318, 332, 333, 338, 420
Knott, James P
  Governor, 38, 100

—L—

Lait, Ed, 81
Lamson, C H, 249
*Land, Shirley*
  of Edenton, 344
Landram, General, 88
*Laws, Evaline*
  of Madison County, 279
Lay, *William*, 72
*Layton, Edgar*
  near Hunter's Ferry, 275
  of Madison County, 279, 391, 405, 407
*Layton, Miss*
  of Hunter's Ferry, 300
Layton, *William*, 300
*Lear, Mrs David*
  and son Thomas, 439
Lear, *Samuel*, 332
Lear, Thomas, 226
*Leonids, The*, 325
Levy, Isaac, 55, 67, 76, 79, 81, 90, 98, 144
Lillard, E T, 119
Lincoln, Abraham, 14, 158
Lisle, Alexander, 31
*Locker, "Buster"*, 261
Logan, J B, 11
Logan, John L, 79
Logan, W A, 187
*Long, J M*, 187
  *of Madison County*, 322
*Long, John*, 358, 389
  of Edenton, 241
Long, Mamie, 228
*Long, Mr and Mrs N B*, 32
*Long, Mrs Napoleon B*, 229, 258
  Allace, 352
*Long, Napoleon B*, 256, 258, 269, 273, 291, 345, 352, 383, 384, 386, 475
  of Madison County, 253
*Long, Susie*
  of Madison County, 288, 289
*Long, Willie*, 241
Lord, Edmund A, 43, 45, 71
*Lovel, John*, 65

Lowens, *William*, 255
Lowery, Hiter, 124
Lowry, *Elijah*, 263, 277, 348
Lowry, *Geo. W*
   *Mt Lebanon*, 199
Lowry, H H, 75, 413
*Lowry, John*, 263
Lowry, Mrs E, 349
Lunger, Irvin, 464
*Lutes, J C*, 259, 312, 325
*Lutes, Mr and Mrs J C*, 290
Lutes, Mrs J C, 267
*Luttrell, James*, 272, 325
*Lutz, Mrs*, 238
Lyne, G W, 76, 179, 287, 444
Lyne, Irene, 197, 215

—M—

M'Afee, Major Allen L, 51
*Mack, John*, 408
Mackey, Henry, 226
*Mackey, Thomas*, 398
*Malear, John*, 267, 274, 281
*Mann, Dr*, 83, 153, 206
*March, Ella*, 34, 73
*March, John*, 354
March, Miss
   of Illinois, 233
March, Mrs John
   of Bloomington, Ill, 367
*March, Ola*, 245
Marcum, J E
   Montana Territory, 37
Marriott, Mrs J H, 370
*Martin, Addie*, 199
*Martin, Mrs*
   of Lancaster, 232
Masters & Son, 76
Masters, Alma, 352
*Masters, Amelia*, 265
*Masters, Bettie*, 318, 352
   of Louisville, 439
*Masters, Elbert*, 27, 32, 158, 251, 355
Masters, Ella James, 251
*Masters, Gabriel*, 251, 253, 283, 295, 367, 368, 387,
   388, 409, 439, 476
   *Cap*, 189
Masters, Gilbert, 251
Masters, Harold, 251
*Masters, Henry C*
   of Madison County, 361
Masters, *James*, 387
*Masters, John S*
   of Lebanon, Ind, 376
Masters, Kate, 352
*Masters, Lizzie*, 27, 28
*Masters, Lulu*, 255, 352

Masters, *Maggie*, 21
*Masters, Matthew*, 411
Masters, Mattie, 352
*Masters, Maud*, 387
Masters, Melinda, 173, 220, 383
*Masters, Mich*, 185, 215, 262, 407
Masters, Mildred, 251
*Masters, Mitchell*, 88
Masters, Moses
   carding factory, 425
*Masters, Mr and Mrs John*
   *Valley View*, 189
Masters, *Mrs John*
   *Garrard*, 80
*Masters, Mrs Wilson*, 200
   Josephine, 352
*Masters, Ora*, 246
*Masters, Robert*, 18, 23, 27, 56, 231
*Masters, Thomas*, 374
   on Hickman Creek, 330
*Masters, William*
   *of Bloomington, Ill*, 160, 245, 376
*Masters, Wilson*, 60, 165, 221, 231, 235, 238, 239,
   246, 253, 255, 318, 352, 476
   *Hokey*, 238
*Masters, Woodson*, 35
*Matthews, Celia*, 86
*Matthews, Joe*, 86
May, E C, 219, 220, 342, 364
May, *Walter*, 310
Mays, Dr Nelson, 226, 235, 240, 263, 476
   residence, 297
*Mays, John*, 274
*Mays, Mrs William*, 226, 476
McCabes
   tannery, 425
McCarty, H M, 118, 120, 121, 129, 130, 131, 136,
   137, 138, 139, 140
   Editor, <u>Jessamine Journal</u>, 42
McCreary, James B, 101, 146, 151, 177
   Representative, 100
*McDonald, Joe*, 65
McDonald, *Mrs Joe*
   *Spencer County*, 41
McDowell, Allen, 448
McDowell, Gould, 102
McDowell, Josephine Masters, 251
McDowell, Jouett, 450
McDowell, Lucien, 450
*McDowell, Wm*, 62
*McGuire, Mrs*
   of Valley View, 236
*McHatton, John*, 228
McKinley, William
   President, 108, 109, 227, 229, 234, 237, 267, 272,
   274, 285, 341, 350, 374, 375
*McMinowey, Miss*
   *Harrodsburg*, 87

*McMurtry, Drummond*, 418
McMurtry, J Hunt, 419
*McQuerry, Dan W*
   of Garrard, 235
McQuerry, George, 203, 324
*McTyre, Mamie*, 28
*McTyre, Nannie*
   Keene, 41
*Merrill, Mrs William*
   of Elm Fork, 291
*Mettemiren, Esquire J*
   merchant of Brassfield, 194
*Miles, A C*, 194, 199, 250, 262, 271, 290, 295, 296, 310, 314, 322, 323, 329, 332, 339, 340, 343, 349, 350, 354, 374, 390, 403
Miles, D V, 184
Miles, *Dan*, 86, 187
Miles, Kittie Hemphill, 476
*Miles, Mr and Mrs A C*, 325
Miles, N D, 94, 105, 300, 304, 328, 337, 354, 382, 387, 476
Miller, Addie Hendren, 117, 134, 163, 168, 188, 191, 198, 200, 202, 205, 221, 225, 232, 273, 283, 287, 293, 305, 312, 320, 324, 325, 327, 328, 351, 375, 384, 440, 444, 445, 447, 448, 449
Miller, Alfred, 445
Miller, Alma, 198, 225
Miller, Bettie Anderson, 76
Miller, Celia Sageser, 5, 9, 76, 152, 160, 257, 336, 420, 428, 443, 477
Miller, Charles Wallace, 162, 172, 174, 208, 250, 256, 266, 292, 333, 344, 415, 445, 448, 449
*Miller, Clayton*, 148
Miller, D B
   of Valley View, 365
*Miller, Dr and Mrs John C*, 391, 442
Miller, Dr John C, 5, 7, 19, 29, 40, 45, 59, 60, 62, 63, 64, 65, 68, 71, 72, 74, 76, 79, 84, 87, 99, 107, 108, 109, 110, 112, 117, 123, 127, 136, 139, 147, 149, 152, 153, 154, 160, 161, 168, 172, 173, 191, 199, 201, 215, 220, 222, 232, 233, 245, 246, 249, 250, 252, 256, 259, 260, 266, 273, 274, 276, 285, 287, 292, 293, 312, 313, 316, 319, 321, 324, 326, 329, 331, 332, 333, 336, 337, 339, 342, 349, 353, 356, 358, 359, 360, 361, 362, 366, 367, 368, 369, 370, 373, 375, 377, 383, 387, 395, 397, 399, 401, 406, 416, 420, 423, 427, 428, 443, 465, 477
Miller, Dr R H
   of Mt Vernon, 449
Miller, Elizabeth Freeman
   wife of Frances M, 477
Miller, Elizabeth Jane, 9, 12, 15, 17, 18, 41, 42, 45, 58, 62, 78, 79, 83, 89, 91, 95, 105, 113, 133, 145, 154, 156, 162, 172, 177, 179, 180, 183, 184, 188, 190, 196, 197, 198, 199, 200, 205, 206, 209, 213, 214, 216, 217, 218, 219, 220, 223, 224, 228, 231, 235, 236, 238, 239, 245, 249, 255, 276, 277, 279, 281, 282, 286, 287, 291, 292, 304, 305, 308, 310, 313, 314, 317, 323, 328, 332, 333, 337, 338, 339, 340, 345, 348, 349, 351, 355, 362, 363, 375, 376, 397, 398, 400, 420, 421, 425, 427, 428, 429, 434, 477
Miller, Emma Reynolds, 191, 201, 353, 443, 444
Miller, Fannie Kimbrough, 315
Miller, Flora Scott, 315, 454
Miller, Forest, 9, 15, 18, 38, 58, 76, 78, 82, 121, 133, 135, 144, 146, 160, 165, 167, 169, 172, 175, 183, 193, 218, 219, 223, 241, 249, 253, 254, 255, 256, 258, 261, 263, 265, 266, 273, 287, 288, 291, 293, 294, 296, 299, 305, 307, 308, 309, 310, 316, 317, 323, 324, 333, 341, 351, 391, 404, 427, 429, 434, 436, 439, 442, 445, 449, 451, 452, 453, 454, 459, 477
*Miller, Forest and Scottie*, 223
Miller, Frances M, 9, 476
Miller, Francis S, 9, 12, 36, 58, 169, 172, 317, 378, 420, 427, 437, 442, 454, 467, 477
Miller, *Frank*, 398
   son, 354, 367
*Miller, Frank P*, 314, 454
Miller, Henry P
   Indiana, 117
Miller, Hon R W
   of Richmond, 426
*Miller, Hugh*, 73, 157, 161, 165, 168, 176, 191, 198, 205, 232, 235, 246, 253, 259, 273, 283, 287, 293, 305, 309, 312, 318, 320, 324, 325, 338, 351, 366, 371, 372, 378, 398, 402, 408, 422, 443, 444, 445, 447, 448, 449, 450, 451, 477
Miller, J W, 57, 66, 239, 241, 279, 283
Miller, James W, 76, 78, 153, 156, 268, 284, 320, 477
   merchant and postmaster, 194, 228, 238, 253, 261, 262, 317
Miller, Jefferson W, 257, 290, 477
   child, 331
Miller, John Pink, 9, 19, 103, 115, 172, 180, 196, 214, 238, 256, 277, 305, 308, 315, 343, 345, 349, 376, 403, 427, 429, 434, 437, 442, 447, 449
Miller, Julia Payne, 326, 328, 349, 370, 386, 396
Miller, Maggie Edwards
   wife James W, 317
Miller, Mahala
   wife of William, sister-in-law of Merriman, 203, 257
*Miller, Mary*, 311
Miller, Mary Anderson, 369
Miller, Mary Benjamin, 309, 337
Miller, Mary Blakeman
   wife of Jefferson W Miller, 477
Miller, Mary Harris, 447
Miller, Mary Talbott, 448, 449
Miller, Mason C, 449, 477
Miller, Matilda (Aunt T), 13, 78, 82, 83, 167, 169, 236, 301, 304, 343, 351, 358, 359, 391, 427, 432, 447, 477
Miller, Mattie, 100

Miller, Meade, 172, 260, 263, 278, 292, 294, 309, 312, 316, 319, 324, 325, 327, 333, 337, 338, 342, 366, 372, 376, 378, 382, 383, 384, 401, 402, 404, 405, 408, 422, 427, 443, 445, 448, 449, 450, 477

Miller, *Merriman (Mann)*, 64, 76, 84, 85, 99, 108, 124, 160, 161, 172, 176, 208, 256, 266, 333, 336, 344, 353, 369, 374, 415, 443, 448, 449, 450, 477

Miller, Merriman F, 5, 7, 9, 19, 29, 30, 74, 76, 82, 152, 156, 160, 257, 336, 420, 428, 434, 443, 449, 450, 477

*Miller, Mr and Mrs Forest*, 358, 453

Miller, Mr and Mrs *Merriman (Mann)*, 447

Miller, Mrs Arminta
   Mt Lebanon, 131

*Miller, Mrs E C*, 296

*Miller, Mrs Frank*
   nee Reynolds, 349

*Miller, Mrs J Wilkes*, 286

*Miller, Mrs Meade*, 401, 402, 403, 442, 447

*Miller, Mrs Squire*, 188

Miller, Nancy, Laura, and John C
   children of Hugh Miller, 309

Miller, Nanie Rice, 5, 7, 191, 443

Miller, Ray E, 219, 234, 250, 281, 346, 351, 358, 367, 397, 449, 452, 453, 465, 467

*Miller, Rice*, 64, 76, 151, 152, 155, 161, 163, 172, 193, 200, 206, 209, 212, 213, 227, 229, 246, 247, 248, 253, 260, 263, 266, 270, 280, 283, 287, 292, 293, 297, 312, 322, 325, 326, 329, 330, 349, 386, 443, 477

Miller, Scottie Hendren, 18, 19, 32, 39, 64, 82, 86, 93, 99, 108, 133, 134, 135, 138, 142, 145, 147, 148, 174, 175, 183, 206, 208, 217, 218, 219, 220, 223, 232, 234, 249, 270, 281, 351, 396, 400, 403, 426, 447, 449, 451, 452, 453, 477

Miller, Squire, 100, 213

Miller, William, 477
   brother of Merriman, husband of Mahala, 257
   died in 1890 @ Little Hickman, 107

Miller, *William Jesse*, 236, 245, 273, 299, 303

*Miller, William R*, 154, 303, 311

Miller, William S
   son of Francis S Miller, 477

Millin, Mrs James
   of Bloomington, Ill, 367

*Million, Elzy*, 193

*Million, Emmett*, 321
   of Richmond, 347

*Million, George W*
   of Madison County, 405

*Million, Viola*
   of Richmond, 183, 211, 228

*Million, Woodson*
   of Madison County, 405

Mitchell & Davis, 75, 81

Mitchell, A P, 185

*Mitchell, Esquire*, 64

Mitchell, J W, 277

Mitchell, Lonzo, 8

*Mitchell, Mrs Nannie*, 390

*Moberley, Mr and Mrs Sam*, 436

*Moberly, Mrs Sam*
   of Edenton, 235

*Moberly, Samuel*
   of Edenton, 289, 377, 391, 402, 405, 407, 409, 437

*Montgomery, William*, 299

Moore, *Elizabeth*, 215, 216

Moore, G R
   Wilmore, 135

Moore, George, 141, 220, 273, 299, 303, 304, 377

Moore, *Moraney*, 72, 75, 220, 225, 477

Moore, Mrs Diana, 116, 160, 186, 220
   wife of Moraney Moore, 477

*Moore, Richard*
   of Bourne, 407

*Moore, W H*
   of East Hickman, 361

Morris, Joseph, 162

Morris, T H, 131

Mosby, Rose, 22

Moseley, *Clay*, 24, 29, 30, 64

*Moseley, Forrest*, 24

*Moseley, George*
   Missouri, 65

*Moseley, Irene*, 64
   *Keene*, 80, 133

*Moseley, May*, 24, 29, 30, 64

*Moseley, Mr and Mrs Tom*
   *Keene*, 65

*Moseley, Mrs*
   *Missouri*, 19

*Moseley, Mrs Julia*, 64

*Moseley, Robert*, 14, 39, 40, 372

Moseley, W G, 47, 75, 172

Mosely, Pete, 61

Moynahan, Bernard, 165, 166

Moynahan, Eugene, 395

Muir, Samuel B, 178

*Mulkey, Constable*, 271

Munday, Mrs, 46

Murphy & Horine, 145, 146, 162, 167

Murphy & Miller, 167, 169, 171, 177, 188, 190, 193, 202, 213, 219, 225, 227, 229, 233, 239

*Murphy, Betty*
   mother of J H Murphy, 40, 238, 240, 280, 284, 374, 394

Murphy, *Edward*, 255, 406

*Murphy, J H*, 14, 19, 21, 22, 23, 24, 27, 29, 33, 35, 40, 44, 45, 55, 57, 62, 65, 73, 76, 79, 86, 93, 96, 115, 144, 146, 152, 154, 162, 165, 193, 200, 204, 209, 213, 228, 231, 240, 248, 254, 300, 308, 317, 321, 325, 341, 342, 347, 349, 352, 369, 374, 390, 395, 396, 397, 404, 419, 442, 445, 446, 451, 477

*Murphy, John*
   of Buckeye, 339

*Murphy, Manfred*, 165, 223, 340, 352, 400, 426, 445, 446, 478
Murphy, Mary Horine, 352
*Murphy, Mr and Mrs J H*, 122
Murphy, Mrs J H
   Mary Horine, 43, 426
*Murphy, Mrs Pencelar*, 327
*Murphy, Woodson*, 410
   near Edenton, 409
*Myers, Byron*
   of Clinton, Ill, 314
Myers, Charles, 352
*Myers, Dr Joseph*
   and family of Clinton, Ill, 314
*Myers, George*
   *Clinton, Ill*, 26, 28
*Myers, Henry*, 283, 352
*Myers, John*, 352
   *of Illinois*, 230
*Myers, Jordon*, 314
*Myers, Joseph*, 220, 230
Myers, Julia, 282, 286, 314, 347, 401
Myers, Lulie, 178
*Myers, Mollie*
   *Madison*, 78
*Myers, Perry*, 194

—N—

Nation, Carrie, 360, 364, 419
Nave, Dr J E, 160, 243
Nave, Dr Peter, 160
*Nave, Ida*, 164
Nave, Jas M, 191
Nave, Matt, 134
*Nave, Moses*, 164
Nave, Susan Miller, 7, 65, 136, 156, 160, 162, 163, 243, 291, 329, 333, 336, 344
Neal, Jesse, 54
*Neal, Louis*, 208, 283
Neal, Pratt, 213
*Neal, W L*, 208
*Neveeya, Mrza S K*
   lecturer on Persia, 374
*Newby, Jessie*
   of Madison County, 365
*Nichols, Henry*, 287
   *Hanley*, 12
*Noel, William*
   of Garrard County, 432

—O—

Oliver, *James*, 405
Overaker, John, 218
Overstreet, *Charles*, 404
Overstreet, *Hillery*, 303

Overstreet, J W, 85, 96, 110, 120, 157, 164, 188, 370, 455, 478. *See* Pomp
   Funeral address, 455
   Poem "When I Am Gone", 457
Overstreet, James Jr, 455
Overstreet, John
   of Minneapolis, 455
Overstreet, John Pink, 13, 19, 29, 30, 45, 159, 161, 232, 236, 446, 478
Overstreet, Mr and Mrs J P, 435
Overstreet, Mrs J W, 227, 229
Overstreet, Sarah Miller, 13, 19, 45, 65, 160, 336, 383, 407, 411, 421, 434, 443, 446, 450
*Overstreet, Syl*, 277
*Owens, Alice*
   of Newport, 370
Owens, Annie Tombs, 319
Owens, Fleming, 319
Owens, W C, 176
   Breckinridge congressional opponent, 176
Oxley, Mary, 82

—P—

*Palmer, Miss*
   *Lancaster*, 56
*Pardee, Sudie*
   of Colesburg, 363
Parish, *Mills*
   *Louisville*, 74
*Parker, Mr and Mrs*
   of Stanford, 290
*Parks, H S*, 17
*Parrish, Capt*
   first Journal editor, 267
*Parrish, Jennie*
   *Cave City*, 28
   Louisville, 69
Pates, C L, 327
*Patton, Sallie*, 73
Payne, Col and Mrs James B
   of Elizabethtown, 292
Payne, Col J B
   of Elizabethtown, 328
Payne, David L
   of Okla, 423
Payne, Julia Blackburn
   of Elizabethtown, 292
Payne, Lena
   of Elizabethtown, 292
Payne, Samuel T
   of Elizabethtown, 292
Peary, Lt William, 158
Peel, Armedia Hunter
   wife of Dr Thomas Peel, 478
*Peel, Calvin*, 336
*Peel, Charles*
   of Leroy, Ill, 289, 290, 330
Peel, *Clarence*, 301

Peel, *Dr Thomas*, 50, 52, 79, 107, 231, 232, 478
*Peel, Dr William*, 340
*Peel, Fabe*, 411
*Peel, Fount*, 336
*Peel, G W*, 340
Peel, *Geo B*, 304, 346, 368
*Peel, George*, 33, 215, 396, 407
*Peel, George Sr*, 294
Peel, Hugh, 109
    of Boyle County, 296
    sons Paul and Claude of Danville, 436
Peel, *Hunter*, 259
Peel, *Irvine B*, 286, 296, 407
*Peel, James*
    child, 293
*Peel, Joe*, 311
*Peel, Louis*, 304
*Peel, McKey*
    daughter, 210
*Peel, Melvin*, 231, 263, 388
    son, 232
*Peel, Milton*, 374
*Peel, Mrs Charles*
    of Leroy, Ill, 274
Peel, *Mrs Elizabeth*, 337
    of Pink, 367
*Peel, Mrs Emaline*, 403, 407
*Peel, Mrs Emily*, 198, 210, 253, 262, 264, 267, 274, 297, 325, 436
*Peel, Mrs Fountain*, 354
Peel, Mrs James, 248
*Peel, Mrs John*, 72
*Peel, Newt*, 308
Peel, *Rhoda*, 181, 300, 311, 331, 338
Peel, *Samuel*, 301
*Peel, Thomas*, 50, 56, 100, 380, 383
*Peel, Thomas Jr*, 231, 232
*Peel, Will*, 24, 333
*Peel, William*, 296
Peel, Wilmot
    wife Melinda Sageser, 434
Peel,*Rhoda*
    *Hanly*, 75
Perkins, *Dr J H*
    *Edenton*, 199
*Perkins, J W*, 271
*Perkins, John*, 314, 355
Perkins, *Thomas*, 261, 262, 263
Perry, *John*, 109
    *Hanly*, 63
*Peyton, Lizzie*, 64, 83, 85
Phillips, Judge, 88, 128, 207, 224, 233, 278, 444
Phillips, Lena, 278
Pilcher, Dick, 66, 71
Pilcher, Emma Dorman, 95
*Pilcher, Louis*, 204, 368, 374, 385
Pilcher, T J, 46
Pollard, Madeline, 173
    Breckinridge lover, 176
*Pollard, Thomas*
    daughter, 331
Pomp, 37, 60, 63, 71, 79, 85, 114, 119, 126, 128, 137, 138, 154, 157, 164, 166, 179, 186, 220, 229, 342, 370, 397, 451, 454, 455
*Poor, J J*
    *Garrard*, 65
*Poor, J W*
    *Garrard County*, 62
*Poor, Ora*
    *Garrard*, 65
Pope Leo XIII, 417
Pope Pius X, 417
Porter, *Dr Phil*
    *Detroit*, 83
*Poston, Henry*, 162
*Prather, Bessie*
    of Edenton, 381
*Prather, Carrie*
    *Spearsville*, 27
*Prather, James P*
    of Edenton, 374
*Prather, Minnie*
    *Spearsville*, 27
*Prather, Mr and Mrs James*
    of Madison County, 289
Preston, *Berryman*, 80
Preston, *Green B*, 78
*Preston, Mary*, 80
*Preston, Sam*
    *Louisville*, 199
*Prewitt, William*
    near Kirksville, 381
*Price, Billy*
    of Buckeye, 434
*Price, Carl*, 287, 368
Price, Dr A D
    of Shelbyville, 400
*Price, Milton*, 162, 287, 347
Price, *Mrs Milton*, 209, 361
Price, Sam, 134
*Pryor, George R*, 280
*Pulliam, Robert*, 86
*Pullins, Leah Stacy*, 286, 304, 305, 358, 439, 449

—Q—

*Quimby, John*, 332
*Quinn, Emma*, 27
*Quinn, Miss Druey*
    *of Madison County*, 324
Quinn, R M, 76
*Quinn, Robert*, 41

—R—

*Ramsey, John*

of Lincoln County, 405
Randolph, Cecile Adcock, 438, 450
Randolph, Mr and Mrs Raymond, 451
Randolph, Raymond, 450
*Ray, Alexander*
   of Cottonburg, 362
*Ray, Beatrice*
   *Buckeye*, 412
Ray, *Bronson*, 15, 22, 24, 30, 36, 43, 447
Ray, Dr William, 43, 48
   of Buckeye, 361, 447
*Ray, Lelia*, 412
   of Buckeye, 406, 407, 412
*Ray, Lindsey*
   of Buckeye, 405
Ray, Lucy, 54
*Ray, Mr and Mrs W B*
   of Buckeye, 291
*Ray, W B*
   of Buckeye, 265, 290, 313, 340, 403, 405, 406, 407, 412
*Reagan, Mrs Sue*
   of Edenton, 402
*Reagan, Robert*
   of Edenton, 194, 319, 341, 403, 407
*Reece, Mr*
   of Hopkinsville, 181
*Reeder, Thompson*, 186
   daughter died, 180
*Renfree, Joseph*
   of Madison County, 241
*Rettig, Annie*, 34
   *Louisville*, 33
*Rettig, Frank*, 16, 19, 22, 26, 33, 43, 57, 58, 63, 65, 75, 103, 317
*Rev Absolom Reynolds*, 188, 193, 254
*Rev B F Jenkins*
   President, Kentucky University, 390
*Rev Baird*, 235, 238, 240, 251
Rev Ben D Bell, 378
Rev C F Oney, 201
Rev C M Humphry, 420
Rev *Collins*, 294
*Rev Crabtree*, 374
*Rev Creighton*, 133
Rev D B Cooper, 413
*Rev Dills*
   of Wilmore, 333
*Rev E C Savage*
   *of* Wilmore, 277, 279, 282, 294, 333, 337
Rev E G B Mann, 359
*Rev Edward O Guerrant*, 259
*Rev F S Haskell*, 303
Rev F W Noland, 13, 167, 294, 326, 336
*Rev G C Calhoun*, 436
Rev G W Neal, 340
Rev Geo W Bell, 211
Rev George Bealer, 300
Rev George O Barnes, 58, 59, 60, 61, 88, 102

Rev H C Bell
   of Springfield, 453
Rev H K Berry, 401
   of Owenton, 401
*Rev Henry Masters*, 261
*Rev J A Sawyer*, 209
Rev J E Moss, 454
Rev J G Perkins, 50
Rev J W Hughes, 219
*Rev James Young*, 88, 89, 122
*Rev Jno P Lowry*
   of Little Rock, 296
*Rev Joe Ison*, 78, 88
*Rev Jos. Ballou*, 164
*Rev M D Reynolds*, 286
*Rev M V B Bennett*, 121
Rev Mann
   of Lexington, 443
Rev *McNeal*
   of Wilmore, 333
Rev Morrisey, 160
Rev Mr Walden, 46
*Rev Owen J Young*
   of Madison County, 343
*Rev Owen Young*, 43
*Rev R D Bivins*, 337, 369
Rev R E Douglas, 326
Rev R H Wilkerson, 453
Rev R L Prunty, 168
Rev Rhodes Thompson, 440
Rev Sam Jones, 60, 61, 143, 145, 157, 195, 316
Rev Sam Small, 60, 94
*Rev Simpson*
   *Lexington Bible College*, 268
*Rev Staley*, 429
Rev T J Anthony, 154, 155, 166
Rev T J Overstreet, 17
Rev T W Watts, 317, 336
*Rev T Warn Beagle*, 73, 110
Rev Timberlake, 433
*Rev Vaughn*, 230
Rev W C Taylor, 200
*Rev W M Zeigler*, 311
*Rev W S Grinstead*, 103, 166, 309
Rev W W Spates, 12
*Rev Walter S Smith*, 246
*Rev Wm Johns*, 65
*Rev. H E Ward*, 57
*Reynolds, Alexander Campbell*, 206
*Reynolds, Buky*, 271
Reynolds, Dick
   tavern, 425
*Reynolds, Eliza*, 271
*Reynolds, Emma*, 40, 77, 78, 195
   *Cincinnati*, 31, 89
*Reynolds, Henry*, 286
Reynolds, *Jefferson*, 225, 271
*Reynolds, John*, 194

*Reynolds, L McL*
   of Stanford, Ill, 331
*Reynolds, Lee*, 432
   of Kansas City, 431
Reynolds, Levi and Henrietta
   of Madison County, 355, 357
*Reynolds, Lilly*, 296
*Reynolds, M S*, 194
*Reynolds, Meda*, 190, 194, 198, 238, 361, 432, 433
*Reynolds, Milton*
   of Silver Creek, 198
*Reynolds, Moses*, 178, 209
*Reynolds, Mr*
   at Black Bridge, 428
*Reynolds, Mr and Mrs J*, 368
*Reynolds, Mrs Bettie*, 365
   of Alva, Texas, 397
   wife of Rev M D Reynolds, 286
Reynolds, *Mrs T C*
   Texas, 122
Reynolds, O P, 202
*Reynolds, Smiley*, 377
Rhodes, Cecil
   Scholarships, 387
*Rice, A L*, 310
*Rice, A N*, 312
*Rice, Belle*, 194
*Rice, J T*
   of Richmond, 321
Rice, *Mrs A N*, 89
Rice, Mrs Al, 98
Rice, *William*, 262
*Richards, W A*
   Land Office, 436
*Richardson, Bailey*, 309, 398
*Richardson, James*
   Irvine, 255
Richardson, *Mr and Mrs William*, 18, 103, 156, 235, 236, 328, 345, 358, 400
*Richardson, Mrs Bailey*
   daughter, 380
Richardson, Susan Miller, 18, 113, 129, 152, 200, 214, 254, 286, 304, 305, 427, 428, 439
   "Aunt Sudie", 183
R*ichardson, William*, 183, 343
*Riddel, Mr*
   of Irvine, 397
Riddell, Harvey
   of Denver, 337
Riddell, Judge Robert
   of Irvine, 337
Riley, James Whitcomb, 154
Roach, Cynthia, 96
*Roberts, Ada*
   of Cottonburg, 289
   of Ruthton, 370
Roberts, *Burton*, 288
Roberts, *Dr Phil*, 178
   of Richmond, 289
Robinson, A W, 377
*Robinson, Allen*
   near Logana, 253
Robinson, *Beatty*, 228
Robinson, Lizzie, 117, 135
   *Logana*, 164
*Robinson, Michael*
   *Garrard County*, 57
Roby, G A, 402
Rock, Capt S F, 171
Rockefeller, John D, 309, 336, 423
Rodenbaugh, H C, 51, 186, 206
Rodman, Dr J J
   Owensboro, 136
*Rolan, John*, 199
*Romans, Mrs Minda*, 432
Roosevelt, Teddy
   President, 286, 287, 289, 290, 292, 341, 350, 428, 435
Rose, Frank, 464
Rose, H W, 75, 95, 98, 221, 254
   clothier and tailer, 202
Ross, Betsy, 266
Ross, James Metcalfe, 266
*Ross, Lilly*, 397
Ross, Mary E, 31
Ross, Maude Miller, 172, 266, 285, 344, 353, 428
*Royce, Mrs Sam*, 429
Ruble, J F
   *Garrard*, 83
*Rue, William*, 274
Runyan, *Richard*, 328

—S—

*Sadler, Mr*
   Tennessee, 83
Sadler, *William*, 251
Sageser, Andrew J, 12, 15, 18, 24, 27, 55, 63, 103, 114, 146, 148, 152, 154, 164, 165, 168, 178, 219, 220, 226, 236, 259, 265, 285, 286, 346, 351, 391, 398, 400, 414, 428, 430, 437, 452, 478
S*ageser, Babe*, 303
Sageser, Catherine Bruner, 152, 257
Sageser, David, 152
*Sageser, Dr N*, 430
   near Hanley, 428
*Sageser, Elzie*, 354
Sageser, Frederick, 152, 257
Sageser, G M, 154
Sageser, Hubert, 236, 351, 452
Sageser, Irene *Bourne*, 78, 279, 295, 297, 359, 360, 382, 399, 411, 451
Sageser, J L, 163
*Sageser, James*, 103, 148, 211, 253, 255, 262, 303, 330, 352, 407, 478
Sageser, Martha Moore, 478
*Sageser, Mr*, 40

*Sageser, Mr and Mrs Andrew J*, 65, 431
*Sageser, Mr and Mrs James*, 418
Sageser, Mrs James
    Martha Moore, 352, 399, 406
Sageser, Oscar, 251, 331, 343, 352, 386, 387, 407, 411, 461, 478
Sageser, R E, 109
Sageser, Rose Miller, 9, 12, 18, 24, 95, 104, 111, 146, 152
Sageser, Susie Hendren, 62, 86, 93, 96, 99, 108, 114, 129, 131, 135, 138, 142, 143, 145, 148, 152, 174, 351
Sallee, *Hannah*, 196
    of Paint Lick Creek, 216
Sallee, *Stephen*
    of McAfee, Mercer County, 196
Sallee, *William*, 196, 251, 399
    of Edenton, 216, 388, 391
    of Garrard, 339
*Sanders, Andy*, 43
Sanders, Granville, 80
Sanders, *Lizzie Masters*
    *Edenton*, 358
Sanders, *Mrs Sallie*, 18
*Sanders, Taylor*
    of Stone, 396, 407
*Sanders, W A*, 418
*Sanders, W S*
    Idalia, 411
*Sanders, Walter*
    *Edenton*, 358
*Saunders, Brutus C*
    of Madison County, 427
*Saunders, Charles*, 181
*Saunders, Giles*, 78, 79, 162, 203, 216, 218, 478
*Saunders, John*
    of Buckeye, 228, 361
    of Garrard, 206
*Saunders, Lucy*, 231
*Saunders, Luther*, 193, 194, 229, 245
*Saunders, Mary*, 18
Saunders, *Mrs James S*, 209
Saunders, *Mrs Sallie*, 12
    wife of Giles, 478
*Saunders, Taylor*
    of Silver Creek, 274
*Saunders, William*
    of Edenton, 340, 396
    of Idalia, 402, 429
Sayer, *Jas T*, 259
Scearcy, Ella, 138
Schenk, John, 79, 117
Schenk, Lulu Miller, 117
*Schneider, Ewalt*, 182
*Schuler, Frank*
    *Lexington*, 199
*Scott, Dr*
    of Estill County, 214

*Scott, Iva*, 192
Scott, J G, 226
*Scott, James*, 339, 343
*Scott, John*, 214
Scott, Judge T J
    Richmond, 84
Scott, Lt Ethelbert D
    of Somerset, 329
Scott, Lucy, 155
*Scott, Lulu*, 183
*Scott, Miss*, 185
*Scott, W L*, 195
*Scott, Wm*, 192, 431
    of Bryantsville, 197
Sea, *Preston*
    *Louisville*, 86
Segal, Adolph
    Philadelphia, 261
Sewell, *George*, 193, 300, 343, 358
*Sewell, John*
    of Buckeye, 436
Sewell, *Lee Annie*, 193
Sewell, *Reece*, 192
Shannon, T W, 141
Shaw, Mrs Ida, 209
*Shearer, Luke*, 374
*Shearer, Mattie*, 203
*Shearer, Miss*
    *Richmond*, 86
*Shearer, Mrs James*
    of Kirksville, 439
Shearer, *Mrs Mattie*, 426, 439
    *Kirksville*, 32
Shoat, *Alexander*, 415
*Short, J Irvine*
    *of Edenton*, 361, 363
*Short, W M and family*
    of Madison, 345
*Short, William*
    of Madison County, 345, 347, 406, 414
*Shropshire, Perry*, 361
Shy, *Mrs Sallie*
    *Texas*, 65
*Sibold, Prof*, 240
Sickles, General, 158
*Silverburg, Luther*, 267
Silverburg, Taylor, 449
*Simpson, Daniel*
    *Edenton*, 391
*Simpson, Dock*
    of Buckeye, 389, 390
*Simpson, Marion*
    of Buckeye, 389
*Simpson, Moses*
    daughter, 339
*Simpson, Norman*, 297
*Simpson, William*
    and family of Teatersville, 314

Small, *Ruce*, 191
*Smiley, Mary*
    of Lexington, 399
*Smiley, T J*, 52
Smith, *Andrew J*
    *Huntington*, 203
Smith, *Austin*, 403, 407, 408, 436
    *Edenton*, 391
*Smith, Earl*
    of Richmond, 342
Smith, General E Kirby, 153
Smith, *Henry C*
    *Harrodsburg*, 124
Smith, Ida
    Harrodsburg, 96, 124, 133
Smith, J Soule, 38
Smith, Mag, 462
Smith, *Marshal*, 312
*Smith, Mr and Mrs A J*
    of Indianapolis, 340
Smith, *Mrs Andy*, 309
*Smith, Mrs Harrison*, 340
Smith, *Mrs Lena*, 311
    *nee Horine*, 431
*Smith, Sid*, 360
*Smith, William*
    of Edenton, 342, 365, 391
*Smither, J B*, 386
Smither, Joe, 378
Snell, George, 52
Snowden, A D, 179
Snowden, Arch, 157
*Snowden, Blanche Askins*, 347, 352, 370, 411, 446, 470
Snowden, *George*, 165, 170, 171, 172, 184, 239, 244, 246, 259, 296, 325, 346, 353, 367, 368, 433, 434, 446, 454
*Snowden, James*
    of Irvine, 258
*Snowden, John*, 223, 351, 355, 381, 454
Snowden, Lucy Miller, 18, 169, 239, 252, 351, 427, 454, 479
*Snowden, Mr and Mrs George*, 190
Snowden, Mr and Mrs *Stephen N*, 103, 452
Snowden, Nora Taylor, 184, 254, 353, 446
*Snowden, Russell*, 309, 351, 454
Snowden, Sarah Butler, 355
Snowden, *Stephen N*, 62, 133, 157, 159, 169, 170, 171, 183, 256, 279, 290, 308, 309, 329, 340, 351, 381, 423, 432, 434, 442, 450, 453, 454, 479
Snowden, Virgil, 351, 452, 453, 454
Snowden, William, 157, 183, 279
*Snyder, Lulu*
    of Nicholasville, 245
*Snyder, Wm*, 401
Soper, *Emma*, 252
Soper, Mrs Ora, 365
Sparks, E R, 163, 249

Sparks, *Jerome*, 56
Spears, Ben D, 136, 149, 183, 374
Spears, *Julia Hare*, 16, 18, 24, 28, 29, 30, 32, 33, 41, 52, 55, 56, 60, 65, 69, 72, 75, 86, 87, 88, 133, 136, 183, 212, 243, 346, 473
Spears, Luther, 48, 373
Spears, Robert, 346, 453
Stacy, Belle Miller, 91, 95, 104, 105, 111, 448, 449, 479
*Stacy, Bertha Askins*, 314, 347, 352, 370, 391, 430, 470
*Stacy, Frank*, 398, 400
    *Middletown, Ohio*, 448
Stacy, Guy, 38, 246, 249, 391, 426, 432, 448, 449, 479
Stacy, J B (Hon), 36, 345, 449, 479
Stacy, Mr and Mrs J B (Hon), 91
Stacy, Vernon, 448
Stafford, B F
    Mt Lebanon farmer, 278
Stafford, *Flariday*, 55
Stapp, *Forest*, 204
*Stapp, Forrest*, 217, 391
    of Garrard, 204
*Stapp, James*
    of Newby, 405
*Stapp, John*, 405
    of Newby, 410
*Stapp, Reuben*, 238
*Stapp, Willard*
    of Newby, 405
*Steele,*, 401
*Stennett, Elijah*, 40
*Stinnett, Mary Jane*, 206
*Stinnett, Morton*, 198
*Stinnett, Rosa*, 302
*Stoker, Elmore*
    of Watts Mill, 430, 434
Stoker, *Thomas*, 433
Stone Mr
    *Midway*, 23
*Stotts, Arch*, 14, 15, 154, 155, 263, 339
*Stotts, W A*, 405
Stotts, William, 242
Stowe, Harriet Beecher, 230
Stratton, J S, 414
Straus, Louis, 146
*Strode, G W*
    of East Hickman, 340
Stull, *Mr L*, 199
Stulz, Ann, 306
*Sugars, Derb*, 87
*Suger, J T*, 430
Sullivan, John L, 86
Sulphur Well Correspondent, 11, 12, 14, 15, 16, 17, 18, 19, 21, 22, 23, 24, 26, 27, 28, 29, 30, 32, 33, 34, 40, 41, 43, 50, 52, 55, 56, 57, 58, 59, 60, 62, 63, 64, 65, 72, 74, 77, 78, 80, 81, 83, 86, 87, 88,

89, 93, 103, 105, 115, 121, 122, 124, 133, 148,
154, 155, 156, 158, 160, 162, 164, 165, 166, 178,
180, 181, 183, 184, 185, 186, 187, 189, 190, 191,
192, 193, 194, 195, 197, 198, 199, 200, 202, 203,
204, 205, 206, 208, 209, 210, 212, 213, 215, 217,
219, 220, 221, 223, 224, 225, 226, 228, 230, 231,
232, 234, 235, 236, 238, 240, 241, 242, 245, 246,
250, 252, 253, 254, 256, 258, 259, 261, 262, 263,
264, 265, 267, 268, 269, 271, 272, 273, 274, 276,
277, 279, 280, 281, 282, 283, 284, 285, 286, 287,
288, 289, 290, 291, 293, 294, 295, 296, 297, 299,
300, 301, 302, 303, 304, 305, 306, 307, 308, 309,
310, 311, 312, 313, 314, 317, 318, 320, 321, 322,
323, 324, 325, 327, 328, 329, 330, 331, 332, 333,
336, 337, 338, 339, 340, 341, 342, 343, 344, 345,
346, 347, 348, 349, 350, 351, 354, 355, 356, 357,
358, 359, 360, 361, 362, 363, 365, 367, 368, 370,
374, 375, 376, 377, 378, 380, 381, 382, 383, 386,
387, 388, 389, 390, 391, 394, 395, 396, 397, 398,
399, 400, 401, 402, 403, 404, 405, 406, 407, 408,
410, 411, 412, 413, 414, 415, 418, 426, 427, 428,
429, 430, 431, 432, 433, 434, 436, 437, 439, 455
Summerall, W L, 401
*Switzer, D*, 206
*Switzer, Daisy*
   of Harrodsburg, 368
Switzer, David, 318
Switzer, *Mrs Fountain*, 72
*Switzer, Samuel*, 332, 337, 374

—T—

Tate, James W, 49, 52, 53, 56, 67, 174
Tate, Mary, 207
*Tatman, C A*, 306
*Tatman, H C*, 310
   daughter, 307
*Tatman, J H*, 388
Tatman, *Mrs C H*, 312, 313
Taylor, *Annie*, 303, 318
*Taylor, Arthur*
   Edenton, 358
*Taylor, B*, 299
*Taylor, C F*, 62
*Taylor, C T*, 11, 15, 17, 18, 22, 31, 73, 162, 178,
   181, 184, 216, 217, 240, 252, 265, 282, 284, 343,
   349, 374, 479
Taylor, *Callie Long*
   *Edenton*, 358
*Taylor, Cordie*
   of Harrodsburg, 401
*Taylor, Emmett*
   of Ruthton, 363
*Taylor, Ernest*
   son, Roy, 433
*Taylor, Eula*, 31
Taylor, F P, 47, 108, 179, 333, 356, 430
*Taylor, Frank*
   of Mt Lebanon, 237

Taylor, *Frank Sr*, 221, 317
Taylor, G B, 18
*Taylor, Groom*, 33, 49, 75, 169, 184, 446
*Taylor, Ike*, 156
   children
      William, Dera, Dela, Jamie, Julie, and Sally,
         352
   *wife* died, 333
*Taylor, Isaac*, 208
*Taylor, John*, 14, 23, 27, 267, 301, 374, 380, 414
   *Lexington*, 33
*Taylor, John W*, 386
Taylor, L B, 171, 217, 264, 301, 401
*Taylor, Leroy*, 414
Taylor, Lewis, 282
*Taylor, Lila*, 164, 165, 231, 342
*Taylor, Lulu*, 33, 62, 68, 283
*Taylor, Mary*, 192, 213
*Taylor, May*, 165, 181, 183, 209, 305, 362, 370
   of Lexington, 219, 230, 252, 297, 317, 337, 342,
      348, 427
Taylor, Misses
   of Richmond, 360
Taylor, *Mr and Mrs*, 28
*Taylor, Mr and Mrs Bart*
   Lexington, 32
*Taylor, Mr and Mrs Cyrus T*
   of Richmond, 328
Taylor, Mrs C T
   Ella Horine, 29, 32, 165, 295, 342, 356, 426, 439
Taylor, Mrs Cyrus T, 475
Taylor, Mrs Groom, 179
Taylor, *Mrs Speed*, 285
   *daughter Hattie*, 322
Taylor, *Mrs Susan*, 311, 336
Taylor, Mrs *Zach*, 282
*Taylor, Sam*, 210, 244, 296, 303, 426
   and family, 426
*Taylor, Speed*, 377
   *Madison County*, 29
Taylor, W S
   Governor, 316, 324, 327, 331
*Taylor, Zack*, 382
*Teater, Allen*, 218
   of Garrard, 338
Teater, *Cyrus*, 360
*Teater, George*
   of Edenton, 409
*Teater, J W*
   of Edenton, 407
   of Giles, 432
Teater, *James*, 301, 322, 431
*Teater, John*
   of Buckeye, 340
Teater, *Leslie*, 340
*Teater, Morton*
   of Buckeye, 308
*Teater, Mr*

*Garrard County*, 62
*Teater, Mr and Mrs John*
   of Buckeye, 288, 344, 356
Teater, *Mrs Cyrus*, 361
*Teater, Mrs Morton*
   of Buckeye, 368
*Teater, W H*
   of Madison County, 281
*Teater, William*
   of Edenton, 431
   of Stone, 404
Temple, *Richard*, 199
*Terhune, Charles*
   *Braxton*, 162
*Terhune, D C*
   of Harrodsburg, 410
Terhune, *James Isaac*, 22
*Terhune, Lee*
   of Mercer County, 430
*Terhune, Mr and Mrs Lee*, 33, 60
Terhune, *Mrs Lee*, 18, 22
   of Mercer County, 77, 78, 434
*Thompson, Charles P*
   of Buckeye, 433
*Thompson, Edgar*, 314
*Thompson, Ike*, 396
   of Buena Vista, 402
   *of Lancaster*, 231
*Thompson, Mary Sue*
   of Paris, 431
*Thompson, N D*, 231, 241, 263, 298
   of Wilmore, 203, 276, 283, 322, 349
Thompson, Phil, 22
Tillett, Samuel, 17
Tipton, Dora, 207
Tolliver, Craig, 25
Toomey, T M
   Silver Creek, 403
Tracy, Smith, 138
Troutman, Florence
   of Lexington, 303
Troutman, Mrs Jacob
   of Lexingon, 303
True, *Mrs Harry*, 209
Tudor, Allen
   of Madison County, 241
Tudor, *D Boone*, 264, 413, 414, 442
Tudor, Fatima
   East Hickman, 95
*Tudor, Fletcher*
   of Madison County, 413
*Tudor, James O*
   of Edenton, 327
*Tudor, Jason*, 203, 240, 341
   *Madison County*, 31
   of Cottonburg, 302
   *Prof*, 305, 308
*Tudor, John*
   of Illinois, 377

*Tudor, Mary*
   of Madison County, 281
Tudor, Mrs
   Madison County, 39
*Tudor, Mrs James O*, 330
   of Madison County, 307
*Tudor, Theresa Hendren*, 375, 402, 403, 411, 412, 442
*Tudor, Thomas*
   of Edenton, 386
*Tudor, Wolford*
   son, of Madison County, 272
*Turner,*, 324
*Turner, Albert*, 381
*Turner, Edna May*, 434
Turner, Ella West, 235, 238
*Turner, Emma*, 28
Turner, *J H*, 65, 66, 81, 105, 162, 178, 197, 231, 238, 242, 250, 252, 253, 265, 289, 290, 300, 313, 314, 318, 321, 323, 325, 338, 341, 347, 348, 349, 351, 354, 356, 374, 377, 383, 384, 386, 396, 398, 399, 400, 403, 407, 411, 439, 479
*Turner, J P*, 22, 28, 33, 40, 41, 45, 52, 56, 64, 65, 66, 74, 88, 89, 105, 110, 154, 157, 162, 165, 194, 197, 210, 211, 213, 217, 219, 220, 221, 235, 236, 238, 241, 242, 249, 250, 253, 254, 256, 257, 258, 261, 262, 269, 271, 272, 274, 286, 293, 297, 301, 309, 318, 320, 321, 322, 333, 337, 338, 339, 341, 343, 347, 349, 350, 354, 362, 370, 374, 386, 395, 396, 397, 398, 399, 400, 401, 402, 403, 404, 406, 410, 446, 479
*Turner, John*
   of Bowling Green, 338
*Turner, Joseph Lynn*, 282
*Turner, Levi*, 346
*Turner, Luther*, 88, 242
   Elma Grinstead, 479
*Turner, Mary F*
   of Wilmore, 217
Turner, *Mayme*, 330, 346, 348
   *daughter of J H*, 250
*Turner, Mr and Mrs J H*, 166, 290, 396, 419, 434
Turner, *Mr and Mrs J P*, 86, 245, 265, 274, 281, 286, 293, 296, 299, 310, 313, 345, 346, 355, 377, 386, 390, 391, 398, 400
Turner, *Mrs J H*, 196, 244, 247, 256, 281, 283, 287, 309, 312, 314, 391, 397, 398, 412, 413, 427, 431
   and daughter Edna Grace, 439
   daughters Mayme and Edna May, 436
   *Elma Grinstead*, 287, 346, 479
Turner, *Mrs J P*, 27, 33, 41, 88, 397, 478
   *Myra*, 286, 290, 307
Turner, *Mrs Tom*, 56
*Turner, Rev and Mrs H G*, 310, 311, 313
Turner, *Rev H G*, 17, 40, 50, 65, 66, 75, 80, 83, 88, 105, 165, 183, 211, 217, 221, 233, 234, 235, 237, 238, 242, 244, 245, 257, 265, 273, 274, 277, 279, 281, 282, 286, 290, 293, 299, 307, 309, 322, 328,

331, 339, 341, 343, 345, 347, 350, 355, 362, 366, 369, 377, 386, 391, 396, 398, 400, 402, 479
Turner, *Suinie*, 65
***Turner, William***
*Bowling Green*, 254
Turpin, *Caryton*, 280, 374
  son, 314
Turpin, *Geo W*, 208, 344
*Turpin, Mr and Mrs Caryton*, 407
*Turpin, Mrs Geo D*, 406
*Turpin, Smith*, 345
*Tutt, Mr*, 197
*Tutt, W C*, 321
  *a butcher*, 325, 377
*Tuttle, Miss*
  of Spears, 308

—U—

*Underwood, Arthur*, 209
*Underwood, John*, 255, 320
*Underwood, Mrs H*, 349
*Underwood, Mrs S N*, 284, 286
*Underwood, Newt*, 225
*Underwood, S N*, 185, 204, 208, 209, 255, 297
*Underwood, William*, 427, 431
*Urton, John*, 263

—V—

Van Arsdale, Jack, 29
*Van Arsdall, Dr*, 263, 267
Van Winkle, Lizzie Hendren, 47, 54, 71, 93, 95, 96, 133, 142, 147, 157, 165, 181, 197, 208, 213, 217. *See* Crosley, Lizzie Hendren
Vanderbilt, Cornelius, 321
*Vince, Mrs Wm*, 65
*Vincent, Allen*
  *Edenton*, 391
  of Cottonburg, 374
  of Edenton, 290, 391, 401, 427
*Vincent, Beatty*, 403
  of Edenton, 290
*Vincent, Caperton*, 303, 340, 354, 374, 377, 382, 389, 397, 403, 405, 409
*Vincent, Capt*, 339
*Vincent, Dr*
  of Edenton, 390
*Vincent, E D*, 164, 165
*Vincent, Ezekiel*, 214, 259, 279, 291, 305, 354, 360, 374, 403, 405, 413
  *Edenton*, 391
*Vincent, James*
  of Edenton, 289, 351, 399, 442
*Vincent, Mrs Caperton*, 377
*Vincent, Mrs James*
  of Edenton, 235, 429
*Vincent, Oliver*
  of Edenton, 347

—W—

Wade, Bob, 120
Wade, *Robert*, 240
Wagers, Annie
  of Irvine, 250
Wagner, *Annie Hendren*, 15, 32, 105, 244, 364, 366, 399, 440
Wagner, Dr George B, 243, 244
*Wagner, Nellie*, 231
*Waide, Robert*, 354
Wait, John, 17
*Waits, James*, 329
*Walker & Cobb*
  thresher, 210
*Walker, Elbert*, 23, 55, 63, 72, 162, 194, 195, 196, 226, 228, 253, 255, 262, 297, 310, 331, 340, 349, 352, 354, 362, 377, 378, 391, 404, 429, 430, 434, 479
Walker, James, 149
*Walker, Janie*
  *Hanly*, 65
*Walker, Jennie*, 12
*Walker, Mr and Mrs Thomas*, 290, 297
*Walker, Mrs W B*
  *Elizabeth*, 63, 282, 349, 352, 365, 399, 412
*Walker, Mrs Wm*, 12, 27, 28
*Walker, Thomas*, 263, 284, 297, 301, 309, 377, 413, 480
*Walker, W B*, 183, 189, 204, 208, 221, 240, 299, 302, 321, 332, 341, 342, 349, 352, 354, 368, 370, 388, 436, 479
*Walker, William*
  near Saunders Ferry, 415
*Wallace, F N*, 226
*Wallace, John*, 225
*Wallace, Mr and Mrs O T*
  of Point Leavell, 342
*Wallace, Newt*, 294
  of Little Hickman, 293, 313, 314
*Waller, John*, 198, 308, 321, 323, 342, 361, 399, 480
*Walls, James*, 418
Walls, *W T*, 17
Walter, Dr L P, 129
*Walters, Fina Taylor*, 287, 288
*Walters, George*, 321, 399
  daughter, 245
*Walters, Howard*, 429
Walters, *Humphrey*, 199
*Walters, Minnie*, 362, 391, 400
*Walters, Mr and Mrs George*, 287
*Walters, Mr and Mrs William*, 331
Walters, Mrs Perry, 352
  Belle, 267, 274, 281, 480
*Walters, Simon*, 357, 400
*Walters, Squire*, 398, 400

*Walters, William*, 352, 377
   of Illinois, 327
   of Virden, Ill, 287
*Walton, George*, 310
*Walton, J C*, 409
*Walton, Joseph*
   Georgetown, 387
*Walton, Mr*
   son, 394
*Ward, James*
   of Buckeye, 357
Ware and Ware, PSC, 466
*Ware, A J*, 194, 274, 338, 352, 396, 480
*Ware, Ed*, 274, 308, 309, 352, 356, 361, 428, 480
Ware, Eunice Dean, 472
Ware, Frank Edward, 249, 441, 450, 459, 480
Ware, George W, 33, 204, 249, 308, 459
Ware, Luther, 8, 38, 213, 214, 249, 250, 288, 308,
   352, 354, 359, 367, 378, 389, 426, 459, 470, 480
Ware, Mary Miller, 441, 450, 453, 459, 461, 465
Ware, *Melvin*, 342, 352, 480
*Ware, Minnie Reynolds*
   wife of Ed Ware, daughter of John Reynolds, 356
Ware, Mrs Julia
   of Lincoln County, 338
Ware, Ray Miller, 8, 120, 462
Ware, Sallie, 352
Ware, Sarah Teater
   wife of A J Ware, 480
Ware, Steven Douglas, 369, 464, 465
Ware, Sue Davenport, 120, 460, 461, 463, 464, 466,
   467
Warfield, *John H*, 355
*Warfield, Josh*, 358
Warner, *Anna Warren*
   Edenton, 358
*Warner, George*
   *of Edenton*, 322
   of Idalia, 382, 410, 411
*Warner, George W*
   *of Edenton*, 432
Warner, Hattie, 242
*Warner, James*
   Edenton, 358
Warner, Lizzie, 242
*Warner, Mr*, 203
   of Buckeye, 203
Warner, Nannie, 242
Warner, Sallie, 212
*Warner, William*
   of Edenton, 374, 404, 405
*Warren, Elisha*, 340
   of Edenton, 380, 382, 391
   of Madison County, 303, 409
*Warren, John*
   of Madison, 348
*Warren, Misses*
   Windom, 43

*Warren, Simpson*, 195
   of Edenton, 382
   *of Madison County*, 194, 303, 380, 409
*Warren, Thomas*
   at Miles Ferry, 410, 415
*Warren, Wm D*, 191
   *Madison*, 193
Wasserman, Max J, 464
*Watkins, Dr*
   of Edenton, 399
*Watkins, G S*, 214, 217, 232, 236, 301, 337, 338
   *Mercer*, 201
*Watters, George*, 148
*Watters, Simon and Willie*, 148
Watterson, Henry
   Editor, Courier Journal, 142
Watts, Allen Clay, 74
*Watts, James*, 274, 297, 302, 328, 337, 340, 343,
   363, 410, 411
   Hunter's Ferry, 303
Watts, John C, 152, 420
Watts, Susan Sageser, 152, 420
Watts, *Tilford*, 197
*Webb, Robert*, 183
*Weber, Chas*, 164
Weil, Simon, 277, 377
*Weisbach, Mr*
   of Lexington, 409
Weiser, Mary Bradshaw, 85, 91, 142
Weiser, Rudolph, 85
Welch, Dr, 17, 81, 263
Welch, Dr John C, 49, 83, 191
*Welch, Dr S D*, 5, 75, 84, 480
Welch, Dr Thomas P, 278
Welch, Henry, 34
Welch, John H, 316
Welch, *Mrs J C*, 63, 65
*Welch, Squire*, 72
*Welch, Tom*, 86
Wells, Beatrice
   of Junction City, 252
Welsh, G W
   of Danville, 292
*Wesren, Porter*
   of Garrard County, 274
West, Arthur, 148, 288, 452
West, Carrie, 186
   Garrard, 134
West, *Clayton*, 73, 89, 115, 122, 166, 178, 237, 243,
   253, 377
West, Dan, 461
West, *Dora Murphy*, 122, 135, 162, 172, 183, 209,
   211, 219, 223, 227, 228, 230, 238, 252, 271, 280,
   288, 297, 311, 348, 352, 360, 362, 370, 385, 427,
   452, 478
*West, Eliza Hendren*, 213, 229, 474
*West, Emma*, 317, 318, 362, 370, 428
*West, James*
   of Edenton, 389

*West, Jennie*, 122
*West, John T*, 45, 88, 182, 186, 204, 210, 213, 243, 268, 321, 329, 355, 360, 396, 398, 400, 475, 480
West, Lizzie Robinson, 243, 252
*West, Mr and Mrs John T*, 32
*West, Mrs John T*, 103, 368, 435
West, *Perry*, 348
West, Turpin, 229
*West, William*
   of Speedwell, 329
*Wheeler, A F*
   of Lexington, 437
*Wheeler, Ben*, 320, 401
   daughter, 361
*Wheeler, Ella*, 28, 87, 103
*Wheeler, Ida*, 341, 418
*Wheeler, Mary*, 28, 418
   of Cincinnati, 229, 233
*Wheeler, Mary and Ella*, 30
*Wheeler, Mary Hendren*, 52, 286, 311, 341, 345, 364, 366, 367, 418, 454
*Wheeler, Minnie*, 103, 122
*Wheeler, Mr and Mrs A F Hendren*, 431
*Wheeler, Mrs A F*
   *Jennie Hendren*, 410
Wheeler, *Mrs Ben*, 344
*Whitaker, M T*
   of Garrard County, 377
White, Mrs James M, 160
*Whitenack, Mr and Mrs John*
   of Mercer County, 219, 265, 283, 291, 295, 317, 341, 345, 407
*Whitenack, Mrs John*
   *Lulu of Mercer County*, 396
   *son*, 396
*Whittaker, Arch*, 190
   Lerny, Ill, 411
   of Garrard County, 272
*Whittaker, B*
   of Madison County, 339
*Whittaker, Connie*, 327
*Whittaker, Eliza Tudor*, 190
Whittaker, Holland, 330
*Whittaker, Mr and Mrs Roy*
   of Madison County, 258, 273, 284, 332
*Whittaker, Mrs Martha*
   of Garrard, 258
*Whittaker, Mrs Willard*
   of Edenton, 405
*Whittaker, of Lancaster*, 115
*Whittaker, William*, 343
   of Stone, 340
*Wilds, B F*, 55, 74, 78
   father of Dr J L Wilds, 480
   Garrard, 174
Wilds, Dr J L, 17, 21, 24, 38, 43, 55, 56, 64, 78, 79, 80, 81, 82, 83, 87, 101, 111, 128, 131, 141, 158, 159, 172, 173, 174, 176, 183, 245, 422, 480

Wilds, Eliza Dismukes, 174
   *Lancaster*, 80
*Wilds, Elizabeth Welch*, 28, 32, 57, 63, 64, 65, 77, 80, 102, 152, 176, 422, 480
   daughter, Dr J C Welch, 174
Wilds, Lizzie
   died, 67
*Wilds, Mrs*
   Garrard, 21
Wilds, Olive, 245
Wilds, Sally, 158
Wilds, *Sybelle*, 27, 28, 31, 52, 55, 58, 64, 70, 80, 101, 112, 113, 131, 146
Wilds, Tom, 158
*Wilds, Welch*, 78
*Wiley, Henry*
   of Bloomington, Ill, 403
*Wiley, Jasper*
   of Madison County, 409
*Wiley, Robert*
   little son, 178
Williams, *Geo. S*
   *Red House*, 156
*Williams, John*, 263
   of Richmond, 299
*Williams, Mrs and little son*
   of Richmond, 208
Willis, Alex, 187
*Willis, Capt and Mrs Irwin F*
   of Shelbyville, 344
*Willis, Carr*, 44
Willis, *Green B and daughter*
   of Edinburg, Ind, 358
*Willis, M*
   daughter, 318
   infant, 317
*Willis, Miss*
   *Richmond*, 86
*Willis, Mrs Green B*
   of Indiana, 295
*Willis, Tom*, 327
Willis, Wilson, 52
Wilmore, Col., 115
Wilson, Captain
   accepted flag Jessamine Institute, 278
*Wilson, Willard*
   of Buena Vista, 405
*Wilson, William*
   of Buena Vista, 407
Witt, Anna Miller, 169
Witt, *James*, 405
*Witt, Mrs*
   of Estill County, 236
Witt, Victor, 169
Witt, W S, 169
Wolf, Bernard, 5, 59, 76, 123, 129, 135
Wolfe, Dora, 378
Wolfe, Mr and Mrs Bernard, 378
Wood, A T

Mt Sterling, 119
Wood, *James*, 206
*Wood, Mrs John*, 426
Woodard, Bobbie, 306
Woodard, Chess, 306
Woodard, Mattie Askins, 306, 348, 352, 436, 470
Woodard, Roberta Wilhoit, 306
Woodford, *Mr and Mrs Jas.*, 18
Woods, A G, 76
Woods, Dr, 125
Woods, Kate Hemphiill, 473
*Woodward, Carrie*, 14, 16, 18, 19, 21, 26, 28, 43, 63, 72, 78, 87, 124, 148, 221, 343, 353, 362, 439
*Woodward, Clint*, 378, 429, 430
*Woodward, Ella*, 74, 124, 155, 252
*Woodward, Henry*, 245, 329
Woodward, *Houston*, 286, 353, 362, 368, 376, 391, 397, 398, 418
*Woodward, James Jr*, 50, 75, 77, 87, 89, 121, 217, 265, 271, 297, 330, 378, 429, 430
*Woodward, James Sr*, 60, 78, 133, 217, 223, 245, 246, 255, 353, 365, 377, 418, 435, 480
Woodward, *Joe*, 12, 23, 33, 35, 43, 49, 50, 55, 56, 170, 312, 353, 359
Woodward, Johnny, 170
Woodward, *Lulu Spruce*, 21, 27, 34, 35, 43, 49, 57, 152, 170, 353, 470
*Woodward, Mattie*, 14, 21, 87, 93, 96, 124, 252, 362, 439
*Woodward, Mr and Mrs James Jr*, 253, 337
*Woodward, Mr and Mrs James Sr*, 427, 429, 431, 434
   *Caroline*, 434

*Woodward, Mrs Henry*
   and daughter of Dayton, 427
Woodward, Mrs James Sr, 439
   Caroline, 353, 435, 480
*Woodward, Russell*, 65
   of Little Hickman, 213
Woolfolk, Annie Lee, 284
*Woolfolk, John*
   of Lexington, 410
Woolfolk, Mary, 279, 284, 405
Woolfolk, Mrs John, 424
Woolfolk, *Sallie*, 71, 72
   *Buckeye*, 12
*Wright, William*
   daughter, 286
Wylie, *William*, 332, 389, 403
   near Giles, 403, 405, 411, 413
   of Edenton, 333, 437

—Y—

Yarnell, *Squire*, 192, 399
*Yates, Mr and Mrs Mike*, 330
Young, Bennett, 71, 202, 228, 291
Young, Dick, 128
Young, *Dr F O*
   *Lexington*, 193
Young, E J, 75
Young, Eliza Sharp, 202
Young, Mrs Mary R, 378
Young, *Richard*, 344, 377

# Descendants of FRANCIS M MILLER

```
 M MILLER  Abt 1748 - 1839
 ETH FREEMAN  Abt 1769 - 1845
 HN MILLER
 IZABETH (FREEMAN) MILLER  1787 -
 ATHERINE (FREEMAN) MILLER  1797 -
 ASON MILLER  1798 -
 ELIZABETH STIGALL
    .. 3 JAMES F MILLER
    .. 3 MILTON J MILLER
    .. 3 MARY (STIGALL) MILLER
    .. 3 ELIZABETH (STIGALL) MILLER
    .. 3 GEORGIANA MILLER
    .. 3 MASON C MILLER JR  1836 -
 OLLY MILLER  1802 -
 ILLIAM MILLER  1803 - Abt 1874
 MAHALA MOORE  - 1897
    .. 3 JEFFERSON W MILLER  Abt 1852 -
    ...... +MARY BLAKEMAN
    ............. 4 NETTIE MILLER  1880 - 1967
    ................. +ELBERT CARTER  1875 - 1934
    ............. 4 MAGGIE MILLER
    ................. +UNKNOWN YARNALL
    ............. 4 ELLA MILLER
    ................. +BURT P EASLEY
    ......................... 5 ELLA MAE EASLEY
    ......................... 5 ALLIE T EASLEY
    ............................. +LUTHER CARTER
    ................................. 6 BOBBY NELMES CARTER  - 1933
    ................................. 6 VIRGINIA CARTER
    ................................. 6 LOUISE CARTER
    ................................. 6 RUTH CARTER
    ................................. 6 ANN CARTER
    ......................... 5 UNKNOWN EASLEY
    ............................. +MARTIN COOLEY
    ......................... 5 UNKNOWN EASLEY II
    ............................. +HARLAN CLOSE
    ......................... 5 JOHN EASLEY
    ......................... 5 ROGER EASLEY  1910 - 2002
    ............................. +WILMA CADDELL
    ......................... 5 JOE EASLEY
    ......................... 5 JAMES EASLEY
    ............. 4 FRANK MILLER  Abt 1875 -
    ................. +ANNA MARIAH REYNOLDS  1877 - 1942
    ......................... 5 AMANDA MILLER  1909 -
    ............................. +WILLIAM J TODD
    ......................... 5 ELIZABETH MILLER  1904 -
    ............................. +JULIAN W THOMPSON
    ......................... 5 HAZEL MILLER
    ............................. +WILLIAM H JOYCE
    ......................... 5 CHARLES M MILLER
    ............................. +ELVA JENNINGS  1902 -
    ................................. 6 CHARLES LOGAN MILLER
 ERRIMAN F MILLER  1804 - 1887
 CELIA SAGESER  1806 - 1882
    .. 3 FRANCIS S MILLER  1829 - 1895
    ...... +ELIZABETH JANE WILLIAMS  1830 - 1904
    ............. 4 MERRIMAN GEORGE MILLER  1853 - 1868
    ............. 4 JAMES WILLIAM MILLER  1854 - 1898
    ............. 4 LUCY CATHIAN MILLER  1856 - 1920
    ................. +STEPHEN N SNOWDEN  Abt 1853 - Abt 1934
    ......................... 5 GEORGE SNOWDEN  1874 - 1932
    ............................. +BLANCHE ASKINS
    ............................. *2nd Wife of GEORGE SNOWDEN:
    ............................. +NORA W TAYLOR  1876 - 1910
    ......................... 5 MYRTIE SNOWDEN  Abt 1876 - Abt 1946
    ............................. +MELVIN DEAN  1860 - Abt 1938
    ................................. 6 MELVIN L DEAN  1914 - 1991
    ..................................... +ELIZABETH WILSON
    ......................................... 7 SARAH DEAN  1944 -
    ............................................. +JOEL L MCGILL
    ................................................. 8 ANDREA MCGILL  1970 -
    ................................................. 8 BRYAN MCGILL  Abt 1973 -
    ......................................... 7 SUSAN DEAN  1947 -
    ............................................. +RICHARD A MITCHELL
    ................................................. 8 LEAH MITCHELL  1973 -
    ................................................. 8 SCOTT MITCHELL  1976 -
    ......................................... 7 MELVIN W DEAN  1952 -
    ............................................. +BEVERLY WISEMAN
    ................................................. 8 MELVIN L DEAN III  1970 -
```

```
........................................................... +ANDREA GAIL LANE  1977 -
..................................................................... 8 JENNIFER DEAN  1972 -
................................ 5 JOHN SNOWDEN  1882 - 1965
................................ 5 VIRGIL SNOWDEN  1894 - 1979
................................... +HATTIE WARNER  1899 - 1985
................................ 5 BESSIE SNOWDEN  1897 - 1984
................................... +RAYMOND HARE  - 1951
............... 4 MATILDA CELIA MILLER  1859 - 1944
............... 4 SARAH BELLE MILLER  1862 - 1890
.................. +HON J B STACY
................................ 5 LEAH STACY  1887 - 1981
................................... +JOHN PULLINS
..................................... 6 SUE PULLINS
................................ 5 VERNON STACY  1890 - 1970
................................... +SARAH HOTCHKISS  1893 - 1987
................................ 5 GUY STACY  1885 - 1957
................................... +BERTHA ASKINS  1884 - 1957
..................................... 6 NANCY STACY  1921 -
........................................ +JOE BREINER  1916 -
........................................... 7 JAMES MEREDITH BREINER  1942 -
.............................................. +LINDA PRATHER
................................................. 8 GUY SCOT BREINER  1964 -
................................................. 8 JAMES STEVEN BREINER  1967 -
........................................... 7 JOSEPH MICHAEL BREINER  1948 -
.............................................. +FRANZETTA STATON  1949 -
................................................. 8 TIFANY JO BREINER  1977 -
................................................. 8 ANDREA MICHELE BREINER  1978 -
................................................. 8 JANA KATE BREINER  1980 -
........................................... 7 RONALD CLAY BREINER  1950 -
.............................................. +REGINA ANN CORMAN  1951 -
................................................. 8 MELISA ANN BREINER  1974 -
................................................. 8 JOHN DANIEL BREINER  1977 -
............... 4 JOHN PINK MILLER  1864 - 1919
.................. +FLORA SCOTT  1865 - 1952
................................ 5 FRANK P MILLER  1888 - 1979
................................... +FANNIE KIMBROUGH  1890 - 1979
................................ 5 ANNA MILLER  1890 - 1976
................................... +VICTOR WITT
..................................... 6 EUNICE WITT  1908 - 1994
........................................ +JOHN WINN
........................................... 7 RHONDA WINN
.............................................. +UNKNOWN HIGGINGBOTTOM
..................................... 6 CLEO WITT  1910 - 1996
........................................ +GILBERT MASTERS
..................................... 6 LEON WITT  1913 - 1995
........................................ +HELEN FRANCES STEVENS
........................................... 7 LEON WITT II
........................................... 7 JOHN WITT
........................................... 7 MARK WITT
..................................... 6 VIRGINIA WITT  1919 - 2000
........................................ +TOM HOWARD SCOTT BONNY  1911 - 1983
........................................... 7 JUNE BONNY  1943 -
.............................................. +JACK GARY WILLIAMS  1937 -
................................................. 8 JULIE ANN WILLIAMS  1978 -
................................................. 8 JARED BLAKE WILLIAMS  1980 -
........................................... 7 TOM HOWARD BONNY  1946 -
.............................................. +FRANCINE FREEMAN  1953 -
................................................. 8 TARA  1988 -
..................................... 6 MARGARET WITT
........................................ +GEORGE PENDERGRASS
........................................... 7 JAMES PENDERGRASS
........................................... 7 JODY PENDERGRASS
..................................... 6 WILLARD WITT  1924 - 1995
..................................... 6 GLENNA WITT  1928 -
........................................ +BRUCE BARRETT
........................................... 7 J PAULA BARRETT
........................................... 7 EDWARD BARRETT
................................ 5 CECILE MILLER  1891 -
................................... +HENRY BENNETT
................................ 5 ELIZABETH MILLER  1896 - 1973
................................... +HOBERT POWELL
................................ 5 RUTH MILLER  1901 - 1983
................................... +GUY CONNELLY  1893 - 1974
..................................... 6 GUY CONNELLY, JR  1926 -
........................................ +MELVA L MADDOX
........................................... 7 MELINDA CONNELLY
.............................................. +JAN SMITH
........................................... 7 GUY CONNELLY III
........................................... 7 JOHNNY CONNELLY
........................................... 7 DAN CONNELLY
........................................... 7 SAM CONNELLY
```

```
            6 JOHN CONNELLY 1930 -
               +GRACIE JOAN WADE 1935 -
                  7 DELIA LUANNE CONNELLY 1955 -
                  7 DEBORAH KIM CONNELLY 1956 -
                  7 JOHN A CONNELLY, JR 1960 -
                     +BETH M SHAFER 1957 -
                        8 TIFFANY S CONNELLY 1980 -
                        8 JOHN M CONNELLY 1987 - 1987
                     *2nd Wife of JOHN A CONNELLY, JR:
                     +CECILIA A SCHOLL 1962 -
                        8 ASHLEY R FREEMAN 1986 -
            6 DOROTHY CONNELLY 1922 -
               +JAMES HURST 1921 - 1989
                  7 SHARON K HURST 1943 -
                  7 JAMES PHILLIP HURST 1951 -
         5 GLENN FORREST MILLER 1902 - 1981
            +BABY JO BARKER
               6 GLENNA JO MILLER 1929 - 2004
                  +DICK BROOKS
                     7 LESLIE ALLISON BROOKS 1955 -
                        +UNKNOWN NORTHERN
                           8 DANIEL NORTHERN 1981 -
                           8 JENNIFER MARIE NORTHERN 1983 -
                           8 LAUREN BROOKS NORTHERN 1986 -
                     7 STACEY CAROLYN BROOKS 1957 -
                        +JIM MARTIN
               6 SUE MILLER
         5 CORALIE MILLER 1903 -
            +CLARENCE CASPAR
               6 BOB CASPER
                  +GLENDA SNYDER
                     7 KIMBERLY CASPER
                        +JOHN WOOD
                     7 JOHN CASPER
         5 SCOTTIE MILLER 1897 - 1986
            +THOMAS BARCLAY
               6 THOMAS GERALD BARCLAY 1925 -
               6 ELINOR BARCLAY 1927 -
                  +EUGENE LEONARD 1920 - 2003
                     7 EDWARD ISERT LEONARD 1947 -
                     7 DAVID EUGENE LEONARD 1951 -
                     7 CAROL SUSAN LEONARD 1955 -
               6 ANGELA BARCLAY 1930 -
                  +KENNETH VANCE
                     7 PEGGY VANCE 1951 -
                        +STEVE BACON
                     7 PAULA VANCE 1952 -
                        +MAX GRIMES
                  *2nd Husband of ANGELA BARCLAY:
                  +GORDON ARNOLD
      4 SUSAN ELIZABETH MILLER 1866 - 1921
      4 NANNIE ROSE MILLER 1870 - 1890
      4 FRANK FOREST MILLER 1872 - 1942
         +SCOTTIE HENDREN 1874 - 1967
            5 RAY EUGENE MILLER 1896 - 1918
            5 MARY ELIZABETH MILLER 1906 - 1988
               +FRANK EDWARD WARE 1906 - 1952
                  6 RAY MILLER WARE 1929 -
                     +SUSAN DAVENPORT 1937 -
                        7 STEVEN DOUGLAS WARE 1961 - 2004
                           +JEANNIE CAROLINE TAYLOR 1949 -
            5 EDITH MILLER 1911 -
               +WILLIAM HERMAN JESSE 1908 - 1970
                  6 NAN JESSE 1939 -
                  6 ALICE JESSE 1943 -
                     +JAMES DONALD KIRK 1939 -
                        7 WILLIAM CLIFFORD KIRK 1967 -
                           +KAREN BINDER 1973 -
                              8 BRANDON JOSHUA KIRK 1991 -
                           *2nd Wife of WILLIAM CLIFFORD KIRK:
                           +ANNA MARIA BOBREK 1964 -
                              8 CHRISTIAN JESSE KIRK 2000 -
                        7 DOUGLAS WAYNE KIRK 1969 -
                           +MELISSA BRITTON 1970 -
                              8 EMILY RUTH KIRK 1994 -
                              8 LAURA ELIZABETH KIRK 2001 -
                              8 CHARLES BRITTON KIRK 2001 -
3 SUSAN MILLER Abt 1832 - 1900
3 SARAH MILLER 1835 - 1915
   +J PINK OVERSTREET
      4 BETTY OVERSTREET Abt 1858 - Abt 1862
```

```
................................ 4 ALNEGIA OVERSTREET  1862 - 1942
................................ +CLINTON S DEAN  1857 - 1910
........................................ 5 JEWEL DEAN  Abt 1879 - Abt 1943
........................................ +HARMON TEATER
................................................ 6 RICE MILLER TEATER
................................................ 6 GRACE TEATER  1904 - 1992
...................................................... +CLARK OVERSTREET  1894 - 1982
................................................ 6 RUTH TEATER  1918 - 1998
...................................................... +ROBERT QUINN  1917 - 1990
........................................ 5 PEARL DEAN  Abt 1881 - 1956
........................................ +W F BEVERLY, DR
................................................ 6 LESTER HOWARD BEVERLY  1913 - 1999
...................................................... +ELNA MCQUERRY  1913 - 1998
........................................ 5 BETTY DEAN  1884 - 1971
........................................ 5 CHARLIE MANN DEAN  1890 - 1973
........................................ +ADA SAGESER  1894 - 1970
................................................ 6 CARL ATWOOD DEAN  1918 - 1975
................................................ 6 DOROTHY DEAN  1920 - 2001
...................................................... +CHARLES LYNN TERRELL
................................................ 6 EVELYN DEAN  1922 -
................................................ 6 ROBERT MANN DEAN  1925 -
................................ 4 BATIE OVERSTREET  1864 - 1878
................................ 4 MYRTIE OVERSTREET  Abt 1867 - Abt 1949
................................ +WALTER D HARRIS  1864 - 1928
........................................ 5 BASCOM THOMAS HARRIS, MD  1900 - 1974
........................................ +KATHRYN FREED  1912 - 1975
................................................ 6 WALTER D HARRIS, MD
...................................................... +BETTY KINSEY
................................................ 6 THOMAS E HARRIS
................ 3 WILLIAM S MILLER  1838 - 1855
................ 3 JOHN C MILLER  1841 - 1908
................ +NANIE RICE  1843 - 1885
........................ 4 RICE MILLER  1869 - 1899
........................ +JULIA BLACKBURN PAYNE
........................ 4 HUGH MILLER  1873 - 1957
........................ +ADDA HENDREN  1873 - 1950
................................ 5 ALMA MILLER  1895 - 1974
................................ 5 TOM TURNER MILLER  1897 -
................................ +PHANIAL BOWEN
........................................ 6 MARY VIRGINIA MILLER
........................................ 6 KENNETH MILLER
........................ 4 ELIZABETH (JOHN C) MILLER  Abt 1875 - Abt 1957
........................ +THOMAS WELCH DOWNING  1870 - 1932
................................ 5 ALFRED P DOWNING  1908 - 1997
................................ +MARIE BUTLER  1912 - 1999
........................................ 6 HENRY DOWNING  1936 -
............................................... +JUDIE ADAMS
........................................ 6 SUSAN DOWNING  1949 -
........................ 4 MEADE MILLER  1876 - 1967
........................ +MAE BENJAMIN  1880 - Abt 1940
................................ 5 LAURA MILLER  1902 -
................................ 5 JOHN C MILLER II  1904 -
................................ 5 NANCY RICE MILLER  1900 - 1980
................................ +FRED DOUGLAS LOWE  1900 - 1977
........................................ 6 FRED LOWE
........................................ 6 ELIZABETH LOWE
........................................ 6 LAURA LOWE  1929 -
............................................... +UNKNOWN FERGUSON
........................................ 6 RICHARD LOWE  1927 -
........ 3 KITTY MILLER  1843 - 1923
........ +SAMUEL BARKLEY
........ 3 MERRIMAN M MILLER  1846 - 1926
........ +BETTIE ANDERSON
................ 4 MARY HARRIS MILLER
................ 4 CHARLES WALLACE MILLER  1876 - 1963
................ 4 MAUDE ANDERSON MILLER  1878 - 1959
```

# MILLER FAMILY CEMETERY
## SNOWDEN LANE OFF HOOVER PIKE, JESSAMINE COUNTY, KY

**WILLIAM MILLER**
1803-1877
Son of
Francis M Miller
and
Elizabeth Freeman

**SUSAN NAVE**
1832-1900
Daughter of
Merriman F Miller
and
Celia Sageser

**FRANCIS M MILLER**
1748-1839

**WILLIAM S MILLER**
1838-1855
Son of
Merriman F Miller
and
Celia Sageser

**ELIZABETH FREEMAN**
1769-1845

**JAMES MILLER**
1854-1899
Son of
Francis S Miller
and
Elizabeth Jane Williams

**BELLE STACY**
1862-1890
Daughter of
Francis S Miller
and
Elizabeth Jane Williams

**FRANCIS S MILLER**
1829-1895
Son of
Merriman F Miller
and
Celia Sageser

**ROSE SAGESER**
1870-1890
Daughter of
Francis S Miller
and
Elizabeth Jane Williams

**ELIZABETH JANE WILLIAMS**
1830-1904
Daughter of
James Williams
and
Matilda Goodrich

**CELIA SAGESER**
1806-1882
Daughter of
Frederick Sageser
and
Catherine Bruner

**MERRIMAN F MILLER**
1804-1887
Son of
Francis M Miller
and
Elizabeth Freeman

# Descendants of DOVEN HENDREN

1 DOVEN HENDREN 1773 - 1848
. +JENNY TAYLOR
.......... 2 TALTON HENDREN
.......... 2 MARGARET HENDREN
.......... 2 LORENZO HENDREN - Abt 1846
.......... 2 OLIVER HENDREN Abt 1804 -
.............. +ELIZABETH HARRIS
..................... 3 WILLIAM HARRISON HENDREN 1856 - Abt 1916
..................... +BARBARA ANN COTTON 1858 - 1931
............................. 4 ROBERT S HENDREN 1874 - 1925
............................. 4 THOMAS E HENDREN 1886 - 1957
............................. 4 WILLIAM OLIVER HENDREN 1893 - 1976
............................. +FANNIE NOE
..................................... 5 JANE HENDREN Abt 1917 - 2002
..................................... +HENRY S HODGES
............................................. 6 CAROLYN HODGES
............................................. +KENNETH CARPENTER
............................................. 6 BARBARA HODGES
............................................. +BENJAMINE CRIPE
..................................... 5 WILLANNA HENDREN
............................. 4 JASPER BRADLEY HENDREN 1895 - 1973
............................. +ETHEL GLENN CORNELISON 1895 - 1979
..................................... 5 DONALD BURTON HENDREN 1925 - 1993
..................................... +MARY ELIZABETH STAGNER
............................................. 6 DONALD BURTON HENDREN II 1950 - 1977
............................................. 6 ELIZABETH SUSAN HENDREN 1946 -
..................... 3 J NEWT HENDREN 1858 - 1937
.......... 2 HARRISON HENDREN 1810 - 1876
.............. +CYNTHIA WEARREN 1812 - 1898
..................... 3 SUSAN HENDREN Abt 1835 -
..................... 3 WILLIAM D HENDREN 1840 - 1891
..................... +LEVISA TUDOR 1843 - 1887
............................. 4 BERTHA HENDREN
............................. 4 ADDIE HENDREN
............................. +ADAM K ADCOCK
..................................... 5 BESSIE ADCOCK 1886 -
..................................... 5 RUSSIE ADCOCK 1888 -
..................................... 5 CECILE ADCOCK 1892 - 1973
..................................... +RAYMOND RANDOLPH
............................................. 6 RAYMOND RANDOLPH II
............................. 4 LIZZIE HENDREN
............................. 4 HARRY P HENDREN 1882 - 1976
............................. +HATTIE UNKNOWN 1889 - 1973
............................. 4 LEO HENDREN - 1934
............................. 4 FOUNTAIN HENDREN 1865 - 1897
............................. 4 SUSIE HENDREN 1872 - 1956
............................. +ANDREW SAGESER 1866 - 1932
..................................... 5 ADA SAGESER 1894 - 1970
..................................... +CHARLIE MANN DEAN 1890 - 1973
............................................. 6 CARL ATWOOD DEAN 1918 - 1975
............................................. 6 DOROTHY DEAN 1920 - 2001
............................................. +CHARLES LYNN TERRELL
............................................. 6 EVELYN DEAN 1922 -
............................................. 6 ROBERT MANN DEAN 1925 -
............................. 4 SCOTTIE HENDREN 1874 - 1967
............................. +FRANK FOREST MILLER 1872 - 1942
..................................... 5 RAY EUGENE MILLER 1896 - 1918
..................................... 5 MARY ELIZABETH MILLER 1906 - 1988
..................................... +FRANK EDWARD WARE 1906 - 1952
............................................. 6 RAY MILLER WARE 1929 -
............................................. +SUSAN DAVENPORT 1937 -
..................................................... 7 STEVEN DOUGLAS WARE 1961 - 2004
..................................................... +JEANNIE CAROLINE TAYLOR 1949 -
..................................... 5 EDITH MILLER 1911 -
..................................... +WILLIAM HERMAN JESSE 1908 - 1970
............................................. 6 NAN JESSE 1939 -
............................................. 6 ALICE JESSE 1943 -
............................................. +JAMES DONALD KIRK 1939 -
..................................................... 7 WILLIAM CLIFFORD KIRK 1967 -
..................................................... +KAREN BINDER 1973 -
............................................................. 8 BRANDON JOSHUA KIRK 1991 -
..................................................... *2nd Wife of WILLIAM CLIFFORD KIRK:
..................................................... +ANNA MARIA BOBREK 1964 -
............................................................. 8 CHRISTIAN JESSE KIRK 2000 -
..................................................... 7 DOUGLAS WAYNE KIRK 1969 -
..................................................... +MELISSA BRITTON 1970 -
............................................................. 8 EMILY RUTH KIRK 1994 -
............................................................. 8 LAURA ELIZABETH KIRK 2001 -
............................................................. 8 CHARLES BRITTON KIRK 2001 -

```
.. 3 LUCY HENDREN  Abt 1842 -
.. 3 JAMES M HENDREN  1842 - 1926
...... +NANNIE BERRY  1842 - 1932
............. 4 CHARLES B HENDREN  1875 - 1952
............. 4 J HARRY HENDREN  1873 - 1944
............. 4 W H HENDREN
............. 4 SAM R HENDREN
............. 4 EMMA L HENDREN
.. 3 LORENZO D HENDREN  Abt 1847 - Abt 1855
.IZA HENDREN  1816 - 1896
TURPIN WEST  1813 - 1882
... 3 JOHN T WEST  1841 - 1921
...... +MARY ELLEN GIBNEY HUNTER  1845 - 1928
............. 4 EMMA DEAN WEST  - 1952
.................. +J TYLER REDDEN
............. 4 LYDE WEST  - 1949
............. 4 DAN WEST  - 1947
................. +ALICE MCGILL  - 1949
............. 4 ARTHUR WEST  - 1954
................ +DORA MURPHY  1875 - 1968
... *2nd Wife of JOHN T WEST:
........ +MARTHA JANE BURTON  1847 - 1873
......... 4 CLAYTON WEST  1870 - 1924
................ +LIZZIE ROBINSON  1874 - 1937
........................ 5 JOHN ALLEN WEST  1901 - 1961
............................. +IVA DAVID QUINN  1900 - 1928
..................................... 6 HOLTON QUINN WEST  1926 - 1981
........................................ +EMMA JACQUELINE CHAMBERS
................................................ 7 HOLTON QUINN WEST, JR  1951 -
................................................ 7 JOHN ALLEN WEST II  1954 -
................................................ 7 DAVID KELLY WEST  1961 -
................................................ 7 JANET SUE WEST  1964 -
............. 4 JENNIE WEST  - 1917
.................. +WILLIAM HUNTER  - 1923
..... 3 WILLIAM WEST  - 1920
.... 3 ALLACE WEST
........ +NAPOLEON B LONG
WILLIAM L HENDREN  1819 - 1901
+ELIZA ANN REYNOLDS  1823 - 1900
..... 3 MARY E HENDREN  - 1919
......... +GEORGE B WHEELER
................. 4 MARY WHEELER
..... 3 ANNA HENDREN
..... 3 LOUISA J HENDREN
..... 3 WILLIAM L HENDREN JR
..... 3 HATTIE HENDREN  - 1921
...... 3 LEVI H HENDREN  1841 - Abt 1906
.......... +LOUISA TUDOR
............ 4 ETHEL HENDREN
................ 4 JENNIE HENDREN
...... 3 GEORGE M HENDREN  1846 - 1924
.......... +MARY E JASPER  - 1922
................ 4 NELLIE HENDREN
.................... +HOWARD KING  - 1922
................ 4 MARY HENDREN
.................... +WALTER K DAVIS
................ 4 ADDA HENDREN  1873 - 1950
.................... +HUGH MILLER  1873 - 1957
........................ 5 ALMA MILLER  1895 - 1974
............................ 5 TOM TURNER MILLER  1897 -
................................ +PHANIAL BOWEN
..................................... 6 MARY VIRGINIA MILLER
........................................ 6 KENNETH MILLER
...... 3 IDA HENDREN  1864 - 1913
...... 3 WALTER SCOTT HENDREN  Abt 1867 - Abt 1943
THOMAS HENDREN  1830 - 1902
```

www.ingramcontent.com/pod-product-compliance
Lightning Source LLC
Chambersburg PA
CBHW081143290426
44108CB00018B/2427